RECKONINGS

RECKONINGS

LEGACIES OF NAZI PERSECUTION AND THE QUEST FOR JUSTICE

MARY FULBROOK

OXFORD
UNIVERSITY PRESS

OXFORD
UNIVERSITY PRESS

Oxford University Press is a department of the University of Oxford.
It furthers the University's objective of excellence in research, scholarship,
and education by publishing worldwide. Oxford is a registered trade mark of
Oxford University Press in the UK and certain other countries.

Published in the United States of America by Oxford University Press
198 Madison Avenue, New York, NY 10016, United States of America.

© Mary Fulbrook 2018

Library of Congress Cataloging-in-Publication Data
Names: Fulbrook, Mary, 1951– author.
Title: Reckonings : legacies of Nazi persecution and the quest for justice /
Mary Fulbrook.
Description: New York : Oxford University Press, 2018
Identifiers: LCCN 2017050473 | ISBN 9780190681241 (hardback : alk. paper)
Subjects: LCSH: War crime trials—Europe—History—20th century. |
Holocaust, Jewish (1939–1945)—Influence.
Classification: LCC KZ1174.5 .F85 2018 | DDC 341.6/90268—dc23
LC record available at https://lccn.loc.gov/2017050473

1 3 5 7 9 8 6 4 2
Printed by Sheridan Books, Inc.
United States of America

Contents

Preface

The enormity of the Holocaust is often summarized in one word: Auschwitz. Yet a focus primarily on this iconic site of evil tends to deflect attention from the myriad ways in which individuals became tangled up on the side of the perpetrators, as well as the diversity of experiences among a wide range of victims as they struggled and died, or managed to survive against all the odds. It also misses the continuing significance of Nazi persecution over time and across continents. The selective memorial landscape of Europe today, and the well-known cultural and public representations of this past, cannot do justice to the variety of subjective experiences and personal legacies of involvement in violence under Nazi rule. Reckoning with a still disturbing past entails a myriad of attempts to rectify continuing imbalances or to address a persisting sense of injustice, whether such attempts take place in courts of law or in personal accounts.

This was not an easy book to write. It addresses the distinctive character of involvement in the collective violence unleashed under Nazi rule and explores routes out of and beyond this period of terror—on both sides of the chasm between perpetrators and persecuted. *Reckonings* tells the stories not only of well-known people and places but also of those who remained largely below the radar of public representations, outside the media spotlight. It explores how people were transformed by their experiences and how, under different later circumstances, they sought to reckon with the continuing implications of this "past that refused to pass away"—even as states and judicial systems failed to bring many of the guilty to justice.

This is a perilous undertaking. The topic is enormous, the material potentially infinite. I have selected a range of examples, case studies illuminating a variety of themes, groups, and places, in order to convey both the broad patterning and varying individual responses to this deeply significant past. I have foregrounded these examples and explored the subjective experiences of those involved while only lightly sketching in the wider historical background, the policy decisions, strategies, and events on which there is a huge and ever-expanding literature. Periodically I have given pointers to relevant secondary sources but have nowhere sought to be exhaustive or comprehensive.

Reckonings paints a vast canvas. I am more than well aware of both the scale of the undertaking and the inevitable insufficiencies of the outcome. Any discussion of these issues will be inadequate to the immensity of the almost inexplicable cruelty and suffering with which it is concerned, and the difficulties of dealing with the long aftermath. It is virtually impossible to do justice to this past—not only in the courts of law or in personal and cultural narratives but also in historical analyses. Nevertheless, it is important to understand the parameters of the persecution and collective violence that affected so many people and the lingering consequences that continue to affect us today.

Scholars at the time of the Hebrew Bible had already noted that "of making many books there is no end, and much study is a weariness of the flesh" (Ecclesiastes 12:12). This, of all books, feels like one that cannot ever, in principle, be finished; no analysis of this topic can be exhaustive or final. But there comes a point when it is important simply to stop, and to pass on the interim outcome of the exploration. It is my hope that, despite the selectivity and omissions that are inevitable in such a vast area, the book serves to map some of the contours of the tip of an incredibly significant iceberg. We are far from finished with these questions; there is far more to be explored.

Acknowledgments

There are many institutions and individuals who have helped in the writing of this book. I am particularly grateful to the UK Arts and Humanities Research Council (AHRC) for a collaborative research grant on Reverberations of War in Germany and Europe since 1945, which underpinned the research for this book. I am grateful also to the UCL colleagues who collaborated on different strands of the AHRC grant: Stephanie Bird, Julia Wagner, and Christiane Wienand, as well as our PhD students on the project, Gaelle Fisher and Alexandra Hills. Although they all wrote on quite different topics, the discussions and intersections proved highly stimulating.

My thanks are due to UCL for hosting the project, and specifically to Georgina Bolton, Cathy Brown, Dania Herrera, and other colleagues in the Faculty Office, all of whom assisted in making completion of this book just about compatible with my UCL duties as dean of the Faculty of Social and Historical Sciences—a highly frustrating combination in terms of competing demands on time, requiring the capacity to lead two simultaneous lives, but each fulfilling in different ways. I would also like to thank the staff of the many libraries and archives I have visited in the course of this research, including the German Federal Archives in Berlin; the Kempowski Archive in the Academy of Arts in Berlin; the German Diary Archive in Emmendingen; the Wiener Library, London; the Houghton Library at Harvard; the YIVO Institute for Jewish Research, New York; the Judith Kestenberg archive at the Hebrew University of Jerusalem; and Yad Vashem in Jerusalem. The work also draws on previous research for an earlier project, carried out in the state archive in Katowice and the Jewish Historical Institute in Warsaw. Except where otherwise indicated (as when footnotes refer to published English translations), all translations in this work are my own.

In writing the book, I have benefited from discussions with individuals in a wide variety of contexts, including conferences, seminars, lectures, and other encounters. Their reactions have been invaluable. I was particularly able to benefit from a term as visiting professor at the Jena Center for

Twentieth Century History in 2013, and many of the general ideas under-lying this book are discussed in essays arising from that stint in Jena. My thanks are due to Norbert Frei and Kristina Meyer for their support and encouragement in compiling those texts into a short book, *Erfahrung, Erinnerung, Geschichtsschreibung: Neue Perspektiven auf die deutschen Diktaturen* (Wallstein, 2016), which is in some ways a brief companion to the more extensive substantive development of themes and stories in this volume. I am also grateful to the following institutions and organizations, where I delivered lectures that are reflected in the current work: the Glasgow Holocaust Memorial Lecture, January 2015; the Vienna Wiesenthal Institute, where I delivered a Simon Wiesenthal Lecture in June 2015; and the conference on "bystanders" in Amsterdam organized by Christina Morina and Krijn Thijs, where I gave a keynote lecture in September 2015. In completing this book, I have benefited enormously from the comments of readers, particularly Jane Caplan and Nicholas Stargardt; their characteristically thoughtful and perceptive comments have been immensely helpful in the final stages of revision. I am also extremely grateful to Emma Parry for her continued support and encouragement for the project, and to Tim Bent at Oxford University Press for his ferociously insightful and proactive editing. While acknowledging that this book could not have been written without the help of many others, I of course take full responsibility for remaining errors, omissions, and infelicities.

My particular thanks are to members of my family, especially to my children, who have always put up with my near obsessive immersion in the past and constantly reminded me that there is so much more to life in the present. Now, as adults, their discussions and diversions remain as interesting and invaluable as ever, and they have been immensely supportive in a whole variety of ways. My deepest gratitude is owed to Julian, who not only supported me in this as in all else and commented on successive drafts as the book evolved but also accompanied me on innumerable trips to what he calls "the most dismal locations" across Europe. He too has had to live with this past. Without my family, this book could not have been written.

RECKONINGS

I

The Significance of the Nazi Past

In January 1942 a man known as Szlamek—almost certainly not his real name—managed to escape from the death camp of Chełmno nad Nerem in the Wartheland, a part of western Poland annexed by Nazi Germany. He recounted to the rabbi and the residents of a nearby small town, Grabów, how he had witnessed the gassing of innumerable local Jewish communities from the towns and villages all around the area, how he had seen members of his own family murdered, and how he had helped to dig the graves for those deported from the large ghetto of Litzmannstadt (as the Germans had renamed the Polish city of Łódź). The murdered included both Jews and members of the Roma and Sinti communities, whom Szlamek, like others at the time, simply termed Gypsies. From Grabów, Szlamek made his way to the Warsaw Ghetto, where on March 25, 1942, his account was taken down in writing by those in the ghetto recording their terrible experiences.[1] He managed to get out of the ghetto and made it as far as Zamość. But, although the details of where and when he was later murdered are unclear, it is certain that he did not manage to survive the war. His account of the horrific events taking place in the Nazis' first dedicated extermination center, recounted so close to the experiences in question, is unique. Szlamek was one of only seven people to escape from Chełmno. Three of the others later gave testimony in the context of investigations and trials.

Szlamek's account is deeply harrowing. He details, day by day, almost hour by hour, the process of murder in the small hamlet of Chełmno and the nearby forest. He gives a precise account of the way in which new arrivals at the Chełmno mansion—often termed a "palace," but simply a manor house—were deceived: greeted in a kindly way by an elderly German, who told them with courtesy how they would need to take a bath before continuing their journey and should undress and hand over their valuables separately, and who then guided them to the stairs leading down to a specially adapted vehicle in which they would, within the hour, be asphyxiated by exhaust fumes. Szlamek gives a terrifying but entirely matter-of-fact description of the arrival of the gas vans in the forest clearing, some four kilometers distant. When people were murdered in these vans, the screams could be heard for around fifteen minutes before the driver checked through a peephole to confirm that all were dead. On pulling out the corpses, some families were so closely embracing each other that the guards had to order the Jewish gravediggers to cut their limbs.

Szlamek provides one of the very few accounts we have of the end of a community of Roma people:

> They were lying in their own excrements, their bodies entangled. They looked as if they had just been put to sleep—their faces were not pale, but had a natural skin color. The bodies were still warm, so the "pit-workers" warmed themselves up staying close to them. . . . Having emptied the van of the corpses, the "pit-workers" went on to remove the excrement. The straw and the wooden strips were removed and the vehicle was cleaned with the "pit-workers'" own shirts before the strips and the straw were put back in the van.[2]

Szlamek also tells of the conditions of work and the eventual fate that faced the laborers in the pit:

> After the van had left and the corpses had been placed in the graves, the "pit-workers" put on colorful Gypsy clothes and sat down on the dead bodies in the graves. They were not allowed to hang around with the other forced laborers. During dinnertime they were left in the graves, where they got only bitter, black coffee without even a small piece of bread.[3]

It was presumably not worth feeding these workers, given that this day would also be their last. At the end of the day,

> The eight "pit-workers" were not allowed to leave the grave. They were told to lie down on the corpses of the Gypsies with their faces down. A gendarme killed them with a submachine gun.[4]

Day after day, hour after hour, vans arrived as Jews from miles around, as well as the huge community of Jews from the Łódź Ghetto—the second largest ghetto, after Warsaw—were brought here for gassing.

A deeply pious Jew, Szlamek also tells us of the agonies that he and his fellow prisoner-workers went through night after night, as some of them sang Psalms or said Kaddish for lost loved ones, as others refuted the very possibility of the existence of God, and as they discussed the various possibilities of escape, the desirability of committing suicide, or of seeking to try to stay alive in the hope of warning the world and engaging in eventual retaliation.

Meanwhile, local Polish peasants were aware of what was going on. So too were local Germans, many of whom had resettled or been moved into this area, some of them to assist in the wider project of "Germanization" and some to provide logistical support. In total, somewhere in the region of 150,000 to 250,000 people were murdered in Chełmno: not a phenomenon easily disguised from view, despite all the mechanisms of deception and attempts at security.

Curiously, the sites where all this happened now remain nearly deserted, barely registering on the tourist map, even for those visitors determined to explore the dark past in Poland. There is bare ground where the mansion used to stand; the church, now back in use, bears little trace of the times when it was used to store the belongings of murdered people; the burial pits in the woodland clearings are now just mounds of earth, some subject to archaeological investigation. Szlamek's vivid memories of the individuals murdered there have few counterparts; there were too few survivors. A few visitors may glance at the painful memorials erected on this site across succeeding years, but the past is sinking here, almost without a trace.

The murders at Chełmno, terrifying and tragic, were just one small part of the massive phenomenon we have come to think of as the Holocaust: a combination of genocide and persecution on an industrial scale, almost without parallel, and yet imaginable only through the individual, the locality, the tiny mosaic of the past that we can still in some way visualize. As the enormity of what took place in Europe under Nazi domination recedes from memory and from view, questions arise about the ways in which this past nevertheless still touches and affects us today.

The Continuing Presence of the Nazi Past

We may think that this past is dead and buried—literally as well as metaphorically. Some three-quarters of a century after the explosion of violence and murder across Hitler's European empire, the vast majority of the participants, eyewitnesses, and survivors are no longer with us to tell their stories. Soon their voices will have been consigned to the archival mountains of testimonies, and they will no longer appear in person in schools, museums, and sites of memory to bear witness to the personal impact of this past. Some analysts, it is true, highlight the fallibility of memory and the selective character of survivors' accounts, and treat their narratives less as historical sources than as testaments to the wounds of survival. Yet even so, many commentators and educators worry about the possible implications of the "death of the witness" and fear that, in the absence of survivor voices providing living testimony, younger generations will no longer care about this history. Even where the stories may be wrong in detail, the survivor provides living proof of the enormity and continuing significance of the past.

As far as wider publics are concerned, however, the very opposite seems to be the case. The Nazi past continues to disturb. And its resonance seems, if anything, to be growing with time. Chełmno may be off the beaten tracks, nearly deserted. But the number of visitors to a far better known site of mass murder, Auschwitz, is now well over a million every year—probably receiving as many visitors annually as the total number of Jews murdered there during the five years of its operation as the largest extermination site and concentration camp of the Third Reich. Perhaps most striking of all is the way the Holocaust has become central to the identity and culture of the Federal Republic of Germany, incorporated into its material and moral fiber. A rash of memorials to victims of Nazi persecution were established in the early years of the twenty-first century, and the memory of the Holocaust has become enshrined in the heart of Germany's capital city, Berlin. The extensive Memorial to the Murdered Jews of Europe was opened in 2005, sited right next to the Brandenburg Gate, a brief walk from the heart of government, with the historic Reichstag building and the chancellor's offices nearby in the Tiergarten. There, too, may be found a smaller memorial, erected in 2008, to the homosexuals who were persecuted by the Nazis. Not far away, a memorial to the murdered Roma and Sinti population of Europe, was opened in 2012. Nearby, at the site of the former headquarters of Hitler's so-called euthanasia program at Tiergarten Strasse 4, a memorial was finally established in 2014 to the victims of Nazi policies in which people with mental and physical disabilities were murdered on the grounds that they were "life unworthy of living." And in streets across Berlin, more in some areas than others, there are little brass "stumbling stones" (*Stolpersteine*) set into the sidewalks and doorways of houses from which individuals were deported to their deaths. These remind even casual visitors of the sheer numbers of individuals whose deaths were caused by Nazi persecution—and of the innumerable neighbors who had looked on, unable or unwilling to intervene. The former nation of perpetrators now bears anguish and shame about the national past, embodied in its landscape for all to see.

Less surprisingly, in Israel—a state founded in the aftermath of genocidal persecution, in which Holocaust survivors found an initially uncertain refuge but created an enormous legacy—Yad Vashem, situated on a hill on the outskirts of the historic city of Jerusalem, is virtually a national shrine. Yet it is not only in the land of the perpetrators and in the country so closely associated with the victims that the Nazi past has a central place. In Washington, DC, the capital of a major world power in which survivor families constitute only a tiny minority of the population, the United States Holocaust Memorial Museum (USHMM) has taken a key place adjacent to the National Mall, alongside other national monuments in close proximity to the centers of government and power. And in many European countries, public memorials resonate with references to glorious resistance or commemoration of victims. Europe even has adopted a Holocaust Memorial Day—although on a quite different day and in a different month from that of Israel.

In Yad Vashem and the USHMM, as well as many other sites, the desire to remember the victims is combined with a mission for education, documentation, and research. The memorials convey a sense that what happened was so enormous, so horrendous, that the message must be transmitted to future generations. The Holocaust has become a defining feature of contemporary self-understandings and values, and the more generic notion of genocide has become a controversial catchword for mass violence in a wide range of contexts, from Armenia, Bosnia, and Cambodia to Rwanda and Sudan. References to Hitler and to Nazism abound; the swastika is a universally recognized and contentious symbol. And younger Germans, even several generations after the end of the Third Reich, still have to counter unwarranted stereotypes about their alleged collective identity.

In some respects, then, the long-term significance of the Nazi past seems to have grown well beyond the original sites of the historical events themselves. Like a mushroom cloud, the initial explosion of Nazi violence not only produced devastation at the time but has also spread an ever-broadening

shadow contaminating later generations and affecting those living well
beyond the initial epicenter of death.

Exploring the Legacies of Nazi Persecution

While the memorial landscapes and the political uses of this past have been
widely explored, the personal legacies for those who lived through it and
those born afterward are less well understood. Literary scholars, psychiatrists,
and social psychologists have focused on personal narratives of trauma. We
know far less about the historical variations in the ways in which people
reflected on their experiences, spoke or did not speak about their past, and
transmitted the consequences of this past—through habits, anxieties, attitudes, and behaviors if not actual stories—to members of the next generation.
How people were affected in the longer term by their experiences under
Nazism, and how they affected members of subsequent generations, varied
significantly not only with categorization and experiences at the time but
also according to later contexts.

People were persecuted on grounds of "race," sexuality, religion, disability, politics, "habitual criminality," and "asocial behavior," or were drawn
into the network of Nazi oppression as forced laborers. Most victims
experienced an absolute rupture in their lives at the time of persecution,
suffering stigmatization and humiliation and facing extreme conditions of
deprivation, exploitation, and mass death. Those who survived had to live
with horrifying memories, even as they sought to forge new futures across
the world. For all the commonalities, however, experiences both at the time
of persecution and in the aftermath varied significantly according to the
ways in which people had been—and in some cases continued to be—stigmatized. While Jewish victims and some political opponents of the Nazi
regime were recognized early on, depending on postwar context, other
groups continued to be marginalized, receiving neither recognition nor
compensation for decades after the war, if at all in their lifetimes. Differing
contexts and audiences affected how people discussed their experiences, or
remained silent; who they chose to talk to, where, and when; and the ways
in which they tried to build new lives after such devastation.

Survivors' strategies of living with a painful past may be compared with
the evasive stories, the cover-ups, and comforting tales told among members
of perpetrator communities. Many people on the perpetrator side later

claimed that they had not been personally responsible for what had happened and sought to portray their own compromised pasts in ways that were acceptable to a later present. Meanwhile, legal confrontations in the courtrooms were partial in every sense of that word, with the patchy records of justice frequently at odds with the public rhetoric of the postwar states established on the soil of the defeated Third Reich. The notion of what it meant to be a perpetrator was relatively narrowly defined, varying with context. Survivor witnesses may have had their "day in court," and for a time they were vital to the establishment of guilt, but they often found it was only to be discredited, their testimony discounted. Where the extermination factories had been most efficient, a paucity of survivor testimony allowed many perpetrators to get away with their crimes. Only with the end of the "era of the witness" could perpetrators be found guilty simply by virtue of the role they had played, the place they had occupied in the machinery of mass murder.

Courtroom confrontations constituted, however, only one element among the innumerable ways in which people sought to reckon with the Nazi past. What is often called "cultural memory"—a misnomer—certainly informed but does not fully represent the continuing significance of the past at a personal level. More important for most people were the ways in which the past pervaded family relationships, with significant emotional legacies for those who came after—including the children and grandchildren of perpetrators, as well as the families of survivors, growing up in the shadow of the past. Whether or not they were aware of specific details, members of the "second generation" embodied the lingering consequences of their parents' experiences in their own identities in a later present. Some explored the past more actively, and for a few it was possible to engage in attempts at reconciliation. With the passage of time a dialogue began to emerge across generations, as those "born after" tried to understand the experiences and elicit the stories of those who had quite different perspectives on the Nazi period. Eventually, new audiences emerged, as the "era of the witness" gave way to the "era of the survivor"—an expanding if continually contested term.

When we juxtapose public and legal reckonings with personal experiences, some surprising patterns emerge. Not least, a significant disjuncture is revealed between official myths about "dealing with the past" on the one hand and the extent to which the overwhelming majority of perpetrators actually evaded the net of justice on the other. We can also begin to understand the ways in which the past remained so troubling for so many people, beyond the public representations of intellectuals, creative writers, artists, and politicians. And we can gain glimpses of how this past has had continuing reverberations, with a generational half-life contaminating the lives of innumerable people who had not themselves lived through the Nazi period but for whom it could never quite become merely "history." The memorial landscape today barely hints at the maelstrom of memories, emotions, and lingering reverberations of this era.

Within the already enormous literature on each of these issues, this book therefore takes some distinctive paths. It sketches an overview of a wide range of distinct but interrelated strands, each of which has its own inherent logics and rhythms. Experiences and legacies of persecution cannot be readily reconstructed as a simple chronological account of policies, politics, and events within clearly defined geopolitical borders. There are multiple chronologies, with overlapping eras of interpretation and communication among different communities affected by the wave of collective violence that had been unleashed across Europe by the Nazi regime. The topography cannot, for the most part, be restricted to accounts of particular states, but needs to range more widely according to the issues and people involved. And the focus requires zooming both in and out: to sketch a broad panorama while understanding implications at a personal level requires combining broad generalizations with selective in-depth soundings. This is therefore a highly complex picture to paint.

In the course of Nazi persecution, distinctive "communities of experience" were formed. We have come to think in terms of a triad: perpetrators, victims, and bystanders, and some who were victims later came to be seen as "survivors." Yet these labels are not always easily applied. Even at the time of persecution, people could move between categories. Many people collaborated or assisted in processes of persecution even though they would not, in conventional terms, be labeled "perpetrators." Many were victims of Nazi policies in one context yet beneficiaries or even perpetrators in another. Polish people, for example, were on the receiving end of Nazi oppression and were victims of brutal occupation policies, yet some also assisted the Nazis in hunting Jews; others might hide Jews for a while, thus becoming "rescuers," but then turn them in when fear or considerations of material gain took priority; some might participate in partisan bands resisting the Germans while betraying Jews who tried to join them. There were also changing uses and meanings of these terms after the war. "Perpetrator" became an ever-narrower category in legal understandings in different states, allowing many who were deeply contaminated to escape justice, while portraying others as the "really guilty" ones. "Survivor," a term that was increasingly used in the later twentieth century, could also be interpreted rather narrowly, excluding many who had been victims of Nazi persecution and who often continued to be marginalized and excluded, their sufferings barely recognized and their stories not heard. On occasion unsavory "competitions of victimhood" developed, with distinctions between those deemed to be real "survivors" and others. Yet for all these qualifications, Nazism undoubtedly created a deep chasm between those on the side of the persecutors and those who were persecuted. While "perpetrator" and "victim" are not necessarily always the best categories to capture the wider divisions created by the Nazi period, they remain vital to understanding the dynamics not only of this period but also the of postwar era of debates and divisions.

Perhaps the most problematic of the terms in the triad is that of "bystanders." This can potentially include an extraordinary range of people, and is in some respects only useful with respect to brief moments of concentrated violence within a wider system, when we know too little about the background faces in the photos or the anonymous people in contemporary accounts to be sure about where they really stood.[5] Some might be better captured in a typology referring to collaboration and resistance, combat and complicity, with distinctions made between fighting or facilitating Hitler's rule. Even when referring only to people who stood, apparently powerless, as eyewitnesses to horrific events going on in their vicinity, the notion of bystanders raises a host of questions. Being unable to act, or choosing not to act, or failing to explore what actions might have been possible is in itself a form of (in)action that influences the outcomes of any particular situation: bystanders are not somehow abstracted from the complex course of historical development but are themselves part of the situation that makes some outcomes possible in the first place. And bystanders were also affected by witnessing the events that took place in their midst; they too faced later challenges about their roles, their failures to intervene, and even their potential complicity. People who had in fact been on the side of the perpetrators often later found it more useful to portray themselves as having been merely powerless bystanders.

Whatever terms we adopt to describe people's behavior at the time or later, some things are quite clear. Few who lived through this period could avoid being involved, at some point, on one side or another—sometimes also crossing sides, in complex, ambivalent, and distressing ways, moving from being a committed Nazi to a member of a resistance group, from a victim to a collaborator, from a doubter to a murderer, and from an upright citizen to a shriveled outcast. In the end, and faced with the ghettos, the gas chambers, and the murder pits, people found themselves ultimately on one side or the other of the fatal fences the Nazis had raised between those who could live and those doomed to die. Both those who were personally involved and those who came after were inevitably affected by longer-term legacies of this violent period.

There is, too, a complex, entangled history of the aftermath of persecution. Different postwar contexts shaped the ways in which people who had been involved in the Third Reich later lived their lives, represented their pasts, interacted with others—and in turn affected members of younger generations who had not themselves personally lived through this period. The lives of people in the second and even the third generation—whether in families of survivors or of perpetrators—remained deeply, inevitably affected by the Nazi past. They did not have personal memories of these times, although there were shadows and reflections in families imbued with the all-pervasive weight of the past. But the past was nevertheless more than just history. It formed and shaped their very being, whether through family dynamics or the implications for the wider community. And many people still feel a strong sense of connection with this past: they are affected by the circumstances of their upbringing; they identify with one or another group; and they position themselves and define their own identities in relation to this past, whether they accept or rebel against the assumed legacies. We may speak, then, of "communities of connection" among those who were, for whatever reasons, intrinsically and inescapably linked to the past through personal ties, and wider "communities of identification" among those who, whether or not they had any personal connections, strongly identified with the issues raised by the past and that remained of enduring significance.

In order to explore these aspects in greater depth over time, specific examples have been chosen, which are pursued throughout the book. The primary focus in Part I is on particular sites of discrimination, persecution, and murder, focusing on selected areas within the Third Reich and occupied Poland that highlight key issues of more general significance. I have not sought to present a general overview or comprehensive account, let alone to reference all the relevant secondary literature; rather, I have chosen to

highlight particular areas, incidents, and issues that are relevant to understanding both the processes of persecution at the time and the long-term
reverberations in different later contexts. Some of the places and people
introduced in Part I are pursued as examples throughout the book. One
local focus, for example, which recurs repeatedly, is the area in southern
Poland around Mielec and Dębica. I have looked at the experiences of those
who were persecuted here and later scattered across the world as well as
following the fates of perpetrators who ended up in East or West Germany,
and have examined the significance of this past for their children and for the
wider landscape of remembrance. The Mielec area takes up a great deal
more space in this book than its wider historical significance—or lack of
it—might seem to warrant, but simply by its very insignificance it illuminates
aspects common to many areas that largely escaped public attention. I have
also sketched wider developments, from the beginnings of persecution in
Nazi Germany, through the institutionalized murder of the mentally and
physically disabled and the growing exploitation of slave labor, the ghettos,
camps, and sites of extermination, to the first attempts to recount these
experiences and make sense of this cataclysmic eruption of violence.

Part II explores issues around attempts to bring perpetrators to justice in the
courtrooms, focusing on selected trials at different stages up to the present—
not only the well-known trials of prominent Nazis and major concentration camps but also euthanasia cases and trials relating to less well-known
perpetrators, including those from the Mielec area. It charts key shifts in
judicial reckonings with the Nazi past from the Nuremberg trials to the
present, when all but the last perpetrators of Nazi crimes have passed away.
It not only traces how the roles of perpetrators and witnesses changed across
what is often termed the "era of the witness" but also examines distinctive
variations in what crime complexes came before the courts and which groups
more easily slid away from legal reckonings in different states. The inadequacies in prosecution and conviction for Nazi crimes are generally glaring, but
for differing reasons across time and place; the parameters and practices of
legal reckonings contrasted markedly in Austria, East and West Germany, and
the united Federal Republic of Germany.

Part III broadens the focus to explore the responses of people living
across the world, for whom personal experiences of Nazi persecution reverberated in multiple ways, including across generations and among wider
publics. For those who had survived persecution, the physical and psychological legacies of sustained maltreatment were further complicated by the

ways in which they were subsequently perceived and treated. Some groups received a sympathetic hearing, whereas others gained neither recognition nor compensation, again depending on time and place. In the "era of the survivor," setting in largely from the later 1970s, there was growing sympathy for victimhood and there were ever-larger audiences for survivor accounts, at least among those groups recognized as such. But at the same time, the vast majority of perpetrators still managed to cover their tracks and evade both public attention and personal acknowledgment of guilt. All these factors complicated the ways in which the children and grandchildren of both survivors and perpetrators addressed the legacies of their family pasts. This era is now drawing to a close, as personal connections and emotional links weaken over time and public remembrance is taking over from personal memory.

Throughout the postwar era, perpetrators have remained largely notable by their absence from the stages of justice in the courtroom, discussions in the family home, and representations in memorial sites. But any "integrated history of the Holocaust," which seeks to insert the perspectives of those who were persecuted alongside the policies of the perpetrators, must now be complemented by an equally integrated account of the reverberations, on both sides, in the aftermath, encompassing the broad range of groups who had to live with the complex legacies of Nazi persecution.

Reckonings

Among the gravediggers of the Chełmno extermination camp, the hope for eventual retaliation was sometimes the only thing that kept them alive. Szlamek, one of the handful of escapees, recalled in the spring of 1942 that on at least two occasions he had prevented fellow prisoners from putting an early end to their own lives. He recounted one such incident that took place on Saturday, January 10, 1942:

> At one thirty in the afternoon, the second transport [of a gas van] arrived. Suddenly, Ajzenstab, also from Kłodawa, started crying quietly and said that his life was now pointless, because he saw the bodies of his wife and his only 15-year-old daughter being buried. He even wanted to ask the Germans to shoot him, because he wanted to be in one grave with his loved ones. We talked him out of it, explaining that there was no point in hurrying and that if he managed to escape there would be time for retaliation.[6]

A day or two later, much the same scene occurred with another of the gravedigger prisoners:

> At one point my friend Gecel Chrząstkowski recognized his 14-year-old son being thrown into the grave. He also wanted to ask the Germans to shoot him, but we persuaded him out of doing so. We claimed he should bear it all patiently and think about future retaliation.[7]

Questions of retaliation, revenge, justice preoccupied those who were suffering, even as they suffered. But neither Ajzenstab nor Chrząstkowski, nor even Szlamek, survived the war. Nor did virtually all the other victims of the Chełmno extermination camp, nor the millions of others who lost their lives as a result of Nazi persecution.

A few of the tiny number, the few dozen in all, who survived the death camps in the east—Bełżec, Sobibór, Treblinka—only managed to cling on to life and keep going after their escape by the thought that they had to stay alive in order to bear witness. One of those who escaped from Treblinka, Yankel Wiernik, wrote his account hiding in Warsaw while the war was still raging. He even begins with an address to future readers: "For your sake alone I continue to hang on to my miserable life, though it has lost all attraction for me." He was tormented by his experiences: "Time and again I wake up in the middle of the night moaning pitifully. Ghastly nightmares break up the sleep I so badly need. I see thousands of skeletons extending their bony arms towards me, as if begging for mercy and life, but I, drenched with sweat, feel incapable of giving any help." He continued: "Phantoms of death haunt me." But, as he put it: "I, who saw the doom of three generations, must keep on living for the sake of the future. The world must be told of the infamy of those barbarians, so that centuries and generations to come can execrate them."[8]

If we do not force ourselves to listen to these agonized accounts and to confront, from this very safe distance, the unthinkable images they convey, we cannot even begin to comprehend later attempts to live with this past. And for many members of later generations, particularly those with close emotional ties to perpetrator communities, it can become all too easy to listen to self-exonerating tales and give people the benefit of the doubt. Any reckoning with the past that cannot confront images such as these will remain only partial, inadequate to the enormity of the task of understanding Nazi persecution and its aftermath.

It was not easy for survivors to find answers to the question of how to deal with the personal legacies of a past such as this, nor was it obvious how to achieve justice on behalf of the millions who did not survive as well as those few who did. Tadeusz Borowski, born in 1922 in the Ukraine and a prisoner at both Dachau and Auschwitz, wrote a series of short stories first published in Poland in 1948 and later collected together, following his suicide in 1951. Drawing on his experiences at Auschwitz, Borowski's stories in *This Way for the Gas, Ladies and Gentlemen* record brutality, violence, survival, and death with a mordant humor, a bitter sense of irony, and an acute awareness of just what it took to survive.[9] Borowski's first-person narrator, Tadek, was a relatively "privileged"—non-Jewish—prisoner. He was able to "organize" extra food and articles that he could either use himself—a fine pair of boots, or a silk shirt—or barter for more food. All around, trains would arrive, selections would take place, tens of thousands of people would be gassed, shot, or thrown alive into the flames and burial pits. At one point, Tadek gets engaged in conversation with a fellow prisoner who asks whether "they"—the perpetrators—"can go unpunished." Tadek responds: "I think for those who have suffered unjustly, justice alone is not enough. They want the guilty to suffer unjustly too. Only this will they understand as justice."[10]

Yet another view is represented in the reflections of Denise Dufournier, a French political prisoner in the women's concentration camp Ravensbrück, situated on a lakeside north of Berlin—now a peaceful, almost idyllic setting, an incongruous place for almost unimaginable evil. But this is not the only incongruity. Shortly after the end of the war, when she was once again a free woman, Dufournier wrote:

> Now that I am again able to relax, to sit down by the roadside and breathe the sweet scents of the air, now that nothing is forbidden me, save what I forbid myself, I am afraid . . . for I could not bear that so much happiness should turn to hatred. "Vengeance is mine," said the Lord. Yet, when, here or there, I hear expressions of indulgence towards our enemies, my heart hardens, for I remember all the agonized faces of all those who will never come back and who were, under our impotent gaze, tortured to their last breath.[11]

Instead of pursuing the idea of vengeance, Dufournier went on to long for a poet who might recount "the monstrous epic of this soulless race"; an epic, in her view, that would haunt subsequent generations "so that every man born of this people, his children and his grandchildren may hear unceasingly, within themselves, from morning till night and from night till morning, from the day of their birth till the moment of their death, this immense cry of Despair, crushing as remorse and forever repeated."[12] In the event, the legal pursuit of justice turned out to be partial and patchy; but the "monstrous epic," the "immense cry of Despair" for which Dufournier yearned, was indeed in some places "forever repeated": a sense of guilt was transmitted from generation to generation across the decades. Whether this will continue to be the case with the further passage of time remains to be seen.

The Nazi past remained and remains disturbing precisely because of the enormity of the crimes, and the enormity of the associated sense of injustice. There seems little or no way in which justice could ever be done to this past, whether in the legal sense of meting out justice to the few or in the wider sense of providing material compensation, however inadequate, to survivors, or in aesthetic creations—from memoirs to monuments, from poetry to academic prose—that can in any way "do justice" to the sufferings of the victims. The impossibility of adequate retribution, recompense, or even representation of the horrors inflicted by Nazi persecution has plagued not only those who lived through it but also people born long after the war was over. There can be no easy resolution of the issues involved. And this discomfort, this failure to achieve resolution, remains with us today.

PART I

Chasms: Patterns of Persecution

2

The Explosion of
State-Sponsored Violence

Recognition of degrees of responsibility and the uneven distribution of guilt must precede any reckonings with the past. We cannot grasp the ambiguities and sheer inadequacy of later reckonings without first tracing what it meant to live through the Nazi period and how different communities of experience were forged in a period of unprecedented collective violence.

Those who were the targets of persecution were deeply, existentially affected by their experiences. This was true not only literally for the millions whose lives were brutally cut short but also for the minorities who managed to survive—the "surviving remnant" of the Jewish community, the still-stigmatized gay men, the marginalized Sinti and Roma, "asocials," Jehovah's Witnesses, and others who had been targets of Nazi persecution. Few had the combination of community support and conviction to sustain them that some—but by no means all—of Hitler's former political opponents managed to find, depending on where they ended up after the war. But whatever their experiences, no one who had been persecuted could come out of this period unscathed. Being personally humiliated, degraded physically and psychologically—and over long periods of time, with little means of sustaining any sense of self-worth—affected people for years. Whatever their later strategies for living with this past, those persecuted by the Nazis had been exposed to experiences that profoundly transformed their lives.

People on the side of the perpetrators were rather differently affected by their participation in Nazi persecution. Involvement in collective violence leaves a different personal legacy from that of individually motivated violence. There were, as we shall see, many strategies for denying agency, evading responsibility, rebutting later accusations of guilt. Whether enthused by the

Führer, mobilized for the national cause, or fearful of the consequences of nonconformity, individuals could argue that they had been constrained by circumstances and bore no personal responsibility for their actions. Conceptions of an authentic inner self, an essentially innocent self, could remain intact, while individuals constructed stories that minimized their own roles. Changing skins under altered political circumstances after the war was for many former perpetrators a viable option.

There was a division of labor, and hence of responsibility and guilt, which eventually made it easier to deny personal responsibility for involvement in Nazi crimes. And, as we shall see, the process of persecution took place in stages across a vast arena, from violence and discrimination throughout Nazi Germany to the murder of vulnerable citizens in sanatoria for the mentally and physically disabled, before it ever reached the killing fields and notorious death camps in the east. Auschwitz was, in some ways, the final and most extreme stage in a long process—an end that needs contextualizing in the wider processes and landscapes of violence that ultimately made it possible.

Auschwitz as the Epitome of Evil

With much of the infrastructure intact and visible, and with survivors from a wide range of groups living across Europe and beyond, Auschwitz has entered the postwar popular imagination through innumerable memoirs, novels, documentaries, and films. The infamous entrance gate at Birkenau, with its watchtower and the extended railway branch tracks taking prisoners right into the extermination camp, and the lengthy "ramp" on which people were selected for exploitation or death, have become symbols of evil. Auschwitz has, in so many ways, come to dominate our perceptions and images of the Third Reich.

There are good reasons why Auschwitz has become the iconic site of remembrance, symbolizing the epicenter of Nazi violence. More than a million people were murdered here—perhaps as many as 1.2 million, an almost unimaginable number, more than in any other single site. Yet this still amounted to "only" around one-fifth of the total number of victims of the Holocaust and was a mere fraction of the more than fifty million deaths caused by Hitler's war. Not merely the overall numbers but also the manner of murder challenge the imagination. People died not only in the infamous gas chambers of Birkenau (Auschwitz II) but also as a result of beatings, torture, "medical" experiments, overwork on inadequate rations, hanging, shooting, starvation, and illness, whether in the main base camp of Auschwitz I, in Birkenau, or at the third Auschwitz camp for the I. G. Farben Buna plant at Monowitz, just a few kilometers away across town, or in the huge network of satellite labor camps across the surrounding areas of Silesia and beyond. For those selected for labor rather than death, life was not necessarily much better, nor even much longer. Countless prisoners were worked to death in a program explicitly entitled "extermination through labor" (*Vernichtung durch Arbeit*). The average life expectancy of an Auschwitz inmate selected for work was around three months—although for some few work did actually mean the chance of survival.

Yet by concentrating our focus primarily on this one site, this one image, we run several risks. One is that of failing to understand how this enormity could come about. To get to "there" from "here" is almost impossible to imagine. The gap between what we consider to be "normal" behavior and what took place in Auschwitz is simply too great to bridge; there is a yawning chasm between any sense of ordinary humanity and the possibility— realized at Auschwitz—of willfully driving innocent people, including the elderly, women, children, and babies, to their death in the gas chambers. When we are faced with these images, the immediate reaction will be to think that we can only condemn and not even try to understand. The later suicides of many Auschwitz survivors—and we know mostly about people who grappled explicitly with what it meant—have only added to a sense that this is simply incomprehensible, or that to comprehend is not compatible with continuing faith in humanity. Yet, with ongoing violence and injustice across the world, it is vital to understand the conditions that made such inhumanity possible.

A related risk is that of displacing attention from other sites of terror, large and small. Evil was ubiquitous in a regime where every last victim was sought out: even a small child hiding in a cupboard, in an attic, or in a "bunker" dug out in the ground; someone who required care for a mental or physical infirmity but was seen by the Nazis as a "useless eater" and a burden to society; loving partners whose same-sex relationship was disclosed by prying and disapproving neighbors; a person designated as a "half-breed," "mixed race" (*Mischling*), neither fully Jewish nor "Aryan," ousted from both communities. Not only the hidden death factories in the east but also "medical" facilities and labor camps throughout the Reich were places of exploitation and premature death; not only those who became SS guards and Gestapo brutes but also doctors, professionals, administrators, employers, and even those who obediently or fearfully turned a blind eye were in different ways implicated.

There were specific nodes—moments, incidents, locations—of extreme violence; times and places where violence was physically visible, concentrated. Such moments of extreme physical brutality were embedded in a wider sea of systemic violence. Those who sustained the evolving processes and structures of discrimination, exploitation, and degradation were ultimately complicit in ways that gave political activists, ideological motivators, and front-line murderers the opportunities to realize more deadly ends.

In focusing attention on the largest, most obvious scene of crime, we may overlook precisely the ways in which "Auschwitz"—and all that it stands for—was able to come about, and how widespread was involvement in the institutions and practices of persecution. It was difficult for any adult to live through this period at close quarters without being tainted by one or another form of complicity or benefitting from the persecution of others; it was even more difficult, and often fatal, to try to resist and challenge a system based on the state monopoly of extreme violence.

There is a further and more problematic aspect of such concentration on Auschwitz. We risk falling into a trap that happens to be convenient for people on the perpetrator side: overlooking the myriad ways in which people assisted in making genocide possible, even well before and far away from the gas chambers of Auschwitz. Guilt and complicity cannot be limited or reduced to acting as an SS officer whipping prisoners into line, a bureaucrat tallying stolen property and gold extracted from the teeth of victims, a camp guard exercising particular sadism and brutality, or a medical orderly delivering fatal injections. These are relevant to legal trials and evaluations of criminal guilt. But this focus can distract attention from the roles of innumerable others who were instrumental in making Nazi crimes possible. Many sought to wriggle out of acknowledging responsibility by distancing themselves from the worst aspects of Nazi crimes. A widespread strategy was to claim that they had "known nothing about it"—where the "it," effectively, was reduced to the gas chambers and killing sites of the east.

However many obstacles there might be to understanding, some things are quite clear. State-sponsored violence radically changed people's lives, as they were caught up on one side or the other in the whirlwind of Nazism. This was a distinctive form of violence: not individual acts of violence arising from personal motives but rather collective violence initiated, sanctioned, and ordained from above and enacted, carried out, and in many ways enhanced by initiatives from below. Moreover, this was violence that was not hidden from sight, tucked away in faraway places, but all around and plain for all to see, even within the heart of the Reich.

State Terror

Right from the very start, the brutality of Nazi rule was evident.[1] Political opposition was rapidly outlawed and opponents intimidated, beaten up, and on occasion arrested; people of Jewish descent were discriminated against; and those alleged to be carriers of "hereditary diseases" or seen as a threat to a "healthy ethnic community" were subjected to compulsory steriliza-tion. Radical measures were taken to silence unwanted voices, to close down independent associations that posed any kind of challenge to the regime, and to bring other organizations and institutions into line with the new Nazi state. It was not long before "Gypsies" (Roma and Sinti), Jehovah's Witnesses, homosexual men, and those designated as "asocials" (including prostitutes) or "work-shy" also became the targets of Nazi campaigns to transform German society.[2]

The political world changed radically. The stages of the Nazi "seizure of power" can be variously dated: from January 30, 1933, when Hitler was constitutionally appointed chancellor, in a mixed cabinet, by President Hindenburg; through the symbolic "Day of Potsdam" on March 21, 1933, and the subsequent passage of the Enabling Act on March 24, 1933, exploit-ing the dubious political fallout of the Reichstag fire on February 27; via the dissolution and outlawing of parties other than the NSDAP (the Nationalist Socialist German Workers' Party—the Nazis) and "bringing into line" of independent associations and organizations over the course of the following months; to the death of President Hindenburg in August 1934, when Hitler pronounced himself head of both party and state as the "Führer" to whom the Army swore a personal oath of allegiance. Despite early hopes in some quarters that Hitler's rule would prove only temporary, the new regime became ever more securely established.

With the Law for the Restitution of a Professional Civil Service of April 7, 1933, people with undesirable political commitments or "racial" heritage—including those who had only one Jewish grandparent—were excluded from professional occupations. Members of the state civil service, the legal and medical professions, and teachers in schools and universities were increasingly brought into line. Few non-Jewish Germans followed the example of the young jurist Sebastian Haffner, who kept quiet during the completion of his legal training and then escaped to the United Kingdom to avoid having to engage in the political compromises that were increasingly required.[3]

Governmental institutions, including ministries from the Foreign Office to the Ministry for Labour, largely went along with the goals of the Nazi regime despite retaining a traditional conservative nationalist profile.[4] Alongside traditional structures of government, new Nazi institutions and organizations developed, edging the country toward increasing racial discrimination, war, and expansion—and state bureaucrats faithfully assisted in the implementation of the required policies.

While Hitler remained central in determining the direction of travel, key political associates carved out detailed strategies, despite squabbling incessantly in personal rivalries that beset the regime. Heinrich Himmler built up ever-greater central control of the police and forces of repression, assisted by Reinhard Heydrich; Joseph Goebbels masterminded propaganda as well as acting as Gauleiter of Berlin; Hermann Göring, who had gained flying experience in the First World War, not only built up Germany's air forces but was also tasked with the Four Year Plan office, established in 1936 to prepare Germany for war "within four years" against the economic advice of the president of the Reichsbank and minister of economics, Hjalmar Schacht; Rudolf Hess was deputy leader of the NSDAP until his bizarre mission to Britain in 1941, when he was captured in an unauthorized attempt to broker peace; Martin Bormann headed the Nazi Party Chancellery; Albert Speer, later to represent himself as an essentially apolitical architect, put his professional skills in service of enhancing Nazi displays of power and building the vision of a megalomaniac new Germany—all these and many others, whose names were to become infamous in one way or another, put their energies into designing and constructing the new Reich.

Physical violence sanctioned by the regime was plain for all to see. The official view and the perception of Nazi supporters at this time was that state-sponsored violence was reimposing "law and order" on the streets and clearing Germany of "undesirables." Hitler's rule was sustained at first by the notorious thugs of the brown-shirted SA (the paramilitary storm troopers, or Sturmabteilung), who were officially demoted after the massacre of its leadership in late June 1934, including its leader, Ernst Röhm, in what is often termed "the night of the long knives." The black-shirted elite troops of the SS (protection squad, or Schutzstaffel) under Himmler became increasingly powerful. So too did the ever more subservient police forces, including the State Secret Police, or Gestapo (Geheime Staatspolizei), supported by an expanding network of camps and detention centers in which potential and real opponents were incarcerated. This apparatus of terror also benefitted from the participation of ordinary citizens who used the new apparatus of power for their own ends, denouncing misfits and informing on nonconformists to the Gestapo and others in authority.

Right from the start there were so-called wild concentration camps—variously located in cellars, houses, stockades surrounded by barbed wire, and public buildings all over Germany—soon followed by the first of the major Nazi concentration camps in Dachau, near Munich, which opened to considerable publicity in March 1933. Many others were to follow, including not only the relatively well-known concentration camps but also a large number of sub-camps and also sometimes relatively short-lived centers of detention.[5] Incarceration served a variety of purposes: punishment, deterrence, destruction of opposition, removal of the "unwanted" from society, and the attempted "reform" of a few.

Following an early wave of terror, primarily directed against socialists, communists, and other political opponents, the early concentration camps started to empty out. In the mid-1930s, it was increasingly prisons rather than concentration camps that were used to incarcerate political and social "undesirables" alongside ordinary criminals. From the late 1930s onward, the concentration camp system began to expand again, encompassing an ever-wider range of groups. These institutions—hallmarks of terror in the Third Reich—continued to be used for political purposes and constituted an ever more valuable source of cheap labor for the SS and German industry. As we shall see, during the war a select few were established purely as dedicated killing sites.

This expanding system of institutionalized violence was not tucked away out of sight of the German people. The major camps were well known, and generally situated close to major areas of population and production. Conveniently located on the S-Bahn line running north out of Berlin, Sachsenhausen was set up when Himmler took over as Reichsführer SS in 1936, replacing the Oranienburg camp that had functioned in the town from 1933 to 1934. Buchenwald, situated amid the woods up on the Ettersberg hill overlooking the town of Weimar, renowned for its associations with

Goethe and Schiller as well as later the Bauhaus school of design, was opened in 1937. Construction began in 1938 for Ravensbrück, which was opened in May 1939 for women and young people, although later some men were also associated with the labor camps there. Ravensbrück was located near a relatively small town, Fürstenberg, with a number of enterprises and training grounds in the vicinity as well as a direct railway line to Berlin (passing Oranienburg on the way). On the outskirts of the major port city of Hamburg, Neuengamme was established in 1938 as a sub-camp of Sachsenhausen, and in 1940 it became a concentration camp in its own right. Following the annexation (Anschluss) of Austria in 1938, the camp of Mauthausen was established near the town of Linz—where Hitler had attended school and sought to pursue art studies—and became the center of an expansive network of camps exploiting nearby granite quarries.

All these camps housed a wide range of groups—political prisoners, Jehovah's Witnesses, homosexuals, "asocials," and others—for purposes of punishment, in some cases supposed "re-education," and labor exploitation. Despite brutal treatment, inadequate rations, and high mortality rates, the camps built in the Reich in the 1930s were not designed for the purpose of extermination—an aim that was to develop only later, in the specialized centers of killing in the east.

This system embodied and made visible the distinctions between persecutors and persecuted, as people were stripped of individuality and had new identities imposed upon them. By the later 1930s, structures and practices had developed that we now associate almost automatically with the camp system. Prisoners were made to wear the classic striped clothing and were categorized into different groups, designated with color-coded triangles, and treated differently according to category.[6] Gay men, wearing a pink triangle, fared worse than, for example, Jehovah's Witnesses with purple triangles or political prisoners with red triangles; they received even less food, were put on harsher work details, and were more likely to be subjected to "medical" experiments than other prisoners. Ostracized, isolated, and widely jeered at by many other inmates, they also did not enjoy much by way of solidarity or help from other prisoners. One estimate is that the death rate among gay men in concentration camps was around 60 percent, almost double the death rate of Jehovah's Witnesses, at 35 percent.[7] "Habitual criminals," wearing green triangles, were often co-opted as assistants in the camp scheme of oppression, becoming Kapos ("overseers") or petty functionaries in the hierarchy of brutality. A heterogeneous category of "asocials," which might include prostitutes, "vagrants," "Gypsies," and lesbians who had been convicted under some other pretext, wore black triangles. Jews, wearing a yellow star, were always at the bottom of the heap. Even so, they did not initially constitute the principal group of prisoners, but they suddenly swelled the ranks of inmates with the mass arrests and imprisonment of adult Jewish males following what became known as Kristallnacht, or the "night of broken glass" on November 9–10, 1938.

Banks and financial institutions as well as industrial enterprises worked together to finance the construction of camps. This system of oppression and exploitation was established well before the massive expansion in the wartime years of prisoner numbers, the exponential growth in the network of concentration camps and labor sub-camps across the Reich, and the construction of the notorious death camps in the east. Those Germans who later claimed ignorance seem to have overlooked the repression and inhumanity that were so evident all around them already, even in the peacetime years, and well before Auschwitz was even conceived. They also underestimated the extent to which their own behaviors contributed to the exclusion and isolation of the persecuted.

Peacetime Persecution

The almost arbitrary nature of arrests, periodic imprisonment, and persecution was evident with rampant terror against political opponents of Nazism from the outset. For some groups it worsened considerably from the mid-1930s onward, with Nazi policies both rooted in and exacerbating pre-existing social prejudices.

For much of the prewar period, Nazi policies to achieve a "Jew-free" Germany were directed at removal of Jews from prominent positions in state service and public life, reduction in their status and standard of living, progressive isolation from the rest of German society, and eventually removal from German soil—but not as yet removal from life itself. The Law for the Restoration of a Professional Civil Service excluded people with Jewish ancestry from a wide range of professional employment; the Nuremberg Laws of 1935 gave them second-class citizenship; the radicalization of anti-Jewish measures in 1938, with the confiscation of assets and forced "Aryanization" of property and businesses, the humiliating insertion of the capital "J" on passports and insertion of "Sara" and "Israel" as new middle names, as well as further reductions in freedom of movement, intrinsically affected their identities and reduced their capacity for physical survival.

By this time, people of Jewish descent in Germany were already socially isolated, ostracized by fellow citizens. But many of them—particularly members of the older generation, and those who considered themselves first and foremost German—did not want to leave their homeland. The violence of November 9–10, 1938, with organized arson attacks on synagogues and smashing of Jewish property, as well as the sheer physical and mental exhaustion of those Jewish men who were released after several weeks of incarceration, dealt a final blow to former hopes of weathering the storm and gave further urgency to desperate attempts to gain the necessary visas, affidavits, and material means to emigrate.

Kristallnacht was not, as Goebbels sought to portray it, a "spontaneous" outburst of the people's wrath. But large numbers of Germans were indeed active participants in this state-sponsored outburst of violence—whether through the SA, the Hitler Youth, school groups brought to assist, or people out to pilfer what they could.[8] Others, however, were shocked at violence. As the Berlin journalist Ruth Andreas-Friedrich noted in her diary on Friday, November 11, 1938: "While the SS was raging, innumerable fellow Germans were ready to die of pity and shame."[9] Andreas-Friedrich recorded carefully in her diary the escalating persecution of Berlin's Jewish population and along with a few others tried to protect Jewish friends and acquaintances. Few could imagine at this time that things could get much worse—but astute observers such as Andreas-Friedrich and like-minded souls were clear about the criminality and inhumanity of the regime's policies of persecution well before the war's outbreak.

For Jews in Austria, the Third Reich came suddenly with the annexation of Austria and its incorporation into the Reich in March 1938. Rapidly losing their jobs, status, and livelihood, forced to engage in degrading public rituals such as scrubbing the streets on their knees while surrounded by jeering crowds, Austrian Jews received a radical, rapid introduction to the excesses of Nazi brutality. Antisemitism was widespread in Austria even before the Anschluss, and this seems to have made the establishment of Nazi rule far easier than the convenient later myth of having been "Hitler's first victim" would suggest.[10] Despite (or perhaps also because of) the extraordinary contributions to European culture and intellectual life made by prominent Austrians of Jewish descent—including the psychoanalyst Sigmund Freud, the composer Gustav Mahler, philosopher Ludwig Wittgenstein, writers

such as Arthur Schnitzler and Stefan Zweig, and so many others—and despite
(or perhaps also because of) the fact that the small minority of Austrians
who were of Jewish rather than Christian heritage were to be found across
all walks of life and not only prominent in the major professions or financial
circles, many Austrians harbored antisemitic resentments. These were readily
fomented and played upon by politicians at times of economic and political
uncertainty, as in the period following the First World War and again in the
economic depression of the late 1920s and early 1930s, and prejudices were
possibly made even worse when the Austrian government of the mid-1930s
attempted to ensure some measure of protection against discrimination.

Following the Anschluss, Austrian Jews were afflicted by fright and terror
and thrown into what one Austrian of mixed descent called a general "pan-
demonium of psychic confusion," having to face a far more sudden incur-
sion into their lives than what German Jews had experienced since 1933.[11]
Many people, including non-Jewish Austrians, were shocked into an
apathetic "dull rigidity" in the face of the "almost superhuman strain of
the situation."[12] This strain affected even the most intimate of personal relationships, as society began to split apart. Miriam A., for example, was an
American married to a non-Jewish Austrian, who up until now had many
Jewish friends. Writing in 1940, she vividly recalled the sudden "sense of
insecurity, of horror, of walking in a nightmare," as Jewish friends of hers
committed suicide. But her husband simply began to accommodate himself
to the new regime—which precipitated the breakup of their marriage and
prompted her own return to the United States.[13] Meanwhile, innumerable
other Austrians went wild with public displays of enthusiasm. In Austria, as
in Germany, there were significant generational differences. As Miriam A.
commented: "It was disheartening to hear so much dissimilitude and always
from older people. The young seemed welded into a homogeneous, swash-
buckling, heroic Wagnerian group, ready and willing to follow Hitler wherever he might lead."[14]

Jews were not the only group to suffer. Roma and Sinti had long been
subjected to suspicion and exclusion from German society. When the Nazis
intensified discriminatory policies, it would appear that most Germans were
indifferent to the fate of those they called "Gypsies"; many even approved
of Nazi measures.[15] There were perhaps thirty thousand people of Roma
and Sinti descent living in Germany and Austria, of whom it is estimated
under 10 percent were "pure" Gypsies and most of whom were products of
"interracial" marriages. The definition was frequently in terms of lifestyle,

although the Nazis characteristically engaged in classifying people according to the extent to which they were deemed to be "mixed race" (Mischlinge,
with the category varying according to the number of grandparents who
were Gypsies) and distinguishing further those not of Gypsy descent but
who led the same itinerant lifestyle, curiously categorized as "NZ" (for
Nicht Zigeuner, or "Not Gypsy"), simultaneously condemning them for their
lifestyle and exonerating them with regard to "race."[16] In the course of the
1930s, Gypsies living nomadically in caravans were concentrated in small
urban camps. In July 1936, as part of the "cleansing" of Berlin prior to the
Olympic Games, local Roma were sent to a camp opened up in the north
Berlin suburb of Marzahn, located next to a cemetery. By 1938, many Roma
and Sinti from across Germany were in concentration camps, where they
were classed as "asocial."[17] In December 1938 Himmler issued an order for
"combatting the Gypsy plague," and, as in other areas of "racial" policy,
measures against this persecuted minority began to intensify.[18]

   Himmler's attitudes toward homosexuality also informed the development of more draconian policies over time. Paragraph 175 of the German
Criminal Code already outlawed sexual relations between men. In the early
twentieth century, and particularly during the 1920s, more progressive views
on homosexuality began to develop, spearheaded by social reformers such
as Magnus Hirschfeld, a clinician and founding director of the Institute
for Sexual Research in Berlin. Hirschfeld appeared in a remarkable 1919
film, *Anders als die Andern* ("Other than the others," generally translated as
"Different from the others").[19] Starring Conrad Veidt, this film was one of
the very first to portray sympathetically the difficulties faced by gay men
and the challenges of "coming out" at this time. The protagonist, losing both
his lover and his career, eventually commits suicide. Hirschfeld's institute
was visited by, among others, Christopher Isherwood, whose novels have
informed the popular imagination of Berlin at the time of the rise of the
Nazis. But, as with so many other developments in Weimar Germany, progressive views on homosexuality rapidly fell victim to the Nazi control of
the state. The institute itself was closed when Hitler came to power, and a
clampdown on the gay scene soon followed.

   Changes in legislation were effected over the following years.[20] In 1935,
Paragraph 175 was extended to include any display of affection between two
men, however minimal; a further decree proposed compulsory sterilization,
including castration. In 1936 Himmler made a speech saying homosexuality
must be "eliminated." Those who had served their prison sentences were

now often sent, on release from prison, straight to a concentration camp for "reform," which in many cases actually meant being worked to death. Capital punishment for homosexuality was imposed in 1942 and applied above all in the armed forces. Himmler's personal doctor, Felix Kersten, noted in his diary on November 10, 1940, a discussion that he and Himmler had held regarding a particular case of a blond, blue-eyed gay SS man whom Himmler had hoped would be able to "keep his word and reform his behavior" but who had failed to change his nature. According to Kersten's account, for Himmler there was "only one answer: further degradation, expulsion from the SS, a prison sentence and finally the concentration camp."[21] Himmler allegedly went on to say: "We mean to get rid of homosexuals root and branch," seeing them as "a danger to national health." In Himmler's view, the Nazis could not "permit such a danger to the country; the homosexuals must be entirely eliminated." When Kersten tried to rebut these views, Himmler responded that "that's quite enough," and added: "They're repugnant to me with their womanish attitudes and behaviour."[22]

Against the background of these attitudes at the top, and given a prevalent homophobia in the wider society, gay men faced grim prospects under Nazi rule. Like Jews, they began to notice the changed atmosphere very early on—as did fellow citizens, in a period in which new divisions were introduced, former social bonds began to disintegrate, and members of previously integrated communities drifted apart. Hildegard Wolf, for example, was an "Aryan" who had married a Jewish husband in 1931, never having thought much about whether, as fellow Germans, Jews were different from Protestants or Catholics.[23] Already in 1933 her husband was experiencing pressures on his business and discussed whether they should leave the country. He was considerably older than she was and had already witnessed German atrocities in Belgium in the First World War. Following a walking tour in 1936 in the Harz Mountains where they had met truly "obnoxious" Nazis, he commented that he knew "how cruel" the Germans could be and decided, "Now I've had it." In the meantime, during the long process of making arrangements for emigration, they continued to run their department store on Berlin's central street, Unter den Linden. One day, the sister of a homosexual Jewish employee came to tell them that "the Nazis" had gone to a well-known gay nightclub and arrested all the young men and sent them to concentration camps. This particular employee, according to Hildegard, was eventually released and returned to work with them "but was so frightened he didn't tell us one word about what had happened," and he "looked awful." Others too who returned from concentration camps at this time were hesitant to talk. Increasingly, Hildegard—who stuck by her husband, unlike some of her acquaintances who terminated their "mixed" marriages—became isolated from former "Aryan" friends and began to feel more at home among the Jewish circles who still welcomed them. Hildegard and her husband were eventually able to emigrate. What happened to the gay employee we do not know from Hildegard's account.

Jehovah's Witnesses (termed "Bible students," or *Bibelforscher* in German) also began to experience discrimination from the start of the regime, with growing oppression from the mid-1930s. Elisabeth Dirks, for example, recalls how she spent her childhood in Saxony.[24] She remembers how her father, a convinced Jehovah's Witness, was arrested almost immediately after Hitler came to power. "Right from the word go," Elisabeth recalled, they were "badly treated." Arrested and held for brief periods before release, Elisabeth's father was rearrested four times in the early years of the regime and forced to do hard labor in a nearby stone quarry. Elisabeth remembered the last time she saw him, in 1936, when the Gestapo stormed in "and at pistol point arrested my father." He responded, "You can put your gun away and I'll come peacefully." Her mother too was subsequently arrested, as she was taking her children to stay with their grandparents. Put on trial, Elisabeth's mother was sentenced to two and half years in prison for her religious beliefs. Elisabeth's father was taken to Sachsenhausen, where he repeatedly refused to renounce his faith. He was given the opportunity to sign papers that would have allowed his release but stood by his principles; one of his fellow prisoners, another Jehovah's Witness, did sign and, just as he walked out of the concentration camp, was shot in the back. Elisabeth's mother did eventually sign the papers to secure her release, because, according to Elisabeth, she wanted to see her children "so desperately." But, Elisabeth felt, her mother "felt guilty until the day she died." Elisabeth's father was never released, and he died in prison.

Of Jewish descent, Ernest Platz was a political opponent of Nazism. Although his experiences are extreme, Platz was an astute observer, and his account, given in an interview in 1956 in Melbourne, Australia, is illuminating.[25] When the Nazis came to power, Platz was living in Berlin and working as a journalist for trade union papers, as well as doing some sports reporting for a midday newspaper. Married to a non-Jewish woman, he was a member of the Social Democratic Party, banned in 1933. In September 1933 a dentist denounced Platz as a "communist" and a Jew. He was arrested and held in the provisional SA prison at Berlin's Papestrasse, close to a trans-port intersection now known as Südkreuz. The screams of prisoners tor-tured here were heard daily by passersby.[26] Maltreatment of opponents of Nazism in this prison still concerned relatives decades later: Gisela Faust, for example, a redoubtable Quaker who had provided assistance to Jews and participated in organizing the Kindertransport (helping Jewish children to emigrate), still talked late in life about her husband's experiences in Papestrasse.[27] Here, Platz underwent brutal interrogations, leaving him with permanent kidney damage. Incarcerated in a basement, a dark warren of rooms with crumbling plaster, brick walls, and pipework, Platz was not alone. He estimated that there were around seven hundred fellow prisoners, primar-ily political: cellmates included other SPD members, members of the German Communist Party (KPD), former functionaries of the Catholic Centre Party (Zentrum) and of the German People's Party (Deutsche Volkspartei), even Wehrmacht officers.

Released in February 1934, Platz had difficulty gaining further work as a journalist. In 1935 he obtained employment with the Jewish League of Culture and applied to the Aid Association for Jews in Germany (Hilfsverein der Juden in Deutschland) for assistance in emigration. The reply was less than helpful. Since the nonreligious Platz was married to a non-Jew, the Jewish Aid Association asserted, "We have to help Jews first of all!"[28] Platz was arrested again twice and now held in the Gestapo prison at Columbia-Haus, next to Tempelhof Airport, alongside about a thousand others, mostly not Jewish.[29] Willing to go to Shanghai, Platz once more sought to emi-grate, but the Jewish Aid Association again refused help. By now suffering severe kidney damage from maltreatment in prison, Platz managed at least to obtain medical treatment without payment. Meanwhile, his flat had been searched and all his books confiscated. His wife had to report to the Office for Racial Affairs (Rassenamt) and was pressured to get a divorce; this she refused, despite being threatened with concentration camp herself.

Arrested again in 1938, Platz was briefly held in Berlin's Police Presidium (Polizeipräsidium), along with around four hundred other prisoners: more than half were categorized as "asocials," including many who were simply unemployed; there were perhaps one hundred "criminals," and around sev-enty were categorized as "politicals," including some Jewish lawyers. From here he was taken to the newly opened concentration camp at Buchenwald. He estimated there were some three thousand prisoners, mostly socialists or communists, while some were from the Center Party; there were also about thirty Jews, a few gay men, and some individuals who had tried to escape Germany illegally. Around thirty of the new arrivals were killed, including a "half-Jew" who had fought back when beaten by an SS man and was trampled to death and a young Gypsy who was held over a block, crying out "Jesus, Maria, help, help!," and beaten until he died. The SS fostered competition between the "politicals" and the "criminals" over control of internal administration. The politicals had an underground organization, meeting at night, which encouraged Platz to exacerbate a wound in order to be relieved from heavy labor duties. Then he was tasked with keeping a tally of deaths to establish an accurate count over a period of months. In the end Platz was among a handful from his transport to be released before war broke out. He managed eventually to leave for Shanghai after all, where a significant German Jewish colony developed, and thence traveled on to Australia.[30]

Toward a "National Community"

After the war, it was highly convenient—not only for those who had also been complicit in Nazi rule but also more widely—to focus attention on prominent individuals at the top, as well as the all too evident forces of repression. In the International Military Tribunal and subsequent proceedings under the auspices of the Allies—widely known as the Nuremberg Trials—it helped to concentrate attention on selected individuals, constructing cases with reference to prominent people rather than attempting the impossible task of being exhaustive. But the circles of those who made mass murder possible were wider than the few who came into the public or legal spotlight.

The work of leading Nazis was made infinitely easier by varying combinations of support, complicity, acquiescence, accommodation, or capitulation among those who, for whatever reasons, did not engage in courageous acts of resistance or organized opposition. These ever-changing shades of involvement with the Nazi regime—on an emotional spectrum ranging from enthusiasm through passivity and grumbling to fright and terror—are hard to capture with any precision. But in view of the longer-term sense of continuing unease about this past, it is important to register how people got caught up in what might be termed a "bystander society."[31]

The Nazi ideal of a "national community," or *Volksgemeinschaft*, defined in terms of a "healthy racial" community, was never realized; it is clear that social, economic, political, religious, regional, and other divisions remained highly significant. But merely to establish that this term is better used to refer to an ideological goal and ideal rather than as an analytic tool for historians is in itself insufficient.[32] The idea of a "national community" attracted some people more than others; but many were caught up in events that fostered a sense of belonging and often engaged in behaviors in everyday life that in effect, even if not in intention, served to further the exclusion of those designated as unwanted. During the peacetime years, people were complicit in practices that laid the foundations for more extreme policies in wartime. This included learning who was included in the new "national community," and identifying and isolating the excluded.

Invidious labels were introduced, whether or not the individuals affected accepted such an identity. Many Germans, for example, only registered now that they had Jewish connections or were of Jewish descent—even if only partially, back in their grandparents' generation—and were therefore excluded from professional roles; they soon realized that imposed labels do not always map neatly onto self-designations or sense of identity. But the imposition of discriminatory labels made a massive difference to their lives.

For those who were not excluded, things changed in other ways. Hitler's coming to power coincided with—and aided, but did not directly cause—an economic upswing after the depths of the Depression had been reached and passed in the summer and autumn of 1932. With economic recovery, assisted by work creation schemes related in part to Nazi rearmament policies, many people who had suffered unemployment were brought back into work. Others found new optimism and purpose, as Germany appeared to be reclaiming a sense of national greatness at last, following defeat in 1918, the humiliation of the Treaty of Versailles, and the upheavals of the Weimar years. Some found new sources of fulfilment, or even small bases of power and authority, through membership in Nazi organizations or participation in state-organized activities. In an increasingly Nazified state, many joined affiliated organizations and enacted displays of fervor for the Führer. Enthusiasm was whipped up by Hitler's well-rehearsed performances and public speeches, culminating in the annual staging of mass support at the Nuremberg Party rallies, captured and aesthetically magnified in dramatic film footage by Leni Riefenstahl. However constructed such events were, the effects on crowds rallied to provide a public display of support was noted by numerous contemporary observers, such as the American journalist William Shirer.[33] And many who had not themselves been victims of persecution later remembered the peacetime period of the Third Reich as being among the best years of their lives.

Evaluations of popular opinion and "mood" reports, produced by Nazi authorities or anti-regime groups such as the Sopade (the SPD, or Social Democratic Party in exile) and other left-wing sources, reveal some general tendencies.[34] There were generational as well as political differences in the ways in which people negotiated the Nazi regime. Younger generations were particularly likely to see new opportunities; older Germans already committed to other views were less easily persuaded to change their colors, although many kept their grumbling to themselves.[35]

It is clear from contemporary sources that a degree of enacting new kinds of self-presentation was involved, as people explored the parameters of the new regime and "tried on" new identities. Even committed Nazis, such as an enthusiastic Nazi party member and minor functionary in Brunswick whom I shall call Herr Lorenz (not his real name), were aware of the learning curve among contemporaries and the consequent need to "grasp what we have to do or not do," as Lorenz wrote in a series of letters to former neighbors who had moved to another town.[36] These letters between Lorenz and his friends interestingly document a shift from a sense of newness to habit, evidenced even in the form of final greetings before signature. The previous standard form of friendly greetings or best wishes changes for the first time in a letter of September 22, 1935, to " 'Heil Hitler,' " curiously marked at this point by quotation marks. The Hitler greeting continues to be placed in quotation marks for a full two years, up until a letter of September 12, 1937, when it is for the first time adopted without any indication of innovation or distancing. From then on, it is taken for granted as the standard way to sign off, without any apparent self-consciousness about it.

In a small way, this signifies wider processes at work in German society over these years. Many adults were aware of the new pressures and social expectations and fell into line one way or another. Some actively seized opportunities to behave in ways that would gain them professional, social, or economic advantages. But not everyone who demonstrated enthusiastic commitment to the new Nazi society did so for reasons of career or personal profit. Some were motivated more by fear of the consequences if they were seen as real or potential "enemies of the national community." This included people who had previously been involved in left-wing politics and were only too well aware of the political terror that had been unleashed on socialists and communists in the early weeks of 1933. Gerhard Mazowsky, for example, was a Jewish German who recalled how some of his former friends no longer "dared" to meet him or other Jewish friends "openly," and they had to "take the strongest possible precautions" not to be seen together.[37]

Far more widespread, however, was simple conformity, under awareness of the new pressures and concerns. Such conformity included dropping what were now awkward friendships in ways that barely affected the "Aryan" side of the friendship but were often deeply painful for the increasingly socially isolated Jewish side. For many people this conformity was rooted in fear of social opprobrium and ostracism, fear of being called epithets such as "servant of the Jews" (*Judenknecht*), rather than fear of significant penalties. It took considerable personal commitment and courage to stick with friends, and indeed also intimate partners, across the newly introduced racial barriers, and not everyone was up to the challenge.

Alongside these exclusionary practices, many were tempted by the attractions of belonging to a community that had an apparently more effervescent, energetic form of expression than had been evident in preceding years. Personal documents of the time exude an at times almost euphoric sense of "building up" a new society. Herr Lorenz, for example, was not only donning the new language of "Heil Hitler" in signing off his letters. He had quite clearly fully internalized the goals and vision of the national community. His letters not only update his former neighbors with personal news of family members and mutual friends but also give accounts of political events and express sentiments about broader developments. And in his letters of the 1930s there is a sense of real excitement. He wrote, for example, on December 22, 1935, of the ways in which there was "everywhere life and activity [*überall Leben und Treiben*], work and more work." He went on: "And what about us? We are part of it [*mit dabei*]—and that is nice!"[38] Again in a letter of February 16, 1936, following ecstatic comments about the successes of the Winter Relief charity (Winterhilfswerk), in which one of his sons was very active, Lorenz again exclaimed, "Everywhere there is life and activity!"[39]

Even people who were not as committed as Lorenz could be on occasion attracted—sometimes to their own consternation—by the temptation of belonging to a community of this sort. This was particularly evident on occasions when there was an orchestrated audience for Nazi displays of belonging. Elisabeth B., for example, was a teenager who came from a staunchly anti-Nazi family. In an essay written at the age of twenty-one in 1940, at a time when she was working as an au pair in the United States, Elisabeth B. recalled how even she had on a couple of occasions unexpectedly experienced the potential attractions of belonging to a national community that was awash with enthusiasm. In 1935, while still at school in Bonn, Elisabeth B. and her classmates had been made to stand and wait for Göring to pass through in a motorcade, at which point they had to wave flags. Despite being utterly opposed to Nazism, Elisabeth B. was surprised to find herself positively affected by the enthusiasm demonstrated by the crowds on the occasion: "Although I kept my lips tightly closed together, somehow I was caught up in the frenzy."[40] She had a similar experience when she found herself among the schoolgirls who were selected to go to watch the Olympics in Berlin in 1936. At first, she was impressed at how unenthusiastic and non-Nazi many Berliners appeared to be, in contrast to people in her hometown.[41] But she was then shocked by her own reactions when, invited to a big festival on Berlin's Pfaueninsel (Peacock Island) at the Wannsee, she was given the opportunity to meet Goebbels personally. She records how, "quite mechanically, just like the others, I spoke with Dr. Goebbels, laughed with him, and shook his hand." Writing from the United States, at a critical distance from Germany, she went on: "It is still a mystery to me today as to how I could bring myself to do this."[42]

Elisabeth B. appears however to have had some understanding for her brother's enthusiasm for the community spirit he experienced in the course of doing Reich labor service by assisting with the harvest in Bavaria. One of her aunts was furious with her brother for his glowing report of his time there, and in the course of the discussion stormed out of the room in anger. But, as Elisabeth B. reflected, "Would life be bearable for a young person if he only saw the negative side of things in life? Mustn't young people look for their own way?"[43]

Unlike so many others of her generation, Elisabeth B. managed to remain resistant to the attempted co-option of young people. Despite strong pressure to join the League of German Maidens (Bund deutscher Mädel, BDM) in order to be allowed to take the high school graduation exams, the *Abitur*, Elisabeth B. refused; she was nevertheless able to take and pass the exam. She was clearly not someone who simply uncritically took the notion of community that was offered to her. Yet even so, her own experience of labor service turned out to be curiously similar to that of her brother. She felt that she initially simply "stopped thinking" for herself or seeing herself as an individual, but just as part of a "mass."[44] She was reduced to what she describes as a "mechanic state." It took her quite a while to realize that she was still an individual who could make a difference, and not just a "cog in a machine" who "carried out the often senseless orders and commands" with which the girls in her group were overwhelmed.[45]

There were many different ways in which individuals negotiated the new roles, demands, and challenges they faced. Some retained a greater sense of inner distance than others, and a few were clearly fully engaged. Whether willingly or otherwise, many people went along with the exclusion of outcast fellow citizens from German society, breaking off friendships, sacking or demoting Jewish colleagues, changing the family doctor from a Jewish to an "Aryan" physician, recategorizing fellow human beings under the "racial" terms of the Nazi worldview, and isolating former friends, neighbors, and acquaintances who no longer fitted in. While not all were genuinely enthusiastic, the majority found it easier to go along with the crowd, variously to cheer or to jeer along with the herd, rather than risk being themselves the object of violence or exclusion.

Some chose to go even further, taking the initiative in ways that went beyond anything that might be required. Melita Maschmann's published memoirs, written in the early 1960s in the form of letters to a former friend, present less an example of what was supposedly typical at the time for girls of her age and class—as they are often presented—than a later attempt at self-justification by someone who had stood out in her group for her active support of the Nazi regime. Maschmann's close friends, Marianne and Gabriele ("Rele") Schweitzer, were of a very different persuasion. Before 1933 they had not been aware that they had any Jewish heritage. Growing up in a Protestant family, attending good high schools in Berlin, they led typical middle-class lives with a wide range of friends. But shortly after Hitler's appointment as chancellor, the Schweitzers' father, a medical doctor, called his daughters into his study and told them he was Jewish by descent, a fact about his family background that had now become relevant in a way it had never previously been. Within the next few years, Marianne found her relationship with Melita Maschmann permanently altered. As a result of Maschmann's eventual betrayal, Rele and her boyfriend, Hans, both active in a political opposition group at the time, were arrested and incarcerated, with long-term consequences for their health and well-being.

In her later account, Maschmann claimed to have been intoxicated with the vision of building a new "national community," effectively blinded by the ideology and aspirations of the Nazi movement and adulation of charismatic local leaders.[46] This later strategy of self-exoneration through the effective abdication of responsibility—blinded, intoxicated—was frequently to be found among those who had been compromised by their attitudes and actions under the Nazi regime. The growing separation between communities, initiated by the breaking or downright betrayal of friendships, had long emotional repercussions in the postwar decades, as we shall see.

People who held formal roles also put Nazi prejudices into everyday practice in ways going well beyond what was actually required of them. Lotte Simon was a "half-Jew" (Mischling) who speaks for many when she recounts her experiences of being forced out of school a year before being able to take the *Abitur*, being refused entry to a place in an more vocational alternative establishment, and eventually being deported to a forced labor camp along with "criminals" and other outcasts. As Lotte summarized the situation, "The measures of the Third Reich went way beyond the laws, edicts, and decrees concerning Mischlinge"; in her experience, "first degree Mischlinge were exposed to this sort of 'special treatment' to a high degree."[47]

Actions on the ground often went far beyond what was stipulated by policy directives, and in the process German society was radically transformed. The exclusion of people and the disruption of their lives and aspirations was a form of largely hidden violence sustained by the behavior of the vast majority of fellow citizens. Those who later professed that they had "known nothing about it" were already learning to turn a blind eye to inhumanity and injustice. Whether this arose from conviction, complicity in pursuit of personal advantages, or unwilling or even terrified capitulation to what was perceived as inevitable varied greatly from person to person and over time; but in the process a society formed that was, for the most part, prepared to stand by as others became the primary targets of persecution.

Even if the Nazi vision of a "national community" was never realized to its full extent in reality, a bystander society developed—a society in which people increasingly turned a blind eye to the violence and inhumanity of a system that, in everyday life, they themselves helped to enact and sustain.

The Parting of the Ways: Expulsion and Emigration

Many Jews sought desperately to emigrate while it was still possible, before the enforced (and entirely unforeseen) deportations of wartime. But even in peacetime, as Nazi policies became more radical, some were expelled from Germany against their will. In October 1938, Jews of Polish nationality who were resident in Germany and their families, including German spouses and children, were rounded up, arrested, and deported over the border into Poland, where they were left to fend for themselves.

Irene Eber, for example, was born in Halle in 1930 and spent a relatively happy childhood there, living in a spacious apartment close to many relatives of her mother, who had grown up in a large family in the nearby town of Leipzig.[48] Things began to change in the mid-1930s, with the 1935 Nuremberg Laws forbidding employment of a much-loved resident German maid, and Irene suffering antisemitic attacks at school. But the most dramatic change in the family's circumstances came in 1938, when Irene was nine years old. Following a night in a prison cell in Halle and a train journey expelling them to the Polish border, the family spent a terrifying night between the German authorities on one side, who refused to let them back into Germany, and the Polish guards on the other, who refused to allow them into Poland. Eventually, they were able to make their way across southern Poland to Mielec, the town from which Irene's father, Yedidia Geminder, had originally come. Here, they made a far more cramped home with their Polish relatives. At first, Irene settled in relatively easily, picking up fluent Polish and Yiddish and attending school. But this new life was not to last long; within less than a year, Germany invaded Poland, inaugurating the Second World War. The Jewish community of Mielec, along with Jewish communities across Poland, was almost entirely destroyed. Only around one in ten Jewish children in Europe would survive—and Irene Eber was one of those few.

The forcible expulsion of "Polish" Jews from Germany created enormous misery and suffering for those involved; and it was an incident related to this expulsion that had provided the immediate pretext and publicity cover for a significant turning point in Nazi policies. A young Jewish man by the name of Herschel Grynszpan, born in Germany to Polish Jewish parents but living with his uncle in Paris, was so distressed that he resorted to desperate measures. On November 7, 1938, Grynszpan presented himself at the German embassy in Paris; hoping for an audience with the ambassador, he was greeted by a more junior colleague, Ernst vom Rath. Grynszpan fired at the unfortunate vom Rath, fatally wounding him; vom Rath died two days later, on November 9. Goebbels, who had been agitating for some time, saw this as a perfect opportunity to unleash the well-orchestrated night of attacks on Jewish synagogues, property, and persons, presented in his propaganda as the supposedly spontaneous outburst of the people's fury.

For many, Kristallnacht proved to be a turning point. Among German Jews, it precipitated a last anguished wave of attempts to emigrate. One who succeeded in emigrating was a young lawyer by the name of Hans Ludwig Oettinger (born Jacobson), who, orphaned as a child, had taken on his aunt's name. Although he had lost his legal career because of the antisemitic laws, he managed to keep a job in Germany up to this point; arrested after Kristallnacht, Oettinger was released after a period of weeks and managed in 1939 to escape to Britain. Here, he changed his name to Henry Ormond. Like Fritz Bauer, Ormond returned after the war to his native country determined to fight for justice for the victims of persecution, combatting those defending Nazis in the courtrooms.[49] The desire for reckoning was born well before the later opportunities for practice.

Refugees in many ways reshaped the new cultures in which they settled, and a few significantly affected the public face of the societies into which they immigrated. No comprehensive account of modernist architecture in the United States or developments in critical social theory, or arts and culture more generally, can overlook the influence of émigrés from Nazi Germany. But most immigrants, and particularly those who had survived persecution in Europe and left only after the end of the war, simply sought to integrate into the new societies by attracting as little attention as possible.

Some prewar refugees returned to Germany after the war and had a major impact on how the legacies of Nazi persecution were later dealt with. Among those who escaped was a young lawyer by the name of Fritz Bauer. Born in 1903 in a Jewish family in Stuttgart, Bauer became a committed socialist and was active in the SPD. He was arrested in May 1933 for his oppositional activities and was taken, along with socialist colleagues, including later SPD leader Kurt Schumacher, to Heuberg in southwestern Germany, one of the early concentration camps. Released from camp but dismissed from his professional post—doubly condemned as both socialist and Jewish, and rumored also to be gay—Bauer emigrated to Denmark in 1935; when, during the war, this too was no longer safe, Bauer managed to leave for Sweden in 1943. Here, he joined forces with, among others, a young man going by the name of Willy Brandt; born in 1913 as Herbert Frahm, the illegitimate son of a Lübeck shop assistant, Brandt was now in exile for his political activities. These two were, after the defeat of Nazism, at the forefront of challenges to the politics of the past in West Germany: Bauer, from 1956 district attorney in Hessen, spearheading the pursuit of former Nazis through the courts; Brandt, as West Berlin city mayor from

1957 to 1966, then in the coalition government from 1966 to 1969, and finally as chancellor from 1969 to 1974, leading the way in a crucial period of national change. It was individuals such as these who effectively changed the face of West Germany after their return, often with considerable difficulty in face of obstruction by fellow citizens who had gone along with Hitler. In postwar East Germany, it was predominantly communists, such as Walter Ulbricht, who had spent the war years in Moscow, who formed the ruling party and government after 1945, backed by Soviet power, crushing opposition to radical change.

Those who were able to muster the material means and emotional energy to seek a new life tended to be young; older German Jews often maintained until too late that Germany was their home and they would stay put. A few managed to survive "underground"—perhaps around 1,500 in Berlin—assisted by friends, acquaintances, and committed opponents of Nazism and reliant on a combination of quick wits, material resources, resilience, and sheer chance, as vividly depicted in the accounts of Marie Jalowicz Simon or Inge Deutschkron.[50] A small number adopted more radical strategies, including working as informers for the Gestapo and betraying fellow Jews in hiding, in the generally deluded hope that this would gain advantages for themselves and help to save their own families, as in the case of the notorious informer Stella Goldschlag (often known by her married name of Kübler).[51] Those who were able neither to get out nor to hide were, from the autumn of 1941, deported to the east.

In the course of the Nazi regime, a chasm was created between those on the side of the persecutors and those targeted for persecution. During the peacetime years of Hitler's rule, the victims were people living within the borders of the "old" German Reich, and from 1938 also Austria. There was widespread complicity and collusion in the stigmatization and exclusion of fellow citizens from the Nazi "national community" during these years.

Germans who later claimed that they had "known nothing about it" effectively sustained a cognitive gap, making no connection between the all too evident violence of the peacetime years and the more camouflaged persecution, exploitation, and murder, even within the Reich, during wartime. Later claims to innocence through alleged lack of knowledge of "it"—generally meaning organized mass murder, sometimes even only the gas chambers— were rooted in an extraordinarily narrow definition of what was held to be truly evil, failing to recognize the system of collective violence that had been constructed from the outset of Nazi rule. Yet awareness not only of wartime atrocities but also of prior complicity lies behind a defensive unease on the part of the perpetrator community and a pervasive sense of shame among members of subsequent generations.

In the process, communities were increasingly divided along lines both introduced from above and enacted in everyday life, as people accommodated themselves to the Nazi regime. Within this system of collective violence, many people were too frightened or simply unable to act; most went along with, and some actively benefited from, the discomfort and exclusion of others; and a few eventually became involved in more concentrated nodes of brutality and terror. And the Jews were not the first victims of a systematic program of organized murder instigated on German soil.

3

Institutionalized Murder

The institutions and specialized techniques of extermination did not start
in the forests of Poland under cover of wartime. Organized killing of
civilians began at home, in the heart of the Reich, before the war even began.
The first systematic program of mass murder, with the construction of dedicated killing facilities, was targeted not against Jews but against those deemed
to be "life unworthy of living"—or, in another ghastly Nazi phrase, "useless
eaters" (*unnütze Esser*), euphemistically framed as eugenic "euthanasia."[1] And
most of the victims of this first round of mass murder were German citizens
who were excluded from the Nazi conception of a "healthy national community" not on grounds of "race" but because of mental and physical disabilities.

The numbers murdered—a few hundred thousand in total—were eventually overshadowed by the millions engulfed by Nazi violence across
Europe, including the attempted extermination of all of Europe's Jews. The
reasons for killing were also different, with pragmatic considerations added
to eugenic theories and closely linked to warfare. But the euthanasia program was significant in paving the way for what was to come.[2] It offers
insights into the mentalities and practices that turned some Germans into
murderers and many more into accomplices to murder. Far wider circles
were tainted by knowledge on which they had not been able to act or were
troubled by the issues the Nazis explicitly raised and the murderous practices that they sought and failed to keep secret. The initial attempts even to
soften up opinion and persuade people of the alleged need to deal with
a self-made "problem" are also striking.

"Life Unworthy of Living"

In the spring of 1935, sixteen-year-old Elisabeth B., whose family was
opposed to Nazism, went with her school class from Bonn on a trip to Bad

Kreuznach, a picturesque town situated among hills around the Nahe River close to where it flows into the Rhine.[3] Her mother had been extremely upset when Hitler was appointed chancellor in 1933, and Elisabeth B. was now relieved to be attending the Bonn school, where she felt the atmosphere was less politically pressured than it had been in her previous school. She recalled how at her earlier school, when Hitler and Hindenburg were competing for the role of president in the summer of 1932, support for one or the other of these candidates had been sufficient to divide the schoolgirls and determine friendship groups or enmity.[4] Antisemitism had been evident among the teachers, and the few Jewish students had soon left the school. Following her family's move to Bonn in the summer of 1934, Elisabeth B. felt that the atmosphere was far freer. Girls in her new school did not rush to join the League of German Maidens (BDM), as they had done in her previous school, and only two of her teachers appeared to be convinced or enthusiastic Nazis. Yet the school trip to Bad Kreuznach in 1935 demonstrated just how Nazism appeared to be seeping into educational institutions and preparing the ground for what was to come.

It was a three-week school trip, and no Jewish girls were allowed to come along. On arrival at their lodgings in a youth hostel, the girls were assigned their beds and had to hand in their pocket money, which would then be issued to them in instalments as time went by. Elisabeth B., writing in 1940, recalled that "one suddenly felt as though one was just a number, and that any personal life ceased in this period."[5] There were many trips and visits undertaken as part of the educational program. Bad Kreuznach is famed for its Roman ruins, its centrality in the wine-growing area around the Nahe, its spa and thermal baths, and its many historical houses, including an early-sixteenth-century house alleged to be the former home of the alchemist Dr. Faust, made famous in Goethe's *Faust*. It would seem that there were plenty of sites for rewarding educational visits. Yet the one that appears to have had the most impact on Elisabeth B. was a rather unusual trip, to what she calls a large "nervous and insane asylum" (*Nerven- und Irrenanstalt*).

The visit to the "insane asylum" left a big impression on Elisabeth B. There were many girls kept there, whom she describes as "half crazy, physically crooked [*verwachsen*], malformed." One girl "with a disfigured, glazed expression" called out "Heil Hitler" to the visitors; the others "concurred with grunts." Elisabeth noted how Nazism had penetrated even into this place of supposed "seclusion from the world" and was occupying the inmates' "crazy minds."[6] It was, although Elisabeth B. could not yet know this, not the only way in which Nazism was to affect the lives of these and other mental patients. Far worse was to come in the following years. And the ground for accepting what was to come was being prepared among the German population at this time, including among Elisabeth B.'s schoolmates.

When they returned to the youth hostel, a "vigorous discussion" developed. They touched on what she called the "hereditary health laws" (*Erbgesundheitsgesetze*), referring to the Law for the Prevention of Unhealthy Offspring, introduced in July 1933, which entailed compulsory sterilization of people suffering from a range of conditions, from schizophrenia and epilepsy to alcoholism. The girls discussed this in the light of having seen the "insane asylum" patients that day. Elisabeth B. recalls that the question was explicitly raised: "Was it right to keep these creatures alive, to take space away from other, healthy human beings?"[7] The teacher, perhaps unsurprisingly, expressed more radical views than the pupils about how best to "solve" the "problem" of these "creatures."[8] In this, Elisabeth B.'s teacher was at this time far from alone.

We do not know from Elisabeth B.'s account precisely which institution they visited: it may well have been Eichberg, situated a little over thirty miles from Bad Kreuznach. At this clinic worked, from January 1936, a doctor by the name of Friedrich Mennecke, who in 1939 was promoted to chief doctor and director of the Institute. He was typical of many medical professionals at the time who had jumped on the Nazi bandwagon and were beginning to think about putting into proactive practice the radical ideas that had already been in the air for some time. As we shall see, he is notable less for anything particularly distinctive about his own contribution—he was one of a large team of ideologically driven Nazi medical professionals who became involved in the killing process—than for the fact that he wrote detailed and almost daily letters home to his wife, providing evidence of both his mindset and his procedures, and that after the war his wife did not, as requested, succeed in destroying all these letters in time.

Nor was Elisabeth B.'s class the only one to be given a guided tour of a psychiatric institute. Others too were at this time being exposed to what was increasingly openly constructed as a problem requiring a more radical solution than therapeutic or palliative care. Whether through propaganda images, mathematics teaching in schools, or visits to care homes, people were urged to confront arguments about balancing the intrinsic value of individual human lives against the overall costs to the wider community of their upkeep. The experience of the compulsory sterilization program suggested that patient welfare and psychological well-being was ever less of a consideration for the medical profession involved. In this context, the maltreatment of other patients became increasingly thinkable, paving the way for systematic murder. By the autumn of 1939, Hermann Pfannmüller, director of the Eglfing-Haar clinic near Munich, was even prepared to brag openly about causing the death by enforced starvation of disabled children. This was achieved by progressive reduction of their rations—a treatment that was in his view preferable to the quicker method of lethal injections, since it was less likely to attract adverse attention or foreign publicity than outright killing.[9]

There were mixed reactions to what was being said ever more openly by those individuals who apparently had little if any sense of crossing an ethical boundary. In the Weimar Republic there had already been a legal and medical discussion forming a supposedly scientific background to Hitler's euthanasia program. In 1920, two professors based in Leipzig and Freiburg, respectively, Karl Binding and Alfred Hoche, had co-authored a book entitled *Die Freigabe der Vernichtung lebensunwerten Lebens* (Permitting the destruction of life unworthy of living).[10] In this they posed the question: Should the premature termination of life be permissible only in cases of suicide, where an individual freely chooses to end his or her own life; or should it be extended to permit the legal killing of other people, and if so, to what extent? This question was very much in the air at the time, but Binding and Hoche were not without critics. One of their most vociferous opponents was Dr. Ewald Meltzer, director of the Katharinenhof care home in Grosshennersdorf and chief medical officer in Saxony.[11] He emphasized the intrinsic value of human life; the Christian virtue of caring for the weak, sick, and disabled; and the ways in which children with disabilities could still enjoy a quality of life and were entitled to appropriate care. He was also of the view that emotional ties would so strongly bind parents to their children, however disabled, that they would be of the same view. In pursuit of his case, in the autumn of 1920 Meltzer carried out a survey of two hundred parents and guardians of mentally disabled children, posing a series of questions concerning the conditions under which they might consent to a "shortening" of the lives of their children. Relevant circumstances that were suggested included the supposed "incurability" of the child's mental health, as attested by experts; the eventuality that parents or guardians would themselves no longer be personally able to care for the child, as in the case of their own demise; and the question of whether the child was in pain. To Meltzer's surprise, 162 of the two hundred questionnaires were returned, and of these nearly three-quarters (73 percent) of respondents expressed themselves in favor of the killing of children under certain conditions, while barely more than a quarter (27 percent) were opposed. This finding—where parental will was still enshrined as central to any decision about the child's fate—perversely gave further credibility to the suggestions in the tract by Binding and Hoche and was later picked up by Nazi proponents of euthanasia.[12]

But parental will and what might be in the best interests of the child were very far from what Hitler had in mind. The "euthanasia" program that developed in the Third Reich was cloaked in secrecy and buttressed by elaborate means of deception, to keep the knowledge of the fact of murder from the families affected and to lead them to believe that their loved ones had died of natural causes. Right from the outset, this program of mass killing was known to be crossing a significant moral and legal boundary.

Vulnerable Victims and Professional Perpetrators

The euthanasia program proved to be one further and indeed crucial step along the road already embarked upon, from the outset of Hitler's rule, as members of the medical profession shifted attention from individual well-being to the supposed health of the wider community. A release from suffering for a person in unbearable and incurable pain, who has freely chosen to put an end to his or her own life but is physically incapable of carrying this out, underlies the idea of individual euthanasia. But this was not what motivated Hitler. Rather, it was a desire to rid the German "people's community" of individuals whose care was deemed to constitute a burden to state and society. This form of "eugenic" euthanasia, prioritizing the supposed welfare of the community over that of the individual, was very different from the type of libertarian conception of euthanasia that puts an individual's preference for assisted dying at its center.[13]

The attack on people considered neither "normal" nor useful to the health of the nation started with compulsory sterilization in 1933 and was stepped up massively shortly before the war, when the murder of disabled children began. Hitler had already discussed this topic with a senior Nazi physician, Dr. Gerhard Wagner, at the Nuremberg Rally in 1935.[14] He was, however, wary of explicitly introducing anything so evidently likely to arouse public outrage and adverse foreign publicity in peacetime.

Probably prompted by official encouragement, in 1938–39 some parents of children with congenital deformities and developmental problems sent in details to the Führer's Chancellery (Kanzlei des Führers, KdF), with requests for "mercy killings" to be brought to Hitler's personal attention. In 1938 petitions were also sent in requesting some form of assisted dying for very ill patients.[15] By early 1939, the first notable case was under consideration: Gerhard Herbert Kretschmar, long known by the pseudonym of "Knauer," who was born blind and with missing limbs. This infant was being treated in the Leipzig University Clinic under the care of Professor Werner Catel, who was a strong supporter of "euthanasia."[16] The case was brought to the attention of Hitler, whose own personal physician, Dr. Karl Brandt, traveled to Leipzig to provide an assessment of the child's condition. Following this visit, Catel was told by Brandt on Hitler's instructions that the child could be killed without fearing any legal consequences. Brandt, or Catel, or possibly one of their colleagues—the details remain uncertain—duly murdered the child on July 25, 1939, and the causes of death were deliberately obfuscated. This case opened the floodgates to a program of mass murder that, while personally ordered and sanctioned by Hitler, never actually became legal.[17]

A systematic program for killing disabled children was agreed to in principle in May 1939, when a cover organization, officially named the Reich Committee for the Scientific Registration of Serious Hereditary and Congenital Diseases and shortened to Reich Committee (Reichsausschuss), was established.[18] The first targets were children, and a process for registering newborn babies and young children under the age of three with birth defects including Down syndrome, congenital blindness, missing limbs, or head deformities was established. The killing of young children was later extended to older children and teenagers. During July and August 1939 Brandt and Philipp Bouhler, who was head of the Führer's Chancellery, also started discussing adult euthanasia with Hitler. Here the key criterion was productivity, or lack of it; and when subsequently carers and medical personnel were asked to classify the extent to which a patient was fit for work, they often mistakenly underestimated the fitness for work of the individual, in the hope that they would be spared hard labor and initially unaware of the fact that this was condemning the patient to an early death. It was only later that the character of the intended "treatment" of such people became well known.

It was clear from the outset that this policy could not be made public; the aims had nothing to do with the relief of individual suffering and everything to do with supposedly racial, political, and economic considerations, including savings on institutional staff and care costs. Hitler appears to have been waiting for the outbreak of war in the hope that public attention would be otherwise occupied and he would have less to fear by way of potential opposition on the part of influential individuals or institutions such as the churches.[19] In the meantime, a group of medical professionals were carefully selected on the basis of their likely agreement with the program. Bouhler invited some fifteen to twenty doctors to Berlin to discuss details, explaining this would free up bed space for the expected casualties of the forthcoming war. In light of potential adverse publicity, Hitler had decided not to pass a law on the matter at this point, but he wanted to assure the doctors that they would be protected from facing any legal consequences from their participation in the killings.[20]

Even so, Hitler did on this occasion—unlike the later program to exterminate the Jews—put his order in writing. In October 1939, Hitler wrote a short note on his personal notepaper, and not in his capacity as head of state, signed and backdated to September 1 (the day the war started), authorizing the killing of people who were deemed to be suffering from mental or physical disabilities. Hitler's letter, addressed to Brandt and Bouhler, consisted of a simple one-sentence instruction: the two recipients were given the responsibility of spreading the instruction to "certain doctors in such a manner as to ensure that people suffering from what appeared to be incurable illnesses should, on critical judgment of their medical condition, be granted a merciful death."[21]

This order was never legalized: it only had the force of Hitler's personal order, not the force of law. It is significant both as a direct written order to kill, despite the evident illegality of the act, and also, given popular disquiet, in heralding Hitler's unwillingness to commit to paper any future such order when it came to the murder of the Jews. Awareness at the time of the problematic character of this order is evidenced by the fact that even those most committed doctors who became involved in the program at an early stage, such as the young and ambitious Horst Schumann, clearly recall the way in which they were sworn to the utmost secrecy.[22]

Among those who were involved, it was quite clear what was going on. Dr. Hermann Pfannmüller, for example, was the director of the Eglfing-Haar clinic near Munich. In late 1939, Pfannmüller held up in front of invited guests, including psychology students, a starving, emaciated child as an exhibit "like a dead rabbit" and commented "with a knowing expression and a cynical grin" that it would only "take two to three more days" for the child to die. He displayed no evident sense of morality or awareness of wrongdoing. For the visitor who recorded this occasion, the "picture of this fat grinning man, in his fleshy hands the whimpering skeleton, surrounded by other starving children," made a lasting impression.[23]

Moreover, even the legal profession knew about these killings and did not protest against what technically, under the laws obtaining in the Third Reich, still constituted murder. In April 1941, the Reich Ministry of Justice called all attorney generals and presidents of the provincial high courts and appeal courts to a conference in Berlin to inform them about the program. Those present received the news "without protest" and committed themselves "to forward all communications in this matter to the Reich Ministry of Justice."[24]

The euthanasia program came to be known as "T4," after the address where it was based. The program was coordinated from luxurious offices in a turn-of-the-century villa in central Berlin, at Tiergarten Strasse 4. This had formerly been owned by a Jewish businessman, Georg Liebermann (brother of the painter Max Liebermann) and inherited by his son Hans, who had committed suicide in 1938 to avoid deportation to a concentration camp. In 1940, the villa was "Aryanized" and seized from the family. The T4 program was carried out under a cover organization called the Reich Working Group of Sanatoria and Care Homes (Reichsarbeitsgemeinschaft Heil- und Pflegeanstalten). The history and staffing of the euthanasia centers in the Reich prefigures the later development of the death camps in Poland, and people with physical disabilities and mental illnesses were among the first to be murdered not only within the Reich but also in Poland.

Following the outbreak of war in September 1939, experimental killings of psychiatric patients took place in newly occupied areas, initially by shooting them into prepared pits or mass graves. Soon, patients were also killed by gassing with carbon monoxide in specially designed vans that had been built in Sachsenhausen in calculated preparation for murder. SS captain Herbert Lange was put in charge of a special unit, or Sonderkommando, in the Wartheland that specialized in the use of specially designed buses, some of which had the misleading inscription "Kaisers Kaffeegesellschaft" (Emperor's Coffee Company) painted on the outside. In December 1939, for example, patients—the vast majority of them Polish—were taken from the psychiatric hospital in Tiegenhof (now Dziekanka), around 50 kilometers from Posen, and transported for killing.[25] This was a forerunner of the actions of the Lange Commando in Chełmno from December 1941, as described by Szlamek, inaugurating the mass murder of Jews from across Europe.

The first two euthanasia centers in Germany were located at the site of a former prison in Brandenburg, to the west of Berlin, and at a former hospital and care home in Grafeneck in southwestern Germany. Brandenburg was a significant town with good rail and road links to the Reich's capital city. Grafeneck, by contrast, appears to have been chosen because of its relatively remote location amidst rolling Swabian countryside, yet it also had good transport links by road and rail. Originally built in the sixteenth century as a hunting lodge or small castle in what was then the Duchy of Württemberg, by the 1920s it had been acquired by the Samaritan Foundation of the religious "Inner Mission" movement, which established a home for people with disabilities. Typically for the way in which civilian administrations worked together with the Nazi authorities, in October 1939 the Stuttgart regional government forcibly acquired Grafeneck from the Samaritan Foundation and turned it over to the Reich to develop it into the first fixed killing center.

A Stuttgart police officer by the name of Christian Wirth was closely involved in the establishment of Grafeneck. Wirth was also present, with a select group of others, in Brandenburg in January 1940 to witness the first use of gas to kill people. The converted room in Brandenburg had not yet had dummy showerheads installed, and the gas came in through holes in pipes around the walls with no pretense of water, so "patients" were told they were to be given "inhalation" treatment and should breathe deeply. This experiment included a crude comparison with other means of killing that were found to be less effective.[26] Following further experience in other euthanasia centers, Wirth eventually became the first commandant of the Chełmno death camp in the Wartheland (often referred to as the Warthegau), and subsequently became inspector of the "Operation Reinhard" extermination camps of Bełżec, Sobibór, and Treblinka in eastern Poland. Others observing the Brandenburg gassing included Brandt and Bouhler, to whom Hitler had addressed his original note entrusting them with putting the program into effect, and a number of senior bureaucrats, chemists, and physicians. One of the doctors present was Horst Schumann, who led operations at Grafeneck from January to April 1940. Later, following a stint in the Sonnenstein clinic at Pirna, he relocated to Auschwitz, where he carried out horrendous and frequently fatal sterilization experiments on prisoners.

The deadly use of gas in Brandenburg was deemed successful, inaugurating the killing program; it was first put into effect in Grafeneck on January

18, 1940, in a gas chamber installed in a garage amidst the other buildings. The Brandenburg experience also highlighted the need for disguise, and this not only for the "patients" who were to be kept compliant by believing they were only going for a shower. As Brandenburg began to routinize the killing operation, the signs that something untoward was going on became evident to the local population. The cremation of bodies, with smoke and flames rising into the sky over the center of town, began to occasion popular concern and unwelcome publicity. While the gassings continued in the specially designed "shower room," the ovens were closed and bodies were sent at nighttime in a post office van to a building on the outskirts of town where they could be burned without attracting so much public attention.

In September 1940 Brandenburg was closed down as a center for the region around Berlin and replaced by Bernburg, a mental hospital in a small town slightly further south. It was still relatively convenient for Berlin and northern and central areas of Germany, with good rail links via the town of Dessau. Members of staff were transferred under the direction of SS-Obersturmführer Dr. Irmfried Eberl, an Austrian psychiatrist. In the summer of 1942, following a stint at Chełmno, Eberl became a short-lived commandant of Treblinka extermination camp, the only medical doctor to hold such a position.

The operations at Grafeneck were, like those of Brandenburg, closed down and relocated within less than a year of starting operations, for reasons that remain unclear. It was possibly because of adverse public attention in the locality. Despite Grafeneck's relatively remote location and the official concern that operations should be secret, the repeated arrival of gray buses full of patients—far too many people to be accommodated as residents—began to create gossip among the local population, and no doubt off-duty staff also chattered too loudly in the nearest inn. But this does not seem to have been a decisive reason, given the apparent insignificance of visibility and the proximity of onlookers in the choice of the next site. It was also perhaps because the "feeder" nursing homes of Baden-Württemberg had already been largely emptied out and patients now needed to be brought in from far further afield. Although some patients were sent in from care homes in neighboring Bavaria and Hesse, this small and isolated rural spot on the borders of the Black Forest was very far from the populous areas of northern and northwestern Germany. In December 1940, by which time 10,654 people had been murdered on the site, Grafeneck was closed down, and a new killing center was found in a large mental hospital and care home in the Hessian town of Hadamar.

Located in hilly countryside north of Frankfurt, close to Limburg and the Lahn River, Hadamar was a small town with good transport links to the areas of central and northern Germany, with the industrial conurbations of Frankfurt and the Ruhr area, from which Grafeneck had been rather distant. Atop a hill named the Mönchberg after the religious foundation located there, the state "house of correction" of Hadamar had been founded in 1883 for the "re-education" through work of recently released prisoners, local indigents, and homeless people. In 1906 it added care of the mentally ill to its functions, and from 1920 it became a dedicated sanatorium and mental asylum. By the late 1920s it was a serious psychiatric institution. Perched on top of the hill, the institution overlooked the town and could easily be seen by townspeople, but this seems to have played little role in the choice of site. Some gestures were made to maintaining secrecy around the details of the killing process. A large wooden garage was constructed around the back of the buildings to house the gray buses on arrival, and a makeshift "corridor" was built between this and the main buildings, so that patients could exit the buses and pass from the garage into the rooms in the main building without being seen by passersby. Once inside, they undressed and were cursorily checked by doctors—largely to establish potentially plausible but spurious "causes of death" to be entered on the death certificates—before being taken downstairs to the gas chamber, from which their bodies were seamlessly taken through to the neighboring crematorium. Between January and August 1941, more than ten thousand people were murdered in the Hadamar gas chamber. Over time, "medical" reasons were progressively displaced by genocide on grounds of "race" and productivity. Victims in Hadamar eventually expanded to include children who were half Jewish, foreign laborers suffering from tuberculosis who were no longer considered to be productive, and mentally ill soldiers and SS officers as well as people who had been so traumatized by air raids and war experiences that they had become mentally unstable.

Keeping these activities out of sight did not mean they remained secret. The stench of burning bodies and the ashes were in the air over the town, and rumors of what was going on spread rapidly among the local population. As one former care assistant at Hadamar recalled in 1948, during her trial, "The gassing of those in care was carried out in such a rigorous way that even the population took exception to these measures. It went so far that even schoolchildren threatened each other, when they had been naughty, with the phrase 'You'll go to Hadamar,' which meant, you'll go from life to death, or that they even threatened each quite openly with 'You'll be sent through the chimney in Hadamar.'" Moreover, "because of the burning of innumerable corpses, the air in the vicinity of the institution was contaminated, so that the population turned to the church authorities."[27] There can be little doubt of the wider knowledge of these murderous activities taking place in the midst of German society.

Meanwhile, other regional killing centers were established. Christian Wirth, who had transferred from Grafeneck to Brandenburg, moved again to oversee the construction of gas chambers in the Renaissance castle of Hartheim, situated in idyllic Austrian countryside near the town of Linz, where Hitler had attended school. Hartheim opened for murder in May 1940. It was close not only to Linz but also to the concentration camp at Mauthausen; local railway lines connected these places. In due course the victims at Hartheim included prisoners of war and inmates of Mauthausen who had become too weak to work. In Hartheim, Wirth worked with, among others, the Austrian Franz Stangl. Stangl later became commandant of the Sobibór and Treblinka camps, replacing Eberl—again demonstrating the close relationship between experiences gained in the euthanasia program and later practices in the death camps.

The extermination center at Sonnenstein in Pirna, a little south of the city of Dresden in Saxony, was opened in June 1940, a month after Hartheim. Again secrecy appears to have played no role in the choice of site. Situated in a network of buildings around the fifteenth-century castle, which dominates the charming town of Pirna on a hill rising steeply above the Elbe River, the mental institution that was established in the early nineteenth century had gained a reputation for its progressive and therapeutic approach. This began to alter when Professor Hermann Paul Nitsche was director from 1928 to 1939. Nitsche, who was among those present at the gassing experiment in Brandenburg, was a long-term supporter of eugenic theories and enforced euthanasia, and became a central figure in the organization of the T4 program. When the therapeutic mental hospital was closed down, one of the buildings had a gas chamber and crematorium installed in the basement, with administrative offices and staff quarters in the higher floors. Horst Schumann, who had helped to establish Grafeneck between January and April 1940, now came to direct operations at Pirna. Over the following years some fifteen thousand or so people were gassed here, and often their ashes were simply thrown over the back wall behind the building and down the hillside toward the river.

Since the victims of gassing in these euthanasia centers had friends and relatives who were not themselves targets (unlike increasingly isolated Jews who had no non-Jewish relatives or remaining friends), and since the killing institutes were located in the heart of the Reich (unlike the later extermination camps), large numbers of Germans became aware of these killings. Disquiet began to grow among members of the population. This should not be overstated; even the churches remained largely acquiescent, and some individual churchmen prevaricated about the theological underpinnings or seem to have been more concerned about church property than the intrinsic sanctity of human life. Some did, however, raise their voices in concern, including the Protestant bishop Theophil Wurm of Württemberg.[28] And one senior figure in the Catholic hierarchy who eventually protested to considerable public effect was the politically conservative bishop of Münster, Clemens August Graf von Galen. In July and August 1941 Galen preached a series of outspoken sermons, copies of which were widely circulated; the RAF even printed off further copies and air-dropped them over Germany.

Uneasy about losing popular support, in August 1941 Hitler ordered a halt to the official euthanasia program. But this cessation was neither an end to the killing of the vulnerable in Germany's psychiatric institutions, nor was it necessarily or solely in response to popular protests. Killing of the mentally and physically disabled continued in what was known as "wild" euthanasia—still orchestrated from the center but now carried out in multiple locations, with a wide number of institutions involved in administering death through medical overdoses or starvation.

The expertise gained in gassing was also deployed to new ends As we shall see, the summer of 1941 was a turning point in the east, and specifically in policies toward the large numbers of Jews who had been encountered following the German invasion of the Soviet Union. At precisely the moment that the specialist gassing personnel were no longer required in such numbers within the Reich, Himmler was exploring the deployment of their expertise in killing Jews on the Eastern Front: there, as he discovered during his own visit in August 1941, the mass shooting of Jewish civilians was taking its toll on the killers. Himmler was in search of what he held to be easier methods of killing at one remove, in which face-to-face shooting of naked men, women, and children would no longer be necessary—and the expertise in gassing of the personnel trained up in the T4 program would prove to be invaluable. So the switch was not entirely one of capitulation to popular protests; it can also be seen as in terms of prioritizing the redeployment of professionals to another arena, and against a far larger number of victims.

The gassing facilities of those euthanasia centers still in business were not closed down at this point, but rather repurposed to cover new groups. In the winter of 1941–42, an extension of the T4 program, known as 14f13, involved the selection in concentration camps of prisoners who were too weak or ill to work, or who were proving politically problematic. Jewish prisoners were particularly targeted. Following a perfunctory examination by a doctor— who often only looked for a moment or two at the paperwork—inmates considered unfit for work were sent to one of the institutes to be gassed. A team of experts from the T4 program went around the concentration camps selecting those to be killed, and they appear to have enjoyed these expeditions, which included social aspects. A photograph taken in September 1941 shows six experts who had visited the Dachau concentration camp—including Professor Paul Nitsche, Dr. Friedrich Mennecke, and Dr. Viktor Ratka— enjoying an excursion to the idyllic Starnberger Lake south of Munich, showing little apparent concern for those they had condemned to death.

Selections were carried out quite openly and, despite being presented as a transport of the unwell to better conditions—which initially attracted some hopeful prisoners to sign up voluntarily for what they imagined would be better care and lighter work—quickly aroused suspicions. A political prisoner at the women's camp of Ravensbrück, Margarete Buber-Neumann, describes the first instance there in early 1942, when women "were put into lorries." She and a friend "already suspected the truth," but when, on the following day a "lorry arrived bringing all the personal effects of the sick prisoners, including their triangles with numbers, their toothbrushes and . . . even crutches, an artificial leg and several sets of false teeth," their "suspicions were confirmed."[29] Despite fearful attempts to believe the soothing deceptions offered, Ravensbrück inmates soon could not avoid awareness of the truth. As Buber-Neuman reports, "Sick Transports went off frequently, and with gruesome regularity one lorry returned the next day bringing back all the effects of the sick prisoners." Soon it was the turn not only of the sick: "Hundreds of Jewish prisoners went the same way." Some were even able to get news back of their destination: "One of them arranged to hide a secret message in the seam of her dress. It was found: 'We have been brought to Dessau. Now we have been ordered to strip. Goodbye.'"[30]

This prisoner's mention of Dessau suggests that she was in fact murdered in the gas chambers in the nearby town of Bernburg.

The 14f13 program continued in Bernburg, Sonnenstein, and Hartheim until 1943, by which time more efficient means of killing large numbers had been developed and put into full operation in the east. Hartheim's gas chamber continued in operation—in close cooperation with the neighboring concentration camp of Mauthausen—until December 1944, by now without any input from physicians.

If the gas chambers of euthanasia institutes were occupied with the task of killing the unwanted from concentration camps, it did not mean that people with mental and physical disabilities were safe. With the development of "wild" euthanasia killings, care homes no longer needed to send their patients in the notorious gray buses to the gas chambers of the major centers. They could instead be transferred to institutions near at hand for death by other means. Transfers were helpful to keep relatives at bay, since they were only informed with some delay that a patient had been moved, by which time it would be too late to remove a loved one at risk; but in principle killing could take place anywhere with a willing staff and readily available means and was no longer dependent on the specialist gas chambers. It could also be more readily disguised.

Methods that had already been used in previous years for killing children were now extended to adults: the administration of injections or poisonous doses of sedatives and medications that induced death within a matter of days, and the withdrawal of food from patients placed on special "hunger wards," which took a little longer but was no less deadly in the end. Whether given fatal overdoses of Luminal (phenobarbital) or Veronal (another barbiturate inducing sleepiness) mixed in with food or deliberately starved to death, the intended outcome was murder. Such methods could be used widely, in institutions across and beyond the Reich. Nor were they any less cold-blooded than the gas chambers.

In the Eglfing Haar Munich clinic, for example, Pfannmüller brought together a conference of directors to discuss policies. No longer able to send adults to the gas chambers of Hartheim, he proposed instead a starvation program. He opened two "hunger houses" with four wards—two for men in House 25, two for women in House 22—in which patients were to receive no protein and no fats, subsisting only on small portions of sauerkraut and potatoes until they starved to death. Some 444 people died on these wards before the end of the war.[31] In the children's ward, known as

1BE, children were given Luminal mixed in with their food, causing sleepiness and difficulty in breathing; as their condition progressively worsened and they were no longer able to eat or swallow, medications would be injected until death ensued within a matter of days. Between 1940 and 1945 a total of 322 children were murdered here, of whom 312 were poisoned and the rest starved to death. One of the nurses, Sister Deutlmoser, confessed her actions to the priest responsible for the clinic, Joseph Radecker, and explicitly freed him from the confidentiality of the confessional. Radecker was so disturbed by what he was hearing—and also seeing, when brought in to give last rites to adult patients—that, evading the Gestapo along the way, he risked going in person to report developments to Cardinal Faulhaber, archbishop of Munich. Radecker apparently managed six such secret meetings with Faulhaber, who expressed personal concern at the news—but to no avail.[32]

Some institutions became particularly significant during the later war years. Hadamar extended the groups of those selected to die, including notably children of mixed descent, with Jewish and non-Jewish parentage (Mischlinge), as well as forced laborers who were no longer economically productive. At Tiegenhof in the Wartheland, a specialist children's department was set up under the direction of Ratka, one of the forty listed T4 medical experts, operating from February 1943 until the arrival of the Soviet Army in January 1945. After the war, Ratka moved to West Germany and retired in Baden, where he died, at the age of seventy-one, in 1966.[33]

The psychiatric hospital in Meseritz-Obrawalde became a major center for "wild euthanasia" killings.[34] Situated in a border region of Prussia (formerly Posen/West Prussia, in 1938 reassigned to Pomerania, and now known as Międzyrzecz-Obrzyce in Poland), in 1939 it was a well-functioning sanatorium with nine hundred patients; within less than a year, its size had more than doubled to two thousand patients, many in a very poor physical and mental condition, as people considered unfit to work were sent in from other institutions. Up until 1941, while the T4 program was in full operation, selected patients were transferred out of Meseritz-Obrawalde "to the east" and disappeared. Over the following years, problems of overcrowding and short-staffing became ever worse, with only three physicians on the premises. Meanwhile, a committed Nazi, Walter Grabowski, became director. In the spring of 1943 he told two hospital employees—Dr. Hilde Wernicke and a care nurse, Helene Wieczorek—that a law had been passed saying that all patients with an incurable mental illness must now be released from their suffering. This was of course a euphemism for murder, but one that appears to have given Wernicke the impression she was doing her best for patients in a terrible state. They were, on threat of punishment, to keep absolutely quiet about this order. Apparently Wernicke agreed immediately, while Wieczorek needed three days to think it over. As a qualified doctor, Wernicke was responsible for undertaking a perfunctory check of the medical history and physical state of patients and selecting those to be killed, while Wieczorek assisted the ward nursing staff in administering overdoses of medication. Patients were first given the sedatives Veronal or Luminal, and some were killed outright by overdoses, while others were killed by injections of morphine-scopolamine. The Meseritz-Obrawalde hospital was responsible eventually for perhaps somewhere between a minimum of seven thousand and probably more than ten thousand deaths. The pathologists who entered the hospital at the end of the war put the total at 18,232, although this figure seems implausible.

The Division of Labor and Diffusion of Guilt

The euthanasia program illustrates the division of labor in the murderous system of the Third Reich. A key feature was the distribution of responsibility: no single person need feel that it was he or she who had made the key decision or committed the decisive action resulting in a patient's death.[35] Numerous people were involved: not only those directing from Berlin but also commissions of "experts," doctors, nurses, care workers, secretarial and administrative staff, and transport workers, scattered across the Third Reich. Some of these played a greater role than others, but responsibility for the final decision and action appeared always to lie with someone else—at least in the self-representations these individuals constructed after the war, when trying to justify their involvement as a small cog in the larger killing process.

Teams of experts evaluated cases; doctors filled out medical report forms; professionals made judgments on reports and entered a symbol in a box on the form that led to the selection of patients either for life (marked with a minus sign) or death (a plus sign). Since no single signature alone sufficed, no one need feel fully responsible for the outcome. Other individuals turned on motors or gas taps and monitored the deaths of patients through small windows in the door but later claimed they were only following orders; doctors prescribed lethal doses, but could interpret this simply as necessary sedation, with death merely an unfortunate "side effect" to which disabled people might be particularly susceptible; nurses administered injections or deadly powders with meals, but could see this as simply medication and claim they had no control over dosage. There are many instances, explored further later, of trying to justify participation in these ways; there are relatively few cases where people successfully objected to cooperating in the process.

We can gain an unusual glimpse of this work in the aforementioned letters written by Dr. Friedrich Mennecke to his wife in the winter of 1941–42.[36] His duties took him on an energetic circuit, selecting prisoners from the concentration camps of Sachsenhausen, Dachau, Ravensbrück, and Buchenwald to be sent to their deaths. Away from home for several days at a time, Mennecke wrote frequent and detailed letters to his wife. These letters suggest pride in the speed at which he worked: he reports the precise numbers of prisoners whom he has "examined" each day—and he himself puts the word "examined" in quotation marks, indicating the cynicism with which this "medical" legitimation was treated. Mennecke notes that it was largely a matter of filling up the requisite forms as fast as possible; he could work a little faster with respect to Jewish prisoners than "Aryans," for whom he had to make more of a pretense of a medical checkup. In his letter of November 26, 1941, for example, Mennecke commented: "A total of 1,200 Jews now followed, none of whom had to be 'examined' first, but for whom it was sufficient to take the reasons for arrest (often very extensive!) from the file and copy these over onto the questionnaires."[37] It is in fact extraordinary just how much effort was put into this paperwork, since overall numbers had been decided in advance. In his letters of January 6, 8, and 9, 1942, written during a stint working at Ravensbrück and staying rather comfortably in the nearby town of Fürstenberg, where he appears to have enjoyed particularly good catering, Mennecke commented to his wife on how many prisoners he still had to select to meet the pre-allotted target. In his letter of January 9, 1942, he summarized his new and more efficient method of working at speed: "I will then just go straight to the evaluation and in the process only fish out those I need to see in person for whom things are still not entirely clear even after making the entry. I am sure that in this way there will not be much left to be 'examined.'"[38]

Mennecke's background demonstrates just how easy it was to become a perpetrator by taking the new opportunities offered by the Third Reich. Born in 1904 to a family of modest means, Mennecke appears to have been somewhat lacking in self-confidence. He was initially unable to pursue his dream of studying medicine and started out in marketing and sales. Finally able to pursue medical studies, Mennecke was not an outstanding student and had to repeat a couple of exams, but he eventually gained his degree in April 1934. He had already joined the NSDAP in March 1932 and the SS in May 1932. Financially and psychologically insecure by virtue of both family background and uncertain intellectual mastery of his subject, Mennecke benefited from the boost that the Nazi state gave to his career. He appears to have recorded in such detail his "achievements"—speed in "processing" people for killing—not only because he wanted to keep in touch with his wife about daily activities but also because he wanted to have a written memento of his and the regime's "glory days."[39]

Mennecke was far from alone in his actions, and the individual biographies of killers do not suffice to explain a program organized on this scale. Like so many other aspects of state-sanctioned violence in the Third Reich, the euthanasia program developed in ways that depended on the combination of practical initiatives and ideological commitment on the part of a few and the development of new structures and frameworks of action that required ever more people to fulfill new roles and accommodate themselves to new norms and demands, irrespective of prior views and experiences. It also depended on the complicity or incapacity to act of the many.

Those taking the initiative and running the program were clearly committed individuals. Alongside them were orderlies, nursing staff, carers, and administrators, most of whom seem to have cooperated willingly in the tasks they were set. But some of those involved in the process at the lowest levels had less individual choice in the matter. Menial care assistants, grounds staff, drivers, and other helpers without medical qualifications had little choice in what they were told to do, and some had even gained these roles as part of the Reich Labor Service scheme, without having personally chosen such positions. A couple of examples may be taken of people who were put on trial in East Germany shortly after the war.[40]

Following basic schooling, Erich Paul S. had learned the building trade but was then unemployed in the early 1930s, like so many others. In 1934 he joined the SS, in the hope that this would assist him in finding work. In 1939, he was called up in the more elite SS Death's Head Regiment (Totenkopfstandarte) as a soldier, but was soon wounded and sent home. At first he worked in a prison as a caretaker and watchman, with telephone service duties. He was then sent to work in Bernburg. Erich Paul S. knew that gaining entry to the SS Death's Head Regiment was harder than entering the general SS; but as the East German judge in his postwar trial noted—clearly aware of Erich Paul S.'s intellectual limitations—he had the advantage of exceptional height and physical size. Alongside him as a defendant in the East German courtroom was Erna Sch., the seventh of ten children of a carpenter. She had attended elementary school (*Volksschule*) but had not even completed this basic education because of the family's financial needs; she had been sent out to work at just eleven years old. On December 23, 1940, she was called up by the police president in Berlin and ordered to do compulsory labor service in Bernburg. These two were hardly diehard Nazi ideologues at the forefront of the killing process, although Erich Paul S.'s membership of the SS made him politically more suspect than the ill-educated and entirely apolitical Erna Sch.

What then did these two do that warranted their postwar arrest? Bernburg, having replaced the original killing center of Brandenburg, was specially designed for the purpose: it had more modern showerheads, not just a pipe with holes as in Brandenburg, so it was easier to deceive "patients," and a totally fictive "Dr. Keller"—in actuality Dr. Eberl—signed the death certificates. Disguise was built into the design of the center, and both defendants were explicitly aware of this. Their roles differed somewhat, although both were relatively menial and tangential.

Erich Paul S. was involved in cementing the new building for gassing and building the garages for the gray buses that brought victims to the site. The garage included an internal door to the building with the gas chambers, so that victims were not unloaded in public view. Erich Paul S. was also a handyman and security man in the "Berlin department" at Bernburg, doing repairs, looking after the heating system, and preventing unauthorized people from entering the grounds. He was not involved directly with killing, although he once watched a gassing because, as he put it, he was curious to see "how this sort of thing went on."[41] He does not seem to have queried what was "going on" in any way, although it would be hard to see him as central to the operation.

Erna Sch. had more personal contact with victims: she was a helper tasked with assisting "patients" and accompanying them to their place of death. She was acutely uncomfortable with this role and repeatedly asked to be released from these duties. She protested and cried so much that in April 1941 Dr. Eberl arranged for her to go away for a few weeks, to look after the children of Viktor Brack, who was organizer of the T4 operations and head of Office II in the Führer's Chancellery. In September 1941 Dr. Eberl again arranged for Erna Sch. to find respite by undertaking household duties, this time for Dr. Werner Heyde, a psychiatrist and neurologist who headed the cover organization for the euthanasia institutes. These short breaks did not change the attitude of Erna Sch. to her situation. In order to secure a more permanent escape, she got herself pregnant by a fellow worker, Gerhard Sch., whom she subsequently married, and by whom she later had a second child. At an advanced stage of pregnancy in December 1942, Erna Sch. was finally able to give up her duties. Her new husband died in the war, so by the time of the trial she was a widow with two young children.

There are many similar cases to be found in the trial records; those who were caught up in the machinery of murder at these lower levels were often also those least able to evade the legal net after the war. Their degrees of guilt are hard to define with precision; they were certainly not the type of target one would have expected to be at the top of any juridical hit list, and yet, for their ease of capture, they paid with relatively high sentences—at least in the East German courts in the early years after the war, but less so in the West.

The group of direct perpetrators was relatively small; but far larger numbers were needed to facilitate the administration of different aspects, including organization of the movement of people and disposal of their remains, the processing of finances, files, and letters. Even more knew about what was going on. Complicity in the euthanasia program spread far wider than the legal definition, contributing to a pervasive sense of unease and unwillingness to confront these issues for decades after the war.

Perhaps most problematically, even when it was widely known that gray buses taking patients for "relocation" in another institute would come back with all their clothes and possessions; and even when it was known that large numbers had died at the same time, despite elaborate deception involving death certificates with false information about dates and causes of death, and sometimes also location; and even when rumors about death by enforced starvation and overdoses of medication had spread—even when all of this was a matter of common knowledge, relatives still entrusted members of their families to the "care" of potentially deadly institutions.

This organized killing of vulnerable civilians was widely known during the first two years of the war—a time of foreign policy triumphs—and disturbing reports spread rapidly. Patients in the clinic of Neuruppin in the Brandenburg area, for example, appeared to be dying at a rate that alarmed their families. Some families were concerned that, within a matter of a couple of weeks of the patients' arrival at Neuruppin, they had looked half starved, and shortly thereafter families were informed that their relatives had been moved to another institution and had died of some illness. Even the person in charge of registering deaths and returning urns alleged to contain ashes of relatives to the families, later said that he was surprised at the sheer numbers and knew that something was amiss.[42]

This sort of murder was discussed within families too, if in somewhat guarded terms. Letters to her brother from a woman whose three-year-old child had died in the clinic in Görden, near Brandenburg an der Havel, in July 1942 reveal that while she was away on a short rest cure in Bavaria, her husband had voluntarily handed over their daughter, giving the clinic "full authority" in the knowledge that the little girl would not return. When back from Bavaria, the mother visited her daughter in the clinic; by this time, she "had already become so thin that she was virtually unrecognizable; it hurt me to the depths of my soul." But it was too late: the little girl died three days later, shortly before her fourth birthday. And, as the sequence of letters makes clear, rather than blaming her husband for having knowingly handed over their child, this mother blamed herself for having gone away for a brief recuperation from her caring duties: she felt that it was she herself who "bore the guilt" of her daughter's death. The question of guilt in this family was even more complex: the daughter had been born perfectly healthy but had probably suffered brain damage as a result of a blow to her head by an elder sibling, in a childish fit of rivalry and anger. The story was hushed up and repressed in the family for decades; even when, much later, a member of the family sought to explore this further and wanted to engage in discussion, there was strong resistance on the part of the siblings of the murdered child.[43]

This partially voluntary participation or knowing acquiescence in quiet disposal of an unwanted relative may have been quite widespread, although we have only fragmentary evidence. On occasion, families who could not cope with a mentally or physically disabled relative at home appeared only too keen to have them sent back to an institution. In the case of Henriette, for example, a perhaps well-intentioned doctor appears to have given the family the opportunity to save her: in April 1941, he let her go home for an extended holiday occasioned by a family confirmation ceremony. Henriette's father, however, who had remarried after her mother's death and had repeatedly sought to put her into institutional care even when professionals considered this unnecessary, was not prepared to keep her at home. Just over three months after Henriette was returned to the psychiatric institute, she was taken to her death in Bernburg.[44] We do not know how many victims might have been saved, had families recognized alarm signals and kept their relatives out of institutional care—particularly when given clear indications by concerned personnel to this effect.

Many families could not adequately care for a person with mental or physical disabilities at home and genuinely believed (or persuaded themselves) that institutional care was the best option. Even so, families of victims later had to live with the knowledge of the part they too had played in this tragedy; it is scarcely surprising that relatives subsequently preferred "not to have known" what was going on, when at the time they could have taken action to try to prevent a homicide in the family.

The group of individuals who crossed a moral threshold in the euthanasia program in the Reich in the first two years of the war was relatively small, but those people then went on to spearhead the killing of European Jews on a massively increased scale in the death camps in Poland. Many others involved at lower levels of the euthanasia program were also to transition seamlessly to staff the killing centers of the east. It has been estimated that around five hundred personnel were actively involved in the T4 program from 1939 to 1941. Of these, at least 121 individuals went on in 1941–43 to work in Bełżec, Sobibór, and Treblinka (known as the "Reinhard Camps" after the assassination of SS leader Reinhard Heydrich in 1942). Following the closure of the Reinhard Camps, at least seventy-eight former euthanasia personnel were sent from Poland to the northeastern Italian coast around Trieste, to combat "partisans" and deport Jews during the last two years of the war, alongside others sent directly from the continuing euthanasia program in Germany.[45]

The protests of the German population against the murder of members of their own community had achieved an effect in terminating the organized gassing program in the summer of 1941, at a time when, for other reasons, it suited the Nazi leadership to transfer these experts elsewhere. Popular protests also played a role in removing killing from the public eye; but they neither halted the killing of the disabled nor put a stop to mass murder as a means toward the Nazi vision of a healthy racial community. On the Nazis' own analysis, from the start of the war up to September 1, 1941, more than seventy thousand people were murdered in the six designated killing centers of the official T4 euthanasia program.[46] Probably a further 230,000 "patients" were subsequently killed by enforced starvation, deliberate medical overdoses, fatal injections, and willful neglect.[47]

Even though the T4 killings ultimately amounted to only a tiny proportion of the total death toll of Nazi mass murders of civilians, the euthanasia program had a significance that went way beyond its immediate impact. In its development of mentalities, networks, and specialist expertise, T4 became central to the organized gassing that, alongside systematic starvation and mass shootings, was to characterize the Holocaust. And growing awareness of inhumanity and murder, while turning a blind eye or prioritizing other concerns, became characteristic behavior of the wider bystander society, making the continuation of mass murder possible despite widespread knowledge—knowledge that might later be repressed or denied.

4

Microcosms of Violence

Polish Prisms

From 1938, the German Reich began to expand. The annexation of Austria in March was followed by takeover of the Sudetenland—the western border areas of Czechoslovakia—as agreed by the United Kingdom, France, and Italy in Munich in September. With the loss of its western defenses, the rest of Czechoslovakia was easy prey to German military invasion in March 1939. Emboldened by western appeasement policies and armed with the Ribbentrop pact with the Soviet Union of August 1939 to carve up Poland between them, Hitler orchestrated the invasion of Poland on September 1, 1939. Within a couple of days it was clear that this now meant war in Europe. In the ensuing blitzkrieg, the Germans conquered much of northern and western Europe; and with subsequent expansion to the south and east, Nazi violence was exported to ever-larger areas. Wanton brutality and murder were the hallmark of German policies everywhere, although the peoples of eastern Europe were treated far more harshly than those in the west, and there were variations according to whether defeated states collaborated or were destroyed. It was to take the invasion of the Soviet Union in June 1941 and the involvement of the United States in what became a world war in December 1941 to begin to turn the tide. Even so, it was not until Allied forces had taken over Germany and many of its cities lay in ruins, with Hitler's suicide on April 30, 1945, that the rump German leadership was prepared to agree an unconditional surrender in early May 1945.[1]

Violence and death came in many forms across Nazi-occupied Europe. But it was in Poland that the major ghettos and death camps were situated. And beyond these well-known sites of suffering, there were many other ways in which the Nazis imposed their rule on the subjugated population, and particularly on the Jews.

Small case studies—microcosms of violence—help to illuminate the variety of victim experiences and the ways in which people became perpetrators. By examining a number of small worlds and local experiences, we can begin to understand the multiple tragedies of this era and lay the foundations for exploring its long and complex aftermath.

The Expansion of the Empire of Violence: Poland

The invasion of Poland was marked by organized violence against civilians. It was not only military opponents who were attacked: members of the local intelligentsia, including priests and intellectuals, were rounded up and imprisoned or murdered; and a campaign of terror against Jews was unleashed under the guise of anti-partisan warfare. *Einsatzgruppen*, or special killing squads, rounded up Jews, humiliated and abused them, and burned thousands alive in synagogues, barns, and houses.[2]

The killing squads were replaced, within a matter of weeks, by German civilian government in German-occupied areas of defeated Poland. Borders were redrawn, with the Soviet Union taking over the eastern parts of Poland as agreed under the Molotov-Ribbentrop pact. In the areas ruled by Germany, a rump Polish territory known as the General Government was set up under Hans Frank, while four other regions—eastern Upper Silesia, the Wartheland, Danzig and West Prussia, and areas of northern Poland assigned to East Prussia—were incorporated into an expanded Greater German Reich.[3]

In many areas, Poles had to make way for ethnic Germans brought in as colonizers from the "Old Reich" or brought "home into the Reich" from elsewhere. Some Poles sought advantages by claiming "ethnic German" status, only later to find that this might mean being called up to fight in the German army. Poles were exploited for their labor and subjected to lower rations. Young people were reduced to basic schooling and forbidden to complete secondary or higher education. The idea was to create a subjugated people capable of little more than manual labor for the Germans. Not all gave up the pursuit of learning; some, like the young poet and writer Tadeusz Borowski, were driven underground, continuing to discuss literature and politics among circles of like-minded people. Even this was a dangerous enterprise; following arrest and imprisonment in Warsaw, Borowski was sent like so many other oppositional Poles to Auschwitz.

Polish involvement in German occupation was not unambiguous. The complicated relationship between Christians and Jews in Poland had for centuries been one of official toleration, punctuated by occasional tensions and periodic explosions of violence. Some three and a half million citizens were Jewish, and Poland was home to major centers of Jewish civilization and culture. Not only the "shtetls," small country towns and hamlets, but also large urban centers had significant Jewish populations. Jews were not only rabbis and teachers or small tradesmen and craftsmen; in some cities they were major industrialists, while in rural areas many were impoverished peasant farmers. Some were religious, others assimilated; some socialist, others Zionist; some highly educated and multilingual, others largely paro-chial. The relationships between Christians and Jews were correspondingly multifaceted and complex, and they could change rapidly according to political and economic circumstances.

Under German occupation, pre-existing tensions were exacerbated. In the course of the war, even many liberal Christians who sought to protect their Jewish compatriots began to envisage a future Polish nation that excluded Jews. While some Poles risked their lives to rescue and hide Jews, many others betrayed them or benefited from their distress and deportation. In areas initially under Soviet control, Poles often portrayed Jews as supporters of the Soviet oppressors; once the Germans ousted the Russians in 1941, Poles were often willing to assist in the rounding up, persecution, and even murder of their Jewish neighbors. In the now-notorious case of Jedwabne, in July 1941 groups acting on behalf of roughly half of the village, the Polish gentiles, effectively murdered the other half, the Polish Jews.[4] An initial outbreak of violence was followed, two weeks later, by burning the Jews in a barn that was doused with kerosene and set alight. Germans played a key role in instigating this massacre; but virulent religious antisemitism, com-bined with jealousy and greed, seems to have motivated the local Poles involved. Deep divisions over this incident terrified people across generations, with heated controversies persisting into the twenty-first century.[5]

Other Polish residents who collaborated with the Nazis were ethnic Germans, or *Volksdeutsche*. Some were involved in the "self-protection" (*Selbstschutz*) groups in the early days of the war, fomenting unrest and assisting the Einsatzgruppen and army. Ethnic Germans subsequently became important in local administration, receiving preferential treatment over Poles.

While non-Jewish Poles were treated harshly, Polish Jews fared far worse. They were ousted from their homes, robbed of their livelihoods and possessions, and forced into ever more overcrowded and substandard accommodation, while Germans took over Jewish businesses and shops as well as the better houses and residential areas for themselves.

The first ghetto was established in the small town of Piotrków Trybunalski in October 1939. From spring 1940 onward, ghettoization spread, patchily and with variations.[6] Some ghettos were established to clear Jews out of better areas so that Germans or Poles could move in; a few were means for controlling and confining people and exploiting Jewish labor; others were relatively short-lived "collection points" prior to deportation. Some ran through a series of stages and functions, while others existed only briefly prior to clearance and destruction.[7] Ghettos could be large—amongst which Warsaw was by far the largest—or tiny, as in country towns and villages; they could last a long time, or only briefly, pending "resettlement," the Nazi euphemism for deportation to death. Jews could be exploited for economic production, or left to waste away from enforced malnutrition. They died from disease or starvation; they were hanged for attempting to obtain enough food to stay alive; they fell victim to mass shootings or were shot "while trying to flee." Some ghettos were "open," but the penalties for being found in areas designated as "Jew-free" were massive, and punishment for breaking the rules on curfews or not wearing the Star of David was severe; people risked arrests, beatings, even being shot on the spot. Everywhere, stigmatization meant restrictions on freedom: whether ghettos were open or closed, controls constituted a form of imprisonment. For some newly arrived Germans, imbued with Nazi ideology, the sight of ragged, starving people in the Polish ghettos appeared to confirm what they had previously been told about "eastern Jews."

The two largest ghettos were, respectively, Warsaw, in the General Government, and Łódź—which the Germans renamed Litzmannstadt—in the Wartheland, incorporated within the Greater German Reich. The Łódź ghetto was significant both for the role it played in the beginnings of the mass extermination of the Jews in dedicated killing sites—in this case, the nearby site of Chełmno—and because of the faint hope it embodied for so long of the possibility of survival through work, or "salvation through labor." It was indeed the longest-lasting ghetto; but in the end here too the Jews were deported and the overwhelming majority murdered.

After the war, former concentration camp guards, members of the SS, Gestapo, or ordinary police forces directly involved in killing, were highlighted as "perpetrators." Civilian administrators tended to remain out of the spotlight, and certainly out of the focus of legal prosecutions. But everywhere, they cooperated closely with the forces of repression. This is particularly evident in the history of ghettos. Exploration of just one case, the ghetto in Łódź, reveals the devastating impact of Nazi policies on personal lives.

Concentrating Suffering: Ghettoization in Łódź

In the 1930s, the Jewish population of Łódź was nearly a quarter of a million (some 230,000 to 250,000), according to a prewar census.[8] This figure dropped rapidly after the German invasion, as many Jews fled, and was subsequently around 160,000–170,000. Over the years of the ghetto's existence this figure fluctuated, with losses through disease, starvation, and deportations and periodic additions through arrivals from other areas of Europe, including Hamburg and Berlin, as well as, briefly, Gypsies from the Burgenland area of Austria.

Under the leadership of the Nazi Gauleiter, Arthur Greiser, the "Germanization" of the Wartheland was initially to proceed by expelling unwanted inhabitants (Poles as well as Jews) over the border into the General Government, in order to make way for ethnic Germans to be "resettled" into the expanded Reich. But this plan rapidly failed, and attention shifted to "concentrating" Jews, whether in small ghettos in rural areas or in the large ghetto in Łódź.[9]

The German occupation of Łódź started with typical practices of humiliation. A teenager by the name of Dawid Sierakowiak was on his way to school on Wednesday, October 4, 1939, barely a month after the German invasion. But he did not make it to class; he was seized for forced labor along the way. This was not productive labor but, in a manner similar to the treatment of Viennese Jews in 1938, a means of public degradation. Sierakowiak, an avid diary writer, recorded in his notebook how he was put to work under the supervision of "a single soldier" who brandished "a big stick. Using rude words, he told me to fill puddles with sand." Sierakowiak was deeply humiliated when, looking through the gate, he "saw the happy, smiling mugs of passersby laughing at our misfortune"—bystanders whom he castigated as "stupid, abysmally stupid, foolish blockheads!" With some difficulty, he managed to retain his self-respect: "It's our oppressors who should be ashamed, not us. Humiliation inflicted by force does not humiliate." Even so, he recognized that "anger and hopeless rage tear a man apart when he is forced to do such stupid, shameful, abusive work. Only one response remains: revenge!"[10] But in the Łódź ghetto, which eventually became entirely closed off from the outside world, sealed more completely than any other, conditions were not such as to make revenge possible.[11]

The Nazi district president for the region, Friedrich Übelhör, discussed plans for a Jewish ghetto as early as December 1939. At this time he saw it as a "transitional measure," already considering that "the final aim...must be to burn out entirely this pestilent abscess."[12] In the spring of 1940, Jews were moved from their homes into a run-down, overcrowded, and depressed area of town, Bałuty, where sanitation and facilities left much to be desired.[13] There was some negotiation of borders: German industrialists were loath to move their properties or suffer adverse economic consequences, the Catholic Church was upset that one of its churches would be marooned within the ghetto, and a route had to be organized to the large Jewish cemetery if local gentiles were not to be disturbed by burials of the Jewish dead.

But eventually the borders were fixed and removals underway, and, following the renaming of Łódź as Litzmannstadt in April, by the early summer of 1940 the ghetto was closed off. Its border fences of barbed wire and wood were continually reinforced; wooden bridges were built over thoroughfares dividing one part of the ghetto from another, and spaces were cleared to provide a cordon of uninhabited wasteland between the incarcerated population, portrayed in Nazi propaganda as carriers of disease, and people living in the surrounding areas. One such area of apparent wasteland was the site where Łódź's great synagogue had stood, destroyed by the Nazis in autumn 1939. The ghetto now became completely sealed, its isolation compounded by the confiscation of radios and loss of access to newspapers or independent information from the outside world. But over time, news came in with each set of arrivals.

The man in charge of the Łódź ghetto administration, Hans Biebow, built up a small bureaucracy to govern its operations and oversaw its day-to-day activities, on occasion engaging in physical violence. Biebow also enjoyed, it would appear from photographs, a relaxed and modestly luxurious lifestyle, with delicacies, champagne, and attractive women posing at his side.[14] Biebow's role was crucial: he was the direct point of contact for the Jewish ghetto leadership and determined the parameters of their work and existence. He was instrumental in working with the leader of the Jewish council, Chaim Rumkowski, in developing a "productionist" approach to ghetto life.[15] Once it was clear that Jews had been bled of all their possessions,

Biebow argued that the Jews must be made to work for the German war effort and through their productivity become both self-sustaining and useful—a strategy strongly reinforced by Rumkowski.

Biebow was not the political head of Łódź. Biebow's ultimate superior was the city mayor (*Oberbürgermeister*) of Litzmannstadt. For two crucial years, from May 6, 1941, to August 15, 1943, this position was held by Werner Ventzki, a committed Nazi who had joined the NSDAP in 1931. A trained lawyer who had studied in the universities of Heidelberg, Königsberg, and Greifswald, Ventzki had been involved in political activities on behalf of the NSDAP throughout the 1930s. Once he attained the coveted status of city mayor, Ventzki devoted his energies to "Germanizing" the city, ensuring that its facilities, parks, public buildings, and housing accorded with the modernizing visions of the Reich.[16] A "cultured" member of the professional classes, Ventzki did not pull the trigger of a gun or beat up Jews, but under his watch around sixty thousand people in the ghetto died of starvation—perhaps one-third of the total population. Most of the others were deported to death by gassing, the vast majority in the nearby extermination camp of Chełmno. Toward the end of the war, the last Jews remaining in Łódź were transported to Auschwitz, where the majority perished; only around fifteen thousand survived the war, following death marches to camps in the west. Well over 90 percent of ghetto dwellers had died.

When reading through the reports, diaries, and memoirs of life in the ghetto of Łódź, it seems in retrospect quite extraordinary just how much people assumed, at least in the first couple of years of the ghetto's existence, that this was a phase that they could in some way struggle through, and how much effort they devoted, despite all, to cultural pursuits, education, and preparation for a better future. Dawid Sierakowiak continued to be a model student, top of his class, intensely interested in literature and politics. A keen linguist, in his spare time he devoted himself to literary translations, noting in his diary on Tuesday, July 22, 1941, that he had recently begun translating a poem by Ovid from Latin into Polish and a poem by Saul Czernichowski from Hebrew into Yiddish.[17] Alongside political activities in a youth group, Sierakowiak also engaged in tutoring less gifted students in order to earn some money to help his family augment their insufficient rations.

Nor, despite all, did emotional lives shut down or questions of ethics and morality get screened out. Already knowing that her father had been murdered in Dachau, and suffering chronic hunger and fear in the Łódź ghetto, Lucille Eichengreen (at that time called Cecilia Landau) sought to look after her mother and her younger sister as best she could. But her mother eventually succumbed to starvation; Lucille and her sister had to carry their mother's body across the ghetto to the cemetery and dig a grave in the hard ground to bury her with what dignity they could muster. Later, Lucille's sister, then age eleven, was deported with other children to be gassed at Chełmno—a fate about which Lucille, at the time, was still uncertain. Despite all this and more, Lucille entertained a romantic relationship with an older married man, with whom she was able to share some emotional intimacy and hope; in her memoir, she tells us that even amidst all the pressing concerns of hunger and death in the ghetto, she worried about the morality of this relationship.[18]

For the vast majority of ghetto inhabitants, there was to be no future. And those responsible for their deaths were not always the visible perpetrators, the immediate wielders of violence and brute force, but administrators at one remove. Death by starvation was one way in which perpetrators could later seem entirely unconnected with tragedies that resulted directly from their policies.

We are used to imagining this period through the accounts of survivors, such as Lucille Eichengreen, with stories of escapes, terrifying experiences, lucky moments, and survival strategies. Some try to add a moral to the story, suggesting "lessons" about courage and humanity. The experiences of the vast majority of those who died in the ghetto or were deported to death elsewhere are not so easily captured in these narratives of survival. Some aspects of the lives of ghetto inhabitants were caught in photographs illicitly taken by Henryk Ross, the ghetto's official photographer, who used the camera and film reels with which he was supplied to take far more than just the identity shots and propaganda images the authorities wanted. He ingeniously set up a three-tiered podium in order to take twelve snapshots with one frame, which could subsequently be cut for the individual faces, freeing up the rest of the film reel to capture the miseries of everyday life, privations, and deportations. Knowing that he was risking the lives of himself and his family if discovered, Ross nevertheless persisted in capturing these images, burying the negatives in a secure box that he was able to retrieve from the ground at the end of the war. He wanted, as he put it, to preserve "some record of our tragedy." He "was anticipating the total destruction of Polish Jewry" and "wanted to leave a historical record of our martyrdom."[19]

It is almost unbearable to look at these images and to read the diary entries of those who did not survive but suffered a long, slow decline, succumbing eventually to exhaustion and disease. These deaths too were directly caused by German policies, imposed and implemented by the civilian government and the ghetto administration. Although Biebow was eventually brought to account, the vast majority of those responsible for enforcing segregation and starvation entirely escaped the notice of postwar reckonings, leaving a significant legacy of unresolved feelings of guilt and shame for the generation growing up in their shadow. This was certainly the case for the Jens-Jürgen Ventzki, the son of the former city mayor, who only as an adult learned about his father's role, and whose life was then overshadowed by the need to come to terms with growing knowledge of his father's past.[20]

Death was a daily occurrence in the ghetto. This was noted in reports solicited and collated by Jewish activists in what was termed *The Chronicle of the Łódź Ghetto*.[21] It was also a constant theme in individual diaries. On Tuesday, May 13, 1941, for example, Sierakowiak noted: "A student from the same grade as ours died from hunger and exhaustion yesterday. As a result of his terrible appearance, he was allowed to eat as much soup in school as he wanted, but it didn't help him much; he's the third victim in the class."[22] A couple of days later, on Friday, May 16, 1941, he wrote about his own health. He was "examined by a doctor at school" who, he wrote, "was terrified at how thin I am. She immediately gave me a referral for x rays." He went on to wonder whether some good might come of this: "Perhaps I will now be able to get a double portion of soup in school. In fact, five such soups would be even better, but the two will do me some good, too. In any case, one soup is nothing." But such thoughts did not banish his fears: "The checkup has left me frightened and worried. Lung disease is the latest hit in ghetto fashion; it sweeps people away as much as dysentry and typhus. As for the food, it's worse and worse everywhere; it's been a week since there were any potatoes."[23] Nor did things improve. On Saturday, May 24, 1941, Sierakowiak confided in his diary that he was "damnably hungry because there isn't even a trace left of the small loaf of bread that was supposed to feed me through Tuesday." He knew that he was "not the only one in such a dire situation," but this did little to help: "When I receive my ration of bread, I can hardly control myself and sometime suffer so much from exhaustion that I have to eat whatever food I have, and then my small loaf of bread disappears before the next ration is issued, and my torture grows. But what can I do? There's no help. Our grave will apparently be here."[24] In this prediction, Sierakowiak was sadly to be proved right—and these diary entries were written well before the first deportations to gassing in Chełmno and other sites of extermination.

Tensions over food could tear families apart, as contemporary diaries document only too sadly. One anonymous young Polish Jewish girl, who did not survive the Łódź ghetto and about whom we know very little, recorded in her diary in late February 1942: "Starvation is terrifying. People die like poisoned flies." She pondered: "Will it ever end? I'm sick of life. We live worse than animals. Human life is so miserable, but still one fights for it."[25] On Monday, March 9, 1942, she recorded the wider indifference caused by starvation: "The deportations are still taking place. People are upset, the atmosphere is very tense. The starvation is impossible, people die like flies." Even faced with the deportations, hunger predominated: "It gives me a headache, I can hardly see. The emptiness haunts the apartment. There isn't even a single crumb there or a little coffee." Hunger affected interpersonal relations: "You may fall and nobody will pick you up. A human being is worthless, dozens of them are not important. People are disgusting. Everybody cares only for himself. Recently, I have become so tough that nothing can move me, not even the worst suffering. I learned this from people."[26] Most disturbing to her were the effects within her own family, as she noted on March 10, 1942: "I have no idea why I don't live more harmoniously with my sister. We fight all the time and scream at each other. I must cause my parents a lot of worry. My sister doesn't look well. She is like a stranger to me."[27] The following day she commented: "There is no food, we are going to starve to death. All my teeth ache and I am very hungry. My left leg is frostbitten." She added: "My Mom looks awful, like a shadow." Increasingly, there were fights within her family, mainly over small scraps of food, as when she took a tiny bit of food too early or ate a morsel that she was not entitled to. On this particular day she had an argument with her father, who "started yelling" at her for having "sneaked a spoonful"; she "became very upset and cursed" him; he "stood by the window and cried like a baby." This was a turning point in her family, and she felt terrible about the incident and about herself: "Not even a stranger has ever insulted him before. The whole family witnessed this incident. I went to bed as soon as possible, without dinner. I thought I would die of hunger, because we have our meal only in the evening." This young girl blamed herself, not the Nazis, for this incident: "We would be a happy family, if I didn't fight with everybody. All the fights are started by me. I must be manipulated by some evil force. I would like to be different, but I don't have a strong enough will."[28] In the event, this young diarist did not survive to understand the wider situation and to blame those who were truly responsible for the family's state.

Sierakowiak similarly records a deteriorating relationship with his father. On Monday, May 26, 1941, he wrote about how both his sister and mother cut off bits of their bread rations and gave them to his father. Nevertheless, as Sierakowiak bitterly commented: "He doesn't know, however, how to appreciate it, and his attitude toward them is bad and reveals unmitigated egotism, just as it does toward me."[29] The situation continually worsened. On Sunday, April 19, 1942, Sierakowiak wrote: "Father's true nature revealed itself today. He is becoming more and more crazy.... He just keeps on shouting, annoying everyone at home."[30] On Monday, April 20, 1942, he commented: "Mom can hardly walk, because of her despair. Father stomps about, constantly shouting."[31]

In the end, neither Sierakowiak nor any of his family survived. Along with more than sixty thousand others, Sierakowiak's father died of starvation, despite the extra scraps of food given to him by his wife and daughter; and along with another 130,000 Jews, both Sierakowiak's mother and his sister, Nadzia, were murdered by gassing—his mother in Chełmno and his sister in Auschwitz.[32] Sierakowiak's last diary entry was on Thursday, April 15, 1943: "In the evening I had to prepare food and cook supper, which exhausted me totally. In politics there's absolutely nothing new. Again, out of impatience I feel myself beginning to fall into melancholy. There is really no way out of this for us."[33] Four months later, on August 8, 1943, just two weeks after his nineteenth birthday, Sierakowiak died of starvation, exhaustion, and disease.

There really was "no way out of this" for the vast majority of those caught in the trap of Nazi persecution. For some, the only way to survive appeared to be to enter what would, under supposedly normal circumstances, be considered morally dubious compromises. Ways of negotiating preferential treatment varied with circumstances, and most were in any event doomed ultimately to fail. The vast majority of those who did not succumb to disease and starvation were eventually killed in other ways.

A key turning point for Jews in Łódź, and for hundreds of thousands of others across Europe, came in September 1941. Nazi policy toward Jews in Germany changed, as any possibility of emigration was finally and fatally replaced by visible stigmatization through wearing of the yellow star, leading to ease of separation, round-ups, and deportation. This was evident to anyone in areas with significant populations of German Jewish residents, such as Berlin. The journalist Ruth Andreas-Friedrich, for example, noted in her diary on Friday September 19, 1941, that Jews were now "outlawed, marked as outcasts by a yellow Star of David that each one must wear on the left chest." She was somewhat optimistic about popular responses: "Thank God, the greater part of the people are not pleased with the new decree. Almost everyone we meet is as much ashamed as we." And she downplayed the significance of "the children's jeering," which she felt had "little to do with serious anti-Semitism. There's no great difference between pulling the legs off flies, sticking butterflies on pins, and shouting at Jews." Even so, the long-term significance was clear: "The yellow star makes segregation easier. It lights the way into the darkness—the darkness called the ghetto."[34] From now on, not only from Germany but from all across Nazi-occupied Europe, Jews were transported eastward. In the process, the ghettos became ever more overcrowded, and disease spread among populations weakened by malnutrition. And the authorities now determined that the way to deal with the overcrowding was to select the weakest and those least able to work, in order to dispose of them more rapidly.

Following an influx of Jews from surrounding areas of the Wartheland earlier in the summer, the Łódź ghetto soon received significant numbers of Jews from the west. Between October 16 and November 4, 1941, some twenty thousand Jews arrived in the already starving and overcrowded ghetto, having been deported from Germany, Austria, Bohemia and Moravia, and Luxembourg.[35] The arrival of these Jews, who often brought with them clothes and possessions that were in high demand by the ghetto inhabitants, unsettled the local economy. The increased numbers made it ever more difficult to cope in terms of both food and shelter.

In November 1941, there was a further influx when several thousand Gypsies were sent to Łódź, most from the Burgenland area of Austria. Following an exhausting journey, arriving on several transports over a period of days, they soon fell prey to disease, including the highly infectious typhus. The ghetto chronicle entry of Monday, December 1, 1941, discussed issues around the "interment of the dead in the Gypsy camp." As of that date, 213 burials had already taken place, and "the Department of Burials [was] obliged to send a hearse to the grounds of the Gypsy camp every day no later than 9:00 A.M."[36] But because of growing numbers of deaths, the chronicle recorded, "there are frequently many bodies ready for interment, the hearses now arrive at the camp by six o'clock in the morning."[37] Stronger people were now also beginning to succumb: At first, "the overwhelming majority of the bodies removed from the camp were those of children. It was only toward the end of last month that there were more adults than

children being buried."[38] Within a matter of weeks, the epidemic was affecting others too: on Friday, December 19, 1941, the chronicle noted the
deaths from typhus of Dr. Dubski of Prague, a Jewish doctor who had been
sent in to treat patients there, and also "one of the directors of the local
branch of the German criminal police."[39] Other deaths followed. There
was clearly a high risk of the disease spreading to the surrounding gentile
population.

The idea, already germinating elsewhere, that it might be easiest to
"select" those too weak to engage in productive work and who were likely
to die anyway, soon became reality in Łódź. The spread of disease precipitated the selection of the first deportees to death in the gas vans of Chełmno.

Already on Saturday, December 20, 1941, the chronicle discussed details
of how to choose ten thousand people to be "resettled" out of the ghetto,
out of the original twenty thousand demanded by the authorities.[40] And
among the first groups to be taken on trucks from the ghetto were those
living in the Gypsy camp, deported in their entirety. In the first week of
January 1942, the chronicle recorded that, following further deaths, over a
period of ten days "the 'Gypsies' have been taken away in trucks." The
writer of this report surmised that the "camp, which is practically deserted
now, will no doubt be entirely eliminated by the end of this week. Apparently,
its elimination was dictated by necessity, since there was a danger that the
typhus would spread."[41] These Gypsies were precisely those who ended up
in the gas vans and pits of Chełmno, as described so vividly by Szlamek.

They were not the only ones to be taken. Deportations of the elderly, the
weak, the ill, followed at intervals over the coming months, affecting the
mood of the population. Rumors as to their fate became ever more ominous,
as deportees were no longer allowed to take possessions or provisions with
them, and their clothing and belongings were returned to the ghetto. Those
left in the ghetto were exhorted to work ever harder, despite exhaustion, in
order to prove their usefulness to the Germans in a desperate attempt to stay
alive. Despite the depression that descended on occasions of deportations,
people even began to get used to the sight. As one entry in the chronicle
noted, somewhat self-critically, on April 1, 1942:

> While formerly the processions of emaciated old people and children with
> cadaverous faces made a macabre impression on passersby, now the eye has
> already grown accustomed to seeing spring-carriages pass loaded with people
> who are more dead than alive. Wrapped in rags, barely visible, they lie motion-
> less on the wagons. Their blank gazes fixed on the sky, their faces bloodless and

pale, hold a silent but terrible reproach to those who have remained behind and are bustling anxiously about the ghetto.[42]

And from spring 1942, it was not only Jews from the Łódź ghetto being transported to death; increasingly, from all over Poland and across occupied Europe Jews were being deported to their deaths in Auschwitz and the extermination camps of Bełżec, Sobibór, and Treblinka.

News leaked out, and rumors of these deaths spread far and wide. By late 1942, the foreign press was running reports on mass killings. Censorship affected the extent to which news was explicitly conveyed in the Reich, but the deadly persecution of the Jews was an open secret. Even observers in Berlin, such as Andreas-Friedrich, were not in much doubt about the fate of deportees. On December 2, 1942, she noted in her diary: "The Jews are disappearing in throngs. Ghastly rumors are current about the fate of the evacuees—mass shootings and death by starvation, tortures, and gassings." And it was quite clear to her: "No one could expose himself deliberately to such a risk. Any hide-out is a gift from heaven, salvation in mortal peril."[43] While she and a few courageous others sought to hide Jews and protect them as best they could, the fate of those who had not evaded deportation was more or less sealed. Once they had arrived in the east, if they were not among the few selected for work, there was little most could do to evade death.

And yet many people in the Łódź ghetto still held out hope that at least those capable of work could yet be saved. This was partly due to the character of the ghetto leadership in Łódź.

There were significant differences between the ghettos of Warsaw and Łódź. Some differences were rooted in the contrasting personal attributes of those appointed by the Germans to be leaders of the Jewish councils. One of the most nefarious of Nazi tactics was to use members of the persecuted groups to organize the care, control, and repression of fellow victims, including not only the distribution of welfare—food, medical supplies, housing— but also responsibility for compiling lists of those to be deported. Jewish councils were coerced into unequal "cooperation" with superior German might. They tried in vain to protect at least some members of their community by repeated compromises in an unpredictable but ever-worsening situation, while members of the Jewish militia were deployed to keep other ghetto inhabitants under control. People were either forced or somewhat more willingly entered into compromising roles, dealing with the situation in a variety of ways.

At one end of the spectrum was the well-respected chairman of the Jewish council in Warsaw, Adam Czerniaków, an engineer by prewar profession. Battling with an insoluble and unbearable situation, he was continually plagued by insomnia and excruciating headaches. A teenager, Mary Berg, who kept a diary, had some sympathy for Czerniaków, commenting perceptively that his "position is far from enviable." She continued: "True, Czerniakow often rides in a car to meet with Governor Frank, but each time he returns a broken man. He carries the heavy burden of responsibility for everything that takes place in the ghetto."[44] Czerniaków was caught between conflicting demands, which it was impossible to meet. Mary Berg noted that he often visited the school that she attended, and it was clear even to teenagers such as herself just what an intolerable situation he found himself in, caught as he was between the demands of the Germans and "the complaints and reproaches of the starving, embittered and distrustful population." Berg noted in her diary on April 20, 1941: "He is always clad in black and wears glasses. He has a sharp but mild look. I have never seen him smile; but this is quite natural considering his heavy responsibilities."[45] Czerniaków eventually could no longer bear the strain of witnessing daily deaths or the burden of complicity. As rumors grew that people were being sent to their deaths by gassing (mostly in nearby Treblinka), Czerniaków was called in to discuss deportation quotas on July 22, 1942. He noted in his dairy: "We were told that all the Jews irrespective of sex and age, with certain exceptions, will be deported to the East. By 4 P.M. today a contingent of 6,000 people must be provided. And this (at the minimum) will be the daily quota."[46]

For Czerniaków, the "most tragic dilemma [was] the problem of children in orphanages."[47] On hearing that the children of the orphanage were to be sent to their deaths, Czerniaków committed suicide on July 23, 1942. His last diary entry ran: "It is 3 o'clock. So far 4,000 are ready to go. The orders are that there must be 9,000 by 4 o'clock."[48] He left a note saying that the SS had wanted him to kill the children "with his own hands."[49] In the event, the children were led to their deaths by those in charge of the orphanage, who were killed along with their charges. Mary Berg observed their departure from her window in the Pawiak prison across the road: "Rows of children, holding each other by their little hands, began to walk out of the doorway. There were tiny tots of two or three years among them, while the oldest were perhaps thirteen. Each child carried a little bundle in his hand. All of them wore white aprons. They walked in ranks of two, calm, and even smiling. They had not the slightest foreboding of their fate." The children were accompanied by nurses and one of the doctors and were led by the director of the orphanage, Dr. Janusz Korczak, who had refused the opportunity to escape and remained with his small charges, comforting them to the end.[50]

Leaders in the Warsaw ghetto tried in this way to maintain some semblance of dignity, to exert what very limited agency they still retained, to choose the hour and the manner of their own deaths, to comfort and to soothe others for whom they felt responsible, in face of the inevitably violent fate that they faced.

At the other end of the leadership spectrum from Czerniaków, however, was Mordechai Chaim Rumkowski, a businessman who became head of the Jewish council in Łódź. Rumkowski appeared to enjoy his limited powers and apparently lorded it over the people under his protection. He developed a reputation for self-aggrandizement, even having the ghetto currency named after him (with what was known as the "rumki" replacing the German mark) and riding around in a cart or car when others had to walk. He was not only suspected of favoritism in the distribution of privileges and foodstuffs to his friends and allies, while selecting political opponents for early deportation, but also accused of sexually abusing young people, including children in the orphanages of which he was so proud.[51] In his desperation to save the ghetto through work, Rumkowski collaborated closely with the Germans in selecting the weak, the elderly, and the young for deportations to death. In one of his most controversial speeches, on September 4, 1942, Rumkowski entreated the Jewish population to hand over their children— who were sent to be gassed in nearby Chełmno—in a desperate bid to keep alive those adults who were still capable of working.[52]

These two large ghettos differed not only in leadership styles but also in the differing purposes of ghettoization and the character of the surrounding society in each case. The Łódź ghetto was exploited for its labor; rations were kept low so that ghetto inhabitants would be forced to hand over their possessions, clothing, and jewelry and would also have to engage in work in order to try to stay alive. Provisioning was rationed according to position, with those doing heavy labor or performing significant duties being given more than those without work, who would more rapidly starve to death.[53] The population in the Warsaw ghetto, by contrast, was simply reduced to starvation, with survival only possible through smuggling.

The Łódź ghetto was more perfectly sealed off from the outside world than Warsaw. This was not merely a matter of having no underground sewer system, as in Warsaw, which could function as an illicit transport network for people and goods, but also because of the character of the surrounding population. Located in an area of the expanded Greater German Reich that was being progressively "Germanized," and with a significant local "ethnic German" population, Łódź ghetto inhabitants had far less hope for much by way of assistance in the immediate vicinity if they did by some miracle manage to get out. German visitors to Litzmannstadt, impressed by "Germanization," seem to have been entirely blinded by their ideological presuppositions—at least, as was claimed in the memoirs of Melita Maschmann, who recounts how she managed to suppress her supposedly instinctive sympathy for the plight of starving people, and was able to "see without seeing, hear without hearing."[54]

In contrast to Łódź, productivity for war-related industries was not as significant in Warsaw, and levels of food provisions were even worse; but the Warsaw ghetto was in some respects more porous, making it slightly easier to smuggle food into the ghetto. Despite heavily guarded boundaries and severe penalties for those caught crossing the borders, including being shot on the spot, children were able to find ways in and out, allowing them to smuggle food such as potatoes into the ghetto from the outside, or even to escape and live under cover on the Aryan side.[55]

And it was not only food that could be smuggled into the Warsaw ghetto: some courageous individuals were able also to smuggle in weapons and mount an uprising against the Germans in late April through early May 1943, before the last remnants of the ghetto were entirely annihilated by superior German force. People in the ghetto had long been vulnerable to random acts of physical violence, as members of the SS rode around in rickshaws, randomly shooting into crowds or killing individuals—demonstrations of physical force that were magnified in the periodic round-ups when Jews were taken to the Umschlagplatz for deportations to Treblinka. This violence escalated massively during the weeks of the uprising. Josef Blösche, a low-level member of the SS whose appearance has become familiar through an often reproduced photograph of a deportation including a small boy with his hands up, later recalled that he had only been able to engage in mass shootings by being permanently drunk; the SS canteen ensured a ready supply of strong alcohol at all times for those involved on the perpetrator side.[56] Jürgen Stroop, who was in charge of the obliteration of the ghetto, prepared a lengthy report, with more than fifty photographs, for Himmler. His report gives a vivid depiction of the ways in which

Germans set fire to buildings and shot at those leaping from windows to escape the flames, and how they used gas to expel those hiding in the sewers, shooting them as they emerged from manholes. The ghetto inhabitants, by contrast, were engaged in an existential battle, with both men and women using any weapons they had managed to acquire to wreak maximum damage on the Nazis even in the moment of their own inevitable destruction. Ultimately, Stroop estimated that the Germans had killed at least 56,065 people whose "extermination" could be clearly counted, and many more had died in explosions and fires. The destruction of the Warsaw ghetto ended with blowing up the synagogue on May 16, 1943. In his report, Stroop listed the names of sixteen men who were killed "in service of the Führer and their fatherland" as well as eighty-five men who were seriously wounded.[57]

Going down in an extraordinary struggle for their lives, the Warsaw ghetto fighters earned an enduring place in history for Jewish resistance. But this was not an option open to many. From the perspective of the times, physical resistance against an infinitely better armed and superior enemy could seem suicidal if there were still some hope of salvation through escape, hiding, or productive labor. Between the two extremes of leadership styles evidenced by Czerniaków and Rumkowski could be found innumerable shades of compromise and desperation. The responses of the Jewish councils to an appalling and unprecedented situation in a time of mass extermination precipitated controversies that still resonate today.

For a few short years, Chaim Rumkowski ensured preferential treatment for the Łódź ghetto leadership and officials. But this did not ensure even his own long-term survival: rumor had it that when he had served all useful purposes for the German administration and was eventually deported to Auschwitz, members of the Sonderkommando did not even wait for him to be gassed before throwing him into the oven, ensuring he was burned alive. Whatever the truth of this story, it indicates the depth of feeling among those who had experienced the inequalities and agonies of ghetto life.

It would be only too easy to move seamlessly on at this point to the analysis of extermination camps. Yet there were many other experiences of Nazi oppression and varieties of involvement on the perpetrator side that require more explicit attention. For this, we turn to another microcosm of violence, situated in the General Government: the southern Polish town of Mielec and the surrounding region.

The Destruction of a Community: Mielec

Mielec finds barely a mention in general accounts of the war and the Holocaust. Yet what happened here happened in innumerable other places in occupied Poland. Precisely because of its relative obscurity, with its combination of distinctive features and yet in certain respects typicality, exploration of this area proves illuminating. And, as we shall see, the Mielec case will serve also to highlight later peculiarities in legal reckonings, as well as the complexity of personal attempts, across generations, to cope with the longer-term reverberations of this period.

Mielec is situated around sixty miles to the east of Kraków, in a relatively flat area of mixed woods and farmland with occasional towns. In the late nineteenth century, the urban population had been predominantly Jewish, but with the growth of industry in the early twentieth century Polish gentiles began to move in. By the 1930s, some 2,800 Jews made up just over half of the total population of 5,500. By now an important manufacturing center, Mielec was particularly significant because of an aircraft production factory built just before the outbreak of war on the outskirts of town. Following the German invasion, this factory was taken over by a company run by Ernst Heinkel. In 1942, a labor camp was established here, which in 1943 was elevated to the status of concentration camp—one of the sub-camps (*Außenlager*) of Plaszów.[58]

The German invasion in September 1939 instantly changed everything for the Mielec Jewish community, who were just preparing for Yom Kippur, the Day of Atonement and holiest day of the year in the Jewish calendar. As survivor Bendet Gotdenker later recalled, a "large group of SS people" rapidly surrounded the bathhouse and slaughterhouse. Having chased the women and children into the slaughterhouse, they "shot wildly" and "brutally beat the men with beards." Entering the bathhouse, they immediately "shot dead all the Jews present, who were left lying dead in the baths." To ensure they had finished off their work effectively, "the SS people poured petrol over the still half-alive and the dead Jews and set them on fire."[59]

Irene Eber, who, as we have seen, had been expelled with her family from her native Germany the previous year, was not quite ten years old at this time. Vivid recollections remained with her, with horrific images still in her mind's eye when she wrote her memoirs more than six decades later. She remembered standing on the balcony and hearing the "inhuman screams of people dying carried through the clear air." Irene and her family "smelled the smoke, the smoke of burning wood and burning flesh," and watched as a "wall of flames slowly engulfed the street in front of us." Soon it was clear what was happening: "We heard shots, mad laughter, and terror-stricken shrieks, and we knew then that a portion of the Jewish part of town was in flames."[60] Their Polish landlord made Irene's family leave, for fear his house too would be torched if it were known that there were Jews inside, and they spent the night cowering in fear in a nearby field. Irene "choked in the smoke-filled air" as "clouds of smoke drifted through the night." She covered her ears, "but in the roar of the fire" she could still hear "the terrible shrieks and the mad laughter." This first experience of Nazi terror had a lasting impact: she was "possessed by an unerasable fear of death" which "would surface time and again, paralyzing, immobilizing, and overcoming the rational person." This fear "had the sound of a thousand shrieks, an unsharable fear that was mine alone."[61]

The following day, Irene witnessed how "pious men from the burial society" sought to give a dignified burial to the "charred bodies and bones," even though most "victims were burned beyond recognition" and it was impossible to tell "which shoulder bone belonged with which skull."[62] Like so many other massacres in Poland, the traces have been lost with the memories of the eyewitnesses. The visitor to Mielec today will find in the town center only a rough stone marking the site of the former synagogue.

Nazi occupation changed things for everyone, not just the Jewish victims. When the Germans invaded his hometown of Kraków, Hillel K. had fled to stay with a cousin in Mielec. Then the Germans arrived there too. As Hillel K. recalled: "Part of the population changed from one day to the other, to *Volksdeutsche*."[63] They built "triumph arches" and started saying "Heil Hitler." Hillel K. ran away the very next morning; his cousin, who stayed, was arrested on the day of the bloodbath. Even when interviewed more than four decades later, Hillel K. could not get over the fact that this slaughter of innocent men, women, and children was "not in '42, '43, but '39."[64] We tend to think of synagogue burnings as having happened across the Reich in November 1938, and we associate the mass killing of Jewish civilians with the invasion of the Soviet Union in 1941. But the German invasion of Poland brought the first wave of terror against civilians in wartime.

Following the first shock, life for the Mielec Jewish community began to settle into a new pattern. In an extraordinarily factual account written some forty years later, Jack (Icek) S., who was ten at the time of the invasion, recalled life with his parents and siblings, who did not survive. His oldest brother, Yisroel, "was about 11 years old," his younger brother, Yosef, was "about 7," his sister Devorah "was probably about 5 years old," and, he adds, "Last came my little sister, Gitel," who was "about 3 years old." Members of Icek's family were able to remain in their own home until March 9, 1942. Although they had to undertake forced labor, queue up for rations, and were not free to travel, there was no ghetto.

This was, at this stage, a just about bearable oppression. As Irene Eber put it: "Life gradually and ever so cautiously took on a certain familiar rhythm," but "fear continued to hover like a giant shadow over the streets where the Jews lived."[65] She recalls the closing of schools for Jews, the growing hunger, the constant fear of the Gestapo, the disappearances of men who were arrested in the street and taken away to labor duties, the sudden absences of others who had sought greater safety by fleeing cast across the River Bug to the Soviet side of occupied Poland, the overcrowding as Jews arrived who had been expelled from other places, and the atmosphere of depression and growing anxiety. Selection for labor duties could mean death. Irene's cousin Hayim, who had been at the academic high school (*Gymnasium*), was sent to the forced labor camp in nearby Pustków, in the SS Troop Training Ground area. As Irene recalls: "Pustkow's guards were known for their brutality." Within a few weeks, "Hayim was dead—beaten to death by a guard when he stepped aside to urinate."[66]

In Mielec, people lived in an interconnected social, political, and economic network: Jews, Poles, and ethnic Germans had been part of a community that was now burst asunder, radically disturbed and reconfigured by the new circumstances. And it was not only the invading Germans who served to destroy the local community.

Rudolf ("Rudi") Zimmermann was a local ethnic German who soon became caught up as a perpetrator. Born in 1919 in Hohenbach, a small German enclave known locally as the "German colony" in the village of Czermin, northwest of Mielec, Rudi Zimmermann was the eldest son of a peasant farmer. He never went to the academic high school—attended by many Jewish children, including Irene Eber's cousin Hayim—but had only basic education in the German "one-class school." Less literate than many neighbors, Zimmermann spent his days tilling his father's fields. On occasion he rode with a cart into Mielec and collected provisions from the store run by Irene Eber's grandmother, as Irene remembered: "Grandmother's German customers from Czermin were treated well.... The Zimmermanns with their dour son Rudi drove up in a horse-drawn wagon from their village, and Uncle Reuven, under Aunt Feige's watchful eyes, carried sacks of flour and fetched and carried sugar and lentils."[67] It seemed to the Jews, in their cramped and constrained circumstances, that the ethnic Germans were extremely well off, and such "large purchases" occasioned arguments between Irene's grandmother and her aunt about whether they had been shortchanged. But from another perspective, the Zimmermanns were a family of very modest means. A local ethnic German called Irma, who later became Zimmermann's wife, recalled that production on the Zimmermann family farm "was technically inadequate and carried out arduously with horses."[68] Largely cut off from the outside world in a community that possessed no radio, no telephone, and no electric lights, before the war they had as their only source of wider information a German-language church newsletter.

The rise of Nazism inaugurated a new era for the Zimmermanns and other ethnic Germans. The whipping up of German nationalist fervor and the development of *Selbstschutz* forces began to radicalize Zimmermann's political views, and the invasion rapidly transformed his personal situation. Zimmermann's father was soon appointed mayor of Mielec, and in this capacity he organized, among other things, a convenient room in which one of the local Gestapo bosses, Walter Thormeyer, could illicitly meet his Jewish mistress. Rudi Zimmermann also benefited: although only semiliterate, he could speak Polish as well as German, and at the age of twenty-one he was appointed as an interpreter by the German Security Police. Soon, he held a position in the Gestapo and began to lord it over the now inferior Poles and Jews. He gained further experience deployed in Reichshof (the Germanized name of Rzeszów) and Stalowa Wola and, always following the orders of his superiors, learned to play a violent role in the Nazi regime of terror. For several years, he was a reliable assistant in rounding up, deporting, and shooting Jews. One of those he eventually shot was Irene's cousin Esther, giving rise to somewhat ambivalent later reflections: as she put it, Esther "never shared food with me when I was hungry, and she never treated me very well." But Irene continued: "Yet, here I am, alive, able to eat my fill of cake and apples, while Esther is dead, shot dead by Rudi Zimmermann, the one whose parents bought provisions in Grandmother Mindel's store before war broke out and before he became a *Volksdeutscher*."[69]

While Zimmermann's personal position improved, the situation for his Jewish neighbors deteriorated. Under the new regime, only a few had enough to eat. Those who did included the Feiners, who lived close to Irene Eber's family. Irene was surprised that the Feiner mother always had sufficient flour to bake a dark, heavy bread. Over time the Feiners' daughter, an attractive blonde who had been engaged to a "handsome" man who had fled eastward, began to lose her good looks and was seen by Irene wearing a "low-cut dress" that was "much too short, showing her heavy thighs." Irene asked herself how it was "that she had grown fat while others were getting thinner daily," and "could not understand what had happened to the once-beautiful girl whose features were now heavy and coarse."[70] On the brink of adolescence at the time, Irene did not fully register that the Feiners' daughter was ensuring the family's well-being, by having, as Irene's cousin Esther would have put it "in plain and unadorned language" become "a prostitute, and that her brother was pimping for her."[71]

We do not know if the Feiners' daughter numbered among her clients the local Gestapo boss, Thormeyer. Given the change in the Feiner family fortunes, this is certainly possible. Whoever Thormeyer's Jewish mistress was, she eventually met a brutal end. When Thormeyer became fearful that his commission of the Nazi-designated crime of "interracial" sexual relations would be discovered, he took his mistress on a walk in the woods and shot her in the back of the neck.

Life and Death in the Heinkel Works

If life under occupation was fragile and infused with fear, with survival entailing a combination of luck and compromise, it took a rapid turn for the worse in March 1942. Mielec became the first site in the General Government from which Jews were subjected to "selection" for death or work. The old, the young, the weak and frail were deported. The rest were sent to work at the Heinkel aircraft factory, exploited in the interests of the German war economy. This selection inaugurated an entirely new stage in the destruction of the Jewish community of Poland; experiences here were to become typical for many other places.

On March 9, 1942 the Jewish community of Mielec was shattered and effectively destroyed. With personal knowledge of the community in which he had grown up, it was only a small step for Zimmermann to assist the Gestapo in identifying where Jews lived and finding any who were seeking to hide.[72] Irene Eber vividly recalled the sound of heavy "pounding boots" coming up the stairs, as though she were reliving the experience. The door to their "tiny, crowded room" was flung open, "and suddenly huge, gray-coated men seem to fill every inch of space in that little room; they seem to breathe all the air there is." Terrified, her family shrank "into the corners." But there was no escape: "Their brutal red faces tower above us, among them that of the hated Rudi Zimmermann, an old family friend who was now a *Volksdeutscher*, a member of the Gestapo and a killer. Neither they nor we utter a word; no words are needed, our lives are in their hands."[73] And from this point on, it was for Rudi Zimmermann like so many others only a relatively small step to obeying orders to kill. Some Jews, like an elderly man whom Zimmermann shot dead in his bed on the orders of his superior, Helmut Hensel, were simply too frail to get up.[74] Others, who had been beaten out of their houses, were forced to assemble in the town square, where, as Icek recalled, "the selection began."[75]

The young, the old, and the unwell were taken to one side for deportation—the first occasion in the General Government when people were selected for gassing in the newly built extermination centers of Bełżec and Sobibór, where in fact Mielec Jews had to wait until construction had been completed, providing some, such as Irene Eber's family, the opportunity to escape.

The selection of March 9 was also significant in that it involved a variety of perpetrator groups. There were of course members of the local gendarmerie, Gestapo, and SS. But also involved in the selection process, according to Zimmermann's later testimony, were members of the Wehrmacht and, significantly, civilian employees of the Heinkel aircraft production company, including one Theume, who after the war lived in West Germany apparently untroubled by his past.[76]

This selection, carried out by the fateful combination of the forces of repression and industrial production, had clearly been in the planning pipeline for some time. From December 1941, Irene recalled later, there had been rumors of impending deportation. News of the gassings in Chełmno also filtered through. Her uncle Reuven was at that time a member of the Jewish council; although unable to predict details, he and his colleagues had a fairly clear inkling of what lay in store.[77] They did not yet know that extermination centers were under construction nearby but were aware that mass murder was on the German agenda.

For some, death came more quickly. Many were simply killed along the way to the aircraft works. Icek recalled how his family at first kept together, but not for long: "Both sides of the road were lined with SS storm troopers and big German Shepherds. About halfway towards the hangars, the Germans took all of the older people out and shot them then and there. That was the last time I saw my father."[78] Those still deemed fit to work were forced to march the few kilometers further to the Heinkel plant. Here, another selection took place, as Icek recalled: "When we finally got to the Airport, they separated us into groups. They took my mother, my younger brother and my two sisters, and they put them on a train. Me and my brother, Yisroel, were still together. After another selection they separated me from my brother."[79] While Icek's mother and younger siblings were on their way to the death camp, his brother Yisroel was taken to Pustków, located not far south of Mielec, in the SS Troop Training area where many Mielec Jews worked. At the Heinkel works, Icek and others were held in the hangar without food and water until a makeshift camp was set up. Condensing several years into a brief summary, Icek later recounted that "they tattooed me with a 'KL' [for *Konzentrationslager*, concentration camp] on my right wrist," rendering any attempt at escape without easy recognition far more difficult. In the camp, the "guards were mostly German SS men, and possibly some Ukraines. At this factory we were forced to build and repair planes."[80]

The establishment of this camp marked a turning point not only in the lives of those who became slave laborers but also in the role of Heinkel—and other German employers—in the Third Reich. Mielec was the first sign in the General Government of shifts in German strategy, and Heinkel was one of the first companies to benefit from these shifts. With so many adult males away at the front, there was a growing labor shortage in Germany. This became particularly acute as the Russian campaign became bogged down. At the same time, the need to boost armaments production was becoming ever more apparent. The winter of 1941–42 was significant not only for the construction of extermination camps but also for the deployment of concentration camp labor for the German war economy.

A number of personnel changes marked the shift. Albert Speer, Hitler's architect, was appointed armaments minister in February 1942. He embarked on a drive to increase armaments production and to boost the political visibility and significance for morale of such production. In his capacity as chair of the Central Planning Committee, Speer worked closely with Field Marshal Erhard Milch, who as air inspector general represented the Luftwaffe, responsible for between one-third and two-fifths of armaments production.[81] There was a related drive to increase the numbers of foreign workers. Fritz

Sauckel, who had been a member of the NSDAP since 1923, was Nazi Gauleiter and regional governor of Thuringia; in March 1942 he was appointed by Hitler to the post of general plenipotentiary for labor deployment, working closely with the traditional civil service in the Reich Ministry of Labor. Sauckel embarked on extensive mobilization of foreign labor, a program already underway since 1939. By the time of its peak in late 1944, the program registered nearly eight million foreign workers as working in the Reich, a staggering figure amounting to around one in five of the German workforce.[82] It could hardly be said that Germans, employing or working alongside these foreign laborers, most of whom were living (and dying) in dreadful circumstances, were not aware of this aspect of the regime's inhumanity.

This drive to recruit millions of non-Jewish foreign workers into the Reich labor force took place at precisely the same time as the shift to a conception of the "Final Solution of the Jewish Question" as extermination, chillingly recorded in minutes of the Wannsee Conference of January 1942; and, indeed, foreign laborers were being brought into Germany just as German Jews were being moved out to the ghettos and camps in the east. But at the same time the SS was changing strategy. Following internal reorganization, on February 1, 1942, two departments were merged to form the SS Central Office for Economics and Administration (SS-Wirtschafts- und Verwaltungshauptamt, or WVHA) under Oswald Pohl, who supported the exploitation of prisoners until they collapsed from exhaustion.[83] The SS developed an economic empire based on the selection and hiring out to employers of slave laborers from concentration camps, including both Jewish and non-Jewish prisoners. This suited employers, who needed only to have a guaranteed supply of cheap workers, not necessarily retaining the same individuals over time. Those who were no longer productive could readily be replaced by the seemingly inexhaustible supply coming from the SS-run concentration camp empire. This was, in effect, "extermination through work" (*Vernichtung durch Arbeit*).

Alongside the simultaneous development of the extermination camps, these new strategies for the ruthless exploitation of prisoner labor radically altered the situation for Jews in Nazi-occupied Poland. And these shifts were reflected right from the start in the Mielec microcosm.

The workers at the Heinkel aircraft factory in Mielec were initially Germans from the Reich, local ethnic Germans, and Poles. But with the deportation of the Jews of Mielec in March 1942, Heinkel's aircraft production enterprise entered a new era—one reflecting the growing links between the SS concentration camps and German entrepreneurs.[84] Along with Field Marshal Milch, Heinkel was instrumental in discussions with Himmler about the deployment of concentration camp labor in aircraft production. By this stage of the war, under the inept if flamboyant management of Hermann Göring, the aircraft industry desperately needed additional labor power to ensure higher productivity.[85] Both state and private companies responded by employing a higher proportion of less skilled workers in an industry that had traditionally involved small-scale production with a highly skilled labor force. Heinkel was eager to seize the opportunity.

At the beginning of March 1942, Heinkel was the first to employ concentration camp laborers within Germany, with the deployment of some four hundred Soviet prisoners of war from Sachsenhausen concentration camp, just north of Berlin, in the nearby Heinkel factory in Oranienburg. Within a matter of days, Heinkel also undertook the first such move in the General Government, with the deployment of Jewish labor in Mielec.

Josef Kahane, a prisoner at the Heinkel Mielec works from June 1942 until its dissolution in 1944, gave testimony to the Central Committee of Liberated Jews, in Munich in 1947, when attempts were being made to bring former Nazis to justice. He remembered the many ways in which inmates were maltreated. One foreman, Philip Schmidt, used to "beat them until blood" flowed. Another supervisor, Ludwig Lang, beat inmates until they were dead. The camp commander at one time, Konrad Drozd, "carried out selections every two weeks, and shot many prisoners personally." One of those shot on the orders of Drozd was Josef Kahane's cousin Jakob, purely "because he was ill."[86]

Others gave similar accounts. Poor hygiene and lack of food weakened inmates and lowered their resistance to disease. When there was an outbreak of typhus threatening to spread to the wider community, drastic measures were taken. The leaders of work groups provided lists of those too ill to work, and the Gestapo assisted by shooting prisoners in the woods behind the factory. Zimmermann helped to select weaker prisoners on the roll-call ground (*Appellplatz*) and then took them in groups into the nearby woods; those too ill to walk were taken in one of the Heinkel factory vehicles. Walter Thormeyer, at this time in charge of the Mielec Gestapo, gave the orders to shoot and also shot selected prisoners himself. He had, according to Zimmermann's later testimony, a particular penchant for shooting female Jews, while leaving the male prisoners to others.

For Heinkel, the Mielec camp was just the beginning. Later in the year, Heinkel opened up another plant under the auspices of the Hermann Göring Works in Budzyń, near Krasnik. This required the opening of a new concentration camp, which eventually became a sub-camp of the Majdanek concentration camp on the outskirts of Lublin. Later, prisoners from Budzyń and Mielec were transferred to underground production in a salt mine in Wieliczka, which became a sub-camp of Plaszów in Kraków. When Heinkel's Rostock works was bombed in May 1942, Heinkel rapidly opened new plants at Barth in northern Germany, using slave labor from Ravensbrück, employing around 1,800 prisoners at any one time. In Austria, he deployed slave labor from Mauthausen to work at the airport of Schwechat, near Vienna. By the start of 1944 slave laborers from Mauthausen constituted a quarter of the Schwechat labor force; when this enterprise was moved to a complex of caves known as the Seegrotte south of Vienna, prisoners made up a majority of workers.[87]

Over the course of the war, in his various aircraft production works, Ernst Heinkel came to employ more than twice as many slave laborers from concentration camps and their proliferating network of sub-camps than were employed by the infinitely better known I. G. Farben in their notorious Buna works at Auschwitz-Monowitz. In Oranienburg alone, Heinkel employed as many as 5,939 prisoners from Sachsenhausen, while I. G. Farben's plant at Auschwitz-Monowitz employed roughly five thousand.[88] By spring 1944, Heinkel employed some ten thousand slave laborers from concentration camps. And as elsewhere, the lives of Heinkel slave laborers were deemed expendable; for example, in the Heinkel works based in the relatively small Ravensbrück sub-camp at Barth, which held approximately 1,800 prisoners at any one time, some two thousand prisoners died between the opening of the camp in 1943 and the end of the war in the spring of 1945.[89]

Accounts by survivors from the Heinkel labor camps in Mielec, Budzyń, and Wieliczka record the brutality and privations of everyday life as well as the frequent shootings, hangings, and deaths from disease, maltreatment, and starvation that were commonplace experiences.[90] The camp commandant of Budzyń for two years was one Reinhold Feix (variously spelled as Feiks), who was a veteran of the Trawniki training camp and had come directly from the death camp of Bełżec to run Budzyń. Not only was Feix personally sadistic, but as survivors such as Jack Terry (born Jakub Szabmacher) recalled, he even trained his six year-old son to shoot people.[91] In the words of another survivor, Jack Eisner, Budzyń "was a nightmare." As he summarized it: "No gas chambers, no crematoria, no striped uniforms. But agony, torture, and starvation. Every day."[92] Feix went around spraying bullets at random within the camp, killing several people at a time, apparently just for pleasure, and he brutally maltreated Eisner following an unsuccessful attempt to escape.[93] Eisner also recalled how one day they were taken to a nearby town with a still-significant Jewish community, and hundreds of "terrorized Jews" were "crammed in the small wooden structure" of the synagogue "until it was overflowing," at which point Feix poured out a can of gasoline and set the building alight, while "roaring with insane laughter."[94]

Other Heinkel works were no better. Jack Terry remembered how, with the advance of the Russians, prisoners were moved from Budzyń to work in the salt mines of Wieliczka. Here, water ran down the walls of the dark cavern in which they worked, and people were often electrocuted when the electric wires got damp.[95] One survivor, Pola Grinbaum-Kronisz of Bełżyce, later testified that she "was completely yellow" after working underground for three months.[96] The lives of these workers were deemed to be entirely expendable, so long as production targets were met and there was a ready supply of new laborers from nearby camps.

Like so many others employers of slave labor, after the war Ernst Heinkel evaded the kind of attention that might have been proportionate to his involvement in the Nazi empire of exploitation, suffering, and death. As we shall see, he succeeded in defending his reputation, battling off lawsuits, and continuing to run a profitable business until his death at the age of seventy in 1958. Meanwhile, those at the receiving end, as so often was the case, knew only their immediate physical tormentors and had little idea about the entrepreneurs, administrators, and politicians who had shaped their fate. The testimonies of survivors—recounting acts of brutality, attempts at escape, strategies of survival—do not reveal the wider forces causing their suffering. But their accounts provide a chilling counterpoint to the later evasions of those who had benefitted from their exploitation and were responsible for the conditions under which so many suffered and died.

The Transformation of the Territory

The airfield and rail links also gave Mielec a wider importance. Himmler acquired a swathe of territory stretching south from Mielec toward Dębica.[97]

Sections were designated, respectively, for the air force, the army, and the SS. A Russian prisoner-of-war camp run by the army was complemented by a concentration camp run by the SS. These extensive grounds grew rapidly in significance, including training the Galician SS division made up largely of Ukrainians. A shooting range for the SS was an important element in the complex around the village of Pustków, which had been cleared of its former Polish inhabitants. From November 1943 to July 1944 the so-called Heidelager site was used for secret missile testing, linked with the better-known Peenemünde rocket research and production facility. Rockets were launched from the village of Blizna, also cleared of its previous inhabitants, and situated within the tightly controlled security ring of the SS training area. The rockets landed in populated areas of Poland, where Polish resistance fighters, members of the Home Army (Armia Krajowa), found bits of debris and leaked details to London. Himmler inspected the site in September 1943, and the German rocket scientist (and later NASA administrator) Wernher von Braun, frequently flew in to Mielec to visit the Dębica base because of its centrality for missile research and production.[98]

Many Germans from the "Old Reich" worked at this base. Their experiences were later suppressed, barely spoken of in the postwar world; but they were crucial to the Nazi system. One such German involved in SS activities in the area was "Peter Müller," whose biographical route is in many respects typical for his generation. Born in 1898, Müller completed a basic technical school education and trained as a forester.[99] He volunteered and fought in the First World War, ending up wounded in the thigh. After the war, Müller became involved in the right-wing veterans' organization, the "Stahlhelm," and probably also in the violence of the Freikorps (Free Corps, paramilitary troops active in the years after the end of the First World War). His father went bankrupt in the catastrophic economic inflation of 1923 and committed suicide—a death that Müller blamed on "Jewish bankers." Once the Nazis were in power, Müller joined the Waffen-SS, while his brother became a regionally significant Nazi. In 1945, this brother also committed suicide, unable to face what might follow. Both of these suicides—of Müller's father and brother—were intrinsically related to major historical upheavals. In the first, the shattering economic consequences of the First World War and his father's suicide were blamed on the Jews; in the second, Müller's brother, a convinced Nazi, could not contemplate life after Hitler. Müller came from a family that shared Hitler's prejudices and supported his endeavors. The private lives of family members were intimately connected to the fortunes of the state, even to the point of their deaths.

Notionally still employed in forestry during the war, Müller later represented his activities in occupied Poland as entirely innocent—at least as later portrayed by his son Hans, whose views were filtered through an idealized image following Müller's own somewhat mysterious and untimely death in a car accident. Müller, so he claimed to his family, had been sent to the Reichshof area to be in charge of forestry for the SS Dębica troop training ground, the Heidelager south of Mielec. "Forestry" sounds like merely a matter of planting, tending, and felling trees; it was not so obvious to a postwar audience that the actual work was carried out by forced and slave laborers who, if they dropped from exhaustion, would likely be killed. Those murdered included the near-dead, too weak to work, commonly referred to as "Muselmänner"—an old-fashioned word for Muslims, but in this usage denoting people destined for early entry to heaven. One Jewish survivor, whose tasks included taking corpses for disposal, recalled that the bodies "included people who had been shot, hanged, and beaten to death."[100] A former Polish worker remembered that "there were particularly hard working conditions in the forestry commando and at the Kochanowka shooting range."[101] Another recalled that "Jews were killed in large numbers in various construction sites," but "above all in the forestry commando that had to clear trees in the ring areas" and added that "Jews were often beaten to death during their work."[102] But these were not the later recollections of members of the SS who, like Peter Müller, had served at the site.

Violence was ubiquitous, and far from out of the ordinary at the time, here and across the territory. In 1943 the Mielec labor camp was given the status of a concentration camp under the control of the SS; clothing was supplied from the Plaszów concentration camp, prisoners were tattooed, and Ukrainian guards were brought in to assist in controlling them. Following a brief period under a commandant by the name of N. Hering (first name unknown), the Mielec camp was run by an Austrian, Josef Schwammberger. Schwammberger arrived from Przemyśl, south of Mielec, where he was reputed to have shot around six hundred Jews in a recent massacre, and had—like Feix—apparently given a pistol to his little son to shoot, too. The survivor who recounted this story, Norbert Friedman, was not sure if it were true but recalled that the son said to him personally something along the lines of, "Hurry up you dirty Jew or I'll kill you."[103]

Schwammberger already had a reputation for being trigger-happy. For example, just after the war Renata Trau recounted how her family in Przemyśl had managed to survive repeated "Aktionen"—roundups and deportations—by hiding in a variety of cunningly devised places, including a pantry hidden behind a wardrobe, an attic, and a cellar. She and her father had even managed on one occasion to hide in an apartment while the Germans were blowing up the attic and cellar; her father, who had been shot in both legs, was too wounded to get out of the bed, and this proved to be a lucky escape. They subsequently found refuge with a local Polish woman. But when her mother, who had hidden elsewhere, had gone to look for them, she encountered problems, as her daughter—still not yet a teenager—recounted in 1946: "On the way to the ghetto she had been stopped by a secret policemen, a Pole, who had taken all her money and jewellery. When she was coming back from the ghetto, she was stopped by a group of Ukrainian policemen and taken to the commandant of the ghetto, SS officer Schwamberger [sic]; he had my mother and sister shot."[104] Here we see all the elements of a typical situation in the area: not only the SS but also Poles who worked as policemen for the Germans; Ukrainian policemen; and a Polish woman who helped to hide two Jews. It was extremely difficult for Jews to know whom to trust, who might prove to be a rescuer, and who would betray them.

How then did the actions of others in the area affect the fates of Jews? There were many cases where people survived in hiding, harbored by gentiles with motives ranging from genuine sympathy to greed—people about whom we know because of survivor accounts, and some of whom were later awarded the title of "Righteous among the Nations" by Yad Vashem. There were probably many more cases where Jews were betrayed, even murdered, and where many Poles participated informally in the Nazi-instigated "hunt for the Jews" (*Judenjagd*). The "blue police"—Polish police forces under German leadership—also assisted in oppression and roundups.[105]

The detailed contemporary diary entries of Zygmunt Klukowski, a doctor in charge of the county hospital in Szczebrzeszyn, situated near Zamość to the east of Mielec, include chilling accounts of how locals laughed at the humiliation and arrests of Jews, while a few participated more actively. As Klukowski recorded on October 22, 1942: "The action against the Jews continues. The only difference is that the SS has moved out and the job is now in the hands of our own local gendarmes and the 'blue police.' They received orders to kill all the Jews, and they are obeying them. At the Jewish cemetery huge trenches are being dug and Jews are being shot while lying in them."[106] Others were loaded into railway wagons for deportation. Vacant Jewish houses were sealed, but robberies nevertheless took place. Klukowski commented that it "is a shame to say it but some Polish people took part in that crime."[107] Other Poles were involved more violently, as Klukowski noted the following day: "Skorzak, a city janitor ... had no gun, only an ax, and with the ax he killed several Jews."[108] This sort of event was witnessed repeatedly, although as Klukowski put it, struggling to record what was going on: "It is hard to describe." He continued: "It is so terrible that it is almost impossible to comprehend."[109]

Irene Eber was in the end among the lucky few children to survive in Poland. Deported from Mielec in 1942, she was held in a village close to the death camp of Sobibór, pending the opening of the extermination facilities, but with the help of family money and connections, she and her parents managed to escape certain death at that time. Not long after this, however, they were caught and ghettoized in Dębica. Here, as the outlook became increasingly hopeless, and knowing about transports to Auschwitz, the twelve-year-old Irene chose to defy her father's wish that the family stay together. With the help of her mother, Irene escaped by digging her way under the wire fence surrounding the ghetto and made it back through a snowstorm to Mielec. She first ran to the house of the Polish family friend to whom they had previously entrusted their money and jewelry and who had earlier traveled to Sobibór to assist their escape. But this woman was no longer willing to help and turned the shivering, frightened child away from the door. Other Polish neighbors, the Orlowskys, proved to be more kindly and gave Irene shelter and a place of safety in a chicken coop. Here she hid, amidst the smell and waste products of the chickens and rabbits who were the legitimate inhabitants of the coop, for nearly two years—the long twenty-two months between her escape from the ghetto and the arrival of the Russians in the summer of 1944.[110] After the end of the Nazi occupation, as Irene emerged from hiding, re-entered the sunlight, and tried to regain a sense of humanity, she could barely account for how the time had passed in the chicken coop, where she was "alone and afraid" and where she "knew only the seasons—the long season of cold and night, the short season of warmth and light."[111] Ultimately, she was able to make a fulfilling postwar life, although not without considerable pain in confronting her past.

With the advance of the Russians, Schwammberger's reign in Mielec also came to an end in 1944. In July Amon Göth, the commandant of Plaszów—

who gained posthumous notoriety from Steven Spielberg's 1993 film *Schindler's List*—came personally to inspect the Mielec labor camp. At this time, there were around two thousand men and three hundred women there. Göth ordered its evacuation, and some two thousand people as well as machinery were sent to the underground Heinkel plant at the Wieliczka salt mines to continue production.[112] Here, they joined workers from elsewhere, including Budzyń. They were moved on again as the front drew nearer; some ended up working in Flossenbürg or other camps in the Reich.

We shall meet some of these people again—not only survivors around the world, including Irene Eber, but also perpetrators at different levels. Rudi Zimmermann made his way to what became the German Democratic Republic (GDR) and reinvented himself as a good East German citizen and member of the ruling communist party, the Socialist Unity Party (SED)—until the GDR system of justice caught up with him. Zimmermann's superiors in the Gestapo office, Walter Thormeyer and Helmut Hensel, made it to the Federal Republic of Germany; here, it would turn out that they had much less to fear by way of legal retribution for ordering and carrying out mass murder. The postwar fates of these three—the underling, eventually sentenced to life imprisonment in the GDR, and his two superiors—illustrate key contrasts between the justice systems of East and West Germany. Josef Schwammberger, commandant of the Mielec camp, after the war fled to South America, like so many other former Nazis, but was finally brought back to Germany and put on trial in the 1990s. His case too marks a significant shift in the character and reception of trials and in the treatment of witness testimony in Germany as both defendants and survivors entered old age. The postwar career of Heinkel, by contrast, illustrates just how easy it was for prominent entrepreneurs and industrialists who had profited from the exploitation of slave laborers to reintegrate seamlessly into West German society, continue to lead profitable careers, and successfully fight off legal challenges while covering the tracks of their Nazi past. And while survivors and their descendants scattered around the world, trying to make sense of their suffering and losses, the sons of Zimmermann and Müller, living in East and West Germany, respectively, were given very different accounts of their fathers' compromised pasts. The ripples from the Mielec area spread far and wide.

The first years of the war were, in different ways according to locality, characterized by attempts to survive through terrifying times. From the winter of 1941–42, however, the challenge became that of surviving in the face of imminent mass murder. Chances of survival were intimately linked to the interests of the German war economy and of a range of beneficiaries, profiteers, and plunderers. Whether held in ghettos or scattered across the wide network of labor camps, Jews who were too weak to work were condemned to a speedier death than those who appeared still useful to employers. In the wider population, individuals might be rescuers at one time, collaborators or even victims at another; very few could engage in resistance throughout. In this maelstrom of violence, it was almost impossible to remain an innocent bystander.

Contemporary accounts and later testimonies illuminate some of the predicaments of the victims; the profiles of just a few of the perpetrators—from civilian administrators and economic entrepreneurs to Gestapo functionaries and SS foresters—can help in understanding the distinctive distribution of guilt. And an appreciation of the sheer extent and visibility of Nazi inhumanity—even well away from the gas chambers of Auschwitz—provides a crucial clue to the widespread unease underlying the later claim "We knew nothing about it."

In this way, it also becomes possible to highlight the patchiness of subsequent attempts to address the legacies of collective violence. Later ways of "mastering the past" left much untouched: vast areas remained under-illuminated, skillfully evaded, or effectively ignored in personal accounts, and the overwhelming majority of those who participated in or profited from the system were never brought to justice.

5

Endpoints

The Machinery of Extermination

A distinguishing feature of Nazi rule was the design and construction of dedicated killing centers. Overall, fewer people were killed in these centers than in the dispersed atrocities—shootings and hangings—as well as in the slower deaths by disease and starvation in ghettos and prisoner of war camps. And far fewer people were directly involved in running these factories of death than in the wider system of exclusion, exploitation, and terror.

But the death camps have rightly captured our attention, epitomizing as they do the cynicism, deception, and horror of Nazi practices. The targeted, industrialized killing of the elderly, the frail, the sick, the very young, at the same time as exploiting the able-bodied until they too were broken, poses in highly concentrated form almost unthinkable questions: about cold-blooded murder of innocent people, and the legacies for those who were perpetrators as well as those few who survived.

Perhaps two hundred thousand people, and possibly closer to a million, were at one point or another actively involved in killing Jewish civilians.[1] And the ranks of those who made this possible were far wider. People become variously involved according to the phases of the war and the scenes of persecution. Some were willing participants; some were pressured by their peers and learned to be brutal once in the role; others felt constrained to act in certain ways, despite inner doubts and hesitations. Most later claimed that they bore no personal responsibility for their actions.

Later landscapes of remembrance only selectively represent the realities of Nazi practices. Mass killing of civilians began before the construction of the extermination camps; murder was carried out in many other places, and it continued after the gas chambers and crematoria had ceased their operations.² In a huge network of camps in Nazi-dominated Europe, violence escalated as forced labor become increasingly vital to the war economy. And the visibility of violence was brought home across the Reich in the death marches toward the end of the war. The "it" about which people allegedly "knew nothing" was raging all around them.

Atrocities in the Open

The organized killing of Jewish civilians began on the Eastern Front in the summer of 1941, following the invasion of the Soviet Union. In the fields and forests of eastern Europe, a massive bloodbath took place, as whole communities—women, children, and the elderly as well as men designated as "partisans"—were murdered in locations where they were found. Perhaps 1.8 million Jews were killed in shooting massacres in this way, along with a substantial number of Gypsies.³

Special killing squads (Einsatzgruppen) were once again put to work, as in Poland two years earlier, but now across a far wider terrain, and with a more comprehensive set of targets. In the first few days after the invasion, an attempt was made to instigate local pogroms, as in Lithuania, with some success. As the leader of Einsatzgruppe A, Franz Stahlecker, commented, it was the "task of the security police to set these purges in motion and put them on the right track so as to ensure that the liquidation goals that had been set might be achieved in the shortest possible time", this should take place "without directions from German authorities being discernible." He initially found it harder than expected to set pogroms in motion, but was eventually pleased with the way things had gone. Stahlecker added: "The Wehrmacht units were briefed and showed full understanding for the action. As a result, the cleaning-up operations went off very smoothly."⁴ Some soldiers were shocked. One commented on an incident in Kovno on June 23, 1941: "I saw Lithuanian civilians beating a number of civilians with different types of weapon until they showed no more signs of life." He noted that the "bystanders were almost exclusively German soldiers, who were observing the cruel incident out of curiosity."⁵ He photographed the incident and had his camera confiscated as a result—but not before he had taken out and pocketed the film, in this way being able to keep the resulting photographs. Others too spoke of the way that a "great many German soldiers as well as Lithuanians watched these people being beaten to death."⁶

As German troops moved eastward, the Einsatzgruppen followed in their wake and, often with military assistance, murdered whole communities of Jews at a time, generally by mass shooting into communal graves that victims had been ordered to dig in advance.[7] Learning on the job, those involved in killing slaughtered ever-larger groups as the campaign of murder grew over the course of the summer. A peak was reached on September 29–30, 1941, with the massacre at a ravine near Kiev, Babi Yar. In the course of two days, more than thirty-three thousand Jewish people were brought here, ordered to undress and leave their clothes and valuables in neat piles, and were shot into the ravine, bodies falling one on top of another. Perhaps twenty people in all survived, some by jumping or falling into the mass grave without having been fatally wounded, initially pretending to be dead and then later managing to crawl their way out through the heaped bodies and earth that had covered them.[8] This site was also later used for killing other groups, including Soviet prisoners of war and Gypsies.

The murder of civilians was not secret; it was not something that people "knew nothing about." Significant numbers were directly involved; others observed atrocities themselves or were told about them. People across eastern Europe were witness to the destruction of whole communities. Even back in the Reich, people were aware that something deeply troubling was going on. Rumors spread; letters and visits from the front brought news to people at home. Soldiers took photographs and sent their footage home to be developed; family and friends saw the snapshots before they were sent back to the front; and soldiers carried such snapshots around with them in their pockets, along with photographs of wives and children. Whether or not they personally witnessed such crimes, they discussed these atrocities, which were also talked about quite openly at home.[9] Yet publication of a small selection of such photographs in the *Crimes of the Wehrmacht* exhibition that opened in 1995 occasioned widespread shock, for the knowledge that had been so common at the time had in the meantime been suppressed.

In retrospect, it is almost impossible to imagine, let alone understand, how ordinary men could be brought to engage in the mass killing of civilians, an act evidently beyond the definition of "normal" violence in wartime. No single explanation is valid for all situations and individuals.[10] People were ordered to kill; once they had started, they could be kept at the job by inducements—extra rations, spoils of conquest—and particularly by the anesthetic effects of alcohol, with copious amounts consumed. They often did not even know whom or how many they had killed. Otto Ohlendorf, head of Einsatzgruppe D, which operated in the southern sector of the army's invasion of Russia, adopted the classic strategy of ensuring that no one need feel personally responsible for the outcomes of mass murder: "I always gave orders for several people to shoot simultaneously, in order to avoid any individual having to take direct, personal responsibility."[11]

The idea of a defensive war against "international Jewry"—whether Bolshevik or capitalist made little difference in this crazy worldview—was central to Nazi propaganda. For those involved in killing, varying combinations of careerism, cowardice, conformity, fear, lust, brutalization, hopelessness, desire for reward, choosing the lesser of two evils, simply "doing one's duty" or "obeying orders," or fitting in with what others were doing could all play a role. The way the task was presented could affect how acceptable it appeared. For some, ideology might seem to legitimate what they had done. Talk of combatting "bands" and "partisans," engaging in "reprisals," or carrying out actions necessary to terrorize a troublesome population could make killing civilians seem a "legitimate" aspect of warfare. It was also argued that women and children had to be killed to ensure there would be no one left to avenge the deaths of others. Many ordinary soldiers, discussing these atrocities later when in Allied captivity, still often framed the killings in the Nazi terminology of "combatting partisans."[12]

Peer group pressure was important where the previously unthinkable became murderous reality. Even when offered alternative duties, those "ordinary men" in Police Battalion 101 generally found it easier to conform by killing than stand out by refusing, let alone protesting.[13] Over time, the initial shock wore off, and shootings became part of a day's work. In other cases, people claimed they could see no obvious way out when the penalties for refusal appeared to be high.

Even so, not everyone managed to keep going in the job, and members of the Einsatzgruppen—which were, after all, dedicated killing units—were often extremely uncomfortable. As one participant in mass shootings in Einsatzgruppe C put it, despite both orders from above and pressure from his peers, it was impossible for him to go on: "I began to feel unwell, I felt as though I was in a dream. Afterwards I was laughed at because I couldn't shoot any more." But it was clear that he "was in no fit state to go on shooting." Someone else took his place, and he was not even reprimanded for his refusal to continue shooting.[14] Perpetrators even saw themselves as "victims" because of the difficulty of the task they had to undertake.[15]

From a Nazi perspective, killing Jews where they found them was not "efficient." The mass shooting of civilians was both public and distasteful for many of those involved. New ways of killing were sought that would be less difficult for the perpetrators, while equally deadly for their victims. This coincided with the formal termination of the euthanasia program in the summer of 1941. August Becker, a specialist in gassing who was now transferred east, reported that Himmler had told Viktor Brack, Bouhler's deputy in the Führer's Chancellery and organizer of the T4 operations, that "the men in charge of the Einsatzgruppen in the East were increasingly complaining that the firing squads could not cope with the psychological and moral stress of the mass shootings indefinitely." This gas van expert himself knew "that a number of members of these squads were themselves committed to mental asylums and for this reason a new and better method of killing had to be found."[16]

The former commandant of Auschwitz, Rudolf Höss, later reflected on the inefficiencies of the killing squads of 1941 when he wrote his memoirs in captivity after the war, before being put to death on April 16, 1947:

> Many gruesome scenes are said to have taken place, people running away after being shot, the finishing off of the wounded and particularly of the women and children. Many members of the *Einsatzkommandos*, unable to endure wading through blood any longer, had committed suicide. Some had even gone mad. Most of the members of these *Kommandos* had to rely on alcohol when carrying out their horrible work.[17]

For Nazi purposes, new methods were clearly needed. A key shift took place when Jews were brought to sites systematically designed for killing. And it is these extermination camps that have come to stand as the symbol of what was distinctive, perhaps unique to the organized mass murder of the Jews on an industrial scale.

The Auschwitz Complex

New methods of murder were being developed with a view to considerations of speed, secrecy, cost, and efficiency. Zyklon B gas, normally a disinfectant, was first tested to murder some nine hundred Soviet prisoners of war and other Auschwitz inmates in early September 1941. Although in his memoirs Höss is frequently hazy or unreliable on precise details, he provides a chilling description of his pleasure in discovering that Zyklon B disinfectant was so much more efficient—even, in Höss's warped view, more "humane"—than other means: "I always shuddered at the prospect of carrying out exterminations by shooting, when I thought of the vast numbers concerned, and of the women and children." He goes on: "I was therefore relieved that we were to be spared all these bloodbaths, and that the victims too would be spared suffering until their last moment came"—an extraordinary display of concern for "the victims."[18]

With the apparent "success" of this experiment, the construction of an extermination camp at Auschwitz II, in the hamlet of Birkenau (Brzezinka), situated just over three kilometers away from the main camp, began in October 1941, with continuing expansion of its facilities over the following years (although the last planned section of the camp was never completed). Zyklon B gas was used in two provisional gas chambers in converted farmhouse buildings until the four dedicated gas chambers at Birkenau, with attached crematoria, came into operation in 1943. In the summer of 1944, in preparation for the arrival of more than four hundred thousand Hungarian Jews, the railway tracks had a spur added to take prisoners directly into Birkenau, where on the now infamous "ramp" or platform selections took place between those deemed fit to work and those who were to die instantly. With ten thousand to twelve thousand people arriving daily at the peak of the deportations, the gas chambers and crematoria could no longer cope with the numbers of victims, and in 1944, as previously in the late summer of 1942, bodies were burned in open pits, sending up plumes of ill-smelling smoke visible for miles around.

It is relatively easy to explain why Auschwitz has become the iconic "site of all evil" in our contemporary landscape of remembrance.[19] It is, first of all—though this would not in itself be sufficient explanation of enduring significance—the site where the single largest number of people were murdered in one place. More importantly, communities with a sense of connection to this site are not only extensive but also diverse. By 1945, the numbers of those murdered included around one million Jews; some 75,000 Polish political prisoners; 21,000 Sinti and Roma, or Gypsies; 15,000 Soviet prisoners of war; and 10,000 other prisoners, including a few British and American prisoners of war. Victims came from all over Europe, not only engaging interest but also ensuring funding for memorials on the part of different states. Auschwitz, including its three main sites and numerous satellite camps, also had the largest overall numbers of slave laborers. The gas chambers and crematoria were only one part of the story. For prisoners selected for work and a slower road to death (average life expectancy of those selected for labor was three months), the "sauna" with its real showers and the humiliating process of head shaving and being tattooed with a number and clothed in striped prison garments and ill-fitting clogs was the start of another journey, frequently ending in one of the many Auschwitz sub-camps, from nearby Blechhammer to the more distant camp of Groß-Rosen in western Lower Silesia. Others toiled in the vicinity of the main camp, working in the farms, fields, factories, and mines of the immediately surrounding area.

People affected by Auschwitz were drawn from a broad range of communities. Polish political prisoners and Russian prisoners of war had from its opening in 1940 been the principal inmates of Auschwitz I. Prisoners included not only communists but also Polish patriots, members of the Home Army (AK), Catholic priests, intellectuals, and ordinary Poles who had resisted Nazi rule. Cults could later grow up around the sacrificial piety of a controversial Catholic priest, Maximilian Kolbe, just as much as around Polish political prisoners or communist resistance fighters from across Europe. French communists and socialists had as much stake in commemoration of those with whom they identified as Greek or Hungarian Jews did; Russia was as interested in commemorating its own prisoners of war as Israel was in remembering the vast numbers of Jewish victims. There were numerous variations and reasons for later identification with a wide variety of victims, "fighters" and "martyrs" for a whole range of causes.

Because it was not only an extermination center but also had an extensive network of labor camps, the Auschwitz complex also had the largest number of survivors when compared with other concentration camps with extermination facilities, such as Majdanek, let alone the dedicated death camps. Despite the enormous number of deaths at Auschwitz, an estimated seven thousand people were found still alive there, too weak to have been taken on the death marches, when the Red Army arrived on January 27, 1945. This compares with tiny numbers surviving other extermination centers: only seven known survivors out of the near quarter of a million murdered in Chełmno; a mere two survivors out of the more than half a million murdered in Bełżec; perhaps a few dozen from the two hundred thousand murdered at Sobibór; and between forty and seventy survivors of the three-quarters of a million or more who were killed in Treblinka.[20]

There was, correspondingly, a relatively substantial body of survivor testimony. People who later recounted their experiences came from all over Europe and represented a wide range of backgrounds. Moreover, a large number of unusually articulate survivors provided compelling accounts. Individuals such as Jean Améry (Austria), Tadeusz Borowski (Poland), Thomas Buergenthal (Czechoslovakia), Charlotte Delbo (France), Viktor Frankl (Austria), Imre Kertész (Hungary), Wiesław Kielar (Poland), Ruth Klüger (Austria), Primo Levi (Italy), Filip Müller (Czechoslovakia), Miklós Nyiszli (Hungary), Rudolf Vrba (Czechoslovakia), Elie Wiesel (Romania), and innumerable others sought to convey what life was like in Auschwitz as well as other camps through which they passed, in works which for readers have come to represent, more generally, "the Holocaust." They wrote from a range of perspectives—philosophical, literary, political and religious, Jewish and non-Jewish—and, whether in autobiographical or fictional form or in some hybrid, they brought their experiences alive for later readers.[21]

Such writings, which have become so widely known, have also contributed to the sense that certain moments and events—arrival, selection, tattooing, the brutality of Kapos, acute hunger, unexpected moments of kindness and solidarity—constitute *the* distinctive "Holocaust experience." Other narratives—stories of hiding, early emigration, and so on—may implicitly be demoted. It appears almost as if the only real "survivors" were those who, by some miracle, survived the death camps. Survivor accounts from Auschwitz also, inadvertently, threaten to drown out other experiences of persecution and death at the hands of the Nazis and their collaborators. The process of "death by bullets" had very few survivors—although numerous witnesses on the perpetrator side—and barely made an impact in the west after the war. With few exceptions, such as Babi Yar, the innumerable sites of such executions were also barely marked, those involved barely remembered.[22]

From a purely physical perspective too, the Auschwitz complex is well situated. It enjoys good transport links to nearby tourist centers and the international airport of the picturesque town of Kraków. It retains much by way of "authentic" remains as well as suggestive and poignant ruins. Extensive areas are open to visitors, including not only the brick buildings of Auschwitz I but also the infamous gate and watchtowers of Birkenau, the railroad tracks, the "sauna" area with showers, some of the barracks, the ruins of the gas chambers and crematoria, and, among the trees where Jews had undressed, huddled together, and waited for their end, the suggestive still waters of the "lake of sorrows" where ashes of corpses were thrown.

Even so, there are also extensive areas not included in the designated museum sites.[23] While Auschwitz I and Birkenau are crawling with visitors, the huge industrial site formerly used by I. G. Farben for the production of chemicals in wartime (including Zyklon B gas) is off-limits. There are physical remnants of the Auschwitz III camp in Monowitz, but the main I. G. Farben Buna site has been reused as a factory, and attention seems to be just as unwelcome to the present Polish incumbents as reminders of their past were to I. G. Farben successor companies in Germany.[24] Similarly off-limits are the outlying labor camps and houses scattered throughout the town of Oświęcim that were formerly used by camp staff, including the former homes of Commandant Rudolf Höss and many prominent SS officers later identified as war criminals. Significant buildings, including the main office known as Canada I for sorting the clothing and possessions of those who had been gassed, are also off the tourist trail. Now reused for other purposes and with other inhabitants, these locations have been absorbed into the modern Polish town of Oświęcim, unmarked, untainted, and apparently relatively untroubled by the ghosts of the past.

In the autumn of 1944, prisoners organized an uprising and succeeded in putting one of the crematoria out of action before being gunned down by the superior force of the guards. Auschwitz continued functioning until late January 1945, when the last inmates still capable of walking were taken off on a death march while the dead and dying were abandoned to be found by the arriving Russian soldiers. They documented what they found in film footage that, even where the scenes had to be reconstructed, provokes emotions of shock and horror.

For all that we now know and can learn through visiting the sites or reading survivor narratives, Auschwitz remains an iconic site not only of remembrance but also of selective oblivion. And, paradoxically, the images of Auschwitz that are most readily available to us—the infamous selections of the Hungarian Jews on the ramp in Birkenau in the summer of 1944— are images of a late phase of the killing program. By the time these photographs were taken, more than one and a half million Jews had already been killed in the other dedicated centers of extermination—death camps that are far less present in our later imagination.

The Killing Sites of Poland

With experience gained in the euthanasia centers of the T4 program since 1939 and the experiments in Auschwitz in September 1941, new camps were designed with the sole purpose of murder by gassing. There was some continuity in practices developed within the Reich, but in ways now less visible to the German public.

Violence was exercised by a relatively small number of German perpetrators, with the assistance of locally trained eastern Europeans, particularly but not exclusively Ukrainian guards. But they could not have carried out their murderous duties without local administrations and police forces, including the gendarmerie, who helped in the rounding up and deportation of Jews. From mid-December 1941, civilian administrators knew of mass murder: the general governor, Hans Frank, explicitly confirmed that three and half million Polish Jews could not be simply shot to death, but other measures would be necessary to accomplish their removal, a goal apparently challenged by nobody.[25]

The arrival of T4 personnel at the death camp at Chełmno represented a new phase in the murder of Europe's Jews: not just shooting Jews in the places where they were found but transporting them to a dedicated killing center. Chełmno began its operations using specially designed gas vans in early December 1941—and it is notable that, like Auschwitz, Chełmno was located within the borders of the expanded Greater German Reich, although, unlike Auschwitz, Chełmno was a small village in an area of poor transport links and sparse population.

In the General Government, three further death camps came into operation over the following months: Bełżec, Sobibór, and Treblinka. Again, experiences gained in the T4 program proved crucial in their design. Viktor Brack was tasked with assisting Odilo Globocnik, SS police leader for the Lublin District in Poland, in carrying out Himmler's orders to achieve a "final solution" of the Jewish question in Poland.[26] Brack duly organized the transfer of T4 personnel from Germany to contribute their expertise in constructing new killing centers. All three camps were equipped with camouflaged stationary gassing facilities, using carbon monoxide poisoning generated by running a motor, and conveniently located in proximity to railway lines.

In total, around one and three-quarter million Jews were murdered in these three camps—significantly more than in Auschwitz, although divided over separate sites. They were later known as the "Operation Reinhard" camps, named after Reinhard Heydrich following his assassination in Prague on June 4, 1942.[27] Heydrich, who had been acting Reich protector of Bohemia and Moravia, was one of Himmler's closest associates and among the chief architects of the "final solution of the Jewish question," with responsibility for the Einsatzgruppen and as convener of the January 1942 Wannsee Conference to coordinate strategies for murdering Europe's Jews. Naming these camps in Heydrich's memory was indicative of their purpose.

The first of the Reinhard camps was established in November 1941 in the small town of Bełżec in the district of Lublin, on the site of a former forced labor camp. Under the control of Christian Wirth—who, as we have seen, had extensive experience from the euthanasia program—killings first began here in mid-March 1942. Bełżec was relatively accessible on a railway line, and situated between the towns of Zamość and Lwów (in the Polish version of the name; Lvov in Russian, Lviv in Ukrainian, Lemberg in German, and Lemberik in Yiddish). Bełżec was in full operation for less than ten months, during which the vast majority of Jews from surrounding areas were murdered in the gas chambers. Perhaps up to half a million Jews were killed, along with an unknown but far smaller number of Poles and Gypsies.[28]

Only two former inmates survived to give evidence after the war. One, Chaim Hirszman, escaped from a train from Bełżec following the closure of the camp but was murdered in 1946, while in the midst of giving testimony in Poland; the other was Rudolf Reder, who after the war emigrated first to Israel and subsequently to Canada. Reder's account is the only full-length testimony we have from a survivor of this camp.[29] Reder had been deported from his native Lwów in August 1942, where news about the forthcoming "resettlement," and what it actually would mean, was circulating already two weeks earlier. According to Reder, a worker had escaped from the "death factory," where "he had been building gas chambers," and news had rapidly spread; a Ukrainian guard employed in the killings had also told his girlfriend about what was going on, and she too had told others.[30] But despite advance warning, the Lvov Jews and others nearby could not escape their fate.

Following a journey on an overcrowded train, deportees were greeted on arrival at Bełżec by shouting and brutality, and then the typical calming welcome speech, delivered here by an SS officer by the name of Fritz Irrman. Irrman addressed the crowd, which included "thousands of educated professionals" as well as ordinary workers, the elderly, women, and children, telling them, "First you bathe, and afterwards you will be sent to work." This was repeated "usually three times a day," as the trains rolled in with one transport after another, providing "a moment of hope and delusion."[31] Irrman "always gave the same deceptive speech," and Reder "always saw a spark of hope light up" in the eyes of those about to be murdered. But it was not long before they discovered what truly lay in store, as "the little ones were wrenched from their mothers, the old and sick were tossed onto stretchers, men and small girls were prodded with rifle butts further and further along the path . . . straight to the gas chambers."[32] Women and girls had their hair shaved, while many people were already corralled in the gas chambers, where some had to wait in the dark for a full two hours before all the chambers were filled. Suddenly the women would realize what was going on, and "without any transition from hope to total despair—laments and shrieks erupted." Around twelve SS men "used truncheons and sharp bayonets" to drive people into the gas chambers: around 750 were crammed into each of the six chambers, which were so tightly packed with people that it was difficult to close the doors, at which point the engine was finally switched on.[33] Reder recalled: "I heard the desperate cries, in Polish, in Yiddish, the blood-chilling laments of children and women, and then one communal terrifying cry which lasted fifteen minutes. The machine ran for twenty minutes, and after twenty minutes all was silent."[34] He and others then had to drag out "corpses of people who were alive just a moment before." They dragged them "using leather straps, to the huge mass graves prepared in advance, and the orchestra was accompanying us. It played from morning till evening."[35] The mass graves seeped with blood; "Our feet sank in the blood of our brothers; we were treading in a mound of corpses. It was the worst, the most terrible experience." Reder and his co-workers "moved around like people with no will left"; they were "enduring this horrible life mechanically."[36]

During the few months in which Reder worked in the camp, from August to the end of November 1942, three transports arrived daily, amounting, he estimated, to some ten thousand people killed on average every day.[37] Sometimes there were incidents where people were killed individually, in a sadistic manner, for some infelicity; sometimes the machine broke down or malfunctioned; at other times the killing operation was efficient, routine. The SS men led a separate life, and, as far as Reder could tell, they were never visited by members of their families. Several individuals held more prominent positions, including not only the camp commandant (Wirth until June 1942, then Gottlieb Hering until June 1943), and the SS officer giving the welcome speech, Irrman, but also an SS-Oberscharführer by the name of Reinhold Feiks. As Reder recalled, Feiks was a father of two who "gave the impression he was crazy" and "who forced people to sing and dance while he made fun of them and beat them."[38] Feiks (or Feix) went on to command the Heinkel camp at Budzyń, garnering a similar reputation for deranged cruelty there. Others, including a man by the name of Schmidt, were remembered as bloodthirsty "monsters."

Reder claims that Himmler visited the camp in mid-October 1942, giving a detailed description of the event, although it is extremely unlikely that the "very important person" who inspected the camp was indeed Himmler himself, as Reder believed.[39] There is, however, some evidence to suggest that Himmler might have visited while on an inspection tour through the General Government in January 1942, on his way between Lemberg (Lvov) and Lublin; the only decent road along this route led directly past Bełżec, and it is likely that he would have stopped by on that occasion.[40] Leaving Himmler's presence aside, according to Reder the inspection group of October 1942 that he witnessed included local dignitaries as well as Friedrich (Fritz) Katzmann, the SS and police leader of the District of Galicia who had organized the deportation and slaughter of tens of thousands of Jews.[41] The team inspected the killing operations with apparent satisfaction; it is difficult to imagine what they were actually feeling, as they surveyed scenes of terror while some of them discussed their own hopes of promotion. Katzmann, at least, was never brought to account for his crimes, despite being the author of a well-known and self-serving report, *The Solution of the Jewish Question in the District of Galicia*, which recounted the killing of nearly half a million Jews and plans for deploying those who remained.[42]

From Reder's agonized description, we can gain some sense of how life was for those "doomed prisoners" who were condemned to work at the camp for the few brief weeks before their own inevitable deaths. He recounted:

> Three times a day we saw thousands of people on the verge of losing their minds. We were close to madness too. We dragged on day after day not knowing how we did it. We hadn't the slightest illusion of hope. Each day we died a little together with the transports of people, who for a few brief minutes experienced the torment of illusion. Apathetic and resigned, we didn't even feel the hunger and cold. Each of us awaited his turn, knew he had to die and to bear inhuman suffering. Only when I heard the children calling: "Mummy! But I've been good! It's so dark! Dark!"—my heart, my heart was torn to pieces. And later we stopped feeling anything.[43]

Reder managed, extraordinarily, to escape while being taken to Lvov under SS guard on the instructions of Irrman to pick up sheet metal plates. He was sent in a truck with four Gestapo men and one guard and spent the day loading sheet metal. At the end of the day those in charge decided to go for a night out, leaving only one to keep an eye on Reder. Noticing after a while that the guard had dozed off, Reder managed to slip out of the truck and find his way to the home of his former Polish housemaid, who sheltered and cared for him for the rest of the war. Reder recounted: "I spent twenty months recovering from the wounds on my body. And not only wounds. I was haunted by images of the horror I had lived through. Awake and asleep I heard the moans of the tortured victims—and the cries of children—and the roar of the engine."[44]

The camouflage was not limited to the words of the welcoming Irrman or the misleading signs about the showers, designated as "bathing and inhalation rooms." It was important not only to fool those about to be killed but also to disguise the operations from anyone in the surrounding countryside or from aerial view. As in the other extermination camps, at Bełżec green leafy branches were used to cover what was going on, with luxuriant tree cover in a net over the gas chambers and twigs and branches woven into the surrounding fences and the wire roofing above the road along which the corpses were dragged.

In early 1943 it was deemed that Bełżec had fulfilled its purpose, having killed the vast majority of Jews from surrounding areas as well as some from further afield, along with some Poles and Gypsies. Bodies from the mass graves were exhumed and burned, and the bones were ground up to fine dust. Further efforts were then made to erase all traces of the death factory. A "farm" was established, and a Ukrainian family was installed to keep locals from digging for further bodily remains and searching for gold teeth or hidden valuables that had escaped the initial round of Nazi plunder. When Reder revisited the camp shortly after the war, local peasants described to him how "the pits were opened, the corpses were soaked with petrol and set on fire. Thick dark smoke rose and drifted for a couple of dozen kilometres around the huge bonfires. The stench and human particles were blown by the wind over far distances for a very long time: for long days and nights, for long weeks."[45] On this visit, Reder observed that "the torn up graves were filled in and the surface of the blood soaked earth was neatly levelled. The sinister German monster had covered the tomb of millions of Jews in the extermination camp in Bełżec with lush greenery."[46]

Many of the individuals responsible—those brought over from the euthanasia program as well as locally trained Ukrainians—managed to escape the postwar net of justice. Some, on being sent with other Reinhard personnel to northern Italy once the other camps were closed, were killed while on duty combatting "partisans" in particularly dangerous areas around Trieste. Those who died in this way included Wirth, former commandant of Bełżec and inspector of the Reinhard camps, who was killed by Yugoslav partisans in 1944. Katzmann, who was so proud of having rendered Galicia "free of Jews," initially headed off north to take charge of the liquidation of the Stutthof concentration camp; after the war, and despite the use in the Nuremberg trials of his report on the murder of half a million Galician Jews, Katzmann lived under a false identity as "Bruno Albrecht" until his death in a hospital in 1957 and was buried under his true name.[47] A few of the Bełżec perpetrators were eventually put on trial in West Germany, but, as we shall see, they were largely exonerated for alleged lack of evidence. One of the former T4 staff, Josef Oberhauser, a faithful assistant to Wirth in Bełżec and later in Lublin, was eventually sentenced for the part he played in 300,000 murders to a mere four and half years—only half of which he actually served.

Far less readily accessible was the killing center established in spring 1942 at Sobibór, in the sparsely populated, swampy woods near the town of Włodawa in eastern Poland. Murder by gassing with exhaust fumes started here in May 1942. The first commandant was Franz Stangl, an Austrian with T4 experience in Hartheim and Bernburg. He was transferred to Treblinka in late August 1942 and succeeded by Franz Reichleitner, another Austrian with a T4 background. As elsewhere, camouflage was ensured by physical means, including the installation of brightly painted signs and boxes of flowers outside buildings that were visible on arrival at the train station. And as in Bełżec, tree branches were woven into the barbed wire fences to create a thick canopy of "natural" coverage. But despite emphasis on strict secrecy, the murder and cremation of tens of thousands of human beings was not so easily disguised. One of the few survivors, Thomas Blatt, recalled that "the fire could be seen for miles around and the stink was terrible."[48] He explained: "In summer, the high temperatures caused the gasses and body fluids from decomposing bodies to seep from mass graves. The stench was unbearable and it spread for many miles. Even the water supply within the camp was affected." Things changed over time, but the signs were still clear: "Later, when the crematorium was built, fire and smoke were clearly visible for many miles, and the camp was often wreathed in foul-smelling smoke."[49] Also, Blatt pointed out, trains entered full and returned empty: "The most conclusive evidence that something murderous was occurring in Lager III was the fact that nobody ever came out alive."[50]

Blatt, who was fifteen years old at the time, was fortunate in being chosen as one of the few working Jews, assisting in the functioning of the camp; the rest of his family was gassed. Shortly after arrival, Blatt met a friend, Jozek, who also came from his predominantly Jewish hometown of Izbica. Blatt could hardly believe how emotionless Jozek appeared to be. Blatt was able to reconstruct his later account from notes he had written at the time, as well as from memory. He reports Jozek as saying to him: "It's because we've become robots; our survival instincts have taken over. If we thought like normal people, we would all go mad."[51]

Gassings at Sobibór continued, with the possibility of trading, speculating, and swapping currency found hidden in the clothing and possessions of new arrivals (who had been stripped) for food from the guards, many of whom were open to speculation and personal enrichment. Knowing that the inevitable end would be death, working Jews concentrated on daily survival. But some decided, against all the odds, that they would rather go down fighting, in an attempt to gain their freedom.

Under the leadership of a few, including notably a Jewish Soviet prisoner with military experience, Alexander "Sasha" Pechersky, a revolt was carefully planned for October 1943. Relying on the German reputation for punctuality as well as greed and desire for well-cut coats or new boots, prisoners lured SS men and guards to come to particular workplaces at specific, carefully staggered times. On arrival, they were rapidly killed, their uniforms and weapons stolen. A mass breakout from the by then less well guarded camp took place, in the course of which many prisoners were shot dead or blown up by mines as they crossed the surrounding death strip. Blatt found himself caught by his coat in the barbed wire; tangled up, he nevertheless managed to slide out of his coat, and as one of the last ran across the mined field, where earlier escapees had already been casualties of exploding mines, leaving the terrain relatively clear. He made it into the woods to join a group of others—a moment that was by no means the end of his escape.

Blatt estimated that there had been some 550 prisoners working in the camp. Blatt's numbers are a little difficult to interpret, with a degree of impressionistic guesswork, but the respective fates of the escapees are revealing. Blatt suggests that as many as 320 were initially able to escape; perhaps another 150 got away later. Around 80 were killed by mines or shot during the escape, while 170 were captured nearby and executed. A further 97 were subsequently murdered "mostly by hostile local elements"—a remarkably high proportion of successful escapees subsequently being killed, it would appear, by Poles—while five were "killed fighting the Germans in partisan units or in the regular army." Only forty-eight survived to be liberated by the Allies.[52] A further ten had survived from two earlier escapes (eight in July 1943 from a group working in the woods), making a total of fifty-eight survivors in all.

Estimates of total numbers killed at Sobibór vary, but the number was somewhere between 170,000 and 250,000. As in Bełżec, after the closure of Sobibór the Nazis sought to remove all traces by planting crops. It took some time after the war to reconstruct details of what had taken place, who the victim groups were, and where different parts of the camp had been located. Sobibór remained off the tourist tracks, and memorialization was slow in comparison with better-known sites. Families of victims, particularly relatives of the Dutch Jewish children murdered there, ensured there were some personal memorials, but institutional and state backing was minimal until recently. Only seventy years after the closure of the camp have archaeological investigations uncovered the bases of the building that housed the gas chambers.

A forced labor camp for Jewish as well as non-Jewish Poles was established at Treblinka, some fifty miles northeast of Warsaw, in November 1941; the following summer, in July 1942, as part of the "Reinhard Action," it was expanded with dedicated killing facilities in Treblinka II.[53] The extermination site here operated between July 1942 and October 1943. Between seven hundred thousand and nine hundred thousand people were murdered here—the second largest total in a single site after Auschwitz. Those killed included some two thousand Gypsies. One survivor, Shimon Goldberg, recalled that the Gypsies had put up a tremendous fight, continuing even inside the gas chambers: "The Gypsies went wild, screamed awfully, and wanted to break down the chambers. They climbed up the walls toward the apertures at the top and even tried to break the barred window. The Germans climbed into the roof, fired inside, sealed off the apertures, and asphyxiated everyone."[54]

In Treblinka, most of those initially selected for work lasted only a matter of days, at most a few weeks. Chil Rajchman was one of the very few who had worked in killing facilities, pulling corpses from the gas chambers to the pits or extracting teeth and fillings from the dead along the way. Shortly after his arrival at Treblinka, having been forced to assist with shearing women's hair and carrying bundles of possessions and clothes of those who were gassed—including his nineteen-year-old sister—Rajchman lay at night in the barracks "in pain" and wept. He talked to the man next to him, who was also groaning: "He tells me a secret, which is that he has been here for ten days." This man went on to confide that "no-one knows this," because every day prisoners died and new ones replaced them: "It is very rare for a labourer to last as long as he has."[55] Workers collapsed daily and were shot when they faltered, did not run fast enough, or had too many bruises and lashings of the whip; starving prisoners who had been set to sorting victims' possessions and were caught pilfering a piece of bread were shot on the spot; some prisoners even jumped into the pit with the dead bodies, hoping for a quicker end to their misery. Every morning, several prisoners would be found hanging in the barracks, having ended their sufferings themselves overnight.

The work was intolerable, and carried out at an unbearable pace. Rajchman's new friend, Yankel Wiernik, was another of the few survivors. Shortly after his escape from Treblinka, while his memory was still fresh, he recalled:

> We had to carry or drag the corpses on the run, since the slightest infraction of the rules meant a severe beating. The corpses had been lying around for quite some time and decomposition had already set in, making the air foul with the stench of decay. Already worms were crawling all over the bodies. It often happened that an arm or a leg fell off when we tied straps around them in order to drag the bodies away. Thus we worked from dawn to sunset, without food or water, on what some day would be our own graves.[56]

Rajchman too wrote his account of Treblinka not long after his escape, during the time he was hiding under "Aryan" papers with the assistance of the Polish resistance in Warsaw. The images Rajchman evokes are vivid. As he put it, for the "dentists" waiting for the corpses to be pulled out, "the scene is an inferno."[57] It was at first difficult to separate the bodies pulled out of the gas chambers: "During their death agonies from asphyxiation the bodies also became swollen, so the corpses form literally a single mass."[58] Once they had been disentangled, it was clear that there were differences between the bodies from the smaller and the larger gas chambers: in the smaller chamber, death took twenty minutes, whereas in the larger chambers it took three-quarters of an hour. As a result, from the smaller chambers there was "bloody foam visible" on people's lips, and their bodies were "covered in sweat" as well as other fluids: "Before dying, people had urinated and defecated." Corpses from the larger chambers "were horribly deformed, their faces all black as if burned, the bodies swollen and blue, the teeth so tightly clenched that it was literally impossible to open them," making the job of pulling out the "gold crowns" all the more difficult for the prisoner dentists.[59]

There were some dedicated work groups who managed to keep their jobs for a significant length of time, working further away from the gas chambers. Richard Glazar, for example, was largely deployed sorting possessions and clothing, and wrote down his experiences shortly after the war. He described how one small group of prisoners, known as "the camouflage commando," were still relatively healthy and were allowed "to distance themselves from the smell of corpses that permeates everything—your lungs, the wood the barracks are built of." Prisoners in this group were "fit enough to climb up into the high trees and trot back to camp carrying heavy bundles of branches." They then wove these branches "into strands of barbed wire, thus maintaining the camouflage green around the entire perimeter of the camp."[60]

As in Bełżec and Sobibór, the outside world was not supposed to be able to see what was going on inside, and arriving victims were not to get a whiff of the fate awaiting them until the last possible moment on entering the gas chambers, having been deceived by instructions to leave clothes and valuables before going for a "shower." As elsewhere, those who had died on the journey and people incapable of walking were taken by truck or carried to the "infirmary," where they were summarily shot or thrown still alive into a pit of burning bodies. Forced on occasion to assist in this process, Glazar had difficulty in maintaining his own sanity: "Handle them like lumps. The moment you look at any one of them as an individual, you're lost. No, you can't do that; you can never not look." It was the "motionless eyes" that particularly caught his attention: "There are eyes everywhere, all of them staring at me, getting larger and larger, already blocking out foreheads, entire faces, resting on chins." His strategy was one of attempted distancing, of forensic observation: "Stop, not like this—okay, look, look right at them as if this whole thing were intensely interesting, as if you were investigating every detail, every single body. How many dead bodies are there anyway? One a waxy yellow, one emaciated, one bloated and unimaginably heavy, covered with small deep purple bullet holes and odd bright puncture wounds."[61]

Glazar also provided vivid depictions of the conditions in the camp, the treatment of arriving trains, and the behavior of SS guards—descriptions of conduct that would prove invaluable when it came, very belatedly, to the trials of some of them. One of the Germans in charge, Kurt Franz, widely known by the prisoners as "Lalka" ("Doll") because of his childish features, was remembered as particularly brutal.[62] He had worked as a cook in a number of euthanasia centers—Hartheim, Brandenburg, Grafeneck, and Sonnenstein, as well as the T4 headquarters in Berlin—before being sent, like so many other T4 personnel, to assist in the death camps. Following a short stint at Bełżec, Franz worked at Treblinka from August 1942, acting as the last commandant from August 1943 and overseeing its camouflage and closure in November 1943. His brutality, and the way he set his dog on prisoners to tear into their buttocks and genitalia and maul them all over, was particularly etched in the memories of survivors.

German guards carried out their everyday duties in slightly different ways; a few were seen, rightly or wrongly, as generally less sadistic and brutal than others. Wiernik, for example, remembered one called "Unterscharführer Herman" (Erwin Herman Lambert), who was "about 50 years old, tall and kind"; he often "surreptitiously brought us some food from the German kitchen." But he kept his distance: "He never talked to the inmates" and "was afraid of his colleagues."[63] Lambert was somewhat unusual—but these appearances were also deceptive, since he had in fact been involved in the design and construction of the gas chambers in the euthanasia program as well as the Reinhard camps.[64]

More typical was the behavior of those perpetrators who were the last ever seen by their victims. Wiernik provides a graphic description of arrivals and beating into the gas chambers: "Parents carried their children in their arms in the vain hope that this would save their children from death. On the way to their doom, they were pushed and beaten with rifle butts and with Ivan's gas pipe. Dogs were set upon them, barking, biting and tearing at them." This had the desired effect of coerced cooperation: in order to "escape the blows and the dogs, the crowd rushed to its death, pushing into the chamber, the stronger ones shoving the weaker ones ahead of them." After this, there was little they could do: "The bedlam lasted only a short while, for soon the doors were slammed shut. The chamber was filled, the motor turned on and connected with the inflow pipes and, within 25 minutes at the most, all lay stretched out dead or, to be more accurate, were standing up dead. Since there was not an inch of free space, they just leaned against each other." Wiernik notes that there "was no longer any beauty or ugliness, for they all were yellow from the gas." Yet the bodies still bore the last traces of strong emotions and human connectivity: "Even in death, mothers held their children tightly in their arms."[65]

Despite desperate attempts up to the very last, people designated for the gas chambers could neither save themselves nor protect their children. In the winter of 1942–43, the scene varied slightly, as "small children, stark naked and barefooted, had to stand out in the open for hours on end, awaiting their turn in the increasingly busy gas chambers. The soles of their feet froze and stuck to the icy ground. They stood and cried; some of them froze to death." While the victims waited, Germans and Ukrainians terrified them: one, known as Sepp, "took special delight in torturing children." Despite the pleading of women, "he would frequently snatch a child from the woman's arms and either tear the child in half or grab it by the legs, smash its head against a wall and throw the body away. Such incidents were by no means isolated."[66]

Reading accounts such as these is highly disturbing; there is an instinctive reaction not to read such memoirs—and not to impose such passages on readers so many decades later. But survivors bore witness in such detail precisely because this "inferno" is so unimaginable, and because they desired justice; this need to provide a detailed account, in the hope of future reckoning, was what kept them going at the time—and which is why we too need to face these almost unbearable accounts.

Wiernik continues the passage about people turning yellow in the gas chambers with the following interjection: "And why all this? I keep asking myself that question. My life is hard, very hard. But I must live on to tell the world about all this barbarism."[67] Wiernik survived in part because, as a trained carpenter, he was useful to the Germans in construction work at the camp; and as a result, he almost blamed himself for assisting in the work of extermination: "I sacrificed all those nearest and dearest to me. I myself took them to the place of execution. I built their death-chambers for them."[68] He was not alone in feeling a sense of guilt at surviving through cooperation with his tormentors.

In August 1943, prisoners in Treblinka too succeeded in organizing a revolt. Glazar was one of the two hundred or so who initially managed to escape; while he succeeded in getting away, around half were recaptured immediately. Like Sobibór, Treblinka was closed down in October 1943. And again, following closure, attempts were made to obliterate all traces of the death camp by disguising the area as a farmhouse. As elsewhere, many of the German personnel who had run Treblinka were sent to northern Italy to combat partisans.

The Reinhard camps might be thought to have been costly to operate, and hence in conflict with other German needs in wartime. But Blatt reports some sobering statistics. When the three camps were closed down, he tells us, Odilo Globocnik did some calculations. The total cost, Globocnik estimated, was around twelve million Reichsmarks, including costs of transportation. But between April 1, 1942, and December 15, 1943, the Reinhard camps had made a clear profit of some 179 million Reichsmarks. This figure included only the valuables taken from prisoners in camp, the value of which was estimated at a low price, but did not include the property, including real estate and other goods, confiscated before deportation.[69] Nor did the figure, presumably, include the valuables that slipped into the many hands of those on the ground who profited from the terror and hunger of the victims and engaged in rich trade with other locals. Whatever the precise figures, the very fact that Globocnik could even think in terms of costs and profits—as did those involved in the slave labor program—without a passing thought about the human beings whose lives were so cruelly terminated defies comprehension.

Many non-German collaborators also profited, including people who had themselves previously been victims of Nazi policies, they seized chances to better their conditions, or had little choice but to cooperate or suffer. Some camp guards were known as "Trawnikis," named after the location of the camp where they were trained, in a small town twenty kilometers from Lublin. Many were Ukrainians initially captured as prisoners of war. If they were prepared to switch to serve the Germans, they underwent intensive training in Trawniki. They were then deployed in rounding up and deporting Jews or were stationed at death camps to assist in moving people off the trains and toward the gas chambers.

One such Trawniki-trained guard was Ivan Demjanjuk, born in the Ukraine in 1920, whose life embodied the historical twists of the century. Barely surviving the appalling famine unleashed by Stalin's policies in the 1930s, he had little formal education.[70] During the Second World War he served in the Soviet Army before being captured by the Germans and retrained at Trawniki. He subsequently served in Sobibór as well as other camps. Captured toward the end of the war, Demjanjuk was able to gloss over his past and, in the early 1950s, immigrated to the United States, where he obtained American citizenship. His past only caught up with him in the 1980s, when he was extradited to stand trial in Israel, and again in the early twenty-first century, when he was extradited to Germany to stand trial in Munich in 2009, in a trial that was to make legal history.

Glazar described the Ukrainian guards in Treblinka as "the slave drivers and hangmen's helpers." He continued: "They are despised by the masters and the master hangmen and by the slaves, the damned, as well. Every one of them is young, somewhere around twenty, and they are all bursting with health and vulgarity."[71] The Ukrainian guards seemed in their element: they would never in their wildest dreams have imagined "that they would be swimming in grub, vodka, and money, that the women, the girls, would follow them into the villages around the camp, about to hike up their skirts."[72] The Ukrainians' one saving grace, in Glazar's view, was their singing: "From the remoteness and the utterly endless distances of their homeland they have brought a rare gift with them: spectacular song. In the heavy twilight and the early morning hours, at the changing of the guard, one single column sends a plaintively wild song soaring into the air above the tightly packed crowns of the pines, finally wrapping all of Treblinka in a multipart chorale."[73] Knowledge of these songs assisted Glazar later on, following his escape, when living under an assumed identity as a forced laborer in Germany; he was able to keep his cover as a non-Jew by joining in the singing with eastern European workers.

Beyond the Reinhard camps, another significant site of killing was Majdanek, on the outskirts of Lublin, which operated from October 1941 to July 1944, when it was captured intact by the Red Army. Majdanek commanded a number of labor sub-camps and was itself a camp to which people selected for forced labor were sent; occasionally people fit for work were taken off trains heading for the death camps and redirected there. Majdanek also had its own gas chambers, although most deaths were caused by malnutrition, disease, and shooting. Around sixty thousand Jews were murdered here, as well as some two thousand Soviet prisoners of war. Unlike the extermination camps, there was no time to obliterate the traces of murder at this site: due to the speed of liberation, the gas chambers remain to this day well preserved.

The almost unimaginable horrors of these camps have rightly commanded public attention; and, as we shall see, a small number of the killers were later brought to account in court for their deeds. Less well noticed, however, is the significance of the civilian administrators who made these endpoints possible. All across the General Government, under Hans Frank, there were committed district leaders (*Kreisleiter*): in the main, men drawn from what is often called the "war youth generation" (*Kriegsjugendgeneration*), who had been too young to fight in the First World War but were committed to completing what they saw as unfinished business.[74] The civilian administrators were not the lower-class thugs who brutally maltreated and killed the victims. The majority were from bourgeois backgrounds, highly educated, frequently trained in law, and often had a higher degree or even a doctorate. They created the conditions that made the camps possible: they oversaw the logistics of stigmatization and degradation; they ensured that Jews wore the star, obeyed the curfew, turned up for forced labor, were contained within ghettos, were hanged for infringements of rules or shot in "retaliation" actions—and they put up the relevant signs to ensure that Jews were in the right place at the right time for deportations to the death camps.

A notable example is Baron Otto Gustav von Wächter, who was born in Vienna into a well-established Austrian family, and whose father was ennobled for military service in the First World War. Wächter joined the Nazi movement early, becoming a Nazi activist when this was still illegal in Austria and moving to Germany to complete his studies, before returning as part of the new government following the Anschluss in 1938. In 1939, with the occupation of Poland, Wächter became governor of Kraków under Hans Frank, signing the ghetto into existence. Following the invasion of the Soviet Union, the areas of Galicia that had since 1939 been under Russian occupation were incorporated into Frank's expanded General Government, and Wächter eventually became governor of the District of Galicia. Here he worked with Katzmann, the SS, and the police forces to ensure the smooth running of the machinery of oppression; he was also active in assisting the cause of the Ukrainian nationalists in their fight against Bolshevism. Unable to face up to the full implications of his father's role, Wächter's son Horst would continue to assert that his father was nevertheless able to remain a "decent man" in these circumstances.[75]

A horrific event marked the end of the Reinhard death camps. On November 3, 1943, in the Lublin region in a massacre the Nazis termed "Harvest Festival" (*Erntefest*), as many Jews as possible were killed. Under the direction of Christian Wirth, some forty-three thousand Jews were shot in the course of a single day—the largest of all such Nazi mass shootings. Killings took place in Majdanek, as well as in a number of other camps and sub-camps across the region, including Trawniki, which had functioned not only for the training of Ukrainian assistants to the SS but also as a labor camp for Jews. Here, Jews had already been ordered in late October to begin digging what they thought were large defensive anti-tank trenches, not realizing that these would soon become their own graves. During a long morning on November 3, twelve thousand Jews were marched to these trenches and shot by, among others, members of Reserve Police Battalion 41. Poles living nearby recalled hearing terrible shrieks and screams, partially drowned by loud music played by the Germans; they noted also that the killers drank copious amounts of vodka. While the killing itself was over by the early afternoon, the bodies were subsequently burned, and the stench of flesh and pall of smoke made life unbearable for inhabitants in the vicinity for another week to ten days. Just as in the death camps that had been closed down, the Nazis then sought to remove all traces of the Trawniki camp. Ukrainian guards disinfected the area, and crops were sewn.[76] Only the old brick sugar factory buildings remain visible today.

Unlike the Reinhard camps, Auschwitz continued its work to the bitter end, when the Russians finally overran it in 1945. The date of January 27, when Auschwitz was officially liberated, was chosen as the date for the Holocaust Memorial Day in Europe. This place and date have had to stand as a symbol for far more than what took place on just this site or at this time.

Extermination through Work: Productivity and Profiteering

It was not only in the fields, woods, and ravines of eastern Europe or the ghettos and camps in Poland that victims of Nazism were visibly subjected to violence. In the heart of the old Reich, the concentration camps that had been established in the peacetime years were enlarged; the network of labor camps and satellite sub-camps expanded exponentially; and the use of foreign forced labor in German enterprises grew as the machinery of war swallowed up ever larger proportions of the adult male labor force. Millions of people, including prisoners of war and civilians from countries across Europe, were caught up in the ever-growing exploitation of forced and slave labor.

The wider Nazi concentration camp network changed significantly in wartime. The system developed from serving the initial purposes of incarcerating political opponents and, from the mid-1930s, seeking to "reform" those who did not conform to Nazi ideals, including homosexual men, Jehovah's Witnesses, and "asocials," to an ever-expanding network for massive exploitation of slave labor for grandiose building schemes as well as, increasingly, war-related industries. Camps provided laborers for back-breaking work in the stone quarries that were essential to Himmler's SS-owned enterprise, the "German Earth- and Stoneworks Corporation" (DESt, Deutsche Erd- und Steinwerke), established in 1938. Major camps were established in 1938 at Flossenbürg in Bavaria, near the border with Czechoslovakia, and in Mauthausen in Austria, following the Anschluss. In Neuengamme, a former brickyard on the outskirts of Hamburg was bought by the DESt in 1938 and a concentration camp established first under the control of Sachsenhausen; from 1940, it became an independent camp. In 1940, a camp was set up in Gross-Rosen in Lower Silesia, also initially a sub-camp of Sachsenhausen, which from 1941 became an independent camp playing a leading role in the empire of Silesian sub-camps run by the SS program Organization Schmelt (named after the SS officer in charge).[77] In the west, Natzweiler-Struthof was established in the incorporated French territory of Alsace, under German occupation from 1940 to 1944. Part of the expansion related to secret weapons production, a project that informed the development, in the late summer of 1943, of Mittelbau-Dora near Nordhausen, initially a sub-camp of Buchenwald. With its underground tunnels in the Harz Mountains, Mittelbau-Dora replaced the more visible rockets production site at Peenemünde, which was increasingly the object of Allied bombing. Mittelbau-Dora developed in importance and size and eventually established its own network of satellite camps.[78]

From June 1943, Mauthausen too began to expand, for similar reasons, from its original core around Mauthausen and Gusen, with new sub-camps involving tunneling into the hillsides for secret weapons production at Melk and Ebensee, and eventually encompassing more than forty satellite camps right across Austria.[79] Mauthausen's prisoner population grew from 14,800 in spring 1943 to around 84,500 toward the end of the war. In total, during the period 1938–44 some two hundred thousand prisoners entered Mauthausen and its sub-camps, of whom around one hundred thousand died. In western Austria there were also some thirteen sub-camps of Dachau. The number of civilian forced laborers in Austria rose to more than half a million (in a population totaling only seven million) in September 1944, in addition to prisoners of war also engaged in forced labor.[80]

In this way, the numbers of camps and sub-camps rose dramatically, in a sprawling network of suffering that left virtually no area untouched. This network was not something hidden away in the east: by the end of the war, there were somewhere between 900 and 1,200 sub-camps of the major concentration camps, spread right across the Reich.[81]

Particularly from 1942 onward, the camp network became a major sup-
plier of slave labor, and, under Oswald Pohl and the SS Economic and
Administrative Main Office (WVHA), this was increasingly significant
for armaments production.[82] In exploiting slave labor, there was willing
cooperation between the SS and key industrialists, including notably the
new breed of managers in companies such as I. G. Farben, Volkswagen, and
Steyr-Daimler-Puch, a subsidiary of the Hermann Göring works, as well as
Heinkel, as we have seen. Far from being constrained by the Nazis, as many
later claimed, these industrialists appear to have been only too pleased to
seize new opportunities. They engaged in networking with leading politicians, currying favors and extracting favorable business deals.[83] Similarly,
even where, as in Melk, there appeared to be conflicts between the local
civilian administration and the new armaments-driven enterprises, these
seem to have been less about conflicts of principle than about parochial
encroachments on territory and clashes of competing interests, as when
land was taken over in a peremptory fashion or a new path was built over a
farmer's land and fruit trees were ruined in the process.[84]

The prisoner population expanded exponentially. It had already leapt
from 21,000 in August 1939, just before the start of the war, to between
70,000 and 80,000 in spring 1942. There then came a rapid jump, more than
doubling by May 1943 to a figure of some 203,000 concentration camp
prisoners. By August 1943 this had risen to 224,000; one year later, in August
1944, it had again more than doubled, to 524,286. By January 1945, within
months of the end of the war—and following the deaths of so many millions—there were as many as 714,211 prisoners in the concentration camp
system.[85] This was a simply massive slave labor force: nearly three-quarters
of a million people, from many nationalities and backgrounds, including
political prisoners, and further augmented by prisoners of war, being held
against their will and often worked to death, frequently in full sight of civilian workers and members of the local population.

The death rate was high, both from disease and starvation and from killing when prisoners were considered no longer productive; they were seen
as useful only so long as they could work. Mortality rates varied according
to conditions as well as categories of prisoners. Mauthausen, with its back-
breaking labor and notorious "staircase of death" from the quarry—which
prisoners were sent up, carrying huge granite blocks, precisely in order to
precipitate casualties—had a particularly high mortality rate; in 1941, more
than half (58 percent) of the prisoners died there, compared to just over one

third in Dachau (36 percent) and just under one in five in Buchenwald (19 percent) and Sachsenhausen (16 percent).[86] But in all camps, death was omnipresent, brutality an everyday occurrence. And in all camps, the system of violence was devolved: from the commandants through the SS men through the guards, right down to individual prisoners selected to work as Kapos. These prisoners, operating in what Primo Levi famously called the "grey zone," were put in charge of other prisoners, meting out punishments and petty privileges, organizing productivity and ensuring conformity, and exercising, in a limited and subordinate capacity, the power to affect inmates' chances of life and death. Having a relatively well-meaning Kapo, who was to some extent able to protect those he favored, could make all the difference to experiences and long-term survival chances; mean, brutish, and thuggish Kapos—many of them purposefully chosen from among imprisoned criminals who were considered to be well-practiced in violence—could shorten life expectancy dramatically.

Prisoners' bodies were used not only for labor but also in the interests of "scientific research." "Medical" experiments were carried out not only in Auschwitz, with Dr. Mengele's notorious experiments on sterilization, infectious diseases, and the use of twins for genetic studies, but also in camps within the "old Reich" (*Altreich*), in the heart of Germany. In Ravensbrück, for example, experiments were carried out on the leg muscles of female prisoners, leading to permanent disability for those fortunate enough to survive. In Dachau, experiments with immersion in icy water or deprivation of oxygen led to the deaths of prisoners in the supposed interests of finding ways to help German armed forces survive extreme conditions in the air and at sea. Human life was simply expendable in service of the Reich.

As the exploitation of slave labor expanded, so too did the range of victims; and as labor gangs were marched from sites of incarceration to sites of exploitation in quarries, tunnels, armaments factories, and construction projects, there were inevitably ever-larger numbers of bystanders and witnesses to their distress. Although it is impossible to give precise figures, it is quite clear that across the Reich, millions of unwilling onlookers, pragmatic conformists, regime sympathizers, and opportunistic profiteers were all too well aware of the violence in their midst. Around Mauthausen, for example, local farmers and other residents could not help but see inmates subjected to brutality. Few dared to query the nature of the enterprise; most preferred to turn a blind eye, hoping not to register what was going on. However, some objected to having to see these sights: for example, a local farmer filed a complaint in 1941, commenting that Mauthausen "inmates are being shot repeatedly; those badly struck live for yet some time, and so remain lying next to the dead for hours and even a day long." The complainant, who was "an unwilling witness to such outrages," continued, "Such a sight makes such a demand on my nerves that in the long run I cannot bear this," and he finally requested "that such inhuman deeds be discontinued, or else be done where one does not see it."[87]

This desire not to see was widespread. But it does not seem to have affected willingness, at the same time, to profit from the deaths of others. The local population benefited from widespread trade in the possessions and gold plundered from victims of the nearby gas chambers at Hartheim, who included not only those brought there in the euthanasia program but also weak and ill prisoners from Mauthausen and its sub-camps.[88]

Moreover, with the expansion of the camp system, more and more people were actively involved in some way. Recruitment and training were crucial to keeping the system going. Yet at the same time, the war was sucking ever more young men into military service. While soldiers were dying at the front, tens of thousands of others were brought into the system at home. In 1942, there were 5,884 SS personnel working in the camps, and 511 other workers. By January 1945, there were 37,674 men and 3,508 women working in the camps, many of whom had been trained and arrived at camps only from 1943 onward, with little prior experience of such organized brutality.[89]

This was a system that depended not so much on individual motivation as on mobilization to perform particular roles. There were of course key movers, shakers, and initiators of policy; but many more people now became actively involved in behaviors that, under other circumstances, they would never have conceived. It was not so much perpetrators who produced the system of violence as the system of violence that produced perpetrators.

There were individual variations in responding to the challenges, constraints, and opportunities. Even people who held the same role differed in how they entered into the system and how they initially viewed their position. But once they were in role, certain behaviors were expected, and they had to accommodate themselves. One way or another, people who had previously led "ordinary" lives were able to turn, within a relatively short space of time, into perpetrators.

The transformation of female camp guards at the women's camp of Ravensbrück provides a good example. Like other concentration camps,

Ravensbrück grew and changed over the years of its existence.[90] It acquired additional significance for production in the war industries and in the local economy; no longer were women simply set tasks of useless manual labor, moving heaps of sand from one place to another, as a penal measure designed to "reform" their behavior. A men's camp was set up just over the boundary from the main women's camp, and a youth camp was established nearby. Particularly in the final months of the war, Ravensbrück became increasingly crowded. With the influx of arrivals from the east in the winter of 1944–45, overcrowding reached such proportions that people were dying in the makeshift tent in which they had been quartered, since the barracks were already full to overflowing. In the final months of the war, a gas chamber was built just outside the wall to kill those thought too weak or sick to be of further use.

The staffing changed, too, over time. From 1942, Ravensbrück functioned as a training camp for female camp guards who, following a course that might last up to six months, could then be sent on to other concentration camps; some 3,500 young women were eventually trained here. From 1943, the SS launched a major recruitment drive for female guards, and in 1943, the Reich Ministry of Labor began to conscript women between the ages of seventeen and forty-five. By the end of 1943, most of those women who showed up at Ravensbrück to be trained as camp guards were in fact conscripts who had little or no idea of what they should expect. By 1944, quite apart from the numbers who had passed through as part of their training, there were around 150 female guards or "overseers" stationed at Ravensbrück.[91]

Who were these women? Some of the female guards had been recruited by advertisements or through personal contacts; they were frequently attracted by the prospect of relatively good wages and the chance of improving their circumstances. In 1944 a twenty-five-year-old unmarried overseer could earn around 185 Reichsmarks per month at Ravensbrück, more than twice as much as an unskilled female textile worker. But as the war developed, there was a growing labor shortage in all areas, and women were urgently needed in a wide range of war-related enterprises. Those who had been conscripted were far less enthusiastic about this job and less willing to adapt their behavior on arrival.

The distinctions between the successive cohorts of guards were not lost on prisoners. Margaret Buber-Neumann recalls that in the early days of her imprisonment at Ravensbrück, "concentration camp staff were recruited along National Socialist lines and the guards were all impassioned Nazi types ... who treated the prisoners badly on their own initiative, and took a delight in tormenting them and making their lives a misery."[92] As the war went on, however, with growing numbers of prisoners and greater shortage of labor, "concentration camp personnel had to be recruited wherever it could be obtained," with the result that "on the whole the types recruited were not so brutal."[93] By the later war years, the "Camp Leader Bräuning used to go out on recruiting drives to factories and other places where there were many women." Promised residential work in a "rehabilitation center" in idyllic lakeside surroundings, with good rates of pay and "ample food," many ordinary young women were attracted to the possibility; others were simply sent there.

It was not only the character of successive cohorts that changed; the women themselves changed too, as they adapted to their new circumstances. Buber-Neumann noted that when new guards first arrived, they "were poorly dressed, rather nervous and hesitant in their unaccustomed surroundings, and more than a little intimidated." They were shocked by what they saw and had to do, and "during the first week almost half of them would come weeping to Frau Langefeld and ask to be allowed to go home." Fearing an encounter with the camp commandant, who was the only one who could give permission for release from the duties to which they had just signed up, most settled into the job and were in the process transformed: "Many of them changed out of all recognition once they got into uniform. Top boots and a forage cap stuck at an angle on their heads gave them a feeling of confidence and superiority."[94]

It did not take very long before the new recruits were fully institutionalized, enacting their brutal roles on the side of the perpetrators—as an *effect*, not a cause, of participating in the system. Part of the induction had to do with the way the new guards were taught to perceive the prisoners, "who were always presented as morally degenerate and worthless" and for whom "they were taught to stifle any sympathy." They faced "dire punishments if they violated the service regulations and had any other than strictly official contacts with their charges." These lessons were reinforced by the company in which the new guards found themselves: "They were always accompanied by the worst of the old wardresses, all brutal, bullying, reporting, ear-boxing types," and daily "had strictness and severity drilled into them." Moreover, "during their free hours their only male companions were SS men."[95] As a result, with few exceptions "these young working women were soon every bit as bad as the old hands, ordering the prisoners around, bullying them and shouting as though they had been born in a barracks."[96] These women, for the most part, were later able to claim—with some degree of honesty—that they had not personally chosen to work in a concentration camp and bore no personal responsibility for what went on there.

And these were not the only people involved in oppression. The deaths of millions of prisoners of war in camps run by the army—deaths caused by willful starvation and poor conditions, as well as disease—have tended to pass relatively unnoticed among the many inhumanities for which the Third Reich was infamous.[97] Soviet prisoners of war in particular were subjected to murderous treatment, and the death rate was accordingly high, reaching perhaps up to three and a half million deaths caused by German maltreatment.

The Many Roads to Murder

Toward the end of the war, the system began to descend into chaos. Death marches were organized from camps that were being abandoned or evacuated as the Russian front advanced. Prisoners were taken from one place to another—sometimes on foot, sometimes in trucks or by train—as those deemed still fit to work were moved to wherever they seemed to be needed the most. Sometimes the marches covered enormous distances, with people dropping dead from exhaustion and illness along the way or being shot and left by the wayside as they stumbled. Even those transported on trains died in transit. It has been estimated that at Mauthausen, for example, as many as 1,500 prisoners who had been on the death march from Auschwitz were found to be dead on arrival, and a further five hundred died in the camp courtyard while awaiting registration.[98]

Camps were often unable to accommodate the increased numbers, and many more died soon after arrival in places such as Ravensbrück and Bergen-Belsen. Bergen-Belsen became a place where emaciated prisoners sat around, dying of starvation and illness; many did not survive very long after liberation by the British troops on April 15, 1945. In Ravensbrück, the huge tent erected to accommodate new arrivals was woefully inadequate, as were the available provisions and clothing, and the gas chamber that had just been constructed was barely able to keep up with the task of putting a speedier end to the diseased and dying prisoners.

The death marches—during which around one-third of the prisoners died, perhaps 200,000 to 250,000—illustrate the absurdity of trying to keep alive those last few prisoners who might still be economically useful while killing those who tried to escape or dropped with fatigue. Even the very character of the marches was itself just another form of extermination. But the killings during this final phase of the war were distinctive in several respects.[99]

First of all, killings took place all across Germany—on the sides of roads and in rural areas, hamlets, villages, towns—and not in the fields, forests, and death camps in the east. Secondly, individuals were involved in decisions to pull the trigger, to kill human beings, simply because they were faltering on the road, stumbling through exhaustion and lack of food and water. This was not a routine matter of obeying orders, processing killings like some form of industrial production, giving in to peer group pressure in extraordinary conditions of wartime, or believing in tales of supposed partisans and guerrilla warfare at the front. The "danger" posed by the starving, emaciated, disease-ridden bodies collapsing in the marching columns clearly could not be translated into any kind of military euphemism. And thirdly, the prisoners themselves were heterogeneous. There were prisoners from many nationalities and many categories, as well as significant groups of Jews. Not all Jews were killed, and not all those who were killed were Jews. These killings did not arise from genocidal antisemitism but from a mixture of other motives, resulting from a combination of general orders with personal initiatives under particular conditions.[100]

Prisoners who survived the marches were still used for their labor—whether for desperate last efforts in industry and armaments production, as in the underground tunnels of Mittelbau-Dora or the Mauthausen sub-camps, in the Messerschmitt or Heinkel aircraft works, in the factories of Siemens and others, or for clearing the rubble in German towns that had experienced war damage. They worked alongside civilians and in full sight of others.

Prisoners who later wrote of their experiences included Lucille Eichengreen (formerly Cecilia Landau), who, extraordinarily, was first deported from the Łódź ghetto to Auschwitz, and from there onward via a series of stages right back to her native Hamburg, where she finally experienced the end of the war and liberation.[101] A significant number of others from the Łódź ghetto also survived in this way. Prisoners who had worked in the Heinkel works were often transported to Flossenbürg to work. As Sigmund Reich, for example, reported shortly after the end of the war: "We were demanded for Germany, because we were good workers." This camp was large and diverse,

and in his view "one of the worst lagers," whose inmates included "professional criminals" as well as Russians "and different nationalities."[102] Arriving
at Flossenbürg after a horrific journey in an overcrowded train so that "by
the time we came to our destination many were dead," Mark Stern was
similarly struck by its diversity, commenting that "there were not only
Jews; there were Czechs, Russians, Poles, German criminals, German homosexuals. We were the minority; we were the slaves. We were mistreated by
everybody—by the guards, as well as by other prisoners."[103] Stern was employed
working on airplanes, and he remembers that he tried to sabotage them by
weakening the wings by replacing good rivets with weaker ones. Nathan
Gottlieb, who arrived in Flossenbürg at the age of nineteen and also recalled
the diversity of groups, felt by contrast that "Jews were treated exactly as
all other nationalities. . . . Myself, I didn't suffer." His father, however, with
whom he had stayed together up until this point, died in February 1945
from starvation and disease.[104] Flossenbürg made a major impact on other
prisoners arriving from labor camps in Poland: Jack Eisner, for example, provides a detailed account (although some features are misremembered).[105]
Jack Terry provides a vivid description of conditions in the camp during the
final months of the war and his liberation by the Americans.[106]

But many prisoners did not make it through the death marches to the
intended places of hard labor in service of the Reich. Everywhere, bodies
could be seen by local residents as well as by Germans on "treks" fleeing the
Red Army. Some notable incidents were the subject of discussion at the
time, but memories faded. Others gained wider audiences, but even this did
not necessarily ensure that perpetrators were brought to justice.

One significant example was that of Gardelegen, north of Magdeburg,
where on April 13, 1945, more than one thousand prisoners who had been
marched from the camps of Neuengamme and Mittelbau-Dora were incarcerated in a barn that was set alight; they were burned alive, or shot dead
if they tried to escape from the barn. The local NSDAP district leader
(*Kreisleiter*), Gerhard Thiele, as well as the SS officers in charge, were apparently trying to destroy the evidence of their crimes and silence potential
witnesses before the arrival of American troops who were already in the
vicinity. But their cover-up was not quite complete; the following day, the
Americans discovered the charred bodies. They were horrified and took
photographs, which soon became widely known: in May 1945 the American
magazine *Life* published an article entitled "The Holocaust of Gardelegen"—
an early usage of the word "holocaust," incidentally, which did not at that

time catch on more widely.[107] A junior officer was sentenced in 1947 by a US military tribunal to life imprisonment, but Thiele, who had ordered this massacre, successfully evaded arrest. And there was later little evidence of any urgent attempt in West Germany to bring him to justice; in 1970 his wife untruthfully claimed, following the opening of legal investigations in the 1960s, that she had not seen him since the day after the massacre, and this statement appears to have been believed. Thiele continued to live under a pseudonym, Gerhard Lindemann, until his death in 1994 at the age of eighty-five.

Gardelegen became particularly well known, but there were many similar incidents of mass murder in this period of what was later called "end-phase violence." And although they did not receive the international news coverage of the Gardelegen incident, similar incidents and deaths were well known in the immediate vicinity. In 1950, for example, the East German authorities dug up a mass grave in the small village of Spohla, now a part of the town of Wittichenau in the Bautzen region of Saxony. The regional police reported that the bodies of many former prisoners who had been on a death march from the Groß-Rosen camp had been buried here on March 1, 1945. In total some 118 bodies were uncovered: 99 in one grave, and a further 19 in another nearby place. The incident had been reported by a local eyewitness at the time, but the bodies were only dug up some five years later.[108] Similar mass graves were known right across the routes of the death marches.

Other killings that were part of this "end-phase violence" took place within camps or prisons, prior to the flight of those in charge. The former concentration camp and prison of Sonnenburg, for example, was well known among inmates for the particular brutality of one SS guard by the name of Heinz Adrian; it later gained wider notoriety when the secretary of state in the Reich Ministry of Justice, Herbert Klemm, was put on trial in Nuremberg as part of the "lawyers' trial" for having been the senior official ordering the mass killing that ended the lives of the prisoners remaining here at the end of the war. During the night of January 30, 1945, with the impending arrival of Soviet Army forces, the order was given that all remaining inmates should be shot to death. Numbers vary, but it seems clear that somewhere between 740 and 819 people were shot that night, before those in charge of the prison fled. Interestingly, according to contemporary eyewitness reports, the prison officials themselves apparently refused to shoot and were told to leave immediately—losing their jobs in the process, and having to flee their homes in fear.[109] The Gestapo were instead called in to assist the SS with the work of killing. This incident later provided fodder for the East German authorities, who in an early postwar trial sentenced Heinz Adrian to death, a sentence carried out in 1948, and who were highly critical of West Germany for predictably failing to convict those more senior perpetrators who had fled west.[110] Klemm, who had initially been sentenced to life imprisonment in the Nuremberg "lawyers' trial," had his sentence commuted to twenty years and—like so many others who had been sentenced by the Allies—did not even have to serve this reduced term of imprisonment; he was in fact released as early as 1956.

The widespread local knowledge of mass killings and the visibility of the columns of ragged and miserable survivors who marched through numerous communities, crisscrossing Germany, meant that the inhumanity of the Reich in its final phase was laid bare for anyone with eyes to see. And not only to see: in many incidents, members of the local community were themselves involved in killing or assisted with the logistics. Participants were drawn from across society, from mayors and others in authority to elderly men and young boys who had been called up in the Volkssturm—hastily trained troops of men between the ages of sixteen and sixty, put together in the autumn of 1944—as well as other locals. One can only wonder, again, what precisely was the "it" about which so many later professed to have known nothing.

Extermination came not only in many forms but also with many faces. Those who actually pulled the trigger or exerted physical violence were not the only ones who were implicated. Persecution could not have taken place without the involvement of large numbers of people, in a wide range of roles. Culpability was broadly if unevenly distributed, between the instigation, design, and administration of different forms of oppression; the execution of brutality on the ground; and the ambivalent complicity of daily decisions to turn away, to not see, not register the inhumanity that was so evident all around. As the network of terror spread, taking many forms and in innumerable variations, a wide variety of people were drawn into local topographies of exploitation and suffering.

Many people became involved in the collective violence initiated by the Nazi regime—and felt that they, as individuals, bore little or no personal responsibility for the murderous outcome. The division of labor was accompanied by a corresponding diminution of any sense of personal guilt. This would later make it easier for those on the perpetrator side to live with their past.

For their victims, however, the experience went far deeper. For all the qualifications that have to be made, for all the compromises and gray zones, there is an enormous divide that should not be allowed to slide out of view. This is the gulf, the chasm, between those who were the targets of Nazi persecution and those who by their actions or inaction sustained or assisted the process of persecution. Those who were on the side of the perpetrators, whether periodically or persistently, later sought to distance themselves from this past, to disclaim responsibility and even knowledge of what had taken place. Those who were victims of persecution by virtue of their assigned identity, whether or not they accepted the categories imposed upon them, were affected quite differently. For the victims, experiences of Nazi persecution defined the whole character and course of their subsequent lives—if they were lucky enough to survive this maelstrom of murder.

6

Defining Experiences

Jack Terry, who following work in a Heinkel slave labor camp lived through the last awful weeks of the war in Flossenbürg, and whose entire family had been murdered by the Nazis, commented in an interview in 2009: "Although I left Flossenbürg as fast as possible, Flossenbürg never left me. For us, the former prisoners, this past scarred us for life."[1] Aaron S., who survived the Dębica ghetto, talked in his later testimony about how the life of a Jew was considered to be lower than that of an animal, and "if they had treated us like dogs it would have been heaven." He, too, was unable to rid himself of this past: "The most horrible scenes remain with you and you cannot forget them"; every few days he had nightmares about running, trying to hide.[2] Thomas (Toivi) Blatt, a survivor of Sobibór, could similarly never escape his past and relived it repeatedly in his thoughts and nightmares, as well as periodically returning in person to Poland to try to ensure adequate memorialization on the site. He recalls that his wife could eventually no longer bear it; when she finally left him, she told him, "I don't want to live in Sobibor any more. . . . I've lived there for 30 years."[3]

Similar experiences and emotions were expressed by innumerable other survivors. The experience of persecution was the defining experience of their life; they could never forget or evade the past, only learn to live with it. It is this that served, ultimately, to create a distinctive community of the persecuted; it is this, the undesired lifelong impact of experiences of persecution, that sets them apart from their persecutors—despite all the differences among individuals and groups of victims.

There were of course many differences between groups targeted by the Nazis. Ultimately, Jews were simply not allowed to be at all: the very essence of their being, their very existence on this earth, was denied. There could be no agency on their part that could change this: the Nazi racial version of antisemitism meant that no conversion, no appeal, no "reformation" was possible. The question for Nazis was more one of priorities around how to achieve a "final solution."

People who were designated "life unworthy of living"—the mentally and physically disabled—also were subject to eugenic and racial theories that subordinated their very existence to the goals of the state. By contrast, those who were persecuted because of their behaviors and outlooks, from political opposition through religious beliefs, "asocial" lifestyles, or sexual preferences, could in principle be reformed, even if in practice harsh treatment actually served to kill them in large numbers.

Yet whatever the reasons why particular groups were persecuted, and whatever the differences within any group (such as between western and eastern European Jews), victims of persecution became part of a wider, overarching community situated clearly on one side of the massive chasm created by Nazi policies. The persecuted faced common challenges that marked them out as a quite distinct "community of experience"—one that was for decades to stand in stark contrast to perpetrators. And they had been persecuted precisely as part of the Nazi vision of a "national community," or *Volksgemeinschaft*, in which they were to have no place.

The Nazi vision was never fully realized, and critical voices—despite horrendous penalties for dissent—were never completely silenced. But it is important also to note that the majority on the side of the perpetrators did not need to support Nazi ideals explicitly or feel personally motivated by ideological convictions. Many were simply mobilized in service of the state and drawn into sustaining a system of collective violence irrespective of personal views and responses. By portraying their experiences as essentially benign, unrelated to specific atrocities, they could seek to obscure the intrinsic connection between the national community and the experiences of the persecuted.

Given the division of responsibility in the structures and apparatus of persecution, the majority of those involved on the perpetrator side could separate "what they were doing" from "who they really were": they could separate their roles from their private lives; they could later assign guilt to others, whose orders they could claim they had "merely obeyed," without doubting their own integrity and morality. As regimes and values changed, people who had been on the perpetrator side were able to develop strategies for living with potentially uncomfortable aspects of their Nazi past. Those experiences that did stamp a defining mark on their lives—particularly the effects of war and the consequences of defeat—could be redeployed to cast them in the role of "victims," without recognition of personal responsibility.

Such a separation between self and experience was far more difficult, and in many cases completely impossible, for most of those who were on the receiving end of violence. Their experiences were life-defining. Victimized for who they were, they experienced an attack on the very core of their being, the essence of their identity. This could, for those who survived, have lifelong psychological reverberations. Moreover, those who were persecuted faced existential extremes, an exposure to death or the possibility of death; and the effects of brutality, maltreatment, disease, and starvation could be long-lasting, again with often lifelong consequences. They faced extreme bereavement, the destruction of their worlds, and the loss of homes, families, friends, cultures, and professions.

There are good reasons why the distinction between "perpetrators" and "victims" has remained so useful, despite all the problems surrounding the changing meanings and the often far too narrow applications of these terms.

Diversity and Shared Experiences

There was of course enormous diversity within the community of the per-secuted, not only between but even within different groups. The distinctive-ness of the Jewish experience has on occasion threatened to overshadow the sufferings inflicted on other groups, causing frictions and controversies; but even within the Jewish community, hierarchies of victimhood emerged. Attempts to compare Jewish sufferings with those of other groups have led to accusations of relativization; failures to compare have equally been rooted in and helped to sustain continued prejudices and marginalization of perse-cuted groups. To understand the postwar complexities and long shadows of this past, we need to be sensitive both to the diversity of experiences and also to the common aspects of persecution.

For all groups who were persecuted, there were inconsistencies in policy and differences in practice. Many persecuted groups—political opponents, Jehovah's Witnesses, homosexual men, "habitual criminals," and "asocials"—were characterized in terms of beliefs or behaviors that, as noted, it was thought could potentially be changed. This made the fate of such victims in principle different from that of Jews, but in practice it did not necessarily mean long-term survival. Gay men, for example, might find on release from camp, sometimes following castration, that they were sent to the front in what was in effect a suicide unit destined for instant death; recanting Jehovah's Witnesses might be shot in the back on departure from camp, having just signed a form renouncing their faith. The mentally and physically disabled, if cared for at home rather than in an institution, were not as easily caught up in the program of ridding Germany of "useless eaters" as those in institutions were, nor would killing them have freed up beds in the same way.

Roma and Sinti experienced a rate of mass murder comparable to that of the Jews. There were both similarities and also differences in the definitions and treatment of those groups designated by the Nazis as "Gypsies" and "Jews." These later provoked often bitter controversies over distinctions between "genocide" and "the Holocaust."[4] It is worth momentarily considering some of the underlying issues.

Jews were seen by the Nazis as a fundamentally "racial" group: under the Nuremberg Laws, religious belief and practice was only significant when making distinctions among people who were "first degree" descendants of "mixed parentage," where religious commitment could eventually make all the difference between death, as someone who "counted as a Jew," or a marginalized life as a stigmatized "Mischling first degree." "Gypsy," by contrast, was a category that always mixed social and "racial" criteria, with an itinerant lifestyle forming an integral part of the definition. However, being of Gypsy descent was often considered sufficient proof of supposedly inherent criminality, even when individuals had a proven income and sedentary lifestyle, suggesting that the racial conception was in a sense prior to the social definition, which was simply part of the wider stereotype. However, unlike Jews, "racially pure" Gypsies were considered by the Nazis to be "superior" to those of "mixed race" parentage (the so-called ZM, or Zigeuner Mischlinge). It was not the "racially pure" Roma and Sinti but primarily those of "mixed" descent who were deported. Himmler's Auschwitz decree of December 16, 1942, led to the deportation of more than thirteen thousand German Gypsies of mixed descent to the special Gypsy camp in Auschwitz. "Racially pure" Gypsies in Germany were exempted from Himmler's Auschwitz order, as were several categories of Gypsies of mixed descent who qualified for reasons ranging from sedentary occupations and "orderly" lifestyles to sterling service in the First World War. It was suggested that those who were exempted from deportation should be sterilized, but this was not carried out consistently.

The murder of Roma and Sinti was not accompanied by the extensive ideological underpinnings characteristic of Nazi antisemitism, and was not presented as an integral part of a broader search for a "final solution" or an explicit policy to eradicate an entire "race." Even so, the ultimate outcome would have been the prevention of biological continuity of an ethnically defined group, a key element of genocide.

For Gypsies, deportation did not necessarily mean, as was the case for Jews, that they had already been targeted for killing in advance. Death was often a consequence of the conditions in which Gypsies were held following deportation. The selection of Gypsies for gassing could be precipitated by attempts to combat disease, particularly typhus, as in the transfer of the Gypsies from the Łódź ghetto to the gas vans of Chełmno in January 1942. Even the Gypsies sent to Auschwitz, with its high mortality rate, were not in the first instance designated for gassing, nor were they sent as part of a plan to obliterate their "race." Selection of Gypsies for gassing at Auschwitz-Birkenau changed suddenly in the summer of 1944, when the Gypsy camp was cleared, perhaps to make space for the arrival of large numbers of Hungarian Jews. Elsewhere in occupied Europe, Gypsies were massacred by shooting, sometimes included as part of the killing of Jewish communities. Policies were pursued inconsistently, however, with wide variations in different places and at different times.

Nazi policies toward Gypsies therefore differed from those toward Jews, even though the outcome for the vast majority in both communities was the same: stigmatization, maltreatment, murder. It is purely a matter of differing definitions as to whether one group or the other is or is not considered to have been the object of genocide; this is now, essentially, an academic question.

For the myriad victims who ended up dead, the question clearly matters not at all; but it matters a great deal to groups and organizations speaking in the name of the dead and on behalf of survivors. It also came to matter massively when, in the postwar decades, continuing prejudices led to repeated refusal of claims to compensation for Gypsies—a group still seen by many German officials primarily as "asocials."

Jews too experienced differences and inconsistencies in treatment. Although in principle designated for total extermination with the radicalization of Nazi policies and practices in 1941, Jewish communities were frequently divided into those who were still fit to work and those to be killed instantly. The Nazi notion of extermination through labor of course indicated the proposed eventual fate of these people, but even so, many did actually manage to survive in this way. How to exterminate the entire "Jewish race" over time was a question that was never quite resolved. The "problem" of people considered to be Mischlinge was repeatedly discussed without resolution, including at the infamous Wannsee Conference of January 1942. The option of sterilization in the short term was considered preferable by some Nazis to that of outright murder, given the sensibilities of the "Aryan," or non-Jewish, side of the "mixed" families. But toward the end of the war, when Mischlinge were deported to labor camps, it seemed only a matter of time before they too would be killed.

This diversity of experiences among victim groups provided a basis for later frictions around the questions of who had suffered the most, who were the "real victims" or the "real survivors," and whether the extermination of the Jews was in some way distinctively different, setting Jewish experiences apart from all others. These debates were not simply arguments about the "uniqueness" of the "Chosen People"—arguments often accompanied by hurtful accusations of inverted elitism, perpetuating invidious stereotypes—but were also related to practical questions, from compensation and reparations to the contents, character, and funding of museums and memorial sites. Even in the 1980s, as the "Holocaust" was firmly placed on the memorial agenda and plans were debated for the foundation of a United States Holocaust Memorial Museum, such arguments complicated proposals for remembrance. The voices of other groups of victims also found themselves competing on deeply divided terrain across the postwar decades, where prejudices remained rife.

Yet for all the differences, groups targeted for persecution had certain experiences in common. They were affected in vast numbers by world historical events. Individuals were classified and treated as anonymous members of groups; they were systematically degraded, humiliated, maltreated, and murdered according to the groups into which they had been categorized by the Nazis. This makes the trauma suffered by those who were victims of state-sponsored persecution a widely shared trauma—distinct from the trauma of an individual event, such as bereavement through a fatal accident or illness or personal violation in incidents such as mugging, physical assault, or rape.

It also makes the act of perpetration distinctive. Perpetrators were engaging in violence ordered from above, not carrying out acts of aggression on their own initiative. Practices of persecution and genocide were bureaucratically organized. Despite individual differences in degrees of discomfort in the role on the one hand and sense of commitment and personal initiative on the other, perpetrators acted as small cogs in a larger machine. Key defining experiences for persecutors may not have been at the time of perpetration but rather much later, after the war, and sometimes only when brought to account in public many years after the events in which they had been involved.

The collective character of Nazi persecution exposed victims to common experiences, forced them to live in similar ways, sent them along similar tracks—sometimes literally, to the labor camps or the gas chambers, but also metaphorically, in terms of having to respond to existential challenges. For all the differences between individuals and groups, the persecuted themselves rapidly became aware of a degree of commonality, of shared experience imposed upon them against their will. As a French political prisoner at Ravensbrück, Denise Dufournier, put it in the preface to her account written shortly after liberation, "I was never anything but a *Stück* [piece] among thousands of other *Stücke*"; her experience was "therefore one of those most commonly shared."[5]

Ruptures: Humiliation and Dehumanization

What defines a community of experience among the persecuted, despite all the differences in background, in reasons for persecution and individual experiences? One notable feature is the radical rupture between the life before—with its previously anticipated yet unlived future—and the life they actually ended up living. Related to this rupture, at the time, are the experiences that marked the eradication of past identities and webs of connection. For those who survived, the traumatic experiences of persecution and the multiple losses and deep wounds continued to scar their lives afterward.

In the process of persecution, people were stigmatized; their individuality was stripped from them; they became simply members of categories for discrimination, exploitation, punishment. Beyond the first moment of shock, when the world was changed by the sudden intrusion of Nazi policies into private lives, there were further turning points. Those who were forced into life in hiding, in ghettos, and in labor and concentration camps were utterly degraded in the eyes of the surrounding world. This made the experience of persecution different from that of being a victim of an individual act of violence in a context that condemns and punishes rather than condones or instigates such acts. Submerged in an ocean of surrounding violence from which there appeared no escape, in which there were no countervailing forces, many victims experienced an overwhelming sense of "dehumanization." This could take place in many ways, in what might be a sudden or a more gradual process.

For those who grew up in Nazi Germany, the process might be one of many stages and initially small steps. Cordelia Edvardson, for example, was the daughter of a Jewish father and a mother who was herself of "mixed" background (the illegitimate daughter of a Jewish father and an "Aryan" mother). Growing up in Berlin as a practicing Christian, with her mother and her non-Jewish grandmother, Edvardson had a sense as a child of being somehow different, but certainly not an outcast.[6] She eventually became part of a new and relatively happy family life, with younger half-brothers and half-sisters, when her mother married an "Aryan" man who looked after and cared for her as a good father. But she was still set apart from her half-siblings by virtue of her Jewish family background on her biological father's side: she was initially ostracized at school and denied entry to the youth organization for girls, the BDM, about which she was quite upset at the time, then forced to leave her school and her Catholic youth group, eventually ousted from the safe family "nest" to live in the "Jewish house," and ultimately deported to Auschwitz. Reflecting later in life on her experiences, in partial response to Primo Levi's implied question in *If This Is a Man*, Edvardson responded in the negative: no, these figures with whom she lived in Auschwitz were no longer human beings, but rather just a bundle of hunger wrapped in rags.[7] There were, in her view, deep long-term effects of the experience. And, as she put it: "The transformation process from a human being to a subhuman, and finally to vermin, was carried out quite intentionally."[8]

For Jews living in areas conquered and occupied by Germany, the experiences were generally far more sudden, taking place after invasion. Eva S., for example, grew up in an affluent Jewish family in the Czechoslovakian city of Bratislava. She had horrific memories of the day when the Germans arrived and was shocked by the unexpected joy of her formerly very friendly German nurse, as well as the brutality with which her grandfather was treated.[9] The family was rapidly cut off by former friends. Almost overnight, so it seemed, "nobody wanted to have anything to do with us."[10] Eva S. recalled: "We were suddenly hated and despised by everybody, and that was a feeling of deception and terrible disappointment that all the people you thought were your friends suddenly were your enemies and disowning you."[11] Her parents could hardly believe her when she came home from school and reported how her brother had been beaten up. Things became worse when they had to wear the Jewish star. On one occasion, Eva S. was kicked and punched on a tram by a Catholic and, instead of receiving aid and support, experienced further discrimination when trying to get home. Even when hiding places were eventually offered, assistance arose not out of solidarity but out of greed: "There was nobody that helped us, nobody that cared, nobody that did it willingly. These hiding places were only secure because my father was able to pay for them."[12] As Eva S. explained decades later, these experiences haunted her. She felt "rejected" and "ashamed, humiliated." She continued: "I felt abandoned, I felt inferior, I felt hopeless and helpless."[13]

Others, too, experienced radical breaks with long-term psychological consequences. Interviewed in Israel in 1979, Niusia A. recalled that, from the moment war broke out in her native Poland, her life took "quite another line."[14] Living in the small southern Polish town of Bochnia, east of Kraków, Niusia and her mother escaped the "Aktion" in which seven thousand Jews were deported from the ghetto to the death camp. Extraordinarily, they had been provided at the last minute—at two o'clock in the morning, as far as Niusia could remember—with special passes arranged by the wife of the district Gestapo chief, which meant that they were among the one hundred Jews who were not to be deported that day. What motives (or bribery) lay behind this provision of passes is impossible now to determine. But what followed were years of shame and fear, which left long-lasting marks on Niusia. She watched the deportation procession from the balcony at half past six in the morning, and someone called out to her, asking why she was not with them. She recalls how she went back into the room: "I was ashamed, I was ashamed, why I, why me?" She could never get out of her mind the images of this deportation, of the people among whom she had lived: "To see the people going, they were going as if for a picnic"; everyone had known what was going to happen to them but did not want to believe it, "for it is impossible to think that you are going to die, it's just inhuman, you can't." Later, in the Kraków ghetto, Niusia and her mother managed to organize false papers in order to escape. For the next few years, they survived in hiding, in disguise, "on the Aryan side" in Warsaw, moving frequently and living in constant fear of discovery. Toward the end of the war,

Niusia and her mother succeeded in making their way to Palestine, where they remained.

This story is not the standard one of maltreatment in the camps, but it had a deep and lasting impact in a different way. At the time of her interview, Niusia was still plagued by the "shame" of not having been "among them," alongside the people who were deported from Bochnia or burned alive as the Warsaw ghetto was destroyed, and at the same time she was disturbed by quite another sensation, that of being designated as different, excluded from the world, destined for unimaginable annihilation. As she put it, describing time in the Kraków ghetto: "You think outside there is another world, a quite normal world"; in contrast, "where you are, in this small place, it is another planet." In both Kraków and Warsaw she had felt totally enclosed, while "through the wall" there were "people on another planet," living a "normal" life as she had once done. And she lived in constant fear of putting a foot wrong—giving the wrong answers to questions, not remembering the assumed name on her forged passport, arousing suspicion by wearing glasses or not appearing self-confident or moving too frequently—but she and her mother had somehow despaired in turns, the one supporting the other through the ordeal. In her afterlife in Israel, she was continually tormented by nightmares in which she was constantly running away, seeing visions of the burning ghetto of Warsaw, of the deportation of her community from Bochnia, dreams in which she was both among her people and not among them.

There are many comparable accounts. Narratives differ in details, but the long-term effects are similar. Separation from humanity was consciously intended and actively implemented by Nazi policies. This was particularly evident in the rituals on arrival at major camps, which emphasized transformation into being simply a member of a subspecies, losing all individuality. People were subjected to processes robbing them of all outward signs of individuality and humanity. In many camps, people's clothing and personal possessions were taken away, their hair was shaved off, and they were dressed in prisoners' clothing and categorized by group identity. There might then follow a short period before they were assigned to specific work duties. Denise Dufournier recalled varied reactions in Ravensbrück, when women were stripped for the shower, had their hair shorn, and were put into striped clothes: "In the revolting shamelessness of this exhibition, some of the young laughed out of bravado, but the older women could not overcome their humiliation expressed in their haggard eyes and in the trembling

of all their limbs."[15] In the death camps of Sobibór and Treblinka, there were
no initiation rituals: individuals were simply lucky if they were one of the
few pulled off a transport who had to begin immediately with the task of
running back and forth with piles of clothing and possessions, cutting wom-
en's hair, or other duties to process at breakneck speed the thousands who
were on their way to the gas chambers. The process of dehumanization
happened instantly. As Wiernik put it: "The day I first saw men, women and
children being led into the house of death I almost went insane."[16]

Once initiated into the new system, often dressed in prison clothing and
with triangles indicating group category and degree of degradation, people
were supposed to lose their individuality. In Auschwitz, workers were tattooed with a number by which they would henceforth be known, losing
even their name. Once absorbed into the anonymized slave labor force, people
became pawns to be exploited and maltreated, with death the almost inevitable endpoint of radical dehumanization. Even small camps had some means
of eradicating individuality and imposing a new prisoner identity. After
ghettoization and losing his mother and siblings (who he later discovered
had all been gassed), Mark Stern ended up working in Mielec. He recalled
that "the gate was under the watchful eye of the SS. To make sure that we
couldn't escape they tattooed KL on the wrist. I still have the KL on my
right wrist. Anybody who walked through the gate—they checked him for
the tattoo and he was trying to escape—he was shot, without questions."[17]

Initiation rituals were severe, but survivors recall how some people managed to accommodate themselves to the new conditions. Within weeks of
arrival at Ravensbrück, according to Margarete Buber-Neumann, a woman
generally "resigned herself to her fate and adapted her being to existence in
a camp." She noted: "Gradually the interest for the outside world and for
other prisoners declines. The reaction to horrifying events grows less intense
and does not last so long. It is a process of hardening, until soon the news of
death sentences, executions, floggings and even atrocious tortures causes not
more than a faint reaction of horror which is over in a few minutes, and
then there is again laughter and talk, and the camp life goes on as though
nothing had happened."[18]

Interpersonal relations changed as a result of camp conditions, and responses
to other prisoners often become more brutal. Buber-Neumann—whose first
marriage had been to the son of the philosopher Martin Buber—commented
critically that "Christian morality declares that suffering ennobles the suf-
ferer," but her own experiences of concentration camp life "showed the

contrary to be true more often than not." As a consequence of being "made to suffer, deliberately made to suffer" and being exposed to "constant provocations and constant humiliations" without ever being able to answer back or strike those in authority, prisoners were tempted to take out their frustrations and anger on fellow prisoners. Among the "asocials" in particular, who had been arrested because of prostitution, petty crimes, or an irregular lifestyle, there was "a fight of all against all," but even the "politicals," who were acutely aware of a common cause and the need to maintain solidarity under adversity, "were envious and jealous of each other."[19]

In her role as block senior for "asocials," Buber-Neumann tried to help them avoid further punishments for infringement of camp regulations. Despite feeling sorry for these women, many of whom had grown up in difficult circumstances and had been forced to make their living on the streets, Buber-Neumann could hardly bear the way in which they were further brutalized by their experiences of supposed "re-education" in concentration camp. "Thieving, mutual accusations and denunciations were everyday affairs" for these women, despite the fact that, as Buber-Neumann pointed out, "friendship and comradeship in prison and concentration camp play an even more important role than they do outside in freedom."[20]

From these and similar accounts, we gain a vivid sense of the differences in ways in which people responded to imprisonment. Some survivors felt they had been aware of the process of dehumanization at the time. Gilbert Michlin, a French Jew imprisoned in Auschwitz, subsequently recalled: "We tried to cling to life and maintain our humanity in this perfect system designed to strip us of everything by reducing us to the level of beasts ready to kill each other, willing to accept anything to prolong our existence." It was most important to try "to remain a man, forget nothing," and "not become an animal or even worse, a nonhuman."[21]

Others only much later became acutely aware of having succumbed to a process of dehumanization, registering this well after they had recovered and established new lives. As Alex H. put it, when interviewed in 1983: "You were reduced to such an animal level that actually now, when I talk about those experiences, I feel more terrible than I did at the time." Physical needs at that time had taken priority: "We were in such a state that all that mattered is to remain alive."[22]

Humiliation and processes of dehumanization were experienced in different ways according to personality, age, gender, and outlook, and varied with differential treatment. Ella Lingens-Reiner, for example, was a non-Jewish doctor from Vienna who was arrested and incarcerated in Auschwitz for trying to help Jewish friends to escape. In her early postwar account of prisoner life within Auschwitz, Lingens-Reiner provides an extraordinary level of detail about the extent of theft, pilfering, and "organising," and the general collapse of external moral codes and systems of values. Members of the SS and prisoners alike engaged in barter, theft, exchange, bribery, and blackmail, to survive and achieve small advantages or privileges or means to other ends. This breakdown in value systems, Lingens-Reiner believed, was worse in Auschwitz than elsewhere.[23] Even so, similar accounts of survival strategies through pilfering and barter are described by, for example, Richard Glazar for Treblinka and Thomas (Toivi) Blatt for Sobibór.[24]

Lingens-Reiner herself barely survived a severe case of typhus and crawled back from near death only by thinking of the small son she had left behind in Vienna, to whom she was determined to return. As an "Aryan," and as a professional woman whose medical expertise was much in need in Auschwitz, she received slightly better treatment than "non-Aryan" prisoners: she was not shaved or tattooed, and was known by her name and not a number. She was even on occasion able to assert her authority and received a surprising degree of respect. Not merely did she not bear some of the physical marks of humiliation and dehumanization, but her personal characteristics—particularly her intellect and medical qualifications—were valued, rather than being absolutely negated as in the case of Jewish prisoners. In this way, although the experience of Auschwitz was physically horrific—she describes shocking incidents, suffering, and deaths all around her—Lingens-Reiner was able to remain strong and to a degree psychically intact despite all. Her son Peter, the child for whom she was determined to stay alive, later even claimed that the personal abandonment she felt when her husband left her for another woman was more deeply humiliating for her, although this is hard to judge.[25]

People of Jewish descent were subjected to far worse treatment than what Lingens-Reiner experienced. Following her early experiences in Bratislava, Eva S. was deported with her sister to Auschwitz. On arrival, Eva S. was immediately struck by the appearance of prisoners, who "looked like insane animals. They were shaven, emaciated. All you could see were mad eyes."[26] Eva S. was herself subjected to medical "experiments" under the control of the notorious Josef Mengele and his team. She was given injections, in the course of which she witnessed horrifying scenes as other children around her died. In the case of one boy who was "screaming with agony," she recounted, "They were doing experiments on him and literally, his side was open and the organs came out." On another occasion, tasked with taking toilet "buckets to the sewer," Eva S. visited the "chamber where they deposited all the people on whom they did the experiments, the dead people." This sight made a strong impact: "They were even playing games with that, so a boy I came with in the transport, he was sitting there fully naked with an ear missing and arm missing and they placed it next to him. And you could see various organs, so I knew they did something very horrific."[27]

Yet even after her horrendous experiences at Auschwitz and a difficult journey home on liberation, the first experiences of humiliation in Bratislava remained vividly in her mind. When asked what was the worst persecution she had experienced, Eva S. replied that it was not only "the experiments, the standing in roll call in the morning and the evening" but also being "demeaned." This she "found most disgusting," including even the pre-deportation "kicking and the pushing off the tram." She repeated the point for emphasis: "To be demeaned I found the most offensive."[28] Being reduced to the status of less than equal dignity as a human being, less valued than other humans, was integral to the experiences of the persecuted—and it was carried out by very many ordinary people, such as the Catholic who beat her up and those who refused her assistance on the tram, as well as by the perpetrators and "medical" personnel at Auschwitz.

Dehumanization was not only a matter of the categorization and loss of individual identity imposed by the Nazis; it was also an effect of living under the appalling conditions into which people were forced. Some consequences were physical, others psychological and indeed moral. Many survivor accounts include stories of people scrabbling for a piece of bread, tearing each other apart in their struggle to claim the valued crumbs from the dirty floor, feeling they were reduced to the status of animals. As Hans Frankenthal recalled of his time in Auschwitz: "Scrounging for food was a matter of life and death. Those who tried to subsist on the rations allocated to them soon became debilitated and died within a short period of time."[29] This often meant that prisoners could only survive if they stole someone else's food, condemning the other to more rapid starvation. Fights would often break out then, sometimes ending in immediate death. Yet, as Frankenthal commented, when "people are near starvation, even the threat of death isn't enough to prevent them from stealing food."[30] It took a quite explicit moral stance to work out some way of allocating food portions to ensure a somewhat more harmonious division of scarcity, or the distribution of starvation rations.

Both physical and psychological effects of starvation, maltreatment, and disease were significant in this process of dehumanization. Some survivors later not only explored their own experience but attempted more systematic studies of the effects of incarceration. Shortly after the end of the war, for example, Lingens-Reiner wrote a graphic, detailed description of the various states of ill health and disease in the camp from her perspective not only as a former inmate but also as a medical professional. Under these incredibly poor conditions, she observed, life expectancy was less than one year, even when it was possible to organize extra rations in some way. Only a few people who came from tough backgrounds—Lingens-Reiner noted particularly the relative resilience of Polish and Russian peasants, in contrast to their urban compatriots—or who were able to receive food parcels from outside or had good networks could maintain a reasonable weight and hope to survive. Others "died at some stage between the fourth and the tenth month of their imprisonment."[31] The food provided in the camp, such as it was—watery black coffee, watery soup, small rations of bread—was not merely utterly insufficient in terms of calories but also tasted simply terrible; sick and convalescent prisoners found it indigestible, which made recovery from illness even more difficult. Under these conditions, too, traditional moral values seemed to many to be entirely irrelevant in the struggle for survival.

Some prisoners who gained for themselves the small advantages of being Kapos occasionally began to copy their oppressors, acting as small tyrants in their own right and oppressing those under their charge. Bruno Bettelheim, a psychologist who had himself been a prisoner at Dachau, published a seminal article in 1943 on what became known as "survivor syndrome." Bettelheim observed that some long-term inmates not only began to ape the conduct of their camp guards but even tried to obtain scraps of uniforms, badges of status as oppressors rather than oppressed, and seemed to have internalized the perverted norms and values of the camp system.[32] Bettelheim's analysis and theoretical conclusions have proved controversial, but there was a wider truth in this observation, noted by many survivors. Those who gained roles as camp functionaries could be brutal, oppressive, and cruel to their charges, using the situation of unequal power within the wider system of violence to obtain advantages for themselves.

Kapos had a great deal of power over those under their charge, and differences between prisoner groups could be exacerbated, and even become existentially significant. In his account of imprisonment on grounds of homosexuality, Heinz Heger recalled that primarily criminals and political prisoners were used as Kapos, who "greatly abused the very real power they had." Moreover, "where brutality was concerned they were in no way behind the SS, particularly in dealing with those of us who wore the pink triangle."[33] Some were, in Heger's experience, particularly homophobic: "It was precisely the politicals who were the most vexatious opponents of their homosexual fellow-prisoners. The majority of them are still so today, under our democracy, where many of them now hold positions of power."[34]

Gay prisoners, according to Heger, were the first to be put on lists for the worst treatment, such as being "prioritized for medical experiments, and these generally ended in death."[35] Gay men were also selected as live targets for SS shooting practice, being forced to push barrows of earth up a mound to build a firing range; within two weeks, Heger recalls, fifteen gay prisoners were shot dead while in this work.[36] As he put it, "The intention was not just to kill us off immediately, but rather to torture us to death by a combination of terror and brutality, hunger and bitter toil."[37] The prisoners' office, headed by the camp senior, also periodically had to draw up a list of one hundred or more prisoners to be sent to extermination camps to be gassed or killed by injections, and here again, homophobic attitudes came into play: "If the camp senior was a political, you could be sure that by far the greater number of those prisoners marked down for extermination would be men with the pink triangle."[38] Gay prisoners remain underrepresented in collections of testimonies and survivor accounts, whether because of enduring prejudices and an associated sense of shame or because collectors of testimony were until relatively recently not as interested in the accounts of gay men as in those of victim groups who had been recognized far earlier. It is therefore not easy to gauge how typical Heger's experiences were, but clearly homophobic attitudes on the part of other prisoners were an additional hazard they had to confront.

Kapos were placed in a situation within the structure where they had to demonstrate brutality in order to retain the role, and they rapidly changed in the process. People giving accounts shortly after the war noted that long-term inmate functionaries had themselves become "animalized," as one survivor put it.[39] Nevertheless, some prisoner functionaries were able to retain their positions while still showing some humanity toward at least a few of those under their control. Prisoners generally knew the reputations of different Kapos, and it could sometimes make the difference between life and death to be under the charge of a sympathetic prisoner functionary. Henry

K., for example, recounts how when he was sent to the labor camp at Blechhammer, a particular Kapo managed to get him preferential treatment with a job in the kitchen, which gave him the access to the additional food that was crucial to survival, and he could even manage to smuggle extra rations to his brother and uncle elsewhere in the camp. Sometime later, when Henry K. was in the camp infirmary with an infection and excruciating ear pain following an altercation that had caused damage to his ear, the Kapo came to tell him to get out fast. Henry K. replied that he had a high fever, but the Kapo insisted. It turned out that the infirmary was being cleared and remaining patients were transported to the Auschwitz gas chambers; the quick warning from the Kapo saved Henry K. from certain death on this occasion.[40]

Even Heger found that maintaining good relations with prisoner functionaries and engaging in a sexually intimate relationship with a particular Kapo helped to save his life. But this was at the expense of his former ethical codes: "My will to survive the concentration camp was uncommonly strong, but any such survival against the brutes of the SS had a high price, the price of morality, decency and honour. I knew this and suffered on account of it, yet without such friendships with Kapos I should not be alive today."[41] There are many similar stories of survival through engaging in compromises that would generally be unthinkable outside the degenerate and violent moral universe of the camps.

But it was not only in camps that those who were persecuted had to enter into moral compromises to secure their survival. Having decided to tear off the yellow star, evade deportation, and try to survive "underground" in her native Berlin, Marie Jalowicz Simon was engaged in a constant discussion with herself about retaining a sense of morality and self-worth despite breaking innumerable previous ethical codes. She was forced by circumstances to act against many of the values of the world in which she had been raised. Like many others in such a situation, on occasion all she had to sell were sexual favors—she was particularly relieved to find that one disagreeable syphilitic Nazi in the event also proved to be impotent—and she had to engage in all manner of deceptions and dishonesty. But she came to the conclusion that although people in hiding such as herself were known as "illegals," it was not she who was engaging in illegality; it was the fundamentality illegitimate regime, with its criminal rule, that had forced her to adapt in the interests of her ultimate and absolute goal: survival. This internal moral debate accompanied her throughout the years of hiding and gives her account an interest going well beyond the details of her narrow escapes, her continual fear and yet occasional moments of happiness, and the staggering decency and kindness of so many ordinary Berliners who jeopardized their own well-being to help her throughout the years of persecution.[42]

Resisting Dehumanization

Stigmatization affected a victim's sense of self and could rapidly result in feelings of personal worthlessness. This varied somewhat according to the reasons for persecution: those incarcerated for political or religious beliefs and moral commitments appear to have had stronger external bases for continued self-belief than did many others. There were also differences relating to personality, age, and background. And the kind of conditions to which people were exposed made an enormous difference in their strategies for retaining any sense of humanity.

We are inevitably influenced by survivor accounts, with their evidence of resilience. But we should not overstate the capacity for resistance. The most typical story among those millions who were persecuted was a story that ended in death, not in survival; and combinations of circumstances, blind choices, and what is often called luck, rather than—or in addition to—resilience, clearly played a role. We also have to understand how those who were persecuted saw their situations both at the time and later.

Although many survivor accounts try to find some wider significance in their suffering, and some seek ways of embedding these horrors in a frame-work providing sustenance or a measure of peace in living with the past, there are no general messages that we can take from this terrible period. As Thomas (Toivi) Blatt put it, in memoirs based on notes he kept of his time at Sobibór and his near-death experiences at the hands of Polish peasants following his escape: "I have read what I call 'positive' books on the Holocaust—in spite of their accounts of human cruelty and suffering, a message always shines through their pages, telling about courage selflessness, great faith, and the survival of the human spirit. My story has no dominant message; it is the story of a Jewish teenager just trying to survive."[43] What follows is simply an attempt to explore some of the ways in which people in different situations of persecution experienced and responded to the challenges, in order just to survive—and to survive with some sense of their self, their humanity, still intact, despite all. The vast majority of others, with similar strategies, did not and could not survive in the face of extreme and overwhelming power.

The omnipresence of torture and death was almost impossible to deal with, as Wiernik related from the death camp of Treblinka, when he entered a particularly ghastly area of Camp no. 2, situated behind the gas chambers, and barely recognized his fellow workers, some of whom he had previously known from Warsaw. "I learned to look at every living person as a prospective corpse. I appraised him with my eyes and figured out his weight, who was going to carry him to his grave and how badly his bearer would be beaten while dragging his body to the ditch. It was terrible, but true nonetheless. Would you believe that a human being, living under such conditions, could actually smile and make jokes at times? One can get used to anything."[44]

But not everybody was as resilient as Wiernik. Although his estimate of numbers of victims is higher than is likely, his account conveys an immensely powerful impression of "periods when as many as 30,000 people were gassed in one day, with all 13 gas chambers in operation," and all the prisoner-workers heard "was shouts, cries and moans." Resilience was severely challenged at such times:

> Those who were left alive to do the work around the camps could neither eat nor control their tears on days when these transports arrived. The less resistant among us, especially the more intelligent, suffered nervous breakdowns and hanged themselves when they returned to the barracks at night after having handled the corpses all day, their ears still ringing with the cries and moans of the victims. Such suicides occurred at the rate of 15 to 20 a day.
>
> These people were unable to endure the abuse and tortures inflicted upon them by the overseers and the Germans.[45]

It is extraordinary that anyone was capable of withstanding these conditions and keeping going; Wiernik managed to cling on in the hope of being able to bear witness.

In other instances it might be not so much, or not only, the physical conditions but also the psychological humiliation that posed the major challenge. Part of the process of resisting dehumanization might be the attempt, not easy under the circumstances, to uphold particular standards of ethics and morality, to exercise agency that was in line with previous beliefs and values.

Commitment to strong religious belief was one way of resisting dehumanization. In Ravensbrück, Buber-Neumann could hardly believe the contrast when she left the "asocials" barracks to become block senior to

Jehovah's Witnesses, in what struck her as a "complicated purgatory of cleanliness and order."[46] The "simple and satisfactory belief" in their own salvation and life after the impending Armageddon, provided they kept to the tenets of their faith, "lent them strength and made them able to stand the long years of concentration-camp life and all the indignities and humiliations and still retain their human dignity."[47] While the "asocials" had fallen over each other fighting for a better portion of food, the Jehovah's Witnesses sought to achieve an equitable distribution of their meager rations and proceeded to an orderly, calm, and peaceful meal together. Because they could be relied on not to try to flee or steal, they were often given jobs looking after the houses and children of the SS officers and female camp guards and led a somewhat less physically demanding life than those sent out on hard labor duties on even less adequate rations. Like other prisoners, Jehovah's Witnesses suffered and died of disease and malnutrition, but they faced their end comparatively tranquilly, since "death had no terrors for them." Buber-Neumann commented: "How much easier it is for a religious martyr to die for his faith, for he believes that everlasting happiness and glory await him on the other side. The political martyr must be content with sacrificing himself that others, future generations, may one day enjoy the fruits of his sacrifice."[48] Those with neither religious nor political convictions had even less by way of ideological supports in their suffering.

Many accounts emphasize "redemption" stories; these are perhaps more frequent when experiences are recounted some considerable time later, rather than in the immediate aftermath of liberation. In the summer of 1943 Norbert Friedman, for example, was in the labor camp at Mielec, which that year became a concentration camp under the direction of the SS. Friedman recalls, "We were already dehumanized," and in the camp "we changed from decent people into animalistic behavior; everything around us, all the laws under which we used to live were upturned, things that were normal, abnormal, and the things that were abnormal were accepted."[49] It was a constant struggle to try to retain a sense of common humanity, morality, decency. On one occasion, the Mielec slave laborers were called together and told that they had to choose twenty people who were to be killed. They debated among themselves: some said that they should choose the weakest; others that they should choose the "trouble makers." Eventually a rabbi intervened, pointing out that under Jewish law they could not do this—no single human being could know whose life was worth more than another's. At that time, Friedman recalled, the other workers all laughed at him, asking, "What God are you talking about, after what we have experienced?" But the rabbi persuaded them, and they refused to give a list to the Gestapo. As Friedman put it, the Gestapo were "furious" because "they did not break our spirit." The Gestapo themselves then selected forty people to be executed—double the number originally requested. In Friedman's view, "The only thing that was accomplished was that they never repeated this request." But, he added, after this incident he and the other prisoners "felt better about ourselves"—even at the price of an additional twenty deaths. There are other similar stories of refusals to be co-opted into participating in the bloodshed—an anguishing ploy frequently adopted by the persecutors. There was a high price to be paid for trying to remain true to non-Nazi values, and it was sometimes a price paid by others, adding to the sense of guilt. But out of such situations people could draw a sense of moral courage, of refusal to be entirely contaminated.

It should be noted that Friedman's interview took place more than half a century after the events recounted. He was clearly now searching for meaning, for any rays of light that could be shed on this dark past. The capacity to exert some agency, some tiny degree of control over an intolerable situation, clearly meant a lot to him. A further moment when Friedman and other survivors were able to exercise and confirm their underlying humanity was, he recalled, during the transport to Flossenbürg, a train journey over several days during a hot period in August 1944. On the third day a man standing next to the window in the wagon was handed a potentially life-saving bottle of water by a kindly and courageous passerby. Rather than downing all the water himself, he did not drink at all, but rather gave it first to the person next to him, telling him to drink only a little and then pass it on. In this way, it passed all the way around the wagon, with each person having a sip. In Friedman's view, the value of this experience reached well beyond the minimal rehydration afforded by the tiny sips of shared water. Rather, they were "transformed": the man's "act of self-sacrifice returned to us our dignity." On the fourth day of the transport, when they arrived at Flossenbürg, they "were different people."

The man who had initiated this act of humanity and commitment to the well-being of the community did not survive to tell the tale: he died in Flossenbürg just a month before liberation. But for Friedman this was a key moment in his own survival, as well as for others: for them, this man's act "was a beacon of hope and faith."[50]

Michlin, a survivor of Auschwitz who had sustained self-respect by choosing not to escape when given the opportunity in Paris and instead staying with his mother to the last—the moment when she was selected for the gas chambers and he was powerless to prevent this—found it increasingly difficult to resist dehumanization. But in the final stages of the war, in the winter of 1944–45, an incident took place that was for Michlin a turning point. On a harrowing death march through Silesia, many prisoners had gone mad, and inmates had beaten other inmates. Savagery overcame any last vestiges of common humanity; the struggle to survive, even at the expense of fellow prisoners, was intense. The remaining prisoners were eventually loaded onto a train bound for another camp in Germany, routed via Prague. Here, the train halted for a while. During this pause in the journey, there was a wholly unexpected experience, as a group of people gathered and gazed down at them. Michlin was initially discomfited, remembering that they were "ashamed of being examined in this way" because they were "so dirty and emaciated," and the onlookers seemed to be shouting at them. The group of onlookers went away but returned shortly thereafter and "tossed us bread, entire loaves of it," and he realized that "their shouts were of encouragement."

As Michlin observed, it was not only the bread that was important, vital though that was to their physical survival: "I had forgotten what a simple human gesture was. I had even forgotten that people could have relationships that were not based on a power struggle, that it was possible to give like this, that solidarity was not just an empty word."[51] Another French survivor noted a similar incident of bread being offered while their transport was halted in Prague, contrasting the supportive behavior of the Czechs with brutish treatment by Poles.[52]

There are many such stories, many such vignettes. Such incidents stick out in the memory of survival, which entailed not only finding sufficient food and water but also re-entering the world of a humanity that cared about them.

Common too are stories of everyday strategies to retain a sense of self—often strategies that did not rely on any sense of higher morality. As Blatt put it, discussing the ways in which he and other prisoners sought to survive as workers in the death camp of Sobibór, the "tactics for survival" could be as simple as maintaining personal cleanliness. "Refusing to give up," some of his fellow prisoners "kept as clean as they could, shaved when they could, and walked erect in the presence of the Germans."[53] Looking strong and in control was important not only for retaining a sense of self-respect but also for avoiding the unwelcome attention of guards who were keen to strike down anyone faltering or weak.

Strategies were sometimes not merely mundane but also potentially in conflict with values previously upheld in the outside world. Blatt himself took a particular pleasure in the dangerous activity of trading valuables taken from the possessions of the dead for food from camp guards—not (or not only) because of the need for additional nourishment but also because of the benefits this transaction brought for feeling human, even exercising a small degree of power. When swapping five gold pieces for sausage and vodka, Blatt tells us: "I felt something strange. The guard who was my deadly enemy, and of whom I was supposed to be afraid, was a human being. I felt, and could see it in his eyes, that he was even more frightened than I. While I had already accepted and come to terms with my fate, and was only trying to postpone my death here, he was free." Yet prisoner and guard had something in common: "For a short time we were both afraid of the same enemy." Moreover, Blatt sensed a degree of strength: "I felt I had some kind of power over my oppressor, and it made me feel good. I wasn't just a 'nasse Sacke' (wet sack) as the Germans called us. He must reckon with me." This was in itself rewarding: "Many times after that I repeated this dangerous transaction, without logical reason, except to see fear in their faces and feel—even if it was just for a moment—that I still counted in some way."[54] This feeling that he "still counted" was crucial for Blatt in retaining a sense of humanity and being able to resist the imposed dehumanization.

Retention of a sense of humanity could even, in the context of extreme conditions under Nazi persecution, be achieved through exercising the willpower actually to refuse food, confirming one's belief in an alternative faith, an alternative worldview. Dr. Hillel K., who later became a psychiatrist in the United States, recalled several such incidents.[55] Suffering from terrible hunger, on one occasion he was speaking with a fellow prisoner who still had a wife and daughters who had succeeded in obtaining "Aryan" papers with which they had some hope of surviving the war. This man was desperate to stay alive, to see them again. Hillel K. gave the man some of his own bread, thinking that by contrast he very likely had no one now left for whom he should stay alive. He later recalled that despite his own appalling hunger "this sharing" of his bread "was important" to him. Similarly, he went on, "As a non-observant Jew I prayed with the others, it was important." In 1944, despite near starvation at the time, he and others chose to follow the Jewish custom of fasting on Yom Kippur, the holiest day in the Jewish calendar, because it was important "not to accept the slavery" that was being imposed on them. A sense of control over one's own body was perhaps the last way of exerting agency, a last defense against being plunged into nothingness. Not only trying to wash and keep clean but even enjoying the basic bodily function of defecation could for Hillel K. be a source of self-assertion. When a somewhat surprised interviewer interjected a question on this point, Hillel K. responded that this was one way of counteracting the terrible "fear of being nothing." He emphasized the significance for retaining a sense of personal identity of being able to feel "that your body is still functioning"; he went to explain "that you are using your own body as a source of satisfaction when there are no other satisfactions" and claimed that people could use their bodies as a source to prove to themselves: "I am existing."[56]

A sense of irony, too, was important to survival, as were friendships. Solidarity with others, allowing them to huddle in a group and keep warm, to hold each other up during roll calls when one or another felt too weak to stand, to walk in step together using the minimum of energy, were key to survival. Songs, hopes, a strong internal life, glimpses from the outside world, a belief that they had not been entirely forgotten—all this mattered and helped to keep him going. On liberation, Hillel K. weighed a mere sixty-two pounds and was seriously ill with typhus—physically barely alive, but spiritually extraordinarily strong.

Distancing oneself mentally from the immediate conditions of imprisonment could be vital in retaining a sense of self. Viktor Frankl, for example, was a neurologist and psychologist born in Vienna in 1905 who, following incarceration in Theresienstadt and then slave labor at Auschwitz, spent the closing months of the war in sub-camps of Dachau, first engaged in hard physical labor and subsequently working as a doctor assisting patients dying of typhus. In a burst of writing following liberation in 1945, he reflected on the period of persecution, on his own experiences and those of fellow prisoners.[57] Prior to the war, one of Frankl's specialties had been giving psychiatric support to people at risk of committing suicide, and this interest informed his reflections. He sought to identify characteristic responses among prisoners during different phases of imprisonment and following liberation. Despite his own deteriorating physical and psychological condition, Frankl was also able to develop strategies for pursuing an inner life that allowed him momentarily to find meaning in life despite the afflictions of his physical surroundings and the torments inflicted on him by the cruelties of Kapos or foremen and the constant hunger, exhaustion, and physical distress. Thoughts of his wife (whose twenty-fourth birthday would have been on the second day he was in Auschwitz, when he had no idea whether she was dead or still alive), a sense of her presence, and an inner conversation with her, imagining her face and her likely responses to his thoughts, kept him going on the trek from the camp to the labor site; moments of acute natural beauty, a sunset or the sudden turning on of a light in a distant farmhouse just as he was thinking of light in the darkness, shafted rays of hope into his perceptions of the gray and apparently hopeless present. He also developed a means of observing, with an extraordinary degree of detachment, the effects of imprisonment on his fellow sufferers. He found his own meaning in suffering by using his experiences to analyze the significance of his and others' responses. In conditions where nothing seemed to be under the prisoners' control, the only freedom that remained to most of them was to choose their own attitude, their own response to their suffering.

A few prisoners had opportunities to work together in one form or another of resistance, and to provide a sign of hope to others. Franz Ehrlich, for example, was a political prisoner in Buchenwald when it first opened. A former student at the Bauhaus, he was tasked with designing the slogan over the entrance gate. In other camps, such as Sachsenhausen, Buchenwald, and Auschwitz, the words that were cynically chosen by the Nazis were "Arbeit macht frei" ("Work sets you free"). But for whatever reason, in Buchenwald the chosen words were—equally cynical in the context—"Jedem das Seine" ("To each his own"). It was intended as a mocking, sneering adaptation from a two-thousand-year-old Latin saying about justice, including the phrase "Suum cuique"—to each his own—that originally meant that each should get his just deserts, according to his guilt.

The Buchenwald camp commandant, Karl Koch, apparently liked this sign, despite having no understanding of Latin. In contrast to the signs at other concentration camps, which faced outward and greeted people on arrival, the sign at Buchenwald was explicitly designed to face inward, where the prisoners would see it daily, facing as it did into the parade ground where roll calls and public punishments, including hangings, took place. Recent research has revealed that it was repainted annually on the inside, with eight layers of paint reflecting the eight years of the camp's existence, whereas the back of the sign, the side that could be seen only on entering from outside the camp, had only the original layer of paint, which had never been retouched. This sign was clearly seen by the Nazis as giving an important message to the inmates.

But there is a twist to this story of willful humiliation of the prisoners. Franz Ehrlich did not just produce any old lettering for the sign: he turned it into a piece of art, demonstrating the influence of the Bauhaus school of design, which had been closed down when the Nazis came to power. The gate itself was designed as a triptych, with a small door bearing the inscription right in the middle of the two wider gates. While the letters in the signs at other camps were crude and ill-spaced, the Buchenwald sign was evenly spaced and beautifully designed.[58] Subtly, Ehrlich used a typeface influenced by his Bauhaus teachers Joost Schmidt and Herbert Bayer.[59] The outcome was a work of art, with dancing letters and significant words facing inmates in a place where all had been reduced to numbers and functions, hunger, suffering, and the struggle for survival. It was a visible reminder of the possibility of artistry, creativity, even beauty, in a place of torture and death. The form arguably subverted the cynical message intended by the SS. The "S S" part in "das Seine" ("his own") was designed such that the two Ss were placed close together, equally sized and long and thin, implying that it was the SS who in due course would get its "just deserts."

How was the gate perceived at the time? Did it actually have a subversive effect, giving hope to the imprisoned? It is difficult to tell. A photograph taken April 11, 1945, now in the Buchenwald archive, emphasizes the significance of the gate as the entry point for prisoners, on first arrival, and after exits for work duties, as they were beaten and sworn at and hit and shoved through the gate. Many survivor accounts mention their arrival but not the inscription; most focus on tortures, misery, and degradation in the camp. We may be reading too much back into the sign now, at this distance. But there is some evidence that it was seen as significant and subversive by at least a few at the time. In 1943 the writer Karl Schnog, who was a prisoner in Buchenwald from 1941 to 1945, wrote a satirical poem entitled "Jedem das Seine," published in 1947 in a collection under the same title, *Jedem das Seine*. The first verse draws attention to the mocking intent, suggesting that their tormentors "really had a sense of humor" in putting this sarcastic sign on the gate. The poem ends with an address to the SS, saying, "Believe me, one day the prisoner will take what he really deserves. And you? You will then get your own just deserts!"[60]

It was perhaps easier for political prisoners to maintain a sense of solidarity and defiance than it was for others, and representation of their struggles often grew in significance in postwar contexts. Buchenwald, in particular, became something of a national shrine in East Germany, and myths grew up around the cult of the communist leader Ernst Thälmann, who was murdered there, as well as around the "Buchenwald child," who was saved by political prisoners—although at the expense of another child whose name was put on the list for deportation to Auschwitz in place of his, causing further controversy even into the twenty-first century. The significance of non-Jewish political resistance also became important in postwar France, tending to eclipse the specificities of the tragedy engulfing Jews both in France and across Europe.

Artistic endeavors could also assist in retaining a sense of another self, a different world. This was notable particularly in Theresienstadt, where attempts to cling on to an earlier normality by engaging in music, theater, and visual arts were inadvertently assisted by the Nazis' own policy of constructing a false portrait for a Red Cross inspection. The inspectors were duly hoodwinked, but the possibility of playing music certainly assisted in the survival of some inmates, such as Alice Herz-Sommer. Before deportation from Prague, she had learned Chopin's etudes by heart; this, along with determination to protect her young son from awareness of the utter awfulness of her situation, played a significant role in her own capacity to survive as well as aiding others in the darkness of the times. As she repeatedly stressed even late in life, she was committed to the idea that she should only think and speak about "good things" and accentuate the positive.[61]

Entirely inappropriately, and fueled by Hannah Arendt's well-known critique of the Jewish councils, Jews gained a reputation after the war for compliance and going obediently to their deaths.[62] This had some basis in instances when councils assisted in the deportation of some in the hope of rescuing others, as in the case of Chaim Rumkowski in Łódź, but it was a grotesque overgeneralization and misrepresentation of the wider picture. Despite all, innumerable people from all backgrounds engaged in direct physical resistance, sometimes on a substantial scale—the Warsaw ghetto uprising; the revolts in Sobibór, Treblinka, and Auschwitz; the resistance to deportations; the partisan bands; the numerous individual refusals to cooperate—and in individual acts of defiance, however futile in face of the infinitely superior forces.

These revolts both demonstrated capacity for resistance and affected German capacity for repression. Led by Mordecai Anielewicz, Jews who still remained in the Warsaw ghetto after the mass deportations in the summer of 1942, mostly to Treblinka, determined to put up a fight until the last. In the course of the autumn, organized groups formed and managed to acquire arms from outside, including from the Polish Home Army. A brief outbreak of armed resistance on the occasion of a deportation in January 1943 appeared to be successful in putting a temporary halt to deportations; but this was not for long. When the final ghetto clearance began in Warsaw, ghetto inhabitants managed to hold out for nearly four weeks—from April 19 to May 16, 1943—and put up massive resistance, causing dozens of injuries and a significant number of deaths on the German side, although the total tally remains uncertain. The uprising was only quelled when buildings were set on fire and the entire area was razed to the ground. Resistance elsewhere included the activities of groups associated with Abba Kovner from the Vilnius ghetto, who explicitly announced in 1942 that they should not go "like lambs to the slaughter," and the Bielski partisans who were active in eastern Europe. There were similar, if less well-known and smaller revolts and acts of armed resistance elsewhere, including in the ghetto of Będzin-Sosnowiec on the occasion of its final clearance in the summer of 1943. It should also be remembered that the closures of two extermination camps were precipitated by revolts, as we saw in Sobibór and Treblinka, and prisoners succeeded in putting out of action one of the four gas chambers and crematoria at Auschwitz-Birkenau in the autumn of 1944.

The persecuted faced insuperable odds, but often just the act of choosing to die defiantly could make some difference in retaining a sense of their own humanity, their own freedom of will. This is hardly captured in the catch-all notion, unfairly popularized in Arendt's work, of Jews having gone "like lambs to the slaughter."

Other groups too mounted resistance in the face of immediately impending extermination, when almost nothing seemed possible. On May 16, 1944, knowing they were about to be sent to the gas chambers, people in the Auschwitz Gypsy camp armed themselves with knives, stones, and spades and refused to leave their barracks to be transported to death. They managed to prevent the planned liquidation action on that day, although they were murdered on a later date.[63]

These comments are not meant to be in any way comprehensive; they are merely indicative of the many ways in which, despite the worst efforts of their persecutors, victims of Nazi policies were able to preserve a sense of their own humanity—even if not, in most cases, their lives. It is remarkable that, despite all, many victims of Nazi persecution managed to sustain hope for the future. "Dehumanization" was never complete: even under the most extreme conditions, and whether or not they were in circumstances that allowed any agency or resistance, people managed to retain their own individuality. But the sense of self was severely challenged, and for those who survived, the surviving "self" was not the same.

Communities of the Persecuted

Experiences of Nazi persecution radically altered people's lives, and each survivor had to seek ways of living with loss, pain, and the search for meaning in a world that had changed fundamentally. To try to develop a hierarchy of victims, let alone indulge in competitions for victimhood, is entirely inappropriate.

Some had undergone extremes of deprivation, depersonalization, and torture in camps; others had lived in hiding, in disguise, fearful for their lives. Survivors of the concentration camps, if they managed to make it through the weeks following liberation, when rampant disease or a sudden abundance of food finished off tens of thousands shortly after liberation, often suffered long-term physical and psychological effects of sustained maltreatment. Those who had survived in hiding frequently had difficulties in readjusting to life in society, to relearning trust and entering into new social relationships; there were also physical consequences of long periods of immobilization, concealment, life in the dark, and malnutrition. There are deeply significant if often hidden implications of having been treated as worthless to the point of not being worthy of living at all.

The identity problems of "hidden children" might be particularly acute, as they had not previously developed any stable sense of identity. The long-term pain of losing loved ones—parents, children, siblings, relatives, friends—to murder, whether in a sudden and violent death or a lingering and painful one, is immeasurable. Many survivors founded new families after the war and later claimed they felt blessed by having numerous grandchildren.[64] But this could never make up for the families they had lost, and this sense of loss, of absence, was transmitted across generations. Others, such as the victims of compulsory sterilization, lost any chance of having a future family. For some victims of Nazi persecution, such as gay men, the fear of exposure and feelings of shame and exclusion continued throughout their lives, particularly where homosexuality remained criminalized. Even where individuals had managed to escape and flee Europe before being caught up in the catastrophe, the destruction of their previous worlds formed a deep, unforgettable rupture in their lives. None of those who were targets of Nazi persecution were able to live the lives they had expected or aspired to before the catastrophe.

For all the diversity and individuality to be found among the victims, the fact that it was a transformative experience, defining the whole of the rest of their lives, was common to all. More important, and not ever to be lost from sight, there was a yawning gulf, a chasm, between those targeted as victims and those who had in different ways supported the Nazi system. Among the former, there was an enormity of suffering and loss. The period of Nazi persecution was inevitably, for its victims, a defining experience, separating them from others who had not survived similar experiences.

A sense of difference from those who had not been subjected to persecution was evident as people were clinging to the hope and possibility of survival, just before and soon after the end of the war. Writing not long after liberation in 1945, the French political prisoner Denise Dufournier recalls the sense of community among her group of political prisoners in Ravensbrück, even in the last chaotic months of the camp's existence: "Amongst us all, however, the living and the dead, there existed a fraternity stronger than anything on earth; it was as if we belonged to an immense community, outside the human race, situated on a mysterious planet, where the macabre, the ridiculous, the grotesque rubbed shoulders and intermingled in a fantastic and irrational chaos."[65] Following the horrors of the selections and exterminations of the final weeks of the camp, Dufournier was liberated and taken by the Red Cross to Switzerland and from there to France. She recalls vividly the mood on the train toward Paris: "With the joy of our return, tempered by the sorrow of being so few in number, was mingled the fear of the unknown which we were to face. It seemed as if we were waking from a long and inexplicable nightmare. This world, into which we had just been so suddenly reintroduced, appeared foreign to us." She went on to ask: "Would our exile continue, then, in the land of the living?"[66]

Dufournier, a woman who seems to have faced the challenges of survival with as much resilience as she did the horrors of the camp, ended this very early account on an upbeat note: she and her little group sang as they entered Paris. For political prisoners such as Dufournier, it seems to have been possible to sustain a real sense of living community with others in the present.

For others, particularly Jews—at this time seeing themselves not as "survivors" but as "the surviving remnant"—the links were more with the dead and with the communities lost in the past, compounded by a sense of enduring difference from all those who had not been persecuted. They did not need to engage in any particular set of social relations—an actively organized community—to know that they had in principle something in common that set them apart from all those who had not gone through comparable life-changing experiences. For them, it was an absolute rupture, a permanent challenge. As Michlin put it: "This monstrosity—this 'experience', as it is usually referred to—is something I have never forgotten. To this day, I yearn to know why and how people could have plunged me into hell simply because I *was*."[67] Saul Friedländer summarized the meaning of these years for Jewish victims as "the most significant period of their lives," one in which they were "entrapped." As he put it: "Recurrently, it pulled them back into overwhelming terror and, throughout, notwithstanding the passage of time, it carried along with it the indelible memory of the dead."[68]

Such persecution lent a degree of uncertainty, a sense of provisionality, to life afterward. In Cordelia Edvardson's words: "We, the survivors, have lost our right to residence in life [*unser Heimatrecht im Leben*]."[69] However lovely the summer's day, there was now no possibility of enjoying it for what it was; there was a constant sense of not being quite part of the present, still belonging to the burnt and desolate past. But if there was no easy identification with the communities of the living who were not survivors, neither was there an easy identification with those already dead. The survivors, the *Überlebenden*, the "still living," were neither entirely of the living nor of the dead, but rather a community apart.[70]

The "still living" were different not only from the dead but even more so from those who had formerly been their tormentors, their persecutors, as well as from those who had remained apparently indifferent to their fate, and even from those who had little or no inkling of what they had been through. Edvardson's sense of difference from the community of the living was underlined even by everyday experiences, such as the sight of railway freight cars rattling through Hamburg central station, when fellow passengers in the 1980s could have no sense of the frisson of fear and unwelcome associations provoked by this sight for a survivor. Edvardson comments: "How should I be able to live among you! To live means to remember, and we have no common memories."[71] A sense of difference was also underlined in wider social relations. Edvardson's half-sister married an Austrian, the son of a Nazi; like so many children of perpetrators, this man did not want to have children. Edvardson was highly conscious of the difference between her own world and that of her half-sister.

The chasm was of course greatest between survivors and perpetrators. Edvardson was even more conscious of the gulf separating her from a person she refers to as "Dr. M.," referring to Dr. Hans Münch (on whom more below), a former Auschwitz doctor who in the mid-1980s appeared frequently on television shows concerning the fortieth anniversary of the liberation of Auschwitz and the end of the war. There were insuperable differences between a scarred survivor and a former Nazi who had made a successful postwar career. These differences were grounded in their respective experiences, which could never be erased or eradicated: "The roles have been firmly established, once and for all." In Edvardson's view, "on this basis, there can be no 'formerly,' neither for him nor for me."[72]

Many Jewish survivors found others with common experiences and were able (if often with considerable difficulty) to integrate into wider Jewish communities in Israel and across the world. Similarly, many political prisoners found postwar political groups, parties, and movements with which they identified, and could seek out the company of other like-minded individuals; in the best case, they could live in places championing the cause for which they had fought and suffered. It was not their personal identity but rather commitment to the wider collective that had been at the root of their persecution and that had given their individual suffering meaning.

But other groups of victims found it far more difficult to talk about their experiences or find sympathetic audiences.

One example must stand for the many thousands who remained silent. In his hometown of Mulhouse in Alsace, a region of France bordering Germany at the Rhine, Pierre Seel had enjoyed a happy childhood until the area in which he lived was taken over and annexed by the German Reich.[73] As a teenager, Seel had become increasingly aware of his homosexuality. He had a growing friendship with a young man of his age, Jo, whom he came to love. One day, while Seel was in a café that was popular among gay men in Mulhouse, a thief had stolen his watch, a precious possession given to him by his aunt on the occasion of his first communion. Seel duly reported the theft to the local police—who, when they learned of the location in which it had been stolen, put him on a list of known homosexuals. At this time, homosexuality was not a crime, and indeed had not been illegal in France since 1792. But when the Germans took over the area and annexed Alsace, matters changed completely. The French authorities, apparently unbidden, handed over the list of gay men in the town, and Seel was promptly arrested. Appalling treatment followed, as the SS sought to obtain a full list of all gay men: "The walls echoed with our screams." Seel describes graphically how members of the SS forced them to kneel down on wooden rods or "rulers": "In their fury, they broke the rulers we were kneeling on and used them to rape us. Our bowels were punctured. Blood spurted everywhere. My ears still ring with our shrieks of atrocious pain.... It was pure violence, the kind that destroys forever."[74] The group was then taken to the nearby concentration camp of Schirmeck, "where horror and savagery were the law."

But "the worst ordeal" was when the prisoners had to report to the roll-call site and watch an execution: "Horrified, I recognised Jo, my loving friend, who was only eighteen years old....Now I froze in terror: I had prayed that he would escape their lists, their roundups, their humiliations. And here he was, before my powerless eyes, which filled with tears. Unlike me, he had not carried dangerous letters, torn down posters, or signed any statements."[75] Seel and hundreds of other prisoners had to stand and watch as "the loudspeakers broadcast some noisy classical music while the SS stripped Jo naked and shoved a tin pail over his head."[76] They then set "their ferocious German shepherds on him": "The guard dogs first bit into his groin and thighs, then devoured him right in front of us. His shrieks of pain were distorted and amplified by the pail in which his head was trapped. My rigid body reeled, my eyes gaped at so much horror, tears poured down my cheeks. I fervently prayed he would black out quickly."[77] The memory of this would, for decades afterward, make Seel wake up in the night, "howling." Seel summarized the legacy: "For fifty years now that scene has kept ceaselessly passing and repassing through my mind. I will never forget that barbaric murder of my love—before my very eyes, before *our* eyes, for there were hundreds of witnesses. Why are they still silent today?"[78]

Seel was but one of so many who suffered and whose lives were so cruelly twisted and distorted by Nazi persecution. His story must stand here for many, to remind us of the diversity of victims and the brutality of the means of imposing Nazi conceptions on the world they conquered. And in Seel's case, as in so many others, the story of victimization and exclusion did not end with the liberation. While postwar French president De Gaulle repealed Nazi antisemitic laws, he did not repeal the homophobic legislation introduced by the Germans. It was not until 1982 that French president François Mitterrand finally repealed the 1942 Vichy laws on homosexuality. More than fifty years after the end of the war, and a decade after he had finally plucked up his courage to speak out about his appalling experiences, overcoming the shame about the reasons for his deportation, Seel had still not received official recognition or entitlement to compensation for his suffering.

The distinctions among the persecuted—whether Jews, Gypsies, asocials, politicals, Jehovah's Witnesses, gay men, or the mentally and physically disabled—should not blind us to the overwhelming significance of this period for all those whose lives were so radically transformed or truncated by the Nazi machinery of death. Those who were persecuted formed, ultimately, a distinctive wider community of experience, separating them from those on the other side of the chasms created by Nazi policies. These chasms continued, not surprisingly, into the postwar period. It would take the passage of decades before attempts at communication, let alone reconciliation—largely among members of different generations—could begin to take place between communities of the persecuted and those who had persecuted them.

7

Silence and Communication

Those who were personally involved in the violence, on either side, could not help but know about and discuss what was going on, even if they had only partial insights into the scale and character of the cataclysm overwhelming Europe at this time. Yet after the war, or so it was assumed for a long time, people fell silent about the recent past—and this silence was supposedly to be found among both victims and perpetrators.

For many years, the "myth of silence" held that survivors were unable or unwilling to talk about their experiences. There is a grain of truth in this—but it is far from the whole picture. The "myth of collective amnesia," by contrast, was more sharply presented as a critique of perpetrators who claimed to remember next to nothing about the atrocities in which they had so recently been involved. People generally, it was held, did not want to talk about or confront their experiences under Nazism but put all their energy into building new lives after the war.

The "myth of silence" has been challenged by documenting just how many survivor accounts were published after the war.[1] Similarly, the "myth of collective amnesia" has been amended by demonstrating just how much people did in fact talk about war experiences and how the past remained a live issue—if selectively talking about certain topics, while suppressing or marginalizing others.[2] These revisions of the old myths are welcome but should not make us lose sight of significant shifts in patterns of silence and communication.

The recent past was in many cases too painful for some to want to talk about it, while others dwelled on it constantly; and in the early postwar years, many had other urgent priorities in their personal lives. But communication patterns changed. At first, people often only talked informally within circles of those with similar experiences. The only others who were interested enough to elicit their accounts were institutions or individuals with close connections with such communities of experience. A significant change in the character of audiences took place from the later 1970s and 1980s onward, when survivors started to talk to younger generations.

Although at first, both during and in the first years after the war, the victims of persecution—not yet venerated as "survivors"—faced widespread incomprehension or lack of interest, there were nevertheless organizations and individuals actively searching for witness accounts. Some testimonies were proactively offered or actively elicited; other attempts at communication were met with indifference or incomprehension; and often survivors chose to talk only selectively, or not to talk at all. Initially there was an urgency about telling the outside world what had happened; there was at first no overall picture of the catastrophe that had befallen the persecuted peoples of Europe, only a mosaic of individual stories. The simple need for information about the events themselves was at the heart of early testimonies. It was only decades later that the whole life stories of survivors came into focus, of interest in their own right, and of interest precisely to those who had not lived through similar experiences.

The struggle of survivors to find or bestow meaning on what they had been through is evident throughout the decades. What changed over time was not only the way in which "talking" related to personal priorities at different stages of life but also the wider frameworks of understanding and the character and receptivity of new audiences. At first, the chasms that had opened between those who had been persecuted and those on the side of their tormentors remained, and the mosaic of individual experiences did not yet amount to a pattern that made any overall sense. In a period of deep emotional rifts and conflicting needs, there was little desire to try to bridge the chasm or to engage in projects of mutual understanding. These tasks would, in the main, be left to subsequent generations.

The Continuation of Parallel Worlds

Some aspects of the phenomenon of "parallel worlds" are by virtue of their very nature hard to document, particularly that of selective silencing. There were many survivors who would talk endlessly among themselves about the past, recounting particular stories again and again, talking about mutual friends and relatives they had lost or about their feelings when they witnessed the murder of loved ones. But they would talk only among themselves.

Even among sympathetic communities, those who had experienced perse-cution might be willing only to talk to other survivors. And there is little way of identifying what they were leaving out of their stories.

Memoirs give us some glimpses of the character of these discussions and silences. Mark Spigelman was born in Poland in 1940 and spent his early childhood either disguised as a girl or in hiding; emerging at the end of the war, his family left for Australia. He describes how in Australia his parents would talk on Saturday evenings with groups of friends and other survivors at length.[3] Spigelman describes this as a form of catharsis, with participants in these in-group discussions being willing to listen, over and over again, to the same stories, the same outpouring of emotions. But the moment a non-survivor was present, the character of the conversation would be quite different. They would never tell these stories or talk in this way. An informal, unseen barrier went up between those who had been through these experiences and those who had not. Although there was no apparent reason for this—there is no suggestion that friends who were not themselves survivors might have been unsympathetic—there was simply no dialogue across the boundaries and borders of different communities of experience.

This seems to have been common wherever in the postwar world survi-vors were living. The experience of feeling no one was willing to listen was widespread; a sense of mistrust and isolation from the host community was common. People chose largely to withdraw into their own families.[4] Similar accounts of survivors talking incessantly, but only among other survivors, are described by, for example, Ruth Klüger in relation to her mother's friendship groups in New York, by Anne Karpf for her family in postwar London, and by Lisa Appignanesi for her parents' circles in Canada.[5] Similarly, Eva Hoffmann, born in 1945 to Polish survivors, describes how, during her childhood, survivors in Poland talked to "fellow survivors, or others whom they could trust" and also to "their immediate intimates, to spouses and siblings, and yes, to their children."[6] Not all survivors partici-pated even in family discussions, choosing for many years not to engage explicitly in confronting the past.

Some survivors felt isolated even among people who might otherwise be sympathetic. When Eva S. returned from Auschwitz to her hometown of Bratislava and rejoined her parents, she found it hard to relax and reinte-grate: "I felt a bit estranged. I couldn't kiss or cuddle. I felt like an animal that hasn't been touched for a long time."[7] Once she became better able to relate to members of her family, they did not want to ask or hear about her experiences at Auschwitz, where she had been subjected to Mengele's experiments. Perhaps, Eva S. thought, her mother was simply too preoccupied by other matters; the situation was complicated by the fact that one of her brothers, having survived the war, tragically died in a drowning accident. As Eva S. recalled: "I came back to Bratislava and was like a lost sheep. I was wandering the streets, sitting on my brother's grave, and writing poetry because I had no one that would understand me, no one I could talk to."[8] When asked if she told her parents about her camp experiences, she replied: "Never, never, they never asked me. So I would just sit on my brother's grave and write poems." And when she went back to school, she "was discriminated against."[9] The continuing hostility toward Jewish survivors experienced by Eva S.'s family precipitated their emigration three years after the end of the war. Similar experiences were recorded by numerous survivors elsewhere in eastern Europe, and particularly in Poland. Far from finding a sympathetic audience in their former homes, they faced extreme hostility, sometimes violence.[10]

    Experiences everywhere were affected by the nature of the communities to which survivors returned or where they resettled. Whether as a young woman making a new life in neutral Sweden, or as an older and by now well-established author and mature woman, Cordelia Edvardson found it hard to communicate her experiences, to convey any sense of what she had been through to those who had not had similar experiences.[11] Even where communities had themselves been subjected to Nazi domination and were aware of what survivors had suffered, it was not easy. Some three-quarters of French Jews managed to survive, often due to the assistance of fellow citizens.[12] This did not necessarily make it easier for survivors to develop ways of recounting their experiences. In France, many early testimonies praise those who had given them help, and in particular those who had assisted children to hide and survive. There were genuine bonds of gratitude and in some cases affection between young people and their rescuers.[13] Yet not all returnees from camps found it so easy. Gilbert Michlin found his former apartment, his former employers, and old friends. But for him, everything had changed. He "could not forget the beatings, the cold, the hunger, the corpses, the smokestacks, and the odour." He was aware that "nothing could ever be as it was before. But I wanted to forget it all. Forget that I was ever there, that my parents died there, and that friends I made had died there too." As a consequence, he never spoke about his experiences, even to his former childhood friends.[14] Michlin came to the view that his very identity in postwar France was at stake: denying his Jewish identity "was not some sort of self-hatred, but simply a method of self-preservation."[15] At his former workplace, Michlin felt isolated and found his colleagues "harder and harder to bear." They had been "mostly indifferent" to the Nazi occupation, "and at times seemed to have approved it." He began to feel that they were reproaching him for having survived, implicitly asking "How were you able to return, if everybody else died?"[16] More broadly, the failure to face up to the ways in which the French administration had cooperated with the Germans and the French police had assisted in the roundup and deportation of French Jews, including Michlin and his mother, was almost unbearable. At a personal level, Michlin could not even get the officials who had arrested him to own up to the enormity of their collaboration: "The famous national reconciliation meant that everyone in the administration remained in place."[17] Michlin chose in the end to leave for the United States.

Even in countries such as the Netherlands, which had experienced bitter oppression under Nazi occupation, survivors were not always given the kind of hearing they had expected. Gerhard Durlacher was a Dutch Jew who survived both Theresienstadt and Auschwitz. Returning to his former home in the Netherlands, he was barred entry by the new occupants who had taken over the house. Even family friends barely listened to him: they each, he recalled, "had their own story of the hardships of occupation which made me choke back the unspeakable."[18] He found that he was a "near stranger who had to listen," and he sought to gain "acceptance" through keeping silent.[19] It was impossible to communicate: "We lacked the language to describe our experiences," and "virtually nobody wanted to listen." His words "would spoil the glow of liberation and expose the self-deceit of many."[20] In the short-term, the only solution was silence: "I learned to live like a human being among people again, found hospitality, sometimes even warmth, and bricked up the past in my memory."[21] It was only four decades later, by which time he had become an eminent sociologist, that Durlacher was finally able to confront his past. Now, "thanks to understanding therapists," he could explicitly begin to confront the "shocking memories."[22]

It was for a whole range of reasons perhaps most difficult for those survivors who lived in Germany, whether East or West, to talk openly about their experiences within the wider community. In East Germany, communists downplayed what they represented as passive suffering, celebrating rather the active resistance of communists and their political allies. This affected even the character of stories told by Jewish survivors within the Association of Persecutees of the Nazi Regime (VVN), with a slightly defensive tendency to try to highlight reasons why active political resistance was less possible among those persecuted on "racial" grounds than it was for political opponents of Nazism.

In West Germany, the dominant community was that of fellow travelers and former Nazis. Dagmar B., for example, describes her non-Jewish father's growing bitterness as he realized that, as a result of standing by his Jewish wife during the war, he would never be able to make the life and have the career he had expected. Former Nazis changed their political colors and continued to be promoted, while he remained stigmatized, marginalized. The discussions within the family always revolved around the possibilities of gaining compensation, but her father's bitterness persisted until his death. Meanwhile, there was a massive rift between him and other relatives on his side of the family who had made their peace with Nazism; in particular, he was barely on speaking terms with one of his uncles.[23] Dagmar B. herself, despite being a child survivor, was also not really told about the past; she only picked up bits and pieces through observation and eavesdropping on conversations among others. Though she accompanied her mother to help with survivors from the camps, she was not told precisely what they had been through or why they looked to her, as a child, so frightening." She recalls how the survivors of the camps "looked like ghosts," with no hair, and spoke Yiddish. She could not understand them, "and they looked so terrifying." She retained very strong memories of how they went on visiting "these monsters for months on end."[24] Dagmar B.'s mother did not explain why the women looked and acted in the ways they did, making their behavior even more terrifying. Dagmar B. was particularly afraid of being touched:"They were desperate to touch little children. I was there, I existed, I can understand that today. I was a piece of the continuity of life. Their children had been murdered and I was alive."[25] But for Dagmar, by contrast, "it was simply terrifying, these skeletons with no hair."[26] There were further barriers to mutual understanding, in that the women were "eastern Jews" (*Ostjuden*), to whom the more assimilated western Jews felt superior, and who spoke largely Yiddish, a language that many western Jews did not understand.

Dagmar's experience was somewhat unusual in that she crossed between the worlds, as a child of a Jewish mother and a non-Jewish father. It is all the less likely, then, that there would be communication across these communities where there was no such close emotional connection. Her parents were also keen to educate her about what had happened elsewhere, to those who had been less fortunate. When an exhibition was put on in Hanover, her parents took her to see it, and it made a huge impression on her five-year-old self: "Photos of the concentration camps were exhibited, with ovens for burning bodies, with piles of corpses, everything."[27] Worst of all, in Dagmar B.'s memory, were the ovens. Yet despite the openness of her mother to the experiences of Jews from eastern Europe, and despite the broader discussions about the Holocaust, there was silence about deaths in her own family: "My Grandma was never mentioned at all. Grandma was gone, and would not come again, she was gone, and she was not mentioned."[28] Even when precious objects—a silver bread basket and a menorah from her grandmother's family—reappeared in the family home, Dagmar had no idea where these came from. An unspoken "vow of silence" held.[29] Losses within the family were simply too painful to be discussed at this time.

Hans Frankenthal and his brother had survived slave labor in the I. G. Farben plant in Auschwitz III, Monowitz, and, following the death march, in the secret weapons production in the underground tunnels of Mittelbau-Dora. After yet another transport guarded by the SS, Frankenthal ended the war ill and unconscious, waking up to find himself in the now-liberated concentration camp of Theresienstadt, where he was reunited with an aunt who had survived by virtue of her protective "mixed marriage." At this time, he had a high fever and was close to death. Nursed back to health—though with lifelong disabilities as a consequence of maltreatment—he returned to his Westphalian hometown of Schmallenberg. Here, he was shocked to discover how little the townspeople wanted to know about him and his brother, and how little they were welcomed when, now orphans, they returned alive after the war. Only seven of the original fifty-one Jewish residents of his town had survived.[30] Far from being given assistance—let alone counseling or therapy—Frankenthal encountered only obstacles in his attempts to start a new life. On trying to set up a new business, he soon realized that there were significant continuities in personnel in the government agency he was dealing with, since "the bureaucrats who manned it were the same people who had staffed it under the Nazis."[31] They were, moreover, still antisemitic and discriminated against Jews: "Now that virtually all the Jews were dead and gone, others should be discouraged from ever coming back again."[32] By contrast, it did not seem to matter if people had been Nazis or what they "had done in the past." People "simply took no notice of our past or us. And when the Cold War began, things got even worse. Denazification was a farce."[33] Attempting to make a radically new start and integrate as best he could into local society, Frankenthal married a Christian woman. He did not want to talk to her about his experiences, although he suffered from dreadful nightmares and "would cry out and scream at night."[34] Under pressure from his wife's family, all three of their children were baptized, but they still suffered from discrimination.[35] Nor did he feel he could talk to his children about his past: "When they asked me about the tattoo on my arm, I explained that it was an important telephone number that I dare not forget."[36] Frankenthal knew others too who not only "wanted to forget the horror" but also lacked a willing audience: "The Germans, of course, never asked the survivors any questions."[37]

Even in Palestine, from 1948 onward the State of Israel, which was seen by many as a safe haven for Jews in a post-Holocaust world, survivors did not necessarily find a sympathetic hearing: the prewar Zionist settlers in the promised land seem to have generally felt that they had little in common with the ragged, starving, disturbed arrivals from postwar Europe.[38] Their evident anguish and tendency to relive rather than narrate traumatic experiences are vividly portrayed in fictional form by the novelist David Grossman.[39] But even those who were highly articulate and keen to bear witness came up against a lack of interest. Yehuda Bacon, for example, left Prague for Palestine at the age of sixteen in 1946. Already committed to bearing witness, Bacon made detailed notes on Auschwitz and Birkenau in the first two years after the war. He was at first bitterly disappointed on finding that no one in Israel wanted to hear about this. He felt that people gradually began to listen in the early 1950s, with the establishment in 1953 of Yad Vashem as a global center for Holocaust commemoration, documentation, education, and research; but in his view it was really only with the Eichmann trial in 1961 that people in Israel began to see that heroism and victimhood were perfectly compatible.[40]

It was not only Jewish survivors who were met with a combination of incomprehension and ambivalence on their return or relocation after the war. Similar experiences were recorded by members of other victim groups, particularly when living among former perpetrator communities. Leopold Engleitner (1905–2013), for example, was an Austrian from a modest social background who had, in the early 1930s, decided he could no longer continue in the Catholic faith and became a committed Jehovah's Witness and conscientious objector to military service.[41] Not surprisingly, the Nazi takeover of Austria in 1938 brought Engleitner into political trouble. A survivor of three concentration camps—Buchenwald, Niederhagen, and the men's camp at Ravensbrück—Engleitner returned to Austria after the war physically and psychologically broken by the brutal treatment he had received. Speaking as someone who had been persecuted for principled opposition to Nazism, Engleitner was asked in an interview how he was "received by society" on his return to Austria. He replied that he had thought he "would be welcomed with open arms," but was shocked to find it was quite the opposite: "We were regarded as asocial elements and were treated like lepers." More generally, people "wanted to hush up the horror and the atrocities and pretend they never happened." He encountered downright denial, with some people claiming "that concentration camps never existed." The hostile reception in postwar Austria made him feel that it "was almost as if we were the culprits instead of the victims."[42] It was not for several decades, until a younger generation came to maturity and began to take an interest in his story, that his courage was finally recognized rather than resented.

Survivors among Gypsy communities were generally met with hostility, suspicion, or at best ambivalence, if not quite the same exclusionary policies as before the war. Official policies at first demonstrated marked continuity with the Third Reich, and hostile attitudes remained widespread among the general population.[43] Sinti and Roma withdrew, accordingly, into their own communities. The claim has been made that, in contrast to Jews, whose collective identity was rooted in stories of collective suffering and survival, Sinti and Roma were not communities that told stories about the past: their culture was supposedly characterized by defiant forgetting rather than remembrance. Whatever the truth of the comment about cultural differences, the suggestion that Sinti and Roma did not also talk about the past does not hold up.[44] Among relatives, Sinti and Roma survivors seem to have talked openly about their experiences of persecution. Many survivors had been sterilized, a matter of considerable pain for those unable to start families while others were surrounded by children and grandchildren. Survivors had often been left with physical and psychological damage that rendered them unfit to work in many of their previous occupations. One man later commented of his mother that she was rendered mentally ill and emotionally scarred as a result of her experiences.[45] Their stories of persecution remained relevant, as members of subsequent generations also experienced widespread hostility and feared neo-Nazi violence. In the stories of these people, the past surrounded them constantly.

One group of those who had been persecuted by the Nazis who barely uttered a word about their experiences, and if at all then only to one another, was gay men. Until the late 1960s (1968 in East Germany, 1969 in West Germany), to engage in homosexual acts remained illegal. There was no way that gay men would be willing to self-incriminate in a society that still viewed their sexual orientation as abhorrent. It was only several decades after the war that their rights to compensation began even to be recognized.[46] In Austria, gay men had suffered particularly badly under Nazism and were not generally rehabilitated after the war. One man, who was five feet ten inches tall, weighed only eighty-six pounds on his release from concentration camp; because of the nature of his "offense," he was not permitted to return to his former employment in financial services but was forced instead into a more menial role.[47] Another, on release from concentration camp, nevertheless had to see out the remaining portion of his sentence in prison. Others too had to complete sentences that had been given to them by the Nazis. In the face of continued ostracism, this did not necessarily make it any easier for gay men to talk, isolated as they often were even among members of their own families. Even when this was not the case, return did not necessarily mean any sense of liberation. When Heinz Heger returned to his native Austria, he was reunited with his sister and mother but found that his father had in the meantime committed suicide because he could no longer take the worry, pressure, and ignominy. Furthermore, Heger found that his request for compensation was denied, since homosexuality was still considered a criminal offense and incarceration in a concentration camp was therefore, in the eyes of the Austrian authorities, justified.[48] It took decades for this situation to change.

Early Survivor Accounts

For all the difficulties that many victims of persecution encountered in talking about their experiences, there were nevertheless both institutions and individuals who immediately recognized the significance of testimony. Some sought to keep diaries and records at the time, or produced written accounts shortly after the war; others recorded experiences of persecution.

Many regularly kept diaries and notebooks, creating records of events that provided invaluable insights into experiences of life in ghettos and under persecution.[49] Many accounts were essentially private musings, ways of dealing with the emotional ups and downs of life under ever more constrained circumstances; some were written specifically with the purpose of letting the wider world know of the catastrophe enveloping them and sealing their fate and providing testimonies for posterity. Those written by people who did not survive to tell the world of their experiences in person included individuals whom we would otherwise likely never have heard of, such as Dawid Sierakowiak, who died from starvation and disease as a the teenager in the Łódź ghetto as well as notable personalities including Adam Czerniaków, leader of the Jewish Council of Elders of the Warsaw ghetto, who took his own life rather than be further party to aiding the Nazis with their killing quotas.[50] Some surviving diaries are fragmentary, and we do not always know their authors.[51] A particularly valuable collection is one that recorded life in the Warsaw ghetto, with crucial contributions by people active in literary circles at the time, such as Rachel Auerbach. Masterminded by Emanuel Ringelblum, when it was clear that the end was approaching the collections were buried in sealed containers, including milk cans; after the war, survivors including Auerbach were able to locate and rescue part of this extraordinary archive.[52] Other diaries were written by people who were not directly targeted by the Nazis. One such is the diary of the Polish doctor Zygmunt Klukowski, who lived in Szczebrzeszyn in the Zamość region of southern Poland, and chronicled events as they unfolded.[53]

Whatever the impulse for recording testimony, the question of who the audience might be remained. In some circles, there was keen interest, both during and immediately after the war; but within a matter of a few years, a filtering process left only a few works standing. One account of resistance in the Warsaw ghetto was penned shortly after the war by Bernard Goldstein, a socialist who had been active as a left-wing Jewish leader already for a couple of decades beforehand.[54] This tale of political heroism and arms smuggling for the 1943 Warsaw ghetto uprising seems to have fallen on relatively deaf ears in the Cold War era; it received almost no attention until it was republished in a small edition in 2005. Another account of life in the Warsaw ghetto, a diary by a teenage girl, might have seemed more likely to garner sympathy across the world—but this was not in fact to be the case. The young Mary Berg (in fact Miriam Wattenberg), whose mother was an American citizen, had been released from the Warsaw ghetto in exchange for German prisoners of war. No sooner had she stepped off the boat in New York than she was met by a journalist eager to hear her story, one S. L. Shneiderman. On discovering that she had kept a diary throughout the years of persecution, he rapidly arranged for its translation and publication. It was published in February 1945, and Mary Berg spoke on numerous occasions to raise awareness of the plight of the Jews incarcerated and dying in Europe even during the war.[55] Plagued by feelings of shame that she had been one of the privileged few to escape, she longed to be able to help save others—but by this time it was far too late. Berg continued her publicity activities for a while, then, in the early 1950s, gave up entirely any public role as survivor and witness. In later years, under her married name, Mary Pentin, she tried to retreat as far from the limelight as possible and was irritated by later attempts to republish her diary.[56]

Berg may have had her own reasons for wanting to cease talking about her experiences. But audiences, too, were melting away in the years after the war; what wider interest there was in such accounts began to wane. The extraordinary immediate success of the diary of Anne Frank, written by a Jewish teenager during hiding in Amsterdam and first published in Dutch in 1947, two years after her death from typhus in Bergen-Belsen, then published in English in 1952, was exceptional. Frank's diary soon became a classic summary of suffering with a human face, representing fate at a personal level. Unlike many other such early publications, her story would eventually go on to achieve worldwide fame, with the house in Amsterdam where the German Frank family had hidden becoming a major tourist attraction, in some way disassociated from the wider history that had given rise to Frank's personal tragedy. Frank's diary, by an introspective teenager in hiding in Amsterdam, displaced the previously published account by an equally articulate teenager, Mary Berg, with its riveting details of daily life, suffering, and death in the Warsaw ghetto. Whether because of promotion strategies or the intrinsic interest of a story of hiding and discovery, Frank's book ensured that it was she and not Berg who became the iconic face of teenage suffering, standing in for "the Holocaust" for generations to come.

Shortly after the war, particularly where states, political parties, interest groups, and social institutions had an interest, cultural representations that could command wide audiences emerged. These were always complicated by degrees of censorship and Cold War considerations—political rivalry, anti-communism in the West, anticapitalism under the rubric of "antifascism" in the East—and it is difficult to know the extent to which they affected wider opinions or stimulated any interest in the testimony of survivors. Films such as Alain Renais's 1955 *Night and Fog*, with haunting music by Hanns Eisler, was among the first to convey the enormity of the crimes while underplaying the distinctiveness of Jewish experiences in the "final solution." An early East German classic, Wolfgang Staudte's 1946 DEFA production *The Murderers Are Among Us* (*Die Mörder sind unter uns*), as well as other East German films such as *Sterne*, also put a distinctive slant on the past, critiquing complicity in Nazism and highlighting political strategies for combatting it at the time and afterward. This was indeed inevitable; it was just a question of where in Europe which angles would be emphasized and what downplayed.

But this did not mean that all accounts found ready release or markets—even when they recounted not only personal stories but events of major historical significance. The debates over Jews allegedly going to their deaths like lambs to the slaughter, for example, might have looked very different had these and similar accounts been published earlier. Richard Glazar, for example—the Czech survivor who had taken part in the Treblinka uprising and survived under a false identity in Germany—was unable to find a publisher in Czechoslovakia for his gripping account, written shortly after the end of the war. It was only finally published in German in 1992.[57] Yankel Wiernik and Chil Rajchman, both of whom had escaped from Treblinka in the 1943 uprising, wrote their accounts of this death camp during the war, while in hiding and active in the resistance in Warsaw. While Wiernik's account was published in limited edition in 1945, Rajchman's was first published only in 2009, in French and German, and two years later in English.[58] Similarly, Thomas (Toivi) Blatt, who had participated in the Sobibór uprising and managed to survive the subsequent months in hiding in Poland, had kept a diary of his extraordinary experiences. While some of his family's former friends and neighbors had helped Blatt, providing food and occasionally also shelter, many had been rather more willing to betray him—and in the case of one initial rescuer, even to attempt to murder him as conditions changed. Blatt had given pages of this diary to Christian friends for safekeeping and was able to find about 40 percent of it after the war; some of the scenes had to be reconstructed, but from fairly fresh memories and with the benefit of the manuscript pages he had recovered. In 1952 Blatt produced a manuscript for a publishing house in communist Poland, but the editors wanted to change too much of it—scarcely surprising, in view of the poor light it shed on the greedy, fearful, and often antisemitic Polish peasants, as well as the political circumstances of the last months of the war and liberation, which did not entirely conform with communist narratives. In 1958, following his emigration to Israel, Blatt gave the manuscript to an

Auschwitz survivor to read, expecting a more favorable reception. But the survivor's response—having apparently neither heard of Sobibór nor believing the Jews had revolted—was that Blatt clearly had a "tremendous imagination." As Blatt bitterly commented, when his book was finally published decades later: "I was whipped many times by the SS in the Sobibor death camp, but I never felt so sharp a pain as I did when I heard those words. If he, an Auschwitz survivor, did not believe me, who would?"[59] Blatt's historical depiction of the Sobibór uprising, as well as his account of his own life story, were not published until after awareness had been raised by the appearance of the 1987 film *Escape from Sobibor*, to which he had contributed.[60]

Even in societies with a supposedly more open publishing industry, and where accounts were sometimes crafted with a high degree of finesse, there was often initial difficulty in finding an audience, let alone one on the scale of Anne Frank's diary. Elie Wiesel's *Night*, for example, has attained the status of a classic Holocaust text. Whether primarily autobiographical, or written as a fictional account only loosely based on personal experiences, *Night* provides a vivid, compelling picture of the horrors of Auschwitz and Buchenwald as well as the protagonist's relationship with his father and agony over his death. But Wiesel found it extremely hard to find a publisher willing to take the risk of producing a book that would, it was thought, have little by way of an audience. First written at length—around nine hundred pages—in Yiddish under the accusatory title *And the World Remained Silent*, then rewritten in French and published in a truncated form by Les Editions de Minuit in France in 1958, it received strong support from the Catholic French writer and Nobel laureate François Mauriac. Yet it was rejected by every major French and American publishing house at the time.[61] Wiesel's international status rose slowly, and after he was awarded the Nobel Peace Prize in 1986, the book finally became a bestseller—thirty years after original publication. Even so, despite or perhaps because of his international fame and the ambiguities of "autofiction," Wiesel remained a controversial figure.[62]

There are other examples. Primo Levi's account of his experiences as an Auschwitz survivor, *If This Is a Man*, published soon after the war, initially sold relatively few copies and did not reach a wide audience until some two decades later.[63] Charlotte Delbo, a member of the French resistance and survivor of Auschwitz and Ravensbrück, wrote the first part of her account of her experiences in the first two or three years after the war. But her full account, *Auschwitz and After*, which was augmented by further reflections, was not published until 1965, some two decades later.[64] Imre Kertész, who became a Nobel Prize winner in 2002, portrays in his novels similar difficulties in achieving both publication and—more important perhaps—understanding on the part of a wider public of the experiences of a Holocaust survivor.[65]

It is due to the efforts of a number of committed institutions and individuals that a great deal more was collected by way of early testimonies and accounts of persecution by people whose voices would never otherwise have been recorded. They were active in eliciting accounts, often from the earliest stages of Nazi persecution onward, as well as during and after the war. There were anguished attempts to communicate almost unimaginable events, in the hope of recording horrific experiences for posterity and eliciting responses from the broader community.[66] Some initiatives had started as early as the 1930s and developed new emphases in the wake of the tragedy that overwhelmed European Jews; others began only after the defeat of Germany. It is notable that the major efforts to collect and preserve testimony and to make it available to a wider audience were largely initiated by European Jews themselves, some of whom were able to find both the material resources and a sufficiently sympathetic environment.

Across Europe, Jewish historical commissions and individuals sought to collect the experiences of those who had suffered persecution.[67] Mostly committed lay persons, with only a handful of trained historians, lawyers, or others with relevant professional qualifications, these activists used a variety of methods, including questionnaires and oral history interviews, to capture the experiences of ordinary people from a wide range of backgrounds while their memories were fresh and immediate. Although the relevance of these materials to the writing of history was not fully recognized for decades thereafter, a number of collections became central in preserving Jewish testimony.

The YIVO Institute for Jewish Research was founded in Wilno (Vilnius), Poland, in 1925, focusing on Jewish life and culture in eastern Europe over centuries. It was moved to New York in 1940 and after the war expanded its already broad remit to emphasize the Holocaust, which in subsequent decades became a central reference point for Jewish identity in the United States as elsewhere. The Wiener Library in London was based on a collection of documents originally started by Alfred Wiener in the 1920s, when he became increasingly aware of the growing threat of antisemitism in Germany.

With Hitler's accession to power in 1933, Wiener and his family fled from Berlin to Amsterdam. Although he was able to save little of his own collection of documents, in that year he set up the Central Jewish Information Office under the auspices of the Board of Deputies of British Jews and the Anglo-Jewish Association. In 1939 the collection moved to London, where it became known as "Dr. Wiener's Library," later simply the Wiener Library. Collecting testimony from a very early date, it was of considerable use in providing documentation in preparation for the Nuremberg trials, which started in 1945.

Other collections were set up specifically to record the horrors of the Holocaust. The Jewish Historical Institute (ŻIH) in Warsaw bases its collection on the original Jewish Historical Commission of 1944, which formed the nucleus of the Emanuel Ringelblum Jewish Historical Institute, founded in 1947. Although its remit now covers one thousand years of Jewish life in Poland, it holds significant collections of documents relating to the Holocaust. These include, most notably, the Ringelblum archive of testimony collected in the Warsaw ghetto as well as very early postwar testimonies from survivors who were interviewed across Poland and whose statements were carefully transcribed. Among other unique collections produced in Poland soon after the end of the war were essays by schoolchildren, recording children's experiences of violence and terror in the years of persecution and extermination.[68]

Poland was not the only center of such activities. The Center of Contemporary Jewish Documentation (CDJC) in France was initiated in April 1943 by the efforts of Isaac Schneersohn and other resistance fighters and members of the Jewish communities in occupied France. Initially based in Grenoble, it moved to Paris when the Germans took over the area previously under Italian occupation in October 1943. Schneersohn, with Léon Poliakov and others, sought to document Nazi crimes and assist later attempts to bring perpetrators to justice. This collection was used in the Nuremberg trials and later war crimes trials in France, and also proved invaluable for research into racist polices and individual experiences of survival and resistance.

In Israel, Yad Vashem was founded in 1953 as a specialist site for both research and commemoration of the victims of the Holocaust, developing a database of victims' names, fostering research into the persecution of the Jews, and awarding the status of "Righteous among the Nations" to individuals who had assisted Jews. In many ways, it has become the globally central archive and Holocaust memorial site.

There were also individual efforts to record testimony. Of particular interest are the extraordinary efforts of an American professor named David Boder to tape-record the stories of survivors in Displaced Persons' (DP) camps.[69] Boder himself originally came from eastern Europe: he was born in 1886 as Aron Mendel Michelson into a Jewish community in the town of Libau, in the Courland, then part of Imperial Russia. Boder went to school in Latvia, speaking German, Yiddish, and Russian, as well as taking lessons in Hebrew, and subsequently studied in Vilna (Vilnius) in Lithuania, before pursuing university studies in psychology under Wilhelm Wundt in Leipzig and in St. Petersburg. He left Russia during the civil war that followed the First World War and by a circuitous journey ended up in Mexico, where he acquired fluent Spanish. In 1926 Boder was finally allowed entry into the United States; here, he pursued postgraduate research in psychology and gained a university teaching position at what was later named the Illinois Institute of Technology in Chicago. In the summer of 1946, Boder traveled to sixteen different DP camps in France, Switzerland, Italy, and Germany and interviewed somewhere in the region of 129 individuals in nine different languages.[70] The result was a unique and remarkable collection of the earliest still extant oral history recordings with survivors from many different communities across Europe. Boder was not only personally sympathetic to the plight of these displaced persons; he was also remarkably well qualified, with his combination of expertise in psychology and extraordinary command of languages. His work was also at the forefront of the technology of the time; these were the first tape-recorded interviews with survivors, so that we are able not merely to read the transcribed—and sometimes also translated—words on the page but to hear the original voices. As with other early testimonies, such as those collected by the Jewish Historical Commission in Warsaw, the contents of the Boder interviews are distinctively different from the survivor testimonies collected in later decades, when there was growing interest in the impact on individual survivors' lives of what was an increasingly well-known general story. In early postwar accounts, by contrast, specific factual sequences are elicited and emotionally significant incidents described, but with little or no sense of a wider interpretive framework shaping the narrative. This still needed to be pieced together, and neither survivors nor their interlocutors had an overview.

For all the unique worth of the Boder collection as we perceive it today, it was not recognized at the time in quite the same way as collections of documents. This was not the stuff the Nuremberg trials were made of; these interviews were seen neither as a form of evidence that could lead to successful prosecutions nor as contributing to Jewish cultural heritage or memorialization. In 1949 Boder published a first series of interviews and analyses in a book tellingly entitled *I Did Not Interview the Dead*.[71] But he found it difficult to secure a publisher for subsequent work on this project. Moreover, when his research grant ran out in 1956, Boder was unable to secure further funding for transcribing and translating the interviews. On his death in 1961, despite all his efforts, the project was left unfinished. Only decades later, early in the twenty-first century, was its value was fully recognized.

Political groups were also concerned to document—and celebrate—their own resistance and to mourn those who could been seen as martyrs to the cause. In East Germany, communist-dominated groups of victims and resistance fighters began to collect accounts of persecution and suffering soon after the war. The League of Those Persecuted by the Nazi Regime (Vereinigung der Verfolgten des Naziregimes, VVN), for example, began collecting accounts of individual experiences as well as representing the interests of those who had been persecuted. Over the following decades, the East German regime made a point of periodically collecting testimonies of people whose political experiences and profiles they wanted to highlight.[72]

Attempts to record testimony were rooted in assumptions that implicitly defined typical narratives and acceptable interpretations. Some accounts were circulated orally, garnished and embellished over the years, and collected by committed individuals only decades after the events to which they refer. This was the case, for example, with the "Hasidic tales" narrated by particularly revered rabbis, other spiritual leaders (rebbes), and their followers (Hasidim).[73] These are short stories, almost anecdotes, sometimes formulaic and generally intended to make a point of wider moral significance—such as defining elements of spirituality, recalling portentous intimations of the future or miraculous moments. They provide a vehicle for retaining faith in goodness and God despite the evidence of massive destruction and devastation; through repetition and reiteration of fundamental values, they retain a link with a spiritual world of the past that was all but destroyed. Their purpose is therefore very different from that of sources collected for purposes of historical record and reckoning. But they provide key insights into subjective experiences and ways of endowing the world with meaning, assisting spiritual and physical survival through appalling times.

Political organizations and Jewish communities were assiduous in their collection of testimonies from an early date. But some groups of victims are notable for their absence from early postwar collections. Victims of Nazi forced sterilization and euthanasia policies, for example, do not seem to have produced much by way of documentation themselves (some for obvious reasons), nor did they have powerful interest groups acting on their behalf at this time. Taboos, sensitivities, and fear of further ostracism affected the willingness of relatives to speak. Lines were moreover on occasion blurred. Some Germans whose relatives had died in the euthanasia program had also been ardent Nazis; others had accommodated themselves in one way or another to the regime. We simply do not have an overview of the families affected by compulsory sterilization and euthanasia, nor more than fragmentary and anecdotal evidence of the complexities and strife within such families. When, for example, friends or relatives of individuals who had died after being admitted to a clinic in Neuruppin sought to inquire more closely after 1945, they were greeted with a wall of silence. There were clearly cover-ups: during investigations, files mysteriously went missing in transit; and while the evidence was disappearing, any wrongdoing was denied by the relevant medical, municipal, and police authorities. In the passive voice, the principal doctor who remained head of the clinic after the war claimed that patients had simply been moved out in order to clear beds, and it was not known what had happened to them subsequently or where they had gone.[74] This set the pattern for many more who rapidly sought to distance themselves from the state-sanctioned violence in which they had been so recently involved.

Forced laborers were among the last of Hitler's victims to have their stories taken seriously. Interest in their fates was expressed by some Western historians in the 1970s and 1980s, at a time when contacting ordinary people living behind the Iron Curtain remained difficult. By the time major oral history projects were devoted to these people, following the fall of communism, a great deal had changed, both in terms of audiences and in terms of wider frameworks of understanding.[75]

Shaping the Past

A striking feature of many early accounts is their sheer factual quality, but a facticity that is sometimes disjointed, unconnected—in a sense more of an attempt at ordering in some form of chronology and linked description of discrete moments and incidents than at offering a coherent narrative. People facing, or newly emerging from, extreme persecution were primarily concerned to record and convey *what* was happening, or *what* had taken place. Although victims describe individual perpetrators, and although some survivors were courageous enough to help to track down their former tormentors and assist in prosecutions, many early testimonies are not primarily about *who* was responsible; for many, that would come later, in the context of the legal pursuit of justice. Nor, again with notable exceptions, are many early accounts about what persecution *meant* in any wider sense for their own lives and the lives of their communities. That, too, would have to wait for some considerable time, and in many quarters it would wait for the emergence of wider audiences and younger generations.

The interviews with Jewish children who had survived in Poland, whose accounts were collected by the Central Jewish Historical Commission in the first months after the war, present evidence of the ways in which young people—some very young indeed, others already teenagers—related their experiences so soon after liberation. Many of these accounts are remarkable for their largely flat emotional tone, recording details of a father being shot, a mother being deported and never seen again, a brother going out from a bunker to drink dirty water from a puddle because he was so thirsty and dying as a result, learning to lie and live in disguise, terrifying incidents in the ghetto or shootings in Jewish cemeteries, being hidden by hostile as well as helpful Polish gentiles, betrayal by locals, starvation, weakness of eyesight and limbs as a result of long periods hidden in dark and cramped conditions, a vagueness about periods of time, a sense of the passing of the seasons because it was unbearably cold, unbearably wet, unbearably hot. There are occasional memories of crying or of moments of kindness and flashes of emotion, but it would take a psychologist, not a historian, to explain the patterns. All we can see are chronicles of misery and death and evidence of the loneliness of these young people as well as the physical and psychological damage done to them, with no explanation for the course their lives had taken other than that they were Jewish.[76] It would be decades before they would be able to set their experiences in any kind of wider picture, if at all.

The "if at all" haunts posterity. David Boder's collection of interviews with people in camps for displaced persons is also particularly interesting for the light it sheds on the raw experiences of adults who had just emerged from the maelstrom, the majority of whom would never come to publish their experiences. People in DP camps were of course a distinctive subset of survivors.[77] Those who came from western European countries such as France or Italy and were able and willing to go home generally did so. The way those interviewed in the DP camps talked is critical in understanding survivor experiences so close to the events narrated. Later, their accounts would be refracted by the circumstances in which they subsequently settled as well as growing knowledge about the wider settings of their stories.

Many stories recorded by Boder were recounted in a disjointed fashion, with both interviewer and survivor unsure about the weight to be accorded to different parts of the story, even uncertain, sometimes, about where particular places were, what had happened there, and how the developments recounted had actually come about. There are uncertainties about timing, about the duration of particular periods, about dates of specific events, and about who was responsible or why certain things had taken place at all.

Some of these accounts are of experiences that did not subsequently make it into the expected frameworks of standard "survivor stories." For example, on September 25, 1946, Boder interviewed a man known only as Joseph because he preferred not to give his last name or further identification, who was staying at the time in a DP camp in Wiesbaden, in western Germany.[78] Joseph told Boder of his wartime movements, including arrival in Przemyśl. Here, as he put it, the "Red Army came in and divided Przemyśl. Half of Przemyśl was red, the Red Army, and the other half of Przemyśl, across the [river?] was German." His wife had tried to join him but was stranded on the other side of the river and not allowed to cross. Later, he discovered that she had been deported to Auschwitz and did not survive the war. Meanwhile, Joseph sought to return to the German side to join his wife, but he found himself instead deported to the Soviet Union, where he worked in a series of camps, spending the rest of the war in areas under Soviet control. The account of his time in these camps is quite bare and disjointed; neither Joseph nor Boder seems to have been able to make much sense of the wider context. Certain details—of food, clothing, work—are clear, and Joseph was also clear about how his poor physical condition, due to malnutrition and illness, eventually meant that he was moved to a camp with better conditions and lighter work duties. He was also given medicine, and, he added, "There things were no longer so awful. One could stand it. We did not go to work so early." On being told they had been "liberated," which in fact meant not the end of the war but rather being released from jail or penal camps, Joseph and others sought to get home: "We were liberated and we traveled to find each other's relatives. We traveled and traveled and traveled. We spent whole months traveling. We became ill. We died from traveling. We became ill on the way." His collective "we" includes those who died, a "we" that continues despite deaths, mentioned not only after a sentence about becoming ill but also before another one.

For a while, Joseph seems to have served in an army, and was in "Central Asia." But there he became even more ill, with typhus and dysentery. Following a period of hospitalization and convalescence, he again began to work and travel. Finally, in July 1946 he was able to make it back to his native Poland. He was not prepared for what awaited him there: "When we arrived in Poland...we thought that we would be able to exist at home. Poland was, after all, our home. We had lived there for so many years...our fathers, our grandfathers. But we were told that we could not go out into the street." On being asked who told them this, Joseph replied: "The Jews who came to meet the train. Jews came out to meet the train said that we should not loiter in the street, because there had been some shooting today. At night a train went through going to Warsaw-Lublin, and four Jews were taken off. No one knew what had happened. In the morning it was discovered that they had been shot."

So Joseph traveled further west and was interviewed by Boder at the DP camp in Wiesbaden some two months after this incident in Poland. He was clearly in no state to provide a full or coherent narrative of his life during the preceding years, beyond the bare bones of movement, work, living conditions, ill health, and fear. This kind of narrative never made it into the mainstream of the sorts of accounts that eventually came to be seen as standard patterns of survivor stories. In Joseph's story, there are no rescue attempts or heroic escapes—nothing but a chronicle of sheer survival, not even this being interpreted as due to luck or friendship or humanity or indeed anything. There is, quite simply, no framework of interpretation at all.

Some interviewees were more willing to provide framing narratives or filled in more details. And a few who were interviewed by Boder did go on to give more detailed testimony later in their lives. By this time, they could see a wider picture; they had more secondary knowledge and information to fill in the gaps and sketch in the background to their own personal experiences. Their narratives now "made more sense," in ways that were not possible right after the war.

Half a century later, certain sorts of stories had become the expected narrative of "Holocaust" experiences. When a selection of Boder's original interviews were revised for publication in 1998, the editor, Donald Niewyk, was quite explicit about his selection criteria, choosing exclusively interviews with "Jews who survived Hitler's genocide and had something important to say," whereas those "who were unable to tell coherent stories" were "excluded." Also excluded were accounts by "anti-Communist Soviet citizens, members of various religious sects, and other Gentile refugees." Diversity of experience was downplayed in favor of prioritizing a standard Jewish narrative. And even the accounts of Jewish survivors that were included were subjected to some reordering "for chronological coherence," while "redundant material" was "excised."[79] Joseph's narrative did not make the cut.

There is considerable value to this later selection, which is complemented by an introduction situating the individual narratives within a wider picture. These edited and readable stories can tell us a great deal about Holocaust experiences, providing detailed insights into deportations, ghettos, camps, and forced labor across many areas; and in this form they can reach the far wider audiences that eluded Boder at a time when there was no market for such accounts.

Yet there is also a cost to such selection. By the late 1990s, while ensuring accessibility for later audiences, such an approach to survivor narratives cannot convey precisely the incoherence and incapacity to narrate that was characteristic of so many who were "displaced" in more senses than the purely geographical straight after the war. What we have in Boder's original collection, as in the children's stories collected in Poland, are snapshots of incomprehensible experiences: they are narrated by people who were in effect suspended in time, unable to make sense of what had happened or where they could or should go next. Their worlds had been shattered, and they had not yet acquired strategies for trying to comprehend what it all meant—if there could be meaning at all—or how they would continue after the destruction, the catastrophe.

Tangled Friendships and Torn Bonds

For those who—whether through active participation or emotional identification—were part of the perpetrator community, the defining moment in their lives occurred not with the advent of Nazism, as in the case of the persecuted, but rather with the end of the war, when they had to face up to the consequences of defeat.

Many now saw themselves primarily as victims. People who had been complicit in a system of terror, who had excluded and benefited from the dispossession of others, or had themselves witnessed or been involved in committing atrocities now saw only the pain they were themselves experiencing in the aftermath. Resentments against their current situation festered, with blame generally laid on the new oppressors.[80] Massive population movements, both during and after the war, also meant dramatic upheavals.[81] Germans who returned from the front or from prisoner of war camps, or resettled after flight or expulsion from eastern Europe, talked bitterly about their suffering. Depending on gender, age, and location, experiences included rape, maltreatment, robberies, hunger, illness, worry about loved ones, difficulties on the treks to the west, brutal hard work or boredom in the internment camps, and injustice or hard labor in the Soviet Union.[82] Diaries record worries about lack of food, coal, and clothing and a longing to return to former homes, where people remembered leading happier and carefree lives.[83] Many were themselves bereaved, often displaced psychologically as well as physically, and utterly unwilling to empathize with the victims of Nazi persecution. These upheavals loomed large in memory for decades afterward. They were often recounted in purely personal terms, with little or no effort to place this suffering in the wider context of German policies and practices at the time.[84] Those who had been supporters of the Nazi regime, in whatever capacity—and however far from the killing fields—subsequently kept silent about their former enthusiasm, or viewed their pasts with a degree of dissociation. There is a hidden history here of transformations of the self.

Seeking to understand or engage in dialogue with former victims and survivors was, in these circumstances, the last thing on most people's minds. This also served to entrench the divisions between former perpetrators and survivors of persecution. There were few attempts to bridge the gap between differing communities of experience. But a few took stabs at reconciliation and tried to pick up the pieces of former friendships where they had left off before the chasm of persecution had opened up.

Melita Maschmann, a former leader and publicist for the Nazi girls' youth organization, the BDM, is distinctive for having published an account in the early 1960s in which she was clearly struggling with the question of guilt.[85] In what she called a "report," an accounting with her past self, written in the form of letters to a former Berlin school friend, Marianne Schweitzer, who was of Jewish descent, Maschmann engaged in a searching inquiry into her former enthusiasm and activities on behalf of Nazism. This account presents an extraordinary combination of self-justification and self-criticism, on occasion bordering on self-laceration: it is a delicate balancing act, trying to acknowledge both the omissions and wrongdoings of the past while still portraying a self with which she could comfortably live—an innocent, betrayed self, a young person led astray by the allure of Hitler, the hopes of "doing good" for the disadvantaged, and the promise of contributing to national greatness and glory. Only later, in retrospect, did she appreciate that the "good" for which she had thought she was working was premised on the exclusion, dispossession, and ultimately murder of countless others who were not part of the German "national community." Maschmann portrays her past self as essentially good, innocent; at the same time, she recognizes the harm to which she had contributed and the murderous consequences of her own willingness to blind herself to the suffering of others, to suppress any sympathy for the starving Polish children or the miseries she had witnessed in the ghettos of Kutno and Łódź.[86]

When it was published, the account stimulated considerable interest in West Germany, although it was not universally well received. One British reviewer, the historian James Joll, wrote it off as a "rather dreary and repellent book," the only real merit of which was to show "how easy it was for ordinary people to fall into a routine in which the most appalling things could happen without being questioned or even noticed."[87] Many historians have subsequently mined it for supposed insights into how Nazism was possible, energizing so many young people into willingness to sacrifice their lives for the cause, and how women assisted in attempts to "Germanize" the Nazi east, part of the attempt to settle German-speaking people in Poland and other places.[88] Yet it is arguably more interesting for the insights it affords into the soul-searching that went on among some West German circles in the 1960s—and the persisting chasms that existed between communities that had been persecuted and those who had contributed to their persecution.

Marianne Schweitzer, the intended recipient of Maschmann's letters, had managed to emigrate to the United States before the war broke out, later marrying an American and becoming a language teacher.[89] Although Schweitzer received repeated letters from Maschmann, after one brief encounter she chose not to respond, trying to turn her energies to the new life in America. She only once ever made contact again with the friend to whom she had formerly been so close.

It was not Schweitzer's brothers to whom Maschmann had drawn the attention of the Gestapo, as Maschmann claimed in her account (which explicitly altered some details in the interests of anonymity), but rather Marianne's elder sister Gabriele, generally known as Rele. As a result of Maschmann's denunciation, in late 1937 Rele was arrested for her opposi-tional activities in an illegal youth group by the name of dj.1.11. and incar-cerated in the newly opened women's concentration camp of Lichtenburg. Rele's then-boyfriend, political soulmate, and later husband was Hans Seidel, whom she was forbidden to marry at the time because he was fully "Aryan" whereas she was of Jewish descent, which her father had only informed her about in 1933. Like many other Germans from what are called "assimilated" Jewish family backgrounds, she was brought up as a Christian. Hans Seidel was also arrested and appears to have experienced horrific treatment during his periods of imprisonment in Sachsenhausen and the police prison in Berlin's Alexanderplatz, precipitating repeated bouts of deep depression that plagued him for the rest of his life.[90]

When Marianne Schweitzer first returned to Germany in 1963, a quarter of a century after emigrating, she went to visit her sister Rele, now married to Hans and bringing up a family in Stuttgart, and was persuaded to meet up again with Melita Maschmann. The meeting did not go well; Schweitzer later regretted that she had not been more open to her former friend's attempts at reconciliation and that following this meeting she had chosen again to break off all further contact.

It was extremely rare for someone to talk in public with this degree of honesty, seeking to communicate across the chasm that had been created by Nazism, and expecting to be able to pick up a friendship again as if nothing had changed. However, it was not at all unusual for former school groups to try to meet up again after the war and to engage in a semblance of normality. Often, to sustain a friendship, relationships had to remain somewhat super-ficial, with no "account rendered" along the lines of Maschmann. Silencing the past and pretending to have been against Nazism was a far more com-mon pattern, one that allowed at least social formalities and appearances of friendship to be observed, provided the past was not probed too deeply. Either way, it was impossible for the former easy social bonds of the pre-Nazi period to be reconnected.

In 1969, perhaps because he could not live with painful memories, or perhaps as a result of deep psychological disturbances precipitated by maltreatment in prison and concentration camp, Hans Seidel—a highly intelligent doctor and politically aware citizen—committed suicide, leaving Rele and their children to face the future without him.[91]

In the early postwar years, people generally talked among themselves, among members of their own communities, and not across the borders of different communities of experience. The effects of the past persisted, and they were far from over. While survivors were seeking to recover as best they could from the injury done to them, the majority of perpetrators were busy covering their tracks and changing their tales. It is scarcely surprising that there was a marked lack of communication between those who had been persecuted and people who had been on the perpetrator side. Their interests were often at odds with one another; deep differences in experience and outlook could prevent attempts at reconciliation. Even talking within each community was not necessarily easy.

After the devastations of total war, most people—of whatever background—were primarily concerned with "reconstruction" projects, at both the private level of personal and family life and in the broader public sphere. The postwar decades were characterized by what were, effectively, parallel worlds. There was much talking within particular communities of experience but a relative lack of communication, and a lack of empathy, across them. The stakes and emotions ran too high for the possibility of meaningful dialogue. In some cases, the need for coexistence meant that any feelings of hatred, desire for revenge, or even hopes for reconciliation would have been too problematic to articulate. As a result—whether or not individuals were aware of this at the time—people were generally unwilling to cross either the boundaries of their own informal networks, bound by ties of similar experiences, or the even less visible borders of what was thinkable, expressible, when discussing the recent past.

To talk primarily of "memory" or to limit the focus to cultural phenomena or political controversies is to miss the continuing personal significance of recent experiences. For those who had lived through this period, the past was not just a matter of representations—important as these are—but rather of persisting physical and psychological pain, of continuing emotional engagements, of personal challenges and readjustments, inevitably inflecting and affecting a later present. Seeking to engage in reconciliation and communication of contrasting experiences was inherently risky, often abhorrent, and in some cases close to impossible. The subterranean levels of personal engagement with the past continued, intertwining at times with more visible confrontations on the public stage.

This situation would only begin to change around a quarter of a century later. In the meantime, however, attempts were made to put those considered most guilty on trial: to engage in reckonings in the courtroom. As we shall see, legal systems and practices were inadequate for the enormity of the task.

PART II

Confrontations: Landscapes of the Law

8

Transitional Justice

In his memoir of Auschwitz, written late in life, historian Otto Dov Kulka recalled a desire for revenge while he was still a child living in the shadow of the smoke of the crematoria. He remembered a fellow prisoner, a "young man with a lean face and the bristles of a beard, named Herbert," who was a formative influence; among other things, Herbert gave him a copy of Dostoevsky's *Crime and Punishment*. Herbert also played "a game of suggesting ideas for the 'solution of the German question,'" deliberately playing on Nazi terminology regarding the "solution of the Jewish question."[1] In considering possible "solutions," Kulka recalled, there was an "aversion" to developing an "identical solution" for the Germans, namely, gas chambers and crematoria, or "banishing" them "from the nations of the world."[2] This, it was held, would go too far and reduce Jews to the level of inhumanity of their tormentors.

Yet after the war, a few survivors were willing to contemplate extreme forms of revenge. Abba Kovner, for example, a former resistance fighter and survivor of Vilna (Vilnius) ghetto, led plans by a postwar Jewish group called Nakam—meaning "revenge" in Hebrew—to poison thousands of Germans through contamination of metropolitan drinking water supplies in major German cities.[3] This plan was foiled only at the last moment. However ghastly the idea of killing vast numbers of Germans in this way might be, it did highlight the scale of the pain suffered and the associated strength of feeling, with some urging that reprisals should be on an equivalent scale. Bringing those responsible for mass murder to justice was never likely to be straightforward.

Revenge, retribution, justice—these words mean different things and have very different implications. There was no one strategy broadly accepted among the survivors and victims or that would seem in some way to right the wrongs that had been inflicted on them. Some survivors did take immediate action against former tormentors when opportunities arose. Others did not want to take revenge, but rather sought to return to a feeling of humanity unburdened by the past, however difficult this might be. Like Herbert, they did not wish to be brought down to the level of indiscriminate brutality characteristic of their oppressors. A few eventually even felt the only way they could live with their experiences was to forgive their former tormentors; this was the path adopted by one survivor of Mengele's experiments on twins, Eva Mozes Kor.[4] It was not a solution that suited many others.

Whatever view was adopted, an underlying sense of outrage remained among most. A desire for revenge or justice had kept some victims going in times of extreme adversity, and after the war it motivated a few individuals to pursue Nazi perpetrators against all the odds. At the same time, the Allies' concern to bring the guilty to court was soon complicated by emergent Cold War tensions. Once new states had been founded on the soil of the defeated Third Reich, now truncated and divided by the Iron Curtain, new elites replaced old and political considerations crosscut questions of guilt. Former Nazis sought to rewrite the past and navigate the transformation relatively unscathed, with varying degrees of success, while emergent parties sought to establish a better future, based in very different ideological views.

Transitional justice entails a complex combination of trials, purges, and attempts to compensate for wrongs suffered and achieve a degree of reconciliation for a different future.[5] Nowhere in post-Nazi Europe was legal reckoning with collective violence and state-sponsored crimes simple or straightforward. In the Third Reich successor states, conflicts continued for decades between those seeking justice and those wanting to put an end to reckoning with the Nazi past.

Transformations

While those who had actively supported Nazism or collaborated with Nazi rule were fearful of possible retribution, victims and opponents of Nazism should have been able to breathe more freely—but the extent and manner of any such transformation in the months immediately following the end of the war depended on rapidly changing circumstances on either side of the Iron Curtain now dividing Cold War Europe.

Clear demarcation lines were drawn between those few who were variously identified as culprits and the larger numbers who could be exonerated as harmless fellow travelers. In many states, previous divisions persisted in new forms, and mutual hatreds and suspicions were rife. Reintegration of the vast majority of those who had participated in, sustained, or collaborated with Nazi rule in Europe was the predominant trend across all postwar states, whether in Western democratic Europe or in Eastern Europe under communist domination. Those selected as heroes of resistance, by contrast, varied greatly with context.

There were early moments of immediate, and often unlawful, retribution. The mass rapes of German women by Red Army soldiers in the closing months of the war and the early postwar period, the shaving of the heads of French and Polish women who had slept with Germans, the brutal treatment and shaming of people deemed to have been collaborators, the spontaneous as well as orchestrated violence accompanying the expulsion of Germans from Eastern European states—all these were evidence of the strong emotions that had been aroused in the course of the war and a widespread determination to seek revenge, whether or not particular individuals targeted were themselves guilty of heinous crimes or collaboration. Some were; many others, particularly young female rape victims, were not.[6]

In some places, there was a rapid imposition of justice on the spot. When the Soviet Army arrived at the psychiatric hospital of Meseritz-Obrawalde on January 29, 1945, for example, they found ample evidence of the thousands of murders that had taken place there under the "wild" euthanasia program. The director, Walter Grabowski, and other members of staff including Dr. Hilde Wernicke and Helene Wieczorek, managed to flee; but in March a nurse, Amanda Ratajczak, was captured by the Soviets and given a summary trial, which included a filmed re-enactment of killing methods. Ratajczak admitted to a role in killing around 1,500 patients, and was summarily put to death, along with another carer, on May 10, 1945.[7] Had she managed to flee west and evade trial for a decade or more, the outcome would have been very different, as we shall see in other cases relating to euthanasia killings.

Bringing individuals to account for their crimes was not the only concern. Across Europe, there were systematic attempts to purge those who had assisted the Nazis, as in the "purification" (épuration) process applied to Nazi collaborators in France. In most countries such purges were used as means of selecting new elites, although continuity was more notable than radical change in Western European states. In Eastern Europe, under increasing Soviet domination from the later 1940s, purges were also used to marginalize opponents of communism, of whatever political hue. Polish patriots who had fought against the Nazis in the Home Army, for example, soon found themselves on the wrong side of history once again. Members of non-communist resistance movements were often targeted for incarceration and harsh treatment by the communist regime. On the other hand, in Poland antisemitism was not discredited as it had been in France, because it was not officially associated with a collaborationist regime, and even some Polish liberals felt the country would be better off as a mono-ethnic state.[8] Many Poles remained antisemites, whether for ideological reasons (which had historically been rooted more in religious belief than "racial" considerations) or because of personal and, particularly, material interests. Some were more extreme. The Kielce pogrom of July 1946, which attracted widespread attention, was but the largest outbreak of violence against Jews returning to their former homes after the war. In 1945–46 some three hundred Jews were killed by Poles; many were resentful about the reappearance of surviving Jews and fearful about the possible consequences of being found to have taken over their property or having been instrumental in deaths and deportations.[9]

Some feared postwar reprisals for having betrayed or murdered Jews. Sobibór survivor Thomas (Toivi) Blatt commented that, following the revolt and breakout from the death camp, many of those who did not ultimately survive the war were not killed by Germans, but rather "most were murdered by hostile anti-Semites, nationalistic organizations, or roaming bandits." He was acutely aware that the "situation of a Jewish escapee stood in sharp contrast to that of a gentile escapee. The latter could simply mingle with the rest of the population and be safe. Not so the Jew."[10] Blatt was terrified after liberation of a farmer named Bojarski, who had attempted to murder Blatt and his two friends whom he had previously sheltered.[11] Blatt narrowly escaped being nearly killed by Polish peasants, one of whom, he wrote, was "my executioner in Bojarski's barn.... Bojarski knew very well that if I survived he would need to go into hiding."[12]

The hostility of the Polish population—despite the assistance and help of a few individuals—was also the reasoning behind the decision of Richard Glazar, who had escaped from Treblinka, to disguise himself as a forced laborer in Germany.[13] Paradoxically, then, Jews did not feel much safer in Poland after the war, despite the defeat of the Germans, the dismantling of their camps, and the determination of the victorious powers to put the worst criminals on trial. This would leave significant legacies both for personal choices about emigration and for later policies and practices of memorialization on Polish soil.

Polish justice was nevertheless harsh: there were at least 193 death sentences and sixty-nine sentences of life imprisonment.[14] The first trial concerning the Majdanek concentration camp began in Lublin a matter of days after the liberation of the camp, taking place from November 27 to December 2, 1944. This was also the first-ever trial relating specifically to a Nazi concentration camp.[15] Further trials soon followed, including subsequent Majdanek trials from 1945 to 1952. The most prominent defendant in early Polish trials was Rudolf Höss, former commandant of Auschwitz, who was handed over by the Allies, tried in Kraków, and executed in April 1947 on the gallows in Auschwitz I, just over the fence from his former home in the commandant's house. Amon Göth, former commandant of the Plaszów camp on the outskirts of Kraków, was put on trial and executed in 1946.[16] Others too were tried and punished for their crimes in Poland, including Hans Biebow, former head of the ghetto administration of Litzmannstadt (Łódź). Having escaped to Germany at the end of the war, he was recognized by a survivor. The Allies determined that Biebow should be extradited to Łódź, where, also in April 1947, he was tried and hanged for his role in exploiting and starving the inhabitants of the ghetto.

But it is notable that others who had been responsible for the suffering and deaths in the Łódź ghetto as well as the deportations to the death camps largely succeeded in evading justice. Those not brought to account in court included the former regional president, Friedrich Übelhör, and the former city mayor, Werner Ventzki.[17] Übelhör had gone missing during the closing days of the war. But Ventzki, like so many other former Nazis in civilian administration, subsequently went on to a career in the West German civil service, putting his personal knowledge of conditions in the occupied east to a new form of service in the Ministry for Expellees, Refugees, and Victims of War. For several decades Ventzki's son—like so many others of the second generation, as we shall see—had no inkling that his father had been involved in anything to do with Nazi persecution.

There were also significant trials of Nazi war criminals across Europe. Postwar states often had to contend with political questions around domestic collaboration as well as victimhood. In France, for example, much attention was paid to attempting to heal the rifts of the Vichy period by emphasizing French resistance and downplaying the specifically Jewish experiences of deportation as well as domestic collaboration. In some places, the period of "transitional justice" extended well beyond the immediate postwar years, as trials continued throughout the later twentieth century, periodically bringing back painful memories and disrupting comfortable national myths.[18]

Trials raising problematic questions around culpability in enforced collaboration took place in a state that did not exist at the time of Nazi persecution but in large measure owed its very existence to Nazism and represented the largest group of victims: the State of Israel, founded in 1948 (building on the controversial Balfour Declaration of 1917, which supported a "national home" for the Jewish people in Palestine, but given impetus and urgency by the Holocaust and the wider international fallout of war).[19] In 1950 Israel's parliament, the Knesset, passed the Nazi and Nazi Collaborators (Punishment) Law. This controversial and harshly worded legislation was targeted primarily at those Jewish victims who had only survived the Holocaust because they had operated in the "gray zone," as Kapos in concentration camps or helpers of the German authorities and ghettos. The details and exact number of cases brought under this law remain uncertain, with records closed for seventy years after each trial, but it is estimated that thirty or forty prosecutions took place between 1951 and 1964. It is also clear that some former Kapos were severely punished for the agonizing decisions they had made when faced with severely constrained choices that would mean the difference between life and death.[20] In view of the way so many culpable Nazis eventually got away with their crimes, these verdicts on prisoner functionaries can raise ethically challenging questions about guilt and responsibility under extraordinary circumstances.

The situation in the territory of the former Third Reich was of course different from anywhere else. Former Nazi concentration camps and prisons, in addition to other locations, were often taken over and used as internment camps by the occupying powers. These camps were frequently criticized by inmates, who claimed they had been unjustly interned. While held with other like-minded and aggrieved souls, some became more, rather than less, sympathetic to Nazi views. Melita Maschmann, whose later attempts to pick up her former friendships were unsuccessful, as we have seen, nevertheless recognized the significance of talking to others with different experiences: she felt that any attempt at "re-education" during her internment was of no use whatsoever and claimed that it was only after she was released and began to be exposed to the views and sympathies of other Germans, including those who had been opposed to Nazism, that she eventually entered a long, slow process of rethinking.[21]

In the Soviet zone of occupation, which in 1949 became the GDR, conditions were far harsher than in camps run by the Western Allies. Ten "special camps" were set up by the NKVD (the People's Commissariat for Internal Affairs of the Soviet Union, with close ties to the police and security forces, which later became the KGB). These made use of former Nazi detention facilities, including the grounds of the concentration camps of Buchenwald and Sachsenhausen, as well as prisons in Bautzen and Hohenschönhausen. More than 120,000 people were interned in the Soviet special camps or similar institutions. Many of them had indeed held significant posts in the Nazi system, but others were ordinary soldiers or even, notoriously, simply young people who had somehow fallen afoul of the new authorities and had been arrested on the streets. Again, this did little to gain the support of the local population or to produce pro-communist attitudes among the vast majority of those affected.

"Denazification" was initially seen as a method of purging former Nazis from the administration and other key areas. The extent to which denazification was used as a means to produce radical changes in structures or personnel varied greatly between the occupation zones.[22] An unfavorable classification might mean a longer or shorter period of internment, a fine, or a ban on employment in certain categories of work. In the Western zones the majority simply got away with it, ending up being classified as a "fellow traveler" (*Mitläufer*) or even "exonerated" (*entlastet*). The most extensive measures took place in the Soviet zone, alongside the construction of new communist political system and a far-reaching social and economic revolution. But even here there was more continuity—particularly in areas not deemed politically sensitive—than the authorities would care to admit. In the East as in the West, the reintegration of those classified as having been only "nominal" Nazis soon took precedence over radical transformation. Denazification in Austria varied with region but as in Germany was patchy, and former Nazis were rapidly reintegrated into social and political life. Everywhere, after an initial flurry of activity the exercise became largely one of rehabilitation. There was a complex interplay between processes of restructuring, shaming and "re-education" on the one hand and reconstruction or the supposed restoration of "normality" on the other, with wide variations in individual responses to Allied policies.[23]

People going through denazification generally saw the procedures as a hurdle to be jumped rather than an occasion for serious confrontation with the past. Biographies were reshaped and facts reinterpreted to fit into whichever framework was most likely to lead to a desired outcome. Stories about minimal and purely formal participation in the Nazi system, having been forced to join the party or to collaborate, having inwardly been "always against" Nazism, or having only gone along with it in order to mitigate its worst effects—all these exculpatory stories and more were widely rehearsed at this time. Nations of non-offenders were born out of the ruins of the Reich and its occupied and incorporated territories. Once the Cold War took precedence over dealing with Nazism and denazification proceedings were handed over to the Germans to deal with themselves, treatment of offenders was even more lenient.

Even so, in the first decade after the war thousands of trials were held in East and West Germany and Austria, bringing to light the widespread involvement of former members of the Nazi *Volksgemeinschaft* in persecuting their fellow citizens. These trials were overshadowed, however, both at the time and in subsequent consciousness, by the major trials carried out by the Allies—seen widely at the time as a matter of "victor's justice."

"Victors' Justice": The Nuremberg International Military Tribunal

In 1945–46, before tensions between the Allies erupted into what became known as the Cold War, they cooperated in the International Military Tribunal (IMT). This brought to account those deemed most guilty by virtue of their former positions at the head of political, economic, and military operations in Nazi Germany. The IMT was held between November 20, 1945, and October 1, 1946, in the Palace of Justice in the historically resonant city of Nuremberg, the city where Hitler had held his annual Nazi party rallies and where he had announced the Nuremberg Laws a decade earlier. A series of twelve successor trials under American auspices were also held at Nuremberg (known as the "subsequent Nuremberg proceedings," or the Nuremberg Military Tribunals, NMT). These focused attention on representatives of different professional groups—industrialists, doctors, lawyers, bureaucrats—as well as the military, the SS, and the Einsatzgruppen. Each of the occupying powers also held separate trials in their own zones relating to specific cases. Some trials of prominent individuals were held to achieve maximum public effect; others disappeared almost without a trace as far as public impact and media coverage were concerned. The Allied trials were also significant for subsequent historical interpretations of the Third Reich.[24]

The Allies had an approach that was partially or entirely lost in later trials, particularly those carried out under West German law. In particular, at Nuremberg the definition of "perpetrator" was not, or not only, defined by a focus on the personal brutality or subjective mentality of particular individuals, as became characteristic in later West German trials using the ordinary criminal charge of murder. The Allies' emphasis was placed on the fact that the state and wider circles were jointly responsible. Trials were designed to draw attention to the complicity of industry and of a wide range of professional groups as well as to the significance of shared responsibility. But this did not mean an amorphous notion of collective guilt. As the French prosecutor, Charles Dubost, put it, by making everyone share it, "Nobody bears the responsibility."[25] The Allies' emphasis on "conspiracy" and the division of labor in a system of collective violence was partially lost over succeeding years.

The most prominent of the Nuremberg trials was that of the IMT, often simply termed the Nuremberg Trial, overshadowing as it did the NMT successor trials.[26] Eager not to be seen to be intruding on matters of "domestic policy," the Americans in particular wanted to ensure that the trials focused on issues relating to the pursuit of war. The Allies had reached agreement in the IMT Charter of August 8, 1945, to bring charges against defendants for three crimes under international law—crimes against peace, war crimes, and crimes against humanity—as well as a fourth crime, conspiracy, which was a distinctive feature of Anglo-American law.[27] Each of the Allies played a particular, pre-allotted role. The United States, with Robert Jackson as chief prosecutor, took responsibility for conspiracy, and the British, led by Hartley Shawcross, for crimes against peace. The Soviets dealt with war crimes and crimes against humanity as far the Eastern Front was concerned, while the French took responsibility for these crimes for western Europe.

There was an attempt to have a broad palette of perpetrators on trial, despite the pragmatic need for selectivity (with the length of the defendants' bench prosaically limiting numbers, allowing some to make a lucky switch of role from potential defendant to that of expert witness). Hitler, Goebbels, and Himmler had already committed suicide in late April and May 1945 and so could not be brought to account. Three intended defendants did not appear in court, including the former head of the Nazi Labor Front, Robert Ley, who committed suicide in advance of the trial, and former Nazi Party secretary Martin Bormann, whose whereabouts at the time were uncertain and who was tried and found guilty in absentia. In the event, a total of twenty-one significant public and political figures of the Third Reich were put in the dock, including Hermann Göring, who sought to dominate proceedings in person and ultimately made a dramatic exit by committing suicide the night before his death sentence was to be carried out.

The IMT had grand aims: in effect, it served not only to try individual defendants but also to display the extraordinary scope of Nazi atrocities. Devastating evidence was presented across a wide range of areas. It is often said that the genocide of the Jews did not figure prominently at this time, and certainly the word Holocaust was not as yet current, but there was full awareness of the enormity of crimes against the Jews and explicit acknowledgment of the distinctive status of the genocide—a word coined by Raphael Lemkin in 1944 and enshrined in the Genocide Convention of the United Nations in 1948. In November 1945 the court was shown devastating film footage of concentration camps, and among the perpetrators called to the stand to give evidence were the former commandant of Auschwitz, Rudolf Höss, as well as Otto Ohlendorf, former commander of Einsatzgruppe D.

It cannot be said that genocide was not an issue at Nuremberg, and on January 28, 1946, the first eyewitness testimony was given by a survivor of Auschwitz and Ravensbrück, the French resistance fighter Marie Claude Vaillant-Couturier.[28] She described in detail seeing "columns of living skeletons going to work," the "stacks of corpses piled up in the courtyard"— some of whom were groaning, still apparently just alive—and the problems of cold, thirst, poor shoes, filthy mess tins, and disease, compounded by the random cruelty and violence of the guards. She described the medical experiments and sterilization, the ways in which pregnant women were made to have abortions, and how live newborn babies were killed by drowning. Vaillant-Couturier underlined how the conditions for Jewish prisoners were "absolutely appalling," far worse even than those for political prisoners such as herself. The 1,200 Jewish women with whom she had been interned in France arrived on a slightly later transport than hers; of these, "only 125 actually came to the camp; the others were immediately sent to the gas chambers," but of "these 125 not one was left alive at the end of 1 month." Based in a block right next to the platform where selections took place, Vaillant-Couturier frequently "witnessed heart-rending scenes; old couples forced to part from each other" and mothers and children being "sent to the gas chambers." Departing far from any purely legal concern with demonstrating the guilt of a particular defendant, Vaillant-Couturier detailed how people undressed and were taken into a place that was "somewhat like a shower room, and gas capsules were thrown through an opening in the ceiling" while an "SS man would watch the effect produced through a porthole." The workers who removed the bodies told her that the victims "must have suffered before dying, because they were closely clinging to one another and it was very difficult to separate them." She added that one night she was "awakened by terrifying cries," and was later told by men working in the Sonderkommando that "the gas supply having run out, they had thrown the children into the furnaces alive." She gave details of Mengele's experiments on twins in the summer of 1944 as well as the Gypsy camp and the family camp for people deported from Theresienstadt before this was cleared and the inmates gassed. Of Vaillant-Couturier's own transport of 230 French political prisoners, only forty-nine returned to France at the end of the war.

In the event, twelve defendants were sentenced to death, including Hans Frank, who was hanged. Three were acquitted, and the remainder were sentenced to prison terms of varying lengths, from ten years to life imprisonment. Hitler's chief architect and later minister for armaments, Albert Speer, benefited from subtle self-representation as an apolitical intellectual and was sentenced to imprisonment in Berlin's Spandau Prison, where he worked on his memoirs and gained an ill-deserved reputation as a repentant and essentially "good" Nazi.[29] As we shall see, the children of some of these prominent Nazis, including the families of Speer, Bormann, Ley, and Frank, would later experience considerable difficulties in coming to terms with the past of their parents, resolving their emotional conflicts in ways that differed markedly from the outright denial of parental wrongdoing that was adopted by Himmler's favorite daughter, Gudrun Himmler.

A few anti-Nazi contemporaries were in retrospect "devastated" at the relative failure of the Nuremberg trials to achieve justice, as Karl Jaspers, an unusually perceptive contemporary, put it.[30] Jaspers was a philosopher and psychologist who, because of having a Jewish wife, had been forced out of teaching at Heidelberg University in the late 1930s. The couple survived the war in Germany and chose to immigrate to Switzerland shortly afterward. Reflecting in the early 1960s on his own earlier discussion of guilt—in lectures delivered in 1945 and published in 1946—Jaspers held that the Nuremberg trials had not lived up to their promise. While they were not "show trials" and had been "impeccable" in the application of law, by the early 1960s Jaspers felt that the trials had "not founded justice, but rather increased a distrust of justice."[31] Even at the time of his lectures, Jaspers made distinctions between different types of guilt: criminal, political, moral, and what he termed "metaphysical" guilt. Criminal and political guilt were easily identifiable. Under his notion of "moral guilt" Jaspers included "living with a mask on," and he criticized how people had behaved in ways at odds with their inner feelings; this allowed them to have a clear conscience, without acknowledging that by conforming to Nazism they had brought about bad consequences for others.[32] The somewhat opaque-sounding concept of "metaphysical guilt" related, in Jaspers' view, to the lack of solidarity of people with other human beings, as in the failure to intervene or raise a cry against the regime when synagogues were set on fire in November 1938.[33]

But Jaspers was unusual in his engagement with guilt. While Germans were not admitted to the court simply as members of the public, the licensed press was under considerable pressure from the Allies to present a particular view of the trial, and press coverage was extensive. Letters to newspapers suggest that those whose letters were selected for publication—scarcely a representative cross-section of the population—were generally keen to reject the notion of "collective guilt," and many commented on the widespread lack of interest in the trials. From opinion poll surveys carried out in the American occupation zone and letters written to the military government, it is clear that other priorities were uppermost in many people's minds. Although opinion was clearly divided—some wanted instant justice, thinking guilt was so well established that there was no need to drag things out, while others rejected the proceedings entirely—most people seem to have simply lost interest.[34]

It is not easy to gauge the views of those who neither published their ideas nor gained a voice in the media and political debates. Even so, private letters and diaries, while unrepresentative, allow us to gain some fascinating glimpses. Dr. Hugo M., for example, was a doctor who regularly wrote letters to his son who had gone missing in Russia; this one-sided series of reports by an intelligent man who had made, it would appear, his own compromises with the Nazi regime, provides insights into changing mentalities. In a letter of October 20, 1946, Hugo M. summarized the views of his compatriots on the sentences passed in Nuremberg. He saw a huge spectrum of opinion, from the criticisms of the communist workers who went on strike in protest against the lenience shown to war criminals to "total indifference" on the part of others, while some refused even to acknowledge that crimes had been committed and would still "die with a 'Heil Hitler' on their lips." In Hugo M.'s view, however, "by far the greatest majority" saw it as a "scandal that the victors were able to stand in judgment over the defenceless vanquished," without the Allies' own conduct and potential war crimes (such as the bombing of Dresden) being considered, and that not only the leaders but also those faithful followers who were simply trying to carry out their duties were being indicted. Finally, there was a comment on popular reactions to the ways in which the proceedings had been conducted, responses that have generally gone unnoticed. According to Hugo M., it was widely rumored that "even Göring's corpse had to be dragged up to the seat of judgment so that the sentence could be at least symbolically pronounced," occasioning much criticism, as was the fact "that the ashes of those who had been cremated should be secretly strewn to the winds." These practices were generally seen as evidence of a degree of "tastelessness against which, in our powerlessness, we cannot even protest."[35] Accusations of "tastelessness" in the treatment of Nazis who had been found guilty and executed might seem to us now a somewhat strange reaction, in view of the heinous crimes they had committed while alive.

A teenage girl in western Germany, Ursula E., engaged with contemporary developments in her diary, providing insights into the views of a younger generation. The first question for her concerned blame for Germany having lost the war. In an entry of June 20, 1945, reviewing the preceding weeks, she noted that while leading his troops in battle in Berlin, "the Führer fell for his Germany that he loved so passionately, and for which he wanted everything good conceivable." She added that it "was not his fault that everything turned out differently from how he had wanted."[36] Even so many weeks after Hitler's suicide and Germany's unconditional surrender, this teenager was convinced that Hitler had "fallen" while leading his troops in battle, and the question of blame was exclusively directed at who had failed Hitler. Nor did she come quickly to any other view. More than a year later, and despite massive public exposure of Nazi crimes, she found it hard to discard her earlier feelings. She saw the death sentence in the Nuremberg trials as "murder" and still considered those who had been executed to have been the leading lights of the nation. She was, moreover, filled with collective self-pity for "us Germans," since there was "nothing to eat, nowhere to live, nothing to wear, many refugees, no law, and [Germans were] despised and detested by the whole world!"[37] The former regime, she wrote, "was and remains sacred for me, and it always hurts me terribly when Adolf Hitler and his supporters are so badmouthed and maligned nowadays." Nonetheless, she seemed to be gaining a degree of insight when she noted that "from our youth onwards these people had been set before us as ideals and role models, in whom we had faith and whom we worshipped, so that it is now impossible for me to think badly of them, let alone say anything bad about them."³⁸

Ursula E. was perhaps unusual in the extent to which she confided such continuing adoration for the Nazis in her diary, but she was clearly not alone in having such feelings. Ingrid P., a fourteen-year-old living in Bavaria, commented in similar vein. She called the Nuremberg trials "the biggest theater in world history." Meanwhile, she was more concerned with the threat of a looming war between the Americans and the Russians; although people spoke of peace, they were "living more than ever in a war."³⁹ In September 1946 she was able to visit her father in a prisoner of war camp and was shocked at how thin and ragged he looked. He was filled with anger and told her that if it came to another war, he would gladly shoot both Russians and Americans. She was reassured, however, that he was sur-rounded by a community of like-minded "comrades" who ensured mutual support.⁴⁰

On October 15, 1946, like others, Ingrid P. recorded her thoughts on the executions at Nuremberg of those designated, as she put it in quotation marks, as "war criminals"; she, however, considered them to be "individuals who had always only wanted the best for the German people [Volk]." She added that she was among many who had been very glad that Göring had not been brought to the gallows; while some might think this had indicated cowardice, it had at least served to annoy the military court. She felt it was inhumane to hang only two individuals every quarter of an hour, so as "to extend the suffering of the others," and she was indignant that "people who had themselves committed the biggest crimes should want to stand in judgment over others!" Presumably she had in mind Allied bombings of German cities such as Hamburg, Dresden, and Berlin, when referring to their supposed "crimes." Meanwhile, any "errors" that the top Nazis might have committed had already been, in Ingrid P.'s view, more than expiated "in the long months of investigation."⁴¹

Within a relatively short period of time, public opinion, at least as measured in the American zone of occupation, shifted massively against Allied justice: while in 1946 some 78 percent of people surveyed by the US High Commission thought the International Military Tribunal trial had been conducted fairly, by 1950 the proportion agreeing with this view had sunk to 38 percent.[42] Even for those who did think the sentences were justified, the selective punishment of significant scapegoats could serve to deflect attention from all the others. For some, it was convenient to see just a few members of the Nazi leadership held up as major criminals, since this served implicitly to exonerate the rest.

More generally, the IMT—this most prominent of the Nuremberg trials— faced three widely held criticisms, shared across a broad spectrum of opinion. First was that of the imposition of ex post facto justice, according to the principle of *nullum crimen sine lege*—no crime without law—such that people could not face punishment for acts that were not explicitly illegal at the time they were committed. This related particularly to the charges of crimes against peace and also crimes against humanity. The second was that it was merely an imposition of "victors' justice," because there were no judges from neutral countries or judges selected from anti-Nazi German jurists, and that the charges were one-sided. This related closely to the third criticism, that of *tu quoque*—"you too." The Allies were concerned to try the Germans and not allow consideration of crimes they themselves might have committed. This related not only to Allied bombing of civilians in German cities but also to the Soviet Union's aggressive role in the first two years of the war, when it had carved up Poland in conjunction with Nazi Germany, as well as its prior record of atrocities and purges. But in the interests of retribution for wrongs suffered, the Soviet record was in some eyes outweighed by the consideration that, between 1941 and 1945, some thirty million Soviet citizens had lost their lives, of whom around twenty million were civilians, and that the Soviet Union had played a decisive role alongside the Western powers in securing German defeat.[43] After the IMT, where tensions and political differences were smoothed over, the Allies were no longer able to cooperate in subsequent trials.

Allied Successor Trials

The Allies' successor trials had somewhat less wide impact but were significant in raising to attention distinctive areas. The twelve trials held under American auspices in Nuremberg focused on particular crime complexes and selected groups of perpetrators. These included trials exploring the complicity of medical professionals, lawyers, and industrialists in the genocide. Members of the Army High Command and the Luftwaffe were also put on trial, as were senior officials from the Wilhelmstrasse government headquarters.[44] The intention was to display a range of aspects of the complex functioning of the Nazi system of inhumanity and to bring some of its more prominent representatives and administrators to justice.

The first of these trials was the "doctors' trial" of Karl Brandt and others. It was named after Hitler's personal physician, Brandt, who along with his co-defendant, Viktor Brack, had been charged by Hitler with responsibility for the "euthanasia" program. Twenty of the twenty-three defendants in the Nuremberg doctors' trial were physicians. Seven were sentenced to death: not only Brandt and Brack but also Waldemar Hoven, the former principal doctor at Buchenwald, and Joachim Mrugowsky, former head of the SS Hygiene Institute. Relatively harsh verdicts were pronounced on the others who were found guilty, and seven were acquitted. The only woman to stand trial here was Dr. Herta Oberheuser, a doctor who had carried out "medical" experiments on inmates at the Ravensbrück concentration camp. Her activities had included killing children in order to extract organs and remove limbs as well as deliberately inflicting painful wounds that were then exacerbated by rubbing in rust and dirt. Horrific details were given at the trial, and one witness, who had survived experiments on her leg muscles, even came to display the disfigurement and disability that had resulted. Oberheuser was initially given a twenty-year prison sentence; but in 1951 Oberheuser's sentence was commuted to ten years, and in 1952, a mere five years after receiving the twenty-year sentence, she was released for good behavior. Remarkably, she then simply returned to medical practice—a renewed career that was cut short in 1958 when a former prisoner from Ravensbrück recognized her, at which point her license to practice was withdrawn.[45]

Responsibility for atrocities by mass shooting was addressed in the "Einsatzgruppen trial." The principal defendant was Otto Ohlendorf, former commander of Einsatzgruppe D, who was sentenced to death by hanging, a sentence carried out in 1951; three other commanding officers were also executed. The majority of the defendants in this trial, however, succeeded in having their sentences substantially reduced and were able to walk free in the course of the 1950s. Among the latter was Heinz Schubert, Ohlendorf's adjutant, whose initial death sentence was reduced to ten years' imprisonment; by the 1970s, he was avowing his innocence in terms that, as we shall see, had by then become typical among so many of those who had been involved in atrocities.

The bureaucracy responsible for running the concentration and extermination camps was placed under the spotlight in proceedings named after the principal defendant, Oswald Pohl, who was tried along with eighteen former colleagues from the SS Economic and Administrative Central Office (WVHA). Pohl talked about the exploitation of slave labor from concentration camps by private companies, noting, for example, that the three largest industries to employ slave labor were the Hermann Göring Works, the I. G. Farben industry, and the armaments manufacturer Hasag.[46] Pohl was sentenced to death in 1947, but other defendants had their sentences reduced to lesser penalties in a first revision of 1948, and in 1951 these were further commuted to lesser terms of imprisonment.

The role of industry in Nazi crimes was a significant element in the American trials, despite the fact that this emphasis virtually faded from view in postwar West Germany. Moreover, many of those found guilty at Nuremberg were able to walk free a mere four years or so after first sentencing.

This was true of those put on trial along with the industrial magnate Friedrich Flick. In his many enterprises in the iron, coal, and steel industries during the Third Reich, Flick had employed somewhere in the region of forty-eight thousand slave laborers, some 80 percent of whom did not survive.[47] A member of the Nazi Party who had initially hedged his bets but rapidly cozied up to Hitler's regime, and deeply entangled in the regime's practices, Flick was found guilty and sentenced to seven years imprisonment. Three of the five colleagues who were put on trial alongside Flick were acquitted, and the other two given shorter sentences, including time already served. Flick himself actually served less than three, having been released in August 1950. Building up a massive fortune in the postwar years, he never paid out a cent of compensation to former slave laborers. Similarly, in the trial of the Krupp armaments manufacturer, use of forced labor was significant. The principal defendant, Alfried Krupp von Bohlen und Halbach, was initially sentenced to twelve years but released with a pardon and restoration of control of his company and assets after only three years, going on to build up massive wealth. Ten of the eleven who had been found guilty had been released early, by January 1951.

In the I. G. Farben trial, the use of slave labor at Auschwitz was a major issue. Of the twenty-four defendants, two received sentences of eight years, and one—Dr. Fritz ter Meer—a sentence of seven years; others received lesser sentences, while ten were completely acquitted. Ter Meer was released early in the general amnesty of 1950–51.[48] He then rapidly rose to the

pinnacles of industrial boards, becoming chairman of Bayer AG (one of the
I. G. Farben successor companies) and taking on directorships at leading
banks and businesses. Like so many other industrialists, he succeeded in
constructing an image of himself as "apolitical," downplaying his membership in the Nazi Party, which he had joined in 1937.

The British held 358 trials in their zone of occupation and convicted
1,085 people; of the 240 death sentences that were pronounced, two hundred were carried out.[49] Those who received terms of imprisonment rather
than the death penalty were subsequently able to benefit, as did so many
other former Nazis, from the wider policies of amnesty that began even
before the foundation of the Federal Republic of Germany and were rapidly
extended under the new government of its first chancellor, Konrad Adenauer.[50]
Notable trials included that of members of the SS and other personnel at
the concentration camp of Bergen-Belsen, some of whom had also served
at other camps, including Auschwitz, and a series of seven trials held in
Hamburg, from 1946 to 1948, of personnel involved in the Ravensbrück
concentration camp for women.[51]

The intertwining of German interests and changing Allied priorities was
always significant. The interplay is illustrated, for example, by the case of
former Luftwaffe general Albert Kesselring, whose military record, although
broadly respected by the British, was marred by his responsibility for brutal
treatment of Italian partisans toward the end of the war. Kesselring was put
on trial by the British in Italy in 1947 in relation to the murder of 335
Italians in the Ardeatine catacombs near Rome on March 24, 1944, which
he had authorized as a mass reprisal for a partisan attack the previous day.[52]
He was further accused of responsibility for the murder of 1,087 Italians as
a result of two orders he had given to the troops under his command.[53] His
defense counsel was Dr. Hans Laternser, a well-known defender of former
Nazis, including in the Nuremberg Trial and in the Frankfurt Auschwitz
trial. Kesselring sought to take credit for having allegedly reduced the
numbers killed in the catacombs and claimed he had tried to "protect" the
Jews of Rome when he had refused Himmler's orders to deport the Jewish
community.[54]

Kesselring's trial was used by Laternser as an attempt to establish the
image of the "decent German soldier," as contrasted with the SS and "asocial
elements" who had actually shot Jewish civilians.[55] The strategy was to present
the Wehrmacht as acting only out of purely military interests, while others
had been responsible for the reprehensible killings of civilians. This myth,

although long challenged by historians, was only punctured in public in the mid-1990s, when the exhibition *Crimes of the Wehrmacht* had a wide impact in Germany. Kesselring also benefited from the rapidly changing "politics of the past," both among the Allies and in Adenauer's West Germany after the foundation of the Federal Republic in 1949. Initially sentenced to death by the Italians in 1947, Kesselring had his penalty reduced to life imprisonment. And like so many others at this time, even a "life sentence" did not in practice mean staying in prison for very long: he was released in 1952, following agitation on his behalf by the British, in the context of Adenauer's policies concerning the possible establishment of a European Defense Force (never ratified). Initially given leave for a medical operation, on October 24, 1952 Kesselring was released completely, in "an act of clemency," occasioning considerable celebration among former comrades.[56]

The general picture is one of harsh sentencing in the early years after the war, followed by a period of revisions and reductions in sentences as emergent Cold War tensions shifted priorities. There was a complex interplay between Allied and German priorities over a period of a few years—beyond the occupation period itself—as different groups jostled in attempts to clear their reputation.

Elite Evasions and New Narratives

Everywhere, those who had been compromised by involvement with Nazism sought to revise interpretation of their past and make new lives. Former perpetrators often met up and talked among themselves about the past—more openly in Austria and the western zones of Germany, subsequently the Federal Republic, than in East Germany, where the claim to being the "antifascist state" was crucial to the attempted legitimation of a repressive communist dictatorship.

Even in East Germany, for a brief moment after 1945 the concept of "antifascism" was applied relatively broadly, encompassing a number of groups who had resisted Hitler, including Social Democrats, Christians, conservative opponents of Hitler, and Jehovah's Witnesses. But the term was rapidly appropriated for the purposes of the leading communist party, from 1946 the SED (Socialist Unity Party), emphasizing particularly strength and active political resistance. The category of "victims of fascism" now excluded not only those against whom there were continuing and widely held social prejudices—homosexuals, Gypsies, "asocials," and criminals, as well as the hereditarily ill and disabled—but even Zionists, despite acknowledgement of Jews as primary victims of Nazism. Communists, by contrast, were deemed to fulfill all the new criteria for "genuine" resistance as defined in the official line. The term "fascism," too, expanded in significance, as ever more enemies in the present were tarred with this label.[57] "Antifascism" served to cover anything and anyone who supported the German Democratic Republic (GDR); "fascism" more or less anything or anyone designated as a "class enemy" of the GDR. Tales of conversion and the possibility of redemption were widespread. The Wehrmacht was officially vilified as the "fascist" army, but even generals who had been tainted by Nazism and then, while prisoners of war, joined the National Committee for a Free Germany (Nationalkomitee Freies Deutschland, NKFD) could gain recognition as opponents of fascism and stand as models for a desired conversion experience.[58] Informal discourses had to be somewhat muted, yet former soldiers were able to talk about their war experiences, so long as they also portrayed moments of conversion and commitment to communist ideals. There was, however, no public space in which to present narratives that did not conform to the constraints of the newly imposed myths. Even so, the aim was widespread reintegration of those who had formerly gone along with the Nazi regime as "fellow travelers" (Mitläufer), so long as they were now prepared to commit themselves to building up the new East German state.

Everywhere, people had to deal with bereavement and face questions about whether injury and death in service of the fatherland could still be seen as meaningful. In Austria and West Germany, by contrast, the war was talked about repeatedly, in pubs and restaurants as well as in the home. But the murder of the Jews was not generally part of the stories people told.[59] While much was silenced, questions were rarely asked. One Austrian commented that her father would never stop talking about the war. She and her siblings repeatedly urged him to keep quiet about it; it was only after his death that she realized she had never dared to ask him if he had actually shot anyone, or seen any atrocities. There were no deaths in his stories.[60] In West Germany the Army was widely portrayed as "clean," untainted by "excesses" that were increasingly associated solely with the SS. This became effectively the "alibi of a nation"—the scapegoat that was the really criminal organization.[61] In this way, a positive notion of patriotic heroism could be retained, and the bereaved could still feel proud of those who had "fallen" for their country (now omitting Hitler from the previous formula of "Führer, Volk, and

Fatherland"). Prisoners of war returning from Soviet camps to West Germany were treated as war heroes—and even those perpetrators who had served sentences for war crimes were now seen rather as victims of communism.

A few individuals explicitly developed the myth of the "clean Wehrmacht" in self-serving autobiographical accounts. As Kesselring put it, in the closing paragraph of his memoirs, his aim was to "contribute something towards a truthful record of a good piece of German history, to the raising of a monument to our magnificent soldiers and to helping the world to recognize the face of war in its grim totality."[62] This myth was closely aligned with the new priorities of the Western Allies in the Cold War: Kesselring's memoir was published in English in 1954 with the full support of S. L. A. Marshall, the official US Army combat historian. Distancing himself from "the mistaken racial policy of Hitler and his associates," Kesselring managed to describe the war against the Soviet Union in 1941 without any mention of the murderous Einsatzgruppen or the assistance given to them by the Wehrmacht.[63] In his defense of the brutal suppression of "partisans" in northern Italy, Kesselring repeated Nazi shibboleths. He vented considerable vitriol on "sabotage troops" who "increasingly violated the laws of humanity" and "who robbed, murdered and pillaged wherever and whatever they could."[64] The Italian partisan war "contradicted every principle of clean soldierly fighting"—in supposed contrast to the Germans.[65] Clearly still determined to justify the massacres of Italian civilians for which he had been forced to stand trial, Kesselring commented that partisan activities were designed so "the southern temperament could run riot"; their "vicious instincts" left "few loopholes for compunction." He spoke of how "they ran amok without restraint, doing their nefarious work" undercover, "but never openly."[66] For Kesselring this provided the rationale for the murder of civilians—including children—in areas where everyone was supposedly a "combatant, helper or sympathiser."[67] Although he was initially in demand at veterans' meetings, by the time Kesselring died in 1960 his reputation was in decline; not everyone in 1950s Germany was willing to believe the image that Kesselring sought to propagate.[68]

The myth of a "clean army" was nevertheless widespread in popular literature and films at the time, which also portrayed the generals as "decent" men who had mounted heroic resistance to the Bolshevist threat.[69] The image of the patriotic Wehrmacht, contrasting sharply with the demonized SS and Gestapo, persisted for several decades, providing succor to those who had lost loved ones at the front.

Economic elites and interest groups similarly sought to sustain their reputation in the West.[70] They, too, developed stories covering their tracks—stories that were barely addressed or critiqued until the 1980s, and sometimes even later. In West Germany, many prominent businessmen were rapidly able to return to positions of influence, chairing the boards of major industries and writing self-serving accounts of their companies' pasts and their own.

One of these early accounts was by Fritz ter Meer.[71] Despite his sentence at Nuremberg, by 1953 ter Meer was already covering the traces of Auschwitz in his published account of I. G. Farben's history. He managed both to distance I. G. Farben from the war, which was allegedly detrimental to the industry's worldwide interests, and to praise the company for having done its duty until the bitter end "for its country, which was fighting for its existence."[72] Ter Meer records that production of "pharmaceuticals and pesticides" (Schädlingsbekämpfungsmittel, which translates as both "pesticide" and "exterminator") had gone up from 152 million Reichsmarks in 1939 to 294 million Reichsmarks in 1944; there is no mention of precisely which metaphorical "pests" were being "exterminated" during the years when production of Zyklon B was at its peak.[73] Readers are told about the establishment of three Buna plants in areas to the west, but ter Meer claims that a planned fourth plant in Upper Silesia "never came into operation."[74] In this way, the Buna plant at Auschwitz III, Monowitz, was wiped from company history. Finally, ter Meer argues that the closure by the Allies of I. G. Farben was entirely for political reasons, at a time when an "objective representation" was not possible; but "today," in 1953, there was "the necessary distance from purely political judgments" to write an objective account.[75]

Clearly the "necessary distance" allowed the silencing of any mention of the misery and deaths of slave laborers toiling for the German war industry and the production of the "pesticide" that killed more than a million people. But to mention this might be "political," and ter Meer was, after all, on his own account purely an industrialist, a trained chemist and lawyer, and a captain of West German industry.

Ter Meer illustrated a new pattern of self-interpretation among elites who had profited from the Nazi regime.[76] They drew a clear line between themselves and fanatical Nazis led by a demonic Führer. They portrayed themselves as "victims" of the constraints imposed upon them by "the Nazis," constraints they were powerless to alter and to which they had to conform. Playing on the dual meaning of the word for "victim" in German, Opfer, which also means "sacrifice," they had supposedly sacrificed themselves for their country in wartime. Rather than engaging in wholesale amnesia, this narrative put a positive gloss on the supposedly patriotic achievements of German industry.

Ernst Heinkel, whose aircraft works had vied with I. G. Farben in their use (and abuse) of concentration camp labor, had managed to get off even more lightly than ter Meer. Heinkel was briefly in Allied captivity after the war but managed to avoid being put on trial, presenting himself rather as an expert witness, given his involvement in rocket production in the well-known sites of Peenemünde and Mittelbau-Dora as well as the far less well-known Mielec. He even succeeded in getting his denazification status reduced to that of "exonerated." In the early 1950s Heinkel, too, produced an influential autobiographical account and company history, setting the tracks for post-war West German self-representations. First published in German under the title *Stürmisches Leben* ("Stormy life") in 1953, Heinkel's memoirs enjoyed brisk sales and frequent republication, also appearing in English translation.[77] Portraying himself as a technocrat who could supply helpful expertise to the Allies, Heinkel added further twists to a sanitized portrayal of the supposed role of industrialists and employers during the Third Reich. Despite having joined the Nazi Party as early as 1933, Heinkel presented himself as anti-Nazi, distanced from and constrained by the Nazi regime, citing minor disagreements and periodic frictions with the authorities. He relates, for example, an anecdote about the very first day of Hitler's regime, when he was allegedly reluctant to fly a swastika over the Heinkel factory, for which he was rebuked by Hermann Göring. He suggests that "this start, which wavered between a veiled threat on the one side and the courtship of reluctant and hesitant men on the other, was probably symptomatic of the whole tempo of this new period, whose dangers and ultimate abyss were hidden at that time from millions, probably from many of the leading Nazis themselves."[78] This little story succinctly intimates the desired combination of political distance and constraint, along with ignorance and hence innocence. The account then provides painstaking details of every twist and turn in the story of aircraft research, development, and production over the following dozen years. Heinkel even musters a technocratic reason to have had some respect for Hitler. Recounting a visit to the Führer in Obersalzburg on May 23, 1943, he noted his "surprising expert knowledge": unlike Göring, Hitler supposedly had "an astonishing grasp of air technicalities down to the smallest details." Heinkel says he often thought about this conversation—

which lasted for seventy minutes—and could "fully understand why great technicians like Todt and Speer" had supported Hitler, who was probably unique among politicians in taking "such a burning interest in technical problems."[79]

Emphasis on technical expertise pervades the account; there is no mention of the brutality and deaths incurred in the exploitation of slave labor. One somewhat awkwardly worded sentence does finally mention other workers, and by both omission and emphasis effectively denies any use of concentration camp labor at all. Heinkel speaks of the way in which, at a late stage of the war, "despite the desperate efforts of not only German workers, but of thousands of foreign workers who were neither prisoners nor forced labor, there could be no more talk of regular output."[80] The suffering of the slave laborers in Mielec, Budzyń, Wieliczka, Mauthausen, Sachsenhausen, Ravensbrück, and elsewhere is simply excised by Heinkel from the German past. The aircraft were made, but in Heinkel's account no slave laborers were involved in making them.

Moving on to the postwar period, Heinkel portrays himself, like so many Germans, as a victim. The British had undertaken their interrogations "in an atmosphere of great politeness and friendliness."[81] But this attitude did not extend to the actions of the Russians and Americans: Heinkel discovered that his Marienehe factory had been dismantled by the Russians, who had also seized his factories in Orienienburg and the Waltersdorf branch of Zuffenhausen, and his Bleicherstrasse works had been simply blown up.[82] Similarly, in Austria "the tunnels, mines and caves in Achensee, Strassfurt and Kochendorf," constructed during the last months of the war to protect them from bombing, had been "destroyed, damaged, or plundered."[83] Other sites too, including those in Poland, "had been scattered to the four winds in the general collapse."[84] Finally, not even in West Germany was the property of former Nazis entirely secure: Heinkel was incensed that the Americans had given the Zuffenhausen branch near Stuttgart to one of those "trustees" who "like spotless blooms emerged in surprising numbers from the slime of defeat." Heinkel no longer dared to cross its threshold.[85]

Soon, however, Heinkel was himself rehabilitated and became yet another of the "spotless blooms" springing up in postwar Germany. He regained his Zuffenhausen factory on February 1, 1950, and began to complain about all he had lost.[86] In this, Heinkel was far from alone. Nor was Heinkel alone when, in 1959, his company successfully won a lawsuit against a former concentration camp laborer, Edmund Bartl; as we shall see, the German supreme court dismissed Bartl's case for being filed too late and ordered Bartl to pay costs. Like so many industrialists who had enriched themselves during the Third Reich and ended up in the Federal Republic, Heinkel appeared to be getting away with it in every respect, with both reputation and profits largely intact.[87]

The same is true of industrialists who had profited from the use of slave labor in Mauthausen and its many sub-camps in Austria, including Gusen, Ebensee, and Melk, as well as around Vienna and elsewhere. But not all who had played a prominent role in the Nazi regime sought to justify their lives in print. Some disappeared quietly from the stage, evading justice through flight to another country or the adoption of false identities. Some met mysterious ends. Georg Meindl, the general director of Steyr-Daimler-Puch, responsible for so much suffering in the Mauthausen sub-camps, initially sought to flee, was arrested by the Americans, and then managed to escape. A few days later a badly burned body was found in a hut and alleged to be that of Meindl, following his supposed suicide; but the charred remains were unidentifiable, and in light of Meindl's determination to escape the Americans were not entirely convinced by the suicide theory.

There were also organized efforts to assist individuals seen as part of an endangered community of wartime comrades. An organization called Stille Hilfe für Kriegsgefangene und Internierte ("Silent assistance for prisoners of war and interned persons"), for example, was founded in 1951 to assist former Nazis who found themselves in difficulties after the end of the Third Reich.[88]

At far lower social levels too, former Nazis living in West Germany were able to associate with one another relatively openly. Hans Müller was the son of the former forester Peter Müller, who, as we have seen, had been stationed in the SS Troop Training Grounds between Mielec and Dębica. Hans recalls overhearing as a child discussions among his father's friends: "I picked up a lot when he was talking to old comrades or war comrades, they automatically began to brag" about their war experiences. But they did not discuss the meaning of the war as such: "It was actually all about showing off their personal achievements."[89] When his father was out engaging in his favorite hobby of hunting and shooting in early postwar Germany, it was not only a sport but also being a "lord over life and death." Despite warning his then small son against pointing a toy pistol at other people, Peter Müller "boasted about precisely this from the war," according to his son, and he was proud of his own capacity for sharp shooting.[90] Symbolically, the medals he had won during the Third Reich were not thrown away; the swastikas were merely covered by sticking a postage stamp over them.[91] It is clear from this and similar accounts that continuities in personal life stories, with an associated sense of pride in wartime achievements, could be combined with a little suppression and cover-up—in the case of the postage stamps, literally—of aspects of the past that were now less acceptable.

Most former Nazis, whether living in East or West Germany or Austria, were able to transform themselves into quiet citizens of the new states. Even those who had been convicted of Nazi crimes could readily rehabilitate themselves and be seamlessly absorbed into the wider society.[92] Occasional stories of the discovery of the Nazi past of an otherwise unsuspected individual occasioned widespread surprise, even scandal. But there is a wider hidden history: that of the slumbering, well-integrated, conformist postwar ex-Nazi, a story that is perhaps more disturbing and certainly less well understood than the occasional revelations and sensations that caught press headlines.

What is surprising, then, is that under some circumstances individuals were willing to be apparently open about their past, provided it was appropriately framed and presented. The individuals who spoke about their experiences generally did so in a defensive, self-exonerating (if on occasion even bragging) way. Sometimes the confrontation only took shape under conditions of imprisonment. Rudolf Höss and Albert Speer were notable because of both their prominent roles during the Third Reich and the ways in which they recounted their experiences. While Höss was put to death shortly after completing his memoirs, Speer enjoyed a lengthy old age in which to indulge in public repentance combined with obfuscation, denial, and refusal to acknowledge real responsibility. Unlike the families of less well-known perpetrators, however, the children of Albert Speer and other prominent Nazis were later better placed to examine the records of what their father had actually known and done. In some ways, this would, as we shall see, make it easier for them to face the challenge of dealing with the family legacies of involvement in Nazism—or at least, less easy to "not know."

The Nazi regime had transformed society and sought to establish a "national community" through racial exclusion, political oppression, economic exploitation, a war of aggression, and genocide. People who only a short time previously had been mobilized in support of the Nazi cause now found themselves subject to the vicissitudes of transitional justice, played out in very different ways according to area. The contrasts become clearer when considering developments over time in each of the Third Reich successor states.

9

Judging Their Own

Selective Justice in the Successor States

The vast majority of all trials for Nazi crimes held in the successor states—East and West Germany and Austria—took place in the first few years after the war. This was still a matter of transitional justice, but now carried out by representatives of the societies from which the perpetrators had emerged, rather than by the victors. Moreover, it was extensive, and it addressed deep internal divisions in each state; trials dealt with crimes often at a local level. More than 99 percent of all convictions in Austria for crimes committed under National Socialism took place before 1955. In East Germany, accurate figures are harder to obtain; but on the GDR's own account, some 95 percent of all perpetrators had been sentenced by 1950.[1] In West Germany, 55 percent of all cases and around 90 percent of all sentences were passed in the 1940s and 1950s.[2] And the predominant focus of all these early trials was on crimes committed within the borders of the Third Reich, evident for others to see and still fresh in local memory.

During the occupation period, Germans were only permitted to prosecute crimes committed against other Germans and against stateless persons on German soil. With the foundation of the three new states that were successors to the Third Reich—East and West Germany and Austria—the remit widened, such that prosecutions could be brought for crimes committed against foreign victims too, broadening the geographical focus across Europe. From 1960 in West Germany, all crimes except those relating to murder or being an accomplice to murder were subject to the statute of limitations, which meant that subsequently the emphasis shifted to the major killing sites in the east. But there was everywhere a more general shift in focus at this time.

In every case, the pursuit of justice was shaped and colored by social considerations and political priorities. All the successor states were keen to distance themselves from their Nazi past, and to be seen to be bringing perpetrators to account. Even so, the records of justice were patchy. Selective emphases on certain types of crime and degrees of leniency in sentencing those found guilty differed markedly both between states and over time. Some groups of perpetrators successfully evaded justice as their involvement in the Nazi system was minimized, while others came into the spotlight. Meanwhile, different groups of victims were variously highlighted or marginalized. Decisions made in the early years set the tracks for later trials, even as the legal profession changed and the political and cultural climate shifted.

Crimes Close to Home: Trials under Allied Occupation

Tens of thousands of cases were brought to trial in East and West German courts and in Austria—significantly more, as a database developed by the Munich Institute of Contemporary History has shown, than those listed in the invaluable compendia of trials for homicidal crimes edited by Amsterdam lawyer Christiaan Frederik Rüter along with Dick de Mildt and colleagues.[3] Early trials shed light not only on official political priorities in raising selected issues while downplaying others but also on local preoccupations and controversies. They provide insights into how members of the former *Volksgemeinschaft* reacted to accusations of complicity, how victims perceived former Nazis who were still at large, and how local authorities sought to adjudicate between conflicting interests. In a sense, through domestic trials in the early postwar years the confrontations of the Nazi era continued to be fought out, but under radically altered conditions: people were forced to confront the past as they had themselves so recently experienced it and to address continuing deep divisions within their own society.

In contrast to the high-profile trials held by the Allies, in German and Austrian courts it was relatively low-level people who were brought to court, and their victims were often those who evoked empathy among members of the population.[4] It was, moreover, not the mass killing sites of the east but rather local crimes that were the primary focus. Despite the evidence presented in the Nuremberg trials, and despite the survivor accounts already available, the mass murder of the Jews was not yet a central focus. Indeed, until the late 1950s the word "holocaust" was used only with a lower case "h," and generally modified by an adjective, as in the phrase "nuclear holo-caust." Instead, early trials addressed domestic divisions.

German and Austrian courts concentrated primarily on cases "close to home," in two sense: geographically close and of immediate relevance. In seeking to explain this parochial focus, there were suggestions that represen-tatives of justice did not "know" about crimes committed in the east, only about those in the courts' own jurisdictions. But a great deal was known, not least because of the details presented in Nuremberg and other Allied trials. Nor does the fact that many judges and lawyers were themselves former Nazis explain much; this was to some extent significant for West Germany—more so after 1949 than in the occupation period—and is also relevant in Austria, but in East Germany there was a radical purge of the legal profession. It has also been suggested that postwar courts and lawyers were simply not equipped to consider state-sponsored crimes of this mag-nitude and simply sought to continue legal practice in terms of "business as usual," pursuing cases that conformed with expectations about "normal" crimes. There was certainly little experience of trying crimes committed by bureaucrats; it was far simpler to deal with those who had committed physical acts of violence. In dealing with the "euthanasia" murders, as we shall see, it was easier to put individual doctors and low-level nursing and administrative personnel on trial, but not the Euthanasia Central Office, which only appeared in national legal procedures once before 1952.

The overwhelming majority of cases in the years when the vast majority of trials took place—years when the crimes were still fresh in recent mem-ory, the perpetrators still relatively young and fit to stand trial, and many witnesses still available—addressed internal social and political divisions, rather than facing up to the challenges posed by putting the mass murder of the Jews on trial.

Consideration was also given to what were deemed to be significant victim groups—notably organized political resistance, particularly in East Germany, and domestic casualties of Nazi violence as well as Jewish victims of violence in November 1938, but not as yet gay men, Roma and Sinti, or "asocials." The crimes in the East remained almost untouched. Despite the fact that hundreds of thousands of victims of Nazi death camps, including Auschwitz, had been German citizens and prosecutions could have been brought even during the occupation period, barely half a dozen of the six to eight thousand people who had served at Auschwitz were brought to trial in West Germany at this time. Little changed even after the foundation of the Federal Republic, when courts could also pursue cases where the victims were foreign nationals; even decades after the end of the war, it was still only a matter of dozens.[5]

In the GDR, because of the experiences of the communists in power, there was significant concentration on Nazi political oppression in 1933 and on individual difficulties under Nazi rule. More than half of cases tried in East Germany up to 1952 related to denunciations. The victims were generally Germans who had ended up in prisons and concentration camps as a result of spiteful, self-interested, or politically motivated denunciations by neighbors and workmates. This remained a priority for East German courts: up until the collapse of the GDR in 1990, some 435 denunciation cases were brought to court. In effect, this continued the political struggles of the Third Reich through judicial means, seeking to mete out a measure of justice for political wrongs suffered under the Nazi regime.

The next largest group of East German cases involving homicidal crimes under Nazism was for "war crimes," involving 172 trials for incidents falling under the definition of "homicidal crimes against soldiers and prisoners of war in so far as they constituted violations of the laws and customs of the international laws of war." There were also 141 trials for homicidal crimes against people in detainment centers, and 118 cases relating to "other NS crimes." In contrast, far fewer trials were devoted to "mass extermination crimes"—the term for "acts of genocide" where victims were targets of racial policies. There were only seven trials for killings by Einsatzgruppen, thirteen trials concerning mass extermination in concentration camps, and sixty-two trials for "other mass extermination crimes." There were also twenty-three trials relating to euthanasia killings.[6]

This profile contrasts interestingly with the selection of issues pursued in West German trials. The violence around the Nazi takeover of power in 1933 and denunciations of political opponents, which played so large a role in cases in the East, did not feature to this degree in the West. By contrast, more than half (53 percent) of West German cases related to "final phase crimes," committed at the end of the war.[7] Often the victims of these crimes were Germans—soldiers and others who had been summarily executed for defeatist remarks, refusing to go on fighting, walking away from their units, or other transgressions in the chaotic closing months of the war.[8] There were 295 cases concerning "final phase crimes," compared with fifty-two cases relating to mass extermination crimes committed by Einsatzgruppen, forty-five trials relating to mass extermination crimes in camps, and 187 for "other mass extermination crimes."[9] There were thirty-four trials of crimes relating to euthanasia killings.

West German courts were particularly busy during the occupation period, from 1945 to 1949, when some 70 percent of all convictions for Nazi crimes were secured. No crimes were as yet subject to the statute of limitations, and so relatively minor offenses attracting short sentences could be tried.[10] In West Germany in the sixty years from 1945 to 2005 a total of 36,393 investigations and trials were initiated, involving 172,294 individuals—of whom only 3.7 percent were women. Of these, fully 13,600 trials were held in the four years between 1945 and 1949.[11] The highest number of guilty verdicts pronounced in any single year was in 1948, with 2,011 convictions; the next highest was in 1949, with 1,474 judgments.[12] Numbers decreased rapidly thereafter, dwindling to double and even single figures in subsequent years.

It is therefore particularly important to understand how Germans addressed the past in trials during these early postwar years. War crimes, crimes committed in concentration camps and prisons, and crimes relating to mass extermination, which later came to loom so large in both trials and public consciousness of the Nazi past, were hardly dealt with at all at this time. Interestingly, crimes against Jews in November 1938—Kristallnacht— were by contrast a major focus of attention, constituting more than 15 percent of cases during the occupation period.[13]

Trials concerning the 1938 pogrom were generally instigated by survivors and relatives of victims, often including émigrés as well as Jewish communities and political activists; often, too, they were initiated by local authorities seeking to find culprits to bear the cost of repairing damage to synagogues and cemeteries.[14] These cases display the sheer extent of local participation in violence against Jews as well as in rituals of public degradation and humiliation, looting, pilfering, extorting goods and money, ensuring the cancelation of debts, and other self-serving ways of profiting from the pogrom that had been initiated from above. Cases demonstrate that even though non-locals arrived in trucks to instigate the violence, they found ready collaborators among the population. The crimes were committed by a broad cross-section of the population, with local enterprises, schools, and individual teachers being prominent. And, unlike all other crime complexes, there were many women, of all ages, among the perpetrators who were brought to court. Trials were not easy. Large numbers had been involved at different times in any given locality, and perpetrators often denied liability for particular aspects of the violence or blamed known storm troopers who were by now dead or had gone missing during the war. People who had taken property claimed it was merely for "safekeeping" on behalf of the victims, not theft. Despite the crimes having taken place locally, with many onlookers at the time, people coordinated their stories in advance of trials and were often reluctant to "remember" much, let alone act as witnesses against neighbors with whom they still had to stay on friendly terms. Courts were generally well disposed toward defendants, and there were many lenient sentences and surprising acquittals even where evidence seemed absolutely compelling. Young offenders were held to have been misled by Nazi propaganda, while older offenders had been inebriated, or merely obeying orders, or carried along by comradeship, all allegedly excusing their behavior. Overall, despite the apparently immense efforts devoted in West Germany during the occupation period to bringing people to trial for offenses against Jews, the record is not one of stringent or consistent justice. Even so, a total of 1,174 trials concerning the November pogrom were held in West German courts in the period 1945–49, with 1,076 sentences passed.

Prosecutions in the West German zones of occupation for other offenses against Jews, such as assisting in deportations, were also relatively unsuccessful and began to display characteristics of later trials in West Germany: prosecuting only when officials appeared to have overstepped the boundaries of what had been ordered by the Nazi authorities, as when they coerced individuals in "privileged mixed marriages" and people of mixed descent (Mischlinge) onto transports just to make up numbers, particularly when there was evidence that they knew that transports would inevitably end in death. Simply complying with Nazi regulations and helping the murder machinery to function did not appear to be a culpable offense.

However dismal the overall record of the occupation period may now seem, there was at least extensive public engagement with the recent past. Courtrooms were apparently packed, and often audiences indicated their sympathies quite vociferously—whether supporting defendants or, on occasion, criticizing the lenience of sentences when they disapproved. This sort of intensive engagement with local perpetration subsided after 1949, as the numbers of trials dropped massively and popular complicity in Nazi violence faded from view.

There were fewer trials in East Germany dealing with the violence of November 1938—perhaps three hundred in total during the period 1945–49, carried out on a different legal basis from that in the West—although the archival material has not as yet been exhaustively collated or studied in

detail.[15] But given both the smaller population size and the regional variations in the size of Jewish populations, it is difficult to draw conclusions
about this comparison. Even so, it is clear that there were rather different
emphases in what was selected for trial under Soviet occupation.

East German courts at this time paid particular attention to the ways
in which workers had suffered under Nazism, or what the ruling SED
(Sozialistische Einheitspartei Deutschlands, the Socialist Unity Party of
Germany, which was formed out of a merger between the Communists and
Social Democrats in April 1946) called "fascist" rule, and to exploitation by
employers.[16] The authorities collected reports, for example, on the exploitation and starvation of forced laborers in the Siemens branch in Ravensbrück
and in the Siemens works in Haselhorst, on the outskirts of Berlin, from
where malnourished, unproductive prisoners were sent to Sachsenhausen to
be murdered. Distinctions were also made between different groups of workers. Jewish women reported that they had to work longer hours, under worse
conditions, than other prisoners; they were not allowed access to the canteen;
and they were not given meat, vegetables, or other appropriate nourishment.
There were also reports on resistance groups, including Christians who gave
help, and French forced laborers who managed to obtain illegal papers.[17]

More generally, the focus on workers did not mean that specifically Jewish
experiences were overlooked at this time. For example, in a trial relating to
the Leipzig-based armaments manufacturer Hasag, which had been the
third-largest employer of slave labor in the Third Reich, there was cooperation between the VVN (Vereinigung der Verfolgten des Naziregimes), the
Leipzig Jewish community, and the Central Committee of Jews in the US
Zone. An account of the "hell of Kamienna" by the East German journalist
Hans Frey was published in 1949, based on this trial and recounting the fates
of the more than seventeen thousand Jews (more likely in the region of
twenty-five thousand) brought in to work in the Kamienna branch of
Hasag. The account noted specifically that Jews were exploited and killed as
part of the Nazi party program, for no reason other than that they were
Jews, and that the extermination of the Jews was "the most repulsive crime
of this criminal regime."[18] Most of the Jews either died as a result of "extermination through work" or were deported to Treblinka at the time the
ghetto was cleared; a minority survived through deportation to other labor
camps and later death marches.[19] Even if the Holocaust proportionately
faded from view in light of the priority given to political resistance, it never
entirely disappeared from East German sights.

If the victims were relatively clear in East Germany, so too were the principal culprits: the enterprise managers, particularly if those in charge were evading justice by coming under Western jurisdiction. This was the case, for example, with the Siemens director Wolf-Dietrich von Witzleben, who, despite his long-term support of Nazism, was "denazified" in 1947 in the West Berlin district of Spandau (the area that gave its name to the prison holding seven of the Nazi war criminals found guilty at Nuremberg, including Albert Speer until his release in 1966 and Rudolf Hess until his death in 1987). A report by one survivor, Hedwig Scholl, commented bitterly that, as far as she knew, the Nazi engineer who had been in charge was still in a leading position in the company, whereas all but one of the Jews with whom she had worked were dead.[20] The apparent white-wash of the Siemens director occasioned well-organized protest strikes in two factories in East Berlin—the Elektro-Apparate-Fabrik in Treptow and the Deutsche Messingwerke in Niederschöneweide—on February 28, 1948.

Selected groups were either mobilized or actively associated them-selves with early trials in East Germany. In January 1949, for example, the Association of Persecutees of the Nazi Regime, the VVN, became involved on behalf of the prosecution in trial proceedings relating to the Goehle Works in Dresden, which had employed forced labor.[21] The VVN repre-sentatives were outraged at the brazen manner (*Unverfrorenheit*) in which defendants refused to admit responsibility for the dreadful conditions in which forced laborers had been maltreated. In their twelve-page document as joint plaintiffs, the VVN also pointed a finger of accusation at wider cir-cles, commenting that "thousands of Dresden citizens were employed in these works, and to put it mildly, hundreds of them were witnesses of maltreatment. But they kept silent and in this way made themselves com-plicit."[22] The typical "good deed defense" was also challenged: even if defendants could demonstrate that they had "done one or another good deed, brought someone bread, tobacco, clothing, or other things," this could not be seen as proof that they had not also committed the offenses of which they stood accused. Moreover, those who had been persecuted knew "from personal experiences that there was no criminal of this kind who was not also capable of humane behavior," and that the perpetrators were "somehow also human beings."[23]

Early emphases in East Germany did not fade from view in succeeding decades. The Goehle Works in Dresden, for example, did not disappear from sight. As we shall see, nearly forty years later, in 1987, one of the SS officers involved, Henry Schmidt, was finally brought to court.[24] This relatively late case illustrates continuity in East German concerns as well as highlights some key changes by the later 1980s.

With the foundation of the GDR in 1949, the ruling SED sought to establish that it had effectively "dealt with" Nazism and that major Nazis had either been punished or had left for the West. In the summer of 1950, in the so-called Waldheim trials, some 3,345 rapid judgments were passed on people who had been interned in the Soviet special camps without any prior legal proceedings. With the closure of these camps in early 1950, it was important to give at least an air of legality to the process. While some of those sentenced were innocent casualties of postwar politics, many of those on whom judgment was passed had indeed been guilty of crimes under the Nazis. Ernst Kendzia, for example, was former head of the Labor Department in the Warthegau. Kendzia had been responsible for the use of forced labor from the ghettos and in late 1941 cold-bloodedly proposed the "evacuation"—a euphemism for extermination—of "unproductive" Jews from the Łódź ghetto, effectively supporting the selection of the "unfit" to be sent to the newly established death camp of Chełmno. Kendzia was in fact the only high-ranking official from the Reich Ministry for Labor to be put to death for his crimes; those living in West Germany largely evaded prosecution and continued with successful careers in the civil service.[25]

The extraordinary speed and dubious procedures of the perfunctory trials in Waldheim meant, however, that the actual deeds of those sentenced were barely given any attention. Penalties appeared unduly harsh: more than 90 percent received sentences of more than ten years, and there were thirty-three death sentences. But the longer-term consequences were paradoxical.

Even in Austria, early justice was quite far-reaching. The provisional government established in Vienna in 1945 immediately set up "people's courts" (*Volksgerichte*) specifically to deal with crimes committed under National Socialist auspices. And a law passed on June 20, 1945 (the Kriegsverbrechergesetz), included retrospective prosecution for war crimes and crimes against humanity, along the lines of the Nuremberg Internal Military Tribunal.[26] The actual profile of cases in Austria again demonstrated predominantly domestic concerns.

As in France, Austrians were particularly concerned with questions of political collaboration with Nazism; a considerable proportion of early Austrian trials therefore concerned cases of people who had illegally joined the Nazi Party in the period prior to the Anschluss in 1938 and who were therefore considered "unpatriotic." Another major issue was that of violent crimes committed on Austrian soil, evident for all to see, such as the maltreatment of prisoners of war in forced labor camps and on death marches. Even so, the gaps are striking. And as in East and West Germany, the Jewish dimension of much of the Holocaust was not as yet explicit, nor were the crimes of mass murder committed in eastern Europe high on the agenda of the Austrian people's courts.[27] Moreover, within three years or so after the end of the war Austrian newspapers appear to have lost interest in cases, and discussion shifted instead to the question of when the special courts would be disbanded and trials would cease—presciently foreshadowing later Austrian lack of interest in bringing Nazi perpetrators to court.[28]

Politicization and Partial Prosecution: East Germany

The GDR's official image entailed not only the pursuit of those (supposedly few) perpetrators still living in East Germany but also trials in absentia of those living in the West as well as periodic high-profile campaigns against former Nazis who were prominent in West German public life. Political instrumentalization and abuses of justice in the GDR attracted considerable criticism in the West; so too did GDR self-representations as the "better" Germany as far as prosecution of former Nazis was concerned. The battle for being seen as the "better Germany" was at its most intense during the Cold War, but the struggle over representations did not go away with the disappearance of the GDR on unification with the West in 1990: more than a quarter of a century later, former senior officials from the GDR Ministry for State Security (MfS, or Stasi) still sought to defend their record in comparison with the West.[29]

The number of people who were prosecuted in East Germany dropped dramatically once responsibility for justice had been handed over from the Soviet Military Administration and placed in the hands of the new regime under the communist SED. From 1951 onward, in a series of amnesties, the vast majority of those with short prison sentences were released; by 1956, only thirty-four of them remained behind bars. And, since they had ostensibly already been tried for their crimes, they could not be put on trial again or face more intensive and extensive investigations for the same offenses at a later date.

From 1957 onward, there were no longer to be amnesties for Nazi crimes, and the Ministry for State Security (MfS) became increasingly organized in pursuit of former Nazis. In the 1960s, in cooperation with other MfS departments, two new MfS departments—Hauptabteilung IX/10 (HA IX/10) and Hauptabteilung IX/11 (HA IX/11)—became responsible for collecting and archiving material and pursuing investigations. Over time, they prepared all details of cases to be brought to court, including recommendations for publicity and media coverage, choice of witnesses—in favor of the prosecution rather than the defense—and proposals for judgment and sentencing. Trials could be orchestrated from start to finish, as essential political performances.

It was not only politics but also the (politically informed) legal system that made it easier to prove guilt in East Germany than in West Germany. Unlike in the Federal Republic, in the GDR the Nuremberg principles were not rejected, and for a case of murder, the fatal consequences of the act generally proved sufficient for conviction. Nor was ignorance of the illegality of the act considered to be an adequate defense. This meant that quite different standards were applied, and people tried in the GDR could be found guilty if they had committed certain acts, irrespective of their supposed subjective state of mind or alleged level of ignorance at the time. Trials were in effect only brought when it was considered that there was sufficient incontrovertible evidence, and there was little by way of effective defense. The legal profession in East Germany was thoroughly overhauled after the war, with political commitment initially compensating for lack of professional qualifications and expertise. Because of the turnover in personnel, sympathies of judges and lawyers lay with those who had opposed or been victims of the Nazis, not with defendants. This played a role, albeit one that is hard to define, and which remains to be explored further on a comparative basis.[30] The mutual goading and moral-political competition between the two German states also developed a momentum propelling attempts to bring former perpetrators to justice.

At the same time, the GDR propagated a theory of fascism that argued that Nazism was rooted in "monopoly capitalism," a system continuing in the West but not in East Germany. As with all images and myths, there was a grain of truth in the contrasts drawn. The radical social revolution that accompanied the installation of communist power in East Germany had indeed weeded out more Nazis from politically significant positions (although not, for example, from the medical profession, where professional expertise was essential) than had been the case in the West.[31] And it is certainly true that many individuals who had been deeply implicated in Nazi crimes did flee from the GDR to the West, assuming—rightly, as it turned out—that they would have an easier ride there. All those euthanasia personnel who had originated in eastern Germany before the war and who had continued their deadly work in the Operation Reinhard death camps, for example, left the Soviet Zone and GDR for the West, some leaving their families behind while they fled justice.[32]

With growing international tensions in the late 1950s and the construction of the Berlin Wall in 1961, the SED started using the politics of the Nazi past in new ways. Not merely did they want to show that Nazis in the GDR had been adequately identified and punished; they now also devoted considerable energy to propaganda campaigns against West Germany, where in 1959 there had been a spate of antisemitic actions including the daubing of swastikas and desecration of Jewish cemeteries. A major focus of East German efforts was on highlighting the continuing preponderance of Nazis in high places in West Germany, with prominent campaigns against high profile politicians and civil servants. Many were named and shamed in what became the infamous "Brown book" (*Braunbuch*), published initially in 1960 and in updated editions in 1965 and 1968 (to which the West German government later responded with its own "Brown book" of Nazis in the GDR).[33]

Individuals who were targeted in propaganda campaigns and trials in absentia included Adenauer's chief of staff in the chancellery, Hans Globke, and Adenauer's minister for refugees and expellees, Theodor Oberländer, who were sentenced in show trials in the GDR in 1963 and 1960, respectively. Oberländer was forced to resign from his post, despite Adenauer's support, because the continued publicity around his Nazi past proved politically embarrassing. Many accusations were simply rebutted in the anti-communist West by claiming these were simply Soviet smear campaigns with little substance. Such counter accusations were given some substance by the fact that incriminating evidence was indeed often fabricated or massaged. This was for example the case with West German president Heinrich Lübke, who in 1969 was pressured into resigning from office three months early amidst East German accusations about his role in assisting Speer's building plans for his rocket base in Peenemünde, including barracks for slave laborers. In some respects, perfectly valid observations about the startling continuance of former Nazis in high places in West Germany were undermined by the distortions and untruths that were used to exaggerate the claims.

At the same time, however, the SED and MfS kept very quiet about known former Nazis in their own state. It would have been something of an embarrassment for the self-proclaimed "antifascist state" to concede that they had not entirely cleaned out their own stable, and some former Nazis could be effectively threatened or blackmailed into the service of the State Security Service (Staatssicherheitsdienst, or Stasi).[34] So the slate was not wiped quite as clean as the SED leadership liked to proclaim. By 1973–74, the MfS had compiled a list of 815 GDR citizens who had belonged to the Gestapo, the SD, and SS-Einsatzgruppen, and who were suspected of involvement in crimes.[35] Careful consideration was given as to who should be brought to court, bearing in mind both the likelihood of a successful prosecution and the potential degree of embarrassment if it were to be discovered that known offenders had not previously been prosecuted. In the case of suppression and protection of war criminals, it was important that news should not leak out to the West.

The Stasi sometimes used former Nazis as "unofficial informers" (inoffizielle Mitarbeiter, IMs), keeping them out of the public limelight, in what has been called a "secret politics of the past."[36] This practice, criticized in the West, has been defended by former MfS officials Dieter Skiba and Reiner Stenzel, who claim that those used as Stasi informers were people suspected of Nazi crimes but against whom insufficient evidence could be found to mount a trial. They argue that many former Nazis in the West were working for what they saw as enemy circles, and that it was important for the GDR to have access to these groups. Skiba and Stenzel assert, however, that this did not protect any perpetrator from being brought to judgment and penalized for crimes under Nazism. Examples of former Stasi informers who were ultimately brought to trial include Johannes Kinder; Franz Timm, alias Neumann; Georg Frentzle; and Karl Gorny. In the cases of others, such as Josef Settnik, who formerly worked in the Auschwitz political department, or Karl Mally, who had worked for the Gestapo, they claim there was simply not enough evidence to bring a compelling prosecution.[37]

Many former Nazis managed to bury their pasts and make new lives, whether willingly or otherwise, as GDR citizens. Most former Nazis adapted, conformed, and led relatively undisturbed lives. Given the relatively low numbers of convictions, it is clear that the vast majority of the hundreds of thousands who had been actively involved in Nazi crimes never even came to public attention, let alone to court.

Occasionally we catch glimpses of the new lives former perpetrators were leading and their transformation into apparently good citizens. In 1965, for example, the Düsseldorf court was seeking one Rudi Baer, a former SS man who had served in Treblinka from 1942, in order to prepare for the Treblinka trial.[38] The West German court requested information from the East German authorities, who did indeed manage to track down Rudi Baer at his home in the East German town of Halle. The Halle local police on June 22, 1965, produced a fascinating character sketch of the quiet life of a former participant in mass murder. He apparently carried out his work as an "independent master carpenter" in a "clean and orderly manner."[39] He conformed to the legal requirement concerning pricing of his products and enjoyed a good reputation in his housing block. Fellow residents said that he was "peaceful" person.[40] His parents owned the housing block that he helped to maintain, and he saw to it that any necessary repairs were carried out "without further ado."[41] He was always prepared to help the residents, and he was happily married. There was a mere hint of criticism in the documents when it came to his political views, however—"a degree of uncertainty about his political opinions." Clearly playing it safe, Baer, it was reported, "does not let himself be drawn into discussions in the house."[42] Moreover, he did not play a role in community activities in the area. Worse still, on August 4, 1961—just over a week before the erection of the Berlin Wall—Baer had sought to leave the GDR illegally but was apprehended. Overall, however, the report concluded that Baer had not as yet drawn any "negative" attention to himself.[43] In general, this report suggests an extraordinary transformation from serving in the SS in Treblinka to becoming a quiescent GDR citizen, breathing not a word of his former exploits even among tenants in his own apartment block. Baer is probably typical of innumerable former Nazis who had managed to integrate quietly into East German society and kept their heads down. Others were far less lucky, as we shall see in the cases of Josef Blösche and Rudi Zimmermann.

The GDR pursued selected perpetrators with assiduity, right to the very end of its existence as a separate state on October 3, 1990; and once defendants had been chosen and trials had been launched, the East German authorities were generally less lenient and less well-disposed to Nazi defendants than their West German counterparts were. Sometimes justice was simply being pursued for its own sake, with little apparent attempt to make use of trials in any political sense. There were many trials of low-level perpetrators whose cases only occasionally aroused much public attention. As in the West, East German policy was a complex balancing act, seeking simultaneously to integrate former Nazis, to expose and harshly punish a few, and variously to ignore and suppress evidence or make use of others, according to what appeared most advantageous in any particular case.[44]

Sympathies, Subjectivities, and the Law: West Germany

From its inception, the Federal Republic of Germany emphasized its status as the sole legal successor to previous German states. This was in contrast to the GDR, which, until recognition under Willy Brandt's *Ostpolitik*, was officially referred to in the West as "the Zone," underlining the claim that the GDR was an illegal entity in the Soviet Zone of Occupation.

For all the continuities in personnel, the Federal Republic wanted to be seen to be making a clean break with the Third Reich and exercising its own sovereignty—which also meant breaking with American policies, and dropping application of the Allied Control Council Law no. 10 in 1951. In particular, it was important that—unlike in the GDR—alleged perpetrators should be tried under the existing German criminal code (which, with modifications over time, was rooted in the 1871 penal code of the German Empire) rather than the Nuremberg principles. This would emphasize that the Nazi regime itself had marked a break with German legal traditions and standards of morality. It would also mean no breach of the principle that justice should not be retroactive: that people should not be tried for acts that, at the time they committed them, had not actually been criminal—one of the major criticism of the Nuremberg trials.

In practice, the West German legal system proved problematic. It meant using the charge of murder, which had remained illegal under the German criminal code even through the Third Reich. But to prove someone was guilty of murder (*Mord*) or the lesser charge of "aiding and abetting" murder (*Beihilfe zum Mord*), rather than merely manslaughter (*Totschlag*), meant fulfilling exacting criteria regarding subjective states of mind. The accused must have personally taken the initiative, rather than merely followed orders; acted from "base motives" (*niedrige Beweggründe*); behaved with particular sadism, cruelty, or ferocity, as an "excess perpetrator" (*Exzesstäter*); and must have been aware of wrongdoing at the time. Subjective elements were crucial to the attribution of culpability for murder. Defense lawyers could appeal, variously, to a range of mitigating factors: that, for example, the defendant had killed only on orders; there was no sign of sadism or personal pleasure in the act, and possibly evidence of reluctance to kill; the accused had been unaware that the act was unlawful; or, if they had been aware of illegality, that it had been necessary to behave in this way, and disobeying orders would have had adverse consequences for them.

These legal criteria for individually motivated crimes were not suited to the task of putting state-sponsored mass murder on trial. There were periodic attempts to consider crime complexes as collective systems in which individuals played different contributory roles, as the Allies had done, but in general West German courts tended to consider defendants as though they had engaged in individually motivated crimes. In effect—as we shall see particularly in the case of the Bełżec trial—individuals who had killed thousands of innocent people could, under West German law, be found not guilty by claiming they were only following orders; they had been so effective that there were no survivors providing evidence about brutality and sadism.

Defendants were increasingly likely to be classified as "accomplices," potentially guilty only of aiding and abetting murder, with correspondingly lenient sentences. During the 1960s, nearly two-thirds (61 percent) of those found guilty were classified as "accessories to murder," accomplices rather than murderers, and given sentences of between three and five years for their part in tens or hundreds of thousands of deaths. Barely one third (31 percent) were given a sentence of between six and ten years, and a mere seven percent earned sentences of ten to fifteen years.[45] This meant that in this crucial decade—when West Germany was gaining an international reputation for "facing up to" its past—people who had been involved in mass murder were being recast as merely obedient servants of the state, blinded by ideology or motivated by fear of their superiors. There were notable exceptions, but many sentences suggested that while mass murder had clearly been committed, the killing had been carried out by people who were not themselves murderers. The ordinary criminal law was clearly not adequate to putting state-ordained killing on trial.

There were further complications. One was the statute of limitations, which held that even for murder a person could no longer be prosecuted once twenty years had elapsed since the crime. By the early 1960s, as the twenty-year timeframe from 1945 neared an end, systematic investigation and prosecution of Nazi mass murder in the east had barely begun. There had been a lull in prosecutions in the mid-1950s. Cases were brought in the Federal Republic's regional states, or *Länder*, where the alleged perpetrators lived or where the crimes had occurred. Since so many of the Third Reich's major crimes had taken place in areas outside the current borders of the Federal Republic, prosecutors were largely dependent on citizens recognizing former perpetrators resident in their own area and then bringing them to the attention of the region's authorities. By the later 1950s, there were moves to coordinate efforts and to have a means for undertaking research into crime complexes outside Germany even before knowing the residence of particular perpetrators. This led in 1958 to the foundation of the Ludwigsburg Central Office of the State Justice Administrations for the Investigation of National Socialist Crimes—a cumbersome title for a small office—based in charming eighteenth-century premises in a town north of Stuttgart. Its tasks were to investigate crime complexes beyond German borders, collate relevant materials, and assist prosecutions by coordinating the efforts of the different *Länder*. It was initially assumed that, in view of the statute of limitations, the work of this office would be relatively short-lived, and it was set up with only a small staff and relatively limited resources. But with the preparation of what became known as the Frankfurt Auschwitz trial, stimulated and fueled by the fierce determination of Fritz Bauer, evidence began to stream in.[46]

It was clear that justice could not be done so rapidly, in face of the enormity of the crimes and the mountains of evidence now being amassed. Frantic debates were now held over the question of extending the time period during which murder could be prosecuted. A first solution was to regard the four years under occupation, from 1945 to 1949, as excluded from the twenty-year rule, since German courts could at this time only try offenses committed on German territory or against their own nationals. The end date was therefore first postponed from 1965 to 1969, in the run-up to which there were further debates.[47] Following heated arguments, the statute of limitations for murder cases was again postponed, this time for a further ten years until 1979; it was then lifted entirely. But this was not the case for lesser offenses, putting an even higher premium on the possibility of reducing a charge from murder to manslaughter.

One of the key legal developments slipped through either by stealth and cunning or error and oversight.[48] In 1968, legislation was passed without an apparently minor amendment in wording being noticed. Instead of stating that "accomplices" to a deed *might* be subjected to milder punishment than those perpetrators primarily responsible for the act, it now stated that they *must* be given lesser sentences if they lacked what were called "characteristics of perpetrators." This change meant a shift in the statutory length of time during which they could be prosecuted: retroactively, given the shorter sentence that was now mandatory rather than discretionary, accomplices were no longer subject to prosecution once the period stipulated under the statute of limitations had run out. In practice, prosecution as an accomplice to a Nazi crime could not be pursued after 1960—and this date was to be applied retroactively. Shortly thereafter, several hundred people who had faced the imminent threat of legal proceedings on grounds of their Nazi past were told that their cases had been dropped—a massive relief, particularly for those hundreds of functionaries of Himmler's central coordinating office, the Reich Security Main Office (Reichssicherheitshauptamt, RSHA), and security police forces whose cases had been investigated in the course of the mid-1960s.[49]

All of these features of the West German legal system played a role in the trials of Nazi perpetrators.[50] But the legal system was itself the consequence of political decisions. The ways in which justice was pursued in West Germany were shaped by wider factors, both domestic and international, in a distinctive social context.

Even during the occupation period, the western Allies' priorities had shifted from dealing with Nazism to securing cooperation in the fight against communism. Powerful voices were raised supporting the release of imprisoned Nazis, who were increasingly portrayed not as war criminals but as political victims of Allied justice. In January 1951 the American high commissioner for Germany, John McCloy, gave amnesty to prisoners who had been convicted in Nuremberg to a sentence of less than fifteen years, while other sentences were commuted or shortened; by 1958, a mere decade after their trials, most of the people convicted at Nuremberg had been released.[51] These commutations were not only a result of shifting American priorities.

For the Federal Republic's first chancellor, the conservative Konrad Adenauer, becoming a key ally of the Western powers and regaining full sovereignty were top priorities. This meant not only taking on the mantle of remorse and responsibility for the Nazi past and making gestures of reparations toward Israel but also defusing potentially destabilizing revisionism from the right in the fragile early years for postwar democracy.

Adenauer's "politics of the past" entailed the reintegration of the vast majority of former Nazis, a strategy aligned with that of the Western Allies but also
resulting from considerable domestic pressure. A coalition stretching from
right-wing factions, small parties, and individuals with Nazi sympathies on the
one hand to prominent representatives of both the Protestant and Catholic
Churches on the other, assisted by a group of right-wing lawyers known as the
Heidelberg Circle, put immense pressure on Adenauer's government to com-
mute the sentences imposed by the Allies, to show clemency to those who had
been imprisoned, and to reduce the burden on those still awaiting investigation
or judgment. By the early 1950s, some, like Werner Best, former Nazi plenipotentiary in Denmark and functionary in the RSHA, were fighting for an
amnesty for all Nazis, denouncing Allied measures as purely "victors' justice."

These views were far from unchallenged, with voices also raised in protest. But ultimately, the balance of power favored Adenauer's distinctions
between the supposedly few "real criminals" who deserved punishment and
the many others who should not do penance for allegedly minor misdeeds
under Nazi rule.[52] This let the vast majority off the hook, effectively reversing much of what the Allies had initially achieved.

Many lesser offenses were, under the statute of limitations, no longer
liable for prosecution after 1950. But there were further legal measures to
take perpetrators out of the sphere of justice. An amnesty law was passed by
the new German parliament on December 31, 1949, applying to convictions
with sentences of less than six months.[53] This conveniently obscured the
distinctions between minor, generally "economic" offenses committed under
Allied occupation—when the black market was rife, with currency and trading offenses a feature of survival in daily life, and when many people found
it convenient to adopt a false identity—and the often violent criminal acts
committed under Nazi auspices. All that mattered under this amnesty was the
length of sentence the offense might attract.[54] A further amnesty law was
passed in 1954, applicable to crimes attracting sentences of up to three years
if committed during the period of the "collapse" from October 1944 onward
and involving what was called a "collision of duties." This, too, obscured
significant differences and emphasized the significance of having obeyed
orders for fear of adverse consequences (the notion of *Befehlsnotstand*), even if
in a period of confusion during the "final phase" many might have been mistaken in their beliefs.

Some four hundred thousand people benefited from this legislation.
More broadly, attempts to penalize involvement in Nazi persecution were

increasingly delegitimized, while the story that people had been under immense pressure to obey orders became ever more current.[55] These self-defensive strategies would continue to be used at all levels, from defendants facing serious charges in the courtroom to relatively insignificant former Nazis trying to justify their past to their children or grandchildren. While a few Nazis were demonized, the rest were effectively exculpated. By the mid-1950s, when Adenauer negotiated the return of former prisoners of war from the Soviet Union, some of whom had been serving well-deserved sentences for significant crimes, returnees were generally greeted as returning war heroes in West German society.

There were other significant consequences of Adenauer's policies for the rehabilitation of former Nazis. In a law passed on May 11, 1951, based on Article 131 of the basic law (*Grundgesetz*, the constitution), former civil servants, public officials, and career soldiers who had lost their jobs as a result of denazification or similar actions (including the disbanding of the Gestapo and other Nazi organizations) were granted reinstatement in their former or equivalent positions, and full pension rights. This law even entailed quotas for compulsory employment of former Nazis, which could only be achieved by excluding from employment those who had not yet completed their training or had not been employed during the Third Reich—which meant excluding, once again, those who had already been excluded on "racial" or political grounds. Article 131 in this way doubly reinforced the effects of Nazi stigmatization and exclusion by giving preference to the reinstatement of former Nazis over the employment of those who had already suffered.

The continuity in some ministries between the officials who had faithfully served Hitler and those who provided support for the Adenauer administration was striking: two-fifths of officials in the Foreign Ministry and in the Interior Ministry were "131ers," while—appropriately enough, given its focus on the lost territories of Eastern Europe—as many as two-thirds of functionaries in the Federal Ministry for Expellees, Refugees, and War Victims (Bundesministerium für Vertriebene, Flüchtlinge und Kriegsgeschädigte) were "131ers."[56]

This had secondary effects for the apparent innocence of the Nazi civil service. District administrators from the General Government, for example, who had played a key role in ghettoization and deportation of Polish Jews to the death camps, as well as overseeing the lethal pursuit of those trying to hide, were barely considered in postwar trials. Coordinating their defenses, they all told roughly the same story: the SS was the real culprit, while they had only been involved in administration. Only one such former Nazi administrator was in fact ever brought to trial, and he was acquitted; the failure to bring others to court assisted the construction of the myth of innocence and the lack of visibility as far as the wider postwar public was concerned.[57] There were very many like Werner Ventzki, former city mayor of Litzmannstadt (Łódź), who went on to a senior position in the West German civil service, while his former subordinate, Hans Biebow, head of the ghetto administration, had been extradited to stand trial in Poland in 1947 and sentenced to death. Most civil servants soon realized they were not likely to be held to account and subsequently felt little need to dwell on the parts they had played in the catastrophe that engulfed so many millions. Some prominent figures were targets of East German propaganda campaigns and embarrassing trials in absentia, as in the cases of Globke and Oberländer.[58] But until the widening of historical investigations in the early twenty-first century, including a spate of commissioned works on the complicity of key ministries, West German civil servants with a Nazi past could generally hide behind a veil of official innocence.

The West German judiciary similarly managed rather rapidly to exclude itself from postwar justice.[59] Some eighty thousand people had been sentenced to death by the politicized courts of the Third Reich; judges who had served in Nazi Germany were swimming in a sea of guilt. Yet many returned to their former positions, with Article 131 contributing to what has been called a "renazification" of the West German legal profession in the 1950s.[60] Perhaps three-quarters of West German judges and lawyers at this time had served during the Third Reich.[61] They now argued that, far from having been political, they had simply exercised their professional obligation to uphold the law of the land, whatever the government of the day. By the late 1950s they had taken measures to exclude the actions of their own profession under Nazism from scrutiny in the courtroom. This meant that judges who had served in the special courts and the people's court of Nazi Germany could not themselves be indicted for the tens of thousands of death sentences they had passed in service of Hitler. Furthermore, given their own accommodation with the Nazi regime, many judges were inclined to regard defendants with considerable sympathy and understanding.[62]

At the same time, there were distinctive sympathies for certain sorts of defendants. Factors such as bourgeois social status or previous suffering as a prisoner of war under communism or as a refugee or expellee from Eastern

Europe were often taken into account in sentencing. Where there was any ambiguity, the subjective state of defendants was generally interpreted to their benefit—often whatever the evidence. Either defendants had been so "blinded" by Nazi ideology and propaganda that, as convinced Nazis, they could not help acting in the ways that they did; or, by contrast, they had acted unwillingly, obeying orders without really wanting to act as they did, similarly diminishing their level of guilt. Furthermore, small acts of supposed "humanity"—examples of which could include shooting more accurately to put an early end to the misery of those being murdered, or successfully deceiving victims so that they had little inkling of their impending doom—could serve in mitigation. Similarly, the defense of having only stayed in post to prevent something worse was often treated seriously, while professing remorse might also help.

The judiciary also demonstrated continuing bias against some groups of victims. There generally appeared to be little sympathy, for example, with Roma and Sinti. Paul Werner, who as deputy to Arthur Nebe (who headed the Criminal Police Department reporting directly to Reinhard Heydrich) had been involved in deporting Gypsies to Auschwitz, was cleared by a Stuttgart court on December 9, 1963, on the grounds that even right up to 1943 Gypsies were sent to concentration camps as a form of "preventative crime fighting" rather than because of their "racial" identity. Moreover, this court upheld the view that, even as late as 1943, those who sent Gypsies to Auschwitz could not have foreseen the high probability of death.[63] Whether Gypsies should have been detained at all does not seem to have been a consideration for the court.

In these ways, judges and juries in West German courts often showed sympathy with the perpetrators and far less often with their victims. Indeed, one judge went so far as to say, a couple of decades after the war, that "time has mercifully drawn a veil of forgetting over the sufferings of victims and the tears of relatives."[64] The outcome was a record of lenient sentences, and even acquittals, for individuals who had demonstrably killed innumerable people.

There has been some discussion of the extent to which continuities in legal personnel adversely affected the pursuit of justice in West Germany.[65] Clearly there was a combination of factors involved. The political profile of the legal profession was, in the long term, less significant than the fact that once significant changes were enshrined in law, subsequent trials were affected whether or not individual lawyers were themselves sympathetic to former Nazis. So the tracks that were set during the Adenauer period, when the government, civil service, and judicial profession were saturated with former Nazis, structurally determined the parameters of later trials, whatever the changing profile of the legal profession over time.

There was also a wider social context in which it was convenient to narrow the range of those viewed as "perpetrators" while quietly ignoring the ways in which professional groups had played key roles. Apart from a few leading Nazis, who were either serving long sentences or were dead, the notion of perpetrator was restricted to refer primarily to ill-educated lower-class thugs who had carried out acts of brutality in roles such as camp guards, many of whom were Ukrainian or of other non-German nationalities.[66] Not even all of these were culpable, especially if they had "only been following orders"; the real criminals, it would seem, were just those whose individual actions had "exceeded" the orderly killing mandated by the state. This came very close to legitimizing the whole system of collective violence and punishing only those who went beyond even the boundaries of what was ordered. Meanwhile, the elites whose supervision, authorization, and enforcement of physical violence remained at one remove from outright force, rather than being a matter of face-to-face implementation, were in the main safely excluded from judicial consideration.

So too, by and large, were those who profited from the Nazi system. The distinctive priorities inherent in West German justice become evident in early cases concerning the use of slave labor—cases that proved important, but have received relatively little attention in comparison with the major concentration camp trials.

In 1952 a case was brought against I. G. Farben by a former Auschwitz inmate and slave laborer, Norbert Wollheim.[67] At the end of the war, fully half of I. G. Farben's total workforce had been slave laborers. In the Nuremberg trials, I. G. Farben had argued "the defense of necessity," which was largely successful except in the cases of I. G. Auschwitz—the Buna works in Monowitz that produced Zyklon B gas—and Fürstengrube, a satellite camp situated in the coal-mining district just a few miles north of Auschwitz, where people selected for slave labor (rather than instant gassing) generally died as a result of the conditions within a matter of three to six months. The Nuremberg verdict had indicated that employment under such conditions amounted to "a crime against humanity" and a "war crime"; it had taken place in full knowledge of the inhumane treatment meted out to inmates by the SS, and I. G. Farben's conditions of employment had exacerbated the misery of the prisoners. Even so, those found guilty had been given relatively lenient sentences and released early, soon rising to significant positions in postwar West German industry—and in the case of the German chemist Fritz ter Meer, rapidly covering up the true story of their company's involvement in slave labor and death.[68] The Allies further-more sought to split up the massive enterprise into successor companies—Bayer, Hoechst, BASF—while a firm entitled I. G. Farbenindustrie in Liquidation (I. G. Farben i. L.) ensured that the successor companies would not have to deal with creditors' claims.

This was soon to be tested. On November 3, 1951, the lawyer Henry Ormond initiated the case on behalf of Wollheim, claiming damages amounting to ten thousand Deutschmarks for twenty-two months of slave labor in the Buna plant. Ormond was no ordinary West German lawyer; like others, such as Fritz Bauer, he had something of a personal interest in seeing that justice was done. Ormond was born under the name Hans Ludwig Jacobson to non-practicing Jewish parents. Both parents died while he was a child, and he was adopted by an unmarried aunt. Here, he took on his mother's maiden name of Oettinger, but subsequently anglicized his name to Ormond when in enforced exile during the war. Trained as a lawyer, Ormond had lost his job under the antisemitic provisions of the Nazi Law for the Restitution of a Professional Civil Service in April 1933. He had managed to find other work and stayed in Germany, enjoying the support of a sympathetic employer, until 1938. Arrested after the November pogrom of that year, he was incarcerated in Dachau before being able to emigrate in 1939. After initial internment in Canada, he relocated to Britain and eventually came to serve in the British army. Ormond returned to Germany after the war and, like Bauer, was determined to try to see justice done in the new democratic state.[69] Not only was Ormond centrally involved in the Wollheim case; he was also a prosecutor in the Auschwitz trial in Frankfurt a decade later.

The Wollheim case opened on January 16, 1952 in Frankfurt. Former inmates testified about the appalling conditions under which they had lived and worked; the defense denied these testimonies so vehemently that the judge even had to issue a reprimand. Judgment was reached in the court of first instance on June 10, 1953, to the effect that Wollheim should indeed be awarded damages for the culpable bodily harm he had suffered. In the meantime, the case had aroused considerable interest on the part of other survivors: by the autumn 1952 some 1,100 other survivors had contacted

Ormond's law office. Concerted efforts were then made by representatives of German industry and Adenauer's government to prevent an avalanche of further cases, which, it was feared, would do damage to German industry and Germany's international reputation—particularly in the United States, where many former slave laborers had settled after the war. The government exerted immense pressure to ensure that there would be no further individual claims, pushing through laws to protect German commercial interests. On February 5, 1957, the I. G. Farben liquidators managed to sign an agreement with the Conference on Jewish Claims Against Germany, providing a fund of thirty million Deutschmarks to compensate forced laborers on condition that the Wollheim judgment was annulled, and that there was a short time limit set for any claims for compensation. This fund provided a maximum one-off payment of five thousand Deutschmarks to slave laborers who had been employed for more than six months—by which time, of course, the vast majority of Auschwitz slave laborers had died, given an average life expectancy of only three months under the conditions to which they were subjected. The payment was proportionately lower if the time served was less than six months, and those who missed the deadline for filing an application were to receive nothing. Although historic exchange rates and average salaries are hard to calculate with any precision, the maximum payment would have equated to approximately $1,200, or £425, at 1957 exchange rates—perhaps one-quarter of an average American annual salary that year. A further condition was that this was understood not to constitute an admission of legal or political responsibility and was a purely voluntary action done from a supposed sense of morality.

The Wollheim case set a pattern that was followed in subsequent decades. Heinkel too, as indicated, was challenged in court. Dr. Edmund Bartl was a non-Jewish German lawyer and political opponent of Nazism who had been arrested and incarcerated by the Gestapo for having told a political joke and after serving a two-year prison sentence was transferred to the Sachsenhausen concentration camp, where he was forced into slave labor in the Heinkel works in Oranienburg.[70] His health and eyesight were destroyed by working in unsafe conditions, and on liberation he weighed a mere eighty-six pounds. During the 1950s, he managed to find the time to undertake the necessary legal research to construct a case against the Heinkel successor company in Stuttgart. In 1959, Bartl duly sued Heinkel for its use of slave labor, arguing that he was entitled to compensation both for lost wages and for injuries and pain suffered. He initially won his claim for lost earnings in the district court, but was told he had filed too late for the other claims concerning pain and suffering, which were dismissed. Fighting this ruling, Bartl went on to the appellate court in Stuttgart, which overturned the district court's decision.

The story might have ended happily there, but the news magazine Der Spiegel carried a story on this case. The article not only noted that pain and suffering are not "time limited" but also explicitly listed by name some fifty-one other firms that could potentially be open to similar claims, adding for good measure the numbers of slave laborers that had worked for each of them.[71] Representatives of the Heinkel company, determined not to lay themselves open to a deluge of further claims, immediately appealed to the Federal Court of Justice (Bundesgerichtshof, sometimes translated as German Supreme Court), the highest court in Germany. And the Federal Court of Justice, under some pressure from both the Ministry of Finance and the industrialists' lobby, prioritized the interests of German companies over those who had suffered: it dismissed Bartl's case on the contested technical grounds that, as a German national, Bartl should have filed the claim within tight time limits—despite his previously successful argument that it had taken this long to establish which was the relevant successor company to sue. Moreover, the Federal Court of Justice emphasized that under the London Debt Agreement of 1953, which regulated the payment of German debts and reparations to other countries resulting from both world wars, any final settlement of debts to foreign nationals would have to await a peace treaty—which was not on the agenda during the Cold War, given the absence of any all-German government with which such a treaty could be concluded. As a result of this ruling, German companies no longer needed to fear being forced to make payments to former slave laborers, whether they were German or foreign nationals. The Federal Court of Justice heaped injury upon injury by not merely refusing Bartl compensation for the lost wages and the pain and ill-health suffered as a slave laborer but even ordering him, in addition, to pay all the court and legal costs. Bartl was left financially ruined. Heinkel—and other companies which had evaded any gesture of justice in this way—was left victorious, yet again.

It is worthy of note, to say the least, that these Federal Court of Justice deliberations in the mid-1960s took place at precisely the time that West Germany was gaining a reputation for "facing up to its past" by putting Auschwitz on trial. It is also astonishing that the associated mentality among industrialists and government circles persisted for years thereafter. In 1970

Tuviah Friedman, a Nazi hunter based in Israel and chairman of the World Jewish Federation of Victims of the Nazi Regime, demanded compensation on behalf of slave laborers. He pointed out that of the approximately two million Jews who had been used as slaves, only two hundred thousand had survived, a mortality rate in service of the German war economy of some 90 percent. This claim for compensation was not merely unsuccessful; it was not even given the time of day. The Federation of German Industry refused even to receive the delegation of the World Federation when it came on a special visit to Germany to press the case.[72]

Some companies nevertheless saw reputational gains to be made by gestures of concession, and a few followed the example of I. G. Farben by making modest payments. These were a relatively small price to pay for winning them a better international reputation and did little to help the vast majority of those who had suffered at their hands. There were also innumerable legal and practical difficulties for claimants, who had to go through the Claims Conference and demonstrate that they had in fact worked for specific companies and had also filed their cases on time, so the amounts actually paid out were even more limited.

Many industrialists were unwilling to concede even the moral case for payment. Friedrich Flick, who had walked free less than three years after being sentenced at Nuremberg, was probably the richest man in Germany, and very likely one of the five richest in the world, by the time he died in 1972. While passing on massive wealth within his own family and contributing substantially to the coffers of right-wing politicians, Flick died without having handed out a single cent of compensation to his former Jewish slave laborers. This may be an extreme example, but in his refusal to admit either legal or moral responsibility, Flick was paradigmatic of a particular approach to the past in the country that was allegedly doing its utmost to face up to its responsibilities.

The overall record regarding prosecution of former Nazis in West Germany is therefore patchy and marked by significant political differences. Those who were particularly proactive in ensuring that former Nazis were brought to stand trial, such as Fritz Bauer, were often themselves former victims or opponents of Nazism, or were members of younger generations. There was, by contrast, much foot-dragging among former supporters of the Nazi regime. The claim that West Germany was not "political" in its approach to the law, in presumed contrast to communist East Germany, cannot be sustained. A widespread desire to put an end to discussions, or "draw a line" under the past ("einen Schlussstrich ziehen") was, however, always countered by other considerations, including an eye to West Germany's international reputation, the perceived need to counter criticism, and constant competition for the moral high ground with the neighboring GDR.[73] There was also growing pressure from left-liberal individuals and groups, who, with the passage of time, became ever more prominent in the media, institutions, social movements, and politics. Dealing with the Nazi past took an increasingly central place in public life. But this development required constant vigilance and active engagement, the significance of which should not be underestimated. Even so, structural and legal factors hindering the trials of people accused of Nazi crimes had been instituted early on and were not easily overcome.

Abstaining from Justice: Austria

Austria was ultimately the least willing to engage in the energetic pursuit of former perpetrators, despite having initially nurtured and subsequently harbored an arguably disproportionate share of them. The sheer extent of Austrian participation in sustaining the Nazi system of terror was totally overshadowed, for a long time even buried, by the politically dominant myth of having been "Hitler's first victim."[74] The phrase had already been used by the Allies during the war, when British prime minister Winston Churchill and his close political colleague Anthony Eden emphasized that Austrians were the "first victim of German aggression"; this was consolidated in the Declaration on Austria of the Moscow Declarations of 1943, signed by the foreign secretaries (or secretary of state) of the United States, the United Kingdom, and the Soviet Union, declaring the Anschluss of 1938 null and void. This declaration also drew attention to Austria's responsibility for participation in the war on Hitler's side, but Austrian politicians after the war chose to ignore this. The provisional president, Karl Renner, even managed to recast the majority of Austrian Nazis as having been "victims" not only of the Anschluss (which so many had in fact welcomed) but also of economic, social, or political coercion by the Germans.[75] Most people were only too glad to accept this convenient fiction, which became deeply embedded in Austrian public culture, allowing what is sometimes called an "externalization" of guilt—placing the burden of guilt on others—leading often to a kind of doublespeak.

In these circumstances, Austrians who had supported or accommodated themselves to Nazism felt no particular pressure to confront their own past. In 1948, an opinion poll in Hitler's former hometown of Linz, close to the Mauthausen concentration camp and Hartheim euthanasia center, revealed that over half the people surveyed (55.2 percent) agreed that "National Socialism had been a good idea badly carried out."[76] Meanwhile, the handful—a mere 1,730—of the two hundred thousand Jews who had lived in Austria before the war and were present again in 1945 found on the whole a frosty welcome.[77] The sense among Jews of being unwanted was compounded by the government's refusal to provide compensation or restitution for losses incurred as a result of actions by Hitler's Reich, which they portrayed as a foreign power. Popular antisemitism continued, although in altered forms, particularly as the numbers of Jews grew to around ten thousand with immigration from Eastern Europe in the later 1940s.[78] Considering the boost that Nazism had given to modernizing the Austrian economy, the benefits many Austrians had gained in the process, and the convenient status of being a neutral country when sovereignty was restored in the Austrian State Treaty of 1955, it was scarcely surprising that most felt little need to address questions of guilt or responsibility for the Nazi past. This approach was supported by a remarkably broad political consensus. The general climate also seems to have affected the pursuit of justice—or relative failure to do so.

An analysis of trials concerned with the Mauthausen concentration camp and its large network of sub-camps found that of the 9,808 people who had worked at Mauthausen, a mere forty-one were charged in Austrian courts with having killed people either there or in one of Mauthausen's sub-camps: some 9,767 people who had worked in these camps were therefore able to walk away unmolested by any legal process. Of those forty-one who were actually charged, twenty-nine were given prison sentences. Only one—Johann Ludwig, a half-Jewish prisoner functionary who had managed to survive Auschwitz—was, on the basis of minimal and unsatisfactory evidence, sentenced to death and executed on February 25, 1948. SS men in positions of far greater authority were, by contrast, given lesser sentences for worse offenses. Franz Doppelreiter, for example, was tried twice and managed with the passage of time to have his initial death sentence reduced to imprisonment, while SS-Unterscharführer Alois Johandl, who had on his own admission engaged in brutal individual killings in the Gusen sub-camp, was given a sentence of twenty years in view of his relative youth and alleged susceptibility to brutalization through exposure to "criminal" prisoners. In the so-called Mühlviertel rabbit hunt (*Hasenjagd*) case, relating to an incident in which around 250 prisoners who had escaped from Mauthausen were rounded up and killed with the assistance of local people in the Mühlviertel area, the court tended to accept the cover stories of defendants and the startling losses of memory among potential witnesses, protecting members of the local community.[79]

Since the Austrian government denied responsibility for the Third Reich, it saw no need to pay any reparations or compensation to victims of Nazi persecution. Individuals in this context also felt well placed to resist any personal demands for restitution and sought to retain property they had acquired as a result of Nazi Aryanization policies or related developments as the Jewish community was squeezed out of Austrian life. More generally, Austrians who had supported or acquiesced in Nazi rule primarily wanted to mourn their own losses and make sense of their own suffering. The real issues for most people were grieving for their own war dead and caring for or coping with maimed and mutilated returnees. Former Nazis were generally able to integrate into the new society with little regard for their past and little need to fear being brought to justice.

As in East and West Germany, the vast majority of prosecutions of former Nazis in Austria took place in the first decade after the war and before Austria regained full sovereignty in 1955.[80] In Austria, however, unlike in West Germany, there was at this time no ban on "retrospective" application of the new categories of offense introduced in the Nuremberg trials, including genocide. But this did not necessarily mean that the mass murder of the Jews was high on the Austrian agenda, nor was the murder of Gypsies. Franz Langmüller, commandant of the Austrian Gypsy camp Lackenbach and notorious for his brutality, received a sentence of just one year for his role in torturing and murdering Gypsies in the camp.[81]

The people's courts were relatively active, given the small size of the Austrian population—which had fallen to below seven million by 1955. Some 137,000 people were investigated in the first decade after the war. Trials were held against 28,000 people, and of these, around 13,600 were convicted and sentenced. There were forty-three death sentences, thirty of which were actually carried out. A total of twenty-nine people were sentenced to life imprisonment, and 350 received prison sentences of terms of ten years or more. There was relatively lenient treatment of lawyers and physicians.

Figure 1. A Jewish shop in Magdeburg after "Kristallnacht," November 9–10, 1938. Some Germans were ashamed, while others profited from Jewish distress. *Photographer unknown. BArch Bild 146-1979-046-22.*

Figure 2. German children playing in the ruins of the Peter-Gemcinder-Strasse synagogue in Beerfelden, destroyed in Kristallnacht, November 1938. Many participated in the humiliation of Jews. *Photographer unknown. United States Holocaust Memorial Museum, 96945, courtesy of the Stadtarchiv Beerfelden.*

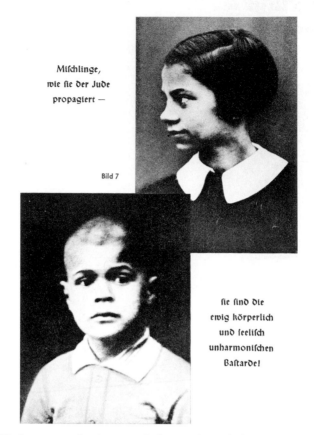

Mischlinge,
wie sie der Jude
propagiert —

Bild 7

sie sind die
ewig körperlich
und seelisch
unharmonischen
Bastarde!

Figure 3. Nazi propaganda pictures of a boy and a girl: the caption reads "Mischlinge [half-breeds], as the Jew propagates them—they are always physical and spiritual bastards!" *United States Holocaust Memorial Museum, 62923, courtesy of G. Howard Tellier.*

Figure 4. A Nazi propaganda poster highlighting the relative costs in 1936 of caring for people with supposedly hereditary illnesses. *United States Holocaust Memorial Museum, 07672, courtesy of Roland Klemig.*

Figure 5. Eugenics poster titled "The Eradication of the Sick and Weak in Nature" from *Hereditary Teachings and Racial Science in Pictorial Representation* by Alfred Vogel. *Photographer of the poster: Lindsay Harris. United States Holocaust Memorial Museum, 94181, courtesy of Hans Pauli.*

ADOLF HITLER

BERLIN, den 1.Sept.1939.

Reichsleiter B o u h l e r und

Dr. med. B r a n d t

sind unter Verantwortung beauftragt, die Befug -

nisse namentlich zu bestimmender Ärzte so zu er -

weitern, dass nach menschlichem Ermessen unheilbar

Kranken bei kritischster Beurteilung ihres Krank -

heitszustandes der Gnadentod gewährt werden kann.

Figure 6. Letter on Hitler's Chancellery office notepaper, signed by Hitler and backdated to the first day of the war, ordering Philipp Bouhler and Karl Brandt to authorize doctors to "grant a mercy death" to patients with supposedly incurable illnesses. The "euthanasia" program was never passed into law. *United States Holocaust Memorial Museum, 67072, courtesy of the National Archives and Records Administration, College Park.*

Figure 7. T4 medical experts at the Starnberger Lake, near Munich, September 1941. Dr. Victor Ratka (3rd from left) led "wild" euthanasia killings in Tiegenhof and participated in the 4f13 selections; Dr. Friedrich Mennecke (4th from left) wrote to his wife about selecting concentration camp prisoners for death; and Prof. Dr. Paul Nitsche (5th from left) moved from Sonnenstein to play a leading role at the T4 Berlin headquarters. *Photographer unknown. BArch, B 162 Bild-00680.*

Figure 8. Staff from the Grafeneck euthanasia institute on an outing in 1940. Many euthanasia workers went on to the "Reinhard" extermination camps and then to killing units in northern Italy, including: Wilhelm August Miete (far right); Willi Mentz (2nd from right); Franz Sydow (front, 4th from left); and behind, Genz and Belitz, who assisted Mentz in Treblinka. *Photograph from the album of Willi Mentz, photographer unknown. Zentrale Stelle der Landesjustizverwaltungen zur Aufklärung nationalsozialistischer Verbrechen - Bildbestand. BArch B 162 Bild-01818 (Old signature: AR-Z 230/59; B 162/3822, Bl. 1198).*

Figure 9. Josef Oberhauser (left), Fritz Irrman (center), and Kurt Franz (right), in Bełżec, ca. 1942/1943. Franz worked in Hartheim, Brandenburg, Grafeneck, and Sonnenstein, then Lublin and Bełżec, and was the last commandant of Treblinka. Irrman "welcomed" prisoners arriving at Bełżec. Oberhauser worked in Grafeneck, Brandenburg, and Bernburg, then Bełżec, and finally northern Italy. *B 162 Bild-Zentrale Stelle der Landesjustizverwaltungen zur Aufklärung nationalsozialistischer Verbrechen, photographer unknown. BArchB 162 Bild-00575.*

Figure 10. Portrait of a Jewish boy, Henius Koplowicz, in Łódź, a year before he was forced into the ghetto and three years before he was murdered in nearby Chełmno. *United States Holocaust Memorial Museum, 23719, courtesy of Regina Kniker Kopelman.*

Figure 11. An emaciated man in the Łódź ghetto awaiting deportation to Chełmno, early 1942. *United States Holocaust Memorial Museum, 37344, courtesy of Sidney Harcsztark.*

Figure 12. Hans Biebow celebrating his birthday in December 1942. In charge of the administration of the Łódź ghetto, Biebow also assisted in deportations and in the final liquidation of the ghetto. *Photographer unknown. United States Holocaust Memorial Museum, 71504A, courtesy of Robert Abrams.*

Figure 13. The suppression of the Warsaw Ghetto uprising, April 19 to May 16, 1943, from the report by SS leader Jürgen Stroop. The SS man, 2nd from right, is Josef Blösche. (See also Fig. 34.) *Photographer unknown. BArch 183-41636-0002.*

Figure 14. The German Colony of Hohenbach, in Czermin, near Mielec, Poland. "Ethnic Germans" from this village, including Rudolf Zimmermann, were involved in Nazi atrocities. (See also Fig. 35.) *Photographer unknown. Deutsches Ausland-Institut, ca. 1929. BArch, Bild 137-030469.*

Figure 15. The Mielec synagogue after the arson attack following the German invasion, 1939. (See also Fig. 36.) *Photographer: Kurt Robert Ferdinand Hippert. BArch, Bild B 162 Bild-00927.*

Figure 16. The Jewish community of Mielec gathered on the town square under the supervision of German soldiers and Gestapo members (including Rudolf Zimmermann), prior to deportation, March 9, 1942. *Photographer: Kurt Robert Ferdinand Hippert. BArch, Bild B 162 Bild-00409 (Old signature: AR 376/63; Blatt 1196; File B 162 / 1429).*

Figure 17. SS–Major (Sturmbannführer) Hans Proschinsky at the SS Heidelager training grounds, Dębica, Poland. Proschinsky was later sentenced to life imprisonment. *Photographer unknown. BArch, Bild B 162 Bild-05508 (Old signature: AR-Z 280/59; B 162/401).*

Figure 18. Hans Proschinsky (left) at the SS Heidelager, Dębica, Poland, with the head forester (called "Peter Müller" in this book), and other members of the SS. *Zentrale Stelle der Landesjustizverwaltungen zur Aufklärung nationalsozialistischer Verbrechen. Photographer unknown. BArch, B 162 Bild-05512 (Old signature: AR-Z 280/59; B 162/401).*

Figure 19. The deportation of Sinti and Roma from Asperg, near Stuttgart, on May 22, 1940, watched by passers-by. Many Germans approved of the removal of "gypsies" from their midst. *Photographer unknown. BArch R 165 Bild-244-42.*

Figure 20. German soldiers taking photographs of "partisans" hanged near Orel, Soviet Union, 1941 or 1942. At least five cameras are visible; soldiers sent photos home, spreading knowledge of atrocities. *Photographer: Koll. BArch Bild 101I-287-0872-28A.*

Figure 21. Jews dig their own grave under the supervision of ethnic Germans from the Ukraine, July 4, 1941, Storow (Slarow), Ukraine. *Photographer unknown. BArch Y 01-3861.*

Figure 22. Jews dig their own grave as people watch, July 4, 1941, Storow, Ukraine. *Photographer unknown. BArch Bild 183-A0706-0018-029.*

Figure 23. Members of Heinrich Himmler's family visit Dachau concentration camp, July 22, 1941. Second on the left is Himmler's daughter Gudrun, who described this outing as "lovely," next to her mother, Margarete (Marga) Himmler (3rd from left). Others include Gudrun's aunts and cousin and Himmler's friend Hanns Johst, Nazi President of the German Writers' Association, with family. *Photographer unknown. BArchN 1126 Bild-16-002 (Old signature: N 1126/16; N 1126-16-02-2).*

Figure 24. The I.G. Farben Buna plant at Auschwitz–Monowitz, 1941–44. Many prisoners worked here; some died on the job, while others were sent to the nearby gas chambers at Auschwitz–Birkenau. *Photographer unknown. BArch Bild 146-2007-0057 (Old signature: Bild 146-1971-034-39).*

Figure 25. Hungarian Jews arriving for selection at Auschwitz–Birkenau, May 1944. *Photographer unknown, but possibly either Ernst Hofmann or Bernhard Walter; taken from the* Auschwitz Album. *BArchBild 183-N0827-318.*

Figure 26. The gates to Auschwitz–Birkenau, just abandoned by the Germans, early 1945. *Photographer: Stanisław Mucha, on behalf of the Polish Red Cross and Soviet investigations of Nazi crimes at Auschwitz. BArchB 285 Bild-04413 (Old signature: Bild 175-04413).*

Figure 27. Death march, spring 1945: prisoners being taken from Buchenwald to Dachau concentration camp. Maria Seidenberger secretly took this photograph from her home near Dachau. She also helped to hide and then forward photos and letters smuggled out on behalf of prisoners. *United States Holocaust Memorial Museum, 99216, courtesy of Maria Seidenberger.*

Figure 28. An American soldier supervising German civilians made to excavate a mass grave at a barn near Gardelegen, where on April 13, 1945, more than 1000 prisoners on a march from a subcamp of Mittelbau–Dora concentration camp had been incarcerated and burned alive. *Photograph taken on April 18, 1945. United States Holocaust Memorial Museum, 17074, courtesy of John Irving Malachowski.*

Figure 29. German civilians, including a woman trying to shield her son from the sight, being made to walk past the bodies of 57 Russians who had been exhumed from a mass grave outside Suttrop, North Rhine–Westphalia, May 3, 1945. They had been shot by the SS shortly before the end of the war. *United States Holocaust Memorial Museum, 08197, courtesy of National Archives and Records Administration, College Park.*

Figure 30. German civilians exhume the bodies of Polish and Russian forced laborers who had been killed at the "euthanasia" institute at Hadamar and buried in a mass grave. *Photograph by an American military photographer, April 1945. United States Holocaust Memorial Museum, 05485, courtesy of Rosanne Bass Fulton.*

Figure 31. American war crimes investigators interrogating Irmgard Huber, Head Nurse at the Hadamar Psychiatric Hospital, May 4, 1945. Despite lengthy sentences (twenty-five years and eight years), like many Nazis, Huber was released in the amnesty of 1952, and lived until 1983 in Hadamar. *United States Holocaust Memorial Museum, 73720, courtesy of National Archives and Records Administration, College Park.*

Figure 32. Dr. Herta Oberheuser being sentenced to twenty years in prison at the 1947 Doctors' Trial, one of the Nuremberg successor trials, for "medical" experiments in Ravensbrück. She too was released in 1952 and returned to medical practice until public protests in the later 1950s. She died in 1978.
United States Holocaust Memorial Museum, 41017, courtesy of National Archives and Records Administration, College Park.

Figure 33. Auschwitz survivor Eva Furth gives evidence on July 16, 1963, in the GDR trial in absentia of Konrad Adenauer's chief aide in the Chancellery, Hans Globke. *Photographer:Eva Brüggmann. BArch Bild 183-B0716-0005-014.*

Figure 34. Josef Blösche, who had assisted in suppressing the Warsaw Ghetto uprising (see Fig. 13), on trial in Erfurt, GDR, March 1969. Following an unsuccessful appeal, he was executed on July 19, 1969. *Photographer unknown. BArch, File DP3 1578.*

VI. Uneven Memorialization and Forgotten Traces

Figure 35. The cemetery in the former German Colony in Hohenbach, in Czermin near Mielec. The 2013 memorial ceremony celebrated the history of the community without mentioning Nazi crimes. (See also Fig. 14.) *Photograph by the author.*

Figure 36. The site of the former Mielec synagogue, destroyed in 1939, now marked by a rough stone defaced by a swastika. There is no memorial in the town square to the Jewish community. (See also Fig. 15 and Fig. 16.) *Photograph by the author.*

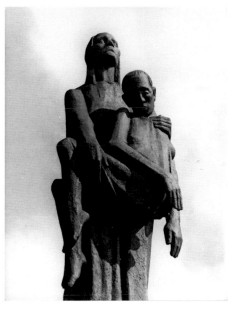

Figure 37. Ravensbrück statue depicting a strong female prisoner assisting a weaker prisoner, based on Will Lammert's 1957 sculpture *Tragende* ("the person carrying"), photographed April 15, 1965. It emphasizes solidarity and the power of resistance, typical themes in East German memorial sites. *Photographer: Heinz Junge. BArch 183-D0415-0016-006.*

20.4.1986.
Wir gedenken des Leides der Opfer des Faschismus, insbesondere der homosexuellen Frauen.

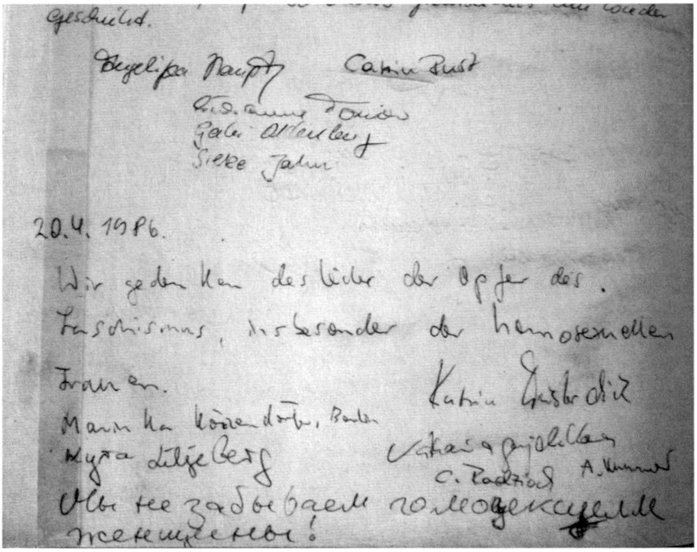

Figure 38. This entry of April 20, 1986, in the Ravensbrück visitors' book, signed by lesbian women, reads: "We remember the sufferings of victims of fascism, in particular of homosexual women." The Stasi confiscated the book to prevent others reading this mark of respect to a still marginalized group. *Ravensbrück Museum display, photograph by the author.*

Figure 39. Gay men also remained marginalized in West Germany until the later 1980s. This memorial reads "Beaten to death—silenced to death. To the homosexual victims of National Socialism." *Nollendorfplatz U-Bahn station, photograph by the author.*

Figure 40. A half-hidden hole in the hillside near Melk, in Austria, a last remaining trace of the extensive underground tunnels of a former Mauthausen subcamp. All across Europe, there are unmarked sites of former suffering and mass death; local knowledge will eventually disappear along with the traces. *Photograph by the author.*

Trials of former Nazis in Austria then more or less dried up completely after the State Treaty of 1955 gave Austria full sovereignty and independence.[82] In December 1955, the people's courts were abolished. Regular Austrian courts took over responsibility for prosecution of Nazis, with what some have summarized as "dismal results."[83] One estimate is that in the more than half century since 1955 only thirty-five sentences were passed in total.[84] With trial by jury in ordinary courts, failure to bring successful prosecutions seems to have had less to do with the legal system than with political will and wider social attitudes to the past.

After a general amnesty for former Nazis in March 1957 only those crimes could be punished that had already been crimes under previous Austrian legal codes. However, the long-standing legal definition of what constituted "murder" was broader in Austria than it was under West German law and did not rely so heavily on subjective elements; it therefore should, in principle, have been able to deal more easily with acts of collective violence. While the emphasis in West Germany was on motives and manner of carrying out the crime, under Austrian law prior to a reform of 1974 it was sufficient to show that a person had acted in such a way that, having an intention to kill, their actions had in fact resulted in the death of a person. This difference in legal definitions of what constituted murder meant that acts that in West Germany would be considered manslaughter could in Austria be treated as murder.

Moreover, in Austria, as in West Germany, there were repeated revisions of the statute of limitations. At first, crimes attracting the death penalty were not subject to any limits, whereas for other crimes, depending on the length of sentence they were likely to attract, limits set in at five, ten, or twenty years, after which people could no longer be prosecuted for their crimes. In 1950, the death sentence was abolished and replaced by a life sentence. In 1965, it was agreed that the limitation for prosecution of crimes that had previously attracted a death penalty should remain indefinite rather than be limited to the twenty years that had now run out. So there was no reason why murders committed under National Socialist auspices should not be prosecuted.[85]

But in practice, these features of the Austrian legal system—a wider definition of murder and no limits on the date of trial—did not entail the energetic pursuit of Nazi perpetrators after 1955. Nor was lack of successful prosecutions entirely due to organizational inefficiency. In 1963 a department of the Austrian Federal Ministry of the Interior was established, with specific responsibility for the coordination of investigations into Nazi crimes. Severely understaffed and overstretched, neither this department nor the legal profession was up to the gargantuan task of tracking down Nazi perpetrators or investigating and collating sufficient evidence to bring a successful prosecution. This lack of adequate resources was not purely accidental: politicians had the responsibility for allocating resources, and— unless there were significant foreign policy considerations in any particular case—the pursuit of former Nazis was simply not a top priority.[86]

Even as public awareness of the sheer magnitude of the Nazi program of genocide was growing, with heightened visibility from the Eichmann trial in Israel and the first Auschwitz trial in West Germany, the pursuit of Nazi war criminals in Austria was faltering. In the 1960s and early 1970s very few individuals were actually brought to trial, and slightly more than half of these were acquitted. In a total of thirty-five trials against forty-eight defen- dants, there were forty-three verdicts: twenty people were convicted, and twenty-three acquitted.[87] Trials in Austria more or less ended entirely at the beginning of the 1970s. This was not merely a result of the legal system; it also came about because Austrian juries appear to have demonstrated remarkable sympathy with those in the dock, perhaps out of shared political convictions and empathy with their plight in being brought to account.

In 1977, an Austrian Ministry of Justice booklet summarized the situa- tion: by 1972, a total of 13,607 persons had been convicted and sentenced for Nazi crimes, including forty-three death sentences and twenty-three terms of life imprisonment.[88] But the overwhelming majority of these sen- tences had been passed before 1955.[89] In 1978 all pending cases in Austria were abandoned. Trials of a few individual former Nazis in Austria restarted only in the 1990s.

The period characterized by an apparently extreme unwillingness to bring former Nazis to trial was presided over, curiously, by the most unlikely figure of Bruno Kreisky, chancellor of Austria from 1970 to 1983. Far from being himself a former fellow traveler under Nazism, Kreisky had, like his West German counterpart for some of the time, Federal Chancellor Willy Brandt, and like many of the East German political leadership, gone into exile during the Third Reich (both Kreisky and Brandt in Sweden, and most of the East Germans in Moscow). Willy Brandt in particular was closely associated with a sea change in West German approaches to Nazism in the late 1960s and early 1970s, and one might have expected a similar develop- ment in Austria under Kreisky.

Ironically, there was a key difference between the two leaders. Kreisky was not only a committed socialist but, unlike Brandt, of Jewish descent. And, perhaps because he was so acutely conscious of the perils of racism, Kreisky upheld a version of Austrian nationalism that could be seen as characteristic of a secular, nonreligious person who wants to insist that there is really no such thing as a "racial" identity. In a manner somewhat reminiscent of the dominant approach in early postwar France—where both Jewish and non-Jewish victims of Nazism were subsumed together under notions of French patriotism and resistance—Kreisky was unwilling to concede legitimacy to notions of an essentialist, racially based Jewish identity. He also continued the long-term policy of prioritizing the integration of former Nazis and downplaying the significance of Nazi-hunting. Inadequate denazification was not an issue to be proactively addressed, nor did Kreisky have much sympathy with the prominent Nazi-hunter Simon Wiesenthal and his activities based in Austria's capital city of Vienna. Wiesenthal was a survivor of several concentration camps, including Janowska (near his native town of Lwów), Plaszów, Groß-Rosen, Buchenwald, and Mauthausen-Gusen, and had lost innumerable members of his family, including his mother, in the Holocaust.[90] Barely surviving liberation, within a matter of weeks Wiesenthal had embarked on his lifelong mission of seeking to bring Nazis to justice, devoting immense efforts to track down those in hiding, including notably Eichmann and Mengele. He was also extremely critical of the ways in which postwar governments, including that of Austria, failed to pursue former Nazis and even rehabilitated them. Kreisky and Wiesenthal had major disagreements when Wiesenthal repeatedly pointed out the Nazi pasts of even members of Kreisky's own cabinet, whose guilt Kreisky had either failed to investigate or had sought to play down in the interests of integration in the present.[91] Kreisky was, furthermore, generally pro-Palestinian and keen for peace in the Middle East.

Austrian identity flourished in the 1970s: the country was widely admired as a neutral, non-EEC, non-NATO or Warsaw Pact state, untrammeled by the difficulties of the Cold War present and relatively untainted by the Nazi past—despite the earlier trials of Eichmann and other prominent Austrian Nazis in countries other than Austria itself. The failure to bring former Nazis to trial in the 1970s and 1980s was rooted not only in the influence of Kreisky's particular background and views but also in broader political considerations and a degree of pragmatism. As we have seen, Austrian juries seemed to show more sympathy with the Nazis in the dock than with their dead victims. It would have been an embarrassment to continue acquitting former Nazis in public; it might indeed be better never to bring them to trial in the first place.

The myth of national victimhood was for the first time challenged in the mid-1980s, although even this backfired to some degree. In the course of the 1985–86 presidential election campaign, the wartime record and Nazi past of the presidential candidate and former secretary general of the United Nations from 1971 to 1981, Kurt Waldheim, was revealed.[92] Across the world, this raised issues of complicity and cover-up in Austria, not only bringing Waldheim's own past to public attention but also the compromised careers of so many others. There was a rather different reaction within Austria, however. In much of the popular press and on the part of prominent politicians—including Waldheim himself—there were slurs about the campaign against him allegedly being coordinated by the World Jewish Congress. An international Jewish "lobby" was supposedly to blame for raking up the past and disturbing the peace and for casting aspersions on the honorable war record of Austrian soldiers, who had—so the myth continued—been equally victims of Hitler's war. So while, on the one hand, the Waldheim affair opened up public debates about the Nazi past for the first time since the war, it also almost immediately foreclosed them by antisemitism.

Whatever its ambiguities and ironies, the affair helped to transform international views of Austria. Within the state, too, new ways of thinking about remembrance and responsibility emerged; this gradually led to more significant changes over the following quarter of a century, although always in face of entrenched opposition and lagging well behind the memorial culture that flourished in neighboring Germany. But these shifts proved to be too late as far as bringing former Nazis to justice in the courts was concerned.

The difficulties of putting state-sponsored mass murder on trial were dealt with in quite different ways in each state. The overwhelming majority of sentences on Nazi perpetrators were passed in the first decade after the war, and most of the early cases were those in which the victims had been Germans, the crimes had been committed nearby, and they were committed in relation to issues of current concern. It took far longer to apprehend and attempt to deal with the enormity of the genocide of the Jews. By the 1960s and 1970s, when witnesses were increasingly brought onto the stand to deal with the mass killings in the east, the reliability of witness testimony and memory was increasingly placed under question, while the defendants' pleas of medical incapacity to stand trial seemed ever more plausible. The omens were not favorable.

The willingness of West and East Germans to continue prosecutions from the late 1950s had much to do with their mutual entanglement and international visibility, as well as the determination of key individuals; it was easier for neutral Austria to subside into a comfortable form of relative obscurity, even despite the best attempts of determined Nazi hunters.

Ultimately, the records of justice in the three states proved to be very mixed. Their criminal justice systems were not adequate to the task of reckoning with collective violence on the scale committed by the Nazis and their collaborators. Vested political and economic interests ensured that some areas received greater prominence and attention, while others were quietly excluded from the spotlight. Trials generally served to reinforce rather narrow definitions of what it meant to be a perpetrator. But they also served to bring some of the victims' experiences to wider public attention, and to stimulate an immense amount of research, uncovering material that has arguably proved to be of more use to historians than to the courts.

In none of the Third Reich successor states was it easy to undertake a legal reckoning with Nazi persecution. When we explore selected trials in more detail, the multiple ways in which justice was attempted and distorted in different contexts become manifest. Despite claims to the contrary, and despite the reputation gained in particular by the Federal Republic, the period of the great trials in the 1960s and 1970s was, as we shall see, far from being the "era of the witness" in anything but the most formal sense of the phrase.

10

From Euthanasia to Genocide

Just as the Nazi euthanasia program had preceded the dedicated death camps, so too trials relating to killings of the mentally and physically disabled within the Reich largely preceded public preoccupation with the mass murder of Jews in the East. It took the Eichmann trial in Jerusalem in 1961 to bring genocide to the center of public attention in Germany. The trials for euthanasia murders, meanwhile, revealed many of the characteristics distorting postwar attempts to bring perpetrators to justice.

Early Euthanasia Trials

In all three successor states, initially, the investigation of compulsory sterilization and euthanasia was a priority; and as in other early trials, the victims had been predominantly Germans, the crimes "close to home." Even so, the records of justice were increasingly skewed: as so often, professionals found it easier to evade justice, and it proved easier to convict the "small fry"—carers and assistants—than more senior medical and administrative personnel.

The first of the Nuremberg successor trials, the "Doctors' Trial" (1946–47), had addressed the abuse of medical expertise, including for inhumane experiments on concentration camp prisoners, ending in illness, disfigurement, or even death. But as in other areas, the outcomes of Allied justice were generally short-lived. Herta Oberheuser, for example, who had been sentenced for her experiments in Ravensbrück, was released early and was back in practice for much of the 1950s. This occasioned isolated protests, as did the release of others convicted of multiple murders, but to little effect.[1] The minister for justice in Hesse, who had pardoned another doctor found guilty of mass murder, even argued that criticism of Oberheuser's lenient treatment was out of place, since so many who had committed similar or worse acts were able to practice medicine without being bothered by the law at all.[2]

The Nazi euthanasia program was an area where pre-existing criminal law should have been simple to apply. Even at the time the program was carried out, it was not considered legal. Although Hitler had issued a personal instruction in his capacity as Führer—a "*Führerermächtigung*"—this had no formal legal status and was never translated into legislation.[3] In technical legal terms, euthanasia killings remained a punishable offense even in the Third Reich. The legal profession at the highest levels had even been explicitly made aware of this.[4] A key issue in some cases, however, was whether defendants had been aware of illegality at the time.[5] People even at the lowest levels had been forced to sign a declaration that they would, on pain of severe punishment, keep the killings completely secret. This played a significant role in early trials, particularly in the Soviet zone, with weight attributed to implied awareness of complicity in an illegal act. But as in other areas, the outcomes of trials varied greatly with jurisdiction and political context.

People who had been involved were brought to trial in all three successor states. Three of the six main euthanasia institutions were on East German soil: Brandenburg, Bernburg, and Sonnenstein in Pirna. Two were in what became West Germany: Hadamar and Grafeneck. One, Hartheim, was in Austria. The locations where defendants were resident generally determined where trials were held, rather than the locations where killings had taken place. Severe sentences were passed in the first two years after the war, but legal pursuit of those involved in euthanasia was variable and became less energetic everywhere as time passed.

One review of Austrian euthanasia cases up to 1955 suggests that the people's courts were relatively effective in bringing euthanasia cases to trial. Cases also seem to have elicited sympathy particularly for the children who were victims.[6] Thirteen euthanasia cases in Austria ended with convictions. Among the thirty-three defendants involved, five received death sentences, one faced twenty years in prison, two were given sentences of fifteen years, and one receive twelve years. The other twenty-four defendants were given lower sentences of between two and ten years.

Given Austria's later record, early cases were notable for their severity and focus.[7] But then all went quiet for decades. It was only in 2000, when a younger generation began to confront the Nazi past, that another euthanasia case was instigated, against Dr. Heinrich Gross. Gross had initially been indicted by the people's court in 1948 for murdering children in a Viennese psychiatric hospital during the war, but his sentence was quashed on grounds of a legal technicality. He then enjoyed a successful career as a forensic psychiatrist and neuropathologist, using the brains of murdered children for his research. But in 1975 a survivor unexpectedly blew his cover, and in 1981 he lost a libel case. Even so, it took another two decades until Gross had to stand trial again for his crimes, about which more evidence had now been uncovered. By this time he had reached the age of eighty-three, and the court was prepared to believe his feigned dementia—even though apparent mental incapacity in the courtroom contrasted markedly with the lively intellectual engagement demonstrated in a radio interview Gross gave shortly after leaving the premises. The case was discontinued.[8] This case was rather typical of later Austrian legal confrontations—or lack of them.

Euthanasia cases were also a focal point of early cases in the western and eastern zones of occupied Germany. But striking differences soon emerged. One example is that of Dr. Alfred Leu. In an East German trial in 1946 relating to the relatively small Sachsenberg Clinic near Schwerin, it became clear that Dr. Leu had been responsible for murdering somewhere between seventy and a hundred children. However, Leu had already fled to the West, where, as we shall see in a moment, he was later to stand trial and receive a remarkably sympathetic hearing.

Defendants at all levels of the professional hierarchy were treated quite severely in East Germany. Shortly after the Nuremberg Doctors' Trial, fifteen people were put on trial in 1947 in Dresden, in connection with the Sonnenstein euthanasia institute in Pirna.[9] The proceedings took place in the shadow of a trial of Nazi lawyers and was treated as a high priority by the SED. A political campaign to influence popular opinion inadvertently revealed the persistence of Nazi views and widespread support for the "euthanasia" of mentally and physically disabled patients, with some people arguing that this was more necessary than ever in current conditions of scarcity and hunger. The defense lawyer was even greeted with spontaneous applause when speaking at a public meeting.[10] On the other hand, witnesses who had lost relatives provided heart-rending testimonies, reporting how they had heard that loved ones, recently in good health, had been moved to other institutions, sometimes twice in rapid succession, and how they had then received news of sudden death from an improbable cause, with instructions about obtaining an urn with the ashes.[11] Press coverage of the trial was wide, and public interest lively. Of those found guilty, four were given the death sentence, including Professor Hermann Paul Nitsche, the former director of the Sonnenstein clinic. Nitsche had been a key player in the organization of the T4 and 14f13 "special treatment" programs and, following a stint as Werner Heyde's deputy, had taken over as director of the T4 department in December 1941. He was responsible for continuing to orchestrate killings after the formal end of the official program, and indeed it was he who had suggested Luminal to induce sleepiness and related medical conditions that would be the proximate cause of death. Nitsche was executed in 1948. One of those sentenced to death was Herman Felfe, a menial care assistant and laborer who had played only a subordinate role; he committed suicide before the sentence could be carried out.[12] Seven others were given sentences ranging from three years to life, and three were acquitted.

Others now found themselves facing relatively severe sentences for even tangential involvement in the euthanasia program. The ways in which people at the bottom of the social scale later paid for sometimes unwilling complicity become painfully clear when looking at what are otherwise relatively insignificant cases, including those relating to individuals we have already met.

In the East German district court of Magdeburg in March 1948, in a judgment later upheld on appeal, the building laborer Erich Paul S. and the carer Erna Sch. were convicted for their roles in Bernburg.[13] As defendants go, these were small fry. As we have seen, Erich Paul S. had helped to build the garage for the buses and to cement the brickwork to the killing chamber, while Erna Sch., once she was aware of what was going on, had tried to escape, even getting herself pregnant to find a way out. The East German court was remarkably harsh in judging these two. They were sentenced for having assisted in actions that they had known to be wrong: Erich Paul S. received a five-year term, while Erna Sch., by now a young widow with two small children, was sentenced to three years, of which she had already served two years and four months while under investigation.

Even harsher treatment was meted out by the Magdeburg court in April 1948 to Käthe H.[14] The daughter of a tailor, Käthe H. was, like Erna Sch., relatively ill-educated, with only basic schooling. She worked on the land until the age of seventeen, and also worked for a while as a housekeeper in Berlin. Reaching the age of twenty, she decided she wanted to enter the nursing profession and in 1921 qualified as a care assistant (*Pflegerin*). Again like Erna Sch., in 1940 Käthe H. was called up to do compulsory labor service and ordered to attend a meeting at the Columbus-Haus in Berlin's Potsdamer Platz, where T4 had rented office space for euthanasia cover organizations, including the Charitable Foundation for Care Institutions. Along with other nurses and carers, Käthe H. was sworn to secrecy and had to sign a declaration that, she claimed, she did not even read. She was then taken by bus to southern Germany, where she was put to work in Grafeneck. She had to assist in sending people to death, and she reckoned that, in total, perhaps two thousand people were killed while she was there. She was then transferred to Hadamar, where she estimated that some ten to twelve thousand people were killed.

Käthe H. was sentenced for "crimes against humanity" to fifteen years imprisonment and loss of all civil rights for a further ten years, but was in fact released early, in 1956.[15] Emphasis was placed on awareness that the operation was built on deception. She claimed she had merely obeyed orders, based on Hitler's proclamation. But the judge argued that she knew it must be criminal because so much emphasis was laid on secrecy, and she did not try to get away or refuse; and even if she simply obeyed orders, this did not relieve her of personal responsibility. The only mitigating fact was that she had no previous convictions.[16]

Similar sentences on ordinary people who had found themselves in low-level positions carrying out crimes ordered by others were relatively harsh. And despite the severe sentences meted out by the courts, members of the local community often appeared to be sympathetic toward defendants. Former Nazi doctors often relatively quickly turned into supposedly good antifascists, supported by neighbors and even local functionaries.[17] Moreover, it was not only local communities that rallied around physicians. Over time, it became increasingly embarrassing to the state to discover significant individuals who had escaped justice. Some prominent medical professionals who had been involved in the euthanasia program were later given protection and apparently allowed, even in some cases helped, to maintain a low profile.[18] The GDR in this way retained its public reputation for stringent sentencing and severe punishment of known offenders and kept as quiet as possible about others.

Developments in West Germany swung in a rather different direction. In Berlin in 1946 death sentences had been pronounced on Dr. Hilde Wernicke and nurse Helene Wieczorek, who were found guilty of killing some six hundred patients in the Meseritz-Obrawalde mental hospital. They were found to have killed in a "malicious" manner, out of "base motives"—in other words, murder in the sense of section 211 of the German penal code as amended in 1941. Defense arguments that they had obeyed superior orders and only wanted the best for the patients were not accepted; their Nazi sympathies and readiness to follow instructions, even with some initial reluctance on the part of Wernicke, were seen as evidence that they had internalized Nazi commands, which they had "made their own." Murder at that time still carried the death penalty, and the two women were duly executed in January 1947.[19] This earned them the dubious honor of being the only two women ever executed in West Germany for their role in Nazi crimes.[20] But things soon began to change with respect to the treatment in West Germany of euthanasia perpetrators.

In the Eichberg trial of December 1946 in Frankfurt, the infamous Dr. Friedrich Mennecke had to answer for his actions in the T4 program, which included sending 2,262 patients to the Hadamar killing center and condemning around 2,500 people to death in the 14f13 selections documented in such detail in his letters to his wife, as well as killings undertaken in the Eichberg clinic.[21] His defense of having been an unwilling participant was undercut by the evidence of his letters, overflowing with enthusiasm for the cause. The court carefully considered both Mennecke's state of mind and that of other defendants. Mennecke himself escaped his death sentence by dying while in custody on January 28, 1947, allegedly from pre-existing illness, more likely a suicide with assistance from his wife, who had visited him some two days before his death. An emphasis on subjective states of mind did not entirely serve to exonerate other defendants who pleaded they were only following orders or had sought to balance conflicting duties, but the tracks were laid for the later lenient sentences and acquittals that rapidly became characteristic in German courts.

The 1947 Hadamar trial in Frankfurt followed an earlier trial of Hadamar personnel in an American military tribunal in Wiesbaden in 1945 and took place at the same time as the American Doctors' Trial in Nuremberg. The American Wiesbaden trial had been specifically concerned with the killing at Hadamar in 1944–45 of some 476 Soviet and Polish forced laborers who were suffering from tuberculosis, since the nearly fifteen thousand murders of German citizens in the T4 program at Hadamar could only be tried by a German court.[22] In the American proceedings in 1945, three defendants received the death sentence, one a life sentence, and the other three lengthy terms of imprisonment. In the 1947 Frankfurt trial under German auspices, the situation regarding participation in T4 was explored in detail, with fine distinctions made between the roles of medical personnel, care assistants, technical assistants, and administrative staff. It was confirmed that people could have refused to participate in the killing process without any dire personal consequences. Yet despite the care taken in the analysis, the sentences were a great deal more lenient than those meted out by the Americans two years earlier. Two of the defendants—Dr. Hans Bodo Gorgass and Dr. Adolph Wahlmann—were initially sentenced to death, having been found guilty of at least one thousand and nine hundred murders, respectively; but these sentences were commuted to life sentences, and, like so many others, they were in fact released early, Wahlmann in 1952, and Gorgass in 1958.[23] Other defendants received much milder terms of imprisonment, ranging from two and half to eight years for nurses who were accessories to murder. Members of the administrative staff were acquitted.

In 1947, the euthanasia perpetrators from Hadamar were the last in western Germany to receive relatively severe sentences. From then on, the situation for perpetrators became far easier. In 1949, twenty-seven people who had been involved in euthanasia activities in Württemberg were investigated, including nineteen people associated with the killing center at Grafeneck, where some ten thousand had been murdered. Of the eight actually brought to court, only three received sentences, of which the longest was five years.[24] West German judges subsequently showed ever-greater leniency in sentencing, and apparently ever-greater understanding of murderous professionals; a Hamburg court in 1949 even opined that "the destruction of completely mentally dead individuals and of 'empty husks of humanity'" was not necessarily "absolutely and a priori immoral."[25] It was not until the later 1960s and early 1970s that such justifications provoked wide public criticism. Even then, however, the West German authorities made it relatively easy for those involved in euthanasia killings to evade justice.

There was a significant development in legal arguments in West German courts.[26] In the early postwar period, the notion that ignorance was no defense was upheld; but over time this ceased to be the case. On this view, if people had not at the time realized that murdering people with mental and physical disabilities was against the law, they were simply misguided, suffering from what was termed "confusion about what was forbidden" (neatly encapsulated in a useful German compound word, Verbotsirrtum). This defense was frequently applied to people in lower positions in the hierarchy—nurses, administrative assistants—helping to exonerate them on grounds of either lower intelligence or lower educational levels.

At the same time, for those in more elevated positions who would have been fully aware of the murderous character of their actions, a new defense was developed: that of a "conflict of duties" (again giving rise to a useful word, *Pflichtenkollision*). Moreover, those in such a position could argue that they had remained there in order to prevent "something worse"; it would, for example, assist their defense to show that, by remaining in post, they had managed to spare other staff from being involved or had marginally reduced the numbers being killed.[27] In what has been described as "jurisprudence based on emotions" (*Gefühlsjurisprudenz*), with an emphasis on the subjectivity of the accused, many defendants could now argue that they had been "inwardly opposed" to killings and had only carried on as unwilling accomplices rather than true perpetrators.[28] As a result, they would not be convicted of murder.

Examples from West German trials concerning the murder of children at the clinic at Eglfing-Haar, near Munich, provide a marked contrast to comparable cases in East Germany, and also illuminate the way in which West German courts became ever more sympathetic to defendants within a very few years. In 1948, three nurses—known in the trial record as "D.," "L." and "S."—were put on trial.[29] They had given massive overdoses of a sedative, Luminal, to sick children on at least 120 occasions, leading to death. When "D."—Sister Deutlmoser—discovered what the white powder was, she refused to administer it and confessed to her priest, Joseph Radecker, precipitating his mission to inform Cardinal Faulhaber of Munich in the forlorn hope of terminating the murder program. Even so, Deutlmoser continued to hand the powder to others to administer. Children generally died within two to three days of starting this "treatment"; some lasted as long as five days before they died.

The nurses had been asked to sign a paper affirming their duty to keep silent about this and registering that it would be punishable by death if they spoke about what they were doing. However, they only signed this paper some six months after they had started administering the fatal doses of Luminal, and it would have possible to ask to switch to other duties at this time. They nevertheless continued to administer the poison to children, knowing its deadly consequences, from 1940 to 1945. They were judged to have been accomplices to murder because commands came from above; they were not personally motivated to kill and did not benefit from the deaths, nor did they kill in a "malicious" manner. Deutlmoser had also, it was claimed, played a role in letting the outside world know about what was going on.[30] The three nurses were not Nazi Party members, nor were they, in the view of the court, particularly inclined to support Nazism. They combined recognition of doing something wrong (and so could not plead ignorance of wrongdoing) with the claim that they thought this was humane because the children were incurably ill and suffering. In defense of the nurses it was pointed out that their former superior, Dr. Hermann Pfannmüller, the director of the Eglfing-Haar clinic, was "a particularly strong personality" in face of whom "everyone in the institution trembled," and they had therefore believed they had no choice but to obey his directions.[31] The nurses were each sentenced to two and a half years imprisonment for their offenses—including Deutlmoser.

At the time of this trial, their former superior, Pfannmüller, a committed Nazi who had first joined the Nazi Party in 1922 and renewed his membership in 1933, was allegedly not medically fit to stand trial.[32] Pfannmüller, as we have seen, had proudly demonstrated the efficacy of his methods of killing children to psychology students; he had also personally initiated the starvation program and established the "hunger houses" for adults, presiding over these throughout the war years.[33] One might think, then, that once Pfannmüller was deemed fit to stand trial, he might be found to have had a far greater share of guilt for the deaths of children in the institution under his care. But this was not the case.

Pfannmüller was brought to stand trial in Munich in March 1951. By now, in the West German climate of clemency, attitudes had changed from when, just five years earlier, Wernicke and Wieczorek had been sentenced to death. Extraordinarily, the Munich court found that Pfannmüller had not acted "maliciously," since the children had been successfully deceived: the fatal powder was sprinkled into meals and delivered at regular mealtimes, and they had died a "gentle" death. On this argument, killing vulnerable victims without their being aware of the process is not really "murder": the more perfect the crime in deceiving the victim, so that all proceeds smoothly, the less it is really a crime. Moreover, it was for what many people continued to think was a good cause.

The Munich court more or less repeated Nazi reasoning, commenting that Pfannmüller did not act from "base motives," because euthanasia was a worldview that, they claimed, still had well-respected supporters. Despite all the evidence of Pfannmüller's active involvement in the Nazi movement for more than two decades, dating back to long before Hitler came to power, the court found that he was merely an "accomplice" of others and therefore supposedly not acting of his own free will. Accordingly, the court found Pfannmüller, who had been responsible for more than three thousand deaths, not guilty of murder, but only of the lesser crimes of manslaughter and being an accessory to manslaughter. His initial sentence of five years was subsequently reduced on appeal and then further reduced to a mere two years to include the time he had already spent in internment, and he was deemed medically unfit to serve the rest of his sentence.[34] He lived a further ten years and died on April 10, 1961.

The remarkable case of Dr. Alfred Leu—the physician responsible for the deaths of up to one hundred children in Sachsenberg, who had initially evaded justice by fleeing to the West—further illustrates the disturbingly understanding approach that developed in West Germany toward those responsible for euthanasia murders. In October 1951 Leu was brought to trial in Cologne.[35] The court found that the killings for which Leu was responsible did not constitute cases of murder but rather the lesser offense of "aiding and abetting murder." The jury furthermore accepted Leu's argument—widespread among former Nazis—that he had only participated in order to prevent something worse. He claimed that he had been instructed to dispose of some 180 children in total and that someone else in his place would have killed the whole group, so by killing "only" around half the children—first seventy, then another twenty or thirty—he had in fact managed to "protect" or even "save" others.

The verdict became even more favorable to Leu in a second set of proceedings that came to judgment in December 1953. The court accepted Leu's claims and even seems to have shared his views, almost justifying such murders. It found that his killings only constituted manslaughter or aiding and abetting manslaughter. His actions were, in the court's view, further mitigated by his claim that he had attempted to sabotage the killing program by continued participation in it. What "sabotage" might be involved in actively supporting a continuing program of murder was not clarified. The court nevertheless believed Leu and his colleagues that he had only adopted the appearance of an enthusiastic Nazi and energetic supporter of euthanasia as a "disguise" in order to carry out this "sabotage" better. This extraordinary verdict seemed to contradict all notions of empirical proof and provided evidence of continuing sympathies with Nazi views in the early 1950s.

What of others who had played key roles in the euthanasia program? Professor Werner Catel, who in 1939 had helped to open the floodgates by requesting Hitler's permission to murder a malformed child, the infant Kretschmar, was never brought to trial at all.[36] He did not have to go into hiding or live under a false identity—nor did he change or disguise his views on "euthanasia," even publishing a book justifying his views.[37] An extensive interview with Catel, giving him the opportunity to expound his views on the "humane" character of killing physically and mentally disabled children, was carried out by the West German weekly news magazine *Der Spiegel* in 1964, creating further publicity and lending a degree of credibility to Catel's position.[38]

Horst Schumann, as we have seen, had first been director of the Grafeneck euthanasia center and had then taken responsibility for the Sonnenstein institute. Here, as well as killing patients with mental and physical disabilities, Schumann was also involved in gassing concentration camp prisoners in the 14f13 action, which made continuing use of the gassing facilities after the formal termination of the euthanasia program. Subsequently, Schumann carried out painful, disfiguring, and frequently fatal experiments in Auschwitz, specializing in sterilization by burning through excessive use of X-rays and castration. Although initially captured by the Americans, Schumann was released and practiced as a doctor in West Germany until he was recognized in 1951. The East Germans issued a warrant for his arrest, but he was nevertheless somehow allowed to escape from West Germany and spent time as a ship's doctor (even renewing his passport in Japan under his own name), working in Egypt, and as head of a hospital in the Sudan—where he was recognized by an Auschwitz survivor—before eventually being extradited from Ghana and returned to West Germany. But with the tardiness of the German police and the support of medical colleagues, Schumann successfully evaded justice. He used his medical knowledge to produce increased measurements of his own blood pressure, arguing that this caused headaches and confusion, and faked serious illness by swallowing some of his own blood, then forcing himself to vomit on the way to court. Taken in by the alarming symptom of blood-flecked vomit and possible internal hemorrhage, the court pronounced him unfit to stand trial. In July 1972 Schumann was released from custody and lived quietly in Frankfurt with his wife until his natural death in May 1983. In the view of the indefatigable journalist Ernst Klee, Schumann had been saved by the collaboration or foot-dragging of the German legal and police forces who had given him ample time to be tipped off and escape when he was first pursued in 1951, and by professional colleagues who wrote the medical reports on him at the time of his trial in 1970–71.[39]

Changing Perspectives

Few of the leading lights of the Nazi euthanasia program were ever brought to trial. Even so, in the 1960s there were changes in public reactions in West Germany. This was a time of generational conflicts and political shifts, with the growth of the student movement and "extra-parliamentary opposition" during the 1966–69 Grand Coalition between the Christian Democratic Union and Social Democratic Party (led by Chancellor Kurt Georg Kiesinger, a former Nazi party member who had joined in 1933). Younger generations as well as left-liberal media elites and opinion formers were becoming increasingly critical of the widespread silencing of the past. One has to wonder, then, whether what is truly noteworthy is the rising tide of critical opinion or the continuing failures of West German judges and juries to bring individuals who had engaged in murder to any kind of justice, even a quarter of a century after the end of the Third Reich. But the balance of opinion was clearly tipping.

In 1967, a Frankfurt court passed verdicts of not guilty on doctors Heinrich Bunke, Aquilin Ullrich, and Klaus Endruweit, with whom Dr. Kurt Borm was also initially accused. Ullrich had worked in the Brandenburg euthanasia center; he recommended Endruweit, whom he knew from student days, to Werner Heyde at T4, and Endruweit also found a position working with Horst Schumann and Borm in Sonnenstein; Bunke worked in both Brandenburg and Bernburg. Using by now well-rehearsed defenses, the defendants claimed they had believed in the underlying legal and scientific basis of euthanasia, based on the book by Karl Binding and Alfred Hoche, published in 1920, *Die Freigabe der Vernichtung lebensunwerten Lebens* (Permitting the destruction of life unworthy of life). They claimed further that they had thought the secrecy surrounding killings was due to wartime circumstances, that the killings were humane, and that patients neither knew what was coming, nor did they suffer. As in other trials, the defendants were perceived not as convinced Nazis but just "weak characters." The verdict of not guilty was received with spontaneous applause from members of the public who had been watching the trial in the courtroom.[40]

Despite this public display of sympathy with the defendants, the federal court reopened the case and returned it for another jury trial in 1970. All three defendants now claimed they were unfit to stand trial because of the stress it occasioned. Despite their alleged incapacity to stand trial, they all continued to practice as doctors over the next decade, Bunke until 1979, Ullrich until February 1984, and Endruweit until March 1984.[41] In May 1987 the case was again addressed, but now only in relation to Ullrich and Bunke. Bunke was now found guilty of aiding and abetting murder in at least eleven thousand murders in Brandenburg and Bernburg between mid-August 1940 and August 1941, and Ullrich was found guilty of aiding and abetting murder in at least 4,500 murders in Brandenburg between April 1940 and August 1940. They were each sentenced to four years imprisonment, revised down to three years in December 1988. The case against Endruweit was closed in 1990 because he was still deemed unfit to stand trial.[42] This case was in many respects typical of the evasions of former Nazis and the tardiness of the legal system; by the time people were brought to trial, and even despite the changing wider climate, it was almost impossible to impose an appropriate sentence.

Meanwhile, in 1972 Borm was put on trial in Frankfurt. He had been responsible for killing 4,696 people in Sonnenstein and Bernburg between December 1940 and August 1941 as well as playing a role in the central T4 organization. A committed Nazi, he claimed he had believed in the legality of the acts and that in adopting an assumed name, "Dr. Storm," and maintaining secrecy, he had been "only obeying orders." Borm's claims were believed, and he was found not guilty. In an attempted revision of this judgment in 1974, the federal court came to the view that the evidence on Borm's state of mind was not conclusive, but even if this was left open, he could at most have been found guilty of aiding and abetting manslaughter (*Totschlag*), for which he could no longer be prosecuted.

Both the handling of this case and the ultimate findings were strongly criticized in an article in the *Süddeutsche Zeitung* of March 22, 1974, as well as in a letter to the *Frankfurter Allgemeine Zeitung* on June 10, 1974, signed by a number of West German public intellectuals, including well-known voices of the conscience of the nation such as Gräfin von Dönhoff, Günter Grass, Martin Walser, and Heinrich Böll.[43] A weighty oppositional voice was finally being raised, protesting against the inadequacies of judicial reckoning with the past. But Borm himself continued to practice undisturbed by his past, and died only in 2001.

In the GDR, the prominent state prosecutor Friedrich Karl Kaul drew Nazi euthanasia murders to East German attention in a book published in 1973, precipitated by his role as a lawyer bringing charges in West German cases against individuals involved in the T4 program. Kaul engaged in critical discussion of the 1967 trial of Ullrich, Bunke, and Endruweit and of the 1967 trial of Dr. Gerhard Bohne, Reinhold Vorberg, Dietrich Allers, and Adolf Gustav Kaufmann, where his own legal interventions on behalf of the prosecution were largely unsuccessful. Kaul's book presented a compelling critique of the lenience of the West German courts, which accepted feeble excuses about supposed ignorance of wrongdoing, were unduly sympathetic to pleas of being too ill to stand trial, and had a tendency to see individuals who had murdered thousands of patients as merely "accomplices" to be given accordingly light sentences.[44]

The Leipzig-based theologian Kurt Nowak also addressed the topic, but from a different perspective, being primarily concerned with the roles of the Protestant and Catholic Churches. His book on Nazi policies of euthanasia and compulsory sterilization was published in the GDR in 1977, and even engaged some attention when it was republished a year later in West Germany.[45]

The wider political context was significant, however, in ensuring that these initiatives at first remained without resonance in the GDR. Despite the isolated efforts of historians of medicine and individuals with an interest in local and regional history, sensitive archival materials were largely inaccessible. In West Germany, conditions were somewhat more favorable to research, but it was still not easy to press this subject There were significant individual interventions in the 1980s, particularly by Ernst Klee; his determination to name and shame was buttressed by vivid accounts of "medical" practices and the fatal consequences for the victims.[46] Klee's politically and morally engaged depictions of the crimes of the medical profession, based on extensive scouring of archival sources, stood in marked contrast to the rather dry tone of many academic contributions at this time. This was true, too, of the work of the journalist and political scientist Götz Aly, who devoted extensive energy to the subject of euthanasia, addressing what was still considered a taboo topic. In West Germany, despite the growth of research, there was a continuing wall of silence around these issues.

The changing of attitudes in the 1970s and 1980s came too late as far as legal trials were concerned. For at least the first two decades after the war, and in many cases well beyond, former Nazi doctors had been able to turn into good postwar citizens. In both East and West Germany, they were frequently supported by sympathetic neighbors and local dignitaries. The limitations of the legal system were buttressed mightily by the protections afforded by members of the wider society.

Similarly, the lawyers who had condoned euthanasia, and others who had been involved at higher levels, also evaded justice. Among his many concerns about the Nazi past (notably the capture of Eichmann and the Auschwitz trial), Hessian attorney general Fritz Bauer was determined to bring senior lawyers to trial for their knowledge of and assistance in the Nazi euthanasia program. Had he been successful, there might have been further implications, including recognition of those murdered in the euthanasia program as "victims of Nazi persecution"—which was still not recognized at the time of German unification in 1990.[47] But Bauer, worn out and disheartened by the continuing fight to gain recognition of the need for a legal reckoning with the past and exposed to numerous personal attacks, including a campaign of pestering phone calls throughout the night, died prematurely in 1968.[48] Bauer's attempt to put senior lawyers on trial for having condoned the euthanasia program while fully aware of its criminality was quietly abandoned by his successor in office, Horst Gauf.[49]

Shifts in Focus

The changing public response was in part related to generational shifts. Meanwhile, however, there was also a significant shift in what crimes were at the center of attention. German trials in the early years after the war had concentrated predominantly on crimes where the victims were also Germans. But from the late 1950s, increasing attention was paid to crimes committed across Europe, and against the largest victim group of Nazi policies of mass murder: the Jews.

In 1958, ten people who had been involved in the Einsatzgruppen unit known as Tilsit were brought to trial in the city of Ulm in West Germany. They had been one of the first units to engage in mass killing of civilians on the Eastern Front, following the invasion of the Soviet Union in late June 1941. While the Einsatzgruppen had been the subject of one of the Allies' Nuremberg successor trials, this trial came about largely by chance.[50] The former police chief in Memel (now Klaipėda, Lithuania), Bernhard Fischer-Schweder, who was responsible for thousands of murders in the area, had been "denazified" after the war and was quietly living in West Germany under an assumed and slightly camouflaged name, Bernd Fischer. From 1955 he had been working as director of a refugee shelter near Ulm. When his identity was discovered, he was asked to resign. Finding it hard to obtain another job, Fischer-Schweder—unfortunately for him, as it turned out— filed a law case requesting reinstatement in public service. Reading about this case in a newspaper report, a survivor from the Memel area identified him and brought a suit against him for the Einsatzgruppen murders. Fischer-Schweder was investigated, and the case escalated to encompass ten former Gestapo and SS officers charged with massacres. Fischer-Schweder himself was found guilty and given a ten-year sentence; he died in prison of a pulmonary embolism in 1960.

The Ulm case was significant for bringing to public attention the atrocities perpetrated by the specialized killing squads on the Eastern Front, although the trial never gained the media publicity of the big concentration camp trials. It was also significant in other ways. It had become evident that relying on ordinary citizens to identify former perpetrators and file prosecutions was hardly the best way of systematically investigating state-ordained crimes or successfully bringing cases to trial. A more centralized pursuit of perpetrators was inaugurated in 1958 in the Ludwigsburg Central Office, with Erwin Schüle, who had been the prosecuting attorney in the Ulm case, becoming its first director.[51] Schüle had himself been a member of both the SA and the Nazi Party, and had served in compromising circumstances on the Russian front. Rumors about Schüle's own involvement in specific acts of violence—allegedly hanging a youth for stealing chocolate and shooting a couple of innocent people in cold blood—were energetically spread by the Soviet Union and the GDR.[52] In autumn 1966, following investigations, Schüle returned to his former work as a senior state prosecutor in Stuttgart, and Adalbert Rückerl took over as director of the Ludwigsburg Central Office.

Tasked with coordinating efforts across the regional states (*Länder*) of the Federal Republic, Ludwigsburg's relatively small office was not hampered only by its limited complement of staff. It was initially also restricted by a relatively narrow understanding or definition of Nazi crimes and by official unwillingness to gain evidence from Eastern bloc countries at a time when West Germany adhered to the so-called Hallstein doctrine, under which it refused to have formal relations with countries that recognized the GDR, reinforced by a wider mentality of anticommunism and distrust and exacerbated by GDR campaigns. A further hindrance in the pursuit of justice was the persistence of organizations assisting former Nazis, such as Stille Hilfe, as well as informal networks (*Seilschaften*) among Nazi sympathizers. These included legal officials and police officers, who on occasion went about their work slowly and in some cases warned suspects in advance of an arrest, effectively assisting them in evading justice.[53] There was at this time an active community of common experience on the perpetrator side—however inchoate and difficult to define this may be—that was willing to assist people who were under threat of investigation and prosecution for crimes committed under the Nazi regime.

Even so, the foundation of the Ludwigsburg Central Office marked a step forward in the pursuit of those involved in Nazi crimes. Over the following decades, assiduous investigations by the Ludwigsburg team amassed an extraordinary quantity of material that would prove invaluable to historians, even if only a tiny part of this material was actually deployed in court. Meanwhile, in the GDR, too, the pursuit of perpetrators was gaining in significance, with an increasingly centralized system developed in the 1960s under the Ministry for State Security. This was not only precipitated by the spate of antisemitic incidents in West Germany in 1959–60 and related international considerations but was also given significant impetus by the Eichmann trial.[54]

In the 1960s, the horizons in both East and West Germany widened dramatically, moving beyond the more parochial focus of the early trials. Yet as the primary focus shifted to the extermination of the Jews, the early confrontation with complicity at home—in denunciations, in Kristallnacht, even in the euthanasia cases—was partially lost, and the notion of what it meant to be a perpetrator shifted again.

The Significance of Evil: The Eichmann Trial

More than fifteen years after the end of the war, with the prosecution of Adolf Eichmann in Jerusalem in 1961, the distinctive nature of Hitler's planned genocide of the Jews finally came to center stage in the courts. But it took the voices of the victims, magnified massively through the prism of the Eichmann trial, to bring this to the attention of people in the lands of the perpetrators.

Fritz Bauer, whose tip-off to the Israeli secret service (the Mossad), led to Eichmann's arrest in Argentina, actually organized this to ensure that Eichmann would be tried in Israel and not in Germany, where Bauer feared the defendant would get far too sympathetic a hearing.[55] If the Nuremberg trials were seen as "victors' justice," then—even a decade and a half later—many Germans saw Eichmann's trial as a form of "victims' justice."

This trial proved to be a turning point, initiating the first public discussions of the Holocaust on a global scale. It allowed victims to speak, giving a public hearing to people who had suffered and fought in intolerable circumstances against their own oppression and the slaughter of their friends, neighbors, and families. And it was the first to put someone on trial for the crime of genocide, a crime carried out on a massive scale by the Nazis but not defined until in the Genocide Convention of 1948. Using the Israeli Nazi and Nazi Collaborators Law introduced in 1950, Eichmann was tried for "crimes against the Jewish people." He was found guilty of collaborating with others in "implementing a plan which was known as the 'Final Solution of the Jewish Question' with an intent to exterminate the Jewish People"—a specification of the more general expression in Article 2 of the Geneva Convention referring to the "intent to destroy, in whole or in part, a national, ethnical, racial or religious group."[56]

The proceedings were used not merely to try Eichmann but also to play a broader, educative role: they were intended by the presiding judge, Justice Moshe Landau (who was himself born in the then German city of Danzig, now the Polish Gdańsk), and the attorney general, Gideon Hausner (born in the then Galician city of Lemberg, now Lviv in Ukraine), to highlight the suffering of victims and to elicit among Israelis a sense of identification with the suffering of the Jewish people, whether or not they had themselves been personally affected by the Holocaust. In his opening remarks at the trial, Hausner spoke passionately of the way in which he was not there just as an individual but was rather speaking in the name of the six million dead:

> When I stand before you here, Judges of Israel, to lead the Prosecution of Adolf Eichmann, I am not standing alone. With me are six million accusers. But they cannot rise to their feet and point an accusing finger towards him who sits in the dock and cry: "I accuse." For their ashes are piled up on the hills of Auschwitz and the fields of Treblinka, and are strewn in the forests of Poland. Their graves are scattered throughout the length and breadth of Europe. Their blood cries out, but their voice is not heard. Therefore I will be their spokesman and in their name I will unfold the awesome indictment.[57]

There could hardly be a more resounding enunciation of a sense of identification with the wider community of the persecuted who had not survived to seek justice for themselves.

Hausner sought to encapsulate the full significance of historical events. It was more than just Eichmann on trial, and just as Hausner spoke on behalf of the persecuted, so too Eichmann's trial was to show to the world the enormity of what had happened:

> At the dawn of history, there were examples of wars of extermination, when one nation assaulted another with intent to destroy, when, in the storm of passion and battle, peoples were slaughtered, massacred or exiled. But only in our generation has a nation attacked an entire defenceless and peaceful population, men and women, grey-beards, children and infants, incarcerated them behind electrified fences, imprisoned them in concentration camps, and resolved to destroy them utterly.
>
> Murder has been with the human race since the days when Cain killed Abel; it is no novel phenomenon. But we have had to wait till this twentieth century to witness with our own eyes a new kind of murder: not the result of the momentary ebullition of passion or the darkening of the soul, but of a calculated decision and painstaking planning; not through the evil design of an individual, but through a mighty criminal conspiracy involving thousands; not against one victim whom an assassin may have decided to destroy, but against an entire nation.[58]

This was, then, a trial of momentous importance. If the Nuremberg Trials had sought to present to the world and record for posterity the sheer scope of Nazi criminality—framing it in terms of crimes against humanity in general—without specifically singling out the treatment of the Jews, the Eichmann trial redefined Nazi criminality precisely in terms of the mass murder of the Jews.

The Eichmann trial was critical in bringing this into the international spotlight, after a decade of near neglect.[59] It was also significant in determining the parameters of debates for decades to come.

The Eichmann trial was pathbreaking in its use of survivor testimony. This was deployed not only to establish guilt but also, and perhaps even more important, to make the Jewish catastrophe vivid, to provide images and stories that brought home its scale and its human significance to the world. Witnesses were allowed to roam widely, telling their own stories, going off script; displays of emotion were common, with one witness—Yehiel De-Nur, who published under the pen name Ka-Tsetnik 135633, his Auschwitz number—memorably fainting in court. The Eichmann trial was a breakthrough in terms of using survivor testimony to tell the world about the enormity of what happened.

Key themes emerged, including notable accounts of bravery among the ghetto fighters and the significance of resistance, as in the testimony of the former partisan leader Abba Kovner. As a young poet and member of the Vilna (Vilnius) Jewish youth group, Kovner had written the first manifesto encouraging Jews to rise in armed resistance, proclaiming on December 31, 1941, that "Hitler plans to destroy all the Jews of Europe," but announcing defiantly, "We will not be led like sheep to the slaughter."[60] Kovner was also passionate about seeking justice and retribution, including the proposal of mass poisoning of German water supplies.[61]

But what many took away from the trial was not so much these accounts of heroism, suffering, and the impact on victims as Hannah Arendt's catchphrase about the "banality of evil." Arendt's controversial commentary on the trial raised key issues and served to reframe views of both perpetrators and victims.[62] Arendt focused attention on "desk perpetrators"—those who gave orders and played a role in the administration of the "final solution." Her comments on the trial were rooted in a historical analysis heavily indebted to the work of Raul Hilberg (whose scholarship, he claimed, she did not adequately acknowledge).[63] And Arendt's perceptions may have been overhasty, failing to understand fully the significance of Eichmann's self-representation: the gray image he presented to court as a conscious defense strategy seems to have influenced her views, but it also served to conceal the more enthusiastic character of his ideology and actions.[64] And while there is indeed considerable mileage in exploring the significance of bureaucratic cogs in the machine, giving credence to views that no one was really guilty, this did not apply to people at Eichmann's level. Furthermore, Arendt's critique of the role of the Jewish councils reinforced the widespread view that Jews had passively collaborated in their own demise. At the same time, her scathing comments on the alleged passivity of most Jews and the compromised role of the Jewish councils deflected attention from the true perpetrators and cast the victims in a highly unsympathetic light, giving oxygen to the flames and igniting further controversies that continue to this day.

Even so, Eichmann's trial gave significant impetus to the process of confronting the past in the successor states to the Third Reich. Intense interest was aroused when the news first broke about his arrest, and the trial itself was followed avidly in the German press. Moreover, extensive coverage in the newspapers ensured that searching questions were raised, and reports brought the Nazi crimes against the Jews into the public spotlight in ways that could no longer be reversed. Despite voices raised in some quarters that the younger generation should be spared a confrontation with these disturbing issues, the silence and repression of the 1950s was well and truly over.[65]

Reactions to the trial in West Germany, as far as these can be measured, present insight into popular opinion just before the start of the first Frankfurt Auschwitz trial. The Gallup polling organization asked the same question in four countries—Great Britain, the United States, Switzerland, and Germany—as to whether Eichmann should have been handed over to a German court rather than tried in Israel. In the United States 6 percent of those questioned agreed that Germans should have been able to try Eichmann, while both in Britain and in Switzerland only 3 percent of people thought this would have been a good idea. By contrast, fully one-quarter of Germans thought they should have been able to put him on trial.[66] He would almost certainly have received a more sympathetic hearing and indubitably a more lenient sentence in Germany—as both he and Fritz Bauer, who we have seen was instrumental in his capture by the Israelis, were well aware.

A further question in the Gallup Poll was whether people thought it was "good" or "bad" that the world was being reminded of the horrors of the National Socialist concentration camps more than fifteen years after the end of the war. Only one-third of Germans (34 percent) thought this reminder was a good thing, compared to 56 percent in Britain, 62 percent in the United States, and 70 percent in Switzerland.[67] The discussions in West Germany were widespread and covered a range of views, but nevertheless betrayed a significant level of continuing sympathy for Nazism. It even seems to be the case that, following a decline in the mid-1950s, there was a rise in the percentage of Germans wanting to put an end to trials for Nazi crimes: at the beginning of the 1950s a majority had been in favor of putting an end to such trials; in 1958, the year of the Ulm trial, only 34 percent wanted this, but during the Eichmann trial it went back up to a slim majority of 53 percent.[68]

One Protestant churchman, Ernst Wilm, aptly summarized contemporary discussions in April 1961. He observed that many people were saying that if Germans acknowledged their guilt, Israel would demand even more by way of compensation.[69] Others were repeating widespread defenses: it could not be true, it was all enemy propaganda, one could not burn so many corpses, that was technically impossible; Nuremberg had been just a matter of victors' justice. Or they advanced more utilitarian arguments: if we cannot deny it, we should at least not talk about it; for the sake of the people as a whole one should not keep mentioning the misdeeds of just a few criminals; above all, children should not be told about it, in order to preserve the honor of the nation. And besides, others too had committed comparable crimes, including the British bombing of Dresden and the actions of the Russians in the eastern territories of the Fatherland. Finally, Wilms reported, people were asking how they could have known about the murder of the Jews and claiming that they could not have even guessed; moreover, they were saying, how could they have believed this possible of those who were in government, people of their own nation whom they trusted?[70]

The rather parochial focus of early trials in both East and West Germany began to be displaced. This was in part inevitable, given the more minor character of offenses, attracting lesser sentences, for which prosecutions could no longer be brought. But it also entailed a wider change in prevailing views. The Eichmann trial both inaugurated a shift in focus to genocide and marked the emergence of the "era of the victim" in the decades when a conception of the Holocaust began to take hold.

Pressure from key individuals and groups was central to legal reckonings, and the testimony of victims—however crucial to the outcomes of trials— was repeatedly challenged. But from the 1960s, the voices of victims could no longer be ignored: survivors now took a central role in legal confrontations with the Nazi past. Even so, unlike in later decades, their voices were not as yet widely venerated; this was an era of continued bitter contestation.

11

Major Concentration
Camp Trials

Auschwitz and Beyond

Held in Frankfurt from 1963 to 1965, the Auschwitz trial has come to symbolize West Germany's attempts to "come to terms with its past."[1] Some have seen it as being at the heart of German reckoning.[2] Often called the "first Frankfurt Auschwitz trial" (to avoid confusion with other trials involving Auschwitz personnel), this trial has assumed a prominent place alongside the Nuremberg and Eichmann trials, effectively overshadowing other trials in the public consciousness. This is in part because of the significance of Auschwitz itself and the extent and horror of the crimes there that were revealed in the course of the trial. It was also because the instigators of the trial specifically intended it to put the whole system of mass extermination on trial rather than merely a few individuals. In this sense it echoes the Eichmann trial—and this is scarcely surprising, given the instrumental role Hessian attorney general Fritz Bauer played in both. But viewed in a broader context, the historical verdict must be somewhat qualified.

The first Frankfurt Auschwitz trial was clearly a turning point in public awareness of Nazi policies of mass extermination. The trial stimulated intense media interest and public debate, polarizing opinion. Among members of a younger generation it precipitated intense involvement with the past, playing a role in the emergent generational clashes of the later 1960s. Moreover, it stimulated detailed historical research, particularly on the part of scholars at the Munich Institute of Contemporary History (Institut für Zeitgeschichte), four of whom produced extensive expert reports specifically for the trial.[3]

Interest in the Holocaust had not up to then been widespread among non-Jewish historians. The Holocaust was of course present in Israel as a live issue even before the Eichmann trial, though research there focused primarily on questions regarding Jewish leadership, resistance, and everyday life, rather than on perpetrator policies, as in Anglo-American and German Holocaust scholarship.[4] Interest in studying Nazi persecution of the Jews was, however, not widely shared even in Eastern or Western Europe or North America in the 1950s and 1960s. Whether or not they were themselves Jewish, scholars who wrote about the Holocaust—including the Austrian-born American historian Raul Hilberg and the East German Helmut Eschwege—experienced initial difficulties in publishing their work.[5] The Frankfurt Auschwitz trial therefore played a role in establishing a place for the Holocaust also among non-Jewish historians and wider reading publics.

As far as any legal reckoning is concerned, however, the Auschwitz trial stands as a measure not of the success of judicial confrontations with the Nazi past but rather of the shortcomings inherent in any such endeavor. First, the trial demonstrates the near impossibility of bringing mass murder to justice in the courts. A system in which people were participants in collective violence initiated and sponsored by the state was not one that was easy to address in terms of the judicial categories of individual guilt, particularly when, as in the West German legal system, there was an emphasis on "base motives" or "excessive" brutality. Obeying orders to shoot or administer fatal injections did not count as murder in the eyes of some judges.

The Frankfurt Auschwitz trial also highlights the crucial role members of different communities of experience—on the side of the perpetrators, and of different groups of victims—played in variously spearheading or blocking attempts to bring former Nazis into the courtroom, particularly at a moment when there was still a chance of garnering evidence and bringing forward witnesses. Yet this and subsequent concentration camp trials illustrate the ways in which the so-called era of the victim during these decades of the major trials was not one in which victims found much of a sympathetic hearing. Courtroom confrontations were less a dialogue than an attempt at mutual defeat; victims' stories were subjected to hostile scrutiny and attempted discrediting by lawyers for the defense.

Unlike the latitude given to survivor stories in the Eichmann trial in Jerusalem, there was little or no desire in the German courts to hear the survivor's full story: victim witnesses were frequently cut off from talking about what was most important to them and belittled for failing to recall precise details with the accuracy necessary for demonstrating legal guilt. Often what was important for the law was not what survivors themselves wanted to say or were able to speak about. Trials may have helped people speak more openly about their past, but for some they merely signaled that no one was willing to listen or believe.

Moreover, while the trials demonstrated the beginnings of wider interest in the Holocaust and growing willingness—particularly on the part of younger generations—to listen to the voices of victims, there was nevertheless widespread failure to bring the perpetrators to any adequate form of punishment. The times were simply out of joint. By the point when the victims began to gain a wider hearing, in the later "era of the survivor," the vast majority of perpetrators had already succeeded in evading justice.

Auschwitz on Trial

Huge numbers of people around the world had an interest in the Frankfurt Auschwitz trial, not least because Auschwitz involved such a wide range of groups and victims, and such a variety of perpetrators and types of complicity. As we have seen, there were a number of camps at Auschwitz: Auschwitz I, the original camp, where many political prisoners as well as Soviet prisoners of war were held; Auschwitz II, or Birkenau, with the dedicated gas chambers and crematoria in which well over a million Jews as well as significant numbers of Roma, Sinti, and others were murdered; Auschwitz III in Monowitz, base of the massive I. G. Farben works in which those selected for work were brutally maltreated and many worked to death; and a huge system of some forty-five satellite camps as well as an extensive further network of work sites, in which further tens of thousands struggled to survive and many more died. While the figure generally given for deaths at Auschwitz is slightly over one million, one recent summary of estimates of the numbers who died in the whole Auschwitz complex lists at least 1.35 million Jews, 20,000 Roma and Sinti, 11,700 Soviet prisoners of war, and around 83,000 political and other prisoners.[6]

This trial was not the only one in which crimes committed at Auschwitz came before a court.[7] Individuals involved in Auschwitz, as we have seen, had already been put on trial in the early years after the war. Rudolf Höss, former commandant of Auschwitz, had been tried by the Polish Supreme

Court in Warsaw and hanged on the gallows in Auschwitz I on April 16, 1947. Some forty others who had worked in Auschwitz were tried in Kraków from November 24 to December 22, 1947. This trial ended with one acquittal, that of Dr. Hans Münch, and a total of twenty-two death sentences, including for Arthur Liebehenschel, who had followed a stint as commandant in Auschwitz with a period as commandant of Majdanek. In the course of other trials in Poland, around seven hundred SS members were sentenced for crimes committed in Auschwitz.[8] In the Allied trials in the West, Auschwitz had similarly been a significant subject, with defendants responsible for crimes in Auschwitz appearing both in the Nuremberg trials and in the Bergen-Belsen trial, one of the first Allied trials held in the British Zone, from September to November 1945. And quite apart from these and other trials, the first Frankfurt Auschwitz trial was itself not the only one to take place in West Germany: it was followed by further trials from December 1965 to September 1966, and from August 1967 to June 1968. Moreover, it was shortly followed by an East German Auschwitz trial that attracted far less international attention, despite the GDR's best efforts, and seems to have backfired somewhat as far as the East German population's reactions were concerned.

The East German authorities were particularly keen to demonstrate the involvement of German industry, in the form of the I. G. Farben Buna synthetics factory in Monowitz, given the existence of successor companies in West Germany. They also focused on Nazi abuse of medicine. Horst Fischer, the former leading camp doctor at Monowitz who participated in selections at Birkenau, was put on trial in 1965, in an effort to parallel the western Auschwitz trial.[9] Local reactions seem to have been similar to those in the West: at one end of the spectrum, agreeing that a person who had done such dreadful things deserved severe punishment; at the other end, arguing that, twenty years after the end of the war, it was time to "draw a line under the past"—to move on and stop discussing difficult issues. This phrase was used repeatedly. One person even commented that Fischer had acted according to an "ethical principle" in trying to rid the world of the Jews—indicating only too clearly the persistence of Nazi sympathies even in the "antifascist state."[10] There were many who wrote letters requesting that Fischer's unblemished record since 1945 and achievements as a country doctor in the Fürstenwalde area of Brandenburg should be taken into account in his favor. Even representatives of the Evangelical Churches put in a request for mercy and reduction of sentence. Stasi reports on discussions among members of the population reveal widespread unease about the severity of the sentence and general understanding for how people had been drawn into supporting Nazism.[11]

But in July 1966, after pleas for clemency had been rejected, Fischer was executed by guillotine in Leipzig—gaining the dubious reputation of being the last person to be executed by this method in Germany. The Fischer case opened up areas for debate that had for some time been taboo in East Germany, revealing subterranean worlds of continuing antisemitism, anti-communism, and perceptions of German victimhood. Despite their best efforts to organize public events and present counterarguments, the GDR authorities were not able to quell popular disquiet and discussion; apart from the severe sentence serving to highlight the contrast with the capitalist West, the trial did not meet the official goals of a prominent show trial.

The first Frankfurt Auschwitz trial was different. Conceived explicitly as a prototype, it was unique in scope and ambition: it sought, through a representative selection of defendants and witnesses, to put the Nazi program of industrially organized exploitation and extermination on trial, in a way that would both deliver justice and inform a far wider public.

It certainly attracted considerable interest in West Germany: it is estimated that some twenty thousand people attended the trial, sometimes for lengthy periods of time.[12] Far more followed the proceedings through the extensive press and television coverage. Leaving aside coverage in the tabloid press, four mainstream daily West German newspapers—*Die Welt*, the *Frankfurter Allgemeine Zeitung*, the *Süddeutsche Zeitung*, and the *Frankfurter Rundschau*—between them published some 933 articles on the trial in the twenty-two months of the proceedings.[13] Although it is difficult to assess public opinion, Germans were not necessarily any more sympathetic to this trial than they had been toward the Eichmann trial; but however ambivalent they may have felt, the Nazi past could not be brushed aside or silenced.

Still, it was not "West Germany" that should receive the credit for the trial but rather particular individuals, most notably Fritz Bauer and Hermann Langbein.[14] Unlike the vast majority of judges, lawyers, politicians, and civil servants, these two had both been persecuted under Nazism. As we have seen, Bauer was a former émigré and resistance fighter.[15] Langbein, an Austrian born in 1912, was a former political prisoner in Dachau and Auschwitz who after the war became general secretary of the International Auschwitz Committee, based in Vienna. He tirelessly sought to expose Auschwitz to the world and to seek justice.[16] Together, Bauer and Langbein sought to ensure that a trial would go ahead despite massive internal opposition in West Germany. Bauer, in public a determined optimist, was in private deeply pessimistic about their chances of success.[17]

The task of bringing Auschwitz to trial was enormous. There had been in total some 8,200 SS men and around two hundred female guards who had at some point in their careers worked at Auschwitz. Only a few dozen of them were ever brought to trial in the West, leaving more than seven thousand who were never brought to court.[18] Prosecutors for the first Frankfurt Auschwitz trial sought to choose individuals for whom they thought they were most likely to secure a conviction. This meant the defendants were selected to represent a variety of different roles and locations within the camp complex; also selected were those who were easily identifiable and who had demonstrated particular brutality and sadism.

More than two hundred survivors were invited from sixteen different countries to give testimony; 101 of them came from Eastern bloc countries, including sixty-one from Poland (with which the Federal Republic of Germany did not officially have relations).[19] While wishing to confirm the horrific actions of Nazi perpetrators, many were fearful of the consequences. Many were scared at having to stay in the same hotel as the accused and their families.

Even Rudolf Vrba, who had shown immense courage in escaping from Auschwitz and bringing details about the camp to the notice of the world, and who was now working for the Medical Research Council in London, was affected by anxiety when it came to testifying at the trial. On March 1, 1963, Vrba wrote to Langbein confirming that he was prepared to come to Frankfurt to give evidence, but added, "Please write to me whether, in your view, my personal safety can be guaranteed in Frankfurt, or whether I should worry about my own protection, since I don't know to what extent the SS might still be active."[20]

Vrba's fears were justified by the continued activities of the right wing in Germany at this time, though there was also growing support for witnesses. Emmi Bonhoeffer, for example, was the widow of Klaus Bonhoeffer, who had been executed on Hitler's express instructions for his part in the plot of July 20, 1944, and other resistance activities, along with his brother, the theologian Dietrich Bonhoeffer. After the war, Emmi Bonhoeffer took an active part in ensuring that Germans would confront this past. Sensing the distress of survivors who had come to testify at the Auschwitz trial, she organized a system of care and assistance. However, the broader community of onlookers was largely indifferent; few West Germans in 1963—despite the Eichmann trial and other cases—appeared interested in the fates and experiences of survivors.[21]

Whether or not the fears of survivors were justified, intense anxiety affected not only the willingness of victims to come forward but also the character of the testimony they gave. Maryla Rosenthal, for example, was a survivor who had worked as a secretary in the so-called Political Department of Auschwitz I, with direct knowledge of the torture inflicted on prisoners and the agonizing deaths caused by the interrogation methods of one of the defendants, Wilhelm Boger. Indeed, one of the instruments of torture, a swing on which prisoners were tied by hand and foot and hung upside down, was named the Boger swing after him. An accomplished translator in a number of foreign languages (Polish, French, German, and English) who moved from Israel to Berlin in the late 1950s, Rosenthal had been interviewed in March 1959. She was still so afraid of Boger that she could only repeat that, for all his acts of brutality and murder, he was a "nice man" who had been kind to her, and whom she defended on a personal level.[22] A letter from her husband explained that she was simply terrified of "the undoubtedly still existing SS organizations."[23]

Many witnesses—including the Viennese doctor Ella Lingens, who had been imprisoned for having tried to help Jewish friends to escape Austria, and the historian Otto Dov Kulka, who had as a boy of eleven been deported from Theresienstadt to the "Family Camp" in Birkenau—were able to provide precise descriptions of brutality and murder.[24] Lingens confirmed that all the personnel had known what was going on in the camp.[25]

The defendants in the trial included not only Robert Mulka, former adjutant to the camp commandant, and after whom the proceedings were officially named ("Case against Mulka and others"), but also twenty-one others, two of whom dropped out due to illness. The accused ranged from those relatively high up in the hierarchies of the camp, Gestapo and SS, through to dentists and doctors, to lower-level positions and even Kapos, in the interests of trying to provide a broad and multifaceted picture of the way the Auschwitz complex worked. Journalist Sybille Bedford described Mulka as "a silver-haired man of 68, dressed in pinstripe trousers and black coat" who "looks like a not undistinguished clergyman in mild distress." Several defendants "look inscrutably ordinary," while "the faces of the rest are dreadful – pinched, closed, hard; carved by cruelty, brutality, vacuity."[26] Most of the accused were on bail, able to walk about freely outside court: "They stamp about with their heads held high. Their photographs and crimes had been splashed over many a front page, yet they were not protected by police when they entered or left court or went to eat and drink in public places." In contrast to the fearful victims, the perpetrators "were not protected because they did not need to be protected. The spectators, the public, never threatened them."[27]

The involvement of experts, particularly historians from the Munich Institute of Contemporary History, assisted in shedding light on the system of organized mass murder.[28] Additionally, an expert from the Ludwigsburg Central Office, Kurt Hinrichsen, confronted the by-now classic defense among the SS of having been forced to obey criminal orders (Befehlsnotstand). Having worked on this topic for years, Hinrichsen stated that he could find not a single case where refusal to follow orders had endangered the life of the relevant member of the SS.[29] On the contrary, there were many examples where there had been few or only minimal consequences when members of the SS had refused to serve in areas where they felt uncomfortable, such as participating in selections on the ramp or working on crematoria duties. In Hinrichsen's view, the obeying-orders defense was in many cases constructed only much later. But it continued to circulate, and its currency retained its value in subsequent trials too.

Despite being known in German as Täter, those who had committed the Tat, or act, the accused appeared to have remarkably little sense of personal agency or responsibility for their own actions. In the pretrial investigations and the trial itself, defendants claimed that they had worked at some distance from the real site of evil, they did not really know what was going on, they were not responsible for killings, they only followed orders, and dreadful fates would have befallen them if they had disobeyed.

When making a statement to prosecuting attorney Joachim Kügler in Hamburg in November 1960, for example, Mulka claimed that he "never knew that gassings took place." He also claimed that "at that time [he] did not know about Zyklon B." Indeed, he claimed, "After the war of course I heard various things about what was supposed to have happened in Auschwitz."[30] This claim was followed by the remarkable assertion that— despite being adjutant to the commandant—he had never been "inside the main camp, in the Birkenau camp, or in any other camp belonging to Auschwitz," and therefore he had "never gotten to know the internal organization of these camps."[31] Moreover, not only physical distance but also "inner distance" could play a role in his defense. On being interrogated by

Dr. Heinz Dux in Frankfurt in September 1961, Mulka spoke of his alleged "political indifference" and inner conflicts while working at Auschwitz, claiming that he found himself permanently "in an unimaginable conflict situation." Additionally, he asserted that he had been known for his "political indifference," which had allegedly caused some concern to Höss and the other authorities in the camp. He furthermore suggested that members of a younger generation could have no conception of how he had felt at the time.[32] During the trial itself, Mulka repeatedly presented himself as ignorant and innocent. In answer to questions about whether he knew that the people taken in trucks from selections on the ramp to the gas chambers were going to be gassed, Mulka claimed: "I did not receive any knowledge of this, and to this extent I did not know it."[33] Yet Mulka had been the co-signatory, after Höss, of a document dated August 12, 1942, ordering SS personnel to keep their distance from the gas chambers, staying at a distance of at least fifteen meters away for at least five hours after gassings, because one SS officer had been partially poisoned by fumes.[34]

Josef Klehr, an SS medical orderly, admitted that he had injected some 250 to 300 prisoners with phenol, causing their deaths—but that he had no choice in the matter. "I found myself in a straitjacket. What could we have said? We were after all just as much numbers as were the prisoners."[35] When pressed, he conceded the total numbers he killed, but "on orders."[36] Klehr's colleague Herbert Scherpe, who did in fact manage to get himself removed from this duty and placed in one of the sub-camps on other duties, provided chilling testimony during the Auschwitz trial on the murders of children. In some self-contradiction with earlier depositions, however, and in contrast to much witness testimony, he claimed that the children neither suffered pain nor knew in advance what fate would befall them; he denied earlier reports of their screams and agonized fear of death, although he did agree that a child waiting outside was crying and calling in vain the names of those who did not come back.[37]

Karl-Friedrich Höcker, who, following a stint in Majdanek, was adjutant to Richard Baer as commandant of Auschwitz in 1944, also maintained stony-faced ignorance: Bedford noted that Höcker "looks neither good nor bad, bright nor stupid, maintains he gave no orders, saw nothing, knew nothing." When the judge pressed him, asking, "You believed that innocent children were killed in order to protect the public?" Höcker simply replied, "Well, they were Jews."[38] Höcker's photograph album of leisure time and outings in the nearby countryside with fellow workers from Auschwitz demonstrates a startling capacity to compartmentalize life and entirely ignore the sufferings of others.[39]

A few of the accused were slightly more believable in demonstrating their own humanity. Dr. Franz Lucas, who was ultimately acquitted, reported how he had managed to evade taking part in selections on the ramp for new arrivals designated for the gas chambers by feigning sickness; he was also eventually able to move to other duties in other camps. Many defendants sought to establish their innocence or intrinsic goodness by recalling small acts of kindness or even attempts to save prisoners, even while denying any knowledge of what was actually going on in Birkenau. Former SS medical orderly and junior squad leader Gerhard Neubert, for example, claimed that he had thought that prisoners who collapsed in Monowitz were being taken off to be cared for rather than gassed; he allegedly only realized in the course of the trial what the truth really was.[40] Simple denials were all that one of the Kapos, Emil Bednarek, was able to manage, despite witness testimony to his brutality and the deaths he had caused.[41] Other defendants, such as the pharmacist Victor Capesius, provided more sophisticated defenses—in Capesius's case by suggesting that he had been mistaken for another SS doctor, now conveniently long dead, who had actually undertaken selections on the ramp.[42] Johann Schobert, who following injury on the Eastern Front had worked in the Political Department in Auschwitz, appealed for sympathy for his whole generation—age ten when Hitler came to power, brought up to be good Nazis, wounded in service of their fatherland at war—and said they should also be considered "victims of National Socialism."[43]

One of the oddest accounts during the trial was given by the Brazilian-born Pery Broad, a former member of the Auschwitz Political Department. While a prisoner of war, Broad had voluntarily written a remarkably factual account of the structure and character of Auschwitz and had made himself useful to the British military authorities in the Bergen–Belsen trial.[44] Intelligent and well-educated, Broad wrote this account in a curiously dispassionate, even critical manner—almost as though he had not himself been there, had not himself played an active role in the horrors he describes. In the trial Broad switched into quite a different persona, denying what he had previously discussed in such detail. Witness testimony suggested that he had been a rather different kind of perpetrator—"clever, intelligent, refined"—than thugs and torturers like Boger who engaged in general run-of-the-mill brutality.[45]

The Frankfurt trial proceedings were marked by aggressive treatment of witnesses, particularly by the defense attorney, Hans Laternser. He had already built up a reputation for himself by defending Nazis in early postwar trials, including the trial of Kesselring in Italy and some of the Nuremberg successor trials. Langbein noted how badly Laternser treated witnesses in the Auschwitz trial, often sarcastically suggesting that they were liars because they could not recall the precise date and time at which particular incidents took place.[46] In contrast, and in line with defendants' self-presentations, Laternser sought to present even the accused as "victims of Hitler."[47]

The extensive coverage of the trial in the press served to bring some of the sickening details of everyday cruelty and killings to the attention of the German public. Moreover, television coverage brought Auschwitz into the living rooms of many families, at a time when television ownership was growing rapidly in the increasingly affluent Federal Republic. The reports were in the main respectful, presenting official views with little by way of independent critique.[48] Hans Frankenthal, an Auschwitz survivor who was among those called to give evidence at this trial, later recalled that two decades after the end of the war people were finally "talking openly about Auschwitz for the first time."[49] And these discussions did begin to make a difference. By the mid-1960s, in the context of the growing student movement and broader generational conflicts, voices were raised demanding serious confrontation with a past that was now becoming infinitely more present, more imaginable.

The trial finally ended on August 20, 1965, with a lengthy speech by the presiding judge, Hans Hofmeyer, justifying the verdicts. Capital punishment had been abolished in West Germany, so death sentences were not an option. Of the twenty accused, only six received life sentences; ten were given sentences ranging between three and a half and fourteen years; one, who had been a teenager at the time, was given a youth sentence; and three were acquitted due to lack of sufficient evidence. At the very end of the trial, journalist Sybille Bedford tells us, "Dr Hofmeyer, the judge who had done so much to keep the atmosphere cool, who had steered the court through so many clashes of temper and had never lost his own, allowed himself to break down."[50]

In terms of bringing perpetrators to justice in the courts, the results were disappointing. Sentences, some of them extremely light in view of the magnitude of the crimes committed, had been handed out to just seventeen of the six to eight thousand people who had worked to make Auschwitz function. Bauer had succeeded in bringing Auschwitz to public attention, but the outcome was far from the justice he had sought to achieve. Moreover, in the course of his efforts it had become clear to him just how significant the continuing opposition to this venture was: as he commented to a colleague, every time he left his office, he felt that he was living in "enemy territory."[51]

Even so, the trial marked a watershed in public perception: given the accompanying exhibition and extensive television and newspaper coverage, it was from now on impossible for Germans to ignore Auschwitz. This was not only a matter of political orientations but also one of shifting generations, as Bedford noted in 1966: "There is a desire nowadays among people who were grown-up during the Third Reich, even, surprisingly, among those who hated it and took risks to defy its worst commands, to be done with it all and not think of it again for the rest of their lives. The young who were born after the events, are more disturbed and curious and shocked. They want to know what happened and how, and why, and they hold their elders to account for what the elders want to forget."[52]

The Frankfurt trial was also significant for those who had lived through it. However painful it was to revisit their memories, the trial acted as a precipitant for victims to speak to a wider audience, and not merely talk among fellow survivors. Six of those who had testified, for example, spoke of this decision when interviewed again in 2005.[53] Three were Polish non-Jews; two were Czech Jews who had immigrated to Israel; and one was a Viennese Jew who had gone to France. One of the Polish interviewees, Ignacy Golik, claimed that he had not spoken at all about his Auschwitz experience until the trial investigations started.[54] A Polish woman, Anna Palarczyk, said that it was a conscious decision on her part not to allow Auschwitz to intrude on her life after the war. She had chosen not to speak about her Auschwitz experience to her husband or her sons, who only heard about the camp in school, and she spoke only to former comrades about their common experiences in Auschwitz.[55] Another Polish survivor, Józef Mikusz, had more explicit political reasons for silence, as he was persecuted even after the war for having been in the Polish resistance. He had had to flee from Zabrze to Wrocław and was only able to return with the political thaw under the new reformist leadership of Władysław Gomułka following the unrest of 1956.[56]

The three Jewish survivors also had rather mixed experiences with their testimony after the war. The only one who said anyone had listened to him in early postwar years was Imre Gönczi, who was asked to speak about his experiences in public, as an official spokesperson (*Referent*) for the state prisoners' organization in postwar Czechoslovakia—but he soon realized that antisemitic comments were being made to the effect that he just wanted to achieve a high status for himself by capitalizing on his experiences as a Jew.[57] Paul Schaffer, a Viennese Jew who returned not to Austria but to his last place of residence in the south of France, was a convinced Zionist who worked in a Zionist organization straight after the war. It was very important to him to talk to fellow survivors, since he hoped that in this way he would be able to "talk himself free."[58]

The testimonies given in the trials that caught public attention were not necessarily beneficial for the victims. In many West German trials in the 1960s and 1970s—the Frankfurt trial and after—victim witnesses often felt that they themselves were being put on trial. The West German jurist Adalbert Rückerl supported the general view—one shared by judges in West German trials—that witness memories were too vague and that too much time had passed for them to be of use.[59] Survivors called to the witness stand in West Germany were asked to give very specific answers to questions phrased in specific legal terms, designed to establish with precision the identities and actions of perpetrators at a particular time, in a particular place. In their absence, perpetrators often had little to fear.

The testimony of victims was even less significant in Austria, despite the influence of the first Frankfurt trial. Hermann Langbein, chair of the International Auschwitz Committee, had played a key role in helping Fritz Bauer in bringing Auschwitz to the West German courts, and he was determined to see a similar trial in Austria. At the time Langbein compiled his major documentation of the trial, published in 1965, he was optimistic that a similar trial—if not an even more important one—could shortly be mounted in Austria.[60] Several prominent individuals were to be tried in Austria because Austrians who had committed crimes in Poland could not be extradited to Germany for trial.

The first indictment had already been brought in March 1960, a couple of years before the Frankfurt trial, against Dr. Georg Franz Meyer, who had served not only at Auschwitz but also in Stutthof, Groß-Rosen, Flossenbürg, and elsewhere, and who was at that time an openly practicing doctor in Vienna. So too were Dr. Karl Josef Fischer (not to be confused with the East German doctor Horst Fischer) and Dr. Erwin Heschl. Also in Austria, and easily found, were the adjutant of the commandant of Auschwitz-Birkenau, Johann Schindler, and the SS leader of the central building team of the Waffen-SS in Auschwitz, Walter Dejaco. Other known Auschwitz perpetrators living and working openly in Austria at the time included the architect Fritz

Ertl, the construction engineer Hermann Töfferl, the former SS guard Roland Albert (whose granddaughter Barbara Albert later made a film about exploring a repressed Nazi family past), Alois Kurz (who also served in Majdanek and Mittelbau-Dora), and Otto Graf and Franz Wunsch, accused of working in the crematoria and gas chambers, as well as a number of others, including a female guard. In view of the significance and range of Auschwitz perpetrators known to be living in Austria and the weight of evidence that was available to mount an effective case against them, Langbein thought that the "Vienna trial" would "be hardly less important than the Frankfurt trial."[61]

Yet despite investigations started in the early 1960s, the first Austrian Auschwitz trial did not open until late 1971.[62] The main proceedings, involving two architects, Walter Dejaco and Fritz Ertl, who were accused of having constructed the gas chambers at Auschwitz, took place from January 19 to March 10, 1972, in Vienna. They were found not guilty, in part because of the assumed unreliability of witness statements. A communist newspaper, *Die Volksstimme*, observed that the verdict was one of many earning Austria the reputation of being "a nature conservation park for Nazi mass murderers."[63]

A second trial was held in Vienna from April 25 to June 27, 1972, with hearings taking place over the course of thirty-one days against two members of the Auschwitz Camp SS, Otto Graf and Franz Wunsch. This trial was also distinguished by attempts to intimidate and discredit the witnesses; the only one who managed to stand up to this treatment, summoning considerable reserves of strength, self-confidence, and humor, was Rudolf Vrba, by then a professor in Canada.[64] Vrba, again concerned for his own safety, needed protection—and was advised that the best protection was simply not to set foot in Austria at all.[65]

When the verdict was announced, both Graf and Wunsch were found not guilty, again largely because of problems with witness evidence as well as the fact that, due to the statute of limitations, the lesser crimes of aiding and abetting murder were by now past the date up to which they could be penalized. The Austrian justice system henceforth more or less gave up entirely on any attempts to put Nazi perpetrators on trial.

The Operation Reinhard Death Camp Trials

By the mid-1960s West Germany was gaining a good reputation—in contrast to neighboring Austria—for pursuit of perpetrators through the courtrooms.

But there was a paradox at the heart of the West German system of justice. The more perfect the extermination machinery, the less likely the murderers were to be found guilty. In the absence of survivors it was easy to maintain a strong defense. The Operation Reinhard death camp trials that took place in 1963 and 1965 (Bełżec), 1964–65 and 1970 (Treblinka), and 1965–66 (Sobibór), illustrate both the significance and the limits of the "era of the witness."[66]

The Operation Reinhard death camp trials took place after the 1962–63 trial in Bonn of twelve people accused of complicity in mass murder in Chełmno, the first dedicated extermination camp. There was remarkably little evidence—neither by way of physical remains nor witness testimonies—in relation to Chełmno, and fully half of the defendants were finally acquitted (three immediately, three on appeal). Mitigating factors that resulted in the reduction of other sentences included claims that one of the defendants had not wanted to work in Chełmno and another had given cigarettes to some of the Jews working in the camp—extraordinary considerations given the gravity of the charge of facilitating the killing of at least 150,000 Jewish men, women, and children and around five thousand Gypsies.[67]

The Operation Reinhard camps—Bełżec, Sobibór, Treblinka—were responsible, in total, for more deaths than Auschwitz-Birkenau. They were built up and run by a relatively small network of people: a total of 121 men who had already gained experience in killing in the euthanasia program had been sent over to the forests of the General Government to build up sites of camouflaged mass murder, and they moved around between camps.[68] It was easy enough for those put on trial to claim they had only been following orders. Where there were survivors who could testify to particular violence, brutality, "excess" cruelty, or sadism, perpetrators might be found guilty. Where there was no such testimony, the defendants could claim they were just little cogs in a machine over which they had no control.[69]

An estimated half million people had been murdered in Bełżec. Only one perpetrator was sentenced for participation in this slaughterhouse. The first trial of defendants who had worked in Bełżec opened in Munich in 1963 and ended with the acquittal of seven out of the original eight, on the assumption that they had only acted as they did under orders. The eighth defendant was Josef Oberhauser, whose trial in Munich lasted only four days, from January 18 to 21, 1965. A mere fourteen witnesses were called to give evidence, of whom no fewer than thirteen were former SS or T4 personnel—hardly likely to want to incriminate their former colleague and in the process risk incriminating themselves, or even provoking the accused into turning on them.[70] Six of these fourteen witnesses had themselves also previously been accused. Five of the witnesses had in the meantime, along with another colleague, become involved in the Sobibór trial.

The absence of witness testimony was crucial to the outcome of the Bełżec trials.[71] By the 1960s, there was only one known survivor from Bełżec, and indeed only two victims were known to have survived this camp at all. One of them, Chaim Hirszman, had been assassinated in 1946 under suspicious circumstances while in the midst of giving testimony to the Jewish Historical Commission in Lublin.[72] The other survivor, Rudolf Reder, had also given testimony to the Jewish Historical Commission in Kraków. Reder's report, given straight after the war, vividly portrays the daily arrival of transports, the shaving of women's hair while the men were already in the gas chambers, pulling out the bodies after the screams had died down and the doors were opened, separating corpses from others to whom they had clung, and dragging the bodies across the terrain to the mass graves that lay waiting. Reder also describes the unspeakable cruelty of the guards, some of whom were Ukrainians and ethnic Germans (*Volksdeutsche*), under the watchful supervision of the SS.[73]

Despite this extraordinary and detailed report on the cruelties perpetrated at the camp, Reder was less helpful by the mid-1960s when it came to courtroom priorities and in particular establishing the putative subjective mentalities of the killers. And he was alone as a witness. In the Cold War context (with the Hallstein Doctrine complicating relations with countries that recognized the GDR), the West German authorities were reluctant to call as witnesses the many Polish workers and local residents who had witnessed what was going on in the camp or former Trawniki men now living in the Soviet Union and elsewhere in Eastern Europe.[74] The Hallstein policy was finally abandoned in the early 1970s with Chancellor Willy Brandt's Ostpolitik, but in the meantime it had a significant impact on the acquisition of incriminating evidence and eyewitness testimonies relating to acts of perpetration on Polish soil.

In the absence of survivor witnesses, there was no one to oppose the defendants' partial and self-serving representations. There was no compelling external evidence about their "subjective" mentality as they carried out acts that they claimed were simply ordered by the state. With the sole exception of Josef Oberhauser, they were all acquitted.[75]

Unlike the others, Oberhauser did not succeed in the "only following orders" defense, since he had been the right-hand man of the commandant and was therefore assumed to have had more leeway for independent initiative. Oberhauser was also unsuccessful in his claim that he had already stood trial and been sufficiently punished by spending eight years in prison in the GDR. On closer inspection, it turned out that the East German case had been for euthanasia killings and not for the murders in Bełżec: the sentence Oberhauser had partially served in the GDR was in fact for T4 crimes in Grafeneck, Brandenburg, and Bernburg. Even so, the West German judge in Munich felt that Oberhauser had already done a form of pre-emptive penance or had a credit balance of suffering, by virtue of his prior imprisonment. His sentence for the crimes committed in Bełżec could, in the judge's view, be reduced because he had already "spent a considerable part of this sentence in penal institutions in the eastern zone under incomparably harsher conditions than in the Federal Republic."[76] He was given a sentence of a mere four and a half years, including time already spent in detention, for aiding and abetting some 300,000 murders out of the 450,000 for which he had originally been charged. In the event, Oberhauser served only half of his sentence before being released.

This was not the only time the West German justice system showed more sympathy for the perpetrator than for the victims. An Italian court later sentenced Oberhauser in absentia to life imprisonment for crimes committed near Trieste, where, like so many other former T4 personnel, he had been relocated after Bełżec had been closed down. The crimes for which he was sentenced in Italy included the murder of partisans and others awaiting deportation. The German authorities refused an extradition request, and Oberhauser lived relatively undisturbed in Munich—ruffled only briefly, during his work as a bartender, by Claude Lanzmann's attempt to film an interview on camera—until his death from natural causes in 1979.

In this way, judicial reckoning with the murders of around half a million people in Bełżec resulted in a single prison sentence of little over two years behind bars. That translates to less than five minutes spent in prison for each murder. This may have amounted to justice in a strictly legal sense—that question must be left to the lawyers—but it is certainly a far cry from any sense of moral justice.

The situation was somewhat different in the trials of the two other Reinhard camps, Treblinka and Sobibór, where revolts and escapes of prisoners had meant the premature closure of the camps and therefore the existence of survivor witnesses.

In the first Treblinka trial, which was held in Düsseldorf from October 1964 to September 1965 against Kurt Franz, the former commandant, and others, more than one hundred witnesses were called. The vast majority of these were former SS or T4 personnel; there were also some expert witnesses to talk about the questions of having to obey orders.[77] However, survivor witnesses also proved crucial to the prosecution.

The Düsseldorf court divided those involved into principal perpetrators, accomplices, and assistants (*Haupttäter*, *Mittäter*, and *Gehilfen*). The principal perpetrators were deemed to be the "initiators" of the crime: Hitler, Himmler, Göring, Heydrich, and a small circle of people high up in the Nazi Party and the SS.[78] This meant, effectively, that anyone actually involved in running the death camp was automatically at most an accomplice and more likely just an assistant. Here, in order to prove guilt it was crucial to establish particular sadism, individual brutality, and base motives. Survivors such as Jakob Jakubowicz and Leo Lewi, both living in Germany after the war, were able to identify Kurt Franz as someone who had been known as "Lalka" or "Puppe" ("Doll") in camp, and they could testify to his personal brutality and specific cases of murder. Another survivor, Samuel Rajzmann, an accountant who flew in from Montreal, was also able to provide crucial testimony about Treblinka, as he had done previously at Nuremberg.[79] An unusually significant witness was Franciszek Zabecki, a former member of the Polish underground who had gained the position of stationmaster for the Treblinka railway stop precisely in order to monitor German trains and their freight. Despite German efforts, as elsewhere, to cover their tracks by destroying all evidence toward the end of the war, in this case quite literally, by dynamiting the Treblinka railway station in 1944, Zabecki had managed to retain waybills and other German railway documentation.[80]

As a consequence of a significant body of witness testimony, four of the accused, including Franz, were sentenced to life imprisonment in the Treblinka trial; five were sentenced to shorter terms, ranging from three to twelve years; and one was acquitted. In 1970, in a further trial relating to crimes committed at Treblinka, Franz Stangl—who had in the meantime been tracked down and extradited from Brazil—was also sentenced to life imprisonment. Prior to his work in Treblinka, Stangl had, like so many others, been involved in the T4 euthanasia program, as well as serving as commandant at Sobibór.[81]

The main Sobibór trial took place in Hagen from September 6, 1965, to December 20, 1966. Twelve people were initially accused of participation in murder at Sobibór, of whom one had to be treated separately because he was ill and one, Kurt Bolender, committed suicide. Dietrich Zeug, one of several Ludwigsburg officials assigned to the pretrial investigations in 1959, was assiduous in pursuit of survivor witnesses, liaising closely with Israeli investigators and prosecutors, and with the World Jewish Congress in New York, to follow up leads.[82] According to GDR authorities, however, the West German investigators—again following the Hallstein Doctrine—were much less energetic about obtaining evidence from Poland, where material and documents were available, including an updated list of former perpetrators with details of their postwar fates or whereabouts.[83] There were, however, significant numbers of survivors who were willing to testify. For the Sobibór trial, a total of 127 witnesses were called, many of them survivors traveling in from the United States or Israel. This made a substantial difference, particularly when compared with the earlier Bełżec trial.

The sentences were clearly less lenient than the acquittals for the Bełżec guards, but still varied. In an earlier trial relating to Sobibór, in 1950, Erich Bauer had initially been sentenced to death for his role in running the Sobibór gas chambers, a sentence that was commuted to life imprisonment. Only one of the accused in the Sobibór trial of 1965–66, Karl Frenzel, was given a similar life sentence for the role he had demonstrably played in at least 150,000 murders; he was acquitted of ten further charges because of what were seen as dubious statements by witnesses. Another defendant, Franz Wolf, who had worked at the euthanasia institute in Hadamar before moving to Sobibór, was given eight years' imprisonment for assisting in at least 39,000 murders, a number that seems to have been plucked almost at random. Two were given sentences of four years, and two were given sentences of three years for their roles in thousands of murders—ranging from 15,000 to 79,000. The other five defendants in the Sobibór trial were found not guilty, including Erich Lachmann, who had also trained Ukrainian guards at Trawniki. Despite his widely known brutal conduct while at Sobibór, he was acquitted on grounds of duress and mental incompetence.[84]

Reinhard trials in Austria were even less successful. More than three hundred SS men had been involved in Operation Reinhard, probably around sixty of whom had also been in Auschwitz, and several hundred had been active in police battalions. Of these three hundred, a mere seven were brought to stand trial in Austria, and not a single one of them was found guilty. Ernst Lerch, for example, had been the assistant to Odilo Globocnik in the Operation Reinhard murders. Despite his elevated position in the SS, his strategic roles in Kraków and subsequently Lublin, and his apparent involvement in the murder of tens of thousands of Jews in the General Government, Lerch's trial in Klagenfurt in 1971 lasted only two days because of an alleged lack of evidence. It was never picked up again, and was dropped entirely in 1976.[85] In the light of these and other cases where acquittal or lenience in sentencing was now becoming widely seen as scandalous, the Austrian authorities appear to have deemed it better not to prosecute at all.[86]

In general, the Reinhard camp trials appear to have provoked less wide-spread public interest than the Auschwitz trial, but at the same time they attracted considerable sympathy for the defendants (and provided fodder for emergent Holocaust deniers).[87] If this was the "era of the witness," as is sometimes claimed, it was not one in which witnesses received an easy hearing.[88] The defenses of the accused to the effect that they had of course only been following orders and had had no alternative for fear of severe consequences if they refused were believed and repeated in judgments. As one of the judges put it, echoing the arguments of the defendants: "They had been forced to follow orders to participate in the extermination of the Jews, because they would otherwise have been disciplined, punished, sent to a concentration camp, shot, or would have received a similar measure against body and soul, and no other possibility existed and could be seen by them to avoid such dangers except by obeying orders."[89] Those found not guilty were "to be excused on grounds of assumed (putative) state of compulsion and necessity" (in German, a single word effectively doubling the force of compulsion—*Nötigungsnotstandslage*).[90] The judges were generally more willing to give credence to the defendants' claimed states of mind than to the facts of their actions.

Yet while the accused were believed, the same was not true of survivor witness testimony, which many West German judges felt to be not entirely reliable. After all, their memories must be hazy more than twenty years after the events. Moreover, judges noted, most of the witnesses had visited or lived in Israel and had periodically met up with one another, swapping stories, such that they might have mixed up "what they have themselves experienced and what they have heard."[91] Furthermore, because they might have lost close friends and relatives, they might have a personal interest in wanting to find someone guilty merely by virtue of their having served in the camp, without tying their guilt to specific crimes. In this way, as a judge in the Sobibór trial noted in a blanket condemnation, survivor witnesses often "emotionally made and perhaps still make all members of the camp personnel responsible 'as murderers' for their suffering, without being able to differentiate according the measure of individual participation and guilt.'"[92]

In this way, there seems to have been more judicial empathy with those who had become perpetrators "under orders" than with those who had been their victims and were desperate for justice. By the beginning of the 1970s, the major extermination camp trials were over. Yet wider interest in the Holocaust and the stories of survivors had barely begun.

The Majdanek Trial

The last major concentration camp trial in West Germany took place at a time when the interest of the broader public, including members of a younger generation, was just beginning to be aroused. Lasting more than five and half years, from November 26, 1975, to June 30, 1981, the Düsseldorf Majdanek trial was the longest war crimes trial held in West Germany and spanned a period of significant changes in public attitudes and views on the past.

The Düsseldorf Majdanek trial was staged more than thirty years after the first Majdanek trial, which had been held in Poland before the end of the war, shortly after the Soviet liberation of the camp on July 22, 1944; a second trial had also been held in Poland in 1946–48. There was no obvious reason for the delay in bringing further trials in Germany,

The Majdanek concentration camp, situated on the outskirts and in full view of the city of Lublin, exploited slave labor on site and was also a feeder for labor sub-camps and the extermination camps. It had its own gas chambers, as well as being the site of mass killing by shooting, including in the so-called Harvest Festival massacre of some eighteen thousand Jews on November 3, 1943. Overrun unexpectedly by the Russians in the summer of 1944, the Majdanek camp leadership had not managed to destroy traces of the murderous activities that had taken place on the site, and the gas chambers as well as copious incriminating evidence remained intact.

Yet for three decades after the war West Germany seemed incapable of putting a single perpetrator from Majdanek on trial, despite having started proceedings against 387 people. Not one was actually brought to court or prosecuted, and for fifty-eight people the investigations were completely terminated.[93] This finally changed in the mid-1970s.

At the belated Düsseldorf trial in 1975, seventeen people were initially accused, but two were deemed unfit to stand trial, and one died before the end of trial. The original defendants included Hermann Hackmann, who had in 1947 been sentenced to death in a US trial for his notoriously brutal crimes committed at Buchenwald, a sentence subsequently commuted to life imprisonment, and Emil Laurich, who had worked also at Sachsenhausen, Neuengamme, and Groß-Rosen. The Majdanek trial also included female defendants. One was Hildegard Lächert, informally known as "Bloody Brigitte," a German nurse who had served in a number of camps, including Ravensbrück, Mauthausen-Gusen, and also Auschwitz, for which she had been sentenced in Kraków in 1947 and was released in 1956 well before the end of her fifteen-year term of imprisonment. Another was Hermine Braunsteiner (Ryan), an Austrian who had moved to Germany following the Anschluss; she worked for a period in Ravensbrück before her transfer to Majdanek, where she was nicknamed "the Mare" because of her cruelty to prisoners, including stamping on them with her metal-shod boots. An Austrian court had in 1948 sentenced her to three years' imprisonment for her crimes at Ravensbrück, but she was released early, after serving only two years. Marrying an American, Russell Ryan, she moved to Canada and then the United States, and clearly never expected to have to return to confront her Nazi past; for the Düsseldorf trial she came back accompanied by her husband, full of outrage at the supposed indignity to which she was now being subjected.

The Majdanek trial is particularly significant for the light it sheds on the changing balance of forces concerning the Nazi past. By then press and television reports were routinely critical of the way West German courts had dealt with trials. Some journalists became aware of the significance of the trial somewhat belatedly but then focused on scandals to increase circulation figures and promote their own reputations as reporters. Many were now prepared to point to the Nazi past and the right-wing sympathies of some lawyers and critique their treatment of witnesses, which they had by and large not been prepared to do in the course of Auschwitz trial a decade earlier.[94]

Moreover, there were significant generational changes at play. Affected by the radicalization associated with 1968, many young people were now becoming journalists, teachers, or other public educators. Not themselves in any way complicit in the crimes of the past, they were increasingly interested in learning about the Nazi period. By the spring of 1977—nearly two

years before the screening of the American TV miniseries *Holocaust* dramatically increased awareness and interest—schoolchildren whose teachers felt
the Majdanek trial was important were being brought in increasing numbers to watch the proceedings. Many were critical of the way in which the
defense lawyers sought to drag out proceedings or maltreated witnesses;
some were also aware of the ways in which the accused—particularly the
female defendants—looked like their grandparents; most were shocked by
the details they heard about the camp.[95] While one pupil of Jewish background felt that she had already heard more than enough about all of this at
home, most said that their parents never wanted to talk about this subject:
"They say that is all past history, after all."[96]

The trial was also notable for the way in which right-wing sympathizers
were increasingly proactive in public. They sought to influence public opinion
by the circulation of pamphlets, including a Holocaust-denial tract, *Die
Auschwitz-Lüge* ("The Auschwitz lie"); they helped to coordinate testimony
for the defense, ensuring that the witnesses on the side of the SS all agreed on
the stories they would present before they appeared in court, and they sought
to vilify and intimidate witnesses for the prosecution.[97] The pro-Nazi organization Stille Hilfe, with which Heinrich Himmler's daughter Gudrun was
closely associated, also became actively and visibly involved. People working
for Stille Hilfe made prison visits, helped in coordinating defense strategies, and
provided advice to defendants. One such was a woman by the name of Josefine
Jürgens, who had been awarded a Federal Service Award (Bundesverdienstkreuz)
for her work with prisoners. Known previously as the "Angel of Prisoners," she
was not only a member of Stille Hilfe but also an honorary representative
of the otherwise entirely respectable Christian-Jewish Society (Christlich-
Jüdischen Gesellschaft). On a television program called *Monitor*, however, she
announced that "justice in the Majdanek trial had to be pronounced in the
name of the German citizen and not in the name of communists and Jews."[98]

The involvement of Nazi sympathizers served to give the trial and the
issues even greater publicity. A WDR program on December 16, 1977, put
together a discussion between Hermann Langbein and the historian and
Buchenwald survivor Eugen Kogon on one side and the former SS man
Thies Christophersen, author of *Die Auschwitz-Lüge*, and Udo Walendy, a
political scientist, Holocaust revisionist, and founding member of the neo-
Nazi National Democratic Party (NPD, on the other. According to Heiner
Lichtenstein, an observer of the trial who wrote about it extensively, this
program was a success "since it reached a public that had until then only

seldom been seen in a courtroom: housewives and pensioners." Lichtenstein noted that in the months after the program "they came in person to experience the trial, about which they had up to then only occasionally seen or heard something."[99]

Nazi sympathizers were active both outside the courtroom and inside. At the start of the trial, there were objections to one of the proposed historical experts, Wolfgang Scheffler: it was alleged that he could not be sufficiently objective since he had studied for his doctorate with a Jewish professor and had spent time in the Wiener Library in London. It was assumed that those with any Jewish connections could not muster the necessary "objectivity," while those with Nazi backgrounds or sympathies somehow could. One of the defense lawyers, Ludwig Bock, was a known right-wing sympathizer who had unsuccessfully stood for election on behalf of the NPD. Bock clearly overstepped the boundaries of his legal mandate in the interests of securing an acquittal for his clients. He traveled to Israel and without letting people know that he was acting as a defense lawyer tried to ingratiate himself with survivors and influence their testimony. He was particularly close to the line with respect to his treatment of witnesses. Bock even went so far as to suggest that one of them, a Polish woman by the name of Henrica Ostrowski, should be put on trial for being an accessory to murder.[100] When she was a prisoner in Majdanek, one of Ostrowski's tasks had been to carry the cans of Zyklon B gas to the gas chambers. Bock's attitude was evident of a persisting mentality in some quarters. In the face of the judge's objections to his attitude, Bock eventually stood down, but he was replaced by a junior lawyer from the same office who apparently continued in much the same vein, if less ostentatiously.

A documentary about this trial, shown in three episodes, aired on West German television in 1984.[101] This included interviews with defendants, witnesses, and people observing the trial (among them the journalist Heiner Lichtenstein, who had reported on schoolchildren's reactions). The utterances of former Nazis were particularly revealing. One who had been a guard at Majdanek, in charge of the dogs, is shown in half darkness, in profile, under a crucifix and candles. He has clearly undergone a conversion experience and is the only perpetrator who shows any regrets. For him, it was evidently a relief to give testimony. The others were defensive. Some claimed they were merely doing their duty, just like soldiers. On November 3, 1943, the day when all remaining Jews in the General Government were to be murdered—some forty-three thousand in total—the shooting of more than eighteen thousand in Majdanek took at least eight hours, with fifty people being shot at a time. By the evening the smoke was already coming from the crematorium; one of the female guards in the documentary talked about the terrible smell of the smoke that lasted for days. A former policeman appeared to feel no responsibility for the event. Both said there was nothing either could have done about it anyway. They had either been forced to obey orders or had been indoctrinated, and either way they should bear no guilt.

The female guards also did not feel responsible for their actions. One, who had assisted in taking two hundred children to be gassed and burned, said she had initially believed the story she was told about taking them to a kindergarten; she maintained that she had later protested about this to the commandant and was told that she was getting too close to the inmates. Apparently untroubled by the scenes they witnessed every day, whether or not they were personally involved in violence, the female guards remembered happy times after the end of the working day. One enjoyed going out riding; another liked to go home to a warm stove and cooking. They took pleasure in visits to the cinema, the theater, and the cultural offerings of the German House—a kind of activities center—as well as drinking coffee, going to the local inns, singing, celebrating birthdays, and other festivities.

Meanwhile, at the Majdanek trial survivors were forced to relive the agonies of their experiences: separation from parents who were sent to the gas chambers; being stripped of their clothes, given tabs with numbers, being shamed; the dirt, filth, lice, hunger; cleaning the latrines, being beaten brutally by Bloody Brigitte (also known as "the Beast"); the reduction to a subhuman state. After their treatment in court—which made Henrica Ostrowski, the witness who was attacked by Bock, even begin to believe he might be right, that she might also be a murderer—they wondered whether it had been worth the pain.

The verdicts, yet again, were remarkably lenient. Five were acquitted, and two more were released on grounds of illness. Six received sentences ranging from three to ten years. Only two received relatively lengthy sentences, one for twelve years and one to life imprisonment. The life imprisonment was for Hermine Braunsteiner Ryan, the only defendant to receive the sentence demanded by the prosecution. Her husband too was utterly unable to accept the verdict and instead blamed the victims; following the handing down of her sentence he commented, "American Jews demand these trials, and this is what happens."[102]

The prominent concentration camp trials that took place in the 1960s and 1970s demonstrate both the determination of some notable individuals to try to achieve at least a degree of justice and the obstacles they faced in terms of both the legal system and the political climate—which in turn had served to shape this system—in the early decades of the Federal Republic. They illustrate also that even in the "era of the witness," where witness testimony could make all the difference, it proved incredibly difficult to prove individual guilt.

West Germany had nonetheless tried to put some of those responsible for murder in the major concentration camps on trial. The same cannot be said for Austria. Efforts to stage a Majdanek trial in the 1960s there came eventually to nothing, and proceedings were terminated in 1972.[103] Other trials that occasioned international outrage included that of Franz Murer, an Austrian—widely known as "the butcher of Vilnius"—who had presided over the ghettoization and destruction of a Jewish community of some eighty thousand people; he was acquitted in a 1963 trial in Graz that lasted merely a week, during which Jewish witnesses were mocked. In the mid-1970s, endeavors to bring known perpetrators to trial were almost entirely abandoned, following a few unsuccessful attempts at prosecution in cases where the evidence seemed clear. Johann Vinzenz Gogl, a former guard at the Mauthausen concentration camp and Ebensee sub-camp, for example, was acquitted both in 1972, in his first trial in Linz, and again when he was retried in Vienna in 1975, despite what one expert has called "overwhelming" evidence against him.[104] Former SS men in court apparently cheered his acquittal in 1972.[105] And we have seen the signal failure of Austrian justice to deal with crimes committed in Auschwitz.

While it proved extremely difficult to put state-sponsored mass murder on trial, under West German criminal law, the trials had at least drawn public attention to the Nazi system, and at times proved educational. But what they did not do was bring the vast majority of those who were guilty of mass murder and collective violence to any form of adequate justice.

Smaller trials revealed much about the differences of being tried on one side of the Iron Curtain or the other, and in one political context rather than another. They also revealed a great deal about the defenses used by perpetrators. As it turned out, much depended on where they had been during the war and where they ended up afterward. This becomes even clearer when looking at the trials of selected individuals involved in the wider system of Nazi violence.

12

The Diffraction of Guilt

The underlying differences in dealing with Nazi guilt in the Cold War era were evident in the major trials of the 1960s and 1970s, which were in the public spotlight at the time and which have remained a primary focus of attention in the half century since. The contrasts become even more striking, however, when considering the cases in minor trials, those involving violence committed outside the major extermination camps and which did not generally attract much public attention. These exemplify key contrasts between East and West German characterization and treatment of defendants. Moreover, the relatively insignificant perpetrators in these smaller trials are in many ways representative of the far larger numbers who were never brought to trial at all. The fates of perpetrators from the areas in Poland explored earlier, around the town of Mielec and the SS troop training ground in Dębica, highlight the significance of postwar location when it came to justice. Along with the contrasting fates of perpetrators from Warsaw, they serve to illuminate not only aspects of Nazi terror but also the differing ways in which perpetrators lived with their past and the longer-term consequences for their families.

These less well-known trials also serve to illustrate another feature: that of the changing role and treatment of witnesses over time. When the former commandant of the Mielec concentration camp, Josef Schwammberger, was put on trial in 1991–92, just after German unification, the situation was very different from two decades earlier. While witnesses were further distant from the events, their memories arguably even less reliable, they were accorded somewhat more respect—and their testimony was less crucial to the establishment of guilt. This development would become even more marked some twenty years later, with the Demjanjuk, Gröning, and Hanning trials. But by then, greater determination to pursue perpetrators and declining reliance on survivor testimony were already too late.

Mielec Perpetrators: Divided Sympathies in East and West

The small cases relating to acts of terror in Mielec, tucked away in the southern part of Poland, did not attract the media attention of the big trials of the 1960s. But precisely because the Mielec trials played little or no role in intra-German reputational competitions—East versus West—and were not publicity stunts, they prove to be highly revealing of underlying differences between the two systems.

The trials in East and West Germany relating to Mielec ran almost in parallel, and many of the same issues were considered on each side of the border. In the West German case, it was one of the Nazi superiors, Walter Thormeyer, the man who had been in charge of the Mielec Gestapo headquarters and giving orders, who was on trial; in the East German case, the defendant was one of his subordinates, the only partially literate ethnic German Rudolf ("Rudi") Zimmermann, who had obeyed orders and carried out some of the atrocities. Their cases were treated in entirely different ways.

On February 10, 1966, the state prosecutor for the Regional Court of Freiburg im Breisgau, in West Germany, wrote to the Central Office for Processing National Socialist Crimes at the Office of the General State Prosecutor of Berlin in the GDR—a country not specifically mentioned in the address of the letter from the Federal Republic, which at this time refused to recognize East Germany as a separate state.[1] The letter contained a request from the West German side to locate Rudolf Zimmermann, who was needed as a witness for the trial in Freiburg, scheduled to start on September 19, 1966, of Walter Thormeyer and others, including Helmut Hensel, Thormeyer's predecessor as head of the Gestapo in Mielec.[2] As a result, Zimmermann was duly located in the small East German town of Altenburg, living quietly with his wife and four children.

By this time, Rudi Zimmermann was a well-integrated GDR citizen who had joined the ruling communist party and the SED as well as the official state trade union organization, the FDGB (Free German League of Trade Unions). He had even acquired a number of merit awards for his hard work and commitment to the socialist system. Such integration of someone who had held a rather lowly position in the Nazi system of terror and had over the course of two decades changed his ways was a typical post-Nazi trajectory. But it meant little as far as the East German justice system was concerned.

Rather than restricting the inquiry to asking Zimmermann to give evidence in relation to the trial of his former boss, Thormeyer, Zimmermann was himself arrested and put on trial in the GDR.

Curiously, Zimmermann appears almost relieved to have been identified and brought to account for his deeds. In a statement given on October 13, 1966, to the committing magistrate in the central Berlin district of Mitte, Zimmermann added (quite unnecessarily, one might think) an unusual confession arising from an uneasy conscience: "I would like to add that I confess my guilt in the sense of the arrest warrant." He conceded that "due to the lapse of time, some of the details of my crimes are no longer in my memory." Even so, "it is correct that I participated in selections and killings." And this had been troubling him to such an extent that, he wrote, "I had already, two or three years ago, considered turning myself in." But, he added, "I already had a family and did not then, after all, have the courage to do this."[3] Once arrested, however, Zimmermann freely gave innumerable details of his participation and provided sketches of the route from the Heinkel aircraft hangar in Mielec to the killing sites in the nearby woods, as well as providing grim details of many other "actions" of mass murder. His occasional difficulties in remembering every detail of his deeds were not a function of selective amnesia; he had clearly felt haunted by his past.

Zimmermann's testimony was refreshingly frank and rather unusual; it seems motivated not so much by any concern about self-incrimination as by a desire to unburden himself of repressed memories, and it is characterized by an apparently genuine tone of remorse. This stands in marked contrast to the self-righteousness, denials, and supposed lapses of memory that were frequent features of perpetrator testimony in the first two decades after the war. Zimmermann talked quite openly of the "liquidation of the Jews" as one of the principal tasks (*Hauptaufgaben*) of the Gestapo offices in Reichshof, Mielec, and Stalowa Wola for which he acted as interpreter.[4] Zimmermann also provided a clear view of the lines of responsibility and orders, as the Gestapo cooperated with higher levels of both the civilian administration and the police and security forces in the area. Hans Frank, the governor general of occupied Poland, gave instructions that were "implemented by the district leaders and county commissioners." There was close cooperation between the repressive forces and civilian administration: the "respective Gestapo offices oversaw all the measures and determined the specifics with the responsible county commissioners or district leaders." Then "the SS or the gendarmerie carried out the deportation," while "supervision was carried out by the relevant Gestapo office in whose district the deport-ations took place."[5] Zimmermann's own role was at the very bottom of this chain of authority and command.

The level of Zimmermann's enthusiasm in carrying out these orders is difficult to gauge from the trial materials alone. It is likely that Zimmermann had at first enjoyed his newfound authority over people to whom he had previously felt inferior—the better educated Jews of Mielec, compared to his own ethnic German farming community of Hohenbach in the hamlet of Czermin, in which he had grown up just a few miles out of town—and exer-cised his new uniformed power energetically, willingly assisting in the iden-tification, roundup, and deportation of Mielec Jews. But he seems to have become less comfortable with his subsequent duties in assisting with selections in the aircraft hangar and mass shootings in the nearby woods. Even so, he went on to participate in organized killings here and elsewhere in the wider area.

The psychological, social, and political considerations brought to bear in the judgment of Zimmermann are significant. Consideration was given to the fact that Zimmermann, unlike so many ordinary perpetrators, did not imbibe alcohol while committing murders, because this was officially forbidden and he was fearful of his superiors. The judge surmised that Zimmermann's "fear of his inconsiderate and brutal superiors [was] greater than his sympathy with his victims." The orders he received appear to have "substituted for human impulses and human empathy." The judge noted that "the accused never drank alcohol during the commission of atrocities, but observed the relevant orders"; it seemed possible, however, that "even the accused would have liked to have had his periodically troubled con-science numbed by alcohol." The judge surmised that "in order not to con-flict with his orders, he only drank after the crimes had been committed."[6]

Much emphasis was therefore given to Zimmermann's relatively lowly status, his inner reservations about the actions, and also his fear of the con-sequences if he disobeyed orders, to which the judge says he "clung dog-gedly." Had his trial taken place in West Germany, these would have been weighty considerations with rather different implications for sentencing—or acquittal.

Due consideration was also given to Zimmermann's changed character and exemplary conduct as a citizen of the GDR. The father of four children now between the ages of ten and seventeen, Zimmermann had worked in Wismut, a major uranium mine in the nearby Erzgebirge Mountains and of strategic significance across the entire Soviet bloc. In 1953 and again in 1955 he had earned the title of "activist" (*Aktivist*), an honor bestowed on those who were particularly productive at work, and in 1954 had even been awarded the higher accolade of "activist of service" (*Verdienter Aktivist*), someone who had met even more demanding criteria of sustained productivity, service, and commitment. In 1958 he was nominated as "master miner of the GDR" (*Meisterhauer der DDR*); in 1960 he received the award of "master of work, second class" (*Meister der Arbeit, II. Klasse*). He was a member of the trade union organization and the Society for German-Soviet Friendship. Following an application in 1955, he was accepted into membership in the SED some six months later. Zimmermann was clearly someone who closely followed orders from above, whatever the political color of the regime. One could hardly hope for a better GDR citizen, as far as his outward record of commitment was concerned.

Against all this, it was noted that Zimmermann had kept quiet about his pre-1945 activities: "Both for his personnel file for SDAG-Wismut [the uranium mine] and also in his application to join the Party, the accused suppressed his membership of the Gestapo and the SD."[7] Moreover, he needed to be held responsible for having "severely affected the life and health of other citizens."[8] Even so, Zimmermann had, in the view of the court, been transformed from the uncertain and ill-educated youngster who had been infected with Nazism and obeyed orders into the mature GDR citizen who had a sense of guilt, in this way holding "a particular place in the ranks of those who committed similar crimes": unlike many other former Nazis, he was "suffering under the burden of guilt that he, as the Zimmermann of an earlier time, has taken upon himself."[9] As "a citizen of our state" Zimmermann had "done everything, but everything, to work off his guilt" and had felt impelled to "put an end to his life's lie." But "cowardice" and "great fear" had in the end prevented him from coming forward. Instead, he had continued "to work secretly on expunging his guilt."[10]

In this way, Zimmermann was represented in court as a changed person—"this is not the same Zimmermann"—and not only a product of his early conditions before and during Nazism but also a person who had converted to socialism very successfully. He had, moreover, actively chosen to live in the GDR rather than the West, having voluntarily returned after an exploratory trip to West Germany. He had worked well and productively, with many awards, and he felt remorse about his past. He was in so many ways a success story for the GDR, demonstrating just how far it was possible to transform people into the desired "socialist personality," even when they had formerly been so utterly blinded by Nazism.

Nevertheless, ultimately all this did not weigh sufficiently in the balance of the East German scales of justice. Zimmermann would still have to be sentenced for his earlier crimes. In the final summing up, the judge concluded that even Zimmermann's impressive contributions to GDR society and his productive work for the Wismut mining company were not sufficient to outweigh the burden of guilt. Nor was the fact that his crimes were committed as a result of "German fascism" sufficient to relieve him of individual guilt.[11] Unlike the successful defenses that we have seen in West German trials at that time, in the GDR having followed orders was no defense and in this case did not serve to compensate for Zimmermann's personal guilt.[12] By West German standards the sentence for this ill-educated underling was very harsh. The judge summarized all the mitigating factors—family background, local circumstances, ideological influences, and postwar transformation—but nevertheless concluded that he should be given a "just sentence": life imprisonment and permanent loss of rights as a citizen.[13]

This was a heavy blow to Zimmermann's wife and four children, although the GDR was scrupulous in ensuring that the children should not be disadvantaged at school or in their further study and employment prospects because of their father's misdeeds. A letter of April 26, 1968, from the party secretary of the Karl-Marx Upper School (*Erweiterte Oberschule*) attended by the two daughters noted that the children's powers of concentration, scholastic achievements, and willingness to learn were being adversely affected by uncertainty over their father's fate.[14] In a reply from the state prosecutor, received by the school a little over two weeks later, it was confirmed that since the children knew nothing about their father's crimes, additional support would have to be provided to help them through the problems they would face; but in a socialist society, children should not be adversely affected by the misdeeds of their fathers.[15]

Irma Zimmermann, who had also grown up in the village near Mielec, remained faithful to her husband to the last, writing to him and visiting him in prison, and doing all she could—unsuccessfully, as it turned out—to try to secure an early release. Not all her letters got through in their entirety. One, dated August 25, 1968, is preserved in the file with a note saying that it was read out to the prisoner on September 10, 1968 with the exception of one sentence that the authorities had underlined, and then it was sent back to the state prosecutor. Most of the letter concerns how much Irma misses her husband and what is going on in the garden, with relatively little detailed news about the children: we hear of summer holidays, lots of fruit, but the children would have to go back to school soon. The relevant sentence that was censored was from the end of the letter. Irma apparently refers back to an earlier comment made by her husband: "You are right, my dearest Rudi, one has to pull oneself together, however hard this may be, life goes on, and there is no justice, no, none at all for the little man."[16] In a later long letter of June 12, 1973, to the general state prosecutor of the GDR, Irma Zimmermann records that the children have made progress: three have passed the final high school examination, the *Abitur*, and have succeeded in entering further and higher education, while the youngest is still at school. But she herself could scarcely bear the burden any more: her health had suffered, and she was close to a breakdown.[17] These and subsequent appeals were to no effect, and the sentence to life imprisonment remained in place until Zimmermann's death in December 1988.

The West German legal process for Walter Thormeyer, former SS *Hauptscharführer* and Zimmermann's superior in the Mielec Gestapo headquarters from summer 1942 until autumn 1943, turned out quite differently. Zimmermann was repeatedly characterized in the West German press as the "terror [*Schrecken*] of Mielec," conforming to the standard notion of the perpetrator as an ill-educated brute.[18] His superior, Thormeyer, who was at this time a senior court secretary (*Justizobersekretär*) in the notary's office of the Freiburg court, gained a slightly more favorable reception.

Thormeyer's former role and misdeeds were clear. He had allegedly been a "favorite" of the relevant SS office in Kraków. He had a wide remit, covering all the Jewish forced labor camps in the area, including the Heinkel aircraft factory and the road-construction company Bäumer and Loesch. He personally ordered, oversaw, and even actively participated in the mass shootings of anyone too weak or ill to work, including incidents in which Zimmermann was involved. It was indeed the fact that Zimmermann was sought by the West German authorities to give evidence in Thormeyer's trial, which began in late 1966 in Freiburg im Breisgau, that had first brought Zimmermann to the attention of the East German authorities; and once the East Germans were in possession of his personal details and whereabouts, his fate in the GDR was more or less sealed. But Zimmermann was really the "little man" in this case, the one who genuinely had only been following orders. In most incidents it was either Hensel or Thormeyer who had actually given the orders. Thormeyer had ordered Jews in the aircraft factory in Mielec, including those whom he considered no longer capable of working, to strip naked in the woods near the aircraft hangar and to witness others being shot dead in front of them before they too were shot into an open grave. According to Zimmermann's testimony, Thormeyer had not only given the orders but had on many occasions carried out shootings himself.[19] Thormeyer clearly looked down on Zimmermann, whom he called a "dumb peasant lout."[20] According to Zimmermann, who was frightened of his boss and tried hard not to rub him the wrong way, Thormeyer did not have a good relationship with his subordinates: "He lorded it over everyone and always thought he knew best. That's why no comradely relationship developed between him and us."[21] As we have seen, Thormeyer had also shot his Jewish mistress once the illegal relationship had become the focus of gossip and he ran the risk of being accused of "racial defilement" (*Rassenschande*).[22]

Zimmermann's testimony provides a chilling description of how such "actions" were carried out, giving a glimpse of how the victims must have experienced the last moments of their lives. Thormeyer would obtain from the leader of the work detail a list of names of those selected for killing, and they would be gathered together to wait on the "Appellplatz," the area where roll call was carried out. Zimmermann recalled that "when the Jewish forced laborers saw us coming, great panic broke out among them because they knew exactly that selections for shootings would be carried out."[23] In the summer of 1943 a typhus epidemic erupted among the workers living in unsanitary conditions on inadequate rations, which meant that there were frequent selections of the weak and the unwell for shooting into a mass grave in the nearby woods. The ones who were too ill to walk had to be taken there in a horse-drawn carriage belonging to the Heinkel factory. On arrival at the execution site, they were pulled out, made to lie on the ground, shot, and then thrown into the pit.[24]

According to Zimmermann, on the occasion of mass killings Thormeyer appeared to prefer shooting the female Jews personally, always selecting them first out of the group and then shooting them himself, while Zimmermann and his Gestapo colleagues Friedrich and Glamann were left to shoot all the male Jews. Zimmermann commented that Thormeyer appeared to derive some enjoyment from this, and that he "shot the female Jews with a certain relish."[25]

Zimmermann also noted the responses of those Jews who had been selected to die, who "behaved extremely anxiously. They wailed, cried, and implored THORMEIER [*sic*] to let them live after all."[26] On one occasion

Thormeyer told them to sit down: "In this way a certain peace was restored. Despite this they wailed and clung to each other. When their turn came, THORMEIER [sic] tore them apart violently, pushed them to the mass grave and killed them with a shot in the back of the neck."[27]

The Freiburg court was aware of all these details when considering Thormeyer's case. Contemporary newspaper reports provide intriguing insights on Thormeyer's trial in what was apparently a packed courtroom. He claimed he was always "uninterested in politics" and had simply been taught in many training courses that "orders must be carried out" without hesitation.[28] Having joined the police force in 1929, he had decided to join the Nazi Party in 1937 and subsequently the SS "not from political conviction but rather in the hope of faster promotion."[29] In January 1959, in order to gain his current position, he had lied about his Nazi past, writing to the Baden-Württemberg Ministry of Justice that he had "taken part in no excesses against Jews and at that time also knew nothing about this."[30] Now called to account for his deeds in court, he sat "pale and shame-faced on the defendant's bench," but once he spoke, he came across as "sure and self-confident."[31] Even so, it was "in a faltering voice" that he described shooting eight or nine slave laborers in the back of the neck; he claimed that he and his three colleagues had found this "harrowing" and had not enjoyed doing it.[32] He even suggested that this terrible "burden" that had been laid upon him would "pursue him for the rest of his life."[33] This self-representation was however countered by many witnesses. One was a man by the name of Glamann (his first name is variously given as either "Wilhelm" or "Heinrich"), a former colleague in the Mielec Gestapo and now mayor of the town of Beckum near Hildesheim, who had assisted in shooting Jewish workers.[34] Glamann recalled Thormeyer's attitude at the time as being "totally unaffected" by what he was doing, "even downright cynical."[35] Other former colleagues in leading positions in the factory claimed to have seen, heard, and known nothing; but in the context, there had been a degree of indifference.[36] Jewish witness statements were more informative, confirming that people were shot not only because they were allegedly too ill to work but also because, for example, they had turned up late to roll call or had "stolen" a potato or had committed other minor offenses.[37]

The West German judge ultimately pronounced a sentence of twelve years' imprisonment. As in the major concentration camp trials, the reasons given for this lesser sentence underline the ways in which a West German judge, more than twenty years after the end of the war, could still appear to have more sympathy with former Nazis than with their victims.[38] As a Freiburg senior court official, Thormeyer was at this time in effect a colleague. In sentencing, the judge explicitly took into account Thormeyer's postwar lifestyle and continued chance of a good bourgeois existence, noting that "a long prison sentence for the accused, in an advanced stage of life, in large measure also destroys his economic existence and makes it difficult to build this up again after the end of the sentence."[39] Furthermore, the conditions of imprisonment would not be easy for someone accustomed to such a lifestyle.[40]

Moreover, the judge's sympathies are evident in a final—quite extraordinary—consideration. In the view of this judge, at least, the way Thormeyer had murdered his Jewish mistress—shooting her in the back of the neck while on a walk in the woods—had been "humane." There could be no doubt about Thormeyer's personal motives for murder, which could in no way be written off as "following orders," since it was entirely selfish, to protect himself against gossip and any charge of "racial defilement." But in the judge's view, the fact that Thormeyer had murdered his mistress without forewarning was deemed to be evidence of "consideration." There are echoes here of the comments in the euthanasia case of Dr. Hermann Pfannmüller, where children in his "care" were unaware of the poisonous powder that had been sprinkled in with their food. According to West German interpretations of the law, killing was a less heinous offense if the victim did not suspect it was about to happen.

The Dębica SS: Rehearsed Defenses and Unreliable Victims

The evident sympathy of judges with perpetrators' perspectives was not confined to this circle, nor was it unique to this case. Former Nazis in West Germany often conferred among themselves on how best to coordinate their stories and prepare their defenses. For example, Werner Best, a former RSHA functionary and Nazi plenipotentiary, was highly active in the 1960s in coordinating stories among former Gestapo leaders on behalf of defendants, as in the case of Otto Bovensiepen, head of the Berlin Gestapo from 1941 to 1943, who had been in charge of the deportation of Berlin Jews. Best wrote around to a long list of former Gestapo colleagues, inviting them to confirm that they had at the time "not known" about the destination or fate of Jews transported to the east; those who replied truthfully that they had indeed been aware of the deadly fate awaiting those transported were crossed off the list of people to be called as witnesses, while others were readied for their duties helping to establish the plausibility of Bovensiepen's highly implausible claim of ignorance.[41] The association representing former members of the Waffen-SS, the HIAG (Mutual Assistance Association, Hilfsgemeinschaft auf Gegenseitigkeit), similarly played an active role in ensuring the best possible defenses through mutual corroboration.[42] And as evident in the Majdanek case, the organization Stille Hilfe provided assistance to former Nazis.

These practices of mutual support and corroboration of stories were well known by West German courts. But this was not seen as a problem comparable to that of survivors meeting up and talking after the end of the war. This probably unconscious sympathy for perpetrator networks became apparent in the treatment of witness and perpetrator statements to the court in the case of Hans Proschinsky, a former SS major (Sturmbannführer) involved in atrocities committed at the SS training grounds at Dębica, just south of Mielec.[43] An oral history interview carried out in 1994 with Hans Müller, the son of one of Proschinsky's former colleagues, Peter Müller, offers some insight.[44] As previously mentioned, Hans Müller had no idea of what had gone on in this area—neither while growing up nor even at the time of his interview. But although ignorant of any specifics, Hans Müller did become aware of increased activity around the time that the trials were being prepared. As he recalls, at some point in the 1960s the Polish authorities had dug up some mass graves, and there was an official "commission" of investigation. Official investigators called on his mother to inquire further about activities in the area where her husband—who had by then been dead for some ten years—had been active. Müller recalled that his mother became "terribly agitated" and maintained that she did not know anything and had "lost sight" of her husband's former friends and "war comrades." After the members of the commission had left the house, her son recalled, "she telephoned around quite hectically," in order to give them "advance warning." She "also tried to agree upon statements with them, just in case."[45]

Hans Müller, still lacking knowledge of SS activities in the area where his father had been stationed, went on to see this in terms of his father's "knowledge" of crimes, rather than raising any questions about what his father might actually have done. His suspicion was therefore only in relation to the question of alleged ignorance: "There is certainly a lot more that my mother either repressed or consciously did not talk about. So I am sure that both of them knew more than they admitted."[46]

Hans Müller's mother had sought to forewarn other perpetrators from the Dębica SS training grounds so that they could make sure their stories corroborated each other. The fact of such collusion was also well known to the judge in the trial that prosecuted crimes committed in this area by Müller's former colleague, Proschinsky. As the judge commented, one former SS leader had in his statements given in 1973 "acknowledged that he had turned to other former members of the SS who had earlier been stationed at the training grounds, in order to contribute to the exoneration of the defendant." This had, moreover, "happened with the consent of the defense attorney."[47] The judge was hence aware that even the defense lawyer was explicitly party to this organized coordination of perpetrator witness testimony. The judge further suggested that everyone knew in any case that former SS colleagues remained in contact with each other. This should not however, he continued, be seen to detract from the value of their testimony, and their "comradely benevolence" toward the defendant was, in his view, "perfectly understandable in human terms."[48] It is likely that similar views were held by West German judges in innumerable other smaller cases and trials that did not enter the public spotlight.

The judgment gives full details of crimes committed in Dębica. A massive camp was built there by the summer of 1941, with barracks to house thirty-five thousand troops and facilities to train in shooting practice. The vast majority of the Russian prisoners of war who were held at a camp at the site had died by the autumn of 1941; they were buried in a mass grave, which was later exhumed and the bodies were burned on a huge funeral pyre. Jewish slave laborers were then put into the barracks where the Russians had previously been held, some of them arrivals from Mielec, a mere twenty kilometers away. The violence was horrific, and prisoners who could no longer work because of malnutrition, exhaustion, and disease were either killed on the spot— shot, lashed, kicked to death—or deported to the extermination camps of Bełzec and Sobibór.[49] The remaining Jewish prisoners were deported in 1944, most of them to Auschwitz, although some were selected as labor for use in munitions factories and were deported further into the heart of the Reich—including to Mittelbau-Dora, near Nordhausen, where they continued to work on Werner von Braun's rocket production program.

This would all seem damning. But the Dębica case again illustrates the significance of the "subjective" aspect in West German law: the state of mind of the person accused was central to demonstrating murder rather than manslaughter. In effect, only "excess perpetrators," who went beyond what was officially required of them under Nazi rule, and not the system itself, were seen as murderers in the sense of the criminal law. The fact that slave laborers in the SS troop training ground at Dębica were shot dead if they collapsed at work or "while trying to flee" or were lashed or kicked to death, hanged, or strangled with a bit of rope carried around for this purpose did not mean that they had technically been "murdered" rather merely having been victims of manslaughter; it all depended on whether the court felt there was adequate proof of the state of mind of the perpetrator at the time of the act.

In the Dębica case, therefore, on each count, the court considered both "the external facts of what happened" and "the subjective state relating to the act." Proschinsky was accordingly found not guilty in certain cases where he had killed workers, including one where the victim died as a result of incessant whip lashings, since the eyewitness to this brutality could not additionally provide any conclusive evidence about Proschinsky's state of mind at the time of this cruel action. As the judge put it: "The statements of the witness Dri. do not entail the conclusion that the defendant wanted to kill the victim who was maltreated with the whip, nor that he saw and approved the possibility of his death."[50] Neither, presumably, could Proschinsky at the time of the trial provide conclusive empirical evidence about his state of mind when he was lashing a slave laborer to death, but he was given the benefit of the doubt and deemed innocent of the intention to murder this particular victim.

There was enough evidence of other incidents under the general charge of "killing of forced laborers by shooting, strangling, and trampling to death" for Proschinsky to be given a life sentence. The verdict seems apposite. Yet even here, with a conclusive overall outcome, witness statements were not seen as sufficient to prove the state of mind of the defendant—which was what made all the difference. Killing purely in the normal course of duties as part of SS activities in occupied Poland was not necessarily murder; perpetrators seem to have enjoyed an enormous benefit of the doubt. This stood in stark contrast to the treatment of witness testimony in West Germany at this time.

The Variable Weight of the Evidence in East and West

For twenty years after the war, despite having received a disfiguring injury to his face in an accident while a prisoner of war in Czechoslovakia, Josef

Blösche enjoyed a quiet life in the small Thuringian town of Urbach.[51] He worked in the People's Own Potash Works Volkenroda (VEB Kaliwerk Volkenroda) in nearby Menteroda, where he belonged to the official trade union organization, the FDGB, and received acclamation as a "master of work." Colleagues remember him as helpful and conscientious. His wife ran a canteen attached to the local cooperative shop, and together they had two children—a son and a daughter. Blösche blended well into East German society. In 1964 he was even able to afford a small car—a Trabant ("Trabi")—a much-desired luxury for which there were long waiting lists. Only when there was a television program or conversation relating to the war did Blösche become agitated, refusing to speak and occasionally leaving the room in some distress. His discomfort increased when his brother Gustav, who lived in Hamburg, told him that he had been questioned about activities during the war. Blösche's own past caught up with him soon afterward.

For Blösche—who, as an ill-educated young man, had held a lowly but violent position in the SS—came to the attention of the East German authorities in 1966, when the Hamburg court requested his extradition to serve as a witness. The West German authorities had since 1960 been investigating the wartime crimes of Dr. Ludwig Hahn, a trained lawyer who as commander of the Security Police and SD in Warsaw had held a position of seniority and initiative.[52] Hahn had been responsible for mass "reprisal" executions in Warsaw, individual incidents of violence, the maltreatment of prisoners in the Pawiak prison. and the deportation in a series of "actions" (violent roundups) of around three hundred thousand Jews to their deaths in Treblinka, which he visited personally in 1942. Hahn was also responsible for the violent crushing of the ghetto uprising during its final "liquidation" in spring 1943 and the Polish uprising of 1944. Josef Blösche—incomparably junior, but since his youth a faithful follower of the Nazi cause—had given assistance, including to Jürgen Stroop, who was in charge of suppression of the ghetto uprising and shortly afterward became SS and a police leader in Warsaw. Blösche is, indeed, frequently seen in photographs of this period, often standing close to Stroop, including in the well-known photograph portraying a young boy with hands held high.

Blösche was initially identified in the summer of 1965 and was arrested in January 1967, the West German extradition request having meanwhile been refused. Held in the Stasi Hohenschönhausen prison in East Berlin, Blösche was repeatedly interrogated by four officers from the MfS.[53] His wife appears to have been particularly concerned by this arrest, having apparently had no inkling of his violent past and confirming that after seventeen years of marriage she had absolute trust in him.[54] She, as well as Blösche's sisters, neighbors, and work colleagues, were questioned, and witness testimonies were obtained from survivors.

Blösche's trial in Erfurt started on March 17, 1969. In his statement Blösche admitted guilt and accepted full responsibility for his actions, saying that he did not remember all the details but that the general picture was correct. He had been attracted to National Socialist ideology as a young person, participating in right-wing youth organizations fomenting nationalist unrest among ethnic Germans in his native Sudetenland, and was later influenced by ideological training in the SS. He had believed that the Jews were an "inferior race," and he had no scruples about using violence to achieve the "final solution." Nor did he worry about the fates of those deported to Treblinka, even though he knew—and was told directly by a Jewish ghetto policeman—that they would be gassed there. He also knew, from an incident where he could not bring himself to shoot a naked girl as Stroop had demanded, that there would be no adverse consequences for refusal to obey orders.[55] The lack of any recourse to the kinds of defense strategies that were typical in West German courts is notable. An appeal against his death sentence was, as expected, instantly turned down by the Berlin high court, with a reiteration of the Erfurt court's findings.[56] Blösche was duly executed on July 19, 1969—a remarkably speedy passage of justice.

This stood in marked contrast to the case regarding Blösche's superior, Hahn, in West Germany, which was what had precipitated the search for Blösche's whereabouts in the GDR. In 1959 a journalist, Günter Koch, had accidentally become aware of the fact that Hahn, who had been responsible for so many deaths in Warsaw, was living quite openly in Hamburg; Koch accordingly brought a charge against him.[57] Little happened, even when Koch gained an offer of support from the Polish embassy in Copenhagen; it was only when a Jewish survivor got involved that Hahn was arrested. Despite being accused of offenses including mass deportations of Jews, violent suppression of the ghetto uprising in 1943 and the Warsaw uprising of 1944, and numerous incidents of ordering shootings and reprisal executions, Hahn was released on bail and continued in profitable employment, buying a plot of land and building a house for his wife and four children. The investigations were remarkably slow, and despite being taken into custody again 1965, he was released in 1967 for health reasons.

The files on Hahn's case had by 1966 swollen to some twenty-two thousand pages.[58] Around two thousand witnesses had testified, and in 1967 the attorney in charge of the investigation reportedly suffered a nervous breakdown due to lack of adequate support in face of the growing mountains of evidence.[59] It was more than clear that, by virtue of his position, Hahn had been responsible for several hundred thousand deaths, whether directly through actions under his command in the Warsaw area or through organization of deportations to gassing in Treblinka. Yet it seemed impossible for the German authorities actually to mount a trial. By the time Blösche was put to death, some critics of West German justice were beginning to ask why, given the overwhelming weight of evidence against Blösche's former boss, it seemed so difficult to put Hahn on trial. Protesting voices included the Holocaust survivor and historian Josef Wulf, who had written extensively on Hahn, Blösche, and the suppression of the Warsaw ghetto uprising in his 1961 book on perpetrators in the Third Reich.[60] Wulf was often isolated in scholarly circles but was here supported by left-liberal journalists as well as by the ubiquitous Austrian Nazi hunter Simon Wiesenthal. Some journalists suggested that Hahn enjoyed the protection of his high-ranking brother-in-law, General Johannes Steinhoff, who played a prominent role in the NATO Military Committee. Finally, after twelve years of intensive investigations, a trial opened in 1972 concerning Hahn's responsibility for the deaths of around one hundred Poles in the Pawiak prison. Found guilty, he received a sentence of twelve years. In 1974, a second trial opened concerning his role in the liquidation of the ghetto, and in 1975 he was found guilty for his part in the murder of at least 230,000 people and sentenced to life imprisonment. In the event, however, Hahn served only eight years, being released in 1983.

These two interrelated cases illustrate a more general pattern, in which a well-organized trial would be mounted in East Germany in direct relation to proceedings in the West. There was a complicated dance in both East and West Germany around mutual willingness (or unwillingness) to assist the other state in requests for extraditions or materials. The Blösche case was also important for the Polish authorities, who assisted representatives of the East German legal team and Ministry for State Security in gaining documentary evidence and witness testimonies, as well as treated them to an extracurricular program of entertainment—sandwiching a trip to Treblinka between a boat ride and a visit to the Warsaw State Opera. The trip was also used to acquire additional materials for the case against Zimmermann. The report on the trip reiterated how both Poland and the GDR wanted to influence the Hamburg proceedings against Hahn as well as the contemporaneous Düsseldorf case against former Treblinka commander Franz Stangl, as well as to expose West German failures to bring Nazis to justice. Additionally, the Polish authorities wanted the case to reinforce their assertion that no Poles had assisted in massacres of Jews.[61]

The GDR authorities on this occasion decided not to make the Blösche case a major focus of publicity. It was agreed that only invited persons should be allowed to attend the trial—and, indeed, photographs of courtroom proceedings show a sober and attentive audience, made up mainly of men in suits and ties with a few demure-looking women. There was to be only restricted coverage by local press and the major GDR newspaper, *Neues Deutschland*—which duly noted that while Blösche was sentenced to death, Hahn was still at large in West Germany.[62] Considerable attention was paid to a reader's letter sent to the youth newspaper *Junge Welt* by an apprentice expressing his concern that former Nazis were still around and might be surreptitiously active in the GDR, despite official claims that all had fled west. On the instructions of the GDR attorney general, a local district attorney was sent to talk to the apprentice in his own home, in order to reassure him that Blösche had been born outside Germany, his crimes committed outside Germany, and that he had only settled in the GDR because of his facial disfigurement and belief that he would remain undetected.[63]

The trial in 1983 of Heinz Barth was, by contrast, a high-profile event designed specifically to highlight and sharpen the contrast with the foot-dragging going on in the Federal Republic.[64] Barth had been involved in the massacre at Oradour-sur-Glane in France, where on June 10, 1944, the Waffen-SS murdered nearly 650 people. Others who had played major roles in this massacre had lived freely in the West, including General Heinz Lammerding, who had authorized the massacre. Lammerding had been sentenced to death in absentia in a French trial in 1953, but West Germany refused a French request for his extradition; he then led a quiet and apparently prosperous life in West Germany until his death in 1971, much mourned by SS comrades.

Similarly, in the context of the trial of Klaus Barbie in France, the GDR again chose to mount a high-profile trial in 1987. In this case it was against former Dresden Gestapo chief Henry Schmidt—picking up again on the trials of the late 1940s relating to forced labor in the Goehle works, but now with new emphases. Deportation was a topic that was rarely touched on in either East or West German trials: in the GDR, there were six trials relating to deportations, all resulting in guilty verdicts; in West Germany there were thirteen trials, but ending with thirty-eight acquittals and only nine guilty sentences.[65] Schmidt's trial highlighted particularly the deportation of Jews to Theresienstadt and Auschwitz, at a time when historical approaches were being opened up and Jewish experiences addressed more directly in the GDR.

Like Blösche, Zimmermann, and innumerable others, Henry Schmidt had led a model life under succeeding dictatorships. From a modest social background, he had made his career under Nazism, gaining experience in an Einsatzgruppe in Poland at the start of the war, receiving training in Ravensbrück and Sachsenhausen, and rising through the ranks of the SS until he was in charge of deportations from Dresden to Theresienstadt and Auschwitz. Having had his SS blood group tattoo removed after the war, Schmidt had subsequently made a new life under his own name in the GDR. He proved to be a model citizen: living with his family in in the East German town of Altenburg (like Zimmermann), Schmidt not only received a variety of honors for achievements in his workplace, including as an "activist of socialist work," but also served stints in an honorary capacity in the voluntary fire service and in the local workers' housing cooperative as well as in his own residential block.[66] And like Zimmermann, but unlike so many perpetrators who stood trial in the West, once confronted with his Nazi past, Schmidt proved to be a model defendant.[67] Perhaps because he knew it would be of no use whatsoever in the East German system of justice, Schmidt did not seek to displace blame to a few scapegoats at the top; although he pointed to the role of the RSHA in issuing the orders, Schmidt did not deny responsibility for his own actions, nor did he deny knowledge of the deadly character of the destinations of the deportations.

The trial was organized down to the last detail, with careful selection of witnesses for the prosecution—none for the defense—and the outcome and publicity were orchestrated in advance. The final judgment by the GDR's highest court of appeal (Oberstes Gericht der DDR) upheld the life sentence pronounced by the Dresden regional court. The facts of Schmidt's biography were noted, including his exemplary postwar life; but unlike in the West, this was not weighed in the balance to mitigate the sentence, and indeed it was noted that he had only been able to participate in GDR society by virtue of suppressing and denying his past.[68] It was noted specifically that "the goal of the persecution of the Jews was their extermination" and that this required the cooperation of a multitude of planners, people who gave orders, and people who carried them out, at all levels within a system of "state-organized murder"; the defendant, as part of this, had a share in responsibility for the outcome.[69] The prosecution attorney, Horst Busse, published an illustrated account of the trial, replete with political arguments. Busse noted that the nearly seventy-five-year-old defendant was always very correct and appeared remarkably unruffled by the proceedings; he was, according to Busse, clearly a "man with two faces."[70] Press commentaries were carefully coordinated to target different newspaper audiences, with the official organ of the SED, *Neues Deutschland*, providing reports, for example, on Busse's speeches. These included his passionate account of how the trial fulfilled the GDR's "promise" and "commitment" to those who had died in the fight against Nazism, and how, "in view of the weight of the crimes and the high measure of personal responsibility," Schmidt should be "forever excluded from society." The GDR would indeed not rest "until the last Nazi criminal" had been discovered and brought to court.[71] Meanwhile people in the packed courtroom, including many young people, were reportedly deeply moved by the witnesses' evidence.[72] The East German state film company, the DEFA, also made a documentary film, including footage of Schmidt's family, with little regard for any personal rights to privacy. The trial effectively destroyed Schmidt's life: his wife committed suicide on the first day of the trial, since she could not face the shame.

Despite the evident distortions of justice, including the failure to bring any witnesses for the defense, when Schmidt appealed in 1992 the verdict was upheld. At the age of eighty-four he was released from prison on medical grounds on April 4, 1996, and he died barely six weeks later.

The Commandant of Mielec: The Fading Significance of Victim Testimony

In March 1990, following the collapse of communist rule in the GDR but prior to the unexpectedly rapid unification with the Federal Republic seven months later, the sorry state of the twenty-three remaining Nazi prisoners languishing behind bars in East German prisons came to the attention of the West German news magazine *Der Spiegel*.[73] At one extreme, a prisoner had been held for thirty-four years; in the case of the most recent conviction, just a few months of the sentence had been served. In the journalist's view, the fact that some Nazi perpetrators who had been given life sentences did indeed remain in prison for life was yet more evidence of the intrinsic inhumanity of the GDR and the politically biased character of its legal system. According to the *Spiegel* article, the SED regime needed the continued imprisonment of "its Nazi henchmen in order to document the cleanliness of the East Republic for the whole world."[74] Some of these prisoners were serving life sentences and would perhaps have been executed in an earlier era when the death sentence was still in use. Whether or not they might have deserved their punishment—as was considered to be the case with Schmidt—was apparently not as important as the alleged abuse of justice for purposes of building an international political reputation. The *Spiegel* article stressed the inhumanity of the sentences in view of the age and ill-health of these former Nazis. Yet again, the voice of the liberal democratic West appeared to be more concerned about the well-being of those who had inflicted death and suffering than with justice for their victims.

Even some forty-five years after the end of the war, the competition between East and West for the moral high ground was still being played out over the treatment of former Nazis. Where one state claimed moral superiority through greater stringency in dealing with perpetrators and overcoming the past, the other claimed moral superiority in greater mercy and humanity shown to precisely those perpetrators.

This was not the end of the story of German attempts—on the whole, failed ones—to do justice to the Nazi past in the courtroom. Trials of just a few elderly individuals took place in the 1990s, after the unification of Germany. These trials effectively marked not only the end of the rivalry and distinctions between East and West German systems of justice but also the petering out of the age of confrontations between persecutors and persecuted. Cases drizzled on, before a surprising legal twist, one that came too late to make any difference at all to the pursuit of justice on behalf of the millions who had been persecuted and murdered.

Another trial relating to southern Poland illustrates the shift in emphasis. The former commandant of the labor and concentration camps of Przemyśl and Mielec, Josef Schwammberger, was finally put on trial in Stuttgart in 1991–92, nearly half a century after he had committed atrocities across southern Poland, including in Stalowa-Wola, assisted by someone described only as an "ethnic German" (*Volksdeutsche*)—possibly Zimmermann, or someone like him.[75]

Born in Austria in 1912, Schwammberger had a typical lower-middle-class background and career, including a period of unemployment in the early 1930s; like so many others, he was then able to find a new status and make a career in the Nazi party and the SS. He gained a particular reputation for brutality in the Przemyśl and Mielec area east of Kraków, where he was active during the war. Stories circulated, including that he had "allowed" his six-year-old son to shoot one of six Jews who were made to stand against a wall, but the son had refused.[76] In another version, Schwammberger had arrived in Mielec fresh from a massacre at Przemyśl, where he had shot six hundred Jews and had given a pistol to his little son to shoot too. The survivor recounting this tale recollected that Schwammberger's son later said to him something along the lines of, "Hurry up you dirty Jew or I'll kill you."[77]

Despite his reputation, Schwammberger was able to escape justice for nearly half a century. After the war, he managed to flee from French captivity and, like so many others, emigrated to South America with assistance from the Vatican's infamous "ratline." The Vatican's relief commission for refugees, and Bishop Alois Hudal in particular, gave many former Nazis help in obtaining new identities, Red Cross passports, and tickets across the Atlantic, assuming they were significant forces in the fight against communism.[78] Before he left Europe however, he had one Dr. Gimpel, an Innsbruck doctor, remove the potentially incriminating SS blood group tattoo on his arm so that he could go underground and evade identification more easily.[79]

Once in South America, Schwammberger was given frequent assistance—including by the German embassy in Buenos Aires, which not only issued a new passport to him in his own name when his old one ran out in 1954 but even issued an extension to his passport in 1963, again under his own name, although there was by this time an international warrant for his arrest.[80] The Argentine government also provided protection. But prominent active Nazi hunters continued to press for his arrest. West German authorities began to seek his extradition in 1973, and he was finally tracked down and arrested in 1987 after the Stuttgart court offered (and paid) a substantial reward for anyone providing information that could lead to his arrest. He was extradited to Germany in 1990.

The trial, which began on June 26, 1991, and ended with judgment on May 18, 1992, illustrated a number of issues. First, it became clear that Schwammberger was in many respects typical of many Nazi perpetrators: a small tool who was used by the system and who allowed himself to be used. He was not a person of much intelligence or initiative, but simply swam with the tide and rose to a position of power. Yet by this point the standard defense of being a small cog following orders seemed to be diminishing in efficacy, and the fact of participation in killings appeared more important.

Second, by the early 1990s the alleged unreliability of witness memories was finally beginning to become less of an issue in determining guilt. Nearly one hundred witnesses gave testimony. Even so, lawyers defending Schwammberger sought to cast aspersions on the statements of survivors, who were still being given a hard time. One witness, for example, was harassed about his apparent incapacity to recall with any consistency the exact details about a particular killing on a particular day. He finally burst out in exasperation: "Every day things like this happened, and this is why I can't remember the particular case."[81] One of the witnesses had to remind the defense lawyer that he was having some difficulty in saying precisely what the time was at crucial moments because all watches had been confiscated in camp and therefore he never knew the clock times at which he was woken, marched to work, or had to stand for roll call.[82] Another witness was repeatedly challenged as to whether he had really seen the murder of a rabbi by the name of Frenkel.[83] The defense lawyer sneered when the witness said he was standing in the front row watching the shooting of Rabbi Frenkel. As the lawyer put it: "Everybody we have heard from so far was standing in the front row. That must have been an incredibly long row." The judge who was chairing the panel of judges came to the aid of the witness by pointing out to the defense lawyer, with emphatic repetition, "We only know from those who survived . . . , from those who survived."[84]

Given this kind of treatment, now half a century after the events, few survivors had much faith in the capacity of German courts to mete out any kind of justice or much desire to expose themselves to the kind of treatment routinely delivered by defense lawyers. Even so, German courts at this point were rather tougher than some had been in earlier decades. Schwammberger was found guilty, among other offenses, of having murdered Rabbi Frenkel on Yom Kippur, the Jewish Day of Atonement, in late September 1942, and of having organized, some three weeks earlier, a mass execution in Przemyśl, in which at least five hundred Jews had been shot. He was sentenced to life imprisonment, and eventually died in prison in 2004 at the age of ninety-two. He might easily have died earlier and never faced trial, like so many other Nazis who were never brought to account for their past.

There was a widespread view among commentators at this time that the trial had indeed taken place too late. The journalist Gerhard Mauz, for example, did not even think the trial was of any help in educating members of a younger generation who knew little about this past. In his view, if anything it might even have been counterproductive, potentially turning young people against the pursuit of Nazis; many seemed to feel they had already had enough of it all and did not want to take on the burden of their grandparents' misdeeds.[85] Moreover, Mauz thought that young people might gain the mistaken impression that only the "little people" were responsible for mass murder.[86] Such criticisms were echoed in other reports, such as that by Hans Schueler in the respected weekly newspaper *Die Zeit*.[87]

It was not only in the big trials, mounted for maximum public effect—whether historical education or political advantage—but also in relatively small and otherwise insignificant trials that time and location made a difference. Even so, over the course of time differing political priorities, social sympathies, and legal approaches affected the nature of the charges, the character of trials, and the severity and significance of the judgments.

At whatever level, questions of when and where perpetrators were brought to trial, and particularly whether they were tried on the capitalist or communist side of the Iron Curtain, radically affected their fates. What was murder on one side might be merely manslaughter on the other; what was personal responsibility and guilt on one side might be merely following orders on the other. There were major differences over evaluations of character and the treatment of convicted perpetrators. In West Germany, people who had been found guilty of significant offenses were often released well before the end of their sentences. In East Germany a sentence of life imprisonment for Nazi perpetrators usually meant precisely that: those convicted generally remained behind bars for life—at least until the unexpected fall of the Iron Curtain, which came too late for prisoners such as Zimmermann.

In the united Federal Republic of Germany after 1990 the ground shifted again as a new generation began to reconsider legal processes and means of bringing former Nazis to justice—by which time very few remained alive and well enough to stand trial. The increasing determination among a younger generation of Germans to see justice done came at a time when it was already too late for the vast majority of both survivors and perpetrators.

13

Late, Too Late

For decades after 1945, survivors of Nazi persecution battled to gain some compensation, however minimal and inadequate, for the pain and losses they suffered. Under growing pressure, some claims were eventually partially and grudgingly conceded, in stages varying with victim group and context. Justice, in this respect, was barely and belatedly done. Arguably, as far as adequate compensation was concerned, it was in principle impossible: that which had been done could never be undone. But the postwar lives of those who had been persecuted could have been made easier, earlier.

Time made a major difference to the likely fate of Nazi perpetrators, to the ways in which witness testimony was received and evaluated, and to what sorts of evidence were seen to count. Following the unification of Germany in 1990, decades after the period of persecution and extermination, a few isolated trials—not only that of Josef Schwammberger but also, crucially, the trials of Ivan (John) Demjanjuk, Oskar Gröning, and Reinhold Hanning—registered significant shifts in legal processes.

These shifts could not bring the truly guilty to account; they serve mainly to mark just how far attitudes had changed over the decades, and just what might have been possible had there been the political will at an earlier stage. By this time, the vast majority of those who had been most responsible had managed to evade justice. A campaign entailed Operation Last Chance II was launched in 2013, pursuing perpetrators under the slogan "Late, but Not Too Late" (*Spät, aber nicht zu spät*). But by this time, it was already precisely that: way past the point for any serious legal reckoning with Nazi perpetrators or for caring adequately for the needs of those who had suffered at their hands.

"Making Good Again"

If punishing the guilty is one side of justice, compensation and restitution to the victims is another.[1] A particular sense of injustice was felt when requests by victims for compensation were rebuffed or levels of payment were insultingly low, while those who had supported Hitler as civil servants, judges, and medical doctors or who had served in the army or SS continued to work in professional employment with high salaries and ultimately received full pensions.

Hans Frankenthal was an Auschwitz survivor who, like so many others, did not live long enough to see the final outcome of lengthy battles for compensation, or *Wiedergutmachung* (literally "making good again") for slave labor. But a wider principle was also at stake for him. As he put it: "I never liked the term *Wiedergutmachung* because I felt that nothing could ever make up for the suffering we had endured."[2]

It is certainly true that nothing could ever "make good again" what the Nazi regime had inflicted, nor could it bring the millions back from the dead. Those who survived faced serious obstacles in the way of gaining compensation that was in any way proportionate to what they had gone through. Frequently, the people officially entrusted with dispensing compensation had themselves been implicated in the former regime. There were further inequalities, based partly on the fact that some survivor groups could command official attention through effective organizations, partly on continuing prejudices and sympathies, and partly on wider political contexts and changing climates of opinion. Details varied, but nowhere in any of the Third Reich successor states was there a clean record of comprehensive attempts to compensate all victims of Nazi persecution and maltreatment.[3]

In the GDR, the official interpretation of National Socialism as "fascism" and the miseries endured by left-wing opponents of Nazism meant that the communist government was unwilling to concede any state responsibility for "making good again." The primary concern of the Soviet Union—which had lost more than twenty-five million citizens in the fight against Nazi Germany—was to gain reparations to help it build its own war-torn and shattered economy, and to this end it also took material, equipment, and people from East Germany after the war. There was also a shift in perceptions of the primary victims. The Association of Persecutees of the Nazi Regime (VVN) was forced to dissolve itself in 1953 and was replaced by the

Committee of Antifascist Resistance Fighters. With the downplaying of Jewish suffering and the highlighting of the significance of communist resistance as well as the very different relationships of the GDR to the United States and Israel, there was little pressure to consider reparations to Jewish victims.

An unwillingness to consider reparations was also evident—for very different reasons—in Austria. Political parties across the spectrum as well as the vast majority of the population were engaged in trying to construct a new "Austrian" national identity that was entirely distinct from and untainted by their supposedly unwilling incorporation into the Greater German Reich.[4] Successive governments and civil society refused to acknowledge responsibility for compensation or restitution to victims of Nazism. It was only toward the end of the twentieth century, with changing attitudes in the wake of the Waldheim affair as well as increasing international pressure, that Austrian authorities began to concede that there were indeed significant claims to be considered and cases to be answered. But it took significant pressure—including individual lawsuits, such as the one brought by the American resident Maria Altmann, a niece of Adele Bloch-Bauer, who was the subject of one of Klimt's most famous paintings—to obtain even the return of art works looted by the Nazis.[5]

West Germany claimed national continuity with its immediate predecessor, and hence official responsibility for making amends for the devastation caused by the Third Reich. It was also mindful of the need to repair its appalling international standing. The early economic miracle, assisted by the Marshall Plan, meant that West Germany was in a financial position to secure a better reputation, and Konrad Adenauer was determined to gain acceptance in the West and become a valued partner of the United States. In 1951 Adenauer's speech to the Bundestag acknowledged responsibility without conceding guilt. In the 1952 Luxemburg Agreement, Adenauer agreed to pay three billion Deutschmarks to Israel to assist the country in absorbing the half a million or so survivors of the Holocaust who had made their homes there, and a further 450 million Deutschmarks to the World Jewish Congress to assist survivors elsewhere.

Adenauer's approach arose as much out of international policy considerations as it did from any sense of moral obligation. And the existence of high-profile international organizations, notably the Jewish Claims Conference (the Conference on Jewish Material Claims Against Germany, founded in 1951), ensured that material support for Jewish victims as well as restitution of stolen properties and goods remained high on the West German political agenda. Even so, compensation was neither adequate nor uncontroversial. And it is notable that in the political climate of 1950s West Germany, those who were perceived as German "victims" of the war—including expellees, refugees, and returning prisoners of war, many of whom had been tangled up in mass murder—appeared to be given a more sympathetic hearing than the victims of Nazi persecution received.[6] The 1952 Law to Equalize Burdens was designed with a view to evening out the disadvantages suffered by many supposedly innocent "victims of history," but in practice it appeared to compensate those who had actively sustained or been beneficiaries of Nazism more generously than those who had been its victims.

Just as the "crimes" of Nazism were being reduced, juristically, to the sadism of concentration camp guards, with a corresponding restriction in the notion of who was a "perpetrator," so too the pool of potential victims entitled to compensation was restricted. As Hans Frankenthal recalled, despite having worked as slave laborers in I. G. Farben's Buna plant at Auschwitz-Monowitz, he and his brother Ernst in total "received 10,000 DM as reparations for slave labor, deportation, our lost youth, imprisonment in a concentration camp, the loss of all our relatives, lifelong physical and psychological problems."[7] He even had to buy back the family house, his childhood home, which had been forcibly "Aryanized" under Nazi rule. Moreover, he and his brother had little "hope of claiming that we had a right to a full pension. My stiff knee, the deep scars on my lower legs, my ruined teeth didn't matter."[8] His brother Ernst, who had also been in Mittelbau-Dora and Theresienstadt and had suffered permanent liver damage as a result of maltreatment, received no pension at all. As Hans noted bitterly, the doctor who examined Ernst was a former Nazi. He added: "We were often confronted with doctors who had either practiced medicine before 1945 or had been Nazis and still believed in Nazi ideology. These were the men who were now responsible for rating us for disability pensions."[9]

There was also a continuation of prejudices against certain social groups, particularly those still designated as "asocials" or "criminals." Anti-Gypsy policies were still in force in postwar Germany, with many of the officials involved being the very same people who had dealt with Roma and Sinti during the Third Reich.[10] In the West German state of Baden-Württemberg, for example, a request for compensation for injustice suffered during incarceration in concentration camps was met with the official response in

February 1950 that "the above-named group were for the most part not persecuted and imprisoned on grounds of race, but rather because of their asocial and criminal attitude"—an astonishing postwar confirmation of Nazi views of "Gypsies" as fundamentally disruptive and lawless, with a tendency toward "criminal" behavior, even without specific evidence of having committed any particular offense.[11] Official policies had changed, and there was an awareness of the sensitivity around continuing Nazi attitudes; yet many officials still saw Gypsies as a problem, even terming them a "plague," and either relocating them or dealing with them punitively. But some members of the Sinti and Roma communities were now becoming more assertive, demanding that they be registered and granted certain rights and benefits.[12]

Under the West German compensation law enacted in 1953 and issued in final version in 1965, people who had been persecuted on "grounds of political opposition to National Socialism or for reasons of race, religion or ideology (*Weltanschauung*)" were entitled to compensation.[13] But Roma and Sinti were held not to fall into these categories; rather, it was argued, they had been treated for "asocial behavior" under pre-existing legislation. On this view, the deportations of Roma and Sinti from 1940 onward had been a legitimate measure to ensure order and security in the "fight against the Gypsy plague," and the West German government disputed the claim that those persecuted as "asocials" or "habitual criminals" were exposed to a specifically Nazi form of persecution.[14] A Munich court in 1961 even sought to justify the deportation of Gypsies to the General Government in 1940 as having been essential to military security. Only those deported following the Auschwitz decree of December 16, 1942, were held to be entitled to compensation.

These views were not challenged in the federal court until December 1963, when it was conceded that Roma and Sinti had been discriminated against for "racial" reasons as early as 1938.[15] But many survivors were still unable to gain compensation because of varying combinations of shame, illiteracy, late applications, exploitation by lawyers, the fact that the authorities did not recognize their marriages, and continuing prejudice by doctors, who wrote medical evaluations intentionally designed to lead to the rejection of claims for compensation.[16] Things did begin to change from the mid-1960s; even so, the West German government was slow to concede even the principle of compensation. In December 1980 the Federal Republic finally agreed to a one-off payment of five thousand Deutschmarks in compensation for compulsory sterilization, which had affected many Gypsies—particularly those married to "Aryan" partners and who were allowed to stay in Germany—as well as others.

Gay men also for a long time received no compensation for their suffering and had no rights to social or financial recognition as people who had been persecuted by the Nazis. In contrast to those who had persecuted them, they also gained no pension rights for their time performing hard labor in concentration camps. The officials who dealt with their postwar claims were again either the very same people who had condemned them under Nazism, or they had shared in and were socialized under the homophobic mentalities of the Nazi era. If anything, official attitudes toward homosexuality in West Germany in the 1960s were worse than they had been in the 1920s. In the Weimar Republic fewer than ten thousand gay men had been prosecuted, whereas in mid-1960s West Germany more than forty-four thousand were prosecuted for their sexual orientation; and these prosecutions, furthermore, were carried out under the sharper version of the homophobic §175, as amended by the Nazi government in 1935, which had not as yet been revised back to the previous milder version.[17]

Attitudes began to change from the 1970s onward, with more open views among younger generations, and increasing pressure exerted by the more courageous members of the gay community who were prepared to come out in public and fight for recognition. Among the activists in Austria was Josef Kohout, better known from his autobiographical account as Heinz Heger, who tried from the 1970s to gain recognition as a persecutee and sought to recover pension contributions for his time in labor camps.[18] Beginning in the early 1980s, the Vienna Homosexual Initiative (Homosexuelle Initiative Wien) organized to look after gay victims of Nazism. It sought to get their prison periods added on to pensionable service and to gain recognized victim status for them. In 1995, Austria finally established the National Funds for Victims of National Socialism, from which a small number of surviving gay men received symbolic financial payments, although they were still not recognized under the Law for the Care of Victims (Opfer Fürsorge Gesetz).

In France, Pierre Seel joined others in attempts to gain recognition and compensation for gay victims of Nazi persecution. As he bitterly observed, the former commandant of the Schirmeck camp where he had been imprisoned, Karl Buck, managed to escape justice. Despite eventually being caught, "after some botched trials, he was able to retire peacefully to his luxurious property in Rudesberg, near Stuttgart."[19] Buck died in June 1977, at the age of eighty. Sickened and saddened, Seel committed himself to more energetic efforts to gain recognition of the Nazi persecution of gay men. By 1993, his request to the French Ministry of War Veterans and War Victims to be recognized as a victim of Nazism had elicited the response that while they had nothing against this application in principle, the ministry would require two affidavits from "eyewitnesses" who could personally attest that Seel had spent at least ninety days in Schirmeck. The affidavits of his brothers testifying to his arrest and deportation did not count in the eyes of the authorities. As Seel pointed out, he had himself been "one of the youngest at Schirmeck," and the likelihood of finding a fellow survivor in their eighties or nineties who would be in a position to testify on his behalf was vanishingly small. In his view, this "administrative demand, a legal requirement, is straight out of a Kafka novel."[20]

As discussed, West Germany had also demonstrated a startling degree of continuity with its Nazi predecessor by initially presenting the exploitation of forced and slave labor as a "normal" aspect of warfare and, as we have seen in the case of Edmund Bartl against the Heinkel concern, hindering claims to compensation. It had at the same time postponed dealing with the issue of reparations to forced laborers who were foreign nationals, on the grounds that this would need to await a peace treaty, which was of course postponed through the period of division. Foreign forced laborers were often doubly disadvantaged in that, following return to their native countries, many of them had been treated as in some way suspicious, potentially having "collaborated" with the Nazis by having worked in Germany.[21]

But in the new climate of the 1980s — increasingly sympathetic to minorities, responsive to identity politics and social movements—a younger generation of historians and political activists started to draw attention to their plight. Emphasis was now increasingly placed on naming and shaming companies that had been involved.[22] Also at this time, the question of whether principled deserters from the German armed forces should be treated as victims of National Socialist policies began to be raised.

Pressure increased following the unification of Germany in 1990—a process that was not in fact accompanied by any official peace treaty to end the Second World War, along the lines that had been suggested. Pressure from a variety of quarters within the ever-litigious United States began to be raised. The collapse of communism also meant easier access for the voices of former forced laborers who had returned to countries in Eastern Europe that had for decades been behind the Iron Curtain. Letters of complaint and demand began to flood into Germany. Equally important, German companies that had used forced and slave labor—Siemens, Volkswagen, and other well-known names—were by the 1990s operating in an increasingly globalized market. They could not afford damage to their international image by refusing to own up to their compromised past or to pay compensation out of their profits to those on whose backs their fortunes had previously been built. Companies such as the Flick Mercedes Benz conglomerate, Deutsche Bank, and Volkswagen came under an increasingly harsh spotlight.

Some companies responded relatively rapidly, but generally through largely symbolic measures, such as erecting memorials to victims and commissioning official company histories that did not gloss over the abuse of labor in the Nazi past in the way the accounts of prominent industrialists in the early 1950s had done. A few companies also made payments to organizations seeking reconciliation and peace. All of this activity illustrated a heightened moral and social sensitivity—or at least it was represented in this way—which could only benefit the international images of the companies concerned. But the question of paying compensation to victims, and the associated recognition of legal liability, was a quite different matter.

Despite its pathbreaking nature, the way in which the compensation deal was finally struck in the Federal Republic of Germany represents, paradoxically, considerable continuity in principle with the ambiguous approach first developed by Adenauer. Again, concessions were only made in the face of fierce pressure by effective organizations acting on behalf of victims. From the summer of 1998, class actions were brought in the United States against German companies that were active in the North American market. In Germany, too, in the increasingly globalized world of the late 1990s, such companies were finding their images attacked in media campaigns; with potentially adverse consequences for sales and market shares, companies had to respond. Major changes arose not only because of increasing international pressure but also as a result of vociferous campaigns within Germany; without the external pressure, however, it is doubtful these would have been successful to the same degree in achieving their aims.[23]

The compromise solution, which also involved the German government, succeeded in combining what was evidently a morally responsible position with continuing support for the interests of German industry. In 1999–2000, a foundation named Remembrance, Responsibility, and the Future (EVZ, Erinnerung, Verantwortung und Zukunft) was established, financed both by individual companies and by the German state. Through it an agreement was reached between the US and German governments about compensation payments. Gesture payments would be made, but only on certain conditions. These included—just as in Norbert Wollheim's case against I. G. Farben nearly half a century earlier—that all future legal demands would be put aside and that no more individual cases would be brought. Moreover, the EVZ adopted a clever strategy with respect to the implications of its own financing. Rather than focusing solely on those companies that genuinely had compromised Nazi pasts, it appealed to the whole of German industry to support the venture on grounds of moral responsibility. While more than three-fifths of the EVZ's money did in fact come from the twelve founding companies, around one-quarter of the total of 6,500 members paid less than one thousand Deutschmarks—symbolic payments in recognition of moral support.[24]

In this way, the German government and German industry together developed a rhetoric of responsibility with, yet again, no explicit or individual admission of legal liability. As in the 1950s, the German government occupied the moral high ground, while significant perpetrators conveniently disappeared behind a veil of apparent responsibility without actual guilt.

Forced and slave laborers only began to receive compensation in 2001, one year after the establishment of the EVZ. In the following six years, some 4.37 billion euros were paid out to somewhat more than 1,655,000 former forced laborers, living in nearly one hundred countries.[25] Not everyone who had been affected in some way was treated equally. A total of 296,740 survivors who had worked in concentration camps, ghettos, and similar conditions were given on average 7,128 euros to compensate them for their suffering. By 2007 this was worth around ten thousand dollars, or roughly five thousand pounds, at the historic conversion rates of the time. For the 561,282 people who had been forcibly deported, detained, or kept in conditions of imprisonment, the payment was set on average at 2,252 euros— considerably less than two weeks' pay at that time for managers in the relevant firms. Some 801,110 former forced laborers who had been held on farms or in households or in occupied territories where conditions were held to be relatively mild, were granted on average 1,196 euros. The claims made on behalf of a further 644,826 applicants were denied completely.[26]

The very last of the new developments was the 2002 Ghetto Pensions Law (Ghettorentengesetz, ZRBG), designed to ensure that people who had worked in ghettos received pensions for their labor, which had actually been paid employment, if remunerated at a very low level, and which was—despite incarceration in the ghetto—supposedly "voluntarily" entered into. This proved in practice to be highly complicated if not actually impossible to demonstrate in ways that satisfied the relevant insurance companies responsible for social pensions.[27] It was estimated that in the first five years after the law was passed, only about 5 percent of the seventy thousand or so claims had been successful, leading to understandable bitterness on the part of applicants in old age.[28] At this time, virtually half of all survivors were over eighty and unlikely to be able to wait much longer for any change in their circumstances.[29]

Making symbolic payments to the relatively few remaining survivors was yet again a way of shoring up Germany's moral reputation for facing up to its past without fully addressing the issue of guilt in a precise and specific way. There was of course progress, but even those who were closely involved in securing compensation and assisting the establishment of the foundation Remembrance, Responsibility, and the Future recognized that this belated justice was not complete. Its historical adviser, Lutz Niethammer, talked of "marred" or "flawed justice" (beschädigte Gerechtigkeit); Stuart Eizenstat, the American under secretary of state and special representative for US president Bill Clinton and Secretary of State Madeleine Albright on Holocaust issues, who was charged with negotiations on behalf of forced and slave laborers, called it "imperfect justice."[30]

The EVZ remains to this day active in sponsoring research projects, bringing to attention the suffering of survivors, and engaging in reconciliation activities; its recognition of victims and concern for both material and symbolic compensation is undoubted. But the sense of diffuse shame without differentiated attribution of guilt is a somewhat lopsided legacy. We shall see the way in which this theme also played out in the extraordinary growth of memorials to an ever-increasing range of victims without corresponding acknowledgement of the variety of roles on the side of the perpetrators.

In the meantime, however, in this new climate of enhanced moral responsibility, there were indeed also energetic if highly belated attempts to bring the last remaining perpetrators to trial. This, too, proved an imperfect form of the pursuit of justice.

After Demjanjuk: The Decline and Resurrection of the Witness

While aging survivors were still desperately seeking compensation for their suffering, a few elderly perpetrators remained at large. And just as wider attitudes toward victims were changing, there was also growing determination to bring perpetrators into the courts of justice.

If the voices of witnesses had only briefly been heard, they had for three decades or so been seen as crucial to establishing guilt. The unreliability of witness memory, or the sheer lack of survivors, allowed many perpetrators to walk away from court with an acquittal, or never to be brought to trial at all. But this shifted abruptly in 2011 with the trial of John Demjanjuk. Suddenly the law no longer required eyewitness testimony to clinch a case. The individuals who were caught by this change in legal practice were, however, of a quite different order from the tens of thousands who had gotten away with it in preceding decades. They were arguably the wrong targets.

Born as a Ukrainian by the name of Ivan Mykolaiovych Demjanjuk in 1920, Demjanjuk first served in the Red Army of the Soviet Union in the Second World. War. Injured several times, in 1942 he was captured and taken into German captivity.[31] Like many other Ukrainian prisoners of war, Demjanjuk was then selected and trained as a concentration camp guard in Trawniki, subsequently serving as a guard in the concentration camps of Sobibór and Flossenbürg. In 1952 he emigrated from West Germany to the United States, where in 1958 he obtained citizenship, suppressing any account of his past. Demjanjuk became a casualty of the country's reawakened interest in Nazi war crimes in the 1970s, when the Justice Department began to look more closely at former immigrants from Eastern Europe and an office of special investigations was set up which was able to draw on documents that were more readily available in an era of détente.[32] In 1981 Demjanjuk's US citizenship was revoked on the grounds that he had lied on his immigration papers. Now effectively stateless, in 1986 Demjanjuk was extradited to Israel to stand trial for his supposed role in Treblinka, as a guard remembered by survivors as "Ivan the Terrible."

The Israeli trial focused primarily on questions concerning his identity, since the Trawniki ID card mentioned Sobibór rather than Treblinka as the camp at which he served, but the prosecution appears to have thought it would be easier to find Treblinka survivors who could testify to the actions of "Ivan the Terrible." As with the Eichmann trial in Jerusalem in 1961, this trial was designed not only to put a particular individual in the dock but also to provide the opportunity for witnesses to testify to their suffering and losses, in the interests of broader Holocaust education.

Sentenced to death in 1988, Demjanjuk nevertheless managed to mount a successful appeal. The fall of communism and collapse of the Soviet Union came to his aid: new documents released from the Russian archives suggested that the Treblinka "Ivan the Terrible" had in fact been one Ivan Marchenko, and not Demjanjuk. Five years after initial sentencing, the verdict was overturned on the basis of mistaken identity, and Demjanjuk was able to return to the United States as a free man; in 1998 he regained his US citizenship.

But Demjanjuk's role in the death camps continued to perplex and irritate the Nazi hunters, who would not let the matter be laid to rest. The authenticity of his identity card as a Ukrainian guard trained in Trawniki had been challenged by defense lawyers, and there did indeed appear to have been another "Ivan the Terrible" at Treblinka. However, documentary evidence seemed conclusive that Demjanjuk had actually served at the death camp of Sobibór. In 2002 his US citizenship was revoked again, and in 2009, despite ill health and advanced age, the nearly ninety-year-old Demjanjuk was extradited to Germany to stand trial in Munich.

Demjanjuk was charged with being an accessory to the murder of 27,900 Jews—the number of Dutch Jews who it was presumed had arrived alive on trains from Westerbork and been instantly gassed on arrival at Sobibór during a specific period of weeks in which Demjanjuk could be shown to have worked there (separate charges related to Majdanek and Flossenbürg). The trial took place over more than ninety days of proceedings, stretching from November 30, 2009, to May 12, 2011; it was periodically held up by Demjanjuk's ill health and incapacity to spend long periods of time in the courtroom. He was pushed into court sitting in a wheelchair, or even lying on a stretcher covered with a blanket, and was periodically administered to by a doctor and medical attendants. For much of the time, he appeared to take little or no interest whatsoever in the proceedings.

Demjanjuk was eventually found guilty despite the lack of irrefutable witness testimony directly linking his actions or state of mind with any particular killings during this time. Precise testimony concerning subjective intentions and base motives—so crucial to earlier German court cases—seemed more or less irrelevant to this verdict. It was sufficient to demonstrate guilt by showing documentary evidence that he had been employed in a specific role at a particular time when a specified number of killings had occurred. Even so, Demjanjuk managed to die as an "innocent" man: moved to a nursing home after the verdict, in 2012 he died at age ninety-one while an appeal was still pending, hence remaining technically innocent under the law.

The Demjanjuk case raised many questions, not least about the advanced age of the defendant and the evidence used. Still, it was of major significance. No longer were eyewitnesses deemed necessary to secure a conviction. Documentary evidence of a particular role and presence in a place of mass murder would suffice. Rather than treating mass murder as an individual crime, for which subjective state of mind was crucial to proof of culpability, the court had finally decided that simple function within a wider machinery of mass murder was sufficient for conviction.[33] A focus on role within a wider system had in fact been present in the Allied trials of the early postwar period, particularly with the charge of "conspiracy." It was also a focus that Fritz Bauer had favored in seeking to bring "Auschwitz" to trial as a broader crime complex, with the defendants illustrating selected exemplary roles; but Bauer had not succeeded in this aim. West German courts generally chose to focus on the personal motivation and "excess deeds" of defendants, who were seen as being accused of committing individual crimes rather than being part of a wider crime complex. But with the Demjanjuk case, finally, the systemic character of Nazi mass murder was recognized in court.

From now on it was possible to try someone merely for having worked at a site where atrocities had occurred. This dramatically altered the scope of those who could be brought to court. With renewed energy and offering the enticement of monetary rewards, the Operation Last Chance campaign—the one with the slogan "Late, but Not Too Late"—sought to ferret out those who might still be prosecuted under the new circumstances. While a few elderly individuals were indeed identified, this campaign, if anything, mainly succeeded only in underlining the long-term inadequacy of attempts to bring Nazis to justice.

Among others, the Gröning case illustrates the last death throes of the cumulative failures of the German legal system to prosecute Nazi crimes in any way adequate to the magnitude of the offense.[34] In 2014, Oskar Gröning was found fit to stand trial at the age of ninety-three. A former bank clerk and member of the Waffen-SS, he described himself as merely a "desk person" and accountant who had sorted the valuables taken from arriving prisoners at Auschwitz. He had kept silent about his Auschwitz experiences for many years after the war, but finally began to speak out when he became increasingly concerned about Holocaust deniers. He even gave a lengthy interview in the documentary about Auschwitz made by Lawrence Rees, in which he made it clear that although he had once witnessed a gassing and had been shocked at the shootings, violence, and selections on the ramp, he had not personally committed any crime. While he abhorred the manner of killing, he said that at that time he had seen it as necessary to deal with an "enemy" in wartime—which is how, under the influence of Nazi propaganda and socialization, he had perceived the Jews.[35] Gröning also gave an interview to Der Spiegel in 2005, in which he stated: "I would describe my role as a small cog in the gears. If you can describe that as guilt, then I am guilty. Legally speaking I am innocent."[36] For all this time, given the state of the law, he did not need to risk prosecution.

But in 2015, following the Demjanjuk case, Gröning was finally put on trial for having been an accessory to some three hundred thousand murders. This was because of the change in the law achieved in the Demjanjuk case: merely by virtue of having worked at the camp at the time, Gröning could be considered to have played a role in the machinery of mass murder. At the start of his trial, Gröning admitted to having been "morally complicit" but left the question of legal guilt for the court to decide. Unlike the situation ten years earlier, when he had given his interview with Der Spiegel, by 2015 the situation with respect to legal proof had changed dramatically. It sufficed to show that he had merely been employed at Auschwitz—even in a non-killing role.

The survivors who were called to give testimony at Gröning's trial were treated very differently from the manner of earlier trials. In addition to the widespread respect and veneration with which they were greeted, survivors were not required to prove anything specific pertaining to Gröning's role at any particular time. Their testimony was very general: personal stories of horror and suffering.

One of the first witnesses to testify was the eighty-one-year-old Eva Mozes Kor. Separated from her parents and older sisters, none of whom she ever saw again, in Auschwitz Eva and her twin sister, Miriam, were subjected to "medical" experiments at the hands of Josef Mengele and came very close to death. Had either one of them died at the time of the experiments, the other would have been killed in order to make a comparison of the corpses.[37] But both managed to survive, although permanently harmed by their treatment. Kor made headlines in the Gröning case with her extraordinary display of compassion toward the accused and her willingness to "forgive" him, demonstrated by an apparently spontaneous hug. This built on two decades of work for peace and forgiveness, during which Kor had founded CANDLES, an organization for surviving twins who had been subjected to Nazi experiments and had also met and achieved a degree of reconciliation with another Auschwitz doctor, Dr. Münch.[38]

Susan Pollack, another witness, traveled from her home in the United Kingdom at the age of eighty-four to testify to her experiences. Deported from Hungary to Auschwitz, she was immediately separated from her mother, who was gassed. As she recalled, "The terror stills my soul. On arrival it was like the terror that stops faculties of thinking." On repeatedly being exposed to Mengele for selections, she commented: "We were regularly marched in front of him, naked. . . . We were dehumanised completely. It was a world I haven't got the words to describe. The fear, the anguish, I haven't got the words to describe. I just wanted to recoil into myself." Following a period of slave labor in an armaments factory at Guben, and toward the end of the war enduring the death marches and a period in Bergen-Belsen, Pollack was finally liberated in April 1945. But she remembers: "For me, it wasn't a joyous experience because I wasn't able to recognise what it means." She was in a state of illness, physical and psychological collapse. As she put it at Gröning's trial, recalling her feelings at the time of liberation: "That feeling of dehumanisation and total despair—it invaded my whole being."[39] This heart-rending testimony barely related to Gröning's role counting the possessions and money confiscated from arriving victims at Auschwitz.

Witnesses had gained a new significance in this trial, testifying not only to actions or immediate consequences of actions but also to indirect, long-term reverberations of the past. They played an essentially educative role—not so much about what had happened (as in, for example, the Lichmann trial) but rather about the long-term significance of what had happened. Some testified on behalf of family members they had lost, and at the same time provided evidence of the continuing influence of this past on the next generation. Judith Kalman, for example, traveled from Canada to talk about the devastating impact of the Holocaust on her family. She focused particularly on the half-sister she never knew, Eva Edit Weinberger, whose name she bore as her own middle name; she also talked about other members of the family, including Eva's cousin Judit Borenstein, who was murdered in the gas chambers at the age of twelve, and after whom her own first name came. As Judith Kalman put it, the death of her half-sister by gassing at the age of six "left me with a burden of inherited survivor guilt that has been a defining feature of my life." The legacies of a past before she was born determined Kalman's whole life, its shadows surrounding her childhood, affecting her choice of profession, her life-partner, her values and priorities.[40]

This kind of indirect testimony about the wider consequences of the Holocaust was a far cry from the way in which survivor testimonies had been solicited or dealt with in the major trials of the 1960s and 1970s. So, too, was the burden of proof—now changed to mere presence at a place whose functions were known at the time of employment there. Had such an approach been in place when so many known former Nazis were still alive, still in their prime and not elderly and frail, infinitely more sentences could have been passed—and passed rapidly. But by the second decade of the twenty-first century, seventy years after the end of the war, and despite the new search for former SS guards, it was impossible to make amends for decades of failure to pursue those responsible for the misdeeds of Nazism.

Oskar Gröning was sentenced to four years in jail. While some survivors welcomed this, Eva Kor was critical. In her view, his remaining time on earth would be better spent talking about the past to groups of young people and the wider public: he should have been sentenced "to community service by speaking out against neo-Nazis." She commented too on her understanding of "forgiveness": "My forgiveness has nothing to do with the perpetrators. It is for my healing alone. The reason I am speaking out is because so many survivors are still suffering emotionally, 70 years later, and they do not understand they have the power and the right to forgive."[41]

Gröning's sentence was upheld by Germany's Constitutional Court at the end of December 2017, rejecting his appeal that at the age of ninety-six he was too old and frail to serve a prison sentence. The rising age of former perpetrators complicated the belated pursuit of justice. The Gröning trial was not the end of trials, but very nearly. A trial was opened in Detmold against former Auschwitz guard Reinhold Hanning, who was charged with being an accessory to the murder of more than 170,000 people, whom he claims he had merely escorted to the gas chambers; he was given a sentence of five years. The planned trial in Hanau of another former Auschwitz guard, Ernst Tremmel, did not take place because he died at the age of ninety-three, just a few days before the trial was to begin. A case against an Auschwitz doctor, Hubert Zafke, was suspended because, at the age of ninety-five, he was held to be too unwell to stand trial.

The Records of Justice

Reputations do not correspond neatly with the complexities of reality. Claims and counterclaims during the period of Cold War division played a significant role in how these states staged trials and represented their reckonings with the legacies of Nazism. The Federal Republic of Germany, as we have seen, enjoyed a reputation for energetically addressing the legacies of the Nazi past. By contrast, prior to its collapse in 1989–90 the communist East German state, the GDR, gained a far less reputable image in the West of abusing the legal system and mounting trials of former Nazis primarily for political purposes. Seen the other way around, from the communist perspective West Germany was portrayed as a haven for former Nazis, while East Germany had, so its government claimed, thoroughly dealt with "big" Nazis at an early stage and reintegrated those remaining "little" Nazis who were willing to convert and turn their energies to building socialism.

But neither East nor West Germany entirely deserved its reputation— from whichever perspective it was viewed. Despite dedicated and valiant efforts in some quarters, and despite the spurs of competition between the two German states for the moral high ground, the overall records of justice were poor on both sides of the Iron Curtain. Following unification in 1990, arguably ever more moral fervor and energy were mobilized in pursuit of perpetrators when it was way too late.

Less buffeted by the propaganda winds of the Cold War, Austria largely maintained its claim to have been "Hitler's first victim," but this too was punctured, if never completely shattered in some circles, by revelations in the 1980s of the Nazi past of its then presidential candidate, former UN secretary general Kurt Waldheim. Only very belatedly did Austria begin to engage with its own complicity in Nazism—and this too remained almost entirely in the sphere of memorialization, rather than in the courts of justice. As we have seen, Austria more or less abdicated the pursuit of justice from the 1970s, while East and West Germany continued the Cold War competition to be the "better Germany."

The biggest apparent success story has a disturbing twist. It is not that West Germany actually was effective in comprehensively reckoning with its past; rather, West Germany *appeared* to be the most effective, with the emergence of open discussions in the public sphere, while powerful interest groups quietly ensured that significant issues were never addressed, or emerged only belatedly when energetic challenges could no longer be successfully confronted or silenced. Key elite groups were never brought to account for their past, and the vast majority of those who had sustained the Nazi system escaped postwar justice entirely unscathed. It was only due to sustained efforts by committed individuals both within and beyond West Germany, and against considerable domestic opposition, that the major concentration camp trials in the 1960s succeeded in opening up public debates in a way that did not happen in Austria until the 1980s and was barely possible under East German political conditions. And yet the emergence of challenges and controversies in West Germany, developing eventually into a massive movement for memorialization of victims, was perfectly compatible with continuing to permit former perpetrators to live almost entirely untroubled by any judicial reckoning with their Nazi past.

The difference was therefore more one of which political system offered public space for open debates, rather than which state actually meted out justice and punished past wrongdoing. The secret of West Germany's reputational success was that, over time, a multiplicity of voices could be heard, not that the majority of former perpetrators were actually punished appropriately for their crimes. Public "reckoning" with the past remained largely a matter of media discussions rather than legal judgments. This may pragmatically have assisted political stability in an emergent democracy: exemplary punishment of the few combined with widespread rehabilitation of the many may have served to spread a moral lesson without fomenting widespread unrest.

Whatever one's views from an ethical or a pragmatic perspective, there is a related paradox. The familiar narrative about public debates and cultural representations in West Germany is one of "facing up to the past" ever more openly and honestly over time, yet this narrative is almost entirely at odds with the actual records of justice in the courtroom as well as with the stories told in the relative privacy of the home.[42]

In none of the three Third Reich successor states were the problems of state-ordained mass violence dealt with adequately through the legal process. The reasons for the inadequacies in each case varied: not only the formalities of legal systems, but also questions of political will and social prejudices played a major role. The passage of generations was highly significant in transforming wider attitudes; those who had not lived through the time of Nazism generally had far less sympathy with defendants. But the balance of factors involved in confrontations in the courtroom was always complex.

What, then, was the overall situation concerning the pursuit of Nazi war criminals, while perpetrators were mostly still alive and well enough to stand trial? The answer has to be that legal systems, political considerations, and social practices were simply not up to the task of dealing with state-sponsored acts of violence on the scale committed under Nazi rule. When looking at the overall statistics and comparing the scale of the murder with the numbers prosecuted and found guilty, one can only marvel at the disjuncture between political rhetoric and the realities of the records of justice.

The Ludwigsburg Central Office was assiduous over many decades, even with very limited resourcing, in collating evidence and undertaking research. What was uncovered in this research represented only a small fraction of what had happened under Nazi rule in Europe, and what showed up in trials in court was but the tiny tip of an enormous iceberg. Arduous investigations over the decades served to amass mountains of paperwork, in a gargantuan effort that was seemingly totally out of proportion considering the small number of cases that actually came to trial.

Oskar Gröning was held to be only the 6,657th person to be convicted in the Federal Republic of Germany.[43] The total number of persons convicted in the Federal Republic for Nazi crimes was in itself fewer even than the number of people who had been employed at Auschwitz alone. Many groups, such as civilian functionaries with administrative responsibilities, industrialists employing slave labor, and judges passing the death sentence in Hitler's courts, were for decades barely even considered perpetrators at all. The focus in trials remained at the level of those directly involved in front-line brutality and individual murders.

The overall records of justice remain contentious. A brief comparison of the statistics for prosecutions and sentencing in East and West Germany points up the significance of the Cold War divide. In making this comparison, it has to be borne in mind that the statistics are not entirely reliable, and revisions to the figures are made periodically. But the general outlines are fairly clear.

It has been calculated that a total of 106,496 people were investigated up to the end of 1998 in the Federal Republic of Germany (West Germany up to 1990, unified Germany thereafter).[44] Of these, fewer than 6,500 people were actually prosecuted for their part in Nazi crimes—an astonishingly low number, amounting to only about one in twenty of those investigated. Recent analyses, which take into account lesser offenses and particularly local trial records during the early postwar years, suggest that in West Germany and united Germany between 1945 and 2005, a total of 36,393 cases were brought to court, involving around 140,000 individuals (some of whose names appeared in more than one trial, accounting for the higher figure of 172,294 defendants).[45] But the overall outcome looks little different: there were only 2.4 percent more convictions than had previously been thought from official figures, with 6,656 convictions and 5,184 acquittals, while the remaining proceedings were terminated.[46] There were sixteen death sentences and 166 sentences to lifelong imprisonment (which, as we have seen, did not often actually mean that). Only 5.5 percent of those found guilty were women, who were disproportionately involved in lesser crimes such as denunciations (two-thirds of sentences of women related to this offense) or involvement in euthanasia crimes (where women made up 27 percent of the accused and 38 percent of those sentenced).[47] The vast majority of sentences—just under five thousand (4,993)—were relatively lenient, with terms of imprisonment of up to two years.[48]

Of those perpetrators actually brought to court in the Federal Republic of Germany before the end of the twentieth century, only 164 individuals were eventually sentenced as perpetrators of murder, rather than for lesser crimes. In view of the hundreds of thousands of individuals who had been involved in the machinery of mass murder and the six million people who had died in what we now call the Holocaust, 164 convictions for murder is not an impressive total. In effect, if not in intention, West German law condoned obedience to a deadly regime and condemned only those who had individually stepped beyond Nazism's already murderous limits.

Figures for East Germany are even more unreliable, but again the general message is clear. The vast majority of convictions in East Germany were between 1945 and 1955, with a particular peak in the period from 1948 to 1950 when a total of 11,274 sentences were passed. This figure included 3,432 sentences passed in the perfunctory proceedings of the so-called Waldheim trials in 1950, when the Soviet administration handed over the remaining inmates of the special camps to the new GDR authorities. This was meant to indicate that the GDR had now successfully dealt with Nazi perpetrators on its territory, although individuals continued to be identified and prosecuted. From the mid-1950s onward, numbers brought to trial in the GDR dwindled, yet a constant trickle continued: with the sole exception of 1984, in every single year until the demise of the GDR between one and eleven sentences were passed on Nazi perpetrators. And these trials were not always simply publicity stunts, although where relevant they were also used for political purposes.

In East Germany between 1945 and 1989, a total of 12,890 judgments were pronounced—nearly double the number of sentences pronounced in the West, and for a population of less than one-third of the size of the West German population.[49] Overall, former Nazis in East Germany had roughly six or seven times the chance of being prosecuted and found guilty than they would have had if living in the West. Even if the large numbers of people prosecuted in the Waldheim trials are excluded, the comparison remains startling: a total of 9,459 sentences were passed in the GDR for a population of around seventeen million people, compared to 6,495 sentences for a population of nearer sixty million in West Germany. And it was not only that former Nazis had a higher chance of being prosecuted in East Germany; they also faced far harsher sentences if found guilty. Penalties in the GDR included 129 death sentences (the last of these being in 1977), 274 life sentences (the last being in 1988), and 3,191 sentences of more than ten years (the last in 1989), as well as a total of 1,924 sentences of between three and ten years and 7,372 sentences of less than three years.[50]

Again, compared to the numbers who had actually been involved in killing, even in the GDR the overall total of those former Nazis who were found guilty of murder remains insignificant but not quite as low as in West Germany. Whether a combined total of 403 sentences to death or life imprisonment in a population of seventeen million is deemed to be "better" than 164 such sentences for a population of around sixty million is a matter of opinion, although the contrast in purely numerical terms is self-evident. The GDR could, however, never really win the argument about the "best" way to deal with the Nazi past. Its own inhumanity—including its treatment of some of those imprisoned for Nazi crimes—rapidly came under widespread criticism as communist rule collapsed in 1989–90.

New generations in the unified Federal Republic of Germany of the late twentieth and early twenty-first century have sought to make amends for the dilatory conduct of previous generations by seeking with renewed energy to try to track down and bring to court every last Nazi. Whether the pursuit of low-level Ukrainian guards or concentration camp accountants in the twilight of their lives constitutes a satisfactory conclusion to the story of the pursuit of justice in the courtroom, when so many had been allowed to get off the hook in preceding decades, remains quite another matter.

The archival records of pain, suffering, and injustice are seemingly unending. The usefulness of all these investigations, all the agonized testimony given by survivors around the world, all the depositions by those being investigated or those who knew them, are now likely to be of more use to historians than to the cause of legal justice.

If the guilty by and large managed to get away with it, it was the innocent who appear not only to have suffered but to continue to suffer. Their day in court was, moreover, not necessarily a time when they could gain a real platform for recounting their experiences.

Trials alone were, however, only a tiny part of the wider story of attempts to reckon with the past. Most efforts to deal with questions of guilt took place not in the public arena of the courtroom but in the relative privacy of the home, in discussions with family, friends, and neighbors, or in personal accounts in memoirs and diaries. Far more people were involved in these private reckonings than in any courtroom confrontations. And unlike the relative clarity and finality of individual judgments in court, such personal wrestling with the past was a process without obvious end, shifting and changing over time.

PART
III

Connections:
Memories and
Explorations

14

Hearing the Voices of Victims

For all their significance in the pursuit of justice, trials barely scratch the surface of reckonings with the Nazi past. Those who had been persecuted had to live with wounds and scars, reconstruct damaged lives, and deal with losses and memories as best they could. People on the side of the perpetrators had to deny or justify in some way their former actions or inaction. And the children of both perpetrators and victims lived under the shadow of a past that continued to loom in their lives in all manner of ways, explicit or repressed, articulated or silenced. Alongside the periodic noise of legal confrontations, there was an inchoate but infinitely significant parallel history of continuous reckonings in the private sphere.

The rhythms of this parallel history of private reckonings related partially, but never entirely, to changing public representations. Cultural phenomena, media events, and political debates were of course important at the level of national patterns of remembrance. But the chronologies of public and private were intertwined in complex ways.

The transition to the "era of the survivor" came not with the Eichmann and Auschwitz trials, nor even with the generational conflicts of 1968, but rather when the life stories of survivors themselves came center stage. A greater willingness not merely to hear but also to actively elicit the voices of victims developed at precisely the time when some were more able to speak openly about painful experiences. This was when the very notion of "survivor" itself began to take hold, awarding a special status to those who had come through hell, bore the marks on their own person, and were alive and willing to tell the tale.

The Era of the Survivor

The era of the great trials in the 1960s and 1970s was an "era of the witness" in a relatively narrow sense. Victim testimony was crucial to the outcome of trials—although survivors were often treated with skepticism, subjected to aggressive questioning, and at times felt as if it were they, not the accused, who were on trial. But even when listened to with seriousness and sympathy, witnesses had to focus on what they could say about the guilt of defendants in the dock—not on what their experiences had meant for their own lives. This began to change from the 1970s.

The focus shifted in subtle but important ways. Survivor accounts now began to be seen as valuable in their own right, conveying experiences over a lifetime, recording not only the period of persecution but also the irretrievably lost world of "before" and the implications of the catastrophe for the life "after." Accounts were significant no longer primarily as a record of horrors but also for what they could say about the survivors themselves.

This was not so much a matter of survivors "finding a voice" as of the emergence of audiences willing to listen. Survivors had always talked, particularly among themselves, and some had written about their experiences. But communication was primarily restricted to particular communities of experience. Now new patterns of communication began to emerge, across different groups and generations, as children and grandchildren—not only of victims but also of perpetrators—wanted to hear from survivors.

Cultural representations both explored and fostered these developments, and in an era of rapid technological change, debates transcended national boundaries. Discussions took place across physical borders as well as between different generations. Developments in documentary filmmaking, recording of video testimony—videotapes, both Betamax and VHS, went into wide use in the 1970s—and the increasing sophistication of oral history techniques among historians strengthened initiatives to elicit interviews for future research as well as public transmission. With new audiovisual media, a growing body of survivor testimony was elicited, making personal accounts widely accessible. No longer were there just a handful of published, literary representations, penned by a few well-known names; now hundreds of thousands of ordinary people were able to "tell their story."

The increased demand and receptivity of audiences did not always make it easier for people who had experienced persecution to talk. Even so, the emergence of new audiences coincided with new phases in survivors' lives. Many had been young adults at the time of persecution. After the war, their primary concern had been to build new lives, found families, and integrate into new societies. By the closing decades of the twentieth century, they had reached a stage in their own lives where they were more willing and able to talk. By now, careers had been firmly established, and many were entering retirement; children whom they had earlier sought to protect from painful knowledge had become adults, and there was a newly felt imperative to pass the message on. These changed personal priorities coincided with a wider context characterized by the emergence of self-help groups, the growth of identity politics, and the revaluation of victimhood in the wake of the Vietnam War. There were variations in the timing and character of these shifts, but similar changes could be observed across North America, much of Europe—both Eastern and Western—and Israel.

There are many ways of trying to explain these shifts.[1] But in Germany the impact was enhanced by the coming to adulthood of postwar generations. Conflicting communities of experience, facing each other across the chasms created by Nazism, were progressively displaced by younger generations with different interests. The newly qualified teachers, journalists, filmmakers, and historians of the 1970s and 1980s did not have the same kind of investment in representations of Nazism as those who had lived as adults through that period. Yet at the same time many had a strong sense of emotional connection, whether because close relatives had been involved or out of a wider sense of shame on behalf of their community. This gave an urgency to their endeavors, propelling their interest while not holding them back from attributions of blame.

Generational shifts were closely related to a changing cultural context, characterized by the emergence of identity politics alongside a search for "roots," particularly in the United States—inspired by Alex Haley's 1976 book, *Roots: The Saga of an American Family*, followed in 1977 by a hugely popular television adaptation. The timing and reasons for the growth of Holocaust consciousness in the United States are disputed. But it is clear that in this, the post–Vietnam War era, trauma and victimhood were being given a new and positive gloss. This shift in perceptions of victimhood was apparent too across Europe, and in 1980 it was marked by the recognition of post-traumatic stress disorder (PTSD) in the official handbook of disorders known as *DSM-III*.[2]

Around this time, too, the notion of the "Holocaust" with a capital H, referring specifically to the Jewish catastrophe, began to gain currency as *the* tragedy or *the* pivotal event of the twentieth century. The TV miniseries *Holocaust*, written by Gerald Green and directed by Marvin J. Chomsky— starring Meryl Streep, James Woods, and Michael Moriarty (as a lawyer turned SS officer and Heydrich's personal assistant)—aired in the United

States in 1978 and in Germany a year later. The show proved to be a watershed both in America and Europe. The series can be critiqued on grounds of inaccuracy and implausibility, but its significance can hardly be in doubt. Bringing the visual horrors of the Holocaust in fictionalized form directly into German homes and representing individuals with whom people could identify and feel empathy, it touched a chord among millions of viewers and stimulated debate about the Nazi past within families and across generations. It also, it seems, precipitated a turning point in the ways in which West Germans spoke about Nazi persecution of the Gypsies, now increasingly respectfully referred to as Roma and Sinti.[3]

West Germany witnessed perhaps the most dramatic impact, at precisely the time when the generation that had supported, tolerated, or at least not actively opposed Nazism was beginning to lose influence in the public sphere. Some historians began to use oral history methods to explore the experiences of ordinary people under Nazism. Such methods were far from new, but the level of engagement in applying them to the Third Reich was distinctive. These historians had been personally affected by the impact of Nazism on their parents' generation, had come of age in the postwar period, and had been involved in the generational conflicts and political tensions of the 1960s. Critical of the generation that had carried Nazism, these historians—not only university-based but also lay practitioners in a growing "history workshop" movement—undertook local history projects illuminating social processes at a level below that of high politics and institutions. They explored traces of nonconformity and dissent and critiqued the narrow official focus on the conservative national resistance of the 1944 July Plot that had received so much praise in West Germany. Shades of gray began to enter the spectrum of analysis of culpability too. No longer were perpetrators seen primarily as either sadistic brutes or banal bureaucrats, pictures fostered by representations of the trials of the 1960s. In some quarters, however, such efforts were seen as politically and intellectually suspect, and there was considerable hostility toward these initiatives. As Alexander von Plato, a prominent pioneer and practitioner of oral history later put it, at that time no one wanted people digging where corpses were buried.[4] Comparable challenges to received views and silences about the past were evident in the different circumstances of Austria in the 1980s, stimulated by the Waldheim affair.

While the 1978 American TV miniseries popularized the term "Holocaust" (which had already been used for some time), the notion of "survivor" now also began to gain currency.[5] This helped many who had suffered from marginalization, exclusion, and fear. But it was not universally accepted. As Werner Weinberg, a former inmate of Bergen-Belsen, bitterly noted, applying the term to people who had survived the Holocaust was different from references to survivors of incidents such as earthquakes or shipwrecks. As he put it: "Holocaust-survivorship is terminal....I have been categorized for the remainder of my natural life." In his view, being categorized as a Holocaust survivor "adds to the damage I have suffered; it is like wearing a tiny new Yellow Star."[6] Many simply wanted to shed this past, this sense of being forever different.

Yet the category of survivor grew ever larger. One controversial scholar and son of survivors, Norman Finkelstein, estimates that at the end of the war there were perhaps one hundred thousand "genuine survivors" in the sense of "those who suffered the unique trauma of the Jewish ghettoes, concentration camps and slave labor camps, often in sequence." But, Finkelstein went on to claim, subsequently the term "'holocaust survivor' has been redefined to designate not only those who endured but also those who managed to evade the Nazis"—a development of which he did not seem to approve.[7] Even so, victims of Nazism who were not in the camps also bore the imprint of this period for the rest of their lives; and the consequences of persecution were often compounded by failures to recognize the long-term significance of experiences of hiding, escape, and displacement without fitting the classic camp survivor profile. Hierarchies of victimhood experience were far from helpful.

The relative victimhood status of different groups, whatever their experiences—in camps or otherwise—also came under discussion. This was of institutional significance. In 1978, Jimmy Carter established a President's Commission on the Holocaust, under the chairmanship of Elie Wiesel, culminating in the decision in 1980 to found the United States Holocaust Memorial Museum (USHMM) in Washington, DC. Wiesel was appointed founding chairman of the United States Holocaust Memorial Council in charge of designing the museum. It was easier to make the decision about memorialization in principle than to work out how to achieve it in practice.[8] Heated discussions arose over which non-Jewish groups should receive a mention—should the exhibition include Gypsies, homosexuals, and others or focus purely on the "final solution of the Jewish question"? And which other genocides might be mentioned for purposes of comparison? The proposed inclusion of the Armenian genocide even led to the threat of withdrawal of financial support by major benefactors. Having suffered in some "unique" way, having suffered "the most," now seemed a desirable status; in a perverse and paradoxical twist, previously marginalized groups were marginalized once again. Yet these acrimonious debates in some quarters also provoked charges of "Jewish elitism," leading the Holocaust historian Raul Hilberg to observe rather acidly that, yet again, "Jews had received a privilege that was becoming a burden."[9]

Despite (even perhaps because of) these controversies, the range of groups that came into the spotlight began to be inexorably broadened. As survivors—however defined—were given a more sympathetic hearing, new projects sprang up, seeking to record and relay the words of survivors "before it was too late." Their experiences were suddenly perceived to have an authentic value in their own right, whether or not they constituted a reliable route to "what really happened" in the past. The ways in which these developments played out varied in different contexts. Initiatives were taken not by "states" but by individuals who had a significant impact in changing circumstances.

In France, the film *Le Chagrin et la Pitié* (*The Sorrow and the Pity*) by Marcel Ophuls was completed in 1969, although it was banned from being shown on French television until 1981. Ophuls was himself a survivor, whose family had first escaped Nazi Germany for France and had subsequently fled France for the United States (dropping the umlaut from the family name in the process). Ophuls returned to France after the war. *Le Chagrin et la Pitié* used numerous interviews to explore the ways in which French people had faced the challenges of defeat and German occupation. While some had resisted, others had collaborated with German policies during the Vichy regime. Alongside the publication of Robert Paxton's pathbreaking history of Vichy France, this film was a significant landmark, affecting discussions in France about compromises made during the "dark years."[10] Louis Malle's 1974 film, *Lacombe, Lucien*, portrays the story of a teenage boy who, unable to join a local resistance group, by a series of accidental events including the breakdown of his bicycle ends up assisting the Nazi occupation authorities. Although fictional, this, too, touched a chord, revealing the almost arbitrary ways in which people ended up on either side of the political divide in Vichy France, the ambiguity of the gray zones, and the role of split-second choices as well as personal emotions in making what eventually proved to be morally laden actions with potentially fatal consequences for those involved. The Gaullist myth of national resistance, so important in the early postwar years, was increasingly fractured.

As the topic of collaboration in France was opened up, so too were the distinctive fates of Jewish victims of Nazi persecution. In the 1970s, Serge Klarsfeld began concerted efforts to document and bring to public attention the sheer numbers of French victims and to restore names and faces to those who had died. Published in 1978, Klarsfeld's book entitled *The Memorial to the Jews Deported from France* contained names of 75,700 Jews deported from France.[11] Another of his works, written in collaboration with others, was a memorial book for deported children, with as many details and photographs as he could collate. Reproducing some 2,500 photographs of the more than 11,400 children deported to their deaths and detailing their fates as far as possible, Klarsfeld saw this documentation also as a memorial for the victims: "This book is their collective gravestone."[12] This assiduous work of remembrance not only assisted families connected with the victims but also helped others to comprehend the character and scope of the tragedy. It took place in a setting where the character of memory was itself increasingly an object of interest, even as waves of memorialization expanded massively in what came to be termed "sites of memory."[13]

Klarsfeld, along with his German-born wife Beate Klarsfeld (née Künzel), also sought to bring perpetrators to justice. This focus was evident too in the work of Marcel Ophuls, whose 1988 documentary film, *Hotel Terminus: The Life and Times of Klaus Barbie,* focused on the cruel treatment Barbie had meted out as Gestapo head in Lyons, his postwar escape to South America, and his belated extradition and eventual conviction. The documentary made extensive use of interview footage with a range of people interpreting these events from differing perspectives.

Even in Eastern European states where the Nazi past had been subjected to official views imposed at the expense of debate and pluralism, there were new tones to be heard by the 1980s. In East Germany, while the significance of communist resistance continued to be the dominant official theme, the Jewish character of the majority of victims came more to the fore. New initiatives were evident in both history and memorialization, within the limits of what was officially desired and the politically possible in the increasingly unstable years of the 1980s. There were pioneering attempts, if necessarily constrained, as in the use of oral history methods to explore narratives that had been suppressed in official representations.[14] In Poland, the question of complicity and silence about the persecution of the Jews, and not merely their own oppression under Nazi rule, was reopened in Jan Błoński's 1987 essay, "The Poor Poles Look at the Ghetto."[15]

Changes were also evident in Israel. Opinions differ as to the extent to which, in the early postwar years, Israelis who had not themselves endured persecution were sympathetic to the plight of refugees from Nazi Europe.[16] Whatever the balance of views about initial ambivalence in Israel, there was a shift away from explicit criticism, by the 1990s, toward greater empathy and understanding. This was coupled with growing recognition that the conditions under which survivors had been humiliated and persecuted had not always made heroism and resistance possible. Failures to resist were no longer judged so harshly, and survivors gained a more respected place as part of "Jewish" rather than "Israeli" society.[17] The Holocaust had by the end of the century gained a place as a marker of collective identity in a long Jewish history of persecution and survival as a community.

A growing focus internationally was on recording the voices of survivors. The Yale Fortunoff Archive was initiated in 1979, the first major collection of video testimonies of Holocaust survivors, many of them still deeply traumatized.[18] This was started by a small group of individuals, including survivors and close relatives: Dori Laub was a child survivor from Romania, and Geoffrey Hartman was married to a survivor who gave one of the first interviews. Interviews allow survivors to dwell on the long-term implications of experiences for their lives, feelings, and relationships. There were no fixed prescriptions about time or emphasis on particular themes, incidents, or places. Rather, survivors could talk at whatever length they chose about what they had been through and what it meant for them now. This is a far cry from the witness statements given in the context of legal trials.

Other collection projects soon followed. Steven Spielberg's Survivors of the Shoah Visual History Foundation was founded in 1994, the year after the release of his film *Schindler's List*, and it collected testimonies intensively from the mid-1990s. Teams of trained interviewers were based around the world or traveled across continents to gather hundreds of thousands of witness testimonies, before it was "too late." From the turn of the century, the Fondation pour la Mémoire de la Shoah began to perform similar functions in France.[19]

There were also projects developed for a wider public, providing only excerpts from survivor accounts. Karl Fruchtmann's interviews with survivors were filmed in 1979–80 and broadcast on West Germany television's ARD channel in 1981. Claude Lanzmann's monumental *Shoah*, first broadcast in 1985, was based on nearly a decade of filming interviews, not only with survivors but also, crucially, with perpetrators and bystanders, including

Polish peasants close to the extermination camps. Many of the latter were, controversially, portrayed as essentially complicit in their passivity and willingness to benefit from the expropriation and murder of the Jews.[20]

This sudden profusion of projects eliciting the testimony of survivors was not a matter of survivors "finding their voice," or "breaking their silence." As we have seen, innumerable victims had spoken of their plight, ever since the very time of persecution and extermination. What was new was, first, the active soliciting of accounts by determined individuals and, second, the expansion of audiences and the changing reception and evaluation of life stories. At the same time, new interactions affected what was said. Victimhood was gradually expanded to become an ever-more encompassing category. But not all victims were listened to equally; some were still heard more than others. And, with few exceptions—particularly the work of Claude Lanzmann—the voices of perpetrators remained notable largely for their absence.

Varieties of Victimhood

As Holocaust survivors increasingly attracted interest and sympathy, their public image was transformed from the initial state of diminution—the wretched, disease-ridden, and dependent creatures who were widely seen as unwelcome burdens immediately after the war—to the more heroic status of "survivors" whose stories were held to carry valuable lessons for all of humankind, acting as an authentic bridge between a horrendous past and a better future. On the personal level, this did not necessarily make for an easier approach to individual memories. But it certainly helped in the formation of certain molds in which stories began to be framed.

Not everyone conformed to acceptable narrative structures. But the new climate of sympathy also allowed somewhat more honesty. Previously sensitive topics could be broached, often occasioning massive controversy when the silence was first broken. This was particularly noticeable in relation to the roles of prisoner functionaries, such as Kapos or members of the Sonderkommandos who assisted in the killing process. Most of these worked for two or three months, then were themselves gassed in order precisely not to be able to bear witness to these crimes. But a handful survived to tell their tale.

Filip Müller, for example, who gave testimony in the Frankfurt Auschwitz trial in 1964, wrote a harrowing account of his experiences in Auschwitz. Charged with herding people into the gas chambers and then pulling out corpses and placing them into the ovens for incineration, he had on occasion been close to suicide. He had persuaded himself out of this by deciding that if he did somehow survive, he should give testimony. Bearing witness proved, however, far from easy. He first published a short account in Czech in 1946, drafted while very ill in the hospital after the war. Following his testimony at the Auschwitz trial, he worked for years to produce a full account. An English version was published in 1979; although it appeared in German a year later, it was barely noticed until he was interviewed by Lanzmann.[21] Müller's account was highly controversial. His work fell into what was known, in Primo Levi's phrase, as the "gray zone," an area of compromised survival that attracted vociferous critique in some quarters. But the publication of Müller's work, and his appearance in Lanzmann's *Shoah*, was significant. It registered a growing desire to understand the complexity and variety of experiences, rather than to condemn those who had faced unpalatable choices and engaged in what to others appeared questionable compromises.

The changing climate provided new—if belated—opportunities for some survivors to gain recognition. A veritable industry of publishing Holocaust memoirs grew, as public appetite for heroic stories of survival apparently became insatiable. As this generation seemed on the threshold of disappearing, so the apparent urgency of capturing ever more interviews and testimonies grew. In addition to the oral history archives of the 1980s and 1990s were now added innumerable late-life memoirs and self-published accounts, while publishers sought out and promoted marketable stories.

It was not only commercial pursuit of profit that drove this industry; there was also a moral desire to make known stories that had previously been underrepresented, and to illuminate aspects that remained inadequately addressed. One such dark corner was that of slave labor. So, for example, former Auschwitz slave laborer Hans Frankenthal gave an account of his exploitation by I. G. Farben's Buna plant at Auschwitz III. Frankenthal's book was based on taped interviews made with him by experts and organized by the German Auschwitz Committee; it was published in 1999, the year he died. This project gave Frankenthal the opportunity to voice concerns about postwar injustice; the editors also contributed an afterword, delineating the legal battles and inadequacies of German compensation to former slave laborers.[22]

On a different scale, and affecting far fewer people but of immense importance to some, was the Nazi looting of artworks and later unwillingness to return works of art to previous owners or their heirs. This also gained momentum from the 1990s. So, for example, a documentary, *Stealing Klimt*, and a related feature film, *Woman in Gold*, were made about the experiences of Maria Altmann in seeking—eventually successfully—to regain from the Austrian government and the Vienna Belvedere Gallery several works by Gustav Klimt formerly owned by her family, including the famous painting of her aunt, Adele Bloch-Bauer, dressed in glittering gold.[23] Despite considerable resistance, and after years of legal battle, the tide was turning.

The enhanced role of victims' voices and the expansion of a market for their stories raised new issues. With the growing involvement of agents and ghostwriters assisting elderly survivors to "tell their stories," questions of authenticity—beyond that of the entirely fake account, notorious from the Binjamin Wilkomirski case—began to arise.[24] In Wilkomirski's case, extreme identification with the Holocaust provided the author with a way of narrating traumatic childhood experiences that he passed off as truthful autobiography rather than the fiction—or, less generously, fabrication—that it actually was. Highly praised on first publication in 1995, it was first exposed as a fraud in 1998, causing a storm of controversy. Something rather different was however at work among the spate of genuine survivor accounts that appeared in increasing quantities from the 1990s onward—raising questions about content, form, and authenticity.

A first-person account might appear utterly authentic, the details unique to the individual. But with professional assistance in writing, the "voice," style, and tone would not be quite that of the survivor whose story was being told. Additional details, wider knowledge, and contextual shading might be sketched in, certainly beyond the knowledge of the survivor at the time and often even later. Literary license might also be taken in describing scenes and narrating conversations word for word in ways that could not possibly be remembered in this detail decades afterward. Other additions by the later writer, arising more from "knowledge" than personal memory, might be particularly jarring when inaccurate. For example, in Jack Eisner's lively account of his experiences, written with the assistance of Irving A. Leitner (an author of children's books whose wife was also a survivor), Eisner appears to remember not only detailed exchanges between people, recounted in direct speech, but also the sign at the entrance gate to Flossenbürg concentration camp—but in fact conflating the sign that was actually there with the distinctive wording at Buchenwald.[25]

Sometimes the survivor insists on use of direct speech, as in the case of Frankenthal's account, in an attempt to convey later memories of scenes that remain vivid in the mind's eye, explicitly portrayed as such by historically sensitive writers.[26] Yet while some aspects essential to understanding the story are added, much may also be lost along the way. What is particularly fascinating about oral testimonies is what might be called, perhaps too grandiosely, a philosophy of life, or at least expressions of wider attitudes and ways of interpreting the world. But in some accounts written by professional authors on behalf of a survivor, the general morals and message of the story are standardized, whether reproducing or challenging expectations. In a sense, plot often seems to take precedence over style; telling a story that will capture the reader's attention appears more important than exploring subjective views, confrontations with the past, or concern with the authenticity of the way in which the story is told. It takes a remarkable writer such as Ruth Klüger to problematize the interplay between the later and the earlier self and to construct the account in such a way that it is clear throughout that there is no simple, unilinear narrative to be recounted.[27] Less literary narratives generally follow more straightforward plot lines, emphasizing moments of heroism, courage, rescue, hope in face of betrayal, danger, anguish, loss; and this is particularly the case when the writer is not the person who went through the experiences narrated.

Such accounts can nevertheless be invaluable in terms of capturing and conveying experiences that would otherwise never be heard even by close relatives, let alone a wider audience. Some of those assisting survivors to tell their story are family members, helping an elderly relative to put his or her thoughts in order and bring memories to paper, or bringing to the world's attention remarkable collections and archives that had lain dormant, untouched, locked up in boxes or attics. Some helpers are themselves also professional people, well equipped and able to bring to the world the stories of a loved one, as in the case of Ann Kirschner's carefully researched and contextualized reproduction of her mother's collection of family letters. Kirschner's mother, Sala, had survived a series of labor camps under the so-called Schmelt Organization—named after SS officer Albrecht Schmelt—in Upper Silesia; the reproduction of these letters, published in 2006, situated in the wider story, is a remarkable document, both giving immediate access to personal experience as it unfolded and simultaneously providing later perspectives that allow a fuller understanding of what the survivor was going through at the time.[28] In other cases, when family helpers were no more professional writers than the person whose stories they helped to tell, the results may be collective efforts that in themselves can be a remarkable account of different perspectives on family experiences. This is the case with the Springer family memoir, published in 2009, where a number of children are involved in telling their own stories of survival as well as the stories of their parents.[29]

In other cases, however, a ghostwriter might take the plot and tell it in a voice that is quite different from that of the person who lived through the events that are being narrated. This is the case, for example, with the memoirs of Sam Pivnik, published in 2012. The frequent interjections to explain the historical context—"I did not know it at the time, but . . ." followed by some historical contextualization—are clearly those of the later, historically informed ghostwriter, somewhat jarring amid the character sketch being developed.[30] The objective tone of voice, which was in fact the product of the ghostwriter rather than the survivor, occasioned some surprise among innocent readers, with comments suggesting amazement at the capacity of a survivor to distance himself so clearly from the emotive events described. This raises questions about the wider impact of the alleged "morals of the story" in supposedly first-person accounts of significant experiences.

Awkward Audiences and Shades of Shame

Contextual changes were also significant. New elements entered the domain of things that could now be spoken about; expectations of sympathy shaped what people were prepared to say, softening previous unwillingness to talk about particular issues. "Shame" became to some extent—it is impossible to gauge how far and among whom—an emotion to which it was possible to admit, at least as viewed from a distance. Josef Baumgarten, for example, who had had a testicle surgically removed during medical "experiments" in Auschwitz, was for the first time able to talk about this openly in his interview for the USC Visual History Archive. He also, stutteringly, applied to himself the not entirely comfortable label of "survivor," as his later self sought to convey some sense of the earlier self who had simply sought to survive for one more day, for one more meal, for one more piece of bread.[31]

The shift in the willingness of younger generations to listen was also significant for some non-Jewish survivors of Nazi persecution who no longer had to fear social exclusion. Leopold Engleitner, a Jehovah's Witness born in 1905 whose story was elicited by a practitioner of oral history in the 1990s, lived long enough to be able to bask in belated recognition of his bravery. In an interview given when he was already in his high nineties, Engleitner recalled how Jehovah's Witnesses had long been "treated as second-class citizens and lumped together with the work-shy and criminal elements" and how "very satisfying" it was "to talk openly about all the things that for so many years were regarded as taboo."[32] Instead of being treated as "something of a pariah," about whom people "used to make derogatory remarks," he was now repeatedly being told by people "how much they admire and respect what [he] did."[33] Near the end of the interview, he summarized his experience as a transformation "from a persecuted, despised concentration camp internee and a cowardly conscientious objector to a completely rehabilitated man who is even regarded as an example to others."[34]

Not all groups found sympathetic audiences. Silence rooted in anxiety about reactions within wider society could be combined with a fear of stigma being attached to relatives, as among families of victims of the "euthanasia" policy. Crucial for this group was the fact that victims were still seen as not "normal."[35] There were often continuing fears that the condition for which the relative was murdered might indeed be hereditary. Many families preferred not to talk about their relatives and tried to suppress their memories. There were often difficulties when a family member discovered or investigated the fate of a relative, with other relatives wishing they had stayed clear of this sensitive area. In some cases, there would be one person who persisted in investigating, while others did not like it being dragged up. In other cases, relatives felt a degree of guilt, or might be accused of having abandoned the patient to institutional care—in due course fatal—when there might have been alternatives. For a few, the pain and loss associated with the murder of a relative was something that had never quite gone away, and facing up to it, however difficult, was a task that could barely be approached.[36]

For different reasons, for decades Sinti and Roma found that few people outside their own community were willing to listen to their stories. This began to change with the airing in Germany of the TV miniseries *Holocaust* in 1979.[37] At this point, it has been suggested, Germans who still could not entirely face up to a sense of guilt in relation to Jewish victims instead became engaged in finding other victims whose causes they could trumpet. An implicit undercurrent of antisemitism was even discernible in some quarters, as accusations appeared to be leveled against Jews for having allegedly cornered the market on claims to attention and compensation. For whatever reasons, Roma and Sinti, along with other marginalized groups, were finally on the list of victims of Nazi persecution. The Central Council of German Roma and Sinti was founded in 1982, and in the course of the subsequent years there was growing awareness of and sympathy for their situation. Even so, they still remained well off the radar as far as most people's perceptions of victims of Nazi persecution were concerned.

Unusually, the Fortunoff Archive contains a unique collection of interviews with Sinti families living in West Germany, filmed just after unification with East Germany, at a time when there were racist incidents in both East and West.[38] This project was carried out by Gabrielle Tyrnauer, a somewhat controversial scholar who clearly enjoyed considerable trust among the families interviewed.[39] These families lived in close proximity to each other, and individual interviews are frequently augmented by the participation of friends and relatives, with partners, children, nephews, grandchildren, and neighbors running in and out at intervals. Virtually everyone in this community was either a survivor or the child or grandchild of survivors. The past had never been suppressed or silenced; the wounds and scars remained so alive that this was not a matter of telling stories about the past, but rather of coping with continuing physical and psychological consequences of extreme persecution. The interviews also strongly reflect the fraught emotional and political context in newly unified Germany, with highly charged experiences of exclusion from local communities and the fear and reality of attacks by neo-Nazis.

For these Roma and Sinti survivors, experiences of persecution seemed to have receded very little, as acute anxiety about racist aggression continued in the early 1990s. Those who were interviewed spoke of their "great fear" as well as the fact that they were constantly being moved on, driven out of places where they wished to settle. Unlike Jews, who had a homeland, they had nowhere to go and felt they were unwanted everywhere. Some mentioned that if they sought to defend themselves against neo-Nazi attacks, it was they, rather than the aggressors, who ended up being arrested. Many felt that their pensions and benefits were pitiful, particularly compared to the pensions of former SS men who had persecuted them. Failing to gain compensation for their sufferings in concentration camps, many felt that Nazi prejudices against "vagabonds" and "asocials" had pursued them through the postwar era.

These comments are confirmed by other sources suggesting they were still widely seen as "asocial and criminal."[40] One woman, Martha E., who had been in Auschwitz, Ravensbrück, and Bergen-Belsen, showed the scars left by beatings by an irate camp guard when, as a ten-year-old, she had stepped out of line to obtain a scrap of food. Still suffering physically from the years of maltreatment and starvation, she felt constantly persecuted and barely dared to go out on the streets. She was constantly suspected of stealing—even of having stolen the flowers she placed on the grave of her daughter, who had tragically died prematurely in a traffic accident. Martha E. also reported a horrific statement allegedly made by a doctor when she sought to go on a rest cure for her medical condition. She claimed that, when he saw the Auschwitz number on her arm, he said: "What a pity, why weren't you gassed? You aren't going to have a rest cure."[41]

Whether or not the doctor uttered precisely these words, the sense of rejection she and many others in her community felt was clearly real. Interviews of this intimate sort, with members of Roma and Sinti communities in their own living quarters, on campsites and in retirement homes, are rare, and are equally rarely integrated into accounts of survivor experiences or the wider literature on long-term consequences of persecution.[42]

Even well after the Holocaust had become a major topic and Jewish survivors a focus of respect, many people had far less sympathy for some other groups of victims. Gay men continued to fear penalties for many years after the war. It was only in 1969 that the Nazi legislation of 1935 relating to Paragraph 175, criminalizing homosexual acts, was finally abolished in West Germany. East Germany had reverted to the pre-Nazi legislation shortly after the foundation of the GDR, but here too homosexuality was punishable until 1968. In predominantly Catholic and conservative Austria, the change in the law came in 1971. But wider attitudes did not change as fast, and it remained difficult for gay men to speak openly about their experiences.

Heinz Heger's frank account of his experiences as a gay man in Nazi concentration camps stands as an exception.[43] This book was written just before homosexuality was legalized in Austria but first published in 1972. It was taboo breaking in a variety of ways, and not merely in the fact that Heger had chosen to speak out at all. Heger had soon found that he was socially isolated in postwar Austria, treated with contempt and discrimination. Nor was his status as a victim of Nazi persecution recognized. The situation only began to change precisely because men such as Heger in Austria, Pierre Seel in France, and a handful of others began to speak out more openly about their experiences.[44] But it was not until 2002 that people who had been persecuted by the Nazi regime for their homosexuality finally had their names cleared. Meanwhile, even despite the cultural changes that came with the rise of social movements and identity politics from the 1980s onward, many gay victims of Nazism did not wish to face further social opprobrium among relatives and in conservative local communities by speaking about their experiences. The few who did often had to face ostracism and derision all over again.

Nor do the main institutions collecting testimony seem to have actively sought them out for interviews. The largest archive, the USC Visual History Archive, initially focused predominantly on the narratives of Jewish survivors, although broadening its focus over time. The Yale Fortunoff Archive has testimonies from a range of groups, but references in the catalogue to homosexuality do not relate to gay men telling their own stories. Rather, they refer to instances recalled by other prisoners of unwelcome homosexual advances, when Kapos sought to engage them in sexual acts against their will. Homosexuality in these cases is seen as an abuse of power, generally recounted with some distaste. Occasionally testimonies will refer to other prisoners who were homosexual, in a rather distanced, third-person manner: objects in the landscape, inmates with whom the person giving the testimony had little personal contact.

Very few gay men who had been persecuted in the Third Reich survived long enough to give their own accounts, from their own perspectives, to a sympathetic audience. In 2000, a documentary film entitled *Paragraph 175*, directed by Rob Epstein and Jeffrey Friedman, gave voice to just five of the remaining handful of survivors of the Nazi persecution of homosexual men.

Cultural shifts subtly affected the extent to which people feared they would be treated with derision and contempt or could expect veneration and respect These fears and expectations varied with the reasons why people had been persecuted, the ways in which they had managed to survive, and the chan ging contexts in which they lived after the war. Not all victims could participate on equal terms in the new era of the survivor; taboos and sensitivities remained, and there were clear hierarchies and patterns of marginalization. The chronologies of silence and speaking varied accordingly.

This was, moreover, communication across generations: communication for the future, to and for younger generations, and not communication between perpetrators and victims. The parallel worlds characteristic of the early postwar decades often persisted to the end. But there were also personal considerations affecting people's willingness to speak and the kinds of accounts they gave of the impact of persecution on their lives.

15

Making Sense of the Past, Living for the Present

Primo Levi observed that there are many reasons for silence about the past, on the part of both victims and perpetrators. The person "who was wounded tends to block out the memory so as not to renew the pain; the person who has inflicted the wound pushes the memory deep down, to be rid of it, to alleviate the feeling of guilt."[1] Difficulties about selective remembering and forgetting are far from new, nor are they limited to Nazi persecution. The sixteenth-century French philosopher Michel de Montaigne made an observation to the effect that nothing fixes something so intensely in the memory as the desire to forget it. The ways a memory is recounted are also affected by time. As Primo Levi put it, "A memory evoked too often, and expressed in the form of a story, tends to become fixed in a stereotype, in a form tested by experience, crystallised, perfected, adorned, which installs itself in the place of the raw memory and grows at its expense."[2]

Yet things stubbornly persisting in memory do not necessarily translate directly into how they are talked about or suppressed, circumnavigated, or evaded. There are many reasons why people remain silent about a painful past. There are also reasons why some talk, almost incessantly, rehearsing certain issues again and again, without apparent resolution; why they remain silent about others, perhaps alluding obliquely to sensitive matters, perhaps confiding only to a few trusted friends or family members; and why some experiences resurface only in nightmares or when unexpectedly precipitated by external stimuli. Psychologists and psychoanalysts have explored in detail the patterns of expression and repression, debating whether traumatic experiences return only as flashbacks and images or can be reframed as—partially controllable, self-distancing, even therapeutic—memory narratives.

Social and cultural contexts, as well as the passage of time, also affect recollections. A few patterns may be observed.

Self-Distancing as Self-Preservation

It is striking how many survivors in some way distanced their later selves from the selves who had lived through these terrible times. The post-Holocaust self lived alongside the self who had experienced the death camps, or the self of the time before the devastation. This has been well portrayed in the extraordinary writings of Charlotte Delbo—both in her raw accounts of fragmentary moments of experience in Auschwitz and Ravensbrück, written shortly after liberation, and in her later portrayals of the fates of other women with whom she had been incarcerated and who were among the few from her group who survived.[3] But it is evident in a wide range of accounts.

The pain of memory can be too sharp, the attempt to portray the past too complex. It may be easier to maintain some form of distance, some sense of detachment. Survivors often convey a sense of not having been quite "there," where it "really" happened. They represent themselves as not having been quite at the epicenter of evil, as having observed from the margins. The "real" victims were those who were murdered: those who returned—in Primo Levi's term, "the saved"—cannot speak on behalf of those who died, "the drowned." And it was only they, the dead, who had the real, authentic experience. For whatever reasons—psychologists are better equipped than historians to comment here—acknowledgment of the full reality might simply be too awful to bear.

Later, once time has put distance between the surviving self and the past life, there may be a growing need to register the loss, possibly on occasion by revisiting former sites of suffering, in order to bring together disparate fragments of a shattered life. Otto Dov Kulka, a historian born in Czechoslovakia in 1933 who only very late in life recorded his childhood memories, was in the so-called family camp of Auschwitz. In his memoirs, he emphasizes that he was never in the gas chamber itself. It was only decades later that he physically walked down the steps into the ruins:

> I descended stair by stair, in the place where all those whose names and images I remembered had descended, and all those—myriads upon myriads—whom I had seen being swallowed up in endless rows into the crematoria and afterwards I imagined how they rose in fire and flames into the illuminated night

sky above the chimneys. Finally I reached the bottom. It was impossible to enter the gas chamber itself, because the roof had collapsed into it and blocked the entrance. So I turned around, finally, and slowly ascended the same stairs.[4]

Part of Kulka's quest is to bring together the divided parts of his self—a division that had made it possible, bearable, to live with the pain of this past, with the recurring dreams in which he is both condemned to die and condemned to survive, in a recurring cycle of the "immutable law" from which he cannot escape.

This quest leads him also to another place from which he had been distant, and which for him was one of the epicenters of tragedy: the place where his mother died. He had last seen her when she was transported from Auschwitz to Stutthof; Kulka later managed to visit the place where she had been a slave laborer, the place where his newborn baby brother—improbably conceived, given the ghastly circumstances—had been killed, the route of the death march from which she had fled, and the site in a nearby village, as he discovered later, where on January 25, 1945, she had died of typhoid fever while in hiding, hoping to survive the last few days before the Soviet army liberated that area.[5]

For many survivors, self-distancing was rooted in a sense of solidarity with the dead: a desire to understand their experience but also a realization that they cannot be brought back and that the distance is unbridgeable. This is evident in Claude Lanzmann's *Shoah*, as he takes his interviewees to the very edge of the experience of death. For others, the passage of time, with a growing distance between former and present selves, was important. Many published accounts by survivors were written only when they had put a great deal of distance between themselves and the past, as in the cases of the historians Saul Friedländer and Otto Dov Kulka and the literary scholar Ruth Klüger.[6]

Some seem to have gained distance by exploring something at two or three removes from their own experiences. Many survivors who became writers—whether of factual or fictional works—wrote about slightly different but closely related topics, not touching too closely on their own experiences but nevertheless in some way relevant to them. Some wrote not only about but also in some sense on behalf of others: Charlotte Delbo's seventeen women on a train; Primo Levi's descriptions of other people in Auschwitz; the analyses of concentration camp life by Hermann Langbein, Viktor Frankl, H. G. Adler, and Ella Lingens-Reiner—all in some way displaced their own sufferings by analyzing strategies of survival or, in part, paid homage to others who did not make it through.

Some chose to write in a different genre, not in a form that could be construed as autobiographical. This could be combined with displacing the "real" story or overarching narrative by using smaller little stories, metaphors, incidents, landscapes, or "something else." The distinctions between "fact" and "fiction" were explicitly addressed by Imre Kertész, both in his fictional but largely autobiographical account of his time in the concentration camps in his novel *Fateless* and in his "interview" with himself in *Dossier K*.[7] Aharon Appelfeld similarly transposed his own experiences into a wider fictional world, in his novels about central European life and the memories of those who survived. Ruth Klüger made quite clear in her own autobiographical account just how constructed, just how much of a literary artifice, every memoir is.

Among those survivors who became historians, professionally committed to evidence-based accounts, flights of literary imagination and creative fiction were not possible. But the act of describing, analyzing, pointing the finger of blame, allowed them to put personal experiences into a wider perspective. Some wrote about places that they had themselves experienced and where close relatives and members of their own families had died, as in the case of Yitzhak Arad's analysis of the Reinhard extermination camps; Arad's parents had died in Treblinka, while he and his sister survived.[8] But it is notable also how many survivor historians—like Otto Dov Kulka—primarily wrote on topics that were not quite those of their own experience. They focused on perpetrators, or on the German bureaucracy, or on something that helped to explain the context and conditions of persecution, without directly confronting their own experiences in the first person.

Survivors' experiences were hard to encapsulate and deeply problematic to convey, whether to somewhat unwilling early postwar audiences or to more sympathetic listeners later on. Among the most difficult to recount, strangely, were not the stories of atrocities but rather how it was nevertheless possible to retain some shred of humanity, or indeed—and even to write this sounds heretical, bordering on outrageous—some capacity for enjoyment of life even under extreme conditions, and to find meaning even in adversity.

Despite all this, there were occasional moments of apparent transcendence. These stand out as significant in some survivors' accounts but pose challenges for discussion and understanding. They can occasion a sense of acute unease; writing about such moments is often self-censored, silenced for decades, before the author dares to reveal what might be quite precious personal moments of memory that do not fit the received narratives and expectations of different audiences.

Recalling moments of tranquility, even happiness, under appalling conditions could even later lead to a sense of what almost verges on nostalgia for a lost world, for a moment during which one had lived in a distinctive way that was, after all, an authentic moment of one's life that could not be denounced absolutely and in its entirety. Kulka recounts in a poetic fragmentary chapter entitled "The Blue Skies of Summer" the happiness he felt in 1944 watching "silver-coloured toy aeroplanes carrying greetings from distant worlds pass slowly across the azure skies while around them explode what look like white bubbles."[9] We now know that these were American planes taking aerial photographs of the extermination camp of Auschwitz-Birkenau, as columns of Hungarian Jews were being sent in the direction of the gas chambers. The Americans in fact then prioritized the bombing of the nearby industrial production plant in Monowitz, rather than the extermination facilities of Birkenau. Kulka includes one of these aerial photographs as an illustration to this passage. He perceived this as a moment of pure beauty, a moment in which he was able to block out the landscape of death all around. All he could focus on was "that beauty and those colours": "The aeroplanes pass by and the skies remain blue and lovely, and far off, far off on that clear summer day, distant blue hills as though not of this world make their presence felt. That was the Auschwitz of that eleven-year-old boy."[10] This moment remained with him as "the most beautiful experience" in his "childhood landscapes." It would remain with him as "the colour of summer, the colour of tranquillity, the colour of forgetting—momentary forgetting—. . . all this [would] remain for all time as a touchstone of beauty" even despite the presence of death all around.[11] For another young prisoner, Gerhard Durlacher, the planes signified the possibility of relief, the hope that the Americans would bomb the gas chambers, followed by the shattering realization that this was not their priority. The question of why the Americans did not destroy Birkenau haunted Durlacher for the rest of his life.[12]

The possibility of happiness and even a sort of nostalgia for time in the camp is also alluded to in Imre Kertész's novel *Fateless*. At the very end, as the young protagonist, Gyuri, has returned to his hometown and leaves his uncomprehending uncles to try to find his mother, he notes the stillness of the evening hour. "It was that peculiar hour, I recognised even now, even here—my favourite hour in the camp, and I was seized by a sharp, painful, futile longing for it: nostalgia, homesickness. Suddenly, it sprang to life, it was all here and bubbling inside me, all its strange moods surprised me, its fragmentary memories set me trembling."[13] For all the recognition of the strangeness of this sensation and the difficulties of his transition, Gyuri senses some continuity and not just the new start that others, on his return, had been trying to impress upon him: "For even there, next to the chimneys, in the intervals between the torments, there was something that resembled happiness." But this was not easy to communicate: "Everyone only asks about the hardships and the 'atrocities,' whereas for me perhaps it is that experience which will remain the most memorable. Yes, the next time I am asked, I ought to speak about that, the happiness of the concentration camps. If indeed I am asked. And provided I myself don't forget."[14] In this seemingly implausible passage, Kertész underlines both the chasm separating himself from contemporaries who had not shared his experiences and the distance from his likely later self.

Readers of Kertész's novel may feel the protagonist is failing to make the points he should be to well-wishers on his return, including the journalist wanting accounts of horror to portray a vivid picture to the wider world and the uncles proposing he should forget his past and start a new life. Readers of Kulka's memoir, and indeed even Kulka himself—who spent a lifetime precisely *not* talking about his past—may wonder at the very possibility of experiencing moments of such intense happiness, such blotting out of the deaths all around; they may question, too, the desirability of talking about such emotions, fearing misuse by people seeking to deny or relativize Nazi atrocities. Both accounts highlight the difficulties of communication, even to sympathetic audiences.[15]

Some memories combined times and places in distinctive ways, registering longing and loss. Irene Eber, who could never settle back in Germany or Mielec, her childhood homes, undertook a trip to Jerusalem in 1994. Her image of Jerusalem was partly derived from a picture that had hung on the wall in her childhood, partly from a song her father had sung that began "Zion, in the green fields, where the lambs pasture." She was struck, despite the ancientness of the setting, by the impermanence of everything in Jerusalem; nor could she feel fully there, in the present: "I watch ageless stones become new houses while others become the dust on which I walk. But I am a stranger here, because when walking in these sunlit, noisy streets,

I also continue to walk through fields of snow and death where Father's song of Zion is no longer heard and where my childhood picture of Zion was long ago torn to shreds."[16]

Life Stages and Changing Stories

The rhythms of private lives did not correspond to those of public representations. But they interwove in complex ways. Priorities altered as people grew older; the desire to build new lives while silencing the past was displaced by the urge to tell new generations; external events could stir up half-buried memories and stimulate renewed concern with the past.

Making sense of the past could not happen over a short period of time. Trying to understand and deal with the consequences of persecution were lifelong endeavors. There could be little closure about the loss of loved ones or the utter senselessness of the suffering. For those old enough to remember a "life before," it was often difficult, even impossible, to bring "before" and "after" into a coherent narrative; for those who were still very young at the time of persecution, it was hard even to construct a sense of continuous identity. Many survivors were left with a sense of being out of place, living alongside others but not really belonging anywhere. No personal reckoning could be considered final, but people developed stories with which they could live. Underlying patterns and key points tended to remain stable, even when the weight of moral reflections shifted.

There were changes in emphasis between the urgent testimonies of the wartime and early postwar years and accounts given later in life, when so many organizations were collecting stories. While earlier narratives focused on specific events and immediate experiences, those from the 1970s onward involved wider frameworks and questions. And because of the passage of time, there was greater awareness of how individual experiences could have a lingering impact over the course of a lifetime.

Psychotherapists recount contrasting responses to trauma, from resilience to incapacity and tragedy.[17] Much of the psychological literature on Holocaust survivors is based on those who sought professional help from psychotherapists or required medical reports for compensation purposes.[18] But many did not. They settled in new surroundings, made new families and friends, and led outwardly secure professional and private lives—and not all wanted their identities subsumed under the category of "survivor."

Some sought to shed the survivor label even after early periods of visibility. This was, notably, the case with Mary Berg: following the publication of her Warsaw ghetto diary, Berg evaded the spotlight entirely from the early 1950s until her death in 2013. When approached about a possible new edition of her diary, she allegedly responded curtly: "Instead of continuing to milk the Jewish Holocaust . . . go and make a difference in all those Holocausts taking place right now in Bosnia or Chechin."[19] Many survivors, by contrast, only began to talk about their experiences late in life, when approached by the growing ranks of interviewers for museums and archival collections of testimony. And the stories of some were neither elicited nor widely welcomed.

All individual memory narratives are affected by cultural and social contexts. Published accounts were subject to commercial as well as aesthetic and personal considerations. In recorded testimonies, the character of the interviewer and the intended audience influenced the stories told and the images projected. Treblinka survivor Richard Glazar, for example, was interviewed for *Shoah* by Claude Lanzmann, who repeatedly pressed for details of reactions to particular incidents. These included how Glazar felt when he first entered a room full of naked women who had been forced to strip before entering the gas chambers, or prisoners' emotions when new transports arrived, after a lull, and they knew that at last there would again be food.[20] Watching the "outtakes" not used in the film, as Lanzmann repeatedly probes Glazar's reactions, we gain a different impression from that left by Glazar's oral history interview recorded during the International Liberators' Conferences in New York and Washington, DC, by the US Holocaust Memorial Council in October 1981.[21] Here, the female interviewer poses limited, factual questions; we gain a chronology of Glazar's life story but hear little of the conflicting emotions and psychological conundrums elicited by Lanzmann. The interview presents a bare summary; the interviewer even on occasion seems to cut off Glazar's thought process, filling a pause rather than waiting for him to continue. Glazar's answers involve factual information that is now available in his autobiographical account, originally written in 1946 but only published in 1992.[22] So we have here in one example the transition from postwar indifference, to emergent interest in the early 1980s, to the eventual publication of the translated memoir a decade after the first interview. Each iteration is different, the presentation shifting with the interests of the survivor, the interlocutor, and the intended audiences.

Some interview projects—particularly those where teams are trained to produce comparable outputs—often predetermine the structure of narratives, allotting proportions of time to different questions, pursuing particular topics and not others, or moving on when an interviewee hesitates. Others, such as interviews for the Fortunoff Archive held at Yale or the Kestenberg archive in Jerusalem, are interested precisely in complexities and ambiguities in response. Some projects are explicitly concerned with reconstructing the worlds that were lost and events at the time of persecution; others are more focused on the significance of persecution for life after liberation. Many survivors express a sense of frustration, feeling the impossibility of adequately representing their experiences. Written transcripts cannot convey nuances of the kind evident in recorded interviews through tone of voice or, in videos, body language, leaving greater leeway for differing interpretations.

In all these ways, contexts affect the self-representations of those survivors who spoke. Far more, however, were barely heard; we catch only occasional glimpses of individuals struggling with their pasts. One such survivor, for example, was leading what sounds like a miserable, isolated existence in Queens, New York, where he talked to nobody about his experiences as a boy in Auschwitz; a somewhat difficult encounter over dinner with this taciturn and irascible man is described by Gerhard Durlacher, who went on a quest to trace the "Birkenau boys" with whom he had been incarcerated as a teenager in the so-called family camp.[23]

There were also people who did not easily fit into the categories for which testimony was sought. Pierre Seel, for example, who had been incarcerated in the concentration camp of Schirmeck (at Natzweiler-Struthof) as a homosexual in his native Alsace, managed to survive the war in ways that did not conform to the script of a venerated survivor story.[24] He had been released on condition he did labor service in the Reich and was called up in the German army as one of those known as "despite ourselves," Frenchmen forced to fight on behalf of their enemy, the Germans. And Seel's postwar life did not lend itself readily to heroization as a survivor either; made to feel ashamed of his sexuality in a homophobic society, Seel married and brought up three children before succumbing to depression, divorce, and drink. It was only in the 1980s, gaining courage from others who were prepared to come into the open (including Heinz Heger), that Seel finally found his voice—but even then, still not always a receptive audience. The circle of those willing to watch Seel's account—as one of the men interviewed for the film *Paragraph 175*—was relatively limited. And his life story still did not fit neatly with those generally thought of as "survivors."

It is therefore not easy, despite the enormous body of material that has been amassed, to make generalizations about how survivors sought to make sense of their past. Even so, some patterns—similar themes, common challenges, and shared responses—emerge, illuminating the continuing significance and personal implications of living with this past among those who did not write published accounts.

Selective Silencing and Individual Differences

Survivors sought to control what they said, to whom, and when. There were many reasons for this. The expression of grief even decades after the events could be part of a healing process—or could simply reopen old wounds and cause new pain. Life stages played a part in personal choices, as did changing relationships, including considerations around telling children.

In some later life accounts, the years immediately after the end of the war are remembered as almost happy. Youth, of course, often appears rosy in retrospect. Yet it is striking how frequently people talk of having enjoyed life in the early postwar period. After the shock of liberation and physical recovery from starvation, maltreatment, and disease, some survivors recollect having had a sense of sheer joy in being alive. Despite all the difficulties and uncertainties of the time, many recalled that there was also happiness and fulfilment, particularly as new relationships were forged that helped in dealing with the grief at losses.

This is sometimes contrasted with later depression and loneliness, accompanied by a sense that at that time one could talk but later could not. Survivors recall how at first people were busy seeking missing relatives and making new friends; there was a lot of talking in camps. Mila P., who was born in Chrzanow in Poland and survived labor camps after passing through Auschwitz, recalls a phase where everyone was asking "Where were you?." But when interviewed in America in 1980 for the Fortunoff Archive, Mila P. felt that "no one wants to talk about it any more." She saw this as largely relating to saturation with information: "Now we know what went on, so nobody really wants to talk about it."[25] She registered a shift in emphasis from fact-gathering and eager exchange of information to a weary sense that people had heard more than enough.

While the emphasis was on physical rebuilding out of the ruins, there was little notion of any need for psychological therapy; one should simply get on with a new life. As Rachel P. put it, interviewed in Sweden for the Judith Kestenberg research project, there was initially no idea that people should receive counseling: "It was not like now, that you should work it out"; rather, they had "to digest it quick," so that "everything should be as usual, as if nothing has happened."[26] Rachel P. did not talk about her childhood in the ghetto, in Ravensbrück, and in Bergen-Belsen, nor of the death of her mother from typhus just after liberation. Referring first to her time as an orphan in postwar Sweden and later as a young adult in Israel, Rachel P. said: "No, I could never talk to anybody. . . . I decided I was young and pretty, I have all this behind me, and now I shall start to live." She wanted to build a better future: "I worked very hard from the beginning to be brave, competent, capable." Her attempts at continued "disguise"—a survival skill acquired in the camps as a child—were successful if problematic: "I was brave, but not as brave as I pretended."[27]

Longer-term strategies often meant neither dwelling on the past nor betraying its influence. There were variations in willingness to confront the past among even members of the same family. This was the case with two sisters and a brother who survived in France, having been taken in by French Catholics, while their parents were deported and murdered. All three immigrated to Australia after the war. Yet only one of the siblings, Paulette G., who was interviewed in 1994, finally made a trip back to France to try to meet up again with the people who had courageously saved their lives when they were children and to find out what had happened to their mother. Despite her best efforts to persuade her brother and sister to travel with her, in the end she went alone. And when she returned, her sister did not want to listen: "She wants to finish and live for today, the same with my husband."[28] Paulette G. found that her own willingness and desire to understand the past was quite different from the responses of her family.

Like Rachel P., Paulette G. did her best to disguise her past and change her identity. As an orphan in Australia, Paulette G. found that others treated her as inferior, a person of whom they could take advantage: "If a boy wanted to kiss and I didn't want to kiss him, he would say: you're only an orphan, you can kiss me, you have to kiss me, you have to act like an orphan, and I didn't like it."[29] She was plagued by the sense of inferiority and victim status: "I always felt that I wasn't as good as anybody else because I was jealous of people that had parents and grandparents, it used to upset me."[30] She was determined not to dwell on the past. It was only when she was in her mid-fifties that she joined a support group of fellow survivors and finally began to confront the long-term consequences of her experiences. Even then, she found it hard to talk. As she put it: "Before when I was blocked out, I felt good and comfortable and happy and merry and everything was just wonderful."[31] But then things changed: "I can't seem to join the past with the present together, it's very hard to join them together because you've got to live for today." Her previous determination to "enjoy the full day today" was weakening: "Since this year, I must say I think it's the first time that I've cried so much. I don't remember crying much before."[32] For other survivors, the only solution was continued silence.

Paulette G. had first married a man from a family with no Holocaust background, and she found it difficult to accept gifts from her mother-in-law. Following an early divorce, she found herself a husband who, like herself, was a survivor without parents. But even after thirty-two years of marriage, she knew little about his past. She did not even know exactly which camps he had been in, and he had only begun to talk after she started attending the support group. But their children still knew nothing about either his or his parents' past.[33] While both Paulette G. and her husband suffered from flashbacks and nightmares, he would not talk to her about this. "I can tell during the day when he says that he's had bad dreams the night before but he's never ever told me one of his dreams. He doesn't talk."[34]

What worked for one survivor might not work for another. In an interview given in Australia in 1993, Eva S., who along with her sister Martha had survived Mengele's experiments on twins, explained how she found it difficult even to talk in a survivors' therapy group. She also no longer spoke much to her sister about the traumatic past they had shared. As Eva S. put it to the psychotherapist who interviewed her, Martha was "more angry" than she was.[35] It was her sister's choice not to talk but to live with her anger as best she could, yet it was not clear that expressing anger in a therapy group was very helpful either.

Even when people did talk, they talked selectively. Eva S. started to recount an incident she had experienced in Auschwitz that had made a long-lasting and troublesome impression on her. She had been given the task—as a young teenager herself at the time—of looking after younger children in the children's camp. The woman in charge of the block, a prisoner in authority as "blockmaster," came in and forcibly took away the milk that Eva S. was going to give to the children, because, this woman said, they would not live anyway. Eva S. could not complete this story, saying only that the woman, now also living in Australia, then said something she would "take to her grave."[36] It is not clear what prevented Eva S. from repeating what had been said all those years earlier: a sense of shame about the woman's behavior, on behalf of the collective identity of Eva's "own people," or because, half a century later, Eva S. was taking into account the woman's place in the Holocaust survivor community where she lived. Shame and social relations after the war both played a role in selective silences. There were also many occasions where shame related directly to a person's own behavior, and in some stories, although unlikely in this case, the actions of which a narrator is ashamed are displaced to others, so that they can be aired without bringing too much disregard on oneself.

Unlike many of those who were truly guilty, survivors were often plagued by a deep sense of guilt, feeling that they could or should have done more to save loved ones, that they had made the wrong choices, that they had perhaps acted immorally in order to survive, that others should have survived in their place. For some, allowing too much pain to resurface did not seem to help. Alex H., interviewed in the United States for the Fortunoff Archive in 1983, remembered how after the war he had other priorities: "I was so involved in the fight for a new existence that I simply could not think of anything else."[37] Raised in the small town of Strzemieszyce in eastern Upper Silesia and having attended an academically demanding high school (*Gymnasium*) in the neighboring county town of Będzin, Alex H. had been forced out of the prosperous family home, sent to live in the ghetto, and eventually was sent with his brother to Auschwitz. The interviewers allowed Alex H. to take his time and concentrate on what was most important to him. Barely fifteen minutes are taken up by the basic "story" of persecution, including details of camps he was sent to, before Alex H. arrives at the questions that plagued him most: the psychological torment of having failed to save his brother; the animalistic state to which he was reduced, and the depression that now overcame him, four decades after the events described. After the war, he had arrived in the United States, unable to speak the language, with no family and no relevant education. His life was taken up by a "daily fight" that "took all his energy and thought." But now that he had achieved these goals, he said, "The time of my past is coming to haunt me."

Following a break to regain his composure, Alex H. resumed the interview, explaining that sometimes "there comes a picture before my eyes and it is so real that I could touch it." When he remembered what happened to people he had known, he said, "I get that depression, and I simply cannot get out of it, it takes days." It was not as if he had previously forgotten the past: "Somehow it was always with me, but always I pushed it away," yet with growing older, even seeing his children and his grandchild, everything "brings up the past." He longed for the help and comfort that might come by talking with others with similar experiences: "I cannot talk to somebody who always lived a normal life," since they would not understand. In place of monuments and memorials, Alex H. thought resources should be devoted to creating a place where survivors could come together, since they "feel comfortable amongst each other," and most had a fear of being alone, of having "no one that they could be close to."[38]

Nearly everyone interviewed commented upon the unavoidable pain of flashback memories. This is the case with survivors who appear outwardly strong and well adjusted, such as Aaron S., a survivor of the Dębica ghetto and the Plaszów and Mielec camps, who eventually managed to jump from a train in which "everybody knew they are not going to live." When interviewed in the United States in 1989, Aaron S. commented that "horrible scenes remain with you and you cannot forget them"; every few days he was plagued by nightmares in which he was running, trying to hide.[39]

Attempts to avoid painful memories were common. "I personally don't want to talk about it," says Mila P., "because it's too painful, it just goes through me, and I get all upset, nervous, and cry."[40] When her children had seen a movie or play that stimulated their curiosity, they would ask her why she cried. "What do I cry about? Why couldn't my younger sister be alive? She would have been forty-nine years old today. Why couldn't my parents— why did they have to go with the dead the way they did? What makes me a better person that I survive?" Thinking about her feelings of guilt, she added that there were "not enough tears any more to cry." As the interviewers switched off the camera, but with the audiotape still running, Mila P. can be heard saying "And now I feel like I want to die."

A frequent motive among survivors to remain silent was a desire to protect their children. How should they explain, for example, the differences between their own family and those untouched by tragedy, their own lack of grandparents and other relatives, while shielding children from too much misery? And how could they talk about their losses without also breaking down emotionally, demonstrating their own grief and vulnerability in front of those for whom they wanted to seem strong?

There was also a widespread desire for children to blend into society without seeming different, as survivors themselves had been. Paulette G. related that she had never talked to her children as they were growing up: "I wanted them to be like everybody else."[41] Every time they had asked her questions, she "would just burst out crying."[42] But, she added, "I wanted my children to think I am normal like everybody else."[43] The appearance of "normality" was very important to her. Fearing she would not be able to give her children the upbringing they needed, she had help with childcare while she worked incessantly to cover the cost. She wanted them to have "a normal person" in the home, so that they could "be brought up like normal children, like Australian children"; she did not want them to have "an accent like me," but rather to "speak a good English."[44]

Eva S. too recounted how she had sought to give her children the best upbringing she could manage: she "never spoke to them about anything that happened." She wanted to "protect them from all that until they were much bigger."[45] Yet even as her children grew up, Eva S. found it difficult to talk directly, and instead gave them "a tape to listen to."[46] Meanwhile, the skills that she ensured her children would acquire as they were growing up related quite closely to her own experiences of what was necessary for survival: "I made sure that they learned Judo, I took them to swimming. Everything pertaining to being able to defend yourself and run away."[47] Despite her concern for her children, her relationship with her children was affected by her own traumatic experiences when experimented upon by Mengele in Auschwitz, and she was uncomfortable with physical expressions of closeness: "My children think I'm not demonstrative enough.... I will never embrace and cuddle and smooch, in fact, it annoys me. They don't think I'm very warm."[48]

A similar concern with trying to ensure that her children would have a good childhood, entirely unlike her own, was expressed by Rachel P. While a young woman in Israel, she met her husband, who was "a dashing young man, a young Israeli." They moved together to Sweden, where she too sought to make as "normal" a life as she could. "I never mingled with people who have been through the war, I was always together with those who were born there, I melted in very well. I knew, I wanted to be like them."[49] Partly this was for her children, to whom she never talked about the past. "I brought them up in a very peculiar way, I loved them very much, and they were not allowed to have any worries. All worries I should care for, everything that was a problem they should leave to me, I would take care of those, and thus all my life, I educated the children in a very unnatural way, i.e. after all I lived through, I wanted that their life should be like a fairy tale, without any worries." She wanted them to be "always happy," and they knew nothing about her past until they were young adults.[50]

This kind of upbringing clearly had consequences. Rachel P.'s children lacked "the dimension of seriousness, of fighting" that she had been forced to acquire at an early age. And they were "different from others, as I have taken away from them all problems, all worries, they should always have it smooth."[51] Moreover, her strategy affected family dynamics, and there tensions could not be avoided, as Rachel P. challenged her husband's desire for her to talk: "I got mad at him. He should never disturb the idyll." She felt that talking about a past that was "so traumatic" would not help her deal with "all that pain, all that disguise"; she did not "want to go on with it" but rather wanted "to live."[52] There was no obvious way to resolve these conflicting needs pulling her in different directions.

Some reacted in quite the opposite direction, as far as telling children was concerned. Aaron S., interviewed in the United States, commented that "like all American children" his own family did not want to listen to his stories at first. Although as they grew up they became "more interested," he felt that time was "against us," and feared that antisemites might get the upper hand.[53] Mila P. too told her children "everything," and they responded with interest: they read books, watched relevant TV programs, and asked her questions, even though "they were not taught anything at school about the topic." Although Mila P. found it personally painful, she felt it important that her children should be educated as part of the wider Jewish community: "As a Jew, they are obligated, they should know."[54]

Olga S., who had survived the war in Czechoslovakia and immigrated to the United States after the war, married a fellow survivor who came from near her own hometown. At first, neither of them talked to each other about their experiences during the war.[55] Fluent in several languages—Czech, Yiddish, German, Russian, Hungarian—she now had to learn English and found "it was amazing how people judged you on the fact that you didn't speak English." It did not matter how educated she was, how many languages she could speak, people were not interested. Wanting to blend into the local environment, she did not talk to her children about her experiences. It was only later, as the neighborhood in which they lived became more Jewish, and following several antisemitic incidents, that her children became more interested and she started to talk more about the past.

For other survivors, the past had to be put to use in some way. Mark Stern, for example, had come from a relatively well-to-do background in Kraków, where his father ran a business. Under Nazi occupation, he became a slave laborer in Mielec and still bore the "KL" tattooed on his wrist. From Mielec he was evacuated first to Plaszów, then Flossenbürg. After liberation, he had planned to go to Palestine but met the woman who became his wife; she had relatives in America, so they immigrated to the United States. In 1981, he gave an interview in Pittsburgh that was taped for the World Gathering of Holocaust Survivors in Israel that year. He explained how he tried to make sense not only of his experiences but also of his survival. He and his wife brought up their children "to believe that we have to be strong as Jews, that we have to fight to survive as Jews and maintain our knowledge of the Jewish religion and Jewish life style." This was in Stern's view why they had survived: God wanted them to "bring children into this world," who "can be the Jewish people of tomorrow." In relation to the Holocaust, "survivors have to hope for one thing, that there was some kind of reason for our survival," and indeed, "the creation of the State of Israel is part of it."[56] Support for Israel was rooted not only in a determination to sustain a place of safety for Jews—a country they could defend and that would protect them like no other—but also, in part, in a desire to give meaning to otherwise entirely meaningless suffering. This was, in turn, reinforced by a wider environment, as on this historic occasion of the first World Gathering of Holocaust Survivors in 1981 in Israel for which Stern recounted his story.

Meaning could also be found in small, personal experiences. Many sought to keep some things entirely private. This was true even for people whose whole professional lives were dedicated to interpretation of the cataclysm that had engulfed the victims of Nazism. Saul Friedländer, both an internationally renowned Holocaust historian and himself a child survivor, suggested that there "are certain memories that cannot be shared, so great is the gap between the meaning they have for us and what others might see in them."[57] He continues: "Even a story complete to the last detail sometimes turns into an exercise in hiding things from ourselves."[58] The most precious memories are often ones for which there is no adequate means of expression. In his memoirs, Friedländer vividly describes the moment that was, as it turned out, to be the last time he saw his parents, when he ran away from the Catholic institution where he had been placed for safety and found them in a nearby hospital, where they were staying prior to their deportation. Even the moment he describes in emotive tones, as he was ripped away from his parents, is recalled as a visual image rather than a recovery of his childhood emotions at the time. "What my father and mother felt at that moment disappeared with them; what I felt has been lost forever, and of this heartbreak there remains only a vignette in my memory, the image of a child walking back down the Rue de la Garde, in the opposite direction from the one taken shortly before, in a peaceful autumn light, between two nuns dressed in black."[59]

In the case of Mark Spigelman—also an academic—the extraordinarily sweet and wonderful first taste of sugar, a present at Christmas near the end of the war when survival seemed more likely, was a childhood memory so significant that that he chose to preserve it as a secret for himself alone; it was only seventy years later that he first spoke about it in public.[60] These were personal images, not necessarily to be shared, deeply meaningful to the individual who did not wish to risk them being trivialized or misunderstood.

The reasons for selective silence were many and various, some more surprising than others, some deeply personal, and others common to wider groups. The dilemma of talking or remaining silent was never easy to resolve. Whether people spoke, remained silent, or spoke selectively, sharing fractured, fragmented memories, perceptions, and reflections depended on many factors. Whichever way survivors tried to reconcile themselves with awareness of losses, pain, and the enormity of what had happened, there was no way of presenting a coherent life story. But all had in common the strong sense that their lives were not what they might have been.

Many felt they did not really belong anywhere, since their prewar worlds had been destroyed. Immigrants had an enduring sense of rupture, of wondering about the lives they might have lived. For Olga S., trying to fit into American life seemed almost more of a challenge than wartime survival. But following the fall of communism, she went on a trip back to her hometown with her husband and visited former schoolmates living in a "terrible situation"; she suddenly realized that she had a "wonderful life in the United States." Yet although she was "comfortable in America," nevertheless her "roots [were] still there."[61]

The uncertainties of immigration and new identities posed challenges not only to those who had survived the camps but also to those who had fled before the outbreak of war. And they, too, could feel a deep sense of guilt about their own survival, while loved ones left behind had perished. Evelore S., for example, escaped Germany shortly after Kristallnacht, first for the United Kingdom and subsequently the United States, where her father had settled.[62] When she left Germany, Evelore recalls, "My mother was broken down." She did everything she could to try to get her mother out, working hard in a series of low-paid jobs, but to no avail. Her mother was deported in 1943, and she never saw her again. Evelore settled in the United States and made the best of things, adopting a positive attitude as best she could. But there was always a sense of displacement. "You go back to Germany, you know you don't like the Germans, and yet somehow in here you still are, this is your home, this is your culture." She tried to suppress thoughts of the life that might have been: "Sometimes I can't help but thinking what would have become of me had I stayed there, I suppose my life would have been entirely different, but you don't dwell on that, I mean you're grateful for everything you have." On a visit in 1958, she decided she was not going to live her life "hating everybody there." She tried not to dwell on the past—"It's no use, you know"—and summarized her approach as making "the best of your life." But by the end of her interview Evelore was fighting back tears.

Self-Discovery: Child Survivors

Too young to pass selections as workers, children rarely survived in camps; those who later gave accounts had generally survived in hiding. The oldest were around sixteen at the war's end; the youngest with any personal memories of the Nazi period were only four or five. Child survivors had known little or no secure life before persecution; their experiences were formative, shaping their identities and lives. And their experiences were distinctive.

They cannot be considered "second generation" like the children of Nazis who had been too young to bear a share of responsibility, even if they were the same age. Child survivors experienced persecution under existential fear for their lives. Jewish children were considered dangerous from a Nazi perspective because they embodied the future of the "race" and because, if left alive, they would grow up harboring a desire for revenge. Many child survivors lost their parents at a young age. Most had to disguise their identity and were confused about who they were or what they should say to whom. All knew they were in some way "different," marked out, and could not play with other children freely and easily nor lead what might, in other circumstances, have been considered a "normal" childhood.

Those who were very young at the time of persecution are sometimes referred to as the "1.5" rather than the "first" generation.[63] It took longer for them to be recognized as "survivors," or even to see themselves as a distinctive group. Unable to tell coherent stories, child survivors for a long time neither were sought after as witnesses nor did they even feel themselves that they had a "story to tell."

Marginality was compounded by geography. Most child survivors had been hidden in western Europe, particularly in France, where the over-whelming majority of all children in Europe who survived the Holocaust had lived. Many of them felt they were therefore not part of the "story" of survival in Poland and eastern Europe.

For those who had in fact survived in hiding in Poland, there were other complications. Some had been cared for by Catholics and changed their identities. They were often fostered or adopted and felt loyalty and love toward their carers. Whether or not this was the case—some had survived in appalling circumstances, abused by those who nevertheless provided shelter and a degree of safety—most wanted only to blend into society after the war, without drawing attention to (or in some cases even being aware of) their Jewish origins. Continuing antisemitism also made it prudent to disguise their background even from their own children, some of whom only found out late in their own lives that a parent was of Jewish origin.[64] It was widely accepted that, as the journalist and psychologist Anna Bikont—who discovered as an adult that she was of Jewish descent—commented, it was "self-evident" that "Jewishness was something shameful that had to be 'revealed.'"[65]

Only gradually did child survivors begin to come together, realizing the deep impact of their childhood experiences. But as they entered middle age or retirement, they began to probe more deeply. Many formed self-help groups; and some published their stories or talked to researchers who realized, belatedly, the value of their accounts both of the time of persecution and the distinctive difficulties in adjustment in different contexts after the war.[66]

Child survivors often registered an ambivalent sense of having lived through the Holocaust and yet not "really" having done so. Particularly if they had been very young at the time, they could not give a coherent narrative of this stage of their lives. They had vivid images of particular scenes or incidents, but not detailed chronologies. Only later, and with considerable difficulty, could they piece together their own stories, weaving fleeting perceptions and fragments into a broader narrative supported by later discoveries, publications, and eyewitness accounts that helped to situate this past. For some, working on their identities and understanding the ways in which historical events had shaped their very being was a lifelong quest.

The earliest real memories of Dagmar B., for example—born in 1940 to a Jewish mother and a non-Jewish father—were of the last two years of the war.[67] She remembered how incredibly calm her mother had remained when their house was bombed and went up in flames and they ran out into the burning street carrying a couple of suitcases with their most precious possessions. She had dim recollections of the families who helped to hide her and her mother in a village near Hanover; her mother going secretly to meet her father, who had remained working in the city while she was left with peasants; and how she was forbidden to play with local children, for fear she would betray her Jewish identity. At some point they had returned to live with her father, cramped up in an attic in a poor quarter of town. Dagmar could recall the terror of the air raids, when neither she nor her mother was allowed into the shelter (which was reserved for "Aryans") and her mother protected her by lying over her, while also being hysterical with fear. When asked about the landscape, Dagmar responded, "I can only ever remember ruins and burning houses."[68]

Of the wider family background Dagmar knew little and only pieced it together, partially, after the war. For refusing to divorce his wife, her father had been demoted and failed to have the career he had expected; after the war he remained bitter about this. Her parents did not tell her, nor did she ask, what had become of her Jewish grandparents; she knew that her maternal grandmother had been deported to Theresienstadt, but had no further details, and this was never spoken about.

Most significant for Dagmar were experiences immediately after the war. The first was when a Jewish uncle who had emigrated before the war returned as a soldier in Allied uniform and was seen giving her sweets and embracing her mother in the streets, occasioning local gossip about consorting with the enemy. This, in turn, aroused envy: "All of a sudden there was something I had not known before, and this was that other children were jealous of me."[69] The family was also now able to move out of the cramped attic and was rehoused in a better area, in a flat previously occupied by Nazis who were ousted to make way for Jewish survivors. Dagmar recalled how her family was greeted with hostility by a deeply antisemitic population filled with resentment that "these Jews" were "now simply getting everything," a population that was "full of hatred, really full of hatred."[70]

For Dagmar—only age five at the time—the worst aspect was how she was now stigmatized and excluded, even after German defeat: "No child was allowed to play with me any more"; there were "exchanges of words, swearing, insults."[71] These experiences were devastating for her sense of self: "I only knew that there must be something about me that was really bad." She added that this was new: "The absurd thing about this is that it took place only afterwards."[72] Right up until her interview in 1995, Dagmar was working on her confused sense of identity and ambivalence about owning up to her Jewish heritage. She retained a sense that to admit to being Jewish was "dangerous" and that there was something deeply wrong with her, which, if others found out, would endanger her existence. She was plagued by a sense of anxiety that, paradoxically, she had not felt during the war when she was physically in danger but had felt secure and protected by her parents. When Dagmar was in her fifties, she finally began to tackle this persisting sense of anxiety. In the meantime, her life had been marked by pervasive silencing, changing identity with context, and feeling stigmatized among Germans who seemed uncomfortable about her existence as a reminder of a burdensome past.

Other child survivors had similar difficulties. Rachel P. was born in the Polish city of Piotrków Trybunalski, near Łódź, in April 1936. She had no memories of any time before Nazi persecution, but had vivid recollections of incidents during the war. "The first thing I remember, 1939, the war has started, and we are on the run, we flee, I do not know exactly how, a carriage. . . . We are on the run all the time. . . . All my childhood consists of running, we sleep once here once there."[73] She was able to piece together fragments from her own memories that she incorporated into what her sister later told her. Her disjointed narrative illustrates in its very style the impossibility of coherence:

> There is no story to tell, bombs falling all the time on Poland, first being closed in a camp in Piotrków, yes, there was a ghetto in Piotrków first, Jews had to live separate, and then we were taken by train, yes that's how it was, by train to Ravensbrück, and I do not know where it started and where it finished, there it was bad, we were treated like dogs, the food, I remember it as a constant chaos around me, the constant fright, my mother was still alive, we were two sisters. The men were taken separate to Buchenwald, and I only remember what my sister told me.[74]

These formative experiences prevented her ever having a secure sense of self, and she repeatedly describes this in terms of "disguise." Her mother "constantly disguised" her by "a dressing up" to make her look older; "The cheeks like this, the cheeks like that, a kerchief on my head, my cheeks rosier, so I should look healthy and fit for work."[75] This early socialization had long-term consequences: "This disguise has stayed with me, I knew I had to be in a certain way to make do, so I have never really become myself, many years later, so the war is not only then and there, but all that it brings with it. It is not only traumatic when it happens, but it continues many, many years." The need for continual disguise was accompanied by feelings of existential anxiety, with "a constant fright that life should be taken from me, because I was so small"—a fright that, she thought, "has stayed with me until this day." At the same time, other feelings had to be suppressed: "I was numb, I did not get any food, I could not stand on my feet. I remember the hunger, people took from each other the bread crumbles, the corpses, terrible things, yes terrible, and I was a child, this is the worst, a child accepts everything. You looked at the corpses and felt nothing, nothing at all. And this is terrible, you get people in a situation to be completely without feelings."[76] Even when her mother died of typhus, she was unable to mourn: "I was completely apathetic."[77] When interviewed in the 1990s, Rachel P. was still working through the long-term effects of her experiences.

A different pattern is evident in the life of Mark Spigelman, who was born in Poland in 1940 and only survived the war because of his parents' skills in deception. At first, because of his blond hair and blue eyes, his mother dressed him as a little girl—whose identity would not automatically be challenged by a physical check for circumcision—and passed herself off as a German mother, dying her own hair blond and riding trams in the sections reserved for Germans, whose identity papers were never checked. On one occasion, capitalizing on her fluent German, Spigelman's mother even managed to have a Polish woman thrown off the tram instead of her, when the woman had challenged her identity. Later, when the ghetto was created, the family hid Spigelman in a "bunker," or hollowed-out dirt hole in the ground; surviving the ghetto clearance, they secured other hiding places, including a closet in the house of a Polish family who hid them as a form of insurance policy, to stock up on moral credentials that might be useful after the war had ended. Only decades later did Spigelman realize that he was himself a "Holocaust survivor." He began to reconstruct his childhood through a combination of the images embedded in recurrent nightmares and the stories told by his parents and others.[78] He became aware of how the experiences of his early childhood had formed him throughout life. As a child with a disguised identity and then in hiding, Spigelman had learned he should always smile and never show fear or cry. He later said that one of his biggest regrets was that he was unable to cry when his parents died—he had learned so early on that he must never show emotions.[79]

Similarly, it had been impressed upon him that he should never attract attention, never trust anyone. "Liberated" at the age of five, he had known no other life; this was for him "normality," and it took him years to learn that he could indeed trust and be friends with other people. In middle age, when delivering a keynote lecture as an internationally renowned professor of paleo-epidemiology (combining forensic archaeology with medical science), he suddenly registered that he was still checking, as he entered the lecture hall, for an alternative means of escape—doors, windows—so that if Nazis were to enter and he would be able to make a rapid exit. The absurdity of this subconscious strategy of self-preservation, learned in childhood and never shed, suddenly dawned on him.[80]

Child survivors who were somewhat older had more explicit memories of a childhood prior to persecution. Lilo C., for example, was born in Berlin just as Hitler came to power.[81] In 1938, her father was arrested and spent time in a concentration camp after Kristallnacht; the family now realized with finality that they had to get out. Coming from relative wealth, they managed to leave Germany for the United States, where they settled. In her interview in New York in 1994, Lilo C. repeatedly highlighted the ways in which she had to adjust from being a "precocious," capable, and self-confident child who had received a good education in Berlin to being a "misfit" with inadequate command of English and a naive view of society in America. When she joined a child survivor group in middle age, she became aware of the long-term impact of her experiences as a young person.[82] Strongly aware of family tensions and discord, she also began to disentangle the issues common in any family from those specifically related to experiences of persecution and relocation.

Irene Eber also experienced long-term uncertainties of identity. Having survived in hiding, after the war she barely knew who she was. She tried a variety of possible identities: the Polish Catholic she was presented as by the family who had hid her, the pious Catholic with aspirations to become a nun, the devout Jew, and eventually the secular Jew, in later adolescence toying with communist ideas. Following reunion with her mother and sister, both of whom survived on Oskar Schindler's famous list, Eber immigrated to the United States, where she was later joined by her mother and sister. In the 1950s, they began to settle down "in the ever-expanding suburbia of Los

Angeles," where they "led quite ordinary lives" and experienced "small joys and petty annoyances." But their identity was never secure: "We learned to appear in daily life as someone other than who we were, and we congratulated ourselves for how well we played the role." This came with a price: it "was important to conceal from others our anxieties, compulsive behavior, strange phobias, fears and nightmares, and the physical maladies such as various intestinal disorders, undiagnosable aches, and fatigue." They soon realized that not everything could be easily disguised, including "skewed emotional reactions to certain situations, when we laughed instead of crying, or reacted stonily when an emotional response was called for."[83] Having lived through a period when survival depended on quick reactions, flexibility, and rapid transformations of identity, Eber was highly sensitive to the impermanence and fragility of life and the possibility of making active choices about who to be, what to do, and what to aspire to. But it was not easy for her to shed her "fears and anxieties," which "were like unwelcome companions on a journey" through life.[84]

Child survivors who lost their parents while still young often had problems reconstructing their parents' experiences or even appearance, with consequences for their own sense of selves. Sylvia Ruth Gutmann, for example, was born in 1939 in Belgium, her parents having fled "their beloved Berlin"; they eventually ended up in France. Her parents were deported from France in the roundups of 1942, leaving their children to an aid agency that smuggled them over the border to Switzerland. Gutmann later received documentation allowing her to piece together her parents' experiences and her own early life: "The parents I do not remember and cannot forget came to me neatly folded in somber gray envelopes." Memories of "that other life shaped by my older sister Rita's stories stir in me the image of a frightened and sad, little black-haired girl" who was once called Ruth. "I have resurrected my murdered parents, and I lovingly recall my late sister Rita now in my senior years. But, Ruth, the name that was dangerously too Jewish, is the figure that never came to mind. She did not allow herself to be part of me."[85] A sense of discontinuity, yet recognition that the unremembered past had dramatically shaped one's whole life, was characteristic of young child survivors who could not remember or identify with the imputed identity of the time of persecution.

For all child survivors, there was a deep rupture between childhood and the later self. In his autobiographical reflections, Saul Friedländer vividly describes the family's flight from Prague, when he was age six, and their experiences in France before his parents were deported, by which time he was ten. But he could barely connect his identity as a child with his later adult self, partially symbolized by significant changes of name along the way—from Pavel to Paul to Paul-Henri, later to Shaul and Saul—reflecting sequential identities.[86] He summarized the fundamental rupture: "For each of us who lived through the events of this period as children there is an impassable line of cleavage somewhere in our memories: what is on this side, close to our time, remains dark, and what is on the other side still has the intense brightness of a happy dawn—even if our powers of reason and our knowledge point to obvious links between the two periods." For that earlier period, "an irrepressible nostalgia remains."[87]

The diversity of experiences among survivors cannot simply be reduced to a few common elements. Age, the circumstances of survival, and the character of surrounding society both during and after the war affected long-term impact; later experiences in different societies were crucial in shaping subsequent identities and affecting degrees of shame, concealment, and long-term strategies of self-preservation. But there are some unifying threads to the manifold variations, including a desire to achieve the impossible and a sense of resolution in face of irredeemable rupture.

"Forgetting" seemed to be a privilege of the persecutors. It is notable that while survivors continued to suffer from their experiences throughout their lives, among perpetrator communities stylized stories grew that allowed people to deal with reproaches—whether explicit or implicit—and to live without too great a sense of unease about their own roles in a deeply disturbing past.

16

Discomfort Zones

Millions of people had in some way supported Nazi rule and later talked about their personal experiences among friends and family, particularly if they had been close to significant events or individuals; it was difficult not to brag about meeting a Nazi leader at a rally or the heroism of particular wartime experiences. But willing participants in Nazi rule were later faced with major challenges in how to tell their life stories. They could not readily justify behaviors or attitudes supporting Nazism, except among other Nazi sympathizers. Nor could they simply leave out or denounce this whole section of their lives; they could not present themselves as having been effectively "absent" for what was—particularly for those who had been young adults at the time—a formative and indeed often enjoyable period of their life. People generally want their lives to have mattered. Those who had supported Nazism or played an active role in the regime, in however small a way, did not want to diminish its importance in their lives. Nor, however, did they want to be judged by it. In what oral historians call a desire to achieve "composure," individuals wanted to bridge the chasm between the life before and the life after, to construct some kind of personal continuity across the divide of 1945. But people who had been enmeshed in Nazism frequently experienced difficulties in telling their life stories, including what were sometimes the most adventure-filled and interesting phases of their lives, tainted as they were by complicity. It was difficult to combine pride in personal accomplishments and happy memories of the "good times" under Nazism with defensiveness about their roles and the consequences of their actions at the time.

Of course the ways in which people told their life stories varied with context and changed over time. The majority of former Nazis went along with the new norms and practices of the successor states after the war, however much they may have grumbled—and however much they may have supported the previous regime, as we have seen in the case of Josef Blösche, for example. Given the taboos around expression of far-right views, it is impossible to quantify the extent to which people really changed their own values or merely learned to mouth new platitudes.

Self-defensive accounts became particularly evident among West Germans, where the public culture rejected the past while accepting responsibility. And as the West German economy boomed and democracy stabilized, people generally came to accept the new system. In East Germany, people were under far greater pressure to conform to the communist regime, which was of course particularly disliked among former Nazi sympathizers. But provided they kept relatively quiet, they generally did not need to account for their Nazi past, discounted as "fascism" was in official ideology as the responsibility of capitalists and militarists who had fled to the West. Austrians, for very different reasons, were also under little pressure to justify their past—although they too wove stories that seemed more acceptable to a later present. When people in any of the Third Reich successor states did talk about their experiences during Nazi rule, a number of general strategies were deployed.

"Ignorance and Innocence": Self-Distancing as Self-Justification

Arguably the most widespread strategy was that of self-distancing—whether in terms of geography, knowledge, or action. When confronted after the war with the realities of persecution and mass murder, many claimed, "We never knew anything about it" (*Davon haben wir nichts gewusst*).[1] The unspoken suggestion is that had one actually "known about it," one might have been able to challenge "it." If one had self-evidently been knowledgeable, other strategies would have to be brought into play.

When using the geographic version, "it" is always situated a little way away from where one was oneself, "somewhere else"—however near or far away. Geographic distance is generally accompanied by an attempt to deny any relevant knowledge. Innumerable accounts emphasize that the death camps were situated far away, hidden in the Polish forests, and that killings on the Eastern Front took place in utmost secrecy. These accounts are—as all plausible stories must be—rooted in the realm of possibility, of potential believability. But people did not need to have been close to have known about what was going on in the east. News traveled, rumors spread, and stories about mass shootings and gassing were increasingly common. So the geographic justification cannot always be taken at face value, even for those tucked away in the picturesque Black Forest in southwestern Germany.[2]

The assumption behind the claim of having "known nothing about it" is, moreover, based in a disturbing distortion. The "it" about which nothing was allegedly known is reduced, effectively, to the gas chambers of the east. But the sheer inhumanity of the Nazi regime was visible all around: the violence and brutality used against political opponents; the stigmatization and degradation of those deemed inferior and outcast; the exploitation of forced labor and the proliferation of labor camps across the Reich and the occupied territories; the horrendous and often fatal penalties for minor infringements—all this and more was evident to anyone willing to see. And indeed, fear of heavy penalties played a significant role in widespread conformity among people who were not enthusiastic supporters of Hitler. It was not as if people did not know about the apparatus of terror.

Even so, the geographic strategy appeared to work as a later excuse for supposedly not having realized the full extent of the horrors. It was possible to claim distance even when located close to atrocities. One sixty-one-year-old West German, for example, recalled that in his youth he had lived in Hindenburg in Upper Silesia; he often visited his grandparents, who lived in Neu-Gatsch (Nowa Gać), which was but "three short train stops away from Auschwitz," frequently staying with them for weekend visits. Even at such close quarters, and even though he often saw "transports" of people being taken to Auschwitz, he claims he was too far away to "know" about "it." From the village where his grandparents lived "one could often see somber clouds in the sky above Auschwitz, and then it was whispered that Jews were again being chased through the chimneys or being burnt." He continued: "No one learned any further details."

What, one wonders, might be needed by way of "further details"? But a good reason for not inquiring further was readily at hand: "Everyone was afraid of being sent there themselves, [if] any comments about Auschwitz or the Hitler regime had become generally known." Moreover, what did they "really" know? As he put it: "An acquaintance from the village was employed in the Auschwitz camp kitchen and said, literally, 'Oh my goodness, if you only knew what was going on in the camp.'"[3]

What is striking in this account is the notion that not enough was yet known. What else might one have needed to "know" in order to be appalled?

The local who worked in the kitchens reinforced the sense that there was more to be "known." At the same time, there is the implication that, even without fully knowing, it would have been dangerous to say anything; a person spreading such rumors would also end up in Auschwitz. Proclaiming ignorance was later the only way to live with the realization that one had actually known enough; it allows the person to maintain self-respect.

Others later claimed that although they had actually witnessed disturbing scenes, they did not really register what this meant at the time. One man, for example, recalled in his memoirs that when, as a youngster, he had been sent via Kraków to serve in the east, he and his companions simply did not want to become aware of what it meant when they saw Jews being transported in a train. He relates that as they came into the Kraków region, they saw "goods wagons, out of which girls wearing headscarves sometimes looked sadly out of the one tiny window." The meaning was clear: "Everyone knew that these were Jewish people who were being transported to the east. But one looked away and repressed this knowledge. There was never any discussion about it." And despite seeing the Jews in transit, there is a retrospective resort to geographical distancing: "That Auschwitz was located very close by I only discovered after the war, when I heard about this terrible place."[4] This claim about only learning after the war is also typical. A relatively small degree of distance is enough to justify ignorance and therefore exoneration.

These individuals were not themselves actively involved in acts of killing at this time and needed only to defend themselves against the widespread reproach (particularly as younger generations matured and challenged them) that they might have been able, had they registered what was going on, to try to do more to prevent it.

Strategies for shifting the burden of guilt to others—moral self-distancing—emerged early on. An implicit definition of what it meant to be a "real" Nazi allowed many former members of the NSDAP to suggest that they were not the "real" Nazis or that they had been forced, in some way, to join the party. Even if they had wanted to join and had enjoyed the activities of Nazi organizations—including the Hitler Youth movement—they had not "really" been Nazis. This was widespread and evident right from the denazification period immediately after the war, where it was essential for pragmatic reasons, in terms of evading fines and retaining professional positions among those who were adults at the time. It took on new inflections with the growth of oral history projects in the late twentieth and early twenty-first centuries, when those who had been relatively young during the Third Reich were now middle-aged or elderly. Interviewees often represent themselves having been only an "80 percent Nazi," contrasting themselves with "100 percent" Nazis. One former Nazi youth leader, for example, presented himself as an expert on everything until it came to atrocities, where his expertise apparently ended: he supposedly knew little if anything about what had gone on.[5] There is a rapid slide from being a supposed expert on the times to professed ignorance on Nazi crimes.

Those who had been Nazi enthusiasts rapidly distanced themselves from having actually exercised any responsibility or agency. The claim of relative powerlessness was common, particularly but not only among female perpetrators, resonating among postwar audiences.[6] A related strategy was to concede that one had indeed been fascinated by Nazism but had been in some way "overwhelmed" by it; the magical powers exerted by Hitler and Nazi ideology had been too great to withstand.[7] One had been, effectively, an innocent victim of the times: used, abused, and unable to act independently or resist being blinded by ideology. This was evident even in the belated concession by Nobel Prize–winning author Günter Grass that he had himself briefly, toward the end of the war, been a member of the Waffen-SS.[8] In the GDR, this argument was quite convincing among younger East Germans, who readily recognized the ways in which a powerful state could coerce people into conformity, in this way easing tensions between generations.

Moral self-distancing involves claiming that one remained "decent" in indecent times and did not do—or want to do—anything that was actually wrong. However implicated in Nazi crimes one was, entanglement was more than outweighed by small acts of compassion: engaging in attempts at resistance, or assisting one of the persecuted, even perhaps saving a person's life. Such isolated acts are held to represent the "real" self.

Postwar German accounts abound in such stories of small acts of compassion or "resistance." Subtly sabotaging ammunition production by inefficiency when working in a munitions factory; allowing forced laborers to eat with the family despite the ban on fraternization; giving them better food or larger rations than they were officially entitled to—all could be thrown into the ledger and added to the moral balance of having lived through the Third Reich and yet remained morally intact. But from the perspective of the victims, there were other possible interpretations of acts of apparent compassion. Dr. Ella Lingens-Reiner, for example, suggested in her

testimony at the first Frankfurt Auschwitz trial that small acts of mercy indicated that perpetrators were indeed complex and multifaceted human
beings, not simply sadists and monsters. There was, in her view, no one who
was simply all bad.[9] In some survivor accounts, it appears as if perpetrators
used the unpredictability of their behavior as a form of power. Lords over
life and death, one minute they could let a prisoner slide by into the wrong
line, permitting them to live, or let them have a small favor, an extra ration
of bread, or other privilege; the next, they might use prisoners for sport,
instructing them to throw their caps toward the fence and run to collect
them, then shooting them dead "while they sought to flee" ("auf der Flucht
erschossen," a supposedly "legitimate" reason for killing). The very capri-
ciousness of their behavior was an act of power. So was the favoritism exercised toward some prisoners, who were then beholden to the perpetrator
who was granting them favors. Finally, as defeat neared, many perpetrators
began a more systematic form of "insurance policy"—even if they did not
call it such—doling out favors and nurturing positive views among prisoners, in the hope of sowing a later harvest of supportive testimony to be
deployed in the ever more likely event of defeat.

For stories about moral distance, much depended on what would go
down well with others—and this varied with context. Reducing the site of all
evil effectively to the gas chambers of Auschwitz in West German accounts
is scarcely surprising. In East Germany, by contrast, the demands and challenges of living under communism seem to have displaced concern with
the Nazi past. The case of Ursula B., a former landowner and Nazi supporter
who became an upstanding GDR citizen, demonstrates how even an individual who had upheld the Nazi "Volksgemeinschaft," the exclusionary "people's
community," could later represent her own life story in ways that omitted
any inconvenient proximity to the Nazi regime.[10] Cases of former Nazis
who were brought to trial in the GDR—Zimmermann, Blösche, Schmidt—
show just how easy it was to keep one's head down for years, even decades,
and make a life as an apparently "good" GDR citizen if one kept quiet enough.
There must have been many more who were never unearthed, and the
Nazi past was not high on the agenda for discussion among East German
families.[11]

Distance in time from the events recalled was also significant, affecting
who was actually doing the recounting and what it was they wanted to talk
about. In united Germany, as survivors increasingly gained attention, the
meaning of victimhood expanded ever wider. Germans who had suffered

the consequences of war and defeat—whether or not they had previously supported Hitler—portrayed themselves too as victims of historical forces. This was not in itself new: the claim of "Germans as victims" had been loud, vocal, and effective in Adenauer's West Germany of the 1950s, with material assistance for the victims of "flight and expulsion" from Eastern Europe and for former prisoners of war. But the primary focus in West German political culture had been on remembering Jewish victims, simultaneously deflecting attention away from perpetrators while supporting those who had gone along with Nazism. At the close of the twentieth century, however, as those who had been young during the war reached retirement age, a new wave of claims about suffering emerged, this time under the banner of "war children" (*Kriegskinder*). People who had lived through air raids, flight, and expulsion when they were still very young now became conscious of shared experiences.[12] Books with a psychotherapeutic angle on the supposedly "forgotten generation," the "children of war," even the "grandchildren of war," sold widely at newsstands in train stations and airports, clearly hitting a chord with many people. And oral history interviews carried out with those who had been young at the time of the Third Reich concentrated more on the by now standard question of "what they knew" than on what they might have done. The schoolchildren who had been taken by their teachers to jeer at Jews on Kristallnacht and to help pick over the spoils in the shops and synagogues that had been destroyed no longer remembered any such actions, merely that they had been at most dimly aware of these events, at a distance.[13]

At the Gates of Evil: A Schoolteacher's Tale

One West German's account of her past reveals how a number of strategies could be combined. Marianne B., a former schoolteacher, was sent as a young woman to teach in a school in the town of Oświęcim (Auschwitz) on September 1, 1943.[14] Late in life, her experiences there were a source of both personal pride and potential discomfort. Her memoirs demonstrate a form of cumulative, partially self-contradictory "collective memory," in the sense that what she imagines others to be thinking has structured and colored her account of her own past, while at the same time some of her language and assumptions betray the persistence of Nazi patterns of thinking from the time.[15] Written in the spring of 1999 when Marianne B. was in her mid-eighties, the memoirs provide an account of the year and a half she had spent teaching at a high school in Oświęcim. They were written for private family purposes, but there is evidence in her somewhat defensive tone of a wider imagined audience. Like so many who lived through Nazi Germany as members of the dominant, "Aryan" community, Marianne B. in old age had difficulty trying to square her own pride in her achievements and experiences with her sense of what was acceptable in the wider culture when she wrote her memories down.

Among Marianne B.'s pupils in Oświęcim were the children of Rudolf Höss, the longest-serving commandant of Auschwitz concentration camp; her colleagues included a teacher whose husband was an SS officer in the camp, and she attended social events and evening gatherings where other SS officers were present. Despite being a teacher in a high school so close to the gates of Auschwitz, associating with parents and colleagues with detailed knowledge of what went on inside the confines of the camp, Marianne B. professes ignorance of what "really" went on there. Yet her account also betrays some evidence of unease, compounded by assumed or actual later criticisms of her inaction. It is not clear from the memoirs whether or not she had actually been challenged, though it is highly likely. The result is a memoir characterized by a tone of self-justification that is at the same time in conflict with her desire for recognition of her distinctive experiences, her proximity to power and the heights of the Nazi regime.

The account therefore operates in multiple directions and exhibits contradictory impulses. Marianne B. portrays herself as an innocent young teacher from Berlin, who had absolutely no idea when she agreed to go east of quite what would await her. Given her proximity to the perimeter of the largest site of extermination in Europe, she cannot help but concede, and indeed almost take pride in, her privileged situation. She intimates a great deal of knowledge and admits that she cannot actually overlook what is going on within the boundaries of the camp. But this requires some adjustment in order to present an acceptable self and sustain self-respect. To have known too much would potentially open Marianne B. to the accusation that she had failed to take effective action or engage in resistance; it would produce precisely the kind of enraged response that people of Marianne B.'s generation had in fact witnessed in West Germany from the later 1960s onward. She therefore asserts that she could not "see" what was going on. Despite her extraordinary proximity to the actual gates of Auschwitz, Marianne B. still manages to claim a degree of physical distance. She could not go for walks too near the actual concentration camp area, she says, because everything was guarded so closely. She could never really "see" inside the barracks or "see" the prisoners properly, with the exceptions of a column of supposedly well-fed, healthy, and suntanned workers marching to road-building duties while singing a German song or the camp orchestra playing music as laborers filed past.[16]

Nor did she "know" what was going on. Like many others, she allegedly only heard indirectly, through intimations by others, that something very wrong was taking place. Even so, it was not sufficiently convincing for her to do more than express a sense of empathy, sympathy, even sorrow. One day, on returning to her room after teaching, she found something that shook her: everything was covered in a fine dust.

> It lay like cigar ash in beautiful white-gray flakes of a quite curious structure on the black wood of my desk. "What on earth might that be?" [My landlady] leaned out of the window. "It can't have blown over from the I. G. Works, because the wind today is coming from the KZ. They are burning there again in the crematorium. So that is human ashes. We have already had that many times!" With that she left me alone. I was shocked and deeply shaken. Was this not a last greeting to me from one of the unlucky ones, an accusation, a moving plea for help from the poor victims?—A proof of mass murder it was not. After all, every big camp had to have a crematorium—even so, I will never forget these curiously beautiful, sad flakes of ash.[17]

Yet she continued to deny that this was evidence of mass murder, despite suggesting that she had seen and known more. Even on her very first day in the town, she had been given to understand that something untoward was going on. On her arrival in September 1943, she had been greeted by the mayor, who allegedly told her, repeating it twice for emphasis: "*Every week more prisoners arrive, but the overall number always remains the same!*"[18] Moreover, even before lessons had begun on her first day of teaching, she had been struck by the ways in which her pupils were suffering from the context:

> Already in the hallway I was greeted by a throng of small, disturbed girls from Class Five; they looked at me sadly and in search of help. "Yet again so many people arrived in a goods train this morning and were unloaded on the ramp," said one of them. I didn't quite register what she meant at first, but then I was appalled and speechless. "What did you see? I've only just arrived from Berlin yesterday. Tell me!" Disappointed, they turned away from me. Then the school bell was already ringing. I was deeply sad. Could one not carry out this

horrible process that they called Selection (choosing those destined for death) out of the eyes of the public, so that little schoolchildren—two platforms away—did not also have to see it?!!¹⁹[19]

Marianne B.'s primary sympathy seems to lie with the young children who had to witness the selections at the train tracks, rather than with those victims who were actually—as she states quite plainly, for once—"destined for death." Instead of protesting at the murderous process itself, she appears to have merely wished it could take place out of sight of the public, so that young children would not be exposed to it. The method, not the murder, was what seems to have been wrong.

At a social event held within the grounds of the concentration camp, she met a colleague of Dr. Mengele—or at least one of the doctors who carried out the selections.

> Next to me sat one of the camp doctors: an Austrian with a lovable charm and definitively cavalier-like manners. He was good-looking, but his eyes had a strange glisten. In a delightful Viennese dialect he entertained the little table.... [After he left], when she came back in my hostess whispered to me "That is one of the worst! He just came from the station, where he led the Selection, and he will now go back and continue with it!"
>
> I shuddered with horror.[20]

Yet despite all the hints and asides—from the mayor, the schoolchildren, and her landlady, as well as the SS officers and their wives whom she knew on social terms—and despite her repeated reactions of distaste, sadness, even "horror," Marianne B. stuck to her claim that she never "really" knew what was going on within the camp. She repeatedly represents herself as innocent, ignorant, and appalled by even the very suspicions that were aroused; but she nevertheless claims that the first time she consciously registered the dire state of the prisoners was only at the very end, when she saw starving, ragged, dying prisoners on a death march.[21]

Marianne B. even sought to maintain distance between what was going on and those who were in charge. She did not hold Rudolf Höss responsible. It was just his "fate." She did consider Himmler responsible, but suggests that even Hitler had not known what was going on.[22]

Several further arguments characterize Marianne B.'s defensive and self-contradictory account. The first is that she believed that the German troops must not hear or know anything about these crimes during wartime, since it could adversely affect their morale and thus the course of the war.

As she put it: "What I was most worried about was that the truth would get out to our soldiers at the front. They must not know about this unworthy action, this ghastly crime, yes, this never-to-be-made-good-again political stupidity."[23] In this way, while condemning the "ghastly crime" and "political stupidity," she was being a good patriot, prioritizing support for the fatherland at war. Moreover, she went on, "No one had ever obliged either me or other citizens of Auschwitz to keep silent about it. Was the regime confident that no one in this difficult phase of the war in 1944 would weaken the government by spreading accusatory rumors? Would it not have been a blow against Germany?" She points out that "it was important to retain a high opinion of one's own people [Volk], in order to survive."[24] Talking about crimes would merely "endanger" the Reich, and in any case "most people either could or would not believe it."[25]

Secondly, she resorts to the defense of lacking agency, asserting that she herself was not in a position in which she could have done anything anyway. Even so, she seeks to rescue the portrait of herself as an inherently good person, indeed even almost a victim herself: "For me, at any rate, who had to live so close to the inhuman crimes, which were after all clearly evident, my conscience was constantly troubled."[26] But she does not pursue the concession implied by the phrase "clearly evident."

Finally, there is resort to the argument about geographical distance, extending implicitly to all Germans. If she and others so close to the gates of Auschwitz could not have "known anything about it," then how could those so much further away?

> It is true that in the course of the years, through rumors and observation of external details, we believed we could put together a vague picture of the tragedy taking place behind this barbed wire and these walls, but an attestation under oath would have been wrong; what could be gleaned from outside was too little, too insignificant, and too uncertain. *If therefore we, as immediate neighbors, could never be witnesses to what happened there, then it is absurd and unjust to make the whole [German] people [Volk] responsible for it.*[27]

We hear the rumblings of a self-defensive conscience, combined with belief that the needs of the fatherland were paramount and self-contradictory comments about what could or could not be "known about it." This uncomfortable combination is common among those who never entirely shed their devotion to the Nazi regime, even while acknowledging the murderous consequences of Hitler's rule.

For all the ambivalence, a preoccupation with guilt—if only to deflect challenges—was a distinctive feature of West German self-reflections. Marianne B.'s memoir demonstrates a widespread preemptive self-defense.[28] It is of course difficult to generalize from individual stories, particularly when there are few means of independently verifying their historical truth. While by the time of the third generation, in the 1980s and 1990s, large numbers of grandchildren may not have believed that their own grandpa was a "Nazi," the burden of guilt had already been shifted—by those who had supported Nazism themselves.[29]

The Guilt of Others

Those whose complicity or guilt could readily be documented were for obvious reasons least likely to concede any responsibility for their actions. They were in principle liable to prosecution and would inevitably present the best defenses they could. Mainly this meant not speaking out at all. Moreover, every setting in which they spoke had its distinctive biases; when they were "overheard" talking among themselves, the effect of peer group pressure among former soldiers, for example, could provoke comments that might not reflect private doubts about disturbing memories.[30] Rarely can we glimpse what they may have been feeling privately or were prepared to say about their past outside the context of legal proceedings.

Much could be at stake in *not* talking, not providing an account. Franz Schalling, for example, was a German policeman who was sent to work guarding the Chelmno extermination camp. Using a hidden camera, Claude Lanzmann surreptitiously filmed an interview with Schalling in which, after describing the arrival of already "half-dead" Jews who were about to be gassed, Schalling explains how he could never talk with either his son or his wife about the terrible scenes he had witnessed.[31] His son would not have understood why he did not rise up and protest against it and would have despised him, and his wife would have called him a murderer. In the interview, Schalling is clearly agitated both by knowledge of what had happened, including his own role in it—even though he did not consider himself a murderer—and by the fact that he feels he can never talk about it with the closest members of his own family.

Among those who were directly involved in atrocities, there are some common self-defense strategies. Heinz Schubert, for example, was the adjutant of Otto Ohlendorf in Einsatzgruppe D. This unit had rampaged through the southern Ukraine and Caucasus in 1941–42, killing Jews, Gypsies, and communist "partisans" on Himmler's orders. Put in the dock after the war in the Einsatzgruppen trial, Ohlendorf was sentenced to death in 1948 and executed in 1951.[32] Schubert, also sentenced to death at this time, was luckier: his sentence was commuted to imprisonment, and he was released as early as 1952. His guilt, one might think, had been amply explored and demonstrated. But when interviewed by Claude Lanzmann in 1979, Schubert employed typical evasion techniques.[33] The interview was punctuated by cautionary interjections on the part of Schubert's wife, who was determined not to let him incriminate himself. This was unnecessary: Schubert himself was quite adept at distancing himself, even evoking Ohlendorf, who allegedly told him: "You should be glad that you have nothing to do with all this."[34] Ohlendorf had of course long since been executed for the crimes for which, Schubert claimed, he himself had not been responsible. Furthermore, Schubert asserts that those who were really responsible were never questioned. Their moment on trial, Schubert claims, was something that he was still waiting for "right up to the present day."[35] When pressed as to whether he himself felt morally burdened ("seelisch belastet"), Schubert accepted a moral burden while refusing to admit guilt. One must feel morally burdened when faced with a large group of people "who have to be executed" without knowing "in individual cases" exactly why.[36] Fearful that things were getting a little too close to an admission of active involvement, Schubert's wife intervened to emphasize that Schubert himself was not actually present at killings. Pressed further by Lanzmann, Schubert replied that he knew lots of others who felt "morally burdened," and he had intervened on their behalf with Ohlendorf, requesting that they be freed from their duties, particularly those who were themselves "fathers of families."[37] Schubert tried to claim the ethical high ground by demonstrating empathy with Germans' suffering because they had to carry out morally difficult acts—not empathy with the victims. Finally, Schubert and his wife emphasized the difference between having had responsibility for and having merely observed acts of killing, a distinction rooted in the linguistic minutiae of similarity in sound but difference in meaning of the words "beaufsichtigen" (to oversee) and "besichtigen" (to see) in German.[38]

Similar tactics are demonstrated by another of Lanzmann's interviewees, Karl Kretschmer.[39] Kretschmer was in the Sonderkommando 4a of Einsatzgruppe C, responsible for the mass killing at Babi Yar, the ravine near

Kiev where more than thirty-three thousand Jews were murdered in the massacre of September 29–30, 1941. Lanzmann was strapped up with a secret microphone and hidden camera, aware that Kretschmer would be an unwilling interviewee. And indeed, Kretschmer insisted that he did not want to talk, arguing that it was so disagreeable that he would rather get away from it. He had already spent three years in internment, from 1945 to 1948; he had then been the subject of legal investigations in 1959, following the establishment of the Ludwigsburg Central Office, and again in 1969, when a Darmstadt court had pronounced him not guilty due to "lack of evidence."[40] Still using Nazi terminology, Kretschmer argued that his group's task was to free the area of "saboteurs." Lanzmann acidly queried the inclusion of Jewish children under the notion of "saboteurs," to which Kretschmer rapidly responded that luckily he had himself never personally had to take responsibility for that. When asked how many Jews he had seen being killed, Kretschmer responded that he did not count them at the time; when asked about the claim that by the summer of 1942 there were no more Jews in Russia, Kretschmer replied that he did not know how many there had been before the war, nor did he know what such a claim might mean. The constant shooting ("Schiesserei") was however difficult for him. But Kretschmer's ultimate line of defense was to say "No comment."

For those close to the atrocities, geographical distance was no excuse. Instead, many perpetrators adopted less literal forms of distance, detaching the self that acted in a particular situation from the "authentic" self and suggesting that the person who acted or behaved in certain ways was not the "real me." The "real" self is the moral inner self; the outwardly visible self that acted was prompted by external considerations over which it had little or no control. The easiest defense was to claim that they had merely followed orders in a situation where there had been no alternatives.

Even for those in positions of authority at the time, there were still ways of distancing oneself from "really" having been involved. Helmut Hensel had been in charge of the Mielec Gestapo at the time of the deportation of the Jews on March 9, 1942, and at the time of subsequent killings, including the "liquidation" of Jewish slave laborers for the road construction company Bäumer & Loesch.[41] Hensel had personally ordered Zimmermann and others to assist in these and other killings, including the shooting of between 100 and 140 Jews in the Jewish cemetery of Radomyśl Wielki on July 19, 1942.[42] But he was never brought to trial in West Germany. Unsurprisingly, Hensel refused to travel to East Germany to testify in the trial against his former subordinate, Zimmermann. But in a statement given to West German authorities on October 6, 1967, Hensel claimed to have been ignorant of what the deportations were about and where the Jews might have been being taken.[43] Similarly, he alleged that he had only "heard" about shootings taking place but had "known nothing more definite" about them. He had been, he claimed, against all these "measures" and wanted "to have nothing to do with them."[44]

Self-distancing through distinguishing between the supposedly "authentic" self and the acting self of the time was a strategy adopted even by Rudolf Höss, commandant of Auschwitz, whose memoirs written in 1947 in Polish captivity contain a remarkable degree of self-reflection—even if, understandably, highly self-serving in nature. He reported on how he himself was transformed in having to deal with a difficult system. Rather than claiming that he was "merely following orders" and hence blaming those above, he adopts a clever twist in which those above were indirectly responsible by having foisted upon him as workers people he designated as criminal elements. He insisted that he was given the worst sort of Kapos and professional criminals with whom to build up the camp. In this way, Höss blamed not only those above but also his underlings. He did not even trust his SS subordinates. As a result, he himself became withdrawn and difficult: "Because of the general untrustworthiness that surrounded me, I became a different person in Auschwitz."[45]

Among medical personnel actively involved in murder, there emerged a distasteful discussion of the relative morality or "humanity" of different forms of killing. Dr. Hans Münch, who had been exonerated in the 1947 Auschwitz trial in Poland on the basis of supportive witness testimony and who gave evidence at the first Frankfurt Auschwitz Trial in 1964, described discussions among camp doctors. Those carrying out selections did not do this "with any enthusiasm." But others took the view that "if it has really been decided that the Jews have to be killed, and that only those still capable of work should first still do the work that they are able to, and only then also should be killed," then under these circumstances, "it is without doubt more humane, if one sends those not capable of work, even if they are children, to the gas chambers." This was, according to Münch, "very much the subject of discussion."[46] Furthermore, doctors frequently discussed "the question of the humanity of gassing" or whether it was better to die by "being injected or by whatever other methods."[47] Münch did not think he had himself done anything wrong, despite participating in medical experiments on those selected by Josef Mengele. During the testimony he gave in 1964, he demonstrated professional pride in the observations he had made, discussing how many months a person could be expected to live on the limited daily calories provided and how much life expectancy might be prolonged if they were able to "organize" additional rations or attain the role of functionary with a little additional power and command of resources.

Like many other medical professionals involved in Nazi medical experiments, Münch appears to have been able to separate his professional interests from the inhumanity of the situation. This compartmentalization seems to have been developed more widely. Among "euthanasia" doctors, for example, a phenomenon of "doubling" has been observed. Professional skills could be used, but for purposes at odds with the previous ethical standards of that profession.[48]

Situations were crucial in affecting how former Nazis portrayed their past. When subject to denazification proceedings or at risk of being brought to trial, they talked very differently than when reminiscing among old comrades. Life stages mattered too. When still young, they might brag among themselves and relive the good times. In the prime of life, career considerations might entail more circumspection. But when elderly, suffering the onset of dementia might entail a lowering of defenses, and there might be reminiscences they no longer wanted to repress. In the memory loss characteristic of old age, long-term memories—and associated emotions and ways of talking—retain greater clarity than short-term memory. Lapses might occur inadvertently when Nazi phrases slipped out, no longer subjected to the self-censorship of preceding years.

An interesting example is, again, that of Münch. Designated the "good doctor" following his exoneration in 1947, Münch made something of a career out of his past. He popped up repeatedly in the press and media, giving interviews in the 1980s as public interest grew. But in the later 1990s his SS past almost caught up with him. The German news magazine *Der Spiegel* interviewed him in 1997, just after he had watched Lanzmann's *Shoah*. The interview, published in September 1998, contained what were considered inappropriate comments. Over marble cake and later slices of bread and meat, Münch reminisced with pleasure about his time at Auschwitz, to which he had become accustomed within a day or two after arrival.[49] A series of antisemitic comments, praise for the good research conditions in the SS medical laboratory, emphatic support for Mengele—all pour out of the old man in this interview, despite his wife's attempts to send the journalist away.

Münch acknowledged he had been engaged in selections, deeming it more "humane" to send people to the gas chambers immediately than let them wait to die; had deliberately infected prisoners with malaria; and had undertaken research on the severed heads of children delivered to him by his friend and colleague Dr. Mengele. Yet he had been able to walk free after the war, going on to enjoy a long life and what appeared to be a pleasant retirement.

The *Spiegel* interview shocked many readers, and a legal investigation was commenced. Ultimately, his son's contention that Münch was suffering from Alzheimer's disease and had lost his short-term memory prevailed, and criminal proceedings were dropped in 2000. Münch died at the age of ninety in 2001. The case raises the question, however, of whether Münch's interview in fact demonstrated not mental confusion, as his son claimed, but rather a declining capacity for self-censorship. As the rose-tinted self-representations of the intervening years slipped away, Münch could no longer keep up the pretense of his postwar persona as the "good doctor in Auschwitz" and instead revealed his previous Nazi "morality" with devastating clarity.

Unlike Münch, most former perpetrators kept a low profile. Those who had suppressed difficult memories wrapped their stories in ways that made them acceptable. The significance in the latter half of the 1990s of the traveling *Exhibition on the Crimes of the Wehrmacht* was that it forced many, for the first time, to face up to the violence in which they had been actively engaged. The photographic evidence that members of the army had been involved in killing civilians challenged the myth of the "clean Wehrmacht" and forced a shift in conversations, with young people now interrogating their grandparents in new ways. Just as members of the second and third generations had been becoming more interested in hearing the tales of the victims, they now also challenged the stories of former Nazi supporters and fellow travelers.

It was not only Germans who began to reassess their involvement in Nazi persecution. Some remarkable interviews have been carried out with people in eastern Europe who were involved in mass shootings, with excerpts available through United States Holocaust Memorial Museum (USHMM). They reveal a curious mixture of empathy, horror, and detachment while representing their own part in mass killings initiated by the Germans or in benefitting from the consequences. Juozas Aleksynas, for example, was born in Makrickai, Lithuania, in 1914.[50] As an auxiliary to

German forces in late 1941, Aleksynas participated in mass killings of Jews in Belarus. Aleksynas claimed he tried to demonstrate some "humanity," describing how he made parents with young children lie in the pit together before he shot them; parents would very often be cradling their children in their arms to comfort them. When asked who he shot first, Aleksynas replied that it was the father. The child would not "feel anything" if his parent was shot, whereas Aleksynas felt empathy for a father having to witness his child being shot while in his arms. He saw it as somehow more merciful to kill the father first. Asked how he felt about killing, he said it was terrible, awful. He could no longer imagine how he had been able to do it. "But then, a person became almost like a robot." After the war, he did not talk about it: "It was shameful to tell anyone, it was a shame. It was shameful and horrible. It was a cruel, horrible situation. Horrible." He was unable to provide any explanation for himself: he simply had to blame God, unable to understand "why he allows humanity to destroy innocent people." He claimed that this was what he also thought at the time, even while he was shooting children.

Even those who were "only" beneficiaries of the murder of their Jewish neighbors found it hard to account for their involvement. In one interview, a Lithuanian woman by the name of Regina Prudnikova described how local peasants had eagerly grabbed as much as they could of the possessions of local Jews who had been murdered: bedding, clothes, shoes, gold rings, even teeth with gold fillings.[51] She maintained that she herself had not been involved: although she had tried to take a couple of pairs of shoes, in the end she had not kept them. One set turned out not to be a pair after all, so she returned them; the other pair had already been chosen by her cousin, who demanded them back, so she returned them. But she still bore a gold filling taken from a tooth of a murdered Jew in her mouth and pointed it out at the end of the interview. She gave no details of how she acquired this gold filling. Trying to square the moral circle of supposed non-involvement—returning shoes not out of guilt but for pragmatic reasons, having someone else's gold filling in her own teeth—was clearly not an easy task.

The postwar history of relations between "neighbors" who had benefitted from the destruction of whole communities and the few surviving Jews was further complicated by envy and suspicion. "Fear," it has been pointed out, was felt not only by survivors who were still potential victims of postwar antisemitism but also by Poles who had assisted Jews and now feared the wrath or greed of neighbors who assumed they must have profited from such activity. This bedeviled Polish-Jewish relations long after the war.[52]

Poles were generally prepared to give evidence about atrocities if Germans were the perpetrators. But when Poles were involved on the side of the Germans, accounts were more problematic. Here, too, strategies emerged to reduce moral discomfort. Among the many Polish eyewitness accounts of the mass murder committed at Trawniki by Reserve Police Battalion 41, for example, only one witness betrays a sense of unease—and this at one remove, for it concerns a distant relative who had collaborated with the Germans. Kazimierz K. reported that he "saw the smoke and was aware of the smell of burning from the burnt bodies, the whole area was drenched through with this nauseating smell."[53] One of his cousins had married a man who worked in the Trawniki camp, wore a black uniform, and bore the German eagle on his cap. But despite working for the Germans, according to Kazimierz K, his cousin's husband "was a decent man and warned the Poles ahead of various actions by the Germans" (no mention of warning any Jews). Like others involved on the German side, including Ukrainians trained at Trawniki to become concentration camp guards, this man fled Poland after the war; by the mid-1960s he and his wife were living in New York. Kazimierz K. noted approvingly that they continued to send packages and letters to their relatives in Trawniki. Though trying to provide a testimonial for a "decent man," Kazimierz K.'s interview provided evidence of complicity, active collaboration with the Germans, and postwar fear of consequences.

Many people benefitted from Nazi policies. Those sometimes termed "bystanders" were in many ways more implicated than this apparently neutral term would suggest.[54] Innumerable Poles became beneficiaries of the murder of Jews, the spoliation of their property, and the destruction of their communities. Some had not only condoned deportations and killings; they had been active participants and accomplices. It became almost impossible subsequently for Poles to face up to this. Moreover, the official communist versions of history, emphasizing a combination of heroism and martyrdom, at times almost brushed the Jews out of Polish history entirely. Decades of relative silence began to be broken in the course of the 1980s—as indeed also in the neighboring communist GDR. In particular, the Solidarity movement precipitated wider discussions and the exploration of new ways of addressing the complex Polish past—debates in which the Catholic Church as well as a more secular intelligentsia and Polish nationalists took part, in the interests of resurrecting a more multicultural Polish past. Lanzmann's *Shoah,* with its unsympathetic portrayal of ordinary Polish people witnessing and benefitting from the distress of the Jews, proved to be highly controversial. The later 1980s saw further publications and initiatives opening up intensive public discussions.[55]

Debates over Poland's past further intensified after the collapse of communism. The publication in 2001 of Jan Gross's book *Neighbors*, on events in the small Polish community of Jedwabne in July 1941, when some 1,600 Jews were murdered by their Polish "neighbors," unleashed a major and long-running controversy.[56] This was carried out not only in the national media but also among ordinary people within the local community. Investigations by Polish journalist Anna Bikont revealed how people lived in fear of reprisals if they spoke too openly.[57] The issues were graphically illuminated in a 2012 film, *Aftermath* (*Pokłosie*), loosely based on the Jedwabne story, written and directed by Władysław Pasikowski. More than half a century after the end of the German occupation, the murders of Polish Jews by their gentile neighbors were still tearing Polish communities apart, with intimidation, destruction of property, and physical violence—even murder—still live consequences of a past that was very far from dead and buried.

When stories of those on the side of the perpetrators are explored, it becomes clear that there was, in effect, a bizarre reversal in the representations of power and agency. While victims often suffered from agonized feelings of guilt—whether about their own survival or their failure to help others—former perpetrators composed defense strategies downplaying their own agency and distancing themselves from what they had known and done. Above all this involved the construction of a "good self" persisting across time despite changing circumstances. But whatever narratives were developed, they did not achieve closure—on either side. The past reverberated not only across the decades but across generations.

17

The Sins of the Fathers

A rnold Speer was the son of Albert Speer, who had been Hitler's architect and minister for armaments and war production. In a documentary about his father, Arnold Speer commented: "Until 1945, he was a father I could look up to; after 1945, he was a war criminal."[1] This expresses, very starkly, what hundreds of thousands of Germans had to face after the war.

The second generation in perpetrator families was not a homogeneous group. It spanned a wide age range: while some were children in the Third Reich, socialized under Nazism, others were born after the war and brought up in a culture condemning the Nazi past. There was wide variation in degrees of knowledge: some were children of prominent Nazis and could not escape awareness of the contaminated past of their parents, while others only discovered by accident, or dimly suspected but barely dared explore their likely misdeeds. The context of knowledge or discovery made a big difference to how stories about the Nazi past were received. And, not least, individuals chose remarkably different strategies in how they dealt with a difficulty legacy: the conundrum of both wanting to love and respect their parents yet utterly denouncing what it was they had done or stood for. This could put them into an almost intolerable psychological situation. Some could no longer trust their parents to tell the truth and broke off connections as best they could. Others accepted parental stories, becoming complicit in convenient cover-ups. Some sought for ways of reconciling apparently mutually incompatible positions. And some, in the process, so disturbed the family peace that they created new problems and tensions.

All of these patterns can be found: at one extreme, sons and daughters uncritically supporting Nazi justifications and defending their parents, through varieties of ignoring or evading difficult questions, to, at the other extreme, making a total break with an intolerable situation, breaking off relationships with the parent, or being nearly destroyed by family strife. But there was no escape, even if "dealing with" meant ignoring or suppressing the past, and trying to get as far as possible away from it; some even preferred to remain in ignorance. The burden of these struggles inevitably affected the second generation. Strategies changed even in the course of one person's life. But whichever way the children of perpetrators turned, there was no way they could entirely square the circle. Some, however, managed to navigate these difficult waters more successfully than others. A few faced up to the significance of the past and put considerable time and energy into working for a better present and future.

Reframing the Past: From Mielec Perpetrator to GDR Victim

The East German town of Altenburg lies in rolling countryside, yet with convenient transport links to the city of Leipzig. With winding cobbled streets, some charming old houses, a spacious market square, a small lake close to the town center, a museum, and a significant church (where Bach once played the organ) alongside a hilltop castle, Altenburg is an attractive town, even if—despite modest fame as home of the popular card game Skat—hardly a major tourist center. Apart from the occasional dilapidated building, it bears little trace today of either its Nazi or its communist past.

It was in Altenburg that, following release from a Soviet prisoner of war camp, Rudolf (Rudi) Zimmermann from Mielec settled with his growing family: his mother and his wife, both of whom had fled Poland, and his four children, born over the course of seven years from the early 1950s.[2] Working hard, Zimmermann established a family home with a garden in which, alongside a wealth of flowers, he grew fruit and vegetables and indulged in beekeeping. Zimmermann's brother and sister had also left Poland; they, however, chose to settle in West Germany and Austria, and although Rudi Zimmermann visited them while the inner-German border was still open, before 1961, he chose to build his life in the GDR. For a while, he seemed entirely successful. Family photographs portray a happy family life, with a good and caring father and holidays at the Baltic coast.

This all came to an end with his arrest, trial, and life sentence. As the judge noted in his summary, Zimmermann had become a model GDR citizen: a highly valued and productive worker, a committed trade unionist, a member of the ruling SED, and a good father bringing up his children in

the spirit of socialism.[3] But despite his apparent transformation from obedient Nazi to committed communist, Zimmermann was still guilty, in the
judge's view, of assisting in roundups, deportations, and murders of Jews—
crimes demanding a life sentence. And in the GDR, this really did mean life:
Zimmermann died in a prison hospital in December 1988.

Klaus Zimmermann was the youngest of Zimmermann's four children.
He was just seven years old when his father was arrested in 1966. Klaus still
vividly remembers how he and other members of the family were held in
one room, while people he describes as the Stasi (the East German secret
police, Staatssicherheitsdienst) ransacked the house and garden, including
Zimmermann's beloved beekeeping facilities. What they were searching for
Klaus did not know.

Following his father's arrest and imprisonment, Klaus barely had an
opportunity to speak with him. Only when Klaus reached eighteen was he
even permitted to visit his father in prison. Even then—not having seen his
father for eleven years—he saw him only briefly, once a year. Visiting rights
were restricted to two people, once every three months. Klaus's mother
went on every visit, and the four children had to take turns. The visit was
far from intimate: his father wore prison clothing and was kept behind
a mesh, next to a guard. It was impossible to hand over gifts or foodstuffs.
Klaus and his father sometimes communicated in Hohenbach Schwäbisch—
the dialect spoken by ethnic Germans in his native hamlet, dating back to
settlers from Swabia who had founded the "German colony" in 1783. Klaus
was familiar with the dialect, since his grandmother and father had spoken
it at home; but the prison guard was unable to understand it and repeatedly
reprimanded them, asking them to speak "proper German." Klaus had little
opportunity to talk openly with his father, let alone explore why he had
been imprisoned, but he retained happy childhood memories of a kind and
loving parent.

Zimmermann's wife, Irma, was a childhood friend from Hohenbach who
married him after his return from the prisoner of war camp. She remained
a devoted and loyal wife. But having to work immensely hard to support her
mother-in-law and four children seems to have exhausted Irma's personal
resources. Her daughter-in-law, Sabine, described her, in carefully chosen
words, as a woman with little time for human warmth. It cannot have been
easy, and yet she succeeded in keeping things going.

But the most surprising success is the way Irma effectively transformed
the story of her husband's Nazi past into one of GDR victimhood. She

knew at first hand his support for Nazism and his work for the Mielec Gestapo; she was also present throughout his trial and heard his own detailed confession as well as evidence presented by survivors. And yet according to Klaus, she told a completely different story at home.

When I went to talk with Klaus and Sabine in 2016, I never expected that they would know nothing at all of Zimmermann's involvement in murder nor have any suspicions of his wrongdoing. I found myself having to tell them details that I thought they would already know only too well.

The story that Irma told her children was that Zimmermann was effectively a victim of an unjust system in the GDR. The Stasi had arrested him for no good reason. According to Irma, her husband had merely been an interpreter for the Nazis and had translated something inaccurately, which had perhaps led to the "wrong" people being killed—and the blame was later laid on the interpreter, rather than on the truly guilty. Moreover, in her telling, it was the GDR authorities and not the "real perpetrators" who prevented Zimmermann from proving his innocence. Zimmermann's two superiors, Thormeyer and Hensel, who could have given evidence on his behalf, were allegedly "refused visas" to enter the GDR—although in fact they stayed away precisely in order not to risk prosecution themselves. Finally, Irma claimed that the sentence was so severe because it was a "show trial"—although reporters had been expressly forbidden to attend the trial and there was no splash in GDR newspapers.

Irma's anti-communist perspective allowed her to recast her husband as a victim of GDR injustice, rather than a man with numerous murders on his conscience. With the story reframed in this way, Zimmermann's children could grow up believing their father was an innocent man who had been wrongly arrested and imprisoned.

Added to this was wider support for the family. The children's school ensured they were not disadvantaged by their father's Nazi past. Neither teachers nor fellow pupils ever made any issue of it. Nor was there apparently any ostracism on the part of friends or neighbors. The only time that his father's past was brought up, Klaus recalled, was when he was being assessed for compulsory military service. He was asked what he thought of his father's activities under Nazism; his response was that it had nothing to do with him. Klaus heard nothing more of it. The practical consequences of Zimmermann's imprisonment were what caused the greatest problems, rather than any emotional or social difficulties associated with confronting his wrongdoing.

There was one odd twist arousing some posthumous suspicion. When Zimmermann died, his personal effects were returned not to his widow or children, as expected, but rather to a son-in-law. This man had already attracted some attention among relatives. At family gatherings he would circulate among the younger children and question them in ways that seemed odd. Following German unification, in some professions employees were "evaluated" and questions raised about collaboration with the Stasi. The son-in-law lost his job at this time. It also turned out that there was a substantial Stasi file on family members, although with names blacked out. The suspicion was that this man had informed on the Zimmermann family because of potential Nazi connections as well as Zimmermann's contacts with his siblings in Austria and West Germany. Whether or not there was any basis for such suspicions, this cannot have made for a harmonious family atmosphere.

Klaus and Sabine accepted that there were challenging issues to deal with. As responsible and well-balanced adults, they recognized that they should explore and discuss this together, with open minds. Klaus was hoping to find a sympathetic interpretation of his father's actions, and he suggested to me the possibility of an exculpatory narrative—that his father might have had to pull the trigger under orders or face being shot himself if he refused. I was uneasy about disabusing him, but also unwilling to participate in a cover-up. I had to point to Zimmermann's own confession, as well as the accounts of survivors. Zimmermann had taken the initiative in using his local knowledge to find Jews and had revealed or killed them even when he could have helped them to hide. I could only portray him as he was, insofar as this can be ascertained—an ill-educated young man who seized what he saw as an opportunity to better himself and then became caught up in escalating violence, resorting to alcohol to keep going. Only later did he appear to regret it bitterly and try to make amends through an entirely new life in the GDR.

I had not expected to have to break the news of Zimmermann's crimes to his son and daughter-in-law; I had not expected that such a perfect veil of silence could have been maintained over the decades by Zimmermann's wife and mother, both of whom knew far more than they had ever admitted to his children. The supportive treatment of the children in the wider GDR context, where such family stories were also not spoken about, similarly meant that their father's Nazi past was never an issue. It was the practical consequences of living in a single-parent family—not unusual in postwar

Germany, with so many fatherless families—and not any emotional challenges posed by their father's record of mass murder that were the biggest issues to face.

This case is unusual only in that Zimmermann was actually brought to court, a matter that had to be reframed by his wife. Given the sheer extent of involvement in Nazi violence and the relative paucity of prosecutions, there must be innumerable other cases that never surfaced, where family narratives could far more easily be adjusted. Unless something brought the involvement of a relative to their attention, members of the second generation could see the Nazi past as an essentially historical rather than personal legacy.[4]

Selective Exploration: From the Dębica SS to the West German Self

Even where little was known, however, there were inevitably some intimations and personal legacies. The case of another perpetrator from the Mielec area, this time one who ended up in West Germany, illuminates a lingering significance without ever really confronting the issues head-on. And if in East Germany the narrative was reframed such that a Nazi perpetrator could become a GDR victim, in West Germany the displacement was toward psychological legacies and the implications for personal identity.

We have already met Peter Müller, a member of the Waffen-SS and forester in the SS troop training ground situated between Dębica and Mielec.[5] Late one night in 1954, when returning triumphant from a shooting championship, Peter Müller apparently fell asleep at the wheel and drove directly into a tree; he died as a result of injuries sustained. His death was traumatic for his son Hans, still a young adolescent; both Hans and his mother clung to an idealized memory of Müller.

Growing up in the shadow of his father's premature death, Hans Müller knew a little about his father's wartime whereabouts. But for decades he did not explore further. Quite by chance in the early 1990s, while taking the place of an absent work colleague, Müller was involved in producing a radio program discussing war damage and the effects on children of the Bosnian war. This had a significant impact on him. He suddenly registered the "discrepancy between parental love and the violence that the same parents exercise as soldiers."[6] This touched a chord, and he volunteered for an interview in February 1994 with a research project examining the personal legacies of Nazism.

By the time of his interview Müller had in fact been dodging this question for years. His father had been released from postwar captivity in 1948; apart from early babyhood, Müller had only known his father when he was himself between the ages of seven and thirteen. He remembered his father as caring, loving, and capable. What he subsequently learned of his father's past had been actively shaped by his mother, the bereaved widow, who burnished his image: an ordinary forester who had only been put into SS uniform because this was a standard career progression route at the time.[7] Müller was somewhat skeptical but unable to challenge the image.

Hans Müller was interested, however, in exploring ways in which he resembled his father. In particular, he saw his father as having what he called "feminine" traits and speculated about his relationships with women. As a young man, his father had separated from an early girlfriend for a trial period, to see whether this really was enduring love; she then got engaged to his elder brother, and Peter Müller married his girlfriend's sister. This rather oddly chosen marriage, which remained childless, ended sadly: Müller's first wife soon manifested symptoms of schizophrenia and was committed to care in a clinic. Under the Nazi laws concerning allegedly hereditary illnesses, Müller divorced her in 1934. Moved to another clinic, she died at an unspecified date in the "late 1930s."

Any death in an institution for the mentally ill during this period inevitably arouses suspicion. Muller's first wife was almost certainly a victim of the Nazi "euthanasia" program; but the question of whether she had really died of "natural causes" at a young age or had been killed was apparently not discussed. The family could almost have been seen as victims of Nazi racial policies—except that Müller had not stood by his mentally ill wife. After a few years, he went on to marry the woman who became Hans Müller's mother. What seems to have concerned Peter's son most of all was the possibility of suppressed homosexuality. Hans's younger brother was openly gay, but a similar inclination on his own part—he had enjoyed acting the role of an adolescent girl in his psychodrama group, including makeup and clothing—was something that Hans himself could only acknowledge with hesitation.

It was the "feminine" side of his father, and his perhaps latent homosexuality, that appear to have concerned Hans Müller most. Curiously, Hans barely explored what his father had actually done in the Waffen-SS in Nazi-occupied Poland. Although aware that his mother presented an idealized image, his own suspicions largely circled around what his father might have "known"—the "ignorance" question. Hans barely addressed the question of what his father might actually have *done*. And although he had wondered about going to Poland to find out more, at the time of his interview Hans Müller had not yet made serious efforts to explore details.

It would not have been so easy before the age of the internet to have found details of the camp and extensive system of bunkers around Pustków, where his father lived for a while, in the extensive SS Heidelager training grounds. It might have been easier to read about the 1972–73 trial in Hanover of his father's colleague, former SS-Sturmbannführer Hans Proschinsky.[8] Hans Müller could have learned a lot very quickly from this case, which provided damning evidence of the violence and deaths in his father's workplace. Proschinsky was sentenced to life imprisonment—unusually harsh for West Germany at this time—and it is highly unlikely that Peter Müller was not also closely implicated in SS violence. Photographs show Proschinsky at the Pustków SS firing range; in another, he stands right next to the "chief forester," whom we know as "Peter Müller." In an elevated position in the camp hierarchy, and with a passion for sharpshooting and the development of the shooting range, Müller surely bore responsibility for the deaths of Jewish slave laborers under his command.

Peter Müller's former SS colleagues and friends had coordinated their stories for the Proschinsky trial. Müller's family would have been aware of these pretrial discussions, given his wife's role in warning comrades about legal investigations. It would not have been impossible, then, for his son to find out more, at least indirectly, about his father's experiences. He had basic reference points from which to start, including key place names and dates. Yet he did not confront these disturbing possibilities.

In his interview, Hans Müller contented himself with speculation about what his father might have "known." So, for example, his father had spoken about "mass graves," and despite fearing that "forestry" might have entailed planting trees to disguise such graves, Hans imagined that his father had been referring to the massacre of Polish officers by Soviet forces in the Katyn Forest. He also worried that his father might have "known" about

Auschwitz. These suppositions seem to have been more palatable than wondering whether the mass graves were actually in the area where his father was stationed and held Jews killed by his father's SS colleagues—and very likely by his father too.

In this way, Hans Müller displaced worries about Nazi legacies onto the question of his father's relationships with women and the possible consequences for his own ambivalent feelings about sexuality. In this way, he stopped short of exploring territory that might have been infinitely more painful to confront.

Nevertheless, Hans Müller highlighted features that, taken in isolation, do not mean a great deal but when inserted into a wider picture begin to make a different sort of sense—and suggest he must have harbored suspicions. Hans recalls the significance for his father of shooting practice during the war and how after the war he enjoyed shooting expeditions with his children as well as participating in championships. Hans Müller outlines what, in retrospect, are chilling details of his father's attitudes. Peter Müller had explained to his son that it was important to "select" the weakest animals and shoot them first, leaving only the strongest to breed. Hans Müller contrasted this approach with that of other hunters, who focused on acquiring the largest heads and antlers as trophies, saying: "My father placed particular value on selectively shooting the ill pieces [*Stücke*]"—using the German word that Ravensbrück survivor Denise Dufournier noted was used to objectify concentration camp inmates.[9]

Peter Müller drove into a tree on the very night that he won the coveted shooting championship in Düsseldorf in 1954. It is likely that attending the shooting championship were former SS colleagues who were apprehensive about potential legal proceedings. One of these committed suicide in the 1960s on hearing that he was to stand trial. Both Peter Müller's father and brother had previously committed suicide at moments when wider historical developments—the inflation of 1923, the end of Hitler's Reich in 1945—had also entailed reversals of personal fortune. We will never know whether this was Peter Müller's way of dealing with the difficulties a Nazi might experience in postwar Germany. Whatever the causes of the fatal accident, it certainly left a difficult personal legacy for his son.

On balance, Hans Müller probably managed to lead a somewhat easier life by not finding out much about his father's SS past. Given the sheer numbers of people involved in Nazi violence, perhaps remaining in ignorance was, after all, the easiest way for the children of perpetrators to live with this legacy.

Public Knowledge: The Children
of Prominent Nazis

Those who did know what their parents had done during the Third Reich had less choice in the matter; their options related rather to how they should deal with the knowledge. The children of prominent Nazis were, additionally, often in the spotlight of media or public attention simply by virtue of their names. The experiences of the children of Hitler's closest associates were distinctive, not representative; they nevertheless form an interesting group and illustrate a range of personal responses.[10]

Most were born during the Third Reich, and some were old enough to remember the days when their parents were in power. The children of Albert Speer were captured in amateur film footage and photographs in the presence of Hitler, enjoying gloriously sunny afternoons on the heights of Hitler's Berghof in Berchtesgaden, against a panoramic backdrop of Alpine scenery. Renate Wald, the daughter of the Reich's labor leader, Robert Ley, was taken along to party meetings with him when she was still a young child.[11] The eldest son of Martin Bormann, Martin A. Bormann (1930–2013), lived for a while in the closed community of Hitler's Berchtesgaden quarters; he also attended an elite Nazi boarding school.[12] They all developed different ways of dealing with the parental past.

Perhaps the most striking example of prominent children who refused to reject the parental mission is that of Heinrich Himmler's daughter Gudrun (who changed her surname to Burwitz on marriage). A recent documentary, based on family papers, personal letters, and Himmler's diary, vividly portrays the idyllic childhood that Gudrun enjoyed in the Bavarian Alps while her father was away for long stints on Reich business, the details of which were kept from the protected and pampered child.[13] It is possible to understand her later claim that she had been unaware of Nazi atrocities at the time. But even after the war, faced with gruesome film footage of corpses in concentrations camps and the shocking details emerging during the Nuremberg trials—in which her mother gave evidence—Gudrun refused to confront and accept the truth. She remained devoted to her father, effectively continuing to fight her father's cause even after 1945. Turning twenty in the summer of 1949, she was already a young adult when the Federal Republic of Germany was founded. From 1951, along with her friend Florentine Rost van Tonningen, she became prominent in Stille Hilfe, the organization assisting former Nazis, particularly those who faced trial or were imprisoned.[14] Following an interview in 1959, in which she outlined difficulties in getting a job given the family name, Gudrun withdrew into her own circle as "an embittered daughter."[15]

Brigitte Höss (who renamed herself "Bridget" in relocating to the United States), the daughter of Rudolf Höss, former commandant of Auschwitz, and four years younger than Gudrun Himmler, similarly refused to recognize the extent of parental wrongdoing. Höss defended her father and claimed, wholly implausibly, that it had not been possible to see over the garden fence and witness the horrors of the concentration camp from their villa next door.[16] Anyone who has visited Auschwitz and has seen the proximity of the Höss villa to the crematoria and the gallows on which Rudolf Höss himself finally met his end knows this claim can only represent a desperate attempt to cling to a childhood picture of a doting father.

Others too found it hard to loosen their ties. Wolf-Rüdiger Hess was the son of Hitler's close associate and one-time deputy, Rudolf Hess, whose mysterious flight to England in 1941 put a rapid end to his Nazi career. In 1959 the German journalist Norbert Lebert interviewed Wolf-Rüdiger Hess as a young man, along with other children of prominent Nazis; some four decades later, in 2000, Lebert's son Stephan reinterviewed them to explore developments in the intervening years. Stephan Lebert describes Hess as by this time "an ailing, embittered, immovable man who even now denies the scale of the Holocaust" and "an ardent admirer of Hitler." He was someone "who doubted that the organized Holocaust had ever happened. An anti-Semite who maintained that if a people were persecuted over a long time, there must be a reason for it."[17]

Himmler, Höss, and Hess were the children of exceptionally significant and high-ranking Nazis, and their explicit defense of their fathers is relatively rare. Others rejected their parents outright. Niklas Frank presents a particularly prominent example. There could be no doubt of Hans Frank's guilt, and he was duly hanged at Nuremberg on October 16, 1946, when Niklas was just seven years old. Niklas was one of five children, all of whom had quite different responses to the Nazi past. Niklas Frank, who became a journalist, wrote a series of books expressing his feelings about his family, including details of the sexual fantasies that his father's execution had inspired in him as a boy. Unsurprisingly, there was a storm of controversy in Germany when the first of Frank's writings on this topic was serialized and then published as a book in the late 1980s.[18] Frank recalled that the majority of personal letters he received "were filled with hate because no son should treat his father the way he had"—apparently without the writers pausing to consider whether the way his father had treated Polish Jews might have justified his account and whether the biblical commandment not to kill should take precedence over the injunction to honor and respect one's parents.[19] Public reactions were however mixed: according to some, Frank's eschatological language undermined the significance of his message, whereas others applauded his emotional honesty. This first book was followed by a second about his mother and, somewhat later, one about his brother Norman.[20] Norman, some nine years older than Niklas and having spent longer with their father as a boy and teenager, would not denounce him with the vehemence and indeed hatred expressed by his younger brother Niklas.

In the course of these books and many interviews, Niklas Frank made clear how his parents' roles had affected his own life and how he had—unlike all four of his siblings—been ultimately able to break their spell. One sister had, by an apparently extraordinary coincidence, died at precisely the age her father had been when he was executed, having vowed she would not live longer than him; another had died in South Africa, still a convinced Nazi who disputed the feasibility of murdering so many Jews in the gas chambers. One of his brothers, unable to deal with his father's death, had obsessively gorged himself on milk and died young from extreme obesity and organ failure. Only with his older brother Norman could Niklas talk openly, despite their very different views. Norman eventually became an alcoholic. The coping strategies developed by Niklas were the only way he could both deal with the appalling record of his parents and protect the next generation—in the person of his daughter—from some of the psychological consequences of their family history. Frank's efforts to leave nothing undisturbed, nothing secret, were apparently beneficial: in a 2011 documentary entitled *Hitler's Children*, his daughter thanks him for having erected a "wall" to protect her and her children from the family legacy, shielding subsequent generations as well.

Niklas Frank started relatively early in his efforts to confront his father's past—well before the wider societal confrontation, in West Germany at least, unleashed by the traveling exhibition *Crimes of the German Army* of the mid- and later 1990s. Public discussions about parental and grandparental guilt were also enlivened by the publication of Daniel Goldhagen's *Hitler's Willing Executioners*, accompanied by televised debates between the photogenic Goldhagen and older historians such as Hans Mommsen.[21] Although poorly received by professional experts, Goldhagen's vehement attack on what he called "exterminationist anti-Semitism" before 1945 found a huge popular readership among generations plagued by self-doubt. The question of "overcoming" the more recent German dictatorship, the GDR, was also high on the agenda in the 1990s, but it did not displace concern with the Nazi era. The question of familial involvement in Nazism was ever more widely discussed and increasingly aired in TV shows, documentaries, and media discussions. This examination of the complicity of a parental gener-ation did not let up in the early decades of the twenty-first century, with the 2013 film *Generation War* (*Unsere Mütter, unsere Väter*) claiming audiences of seven million for each of its televised episodes on first viewing. This public confrontation with parental complicity was muted and partial, in some senses self-serving, empathizing almost to the point of exoneration. And it came very late, in comparison with the children of prominent Nazis, who had to confront the realities of parental guilt for decades.

For Horst von Wächter, son of the former governor of the district of Galicia who had been in charge of civilian administration at the time the last Jews were murdered, it seemed relatively easy to incorporate the Nazi period within a far longer view of history. Living in a cold and draughty castle in Austria, reminiscent of the Knights Templar, Wächter managed to evade serious confrontation with his father's responsibility for war crimes. When repeatedly confronted with the evidence of his father's involvement in the deportation and murder of the Jews of Galicia—as in the filmed journey, together with Niklas Frank and Philippe Sands, back to the area around Lvov—Wächter seemed simply unable to accept the implications and escaped to what for him were apparently more comforting thoughts of the ways in which his father had assisted Ukrainian nationalists in their fight against Bolshevism.[22]

Some children of prominent Nazis found some degree of solace in reli-gious or political commitments. Martin Bormann Jr., for example, was the son of the former head of the Nazi Party chancellery and private secretary of Adolf Hitler. In interviews carried out by Norbert and Stephan Lebert early and late in his life and in between by Israeli psychologist Dan Bar-On, Bormann outlined how he had been able, through his religious faith, both to acknowledge his father's guilt and yet continue to love him.[23] Bormann recalled, according to Bar-On, that Gudrun Himmler had "once phoned him in a rage. She screamed at him: how could he make such terrible remarks about the old times?" Bormann tried to draw the distinction between a father and his deeds. But apparently Gudrun Himmler did not understand this point: as Bormann put it, she had not "quite got that far yet."[24] Bormann also criticized Frank's way of dealing with his father for being largely one of anger.[25] Similarly Werner Oder, son of Wilhelm Oder, who as deputy commandant in the Rabka training school for SS and Ukrainian extermination squads had given instruction on how to shoot Jews in the back of the neck, eventually found that a fervent Christian faith could assist him in living with the "curse" of his father's past.[26]

Some simply had to continue parental strategies of distancing themselves from real evil. Even offspring whose views were entirely in line with postwar morality found it hard to acknowledge the full extent of parental guilt. A notable example is Renate Wald, whose father was Robert Ley, who had joined the NSDAP in 1923. As leader of the German Labor Front, Ley played a key role in Nazi Party organizational and educational activities, alongside Martin Bormann and Rudolf Hess. Facing trial in the Nuremberg International Military Tribunal in 1945, Ley evaded justice by committing suicide (asphyxiating himself in his cell) before proceedings began. His daughter Renate, who explicitly identified herself as a left-liberal, was born in 1922 and had a close relationship with her father during the Nazi years; afterward, she was never quite able to reject him.

As an adult in West Germany, Renate Wald became a sociologist, interested in labor market issues, a continuation of her father's interests. Her own academic work continued to explore some of the themes that had fascinated her father, while she rejected the political system that his work had served. When interviewed by Bar-On in the mid-1980s, Wald was still trying to protect her own anonymity; she did not want her father's name to feature in Bar-On's account.[27] But the interview precipitated—or at least coincided with—a more active phase in Wald's long process of addressing her family past. Some twenty years later, by now in her early eighties and shortly before her death in 2004, Wald seemed at last ready to confront the past in public and published a memoir of her father.[28] In this final assessment of her father's life, she combined a critical account of his historical role with a strong sense of personal attachment and love. Even sixty years after the war, Wald still sought to portray him as essentially innocent, pursuing the right goals, and ignorant of the worst excesses of the regime. She could not squarely address some of the issues around his antisemitism, indulgent lifestyle, and embezzlement.[29] It was the old refrain: that her father did not know what was going on in the regime that he so loyally and actively served. This is a portrait that is less a painful leave taking than a continuing defense by partial denial.

A few individuals managed to accept the guilt of the parent, seeking in some way to atone for it while still retaining a loving relationship. Hilde Schramm, the daughter of Albert Speer, provides a striking example of "compensation strategies." Born in 1936 and a child during the Third Reich, Hilde became well aware of her father's role during his lengthy imprisonment in Spandau following the Nuremberg Trials.[30] In 1952, as a sixteen-year-old, she spent a year in the United States as an exchange student. Initially refused a visa by the US authorities, Hilde Speer, as she was then still called, benefited from protests on her behalf—including by Jewish families—and was able to study in the United States, staying with Quakers who had also hosted Jewish victims of Nazism. Schramm subsequently returned to Europe with a new sense of purpose and mission about ways of dealing with the past. She campaigned—unsuccessfully, thanks to Soviet opposition— for her father's early release from Spandau prison, and she also became actively engaged in left-wing politics and the peace movement. In the later 1980s and early 1990s she represented a small left-wing political party in the Berlin city government, the Alternative List in West Berlin (not to be confused with the right-wing Alternative for Germany founded in 2013). In the changing political landscape following German unification, Schramm became involved with the Alliance 90 / Green Party from 1993, holding a leadership role in the Greens. Her personal and practical contributions to dealing with the past—in addition to seeking to shape a better future— included the organization named Giving Back (Zurückgeben), supporting Jewish artists through grants and scholarships. This organization specifically asks people who had benefitted from the Nazi expropriation of Jewish property to make a material contribution.

Schramm is aware that the symbolic gesture may in effect simply make those who "give back" feel better about themselves, while barely improving the lives of others. The conundrum is real, and the challenge not an easy one—but it is significant that Schramm raises these questions and deals with them head on.[31] When asked in 2005 about whether she felt a sense of guilt, Schramm responded that she had "finished digging into her own past many years ago." She commented: "Instead of using guilt, there is a better word to describe my feelings, and that word is shame. I feel ashamed of what happened in the past, and of course I feel ashamed that it happened so close to me, in my own family. For that I still feel shame."[32]

Schramm channeled her emotions into social and political engagement, in ways that few others could manage. The issues of guilt and shame— including the distinction between the two—are not easy to disentangle, and many children of Nazis grappled with them over the course of their lives, with changing resolutions at different times.

The Rhythms of Shame

Irene Anhalt was a psychotherapist involved with Hilde Schramm at the Zurückgeben foundation. Her reflections demonstrate the psychological complexities and continuing emotional challenges, however successfully she managed her responses to her father's Nazi past.[33] Anhalt's father (whose name she does not reveal) was in the SS, which he had joined as early as 1929, and was promoted to first lieutenant of the SD, the intelligence and security service of the SS. He was based for several years at Berlin's notorious Gestapo headquarters in Prinz-Albrecht-Strasse, and from 1942 he took on a significant role as Berlin city director. Relatively late in her father's life, Anhalt undertook research that demonstrated conclusively that her "illusion" that her father "could have been ignorant of the death camps collapsed utterly." Moreover, as city director he had not "been involved only with the administration and official functions of the city"; he had "taken on that position not as a civil servant, but as an SS official of high rank," with all that this entailed.[34] Although Anhalt is reticent with details, still in effect protecting her father, she intimates that, among other actions, he had been involved in the arrests of SA leaders leading to their murder in June 1934 and had a role in ordering the murder of five thousand people following the attempt to assassinate Hitler on July 20, 1944.[35]

Anhalt shared with Schramm a capacity to love her father while simultaneously rejecting what he had done and stood for. But it was a lifelong struggle, right up to her father's death, to come to an understanding that she could accept. Anhalt's reckoning with her father, in the form of a published first-person letter directly addressed to him (but after his death) captures the complex ways in which confrontations with the past are multilayered, changing over time, and affect both sides in a relationship filled with love and rage, loyalty and guilt, shame and anguish.

Anhalt had enjoyed a happy childhood in a secure and loving family, but her relationship with her father was cut short when she was only four years old. Captured toward the end of the war, Anhalt's father was a prisoner in the Soviet Union and initially condemned to death, a sentence then changed to twenty-five years of hard labor in Siberia. In the end, he was able to return to Germany at the end of 1955. Like so many of the prisoners returning from Soviet captivity under Adenauer, Anhalt's father was "received like a hero." Anhalt recalls how the "little city" where they then lived had greeted him: his "return was celebrated like a holiday"; the "state council honored [him] with a reception, speeches were given, an orchestra played." The mayor even assured him of his help in finding a suitable position. Anhalt, who had engaged in self-harming while her father was in captivity (even scratching swastikas into her shins), now reproached herself: "I was ashamed of myself; how could I have doubted you?"[36] This faith in a loving father, this willingness to believe his stories and interpretations, this irritation with oneself for having been so silly as to think otherwise, is a common pattern among children of perpetrators.

Parental stories can, however, be challenged, or at least come under closer scrutiny in the light of evidence from beyond the sphere of family narratives. Anhalt was jolted when, at a friend's house in Hamburg, she first consciously looked at a book with photos of Auschwitz: "I was bewildered; this was what I had suspected all those years, the dark secret, an unimaginable crime." But it was not easy to confront her father openly, as she recalls in her letter to him:

> After days of inner torment I asked you about Auschwitz. You reacted gruffly and evasively; I had never seen you like that. You had nothing to do with that, was your answer. As I tried to show you and Mama the pictures, you pushed them aside angrily; you wanted to forbid my pursuing this. Mama was pale; she said nothing. In other words, you knew the pictures, you knew what happened in concentration camps; only you had hidden your knowledge from me. Why? For the first time I felt let down by both of you, betrayed.[37]

She believed her father when he claimed he "had nothing to do with the murder of the Jews" and that he could never have known about it at the time. It was instead she who felt culpable: "I was filled with the old feeling of guilt that had run through my childhood. Now I had proof of my guilt at last: I had been indifferent to the suffering of the Jews." Later she could put this into perspective: "I was not aware at the time of how my readiness to take guilt onto myself protected me from seeing the guilt in you. I divided my conscience between sympathy for the Jews as victims of fascism and loyalty to you—you, the champion of law for the good of the majority."[38]

In this way, she gained the trust of her father; she became, in effect, complicit in supporting his interpretation.

But taking the burden of guilt onto herself and believing her father's version of his past could not be sustained for long. This enjoyment of being his confidante and believing in him was once more rudely jolted when, by chance, Anhalt discovered that her father was now a member of the West German secret service. She suddenly realized that he had been deceiving and manipulating her in just the same way that he had deceived and manipulated others. This second moment of recognizing betrayal was not one that could so easily be brushed aside by internalizing the blame.

As a practicing psychotherapist, Anhalt became increasingly aware of all of the strategies and emotional entanglements involved. This did not necessarily make it any easier: the struggle was not readily resolved. Anhalt recalled that in her conversations with her father about his involvement in Nazism, much could not be said. It was far easier to displace the focus of the conversation and talk about sensitive issues in the third person—in terms of interpretations in books, stories about other people. Her father's past was too sensitive to talk about directly.

Two forms of reconciliation eventually came to alleviate Anhalt's difficulties, late in her father's life. One was the unconditional love of her own daughter, Andrea, for the old man who was her grandfather: the "third generation" came to the rescue. As Anhalt saw it, still addressing her father posthumously: "Her love for you, her grandfather, reminded me of those first happy years with you; through her I could experience your many-sidedness again, to which I had blinded myself in my anger and disappointment."³⁹ Total rejection could be replaced by a more complex, partial understanding.

The second was in the form of a near confession by her father on his deathbed. In their accustomed manner, they talked about books and the lessons to be gained from other people's experiences. Anhalt recalls the conversation with her father as he lay dying: "With infinite effort as if you had to call up the words from another world, you spoke: 'it was wrong of the Spaniards to murder the Incas and steal their land.' My throat tightened with tears as I answered you: 'Yes daddy—thank you'."⁴⁰ Whatever the meaning of this statement on the part of a dying man, for Anhalt at least it represented a form of confession, and for her a degree of closure, a possibility of reconciliation with a now finally, so it would seem, repentant former Nazi.

Family Dynamics: Revelations and Tensions

Tensions within a perpetrator's family generally worsened when someone challenged a previously accepted narrative and accused a parent of wrongdoing. The Germans even have a term for such a person: "*Nestbeschmutzer*," someone who "soils the nest."

The Ludin family presents a particularly articulate example of this. Malte Ludin was the son of Hanns Ludin, a committed Nazi and Hitler's ambassador in Slovakia. Implicated in the deportation of thousands of Jews to their deaths, Hanns Ludin was put on trial in Czechoslovakia and executed in December 1947. Increasingly frustrated by complicity in the family legends around his father, Malte Ludin recorded the tensions between himself and his sisters in his 2005 film entitled *2 or 3 Things I Know about Him*.[41] He had waited until the death of his mother to make this film, which so clearly accused her of defending the indefensible. One of Ludin's siblings, Erika, was unable to deal with the tension between love for her father and awareness of his misdeeds. She succumbed to bouts of depression and alcoholism, eventually suffering an agonizing death when, under the influence of alcohol, she stepped into a bath of boiling water and suffered fatal scalding. Her daughter, Alexandra Senfft, found the courage to confront the family legacy and its consequences for her mother—and for herself—in her book *Schweigen tut weh* (Silencing hurts).[42] For both Malte Ludin and Alexandra Senfft, the problem was not only the Nazi past but also the complicity of the family in silencing it. Both Ludin's film and Senfft's book indicate, in their subtitles, the significance of their work: *Die Gegenwart der Vergangenheit in einer deutschen Familie* (The presence of the past in a German family) and *Eine deutsche Familiengeschichte* (A German family history), respectively.

Senfft devoted considerable effort to reconciliation with survivors and descendants of those whom her grandfather had persecuted. She went with a survivor, Tomi Reichental, to Bratislava, both to Ludin's burial place following his execution and to Reichental's nearby birthplace, from which his family had been driven by Nazi policies. This journey to resolve lingering strains was filmed in a 2014 documentary by Gerry Gregg, *Close to Evil*. But not all reconciliation efforts on this journey were successful. Hilde Michnia, the former Bergen-Belsen female guard who Reichental had hoped would take the opportunity to express remorse, not only refused to see him but even mouthed Nazi phrases. This provoked a response across generations:

Hans-Jürgen Brennecke, a social worker and son of a perpetrator, saw the film and was outraged by the comments made by Michnia, seeing this as unacceptable in the Germany of the twenty-first century. As a result of his accusations, a court case against Michnia was filed.

Time and growing distance from any personal connection with the perpetrator certainly helped. While Gudrun Himmler remained committed to her father throughout her life, Himmler's great-niece Katrin Himmler—her grandfather was Heinrich Himmler's brother—was sufficiently removed to confront the family past with courage and honesty. In her quest, she found a companion and kindred spirit, Dani, an Israeli whose Jewish family had been persecuted; eventually, they married and had a son. Writing while their son was still very young, Katrin Himmler commented: "I am still afraid of the moment when he will learn that one side of the family made every effort to wipe out the other. The only thing that makes it easier for me to contemplate that moment is that it will be possible for me to answer his questions and give him clear information on the extent of guilt and responsibility of my forebears."[43] The nephew of Reinhard Heydrich also felt relatively unscathed by the family name, and indeed made explicit use of it in his work as an actor. He was nevertheless affected by a sense of remorse.[44] This infused his work, such that he could act it out, quite literally, in satirical and critical drama. Heydrich's nephew was critical, moreover, of those who, as he saw it, sought to deal with their problems by excessive identification with the victims.[45] And Rainer Höss, grandson of the former Auschwitz commandant, is the sole member of his family to have explicitly confronted and denounced the role of Rudolf Höss. He now devotes considerable efforts to talking in schools and seeking to counteract Nazi legacies in contemporary right-wing movements.[46]

The Nazi past might be unavoidable in families where the repercussions were evident and dramatic, whether because the father had been tried and sentenced or had committed suicide. For those children of perpetrators who only learned at a later date what their parents had done, confrontation took on a rather different quality. Often a child of a perpetrator grew up more or less unsuspecting of that past, and the shock of discovery happened as a result of an external stimulus—an exhibition, public speech, trial, film, or book.

Jens-Jürgen Ventzki, for example, grew up in relatively privileged and affluent circumstances, as his father made a seamless transition from serving the Third Reich as city mayor of Litzmannstadt (Łódź) to civil servant in Adenauer's Federal Republic. The family moved from Berlin to Bonn when

Ventzki was a child, and he dimly knew that his father was worried about legal investigations and possible revelations, but he loved and respected his father and did not pursue these issues. Even so, there were lurking suspicions, and as an adult he circled around the question, seeking to find out more about his own birthplace of Łódź. It was this that brought him face to face with evidence of his father's guilt. Ventzki recalls with horror the shock when he first registered the significance of his father's role. In 1990 he went to see an exhibition about the Łódź ghetto that had just been opened in the Jewish Museum in Frankfurt am Main.[47] This exhibition included not only recently discovered photographs of the ghetto but also a letter of May 1942 signed by his father, in his familiar and unmistakable handwriting. The letter quite prosaically dealt with the disposal of "used textiles" that had been gathered "in the course of the Jewish action"—a euphemism for extermination—in the death camp of Chełmno. As though it were a quite ordinary piece of daily business, Ventzki's father had discussed the costs of disinfection and potential reuse of the clothing and possessions of those who had been murdered in the gas vans. This document was, Ventzki tells us, "the blow" that he had hoped would never strike him.[48] Ventzki subsequently devoted years to learning the truth about his father, reaching out to others with perpetrator parents and engaging in efforts at reconciliation with victims, as well as education of future generations.

Monika Hertwig only registered the truth about her father as an adult, in her case as the result of a book and a film. She was the last and illegitimate daughter of Amon Goeth, the now notorious former commandant of the concentration camp of Płazsów-Kraków, whose misdeeds were portrayed by actor Ralph Fiennes in Steven Spielberg's *Schindler's List* (1993). Goeth was responsible for ordering the killing of more than ten thousand Jews in the course of running the Płazsów camp, the liquidation of the Kraków ghetto, and closing down the Szebnie forced labor camp. He was well known for his sadism, setting dogs on prisoners and personally shooting several hundred Jews, including children. Tried after the war in Poland, he was found guilty of having tortured and killed "a substantial number" of people and was duly hanged in September 1946, when his daughter was still less than one year old. Growing up, Monika was told by her mother that her father had been a good man, and she continued to idealize him in face of all the evidence. Even so, Monika realized that something was not quite right and repeatedly asked her mother how many Jews her father might have shot.[49] Despite constant questioning, she never got more than a vague answer that implied it was a matter of one or two, perhaps three or four, certainly not more than a dozen. It was only a chance encounter with a man in a bar who had been a prisoner in this camp that brought her to realize, with horror, that the situation was infinitely more serious. Her mother, forced finally to confront this past, committed suicide in 1983, shortly after the publication in 1982 of Thomas Keneally's book *Schindler's Ark*, on which Spielberg's later film was based.[50] But it was only after Monika Hertwig had watched the film herself that with a shock she realized the full horror of her father's actions.

It was not only families of well-known or high-level Nazis who had to contend with the continuing shadow of the past. Some had suspicions based on general knowledge of their parents' experiences, roles, or war-time locations but had little by way of specific details; others could only guess at what their parents might have done. Often a search for evidence that fathers in compromised places had made an effort to "get away," had "tried to save a Jew," or had "known nothing about it" would preoccupy members of the second generation, seeking to reassure themselves about parental innocence. But there were always unexpected twists.

Given how few Nazis were brought to public attention, let alone to trial, members of the younger generation might be unwillingly haunted by suspicions about their parents' possible former involvement in the Nazi system. This could endure for years before reaching any resolution, if at all. Sometimes suspicion could be displaced by just a little knowledge, and only selected aspects of a parent's past were explored, so that a mutually acceptable story could be woven—in this way choosing which family legacies to pass on. Such narratives contained references to indisputable facts but glossed over inconvenient details. It could be sufficient for family members to think they knew as much as there was to know with no need to inquire further. Much of the research on perpetrator family narratives suggests a degree of vagueness and distortion; but without external evidence from independent sources, memory researchers can only speculate about the meanings of family tales and never be quite sure about what stories were reflecting or serving to marginalize and obscure.[51]

The most common experience—shared by hundreds of thousands of Germans, given the scale of involvement in the Nazi system—was that of not really wanting to know about parental involvement in the crimes of the Third Reich. "Dieter Henning" (not his real name), born in Hamburg in 1936, was probably typical of many who did not follow where obvious leads might have taken him.[52] His father was born in 1907 and during the Third Reich was a member of the Waffen-SS, stationed near Prague among other places. After the war, he had been a prisoner of war in an American prison in Nuremberg. When he was released in the late 1940s, he picked up his prewar job in a Hamburg bank. But his attempted reintegration into civilian life was not successful, and a combination of problems—heavy drinking and irregularities concerning cash removals from the bank—led to his being fired without notice. He lost his case for unfair dismissal in 1961, in his son's view because the judge took a dim view of his Nazi past.[53] He died soon afterward, in 1962, still only in his mid-fifties. Henning did not follow up on any of the clues he had about his father's Nazi past, saying that he "just didn't ask."[54] The interviewer asked when he had learned about the mass murders committed by the Nazis, commenting that "obviously this was absolutely not a topic of discussion within the family."[55] Henning thought he probably learned about this in his West German school, although he noted that history lessons ended with 1933. But he did not appear particularly concerned to match up his wider historical knowledge with his own father's past. The few key facts that Henning did know clearly caused him some discomfort, but as troubling thoughts arose he tended to trail off into generalizations. "He was last employed near Prague. And then thoughts occur to one, what might he have been up to there? Was he perfectly normal . . ." He went on: "In Czechoslovakia there was a sort of German occupation. I don't know exactly, if something like that . . ."[56] Trailing off at the end of sentences, raising thoughts only to leave them incomplete, Henning effectively chose to remain ignorant, citing his own relative lack of historical knowledge. He stated but did not make links between disparate facts. "I'm not really up to scratch on history. There was also a concentration camp nearby. He was in the Waffen-SS. But those are all things that I haven't really bothered about before."[57] He did not do basic reading on SS activities around Prague, including in the "concentration camp nearby" of which he was aware (very likely referring to Theresienstadt). Anything that came out now, Henning thought, would be merely a matter of "conjectures." In retrospect, he admitted, he probably should have asked questions when there was still opportunity. But he had married young and left his parents' home at the age of twenty-one.[58]

A more frequent response was a simple denial that there was anything to explore, sometimes accompanied by attacking others for making unfounded accusations. A generalized anger against the accusers could take the place of an honest confrontation with the parent's past. Horst L., for example, looked back half a century later on his father's experience of denazification and failure to regain his former position as high school director. Still enraged about this, he laid the blame for his father's misfortunes not on his guilt as a former Nazi but rather on the response of the "younger generation" (although his identification of relevant generations was rather muddled), which "damned" all Nazis as "devils, criminals, murderers." He complained that for younger generations, everything "was seen through the terrible events of the Holocaust." In this way "the whole generation of National Socialists looked away ashamed and kept silent. And we, the direct follow-on generation, we lived on with this taboo, we were ashamed of our parents." The children of Nazis "also saw the whole history of the so-called Third Reich through the lens of the Holocaust and kept silent."[59] These were the words of a by-now angry old man, writing his memoirs in the 1990s, but they register his continuing sense of injustice about the way his father had been treated after the war and demonstrate his own willingness to dissociate his father's role from "the Holocaust"—repeating the self-distancing of the perpetrators themselves.

Yet denial often proved difficult. And where some involvement with Nazism was evident, however minimal, family dynamics were inevitably affected. Rainer L., for example, had been fifteen years old when the war ended. His father had joined the NSDAP in 1937 and had accepted small party functions in the locality.[60] Living in West Germany after the war, Rainer L.'s father lost his job because of his Nazi Party activities, despite the fact, according to his son, that "an anti-Nazi attitude was taken for granted in our house, as among our entire circle of acquaintances." This loss of status affected his outlook for years: Rainer L.'s father "simply went dumb. Humor and irony were no longer possible in his presence." He no longer spoke at mealtimes and threw himself bitterly into excessive gardening.[61] This atmosphere pervaded family life. Rainer L. was not clear whether his father felt ashamed about having taken on Nazi Party functions without being under duress. But the "question of [his] father's guilt" was never spoken about. It was "left shrouded in mist," perhaps because it was not a question of "guilt in any sense that could be debated, but rather of human weakness," and so fundamentally questioned his very character and personality. Yet silence prevailed until his death. Only then did Rainer L.'s mother criticize her late husband "with pitiless clarity," accusing him of being one of those who had needlessly prolonged the war.[62] These reflections, written in the mid-1990s when Rainer L. was in his early sixties, indicate just how deeply a Nazi parent's past, however insignificant in the wider scale of inhumanity, could afflict family life across decades after the war. It was in this case not so much any specific acts as the broader light cast on a father's character and his own incapacity to deal with the humiliations consequent on defeat—undermining his authority—that were at the root of decades of family tensions.

Not all parents were as bad as some of their children feared. Generational dynamics could take quite a different twist. One of the most extraordinary accounts in Bar-On's research on children of perpetrators is that of "Rudolf," born in 1930 and, like so many of the generation that was entirely socialized under Nazism, an ardent member of the Hitler Youth.[63] While Rudolf was gaining a sense of self-importance in a leadership role in the youth organization (singing songs with such titles as "The Flag Is Greater than Death"), his highly religious father was working on railway construction in the east. There, Rudolf's father made close friends with members of the local Jewish community. As rumors grew of their impending fate, he went into the ghetto to pray with them that God would protect and save them; but the very next day he witnessed the mass murder of the entire ghetto, including those with whom he had prayed so ardently the night before. Unable to absorb his horror at what he had witnessed, Rudolf's father suffered a complete physical and mental breakdown and had to be hospitalized out of the area. He never completely recovered, although he wrote a graphic account of his experiences in mid-May 1945, once he felt it was safe to commit his anguish to paper. His son Rudolf was then still a teenager and entirely committed to the Nazi cause. It took a long while for Rudolf to recognize the extent to which he had himself been caught up in Nazi organizations and ideology; he had to address his own complicity before he could begin to understand the experiences of his father.

Uncomfortable Identities and Missions for the Future

A diffuse sense of the burden of the Nazi past, even when the parent had been merely complicit, a witness to rather than active perpetrator of Nazi crimes, often informed the lives of the next generation.[64] In many cases, historical awareness affected life choices.

Many children of perpetrators engaged in professions where they felt they were shaping a better future: teachers, social workers, psychotherapists, historians, journalists. As one of Bar-On's interviewees put it, her choice of profession was "a small personal contribution, a form of reparation, the fact that I help people and protect them as far as possible from misery and suffering. I see my profession very much in terms of a struggle against authority and the exercise of power, state power."[65] Others chose their profession precisely *not* to follow in their fathers' footsteps, as in the case of "Peter," the son of a physician who had served at Auschwitz, precisely by refusing a university education himself. The fact that his father had served at Auschwitz was never discussed; in fact the whole Nazi era appeared to have been successfully suppressed in his family, his school, and the wider environment in which he grew up. He only discovered some of the details about his father through a program he happened to watch on television. Yet his entire life was shaped by a refusal to follow the path of his father.[66]

Others followed Hilde Schramm's lead in engaging in "recompense" actions of some sort, including reconciliation activities, such as Action for Reconciliation (Aktion Sühnezeichen) and work related to the memorial landscape of Europe, as well as alternative military service. Many were concerned about having children, choosing *not* to reproduce (even to be sterilized), in order not to perpetuate what they saw as a contaminated family line. As Bar-On points out, this may be a key difference between children of survivors and children of perpetrators: "The former were charged with the task of biological survival; the latter seem afraid that they will pass on a 'bad seed.'"[67]

A significant number engaged in "personal projects" including identification with the victims. This often led to a heightened interested in Judaism, possibly conversion to Judaism, and, for many, friendship with or even marriage to a Jew. One perpetrator's son, who renamed himself Menachem, even became a rabbi and moved to Jerusalem.[68] Another, Viktor P., had a father who had worked in Dachau. They had a stormy relationship until Viktor P. eventually started to develop some empathy with his father and could see him more fully as a person. Yet he also came to identify so strongly with the victims that he developed an interest in Judaism and even for a while pretended that he himself was a Jew.[69]

A particularly curious case is that of "Hannelore Klingenbach," who exemplifies in extreme form some of the issues faced by third-generation Germans.[70] When interviewed in Australia in the mid-1990s, at the age of twenty-six, she commented that it had taken her years "to realize that it wasn't a criminal offense to be born German."[71] Seeing herself as an "ethnic German," she felt she was not accepted by "real" Germans because she had a Slavic background, and at one point she explored the possibility of conversion to Judaism.[72] She knew this would be greeted with skepticism. As she put it: "Look, I am German. People sometimes ask are you wanting to convert to Judaism because of the Nazi past."[73] Klingenbach's account is pervaded by an unresolved sense of violence, anger, suspicions, and family tensions. Of her grandfather, she remarks that he was "one of the most antisemitic people I know."[74] Her father is "a racist and a nationalist and he has pro-Nazi views."[75] She had nightmares about her family. Her rambling interview betrays many signs of emotional disturbance, but whatever the underlying psychological issues, the manifestations of her disturbance reflect the challenges of postwar German history and identity.

Klingenbach faced particular issues being a German in a non-German context, Australia, where her family had moved. Some Germans of the second generation independently chose to leave Germany and make new lives in other countries. While higher education, employment, and career prospects certainly played a major role in such decisions, for some an added factor was that of gaining distance in order to "deal with" their German past. This did not mean getting away from it entirely, since gaining distance gave them the freedom to be more open, to "break the silence" and escape the suffocating atmosphere of complicity in which they had grown up.[76]

It is probable that many—if not most—children of perpetrators never explicitly talked about their parents' guilt. Yet the Nazi past still disturbed them. Fears and fantasies of death and violence seem to have been a common if not widespread consequence of growing up in the family of a perpetrator. The fact that a close relative or father was involved in mass murder could cast a dark shadow over the lives of the second generation, in some cases with sufficiently serious consequences to require psychiatric intervention.[77] One of Bar-On's interviewees was plagued by fear of being killed. His Nazi father had in fact committed suicide, having previously discussed with his wife a possible plan to kill the whole family.[78] Whether or not this family background played a role, the interviewee's son also in due course committed suicide.

Some children of perpetrators saw themselves essentially as victims, by virtue of their family background, claiming they suffered even more than children of survivors. Some were jealous of the second generation in survivor families, given all the attention that had been focused on them. The war, they claimed, had ended for the victims but not for perpetrator communities. Many resented not being completely accepted; such resentment was particularly acute if attempts at reconciliation with victims had been made and were rejected. They also felt they had in some way suffered the loss of their "own" family identity and heritage. Some attempted to defend their own parents while at the same time working toward a different sort of future by, for example, emphasizing an anti-authoritarian upbringing for their own children.[79]

Despite all the diversity of stories and variations in individual responses, there are some wider patterns that emerge, changing with context and over time.

Themes and Variations in Living with the Family Past

Much has been made of the significance of 1968 and the generational clashes that it entailed. In the United States, it was about the Vietnam War, combining the personal with politics, encapsulated in the injunction to "make love not war"; in the GDR and other communist states around the Prague Spring, it was about dictatorial repression and political reform; in West Germany, generational conflicts in 1968 involved heated confrontations over the Nazi past. Yet with a few exceptions, in both East and West Germany, those protesting in 1968 focused on wider social and political issues and did not directly address the involvement of their own families in Nazism. Moreover, many had only indistinct knowledge. Selective silencing maintained family secrets, even when individuals were aware that there were secrets to begin with.

By the end of the twentieth century, despite awareness of the sheer scale of perpetration and heightened sensitivity to the plight of victims, members of the second and now also third generations often still kept the public record and private narratives largely separate. They had, it seems, found ways of accommodating an expanded historical knowledge with simultaneous belief in their own family's relative innocence.

When looking at ways of living with the Nazi past within families ignorant of details, it is important to remember that this is not exceptional; all we have are narratives that justify, deny, or camouflage events of which the family is not proud; and few have the resources, resilience, and desire to probe beyond acceptable stories with which all can live.[80]

How this worked out over time and place varied. Children of Nazis growing up in Austria were often socialized in a milieu that was more open to continuities in Nazi attitudes than either of the two German states were. In certain circles among former Nazi families, young people were sent to summer camps at one of Austria's idyllic lakes and were surrounded by other like-minded souls, where the Third Reich seems hardly to have been rejected.[81] Although their parents in public had to adopt strategies of denial comparable to those found elsewhere, within the family the dynamics were different.

West and East Germany explicitly rejected the Nazi past in contrasting ways, with striking implications for younger generations. These differences became evident around the time of German unification in 1990. Younger generations of East Germans had grown up with the rather comforting myth of antifascist resistance. Annette Leo, for example, recounts how as a young woman she simply took it for granted that most Germans had been victims or opponents of Hitler—her own grandfather was in fact murdered in Auschwitz—and thought that families with genuinely Nazi backgrounds must have been the exception. Only gradually did she come to realize that they were the rule: people had only "become" antifascists *after* 1945, irrespective of their earlier participation in the Hitler Youth and other Nazi organizations and support for the Führer, the fatherland, and the fight against communism in the Wehrmacht and other institutions.[82]

More generally, younger generations in the GDR could readily understand and empathize with parents or grandparents who had been members of the Nazi party. A study by the Central Institute for Youth Research in Leipzig in the late 1980s—the dying days of the GDR, as it turned out—explored the views of young people who had little choice about joining the state youth groups, mass organizations, the ruling SED, or one of the allied bloc parties.[83] In the light of their own experiences of conformity and coercion, with significant penalties for trying to stand out against what was expected of them, they sympathized with grandparents or parents who said this had also been the case in the Third Reich. Their school education as well as the "antifascist myth" also relieved them of any burden of inherited guilt. The public culture of pride in the "antifascist state" might not have been really believed, but it was accompanied by a sense of family solidarity and understanding for perpetrator parents or grandparents.

By contrast, members of the second generation in West Germany grew up in a public culture of shame, leading to a diffuse sense of undeserved guilt. A study in 1989 of 113 West German schoolchildren, members of the second and third generations, found that as many as two-thirds (65 percent) experienced feelings of shame when the mass murder committed by a previous generation was the topic of discussion, and two-fifths (41 percent) even personally felt guilty, although they themselves had nothing to do with the murders.[84] Yet even so, they too tended to find ways of excusing or justifying the conduct of the generation that was actually involved.

Differences between members of the younger generation in East and West Germany prior to unification were further confirmed by studies of working people in eastern and western areas of united Germany in the 1990s.[85] In western regions in the 1990s, the Nazi period was strongly associated with the Holocaust; many West Germans adopted a defensive stance, anticipating accusations around what it meant to be German. In eastern regions, by contrast, the pre-1945 period was primarily associated with war and the personal consequences of war; the perspective was largely that of their own family's experiences as victims of war and its aftermath, with references to rapes and pillaging by Red Army soldiers, the deprivations of occupation, fears of arrest, and the forcible imposition of communism.[86] On this basis, younger generations were skeptical about the official line in schools and memorial sites, and there was little identification with official myths of antifascist resistance. Yet after unification in 1990, young East Germans still tended to use the communist concept of "fascism" unproblematically. And their lack of any sense of national guilt or shame allowed them to recognize the suffering of their parents' generation without engaging in self-defensive strategies around parental support for Nazism, again in contrast to young people in the West.

Nor was the period before 1945 even as important in the East as it was in the West. East Germans born after the war were far less likely than West Germans of the same generation either to have a sense of connection with the Nazi past or to argue that it was time to "put a line under it"; they were simply less concerned with it in any way at all.[87] Many of the issues of the "second generation" in perpetrator families were specific to West Germans socialized in an atmosphere where a sense of national responsibility for a shameful past was prevalent, indeed inescapable. For East Germans, the turning point of 1989–90, with the collapse of communist rule and the disappearance of the GDR, was a far more significant event than the war.

When the Nazi period was referenced, West Germans would tend to focus on topics such as the violence of November 9–10, 1938 (Kristallnacht), whereas East Germans would readily leap to the questions of flight and expulsion from Eastern Europe at the end of the war. The Nazi period had, in short, become a central orienting category for younger West Germans, but not among younger East Germans.[88]

Family stories were negotiated and shifted across generations, as did the types of justification used to render the past harmless. A study based on 182 qualitative interviews found significant differences in the ways in which the generation that had experienced the war remembered and recounted their past and the ways in which their involvement was represented by children and grandchildren. Fascination with Nazism and recognition of the benefits of the economic upswing in the 1930s for which Hither took credit were prevalent emphases among members of the older generation. Younger generations emphasized rather the constraints and pressures to which their parents and grandparents had, so they thought, been subjected; they saw them as having been forced to act in certain ways, rather than having wanted to do so.[89] Self-justifications around the persecution of Jews were generally in terms of "having known nothing about it," a claim that children and grandchildren tended to believe. If their relatives had in fact "unavoidably" seen anything, younger generations tended to believe they must have suffered terrible fear about the possible consequences of trying to resist and could therefore not have acted differently.[90] Some events were not interpreted as relating to "the Holocaust" but were represented as unproblematic, using Nazi legitimations in terms of "fighting partisans" or similar phrases; this often served to perpetuate across generations Nazi stereotypes of what was seen as normal, legitimate, and acceptable, of who belongs to the in-group and who does not.[91]

The children of former Nazis, aware of at least some details of parental involvement in Nazi crimes, had considerable difficulty confronting their parents' past. Some began to face up to and discuss their heritage over the course of time. This was a slow, faltering process, hedged around with difficulties. At a personal level, it often meant unbearable conflicts between continuing devotion to, or rejection and even vilification of a parent; it also might mean examining one's own potential for violence or fearing a parent's violence against oneself. Family explosions had to be countered, public disapproval faced, the potential for shattering alibis and comfortable lies— and the destruction of family peace—had to be taken into consideration.

At the same time, however, there were attempts, among a minority, to seek a kind of cross-generational "ersatz reconciliation" with communities related to the victims. None of this was easy.

It could take decades to confront these issues with honesty and to attempt to gain greater understanding. This became easier in the third generation. The historian Moritz Pfeiffer, for example, made a concerted effort to compare the stories told by his grandfather, and within his family, with what could be discovered by independent research. Pfeiffer confronted comforting family tales with facts gleaned from archival documents and family papers, reconstructing where his grandfather, Hans Hermann, and his grandfather's brother, Siegfried, had been stationed during the war and exploring what they had likely witnessed and done. The most interesting revelation, discovered only as Pfeiffer's grandfather was nearing his death, had to do with Siegfried's hushed-up career in the SS before he had volunteered for action on the Eastern Front and gone missing, later presumed dead.[92] The grandfather, who professed not to have known anything but clearly did not want to talk about his brother, suddenly told Pfeiffer that Siegfried had at some point been stationed "there"; on further pressure, he admitted that by "there" he meant Auschwitz-Birkenau. This initially shocking revelation turned out to be unsubstantiated: Siegfried was not on lists of those who had worked at the camp, although it was possible he had visited it. Other sources, however, pointed clearly to Siegfried's duties in the SS-training ground of Dębica from April 16, 1942, to February 8, 1943, where Peter Müller and Proschinsky had worked. Siegfried had likely also been involved in the clearance of the Dębica ghetto, from which Irene Eber had so narrowly managed to escape and from which some twelve thousand Jews were deported to the gas chambers. And it was during his time in Dębica that Siegfried had apparently seen and done things that troubled him so deeply that he volunteered to fight on the Eastern Front; he never came back.

Knowledge that a family member had been so closely involved in the Holocaust was kept a dark secret for decades. Unable to digest the details regarding his own brother, Hans Hermann, Pfeiffer's grandfather, resorted instead to reading and recommending Uwe Timm's autobiographical novel about the somewhat similar fate of a brother in the SS who did not return from the war.[93] This dark secret, involvement in the mass murder of the Jews, was for Pfeiffer's family intrinsically associated with the name Auschwitz; they silenced it and chose not to explore further. Just like Hans Müller, they did not want to learn more about the atrocities committed in the Dębica

area. It took the objectivity and curiosity of a member of the third generation, a trained historian, to pursue this in depth—and to succeed in retaining his love and respect for his grandparents while recognizing and
acknowledging in detail their deep involvement in Nazism.[94]

The emotional links with this past and the ways in which it was not merely
of intellectual interest but intrinsically affected how people were brought
up and the kinds of adults they became—shaping their ideals and aspirations, their moral and political choices, their marriage partners, their professions, and the ways in which they treated their own children—are key to
understanding why the Nazi period could not simply "become history"
even long after the Third Reich itself was politically consigned to the past.

When they had few details to go on and only vague family stories, many
members of the second and third generations found ways of excusing or
reducing the guilt of their forebears. Emotional legacies varied with the
wider context. A sense of collective identity as "Germans"—understood as
a community persisting across time—brought with it, in the West, a sense of
continuing unease and heightened moral responsibility based in a diffuse
sense of shame and often also guilt. Such feelings were less prevalent on the
eastern side of the inner-German border. Yet, so far as we can tell, on both
eastern and western sides of unified Germany members of younger generations made a distinction between what they "knew" about the Nazi period
as presented in schools, museums, and memorial sites and what they gleaned
from or interpreted into family stories, where trust and affection generally—
though not always—supported a more understanding attitude toward close
relatives. By the fourth generation, when only the historical knowledge
and not the personal and emotional connections remained, there would no
longer be the dissonance that made the second and third generations feel so
uncomfortable about challenging family stories.

On the perpetrator side, this was a past that clearly had a generational
half-life, one that would decline and fade over time. The generational dynamics were rather different among families of survivors.

18

The Long Shadows
of Persecution

Born in Prague in 1947, Helen Epstein grew up in the United States. From her early childhood onward, she was aware that her family was not like other families in her neighborhood, not even like most other Jewish families in the area of New York City where they lived.[1] Her parents spoke with foreign accents and did not have the same confidence as other people's parents. She felt that she too was somehow different from most other children, including the "all-American" Jewish children in her school and the synagogue to which she rather unwillingly went on the Sabbath.

Only a couple of other children at school seemed to have similar backgrounds: their parents "read the newspapers as avidly" as her parents; one friend "never spoke about family, or history, or how her parents came to be living in New York City."[2] Epstein immediately sensed some affinity:"When I visited them, I felt at home. There was an intensity there, a kind of fierceness about living that was absent from the more casual, easygoing atmosphere of other homes. There was mystery of great consequence."[3] One friend's parents never left their house, because "they were afraid it would burn down or be looted if they left. I accepted that without question, as if it were a natural consideration."[4] For Epstein's own family, any sense of freedom and being at ease seemed only to be at weekends when they went for a picnic in a country park, met with other survivors, and spoke in their native tongues rather than the guttural, accented English they used throughout the working week.

From an early age, then, Epstein was aware they were in some way distinctive—which she recognized without explicitly talking about it at the time: "We children were not like other American children. That fact was so obvious it did not require discussion."[5] There were, furthermore, good reasons for not talking: "Friends, like family, are quick to shield each other from pain and although we all knew that a great deal of pain pervaded the households in which we were raised we never addressed it by name."[6]

Epstein was of course a child of survivors. As a young adult in the 1970s, she began to compare her experiences with those of other children of survivors—and discovered that, for all the differences, they had much in common. Others too discovered this at around the same time, including a group of five children of survivors who in 1975 first published the outcome of their discussions in a Jewish journal, *Response*, registering their sense of collective identity.[7] These children of survivors came of age with the growth of identity politics and self-help groups in the 1980s, and the time was ripe for exploration of "roots," heritage, and legacies. As one pioneer in this area, Lucy Steinitz, put it in an early collection exploring the topic: "Our common origin yields a collective identity."[8]

Members of this self-aware second generation were all much the same age, coming from a relatively narrow generational cohort. Nazi procedures meant that the very young and the elderly were far more likely to have been selected for killing than young adults, who could first be exploited for their labor power and had a better chance of survival. At the time of liberation, the majority of those still alive were young adults. They tended to start—or restart—families in the years shortly after the war, finding partners and having children in the DP (displaced person) camps or on new shores in the later 1940s and early 1950s.[9] In contrast to the children of perpetrators, among survivor families those who were children at the time of Nazi persecution also count as survivors, the "1.5 generation." The second generation in survivor families had no personal experiences of the Nazi period but grew up in the shadow of an all-encompassing past, and they were deeply affected by parental experiences.

Defining the Second Generation

These, at least, are the people who initially defined themselves as "second generation." Children of refugees who had escaped early and who suffered the psychological consequences of stigmatization, uprooting, relocation, and guilt but did not bear the physical marks of ghettos and camps were at first somewhat marginalized and only later recognized as being deeply affected by their parents' ruptured past. Even so, children of Jewish émigrés, whenever they had left Europe, shared in the wider narrative: belonging to a historic group that had suffered and might again be at risk of suffering persecution simply on grounds of being Jewish, a long-term community of fate that had persisted over centuries of persecution, expulsion, exile, and continuity. The borders of the community were tightly defined in ethnic, religious, and cultural terms, persisting over millennia, however scattered across the world. The Jewish year, with its celebration of Passover, had memories of suffering, exile, and survival built into the annual calendar.

The same was not true of other groups persecuted by the Nazis. Many victims of the Nazi euthanasia program were children at the time of their deaths and hence did not themselves have offspring. People who were sterilized had also often not had children at the time of sterilization, and the few who had generally did not want attention drawn to their condition. Understanding or commemorating a relative who was killed or maimed for "medical" reasons under the Nazis was often difficult for families.[10] For rather different reasons, gay men too tended neither to have children nor families who wanted to draw attention to the cause of their relatives' incarceration. "Mischlinge," those of a mixed Jewish and non-Jewish background, might be doubly excluded—from both the Jewish and the non-Jewish communities—and had little sense of belonging to a second generation. Children of those who had been persecuted for political activities similarly did not necessarily see this as a defining experience, even if they had a sense of being "different." This was the case, for example, with Peter, the son of Ella Lingens-Reiner, who had been imprisoned in Auschwitz for assisting Jews to escape Nazi Austria.[11] Peter was deeply affected by his mother's experiences of persecution; but at the same time, he was not accepted as part of the community of children of survivors. A former Jewish girlfriend even disputed the significance of his mother's Auschwitz experience, commenting that he would "never understand"; he observed that, indeed, he could not understand.[12] The very title of his autobiography aptly referred to his sense of being an "outsider" in many respects in postwar Austria.

So the label of "second generation," until recently, was claimed largely by those who were the postwar offspring of survivors of the camps and ghettos of Nazi-dominated Europe. An increasing body of research and discussion focused on the implications of growing up in these survivor families. This research was given a broader impetus in the years following the Vietnam War, when post-traumatic stress disorder was high on the public agenda, but it had started well before. And it was enhanced as the group reached adulthood and became increasingly organized and self-aware. Crucial to the development of collective awareness were individual activists, self-help groups, and social movements. A few key moments stand out.

During the 1970s, when Epstein and others were in their twenties, it began to dawn on them that there were many who had shared similarly distinctive childhood experiences, and that their identities were shaped by growing up in a survivor family. In the following decades, they began to think that talking with people who shared similar challenges would be of personal benefit. Epstein sought out and engaged systematically in conversations with other young adults across the United States and Canada. Her 1979 book, *Children of the Holocaust: Conversations with Sons and Daughters of Survivors*, along with the work by Lucy Steinitz and others, marked a turning point in defining the second generation.[13] This was the formation, in effect, of an explicit community of connection—those who shared a sense of deep personal connection with a specific past, and also a broader connection with one another by virtue of that common past.

From the 1980s onward, groups devoted to exploring second-generation issues also sprang up in Israel, the United Kingdom, and continental Europe. In France, in 1979 Serge and Beate Klarsfeld established the Association des fils et filles des déportés juifs de France (FFDJF, Association of the Sons and Daughters of Jews deported from France), a body primarily focused on attempting to achieve justice by identifying perpetrators and others responsible for the deportation and deaths of Jews. France was unusual in having a relatively high proportion of children who had been hidden and protected and later grew up in the knowledge they were orphans; there was thus a considerable felt need for bringing their parents' murderers to account. The youngest among these, with no personal memories of the period but deeply scarred by the loss of their parents, generally saw themselves as second generation rather than "survivors."

In an increasingly mobile world, members of the second generation became involved in international networks. In June 1981, the first World Gathering of Holocaust Survivors was held in Jerusalem. This included not only survivors but also around one thousand members of the second generation, who "accepted the legacy of their parents to bear witness to the world."[14] Later in 1981, an International Network of Children of Jewish Holocaust Survivors was established, with Menachem Z. Rosensaft as founding chairperson. The first International Conference of Children of Holocaust Survivors was convened in New York in 1984, addressed by Rabbi Gerson

D. Cohen and Elie Wiesel, and the first International Conference of Children of Holocaust Survivors in Jerusalem took place in 1988. In the United Kingdom, the first such conference took place in 1994.[15] Members of the second generation in Britain, perhaps because of their comparatively small size, were somewhat slower to come to realize commonalities and shared concerns than were their counterparts in North America, Israel, and France. The London conferences of 1994 and 1995 for children and grandchildren of victims of Nazi persecution eventuated in the formation of the Second Generation Network, and in 1996 Katherine Klinger set up a group known as the Second Generation Trust.[16]

Interest in the long-term legacies for children of survivors grew as even the second generation aged and began to reflect on the impact on their own lives of their parents' and grandparents' experiences. And the impact was indeed striking, more extreme in some cases than others, but always significant.

Inescapable Legacies

Worldwide, there are currently several million people descended from Holocaust survivors; only a tiny minority has explicitly explored their own identities as members of a "second generation." Among those who have, there are many variations, but a number of common themes stand out. Their accounts reveal how historical events they had not themselves actually experienced remained of intrinsic, inescapable importance.

Growing up in a household overshadowed by the Holocaust posed a variety of challenges for children. Some related to the long-term psychological and physical impact of Nazi persecution on the parents; others were rooted in the later contexts. There were variations depending on whether both parents were survivors or only one; how they had managed to survive; when they had emigrated; and individual personalities, beliefs, and degrees of resilience.[17] Some were refugees who had fled Nazi persecution before the outbreak of war; they had not gone through the experiences of ghettos, camps, and death marches but were nevertheless immigrants who had lost close members of their families and communities, and often felt guilty about having left loved ones behind. Others had been brutally and tragically uprooted in the violence of wartime. They had endured extreme experiences and often suffered long-term physical and psychological consequences of prolonged persecution. Most survivors settled in new countries, learning new languages and skills and adapting to radically different circumstances, adding new issues around immigrant identity to traumatic experiences of persecution, deprivation, and loss.

It is scarcely surprising that the family lives of these people differed from those of other families in the neighborhoods where they settled. This inevitably affected family dynamics. One daughter of survivors, Paula Fass, describes how as a child in Brooklyn in New York she spoke Yiddish at home and when outside had to act as translator and interpreter for her father, whose English was a cause of embarrassment and shame: "I hated doing it, not only did it burden and imprison my childhood in adult responsibilities, but it also exposed the vulnerabilities and inverted the power relations of our household. This made me feel both painfully uncomfortable and endowed me with competence I did not really feel."[18]

Sometimes a parent would succumb to feelings of helplessness or anger and would fly into uncontrollable rages or collapse in fits of weeping, or simply become withdrawn and silent, as if inhabiting another world. Eva Hoffmann, whose family remained in Poland for a few years after the war, recalls how in her childhood the past punctuated life in the present: "In the midst of her daily round, my mother would suddenly be overcome by a sharp, terrible image, or by tears. On other subjects she was robustly articulate; but when the sudden recall of her loved ones punctured her mind's protective membrane, speech came in frail phrases, in litanies of sorrow." She could not escape terrible images, including how "her sister—this was the heart of grief—had been murdered."[19] Such outbursts could be frightening for children. Many felt that they had in some way to try to heal their parents' distress, inverting the relationships of care from a very early age.

At the same time, children did not want to hurt parents' feelings by refusing their care, even if it was inappropriate. Parents who had suffered extreme deprivation and starvation sometimes made a major issue of eating everything up at mealtimes, whether or not they were actually hungry. Children reacted differently to such pressures, even within the same family. Noam and Joel, for example, were brothers growing up in Israel.[20] Their parents had both survived the Łódź ghetto, but their father had spent less time in Łódź, being sent in 1940 to a labor camp and then to Auschwitz, where he worked for I. G. Farben in Buna. After the war, he was able to talk easily about his own experiences but unable to confront his inability to save members of his family. By contrast, their mother, whose own father was a member of the Jewish council in Łódź, remained in the ghetto until the final clearance in August 1944, when she was sent to Auschwitz and then to Bergen-Belsen; she was almost unable to speak about her traumatic past. Both parents were overprotective, forcing their sons to eat, fearing that otherwise they were at risk of dying. Joel complied and became a fat child; Noam, however, became terrified at mealtimes and was unable to swallow his food, as a result receiving beatings from his father, who could not control his anger—in the process reinforcing Noam's fear of food. Noam became very thin, passing on issues around food to his own son, Ronen.[21] Noam and Joel, as children of survivors, and even Ronen, a grandchild, did not need to be told stories about their family's experiences to be personally affected by the implications; they literally embodied the long-term reverberations of Nazi persecution. This is a stark example of how a focus on "memory" alone cannot fully grasp the intrinsic connections between a period of persecution and a later present.

Children often did not know what exactly their parents had been through. They heard the fragments, the stylized stories their parents were willing to repeat, but often these did not form a coherent narrative. Hoffmann spoke for many as she recalled "the torn, incoherent character of those first com-munications about the Holocaust, the speech broken under the pressure of pain." She remembers how the "episodes, the talismanic litanies, were repeated but never elaborated upon." She indicates that it "was precisely the indigestibility of these utterances, their fearful weight of densely packed feeling, as much as any specific content, that I took in as a child."[22]

How parents interpreted their past made a difference; so did the strat-egies that had helped them to survive, or at least the strategies they later played up as having been significant. One psychologist, Yael Danieli, analyz-ing families in New York, identified four different types of adaptation: what she calls victim families, fighter families, numb families, and families of "those who made it." But whichever way they represented the past, there was, in all households, an "omnipresence of the Holocaust."[23] Scholars and practitioners have studied the psychological symptoms demarcating offspring of survivor families from others of their age group; this research remains contested, although psychiatrists from the late 1960s did think they could discern distinctive patterns.[24] More recently, there have been suggestions about possible epigenetic changes, such that parental experi-ences of trauma could be "inherited" across generations through the ways in which specific genes regulating responses to shock could be switched on or off; this, too, remains controversial.[25] But it is clear that there were significant implications in terms of cultural interpretations and individual self-understandings.

As Fass put it, this was "a historical generation, singed by the conflagration at the center of the twentieth century which destroyed their families' Europe and forced them to become engaged in the creation of a new postwar world." Members of the second generation were "at once part of the abomination of the Holocaust" but were "rescued into a much better life."[26] The ways in which they conceived of their lives could never be separated from the past, however much "better" this new life was than the one their parents had managed to escape. And many felt they had to confront what it was that the escape had entailed, what was missing and might have been.

The experiences of the second generation were both diminished and imbued with meaning by the legacies of survival. Parents' experiences shaped the lessons they sought to teach their children: urging them to wear warm clothes whatever the weather, to eat up everything on the plate, to be vigilant and fearful of every danger that might lurk in the outside world—all these feature frequently, along with a pervasive sense of the impermanence and fragility of human life. But they were not only overprotected; children of survivors often found that from a relatively early age they felt they needed to "parent" their parents. They sensed the losses and mourning, the fragility and pain, in their parents' lives and felt that they should in some way try to make up for this. The enormity of what had come before relativized the children's experiences in the present. Some felt they could never express pain and unhappiness themselves, either because it would further upset their parents—living in a world of false gaiety—or because no current pain or unhappiness could in any way compare with what survivor parents had been thorough. There was no authentic emotion of their own to be expressed—fear of the dentist was nothing compared to fear in the camps.

Afterness

The sense of not quite being present in their own lives, but rather an appendage to an infinitely more significant past, was pervasive. Anne Karpf, who grew up in London as a child of survivors, reflected on a moment at Yad Vashem when she was overcome with emotion: "It seemed then as if

I hadn't lived the central experience of my life—at its heart, at mine, was an absence."[27] Common among the second generation was a sense of somehow "coming after." Everything that was truly significant, shaping and forming their lives, had happened before they even existed. As Fass put it: "Hidden behind everything we were and almost everything we did was an earlier life, only partly lived, of which we were either the afterward or the substantiation, or possibly the redemption, but without which our consciousness was incomplete."[28]

A sense of "afterness" pervades Hoffman's aptly entitled *After Such Knowledge*, which opens with the sentence: "In the beginning was the war."[29] For her, born into the ruins of Poland in 1945, "The world as I knew it and the people in it emerged not from the womb, but from war."[30] Only as an adult did she begin to comprehend what had happened: "The Holocaust, in my first, childish reception, was a deeply internalised but strangely unknown past."[31] She knew of its significance before she knew what had actually happened: "The postgeneration's trajectory is the opposite of the more general trajectory of response to events." Reversing the usual order, "those who are born after calamity sense its most inward meanings first and have to work their way outwards towards the facts and the worldly shape of events."[32]

Such "afterness" was engrained even in the personal identities given to children by their parents. Many children born after the war to survivors were given names of lost relatives. This made them feel they had to live up to often idealized pictures of those who had been killed, to compensate for the losses.[33] They were not truly "themselves," but were seen as replacements of someone else, or the supposed "reason" why a parent had survived. Children were often also given "missions" to carry forward the family legacies. Frequently only one of several siblings developed a strong connection with the past—or had such a connection imposed upon them. Dubbed "memorial candles," they had a particular burden to bear, while other members of their families could lead "ordinary" lives in the present.[34] Often, they could hardly bear this burden—which is how they came to enter therapy. As Hava, one such "memorial candle," put it: "I am concerned about the Holocaust and my brother is concerned about my new refrigerator."[35] This legacy often threatened to swamp any emergent sense of individual identity. Arye, born in 1946 to two survivor parents, was given three names of dead relatives. He felt, "I am actually carrying the whole family around on my shoulders." He added, "They piled on me all the names of dead relatives." Now, he felt he had "no choice but to carry the dead on [his] back."[36]

Devorah, also born in 1946, was named after her father's sister. "It's hard for me to drag their dead around with me all the time." She commented, "I'm not the family hearse, yet after all that's what I am."[37] Her father emphasized her resemblance to his dead sister Devorah, after whom she was named, yet he repeatedly told her that she would never be as pretty as his sister had been. Another child of survivors, Baruch, also saw his identity constructed in terms of dead relatives, including a brother whom his father had adored: "I was my father's father, I was his brother, I was his opposite, whatever you want, except for really being myself."[38] He explained: "I've often felt that my father expected me to be what he couldn't be." As a result, he felt, "I was never good enough for him."[39] In the analyst's view of these and many similar cases, the perished were idealized, and children could never measure up to the images of those who had been lost.

Not all children of survivors faced experiences such as these. But many sensed a wider legacy of "coming after." The intangible, "unexperienced," yet vivid imagining of what came "before" is captured by Marianne Hirsch's term "postmemory," conveying the vivid sense of a past that could not actually be remembered yet which was very alive in the family atmosphere. She defines it as "the relationship that the 'generation after' bears to the personal, collective and cultural trauma of those who came before—to experiences they 'remember' only by means of the stories, images and behaviors among which they grew up." Hirsch suggests that the connection to the past is "thus actually mediated not by recall but by imaginative investment, projection, and creation."[40] Hoffman felt that she "was a receptacle of a historical legacy." As the survivor generation was passing away, she "felt more and more palpably that the legacy of the Shoah was being passed on to us, its symbolic descendants and next of kin."[41] For her, the second generation played a crucial role in transmission, as the "guardianship of the Holocaust" was passed to "the hinge generation." This second generation had the crucial ability to "think about certain questions arising from the Shoah with a sense of living connection."[42] This did not result from specific stories; it was simply because of the sheer emotional weight of a past that was often not even spoken about.

Coming after meant imbibing often misplaced lessons for the present. Karpf documents her struggle to understand the impact her parents' experiences had on her as a child, shaping her relationships to them, to herself, and to the wider world. She had, for example, to confront the issue of death and its centrality for her own fears and feelings repeatedly, despite growing up in the relative safety of postwar London. Karpf's anxieties were widely shared in families with experiences like those of her parents—who had variously survived labor and extermination camps, in Russia, in the case of her father, and Plaszów and Auschwitz, in the case of her mother, and who had managed to escape postwar Poland to arrive in Britain. As Karpf put it, the war "just seeped into our home, like some peculiarly mobile fog, and took up residence. The house and our parents seemed layered with a kind of subcutaneous sadness."[43] Death was ever-present, as her parents pored over "rescued pre-war photo albums containing group pictures of chillingly merry people" who "were spoken of vividly, as if they might walk through the door at any moment"—but who had gone forever.[44] This only served to underline the sharp break.

Parents' experiences inflected a child's view of the world from an early age. Judith Kalman writes of her secure Canadian childhood: "Early on, through my father's stories and my mother's startling revelations of horror, I absorbed the knowledge that innocent children could be murdered and whole families and communities eradicated by forces beyond their control."[45] She continues, "I might be playing with a doll that said, 'Mama.' When I removed the doll's clothes, the mechanical voice box lodged in her back was exposed. My mother would exclaim, 'Don't show me that thing. It reminds me of my cousin Blanka when we were running under the bombs like ants, and I ran by her, her back blown open from shrapnel.' Such explosions were not uncommon for my mother." One of the most difficult aspects to deal with was the unpredictability of such outbursts: "We didn't know when my mother's memories might detonate, or what might trigger them. It felt like setting off a landmine just when one had assumed the field was clear. The world plainly could be a scary place."[46] Eva Hoffman, too, recalled how in her home "wartime experiences kept erupting in flashes of imagery; in abrupt, fragmented phrases; in repetitious, broken refrains." These eruptions of the past had "a frightening immediacy in that most private and potent of family languages—the language of the body." Rather than in stories, "the past broke through in the sounds of nightmares, the idiom of sighs and illness, of tears and the acute aches that were the legacy of the damp attic and of the conditions my parents endured during their hiding."[47] There was no way to ignore a past that so interrupted the present, even if little was actually known about it.

Certain aspects of life appeared particularly fraught with danger—even in the most unlikely places and ways. Lisa Appignanesi, for example, recalls her childhood in postwar Canada, when her parents repeatedly moved her from one school to another and kept reinventing their story; on registration in each new school, she was most terrified of the inevitable question of where she was born, not knowing whether to say Poland or France, since this was a feature of her parents' story that was altered depending on what they thought would go down better in different contexts.[48] Survivors often reacted in ways that were crucial to survival during the war, but no longer so apposite in postwar conditions. Appignanesi recalls how her mother and father reacted differently—but entirely in keeping with their respective earlier survival strategies—when approaching the border between Canada and the United States on family vacations in the 1950s. Her father, on sight of border guards in uniform, would freeze in terror; her mother would put on her most flirtatious, coquettish ways to charm her way through.[49]

For the second generation, it has been said, "the Holocaust means the eternal *presence of an absence*."[50] A major absence was that of living relatives. The dead were, in some families, almost more "present" than those around them—even for children who had never actually met their murdered relatives. Kalman recalls that her father "filled her head and heart with frequent narratives about his dead loved ones" to such a degree that she could identify their photographs, reciting like a catechism the names of the dead. "I cannot imagine how he was able to start a second family so soon upon losing everyone. I think that the guilt of survival my father carried in him, threatening always to drag him under, could be measured by the flow of narration and remembrance that poured out of him almost uninterruptedly over the years."[51]

Despite this omnipresence of an absent past, there was at the same time a sense of total rupture with that past. This contrasts markedly with a sense of continuity in most perpetrator families, who lived with a past about which, to be sure, much had been silenced, but which was not separated from the present by such a deep and unbridgeable chasm. But for survivor families, there was a terrifying void, a black hole of destruction and death. As one child of survivors, Lisa Reitman-Dobi, put it, she "knew that an isolated, distant horror" had "severed the past from the present without a trace."[52] Yet at the same time, freighted silences were omnipresent; Fass describes "the picture no one ever saw and the names no one ever uttered" as "unseen images and unspoken words haunted our lives."[53]

Parents who had previous marriages, with former spouses and children killed in the Holocaust, generally found it difficult to integrate their earlier lives with new relationships. Former families were often kept secret. Fass, for example, knew about her mother's first marriage and her son, called Wolf Leib Kromolowski, born in Łódź just before the war broke out. At age three, Wolf was handed over during the "Children's Action" at the beginning of September 1942, when the controversial leader of the Jewish council, Chaim Rumkowski, ordered Jews to surrender their children for deportation, in a desperate effort to preserve the lives of those who could work. Fass's mother told her about her little half-brother who had been deported to Chełmno in this way: "She sent him off with a piece of bread for the journey placed in a little sack around his neck, which she had sewn."[54] Her father, by contrast, did not talk about his former family. Fass recalls her shock when, age seven, she first learned that her father had previously had another wife and four children.[55] He had managed to protect them throughout the existence of the Łódź ghetto, bribing ghetto officials and hiding the two youngest during the Children's Action in September 1942, but ultimately he could not protect them from the gas chambers of Auschwitz. He had refused to keep the one photo he still possessed of this family, with his four children of whom he had been so proud; the photo had gone with an aunt to Israel, and the secret and silence was preserved. For the young Fass, growing up in America, this shadow family was perplexing. "No one I ever went to school with had siblings who had died. And what were the dead husband and dead wife of your parents called? Were they stepparents once removed, almost parents?"[56]

Born into marriages founded on tragedy, these children grew up almost suspended in time, haunted by a past they had not themselves experienced, brought up with attitudes bearing the marks of survival tactics from another era, and burdened with missions for the future that they had often not themselves chosen. Many defined their identities in terms of the ways in which the unexperienced past had shaped them. A few turned to creative writing and the visual arts to express their feelings; tens of thousands wrote in journals or, later, as the internet developed, set up personal websites exchanging experiences or participating in discussions.

The past also affected their choices for the future. There was a sense that they had to excel in order to make up for their parents' sorrows and losses. This might be in professional terms—becoming a doctor, lawyer, or other high-status professional. It might be in terms of private life, through procreation and having a large family, ensuring the continuation of the Jewish people that Hitler had sought to exterminate. Parental reactions against "marrying out," even among those who were not religiously observant, were undoubtedly strengthened by heightened fear and mistrust of gentiles.

The second generation therefore labored under additional pressures with respect to leading their own lives. Failure to achieve or actions of which their parents disapproved might evoke the pained comment "For this I survived the camps?" Emotional entanglements and family tensions in the struggle to break free from parents and develop a separate identity, unencumbered by Holocaust legacies, could be complex and problematic.

Unplaced

The wider postwar context had a significant effect on how parents adapted and therefore how their children experienced growing up. Young North Americans in the 1970s and 1980s were shaped not only by their own family's past but also by the wider culture, marked by identity politics and "hyphenated identities." Survivors' children searched for new configurations that mapped onto their own sense of hybrid identity, at a time when the Holocaust was attaining a prominent place in national consciousness.

It was a very different matter to grow up as the child of survivors in one of the "lands of the perpetrators" in central Europe. Even in Europe, there were major contrasts between the situation of survivor families—as with all other aspects of the Holocaust—in the Third Reich successor states of East Germany, West Germany, and Austria, or in the complex situations of formerly occupied territories such as Poland. It was very different again to grow up among other survivor families in Israel or in distinctive Jewish communities in North London, Australia, and elsewhere around the world. Each of these contexts posed different challenges for members of the second generation, and in each there were greater or lesser degrees of awareness of what it meant to be born into such families.

Israel was of course distinctive in many ways. Dan Bar-On has described it as having developed a "victims' culture" that "exerted constant pressure on us to 'learn from the Holocaust.'"[57] This culture developed over time, changing significantly following the Eichmann trial.[58] But even before this, the Holocaust was everywhere, inescapable, with palpable consequences in everyday life.[59] In Israel, there is a word for individuals who have been indirectly wounded by the past: the "scarred ones," those who bear traces of violence that was wrought not on themselves but on others, those marked by a sense of self as a "sarut," one of the "srutim"—the "scratched," the "wounded"—as a child of Holocaust survivors.[60] Israeli ethnographer Carol Kidron explains this in terms of two Hebrew words, *machuk* and *sarut*, meaning, respectively, "erased" and the superlative "scratched out," as a way of describing "those who cannot cross back completely into their civilian roles after experiencing trauma."[61] This is not necessarily always interpreted negatively. Some of Kidron's interviewees disputed the medical or illness metaphor and felt pride in bearing the wounds of history, rather than being damaged or scarred.[62] More widespread, in the last few decades, has been a rather less freighted approach, exploring and sharing common experiences with others in a similar situation.

The second generation is everywhere in Israel, and many actively and willingly participate in the activities of associations and societies keeping alive memories and transmitting knowledge of lost worlds without being "scarred" by them. Adults who were active in professional and private lives in the late twentieth century were able to recognize a common past without being either reduced to this identity or hampered by its consequences. Yet despite an active interest in a European family heritage, many still sensed a lack of any personal connection with a particular place. And they often identified with the difficulties of their survivor parents, understood their loneliness and the characteristic mistrust that survivors often still felt—even in Israel—creating a rift within the larger Jewish community.[63]

While in Israel the features shared by the second generation may have been self-evident from the outset, in societies where survivor families lived in a predominantly non-Jewish community or where there were few prewar refugees or postwar immigrants, such awareness emerged rather more slowly and sporadically. Karpf portrays the generally quiescent British Jewish community, with its historic desire not to draw undue attention to itself, and the British government's relative unwillingness to take in too many refugees for fear of fostering antisemitism—in a bitter irony, blaming the victims for any unpleasantness that might arise.[64] As a result, although her parents had a network of fellow survivors, and Karpf knew many of their offspring while she was growing up, she continued to feel relatively isolated from the dominant surrounding culture. The notion of a second generation arose around a decade later in Britain than in the United States.

In East Germany, children of Jewish survivors may have been barely aware of their parental legacy at all. They may also have been barely aware of the fact that many of their classmates had parents who had gone along with Hitler. The myth of the antifascist state lifted a huge burden from the shoulders of the next generation, whether among the communities of those who had been persecuted or those who had been on the side of the perpetrators. This was very different in West Germany, with its official emphasis on public responsibility for the Nazi past (even if, as previous chapters explored, with limited legal repercussions). Yet here, Jewish families felt particularly isolated as children grew up in a society where former perpetrators might be all around. They could not overcome a sense of difference, as other children celebrated birthdays among relatives and they remained alone, and as neighboring families treated them with hostility and suspicion or, conversely, an exaggerated philosemitism. Whatever they did, they were permanently marked as "different": the deep chasm between "Jews" and "Germans" created by Hitler persisted long after the demise of the Nazi state. And survivors who stayed in Germany often felt not only uneasy about their own location but also compromised and somehow inferior to those who had immigrated to Israel.

In Poland, the wider community was deeply divided over the Nazi past. While numerous Polish gentiles had hidden Jews during the war, whether for personal gain or out of intrinsic kindness, many more had betrayed Jews and collaborated with the Nazis. Some—and not only in the notorious case of Jedwabne—had killed Jewish neighbors. Whether or not they had been personally involved in violence, large numbers of Polish gentiles had been beneficiaries of the disappearance of some three million Jews from amongst their midst and had taken over formerly Jewish houses, property, stores, and farms. In an economy where so many suffered from poverty and disadvantage, suspicion and envy were ever-present reactions. Surviving Jews who sought to make a life in postwar Poland were often accused of complicity in communist oppression, further fueling popular distrust. In such circumstances, few people of Jewish origin who had not fled following the pogroms and antisemitic crackdowns were enthusiastic about making their identity known.

A research project on members of the second generation, carried out shortly after the fall of communism, noted that no register of Holocaust survivors had been kept in communist Poland, making it difficult for them even to find families with members of the second generation.[65] People were also initially somewhat suspicious of the researchers' intentions and unwilling to participate in the project. When they did eventually identify suitable families, they found that in all cases the survivor had married a non-Jewish person. Only six out of the twenty children in the sample had been aware of their Jewish origins since early childhood, while fourteen only became aware of their Jewish heritage in later childhood or even young adulthood. Survivor parents had often already hidden their identities as a means of survival under Nazism and simply continued this in order to integrate better into a postwar society that remained largely hostile to Jews. They often found it easiest to assimilate as far as possible without drawing attention to their Jewish origins. Fully half of the second generation interviewed in this survey saw the Holocaust as being a secret between their parents, hidden and private. In addition to the silences about the past that were characteristic everywhere, the Polish survivor families had an additional layer of taboo: that surrounding their own identity. In the view of the researchers, the second generation was burdened not only by the question of what had happened in the past but also that of who they actually were and what their own identity in the present was.

This of course changed with time, as elsewhere. Most members of the second generation in survivor families in Poland became fascinated by Jewish identity and culture, beginning as they reached young adulthood in the 1970s. In the post-communist era, twenty years later, interest in the Jewish cultural heritage grew exponentially in Poland, making this far easier than it had been for their parents' generation, who had lived through an altogether more hostile environment.[66] Even so, members of the second generation, while recognizing that they were entirely Polish, sometimes also ended up feeling that they did not truly belong anywhere.

Members of the second generation, wherever they grew up, often had an uneasy sense not of being "displaced"—like their parents—but rather "unplaced." They felt they did not really "come from" the place where they were born and grew up and, depending on circumstances, did not necessarily identify with it. Often as they grew into adulthood they began to engage in a search for roots, even though they did not and could not identify with the places from which their parents came.

Returns to the Unknown

Members of the second generation, uneasy in their haziness about family background while aware of the enormity of its significance, sometimes engaged in exploration of historical landscapes, both literal and figurative.

In North America, for example, members of the second generation explored family legacies and the significance for their own identities through cultural and artistic media. However unrepresentative such voices may have been, their works registered the cultural and social birth of the "second generation." Publications in a range of genres—from Art Spiegelman's graphic novel *Maus*, published in November 1996, through the imaginative use of magic realism in Jonathan Safran Foer's 2003 novel *Everything Is Illuminated*, to Daniel Mendelsohn's 2006 journalistic and autobiographical *The Lost: A Search for Six of Six Million*—engaged not only with the past but also with the lives of those who "came after."[67] They touched a chord among large numbers of readers, and arguably spoke for many in that infinitely larger sea of those who did not express their feelings in public. Such explorations of family pasts, however incomplete, were increasingly widespread.

There were also physical "returns" to the unknown lands from which their families had come. Survivors had complex relationships with former homelands that had been destroyed by Nazi rule. Many German Jews who had settled elsewhere refused to go back to Germany or to speak German; those who did often felt ambivalent and distanced on their visits. Polish Jews, too, while continuing to speak the language and sustaining cultural traditions, rejected a sense of identity rooted in the country in which they had grown up. This partly had to do with the very history of that country and the period into which they were born. Fass discusses how her father, who hated Poland, considered himself a "Jew" and not a "Polish Jew": "His Polish identity meant little to him, and it could hardly describe his relationship with a nation that came into existence two decades after he was born and then disappeared when Hitler occupied the western half of the country and incorporated Lodz, my father's birthplace, into the German Reich."[68]

Others tried through regional associations and social networks to sustain a sense of place and tradition. Sometimes members of the second generation reacted against their parents' determination to cling to elements of the culture of the "old country" that they had been forced to leave. This is evident, for example, in the "Germanness" of the grandparents' flat depicted in Arnon Goldfinger's 2011 film *Die Wohnung (The Flat)*, as contrasted with the modern, placeless, rather antiseptic flat of their daughter, the second generation.[69] It was only in the third generation, with the grandson, that the family past could be explored. But for most, there was a sense of a place from which the family had come, which was much talked about, and which was the location of innumerable stories, but which it was difficult to imagine.

This often gave rise to a sense of needing to "go back," to explore the past, to see the places from which parents or grandparents or other relatives had come.[70] Most "returns" to ancestral homelands resulted not in a sense of resolution but rather a registration of loss. Traces of the past might still be found, but the places were not the same as before the catastrophe, before the old society was destroyed. Even if the physical remains were well preserved and the topography relatively easy to read (not always the case), there was often a sense of disappointment, of the place not quite corresponding to the ways in which younger generations had imagined it to be. Many engaged in detective work or imaginative reconstruction, or found witnesses who could fill in missing links. Simply walking through areas well known from parents' stories, finding street names they had heard about in childhood, could also help. As Fass put it, referring to her first visit to her parents' hometown of Łódź, here she "felt most connected to the past."[71]

Sometimes such journeys had additional missions: to collect photographs or pieces of memorabilia for survivor parents, to erect a memorial at sites where relatives had been lost, to visit graves and pay respects to the dead. At an individual level, there might be a sense of building bridges to the past, being able to understand, reconstruct, and reconstitute a "heritage" by trying to situate an identity, having been born into a displacement. There was a widespread need to see "where it happened" in order to "put it behind oneself" and "move on"—all spatial metaphors that are often used topographically, temporally, and psychologically.

Visiting sites of former life and death could assist in the resolution of anguished emotions. Solly Kaplinski, for example, produced a book of poetry and drawings based on his trip to Poland in 1988, following the deaths of his survivor parents in 1987.[72] The book is full of anger and emotion. Kaplinski's parents had been partisans, constantly on the run. As Kaplinski put it, while his parents almost never spoke of their experiences, in an attempt to protect their children, they nevertheless "carried the scars and were often prone to bouts of anxiety, panic and depression." Kaplinski writes that in his own way he too tried to protect them by not mentioning the past, turning him, as he put it, into an "emotional cripple." The 1988 trip to Poland, as part of the March of the Living program, he wrote, "was a cathartic moment for me: it released a gush of hitherto repressed and unabridged emotional responses."[73]

Clearly there was a huge emotional legacy to be dealt with. Journeys "back" to unfamiliar and previously unknown places where things had happened that radically transformed the history of a family, that dramatically affected people's lives and influenced the lives of subsequent generations, could prove therapeutic.[74]

But like their parents, the vast majority of the second generation simply got on with life. Barry Eichengreen, the son of Holocaust survivor Lucille Eichengreen, became a distinguished professor of economics and political science; he has said little or nothing in public about the personal impact of his mother's experiences as a survivor of the Łódź ghetto and concentration camps, including Auschwitz.[75] Alan Steinweis, a distinguished academic in the field of Holocaust studies, equally decided not to self-identify as second generation or attend groups devoted to exploring the significance of this identity.[76] Many children or grandchildren of survivors have sought to acquire more details out of an interest in family history but not as a part of their own self-definition.

Not every child of survivors developed a sense of identity in the terms of a "second generation." For some, however, belonging to such a group became important in enhancing self-understanding. Still others were burdened with the weight of family history whether they wanted it or not. And all were in some way affected by their parents' experiences: few could follow a path unaffected by parental pressures, constraints, and desires, whether seeking to fulfill or to react against their parents' wishes. There was a powerful field of forces within which they grew up, with which they might conform or against which they might strain, but which they could never ignore.

But what is perhaps most extraordinary was the growth in attempts, among a few, at reaching out across community borders, with efforts to establish a dialogue between the children of victims and the children of perpetrators.

The Quest for Mutual Understanding

Growing self-awareness among children of victims assisted in what might be called the "outing" of children of perpetrators. There was an assumption of public sympathy for the children of victims, whereas the children of perpetrators were both deeply ambivalent about their family past and unsure of any benefits of going public. In West Germany, changes occurred in the 1980s, including the landmark speech by the then president Richard von Weizsäcker—himself the son of a prominent Nazi—in 1985, on the occasion of the fortieth anniversary of the end of the war. This speech encapsulated and signaled the willingness of children of the persecutors to identify with the victims without denying the guilt of their own parents and what they saw as the special responsibilities of the next generation. The debates from the later 1980s onward demonstrated the extent to which this was still a highly sensitive and difficult topic for West Germans to address. But it began to be addressed in public and no longer merely grappled with in private. And it began to be addressed in dialogue with the children of victims and survivors. Again, activists from within this community were crucial in precipitating new developments.

In the mid-1980s, as we have seen, Israeli psychologist Dan Bar-On began to wonder about the experiences of people growing up in Nazi families. In a series of research trips to Germany—a country he was at first highly apprehensive about visiting—he sought out and interviewed children of former Nazis, some of them very high ranking. He noticed that by the time of his third visit in 1987, there had been a notable shift in atmosphere.[77] Bar-On's visit came shortly after the publication of a book based on interviews with children of Nazis, carried out by Peter Sichrovsky, a journalist and child of survivors who had returned after the war to their native Vienna.[78] Some of Sichrovsky's interviews had been published in advance in Der Spiegel. At around the same time, Dörte von Westernhagen—herself the daughter of a perpetrator—published a similar collection of interviews with children of perpetrators, exploring the issues they faced in common.[79] Just over a decade later, a collection of interviews with children of prominent Nazis was published, as Stephan Lebert approached the now adult sons and daughters who had first been interviewed by his father, the journalist Norbert Lebert, as early as 1959.[80] Meanwhile, in the course of the 1990s an increasing number of researchers—social psychologists, political scientists, sociologists, historians—began to concern themselves with the ways in which stories were told in families and the significance of intergenerational dialogue. By the 1990s, half a century after the era of persecution, there were signs of growing willingness to engage in dialogue on both sides.

Research by Gabriele Rosenthal and others highlighted similarities in strategies deployed for dealing with a difficult past in the families of both victims and perpetrators.[81] Focusing on case studies of families living in East and West Germany and Israel, Rosenthal and her colleagues distinguished between perpetrators and accomplices on the one hand and those who had fled their home countries prior to the war and survivors who had lived through the period in camps or hiding on the other. In both sorts of families, "biographical repair strategies" were deployed so as to be able to live with an uncomfortable past. But selective silences on the part of survivors, who wanted neither to relive the pain and suffering nor impose this burden on their children or grandchildren, were very different from the silence of perpetrators covering their tracks and avoiding accusations of guilt, and the anxieties of the descendants of survivors differed from the fears and fantasies of children and grandchildren of perpetrators.

Members of the second generation in survivor families were able to confront the past more easily than the children of people in perpetrator communities were. Interviews were carried out with students in Berlin, for example, comparing those who had a resistance or Jewish family background with those from a Nazi perpetrator or "follower" background. In the former group, the Nazi past was spoken about openly and frequently, and there were points of positive identification. In the group with family connections to Nazism, clichés were trotted out as covers for failure to confront questions honestly; the topic of conversation was rapidly changed; there was haziness about details; and emphasis was placed on their own family's sufferings rather than those of the victims of Nazism. The majority of the members of the second generation appeared to sympathize with their parents.[82] Similarly, Harald Welzer and other researchers looked at family strategies for smoothing over the compromised Nazi past of a beloved grandparent, leading Welzer and his colleagues to summarize their work under the phrase "Grandpa was not a Nazi."[83] The question of the lingering significance of the Nazi past was very much in the air well into the twenty-first century.

Such an approach within families could not always be sustained without active discussion. The increasing openness of debate, accompanied by publications of interviews with individual children of lower-level as well as high-ranking perpetrators, brought many more members of the second generation in perpetrator families out of their previous isolation, realizing the possibly beneficial consequences of finding people with similar backgrounds and exploring emotionally difficult issues with others who could sympathize and understand. One such was Dirk Kuhl, son of the former head of the Gestapo in Braunschweig. Kuhl wrote an open letter to the press that was picked up by Bar-On, among others. Kuhl subsequently became a key participant in the efforts to achieve understanding and dialogue—efforts that were otherwise, notably, generally initiated from the side of the sons and daughters of survivors, with Bar-On playing a prominent role.

From the late 1980s, Bar-On not only explored the psychological issues facing individual children of perpetrators but also precipitated encounters between members of the second generation on both sides. The first such conference was held in Wuppertal in 1988. Bar-On soon found others whose interests were similar. Samson Munn, a Boston-based professor of radiology and son of two survivors, became involved in Bar-On's groups, as did Dirk Kuhl. These two soon formed an unlikely friendship, finding to their initial surprise that despite contrasting parental backgrounds they had much in common. Their growing collaboration and interaction were the subject of a documentary film.[84]

Munn went on to play a key role in facilitating further encounter groups, taking up the initiative started by Bar-On. He was centrally involved in the groups that became known as TRT, To Reflect and Trust, and later also in Austrian Encounter as well as participating in groups in other conflict areas, including Northern Ireland. The possibility of developing mutual understanding and engaging in dialogue was increasingly on the agenda, but it was never an easy process. Some potential participants felt unable to attend, due to fears about threats to their security (as in the case of four members of the Austrian Roma and Sinti communities, following a bombing attack).[85] Others were afraid of being overwhelmed by feelings of rage, hostility, and anger as well as anxiety. Discussions were emotionally laden, often attended by considerable tension; yet even if the numbers involved in any one gathering were very small—a dozen or so at any one time—their significance for participants could be immense, potentially life-changing.

In North America, a figure who attracted considerable media attention was Mona Weissmark, a psychology professor whose parents were both Holocaust survivors. Concerned with the inadequacies of legal systems, she became interested in the ways in which a sense of injustice is transmitted across generations, creating tensions and hostility between people coming from families of survivors and those related to perpetrators.[86] With some trepidation, Weissmark, in association with a friend from a perpetrator background, organized a meeting between individuals from both groups in 1992; the following year, they repeated the experiment on German soil. The filmed records of these encounters provide glimpses into the emotional turmoil faced by participants. Both sides had to renounce, in effect, aspects of their heritage. For children of perpetrators, this was already something they had faced, in coming to terms with the reprehensible deeds of individuals with whom they felt strong emotional connections. More surprisingly, some children of survivors also felt they had to wrench themselves away from commitments to their own community. One woman, a child of survivors, was confronted with a former Nazi, Otto Duscheleit (a "perfectly normal SS-man," in his own words). On seeing his distress about his past and beginning to understanding the ways in which, as a child, he had been swept along by Nazism in the Hitler Youth, she realized that he "didn't fit the stereotype" that she had expected: he was "gentle and sweet, not aggressive, certainly not ten feet tall"; and, despite feeling like "such a betrayer of my mother and father," she impulsively wanted to hug him. Yet she also registered that this act of personal reconciliation would mean failing to fulfill the implicit pledge to take revenge for her murdered relatives and the wider Jewish community—as she put it, the "ghosts, spirits" behind her, "saying 'Avenge me!'" In tempering her initial inclination to express anger, to spit at him, she too had, in some way, to renounce her past.[87]

Such groups were not limited to initiatives from the United States, West Germany, and Israel but also sprang up elsewhere and became entwined in wider developments. Although targeted largely at the children of refugees and survivors, Klinger's London-based Second Generation Trust was also addressed to the children and other close relatives of Nazi perpetrators. Dialogue and reconciliation among members of the second and third generations was one of its aims. This organization played a significant role in a number of initiatives, including—eventually with the support and cooperation of other organizations—an international conference in Austria in September 1999, on the occasion of the sixtieth anniversary of the outbreak of the Second World War. It was entitled The Presence of the Absence: International Holocaust Conference for Eyewitnesses and Descendants of "Both Sides" (in German, Die Lebendigkeit der Geschichte: Internationale Konferenz für Überlebende und Nachkommen von Opfern und Tätern des Nationalsozialismus). This conference was held to be one of the key moments in opening up a larger debate between those connected with the victims and those connected with perpetrators, a debate that had not as yet taken place in Austria, even after the Waldheim controversy of the 1980s. In the view of Samson Munn, it was "the first time that such a large and public yet still personally felt meeting had taken place in Austria related to the Holocaust."[88]

For none of the participants in such groups was this dialogue an easy one. Even language played a sensitive role in these encounters: speaking and

listening to German and physically setting foot on German soil were difficult for some of the children of survivors, while children of perpetrators
often felt unable to express complex emotions adequately in a nonnative
language, however fluent their command of English might be. But the few
who participated were already aware of the baggage they carried from the
past and had the material means, determination, and time—such encounters
usually lasted for several days—to commit to working through their emotions together.

Not everyone who was conscious of their Holocaust heritage was prepared to engage in such encounters; indeed, some children of survivors
were actively opposed even to sharing the pages of a book with Germans
who were descendants of perpetrators. In the introduction to their edited
collection of essays by children from both sides of the divide, Alan L. Berger
and Naomi Berger recount how two of the contributors, Melvin Bukiet
and Anita Norich, wanted to withdraw their essays when they found the
book would also include Germans, and a third, Barbara Finkelstein, "expressed
deep reservations about 'bridge-building' exercises" and viewed "any implied
community between these two groups as perverse and disrespectful to the
martyred dead." Norich, the Bergers report, was also against "dialogue,"
believing "that such attempts to create a false and necessarily shallow sense
of connectedness between the heirs of Holocaust victims and their murderers is an insult to history and to the Jewish people whose loss we continue
to mourn." Bukiet did "not keep company with the descendants of his
ancestors' killers." But because of their "contractual obligations to the
publisher and their personal affection for the editor, they all agreed not to
remove their work in return for this paragraph."[89]

Continuing sensitivities and deeply felt viewpoints such as these clearly
complicate ongoing attempts to engage in dialogue and contribute to the
perception, among second- (and now third-) generation Germans, that they
will never be freed from an obligation to apologize, over and over again,
for deeds for which they bear no personal responsibility. Even so, attempts
continue to bring the two sides closer across the generations. Rainer Höss,
grandson of the former camp commandant of Auschwitz, has repeatedly
sought to make connections with survivors, including with the forgiving
Eva Mozes Kor, who had been subjected to Mengele's experiments; following previous visits to Auschwitz, he also hoped to attend the ceremony
marking the seventy-fifth anniversary of its liberation alongside survivors,
their descendants, key cultural figures, Jewish leaders, and world political

representatives. Höss's agonized personal attempts to deal with a family legacy of guilt and to educate the next generation, making bridges across different communities, remain, like so much in this emotionally fraught area, deeply controversial.[90]

The growth in the numbers and activities of groups from contrasting backgrounds seeking enhanced self-awareness and mutual understanding in the shadow of the Nazi past was striking. People with direct emotional links to a divided past now sought to make new connections across communities. But even if members of the second generation began to talk to each other, the perpetrator generation remained curiously absent; those who had been complicit in the violence that had destroyed so many and scattered survivors across the world still remained largely out of sight, including in the ever-expanding memorial landscape of Europe.

19

Oblivion and Memorialization

The soil of Europe is drenched with the blood of millions, pockmarked by innumerable sites of suffering and brutality. The landscape bears traces, some strikingly evident and others far less visible, of the Nazi architecture of exploitation and genocide. Those physical legacies still raise serious questions today.[1]

Some sites were already partially destroyed by the Nazis, who sought to cover up their crimes; others were pragmatically repurposed at the end of the war, occupied and reoccupied by subsequent inhabitants; and some became, over time, places for remembering the victims—almost hallowed ground for those who came to pay their respects to the dead: to light candles in their memory, to mourn, and to emphasize lessons for the future.

The landscapes of remembrance that we see today tell us as much about shifting priorities and contemporary concerns as they do about the Nazi past that they seek to preserve or portray. Evident everywhere are memorials to victims. But as in all things involving the Holocaust, not all victims have been equally remembered, and memorials to some groups came far later than others.

Notably absent, however, is adequate coverage of perpetrators. This is perhaps understandable. Perpetrators were all too present in the consciousness of survivors; they did not want former tormentors to sully, posthumously, places that were essentially graveyards, cemeteries for whole communities, sacred ground. With the passing of time, social, political, and educational functions began to assume larger dimensions, alongside the primary purpose of remembrance. And there was and is no easy strategy for the depiction of perpetrators, between the extremes of demonization on the one hand, which risks making the crime unintelligible and "abnormal," and humanization on the other, which risks opening the possibility of misinterpretation and even exoneration. It may only be now, as the last Nazis are passing away, that a portrayal of the ways in which people became involved in the system of persecution, and that evaluates degrees of guilt and responsibility for their actions, will even be possible.

The last few decades have seen an explosion of memorialization, in some places more than others. Berlin has arguably become the world capital of Holocaust remembrance, as memorials and museums devoted to a combination of remorse and representation of the Nazi past have proliferated exponentially. Indeed, the road through Berlin's central park, the Tiergarten, passes from a nineteenth-century monument celebrating national unification through military triumphs, the Victory Column (Siegessäule), to one monumentalizing national shame and genocidal crimes, the Memorial to the Murdered Jews of Europe, passing smaller memorials to other groups along the way.

Other places, too, have become remarkably concentrated sites of remembrance, with the opening up of Europe and the growth of "dark tourism." Yet despite ever-increasing numbers of visitors to some sites, others have fallen into near-oblivion.

There are no easy solutions, as conflicting interests collide. Early attempts to destroy the remnants and cover the traces served many interests: to draw a line under a past that many longed to forget (for very different reasons among survivor and perpetrator communities); to make use of scarce resources in a war-torn, economically devastated landscape; to house the dispossessed and displaced millions; to build new societies using the ruins of the old. Against this was a desire to mourn, to remember, to ensure that the names of the dead would not disappear along with their physical remains.

But with the passage of time, questions around memorialization began to take on new dimensions. Should later generations have to live with constant reminders of atrocity, or do they have some right to walk this earth untroubled by the ghosts of a receding past? What should be the balance between memorialization, education, and other later interests? There is also the unsettling question of whether an almost obsessive remembrance of victims is primarily a means for communities connected with perpetrators to work off feelings of inherited guilt. Such commemoration allows them to demonstrate identification with victims publicly and express remorse on behalf of their forefathers—but still permits the perpetrators to escape unnamed, unshamed, unpunished.

The landscapes of remembrance that we see today do not represent an adequate picture, nor do they display the full measure of responsibility for persecution across Europe under Nazi domination. The topography of memorialization prompts us rather to think about this past in particular ways, focusing on selected aspects and downplaying or even ignoring others. The selectivity has to do not only with location and with particular victim groups but also with the division of guilt.

International Symbol and "Site of All Evil": Auschwitz

Yet again, Auschwitz is the iconic site of memorialization. In the early twenty-first century, the museum encompassing the sites of Auschwitz I and Birkenau attracted around one and a half million visitors annually.[2] In the summer months, the crowds can be overwhelming: a ticketing system of timed small group tours had to be introduced to control the flow through the grounds of Auschwitz I. Headsets relay the well-rehearsed talks of guides commanding an impressive range of languages. Inevitably, some aspects are emphasized, while others are marginalized or silenced.

In Auschwitz I, the large brick buildings that had served as barracks, places of "medical" experimentation and torture, punishment cells, and antechambers of death have been transformed into "pavilions" displaying different facets of horror. Shuffling through as part of a group, unable to control the pace or focus of interest, interested tourists as well as visitors with personal connections, coming to remember members of their families or communities, may find it hard to gain space for contemplation. In Auschwitz II, Birkenau, with its far more expansive terrain—the remaining barracks separated by vast empty spaces between the watchtower entrance gate at one end and the ruins of the gas chambers and crematoria at the other—it is easier to gain a sense of the sheer scale, the magnitude of this enormous factory of death. Even here, in the summer months, visitors crawl; busloads are shipped in on package tours starting from Kraków, taking in the salt mines and the historic Wawel Castle—former seat of the Nazi governor of Poland, Hans Frank—as well as the old Jewish quarter of Kazimierz and Schindler's enamel factory made famous in Spielberg's film *Schindler's List*. Auschwitz I, with its infamous sign over the entrance, *Arbeit macht frei*, is firmly on the twenty-first century tourist trail. And the infamous watchtower entrance to Birkenau, with the railway tracks constructed in 1944 to deliver Hungarian Jews directly onto the platform or "ramp" close to the gas chambers, has become an image recognized around the world.

On the other hand, the former sites of slave labor have more or less disappeared from sight, whether in Auschwitz III, the I. G. Farben plant at Buna-Monowitz, or the numerous labor sub-camps across the surrounding countryside. This selectivity has been evident throughout the postwar period.[3]

The very multiplicity of groups associated with this site allowed a variety of forms of remembrance under changing political conditions. The State Museum at Oświęcim-Brzezinka was officially inaugurated on June 14, 1947. A mere two and a half years after liberation, the area covered by the museum was already a very different place than that abandoned by the Nazis and discovered by the Red Army in January 1945, and the museum transformed the site further over succeeding decades. The memorials built during the communist period emphasized the diversity of "nations" subjected to Nazi persecution, underplaying the fact that the vast majority of victims were Jewish. The site became a center for celebration of Polish heroism and martyrdom, including communist resistance, rather than a site of Jewish suffering. Memorialization became more internationalized in the 1960s, and there were key further changes with the visit of the Polish-born Pope John Paul II in 1979, although the communist narrative remained dominant until 1989.[4] Even in the late 1980s, Birkenau, the principal site of Jewish suffering, remained neglected, covered in weeds, and nearly deserted.[5]

This changed dramatically following the collapse of communism, with the growth of international tourist trade in an era of cheap flights. The predominantly Jewish character of Birkenau rose to prominence, albeit never displacing other narratives, including the cult of Polish Catholic suffering, a continuing point of contention. Debates over the renewal of exhibitions in the barracks, or "pavilions," were usually protracted, with at times extensive delays.[6] Was the primary purpose of any particular "national" exhibition to educate people or to evoke emotional responses and facilitate remembrance? The new Jewish exhibition, supported by Yad Vashem and using the latest technology, including music, art, and mood lighting to establish atmosphere, was particularly controversial.[7]

The selection of artifacts could also be controversial. How should examples of particular individuals be deployed, against the backdrop of anonymity and mass death—the piles of hair, discarded shoes, battered suitcases, eyeglasses, and personal effects? These objects contrasted with individual sites of veneration, such as the one to the Catholic priest Maximilian Kolbe, consisting of a display in a small "stand-up" punishment cell in the infamous Block 11, situated next to the Wall of Death where many executions took place. Kolbe was killed after having stepped forward to take the place of a condemned prisoner, Franciszek Gajowniczek, who had cried out that he had a family. Gajowniczek survived the war while Kolbe perished in his place. For his act of self-sacrifice, Kolbe was canonized by Pope John Paul II in 1982. The prominence of this display, while clearly moving, might be seen as something of an affront by anyone aware of Kolbe's prewar editorship of a journal that gave space to antisemitic articles.[8] And without relativizing Kolbe's sacrifice, one might wonder why the same treatment was not given to others, such as the women who had assisted in blowing up one of the crematoria and who were hanged in early January 1945.[9] One of these women, Ala Gertner, did indeed have her photograph included in a dusty corner of an old area of the exhibition, but labeled with the wrong name (at least on the occasion of my latest visit); another photograph was mistakenly designated as Gertner. Given the number of cells in the block where Kolbe's is located, one has to wonder why they are not more representative of the range of victims. These may be questions for curators rather than historians.

For most Germans, Auschwitz—embodiment of the "it" about which they claimed to know nothing—remains in their minds far from the heart of Germany, despite being located on a major railway line in an industrial area that was within the Greater German Reich, rather than tucked away in eastern Poland like the Operation Reinhard camps. Even so, "it" can conveniently be reduced to the gas chambers here, behind the barbed wire and watch towers, rather than also including the killing sites that moved with the army and the Einsatzgruppen along the Eastern Front, or the euthanasia institutions spread across Germany and Austria, or the factories and building sites and farms in which slave laborers were exploited. Auschwitz, the heart of all evil, was far away and had nothing to do with those who professed to have known nothing.

Auschwitz serves in so many ways to epitomize the industrial machinery of mass killing. But at the same time the prominence of Auschwitz in the contemporary landscape of remembrance risks deflecting attention from the ways in which so many were involved in the wider system of violence and the overall machinery of destruction.

Varieties of Remembrance and Neglect:
Killing Sites in Poland

The concentration of remembrance in major sites has been accompanied by the relative marginalization of others. People who were personally connected with victims or who closely identified with certain groups were often active in trying to keep alive their memory, but unless they were wealthy or had powerful backing, it was difficult to do more than place a pebble, a candle, a wreath. And without political support, the meaning of potential memorial sites could be lost. A glance at the postwar fates of the dedicated extermination sites in Poland reveals that the landscapes of memorialization do not adequately map the topography of the past.

Even before the end of the war, Majdanek, Stutthof, and Auschwitz-Birkenau had been declared by the provisional Polish government to be memorial sites, and by 1947 the Polish Parliament had placed them under a "Council for the Protection of Memorials to Struggle and Martyrdom" (Rada Ochrony Pomników Walki i Męczeństwa).[10] The question however arose of what were to be considered "similar locations." Not all sites associated with atrocities were sustained with the levels of resources and attention, both by authorities and visitors, that were devoted to Auschwitz-Birkenau and, to a lesser extent, Majdanek. Political considerations in Cold War Europe inevitably affected decisions.

Curiously, wartime Jewish resistance was less of an issue in early postwar Poland than were other kinds of resistance that did not suit the dominant communist narrative. The 1944 Warsaw Uprising, during which the Red Army had waited at a distance while the Germans crushed Polish nationalist resistance, leaving Warsaw largely destroyed, was particularly problematic for communists. Rather than remembering the Warsaw Uprising heroes, including their nationalist rivals in the Home Army, they focused attention instead on the 1943 Jewish Ghetto Uprising. Amidst the ruins of Warsaw, a memorial designed by Nathan Rapoport was unveiled in 1948, celebrating the courage of the ghetto's inhabitants.[11] Despite continuing antisemitism in Poland, the Rapoport memorial remained significant: it was here that in December 1970 West German chancellor Willy Brandt dropped to his knees, in that apparently spontaneous gesture that became symbolic of German remorse, desire for reconciliation, and the establishment of new relations with the Eastern bloc. A state-of-the-art museum and memorial to the 1944 uprising was only opened in 2004. The tension between commemoration of Jewish suffering and Polish martyrdom was also evident in many other locations. As government priorities shifted, the balance was tipped.

The former slave labor and extermination camps of Treblinka were officially declared national monuments in 1964. Relatively well-funded by the regional government and readily accessible from Warsaw, Treblinka nevertheless remained, in contrast to Auschwitz, a somewhat marginal site. A monument to the murdered Jews was designed by Adam Haupt and Franciszek Duszenko and opened in May 1964. A vast field of jagged stones, reminiscent of a graveyard of broken headstones, bearing the names not of individuals but of whole communities, sprawls across the terrain. A carved menorah highlights the fact that the victims of extermination were overwhelmingly Jewish. Yet at the unveiling of the memorial, journalists covering the event stuck with the politically dominant line in mid-1960s Poland, referring to "nationalities" rather than religion, with press coverage speaking of "citizens of European nations" who perished there.[12]

Jews from around the world subsequently contributed memorial stones, demonstrating a sense of connection internationally. It is now estimated that somewhere between 780,000 and 800,000 Jews died at Treblinka—the second largest number of Jewish victims after Auschwitz-Birkenau. Today, Jewish groups, organized for example through March of the Living, often visit Treblinka—but usually on the way to Auschwitz. Those who walk along the trail beyond the site of the extermination camp—a trail scattered with the ashes of the dead—to the separate labor camp will see a field of traditionally Christian symbols. Crosses, fresh flowers on graves, sometimes photographs of the deceased, bear witness to active commemoration by relatives of the ten thousand Catholic Poles who lost their lives in the quarry here. While communities with a personal connection to the site therefore clearly remain active, there does not appear to be much by way of wider international interest. Despite Treblinka's significance, it has relatively few visitors compared with Auschwitz and has not become an international site of remembrance of the same order.

Even further off the tourist trail, buried in the forests and far from view, is the Sobibór extermination camp. Tucked away close to the contemporary border of Poland with Ukraine and Belarus, the site is accessible by a bumpy, potholed single-lane road through dense woodland. Its isolation supports the prevalent German claim that they "knew nothing about it." Sobibór was not merely relatively inaccessible; it was also barely present in public discourse for many years after the war. This was partly because it had already been closed down following the uprising of 1943. Unlike camps liberated by British, American, and Soviet troops—Bergen-Belsen, Dachau, Majdanek, Auschwitz—where photos and news stories drew attention to atrocities, the mass killings in Sobibór did not become more widely publicized until the Hagen trial in 1965–66. In the 1980s, a number of films and documentaries were made about the uprising; audiences now gained a glimpse into the difficulties of revolt and confirmation that Jews did not, as one critique would have it, all go "like lambs to the slaughter." A 1987 British film, *Escape from Sobibor*, directed by Jack Gold and based extensively on the account by the survivor Thomas (Toivi) Blatt, offers one prominent example.[13] Less well known is the film produced by Lily van den Bergh and Pavel Kogan, released in Germany in 1989 under the title *Aufstand in Sobibor* (Uprising in Sobibór), using interviews made on the forty-fifth anniversary with key participants in the revolt, including Alexander Pechersky, the Soviet soldier of Jewish descent who had provided the crucial military leadership. Claude Lanzmann, who had filmed in Sobibór while making his epic *Shoah* (1985), subsequently released a film on the uprising, entitled *Sobibór, October 14, 1943, 4 p.m.*, first shown in 2001. In different ways each of these gave Sobibór a place in popular historical consciousness.

Yet even while the uprising entered the public imagination, memorialization at the site itself did not reflect this. The sign erected by the communist government spoke of nationalities, rather than Jewish identity, and the Catholic Church used some of the terrain. In 1986 the Capuchin order opened a church on the site, including a life-size wooden statue of Father Kolbe.[14] A kindergarten and a children's playground were also built. As Blatt commented, "Not only had life been taken from the Jews at Sobibór, but now the memory of their very existence was being erased." Blatt and others were determined to rectify this situation. In 1987, he founded and became chair of the Holocaust Sites Preservation Committee. Seven years later, Blatt and his colleagues managed to have Sobibór designated as a historical landmark; the kindergarten was closed and its building repurposed as a museum. They finally also succeeded in having the commemoration plaque altered—which was, in Blatt's view, "the most difficult task."[15] And in 1993, on the fiftieth anniversary of the revolt, there was a commemoration ceremony attended by members of the Polish government. Letters were read out from, among others, the Polish president and former leader of Solidarity, Lech Wałęsa, as well as the prime minister; speakers in person included, as Blatt proudly recalled, "Marek Edelman, second-in-command in the Warsaw ghetto revolt, representatives of the government, military commanders, a rabbi and a Catholic bishop."[16]

Blatt and others managed to rectify memorial activity at the site. Even so, for the next two decades, Sobibór did not attract wider public attention. At the time of my visit in 2013, the site was relatively deserted. The small building of the former kindergarten—little more than a wooden shack—that had then served as a museum had been temporarily closed in 2011, with a sign directing visitors to call the district museum in Włodawa, the county town several miles away. Other than a couple of locals drinking beer, there was no one at the railway sidings that had brought some two hundred thousand or more people here to be murdered. Within the campgrounds, there remained the memorial erected in 1965, and there were some signs of work by the Włodawa Museum's Sobibór branch. Recent personal memorialization largely came from the Netherlands, from where more than thirty-four thousand Jews had been deported to Sobibór in the summer of 1943, including 1,200 children from the camp of Vught. Dutch families had erected small stones along a pathway through the camp; the Dutch government also provided financial support.

In 2012 Sobibór became a branch of the Majdanek State Museum, which meant an injection of new resources and professional attention. Long-overdue archaeological investigations were launched, and a new visitors' center was designed. By 2014, archaeologists had uncovered the foundations of the gas chambers, adding further "authentic" remains of public interest. But it remains doubtful that Sobibór will find an easy place on the tourist tracks, given its location and lack of easy access.

A speedier and more prominent outcome can be traced for the third of the Operation Reinhard camps, Bełżec.[17] After its closure, the site was looted by local people looking for valuables—gold teeth, money—that the Nazis might have missed. There were only two known survivors, neither of whom was subsequently in a position to urge memorialization—Chaim Hirszman was murdered in 1946 before he could complete his testimony, and Rudolf Reder, who had written a report in 1946 and made a deposition for the Bełżec trial, was elderly and living in Canada, dying at the age of eighty-seven in 1968.[18] Neither of them, nor relatives of the half million or so people murdered there, had the opportunity or desire to erect a memorial on a site where the buildings had been razed and grassed over, then dug over and over again by local treasure hunters.

Bełżec lay abandoned for decades. As was the case with Sobibór, the 1965 Bełżec trial brought the site greater attention and prompted the erection of a small memorial. Again, though, it promoted the idea of "nations" and underplayed the fact that the vast majority of its victims were Jews.

Fuller recognition accompanied the collapse of communism and was again spearheaded by people with a sense of personal connection. In 1995 the American Jewish Committee and the Polish Council for the Protection of Memory of Struggle and Martyrdom signed an agreement to erect a new memorial. This was an initiative prompted largely by Miles Lerman, a member of the advisory board of the United States Holocaust Memorial Museum, whose family had originated nearby; most of Lerman's close relatives had been murdered in Bełżec.[19] On January 1, 2004, Bełżec was formally incorporated into the Majdanek State Museum, and on June 3, 2004, a state-of-the-art memorial and museum at the site was opened, combining high quality aesthetic and poetic memorialization with an informative exhibition. Overall, in 2016 the sites run by Majdanek had 213,237 visitors; although no separate figure for Bełżec is given, it is unlikely that many of these visitors will have made it that far. Despite organized school trips and visits by youth groups, Bełżec generally appears relatively deserted.[20]

Another key site is Chełmno (Kulmhof). Despite its historical significance as the first dedicated extermination facility located in one place, and despite the number of victims—probably in the region of a quarter of a million, similar to the numbers killed in Sobibór—Chełmno remained a marginal site of remembrance. As with Bełżec, there were very few survivors—perhaps seven in all. And there were very few remaining physical traces. The mansion (or "palace") into which people had been herded, and from which they entered the gas vans, had been destroyed by the Nazis in April 1943. Local residents soon scavenged materials from the remnants of the building.[21] The significance of this site was at first not recognized, and the last remaining gas van was not even preserved. When a memorial stone was placed there in 1957, the inscription, once again, did not mention the predominantly Jewish character of the victims. The mass graves in the nearby forest did however attract attention, and there were early memorialization initiatives, particularly on the part of local communities. Even so, these were poorly funded and uncoordinated. Eventually, in 1964—coinciding with the twenty-fifth anniversary of the outbreak of the Second World War, and at around the same time as the erection of memorials in Sobibór and Bełżec—a large monument was unveiled. In 1987 a museum was finally established, and serious archaeological investigation of the site began. The museum formally opened in 1990.

A striking feature at Chełmno is the long, high Wall of Remembrance, on which it is possible to put up photographs and plaques commemorating individuals and families. Many of the victims brought from the Łódź ghetto had initially been deported from further afield, including German Jews from Hamburg, and the circles of remembrance began to spread across borders. Israel's chief rabbi and the Israeli ambassador in Poland visited on the occasion of the fiftieth anniversary of the liquidation of the Łódź ghetto, further attracting international attention to the site. The Chełmno Museum claims some fifty thousand visitors annually.

The Jewish heritage in Poland has also attracted increasing attention. In Warsaw, the POLIN Museum of the History of Polish Jews opened its exhibition in October 2014. All across Poland, there have been movements to revive Jewish culture and to engage in projects recognizing the Jewish contribution to Polish life over the centuries. The lively tourist trade that has sprung up in some areas, such as Krakow's old Jewish quarter of Kazimierz, has stirred controversy. Lisa Appignanesi's novel *The Memory Man*, for example, depicts the contrast between the genuine "memory journey" of the principal protagonist and the brash realities of the tourist trade.[22] Public interest in this area was boosted by Spielberg's film *Schindler's List* (1993), based on Thomas Keneally novel *Schindler's Ark*.

However, it is the sites of extermination and resistance that have attracted most attention, while slave labor sites, such as Heinkel's works for aircraft manufacture in an underground salt mine, remain in oblivion. Similarly, most of the thousands of labor sub-camps—some larger, some very small, and some longer-lived than others—remain unmarked, only the most assiduous historical tourist with detailed prior knowledge can hope to find specific locations.

One issue involves the problematic legacy of ambivalence among Christian Poles, who under the Nazis had been caught between oppression and collaboration. The massacre in 1941 of Polish Jews by their Christian neighbors in Jedwabne, described in Jan Gross's 2001 book *Neighbors*, prompted a storm of controversy.[23] A film inspired by this story, *Aftermath* (2012), directed by Władysław Pasikowski, reignited bitter debates. Memorials to the Jews killed in Jedwabne were defaced with swastikas, and one of the (non-Jewish) actors in the *Aftermath* film was subjected to antisemitic attacks. The debate on how the memorial should refer to the perpetrators (Germans?

local Poles?) was bitterly contested.[24] Gross and other scholars have been subjected to police investigations, challenging historians' attempts to pursue the truth about the past.

Elsewhere in Poland, there is often little or nothing to record the events of the Nazi period. Where there are memorials, they generally involve personal connections and community identification. In Trawniki, a small obelisk stands near the site of the former camp and the fields in which thousands were killed. There are two plaques on the memorial. The one placed by the communists speaks of the "international" character of the labor camp. The other pays tribute to the Jews killed in the so-called Harvest Festival massacre of November 3, 1943, when between six thousand and ten thousand Jews were shot into long trenches and their bodies subsequently burned, with the smoke and stench blighting the area for days afterward. This memorial was funded by one of the few survivors of the camp, David Efrati, who later made his way to Israel.[25] This double commemoration—the communist-era reference to workers of numerous nationalities and the individual Jewish initiative to remember the Jewish victims—is fairly typical. But this site—where there is really nothing more to see, and which requires the use of old maps and photos to figure out what might have happened where—is not a landscape where the past can become present for casual visitors. Even the monument itself is easily overlooked.

The former Łódź ghetto is now a somewhat rundown area of the modern city; current residents appear to have little interest in being burdened by the ghosts of a past for which they were not responsible. There are individual plaques on significant buildings of the former ghetto and a massive communist-era memorial to murdered Polish children; there are also small memorials in the area where the Roma and Sinti were held. A far more substantial memorial is on the edge of the ghetto at the small railway station, now no longer in use, of Radegast, from which Jews were deported to Chełmno, Auschwitz, and elsewhere. Built through a largely private initiative, funded by a major Jewish benefactor, Josef Buchmann—himself born in Łódź and whose family perished, while he survived Bergen-Belsen—this includes a museum as well as an authentic railway wagon, and it supports commemoration as well as research into individual fates.

Similar initiatives are to be found across Poland. But in the face of the enormity of the crimes and the sheer extent of the terrain over which terror reigned, there is no way that all sites could be adequately memorialized. When Irene Eber returned to Dębica in September 1980 to search for traces of the ghetto from which she had escaped and where she last saw her father, she found nothing.[26] The former marketplace had become merely a park; no one seemed "plagued by unerasable memories" of the sort from which she suffered.[27] Eber searched in vain for any sign of the former ghetto, a plaque or marker. It was only as she smelled "the unmistakable aroma of fresh bread" emanating from a bakery that she realized, suddenly, that this street "had been the dividing line between the Polish section and the ghetto, with the fence running down the middle."[28] She was suddenly certain that "directly across the street from the bakery is more or less exactly the spot where our rat-infested shack must have been." She wondered "whether any of the elderly people in the park still remember the ghetto and its suffering humanity." She concluded that, unlike her, they probably did not: "For some, forgetting is easy."[29] All other signs had been obliterated.

Not even physical markers on selected sites could preserve a past that had been terminated, a past that had held no future. Eber's depiction of her child-hood friend Tośka, who as a young teenager had been gassed in Bełżec, serves as a more powerful reconstruction and preservation of a unique human being than any plaque simply bearing her name could have been.[30] And there is nothing that can be said or displayed that makes up for these losses.

And what of Mielec, where on March 9, 1942, the first selection for slave labor or deportation to a dedicated extermination site in the General Government took place? In the town's marketplace, where the people were gathered and the first selections made, there is nothing at all to alert visitors to its past. Where the synagogue once stood, there is a large memorial stone with no inscription (and defaced, when I visited in 2014, with a crudely reversed swastika). Somewhere between the town center and the Heinkel aircraft works, a vacant plot was bought in what is now a housing develop-ment, located where a group of stragglers had been shot during the deport-ation. On this plot, which appears only occasionally tended—grass and bushes were growing wild when I visited—Jewish families from around the world have erected memorials to relatives and the Mielec Jewish commu-nity. And near the former Heinkel aircraft factory—now the Euro-Park—there is a lone memorial, difficult to find among the bushes, erected in the mid-1970s by a Polish youth group to commemorate young workers who had died there, a sign of identification with a similar community of young laborers across the years. There is nothing, as far as I could discover, to record the location of the concentration camp over which Josef Schwammberger had reigned. I was told by a helpful local worker that members of the older generation still know the sites of mass graves in the nearby woods and take their grandchildren to see the places, but with the passage of generations, this knowledge will die. It is unlikely that any memorial will be constructed to mark the graves of the victims shot by Rudolf Zimmerman and others.

Oblivion is the price of reconciliation. Nearby, in Czermin, a polished stone was erected in the German graveyard to commemorate the Hohenbach German Colony, 1783–1944. In this cemetery, the gravestones—all lying sideways, as if flattened by local anger at some point—mark the graves of ethnic Germans from this colony, including members of the Zimmermann family. The speech delivered on May 11, 2013, by an American descendant of Hohenbach Germans, Alfred Konrad, on the unveiling of the memorial, emphasized the sufferings of Germans who had been forced to flee as the Red Army advanced, and also mentioned the "madman" Adolf Hitler.[31] But the involvement of members of the German colony in the roundups and murder of the local Jewish community received no mention at all.

It is, after all, always easier to remember victims than to cope with the difficult issue of perpetrators.

The Commemoration of Shame: Berlin and Beyond

Heinz Heger, who had been sent to Flossenbürg because of his growing friendship with another young man, was made to work in a quarry for granite for German motorway bridges. Writing of his experiences and reflecting on the affluent Germany of the late 1960s, Heger was bitter about the hidden significance of the environment:

> What car driver today, hurtling along the German motorways, knows that each block of granite has the blood of innocent men on it? Men who did nothing wrong, but who were hounded to death in concentration camps solely for reason of their religion, their origin, their political views or their feeling for their own sex. Each of the granite pillars that hold up the motorway bridges cost the lives of untold victims—a sea of blood and a mountain of human corpses. Today people are only too willing to throw a cloak of silence and forgetfulness over all these things.[32]

The situation is now very different. Germany's capital city, Berlin, has become the commemoration capital of the world, certainly as far as public displays of shame, remorse, and responsibility are concerned. Most nations commemorate their heroes and martyrs; contemporary Germany, by contrast, displays the enormity of its crimes. But even as memorials to the victims spread across Germany, there remains a difficult issue, only slowly being addressed: the representation of perpetrators.

Public responsibility for the Nazi past was established in West Germany under Konrad Adenauer in the 1950s. As we have seen, this was not entirely realized in practice as far as justice through the courts was concerned, nor were all victims recognized as entitled to compensation. Over time, the generally conservative members of the 1944 July Plot to assassinate Hitler were celebrated, along with selected individuals, including the predominantly Catholic White Rose youth group around Sophie and Hans Scholl, and the significance of "civil courage" in assisting or hiding Jews was increasingly emphasized. Yet even if responsibility for the Nazi past became central to West German identity and public culture, questions of guilt did not become a significant feature of topographical landscapes of memory until the 1980s.

While West Germany tended to evade the question of guilt by focusing predominantly on shame and responsibility, East Germany had a political script centering on resistance rather than remorse. Styling itself the "antifascist state," the GDR emphasized communist heroism, as in the ubiquitous memorials to the murdered communist leader Ernst Thälmann. Memorials at former concentration camp sites within the GDR—Ravensbrück, Sachsenhausen, Buchenwald—prioritized heroic sculptures and memorials to communist resistance, including Fritz Cremer's massive 1958 sculpture in Buchenwald, which somewhat unrealistically portrayed heroic resistance even on the part of prisoners barely able to rise from their knees. But commemoration of Jewish victims was downplayed, and until the 1987 Olof Palme Peace March to Ravensbrück there was barely a whisper of recognition regarding victims on grounds of sexual orientation. Nor did other victims tend to feature much in the memorial landscape.

Such emphases on both sides allowed very narrow definitions of guilt, and a correspondingly limited portrayal of perpetrators in East and West— monopoly capitalism and "fascism" on the communist view, or the demons around Hitler and the SS in Western portrayals. The roles of far larger segments of the population were not easily incorporated in essentially dichotomous portrayals of victimhood and resistance.

This started to change when, following unification, Berlin was chosen as the capital of the new Germany.[33] Along with debates over how to "remember" the recently defunct East German dictatorship—largely symbolized by the Berlin Wall and the hated State Security Service, or Stasi—came a wave of confrontation with Nazism. The mid-1990s saw a renewed concern with perpetrators, including debates over Daniel Jonah Goldhagen's *Hitler's Willing Executioners* and the provocative traveling exhibition *The Crimes of the Wehrmacht*.[34] Yet despite such openness, such apparent eagerness for discussion and willing confrontation with challenging questions—often covering ground long familiar to historians—the translation of scholarly research on perpetrators into the more enduring memorial landscape remained problematic. It was easier to continue the emphasis on resistance and remembering the victims, fueled by a culture of shame and remorse.

Right in Berlin's center, close to the Brandenburg Gate and the Reichstag, the controversial Memorial to the Murdered Jews of Europe opened in May 2005. Arising from an initiative spearheaded by Lea Rosh—who had changed her name to one that sounded more "Jewish"—and in collaboration with the historian Eberhard Jaeckel, this vast arena of 2,711 concrete blocks of varying sizes set in undulating terrain disorientates visitors and recalls for some a massive cemetery. It demonstrates strong identification on the part of significant numbers of the descendants of Nazis with the Jewish victims of their forebears.[35] The relevance for other groups, such as Germans of Turkish descent, was not always clear, as a distinctive "ethnic" sense of what it meant to be German was implicitly embodied in this emphasis on inherited shame.[36] The memorial is accompanied by an underground exhibition portraying victims' fates across Europe. While it clarifies precisely *what* happened, with well-selected examples, it does not seek to answer comprehensively the questions of *how* this was possible, or *who* was responsible. Nor was this necessarily its aim. Both this memorial and the building designed by Daniel Libeskind for the Jewish Museum Berlin serve to evoke the magnitude of suffering and induce a sense of imbalance and disorientation, provoking visitors to reflect on the fractured experiences of the victims. More broadly, such memorials may arouse emotions and stimulate collective engagement, with intellectual curiosity about details satisfied elsewhere. Conversely, however, they may through the concentration of collective remembrance risk displacing individual engagement with the past.

These are not the only forms of memorial. On a far smaller scale, the ubiquitous "stumbling stones," or *Stolpersteine*, remind passersby of former residents who were victims of Nazi persecution. Originally conceived by the artist Gunter Demnig in 1993, the first stumbling stone was laid in

Berlin's Kreuzberg district in 1996. Initially deemed illegal, this single small sign combining personal tragedy and historical enormity was subsequently given permission to remain—a very German procedure. Since 2000, the movement to install the little square brass plaques into pavements spread widely; by the end of 2017, there were innumerable Stolpersteine not only in Berlin but also in around 1,100 other places in Germany and twenty other European countries.[37] These inscribed brass stones replace cobblestones in the pavements, bearing names of individuals who formerly lived there, their birth and death dates (where known), and a brief indication of their ultimate fates. These stones not only reinscribe individual names at a place that was a home of their own choosing but also implicitly indict former neighbors—those who, watching from windows all around, must have been able to register the violent uprooting and sudden disappearance of fellow residents.

Berlin also was, of course, the capital of the perpetrators. A few sites serve to remind people of ways in which the Reich functioned and the machinery of mass murder was put into operation.[38] The Topography of Terror is based on the site of the former Gestapo headquarters in Prinz-Albrecht-Straße. This was initially established as a temporary exhibition, mounted despite significant resistance, when the cellars of the Gestapo headquarters were discovered in 1987 on a piece of land hard up against the Berlin Wall. It has since established itself as a major center, housing not only a permanent exhibition, including details about the notorious Reich Security Main Service (RSHA) headed by Heinrich Himmler, but also changing exhibits, accompanied by book presentations, public lectures, and other events. And on the leafy, lakeside outskirts of Berlin, at the so-called House of the Wannsee Conference, there is a museum focused on the fateful meeting in January 1942 when the details of the "final solution of the Jewish question" were discussed and coordinated among a group of senior bureaucrats, including Adolf Eichmann, and chaired by Reinhard Heydrich.

Beyond these sites, perpetrators do not tend to take center stage in the memorial landscape of Berlin, nor elsewhere in Germany or Austria. There are significant places associated with perpetrators, including notably Hitler's former Eagle's Nest high up in the mountains in Berchtesgaden and sites in Munich associated with the NSDAP, not to mention the landscapes of power designed for the Nazi party rallies in Nuremberg. For decades, a careful balance had to be maintained between desires to obliterate potential shrines for continuing admirers of Nazism while not destroying all traces of "authentic sites" in service of education for the future. Different political parties and groups had conflicting interests, and local power struggles determined the outcomes; and again, generational shifts played a role. Despite more open confrontations with an ever-receding past, memorialization at significant "perpetrator sites" and "places of National Socialist self-representation" remains deeply contentious.[39]

Former concentration camps continue to place the emphasis on violence and the suffering of victims, and the portrayal of perpetrators remains problematic. Experts are sensitive to questions about the implications of misrepresentation, and particularly questions around data-protection laws and personal privacy. There is a fine line to be drawn in seeking to avoid the obvious extremes: portraying perpetrators as "monsters" whom we condemn but cannot understand, or presenting empathetic portrayals of "ordinary" individuals that might "normalize" violence or garner misplaced sympathy. Some sites, notably the former concentration camps at Neuengamme and Ravensbrück, have taken significant initiatives toward a fuller representation of perpetrators. Ravensbrück, for example, includes individual profiles of female guards in an exhibition within one of the former SS blocks. Neuengamme displays selected perpetrator profiles and also, recognizing the significance in personal and family life, devotes time and resources to working with descendants of perpetrators.[40] Increasingly, too, concentration camp exhibitions, such as the one that opened at Buchenwald in 2016, seek to highlight the ways in which camps were embedded within wider networks of exploitation, with sub-camps and the use of slave laborers in agricultural and industrial production—not merely known to locals, but also profitable to many of them.

In Austria, the Mauthausen concentration camp displays individual profiles of SS guards, including details on postwar fates, with a related publication in 2016—the first of its kind for this camp.[41] Notably, the Melk sub-camp already began to develop an exhibition including perpetrator profiles in 1992—the first sub-camp in Austria to do so.[42] Others now also have exhibitions that point the finger at those responsible, including one sited within the dark, cold entrance tunnel to the underground works in Ebensee, another of Mauthausen's sub-camps. Here visitors feel the chill and are exposed to the moisture constantly dripping from the walls and roof—an experience in marked contrast to trying to imagine the former camp outside, the traces of which have been largely obliterated by a housing development built over the destroyed grounds of prisoners' barracks. Only the former camp entrance gate remains—an odd way for contemporary residents to enter their housing quarter.

This is a transitional moment in terms of the passing of the perpetrator generation and growing public representation of those who were responsible for violence or sustained the system. Even highly sophisticated representations, however, raise questions around the balance between remembrance, education, and the rights of those living later in what are still historically resonant places.

Nothing in this area is straightforward. The focus on the most significant concentration camps and public memorials as sites for remembrance of victims, along with specific "perpetrator sites" for pointing the finger at leading Nazis, may run the risk of reproducing easy contrasts while still deflecting attention from the range of people involved on the perpetrator side. But many sites, including large concentration camps as well as a multitude of sub-camps, raise the question of the roles and reactions of local bystanders at the time. The significance of the bystander society is not so easily represented.

There is also the question of how many sites can serve as exemplary or representative, standing in for so many more, and how much should remain unmarked across the "contaminated landscapes" of the European continent.[43] Throughout eastern Europe, for example, despite local narratives and vivid depictions of the swathe of tragedies in these "bloodlands," such sites have only recently attracted attention.[44] Nor were these the only sites of killings in plain sight. Within the heart of the former Reich, in Germany and Austria, at the sides of roads and fields, in barns and in villages, where victims of the death marches collapsed or were shot, there are innumerable unmarked places where thousands of people died in the last months of the war. There are growing efforts by concerned citizens to erect small memorials at such sites, but there is again a compromise between the competing demands of remembrance and the present. Visitors and residents in southern Bavaria today will want to enjoy the beauties of the Starnberger Lake, the picturesquely painted old houses with balconies bedecked with flowers in Wolfratshausen or Bad Tölz, the idyllic cycling and hiking paths along the banks of the "green Isar" river in the foothills of the Alps, without constant reminders of the murders that happened there. And cyclists along the Danube path in Austria might generally prefer to enjoy stopping to admire the Melk monastery without necessarily also visiting the crematorium of the former Mauthausen sub-camp, let alone heading out to a nearby village and exploring through deserted undergrowth to find the half-covered and strictly forbidden entrance to the former tunnels in the hillside, where so many labored and died—and to whom there is no memorial.

The same is true of industry in Germany, powerhouse of the European economy. There is relatively little memorialization of forced and slave laborers at the sites of their exploitation. The vast majority of enterprises that made their profits on the backs of slave laborers managed to avoid admitting legal liability, and some even evaded acknowledgment of moral responsibility or obligation to provide compensation. Only belatedly did some commission company histories that opened up the Nazi years to honest scrutiny. In major enterprises with a Nazi heritage, small plaques may now remind a visitor who has managed both to gain entry and to locate the signs that these businesses profited from the exploitation, oppression, and suffering of slave laborers. So while the little *Stolpersteine* draw awareness to the ubiquitous presence of "bystanders," there is little in the memorial landscape to raise awareness of the significance of profiteers, industrialists, and commercial beneficiaries.

There are some more complicated categories of victims, as far as remembrance is concerned. The German Army today sees its mission as primarily defensive and democratic, combining responsible citizenship with support of peace. There is little to draw public attention to the role of the Nazi Wehrmacht at the prisoner of war camps for which it was responsible and where, in particular, Soviet prisoners died in horrific numbers because of poor conditions, disease, and willful starvation.[45]

Memorials to those Germans and Austrians who died—willingly or unwillingly—as soldiers in service of the "fatherland" also remain problematic. Even so, lists of the "fallen" are to be found in innumerable villages and towns, particularly poignant in small communities where it is clear that a whole generation of fathers, brothers, and sons disappeared in the maelstrom of war.

And now, even deserters from the German army, shot in the last days of the war, are receiving belated recognition as victims of Nazism. There appears to be little end in sight to the wave of memorialization.

Contested Victimhood and Marginalized Victims

An increasing number of previously marginalized victim groups have come into view. While from the 1970s onward the Jewish catastrophe, the Holocaust or Shoah, has received an overwhelming share of attention, internationally as well as in Germany, the fates of other victim groups remained less visible for a while longer. Attitudes toward homosexuals, Roma and Sinti, and people with physical and mental disabilities changed only relatively slowly, and associated sites of remembrance raised different questions than those for the Jewish victims of Nazi persecution.

Victims of Nazi homophobia continued to suffer discrimination after the end of the war and remained "in the closet" while same-sex relationships were still subject to criminal proceedings. Public remembrance of their fates under Nazi rule was understandably not on the agenda while these laws remained in force. From the 1980s, however, activists began to urge the erection of memorials to victims of Nazi homophobia. These activists were largely members of younger generations from communities who identified with the victims; victims of homophobia generally had neither families nor powerful interest groups willing to speak up for them. Even in the still-communist GDR, there were activists seeking wider acceptance in the present and belated recognition of persecution under Nazism, as on the 1987 Olof Palme Peace March to Ravensbrück.[46] It was far easier, however, to demonstrate in public and demand recognition and remembrance in the West.

Even so, there was opposition—including, remarkably, from other victim groups. In Dachau, attempts to get a memorial to murdered gay men were opposed by the Comité International de Dachau until the mid-1990s. In 1985 the aptly named Protestant Church of Reconciliation (Versöhnungskirche), located within the Dachau memorial site area, agreed to erect a pink triangle with the inscription: "Beaten to death—silenced to death. To the homosexual victims of National Socialism" (*Totgeschlagen—totgeschwiegen. Den homosexuellen Opfern des Nationalsozialismus*). Only in 2002, with a new exhibition at the Dachau memorial museum, did gay men finally get explicitly named alongside other groups of victims.[47] The period from the mid-1980s to the mid-1990s was crucial in other places too, where similar pink triangle memorials bearing variations on this inscription were placed, including one in Cologne that arose from the initiative of a local lesbian and gay rights group. A small memorial plaque to homosexual victims of Nazism, similar to the one in Dachau, was erected in 1989 at Berlin's Nollendorfplatz, the center of a formerly flourishing gay culture in the 1920s immortalized in the writings of Christopher Isherwood—but only after some considerable opposition on the part of Berlin's transport authority, the BVG, about the use of one of its buildings for this purpose.[48] People who had been criminalized on grounds of their sexuality were retrospectively pardoned in the twenty-first century, encouraging some by now very elderly survivors to tell their stories.[49]

The government of the Federal Republic was finally receptive to demands for a memorial, and, despite controversy, plans got underway in Berlin. The official memorial to homosexual victims of Nazi persecution, a four-meter-high rectangular block sited on the margins of Berlin's Tiergarten, just opposite the Memorial to the Murdered Jews of Europe, was opened in May 2008—appropriately enough, by the first openly gay mayor of Berlin, Klaus Wowereit. Its slightly hidden location is arguably apposite, as is the scale of the memorial. Even so, it inevitably aroused controversy. The glass pane through which visitors have to peer to see film footage of same-sex relationships was smashed by vandals on a couple of occasions after its opening. Those identifying with other victim groups also challenged its presence at this location. The Jewish historian and Holocaust survivor Israel Gutman, for example, felt it was inappropriate to link the suffering of homosexuals with the mass murder of millions of Jews by topographical proximity.[50] Furthermore, the way in which viewers are invited to challenge their own possibly persisting prejudices by "peeping" through a viewing hole at scenes of gay and lesbian couples remains contentious.

These developments were not limited to Germany. In 2003, the United States Holocaust Memorial Museum finally drew attention to this as yet underrepresented group with a traveling exhibition about gay victims of Nazi persecution.[51] And in 2014 Israel too erected a memorial.[52]

Roma and Sinti victims of Nazi persecution also belatedly received recognition and physical commemoration. From the 1980s, there were a number of local initiatives, stimulated and realized by the insistence of individual persons. In the GDR, a campaign led by Reimar Gilsenach led to the opening, in 1986, of a memorial near the site of the former camp in the north Berlin suburb of Marzahn where Gypsies were held and from which many were deported to Auschwitz. Though Gilsenbach was not entirely happy with the phrasing of the memorial plaque, which had been designed by the communist party and predictably praised the role of the "glorious Soviet Army" in "liberating our people," this was a significant achievement in the circumstances. Even so, sited toward the back end of a side path of a large cemetery, it remains difficult to find and hardly commands wide attention.

A more informative display on the partially built-over site of the former camp, in a remaining small open space near the Marzahn S-Bahn station, now provides more details on the camp and the lives of some who suffered there. Plaques were also put up in significant locations in Western Germany in the mid-1990s, again as a result of individual initiatives, including school competitions; and in 2001, in both Cologne and Hamburg, plaques were erected at the sites of former camps to remember Roma and Sinti victims.[53]

A national memorial for the Roma and Sinti was opened in Berlin by Chancellor Angela Merkel in October 2012. Located in the trees near the Reichstag, with a tranquil pond surrounded by stones bearing the names of places where Roma and Sinti perished, the memorial is peaceful. *Mare Manuschenge*, an evocative piece of violin music composed by the musician and activist for Roma and Sinti rights Romeo Franz can be heard when visitors enter the open spot among the trees. Yet despite strenuous efforts by many concerned citizens, Roma and Sinti remain marginalized, and the memorial was desecrated in October 2015 with the daubing of a slogan accompanied by a large swastika.[54]

In September 2014, a memorial to the victims of Nazi euthanasia polices was established at the edge of the Tiergarten, at the location of the building in which the policy had been masterminded and after which the T4 program had been named.[55] The first two memorials on this spot dated back to 1989. One was an inscribed paving stone—much like a flat gravestone—on the ground at the back of a bus stop, easily overlooked by passersby and often covered in leaves. The other was Richard Serra's sculpture entitled *Berlin Junction*, originally intended to signify the division of Berlin but relocated here after 1989; it bore little evidence of relevance to euthanasia. Those with personal connections to euthanasia victims began to raise their voices, and the Topography of Terror (the institution in the former Gestapo headquarters) invited a round table discussion in 2007.[56] The debate included Sigrid Falkenstein, who had undertaken research on an aunt, Anna Lehnkering, who had been murdered in Grafeneck. In these and further discussions, representatives of the League of Those Affected by Euthanasia and Compulsory Sterilization (Bund der "Euthanasie"-Geschädigten und Zwangssterilisierten) suggested that a memorial to the victims would not in itself be sufficient. Although they were not given permission to erect a new building, they succeeded in ensuring that an informative display case was placed there, providing details on those involved in masterminding and executing the policies of compulsory euthanasia and sterilization. They also interpreted the notion of victimhood broadly, wanting a memorial to all of those who had been oppressed, humiliated, and murdered by the Nazis and who did not have strong representation by later interest groups, families, or wider communities.[57]

The euthanasia memorial may well prove to be the last of the Tiergarten memorials in what has become an almost congested landscape of remembrance in central Berlin. Meanwhile, memorials to euthanasia victims in the dedicated killing centers still fail to attract much attention.

Chełmno is now relatively deserted. As it is a small village well off any public transport routes and situated in a part of Poland boasting few tourist attractions, it is hardly surprising that there are so few visitors. The same is true for Bełżec or Sobibór, as we have seen. But the small town of Brandenburg on the Havel, where experiments with a stationary gassing facility were first carried out, lies a mere forty or so miles west of Berlin. It is barely half an hour by train from the West Berlin lakeside suburb of Wannsee. Brandenburg, though considerably larger than Chełmno, also has little to attract the tourist. In the quarter of a century after the collapse of communist rule, the town's population dropped by more than one quarter, from over one hundred thousand to a mere seventy-one thousand, as young people moved out in search of better prospects elsewhere. Streets lined with some nicely restored buildings nevertheless remain pockmarked by dilapidated, crumbling facades reminiscent of the dying days of the GDR. The memorial to the victims of Hitler's "euthanasia" program, located at the site of a former prison (and a near neighbor of the former local Stasi headquarters), is not the focus of much attention. Despite its historical significance as the first site in Germany to experiment with mass gassing of victims, the museum at this memorial site was only opened in 2012 and is relatively modest in scope. The space is small; it even begins to feel crowded when two or three other visitors enter. The exhibition provides background information and detailed case studies, complementing the memorial plaques in the former prison yard, now a municipal car park. Yet this was where the use of gas chambers for mass murder that infamously expanded in the extermination camps was first trialed. This is where a specially designed gas chamber was first used within the borders of the Reich to murder people held to be "ballast existences," burdens on and threats to the "racial health" of the Nazi "national community." And this site was in all likelihood chosen for the first experiments in gassing in Germany precisely because of its convenience and proximity to Berlin.[58]

Everywhere, both in the formerly communist East Germany and in the democratic West, there was a lengthy delay in erecting memorials in euthanasia institutions. The different political systems affected the character of memorialization efforts, but both sides showed a marked unwillingness to address this area. With some variations, the sequencing is largely similar: local initiatives for remembrance on a small scale were only much later enhanced by often state-sponsored establishment of official memorial sites. In this way, those who had a sense of responsibility for the past partially displaced or complemented those with personal connections who had first spearheaded projects for remembrance. But this only became possible once those who had been deeply implicated in Nazi crimes had begun to pass from the stage.

Generational changes were highly relevant. After the war, there was minimal denazification of the medical profession in both East and West Germany. Where psychiatric hospitals had continued in use, there were significant continuities in personnel; more broadly, the highly Nazified medical profession was less than willing to examine critically its recent past and continuing mentalities. This meant that murderous practices under the Nazi regime constituted a highly sensitive subject on a personal level, calling attention to the tainted past of professional colleagues. There were early initiatives, but these generally did not go beyond the commemoration of victims. The construction of broader exhibitions often did not begin until the 1980s—which was not only when "hearing the voices of victims" began to take off but also, notably, the period when many professionals whose careers reached back to the Nazi period entered retirement.

These factors were reflected in the histories of memorialization in individual euthanasia centers in both East and West. The regional mental hospital of Bernburg was from 1949 to 1990 located in the GDR. In 1952 the association representing people persecuted under Nazism, the VVN (Vereinigung der Verfolgten des Naziregimes), placed a small urn of ashes in the cellar that had housed the gas chambers. But this received little attention, and there was no public access or display. In the 1960s the director of the Bernburg Hospital for Psychiatry and Neurology, Dr. Jochen Quandt, established a room for remembrance in the cellar and talked with colleagues about what had taken place there during the Nazi period.[59] By the early 1980s—notably, well before the collapse of the GDR—attempts were made to develop a small exhibition, although still not open to the general public. This was expanded in 1988 and reopened in September 1989—at a time of growing debate and political ferment in the GDR, just two months before the fall of the Wall.

Bernburg, still housing a specialist psychiatric clinic, opened a new exhibition in 2006. Conceived as serving educational as well as memorial purposes, it claims to be visited primarily by organized groups in a pedagogical context. Despite its presence on a "dark tourism" website, it does not figure high on itineraries of historically significant sites.[60]

In Sonnenstein-Pirna, changes also took place in the later 1980s. The Sonnenstein euthanasia center was prominent and visible from the town of Pirna, situated on the castle grounds atop a hill above the Elbe River. Yet once the 1947 trial in Dresden had ended, Pirna's murderous past lapsed into relative obscurity. An easily overlooked official memorial plaque was placed by the steps up to the castle in 1973, remembering the "victims of fascist crimes" with no explanation of the specific crimes in Sonnenstein. A schoolteacher in 1987 told one of her pupils, Thomas Schilter, that remembering antifascist resistance fighters had to take priority over other victims. Not satisfied, the young Schilter went about asking local residents of a certain age what they could remember and was astonished at their detailed recollections of the gray buses, the smoke from the chimneys, the sweetish smell of burning flesh, and the SS men patrolling the road up to the castle; they also confirmed that this had been widely spoken about at the time among the townspeople, even if with some caution.[61] Meanwhile, ever since he had taken up his post in 1970s, local pastor Bernd Richter had been concerned at the number of people whose consciences were troubled by what they had seen, known, and in some cases been personally involved in, and who felt they had to talk to someone in complete confidence, without fear of the consequences.[62] Schilter was able, through Leipzig theologian Kurt Nowak's connections in the West (this being before unification), to make contact with the West German journalist and political scientist Götz Aly. Schilter, Richter, and the local Protestant church—which made its community center available—were instrumental in establishing an exhibition and memorial site. In the context of growing debate and a proliferation of grassroots activity in the early autumn of 1989, this initiative even attracted, rather surprisingly, the support of some local politicians. The first exhibition, using documentary materials supplied by Götz Aly, was opened with a lecture by Kurt Nowak on September 1, 1989, exactly fifty years after the date Hitler put on his order "empowering" doctors to kill—and just over two months before the fall of the Wall.[63]

An association of concerned citizens in Pirna as well as relatives of those who had been murdered formed a steering group and advisory board in

1991, and a memorial center was opened in 2000.[64] In order to locate where the gas chamber had been, it was necessary to talk to older citizens, including the widow of the former pastor who had been forced to move because his residence had overlooked the premises. In October 1992 Schilter and West German journalist Ernst Klee explored the cellars; an archaeologist later identified the exact location.[65] By the time the twenty-fifth anniversary of the center was celebrated in 2014, the exhibition was well developed and documented in detail the prehistory and history of the treatment of mentally and physically disabled people on the site. Yet—like so many other centers—despite widespread local interest on its initial opening, it seemed to attract few visitors from further afield.

Despite the different political circumstances in West Germany, the sequencing—from early memorialization of victims to later educational exhibitions drawing attention also to perpetrators—was roughly similar. Hadamar claimed to be the first to have established a memorial to victims of euthanasia in the form of a relief placed in the entrance in 1953 by Dr. Friedrich Stöffler, who later became the second director of the Welfare Association of the State of Hesse (Landesdirektor des Landeswohlfahrtsverbandes Hessen, LWV). In 1964 it was agreed that the cemetery on the hill above the building could be used as a memorial area: some 3,500 victims of euthanasia killings had been buried here in mass graves, beneath a few rows of individual gravestones intended to deceive visitors at the time. This site was cleared and more worthy memorials erected. But, as elsewhere, the real initiative for developing an exhibition open to public viewing was undertaken in the early 1980s, under a new director and with input from university students. In 1983 key rooms in the cellar—gas chamber, dissecting room, and crematorium—were made accessible, in what was claimed as the first memorial site in Germany for euthanasia victims, and in the following years the exhibition was expanded. It has educational as well as memorial functions, focusing on the history as well as providing individual profiles, and drawing attention to the range of people involved in different ways in the hierarchy, as well as postwar failures of justice.[66] Relatively accessible from major cities, including Frankfurt, Hadamar had around eighteen thousand visitors in 2014, a majority of whom were schoolchildren and members of other organized groups.[67]

Similarly in Grafeneck, memorialization was relatively late. Although the cemetery was used as a site of remembrance from 1962 onward, the building that had housed the gas chambers was demolished in 1965. A memorial site was opened in 1990, and from 1995 it established a book of names, seeking to restore some posthumous identity to as many victims as possible. In 2005 a memorial stone was put up to remember the 10,654 people who had been gassed there. In a small exhibition, Grafeneck enumerates some of the perpetrators and provides details of their lives after the war. Still functioning as a site for the care of people with disabilities, Grafeneck also challenges contemporary visitors to confront their own responses to current residents, even as it asks them to learn about the past.[68] In 2014, despite its rural location and relative inaccessibility by public transport, Grafeneck claimed to have somewhere in the region of fifteen thousand visitors annually.[69]

In Austria, the Hartheim Castle euthanasia center first allowed visitors to look at the gas chamber in 1969, but it was only in 1997 that the state of Upper Austria and the Upper Austrian State Welfare Society designed a full exhibition, with research and visitor services. Displays provide evidence of the wide variety of victims here, including plaques to Italian prisoners of war, as well as Protestants and Catholics from Poland as well as Austria and Germany, highlighting the fact that many victims were brought from the nearby Mauthausen concentration camp and far from all were selected for mental or physical disabilities.[70] Considerable controversy was aroused by the decision to complement the main exhibition, which was specific to the crimes committed at Hartheim, with an exhibit on the upper floor entitled *Value of Life*.[71] This explores attitudes and practices toward those designated as "abnormal" from the Enlightenment to the present day, including the prenatal identification of fetuses with abnormalities, raising ethical questions around abortion. Some have seen this as overly Catholic and proselytizing, and inappropriate for a memorial center concerned with Nazi mass murder.

In 1995, on the occasion of the fiftieth anniversary of the end of the war, the Austrian government also provided an official fund to give a "symbolic compensation payment" (*Gestezahlung*) of just over five thousand euros to victims of Nazi persecution from all groups—explicitly mentioning, among others, Sinti and Roma and homosexuals—and including also children and close relatives of victims of Nazi euthanasia and forced sterilization.[72] Associated with these symbolic compensation efforts was an attempt, belatedly, to gather the life stories and "traces" (*Lebensspuren*) of those who had been persecuted.

The reasons for the belated recognition and memorialization of the victims of Nazi euthanasia policies are complex. So many people at the time had suspected what was going on that it is surprising that they continued to entrust their relatives to the dubious care of these killing places—and some subsequently clearly felt a degree of guilt. For other families, memories of lost relatives were still painful and raw. But given so many other priorities, including other wartime bereavements, there was little desire to mark the institution as well as to tend a personal grave, if the ashes had been laid to rest. Added to this, however, is a more compelling reason why, after the war, such institutions did not want to put up plaques and memorials to the tens of thousands who had been murdered in them. The medical professionals and other staff who had worked there during the Third Reich had, as we have seen, barely been affected by postwar attempts to bring them to justice for their misdeeds. The vast majority escaped investigation, let alone legal proceedings or sentencing for their crimes. So when the physicians in charge continued to run their institutions, when the doctors and nurses continued to staff the same wards, when the cooks and builders and transport workers continued to assist in the daily lives of patients, it was scarcely likely that there would be a sudden rush for self-incrimination. Public trust and the continued admission of patients also depended in large measure on a heavy dose of repression and denial. It was only with the passing of generations, as those who had been immediately involved were no longer present, that others began to rescue victims of euthanasia from oblivion—and to point a finger at those who had been responsible for their murder.

Situating the Sites

Place is important only insofar as it has meaning—and meanings are multiple and deeply contested. Places need not even be marked within public landscapes of remembrance for them to be endowed with subjective meaning by those with personal connections to the site.

Philippe Sands, whose grandfather was the only one to survive of a family of some eighty people, made a film, *My Nazi Legacy*, in the company of two men whose fathers had been high-level perpetrators in the region where Sands's family was murdered: Niklas Frank, son of Hans Frank, Nazi governor general of Poland under German occupation, and Horst von Wächter, son of Baron Otto von Wächter, governor of the district of Galicia at the time of the mass murder of the Jews.[73] Together they visited his grandfather's hometown near Lviv (formerly Polish Lwów, German Lemberg) and stood inside the empty, deserted shell of the former synagogue where generations of Sands's family had worshipped. For Sands, this was the place where his family, along with friends and relatives, had last attended Jewish religious services before it was set on fire by the Nazis in 1941; for Niklas Frank, it was a deeply meaningful emptiness, symbolizing the richness of Jewish life and culture that had been extinguished by the Nazis, including his father whom he vehemently rejected; for Horst von Wächter, it was just a building, a physical structure that had endured and would continue into the future. By focusing on the physicality of the place, von Wächter evaded considering both the fates of those for whom it had been a sacred space and the guilt of those in charge of Nazi policies. Responsibility for their fates had for Wächter not been a question of individual choice or legal culpability: when viewed in the long sweep of history, developments here had simply been a matter of "inevitability." Von Wächter's father, on this view, had—like so many Nazis—apparently possessed no agency.

The contrasts between the approaches of the three men became even more striking when, shortly thereafter, they went to a quiet grassy site not far from the town, where the bodies of some 3,500 former Jewish residents still lie in the mass pit into which they were shot. Among these 3,500 are members of Sands's own family, and holding overall command responsibility for the shooting was Horst von Wächter's father. While Niklas Frank was able to confront his own father's guilt, von Wächter, becoming visibly more uncomfortable, still could not acknowledge his father's role. On the occasion of a reunion and ceremonial burial service, von Wächter briefly basked in the warm reception given to him by members of the Ukrainian Galicia SS division established by his father in 1943, which is still seen by some Ukrainian nationalists as significant in the fight against Russian domination. In a deeply problematic moment, in the presence of a person wearing a pendant displaying a swastika, von Wächter reassured himself of his father's fundamental "decency." And while Niklas Frank was willing, in some scenes, to stand or sit in the very places where his father had been, including in the cell in Nuremberg where he had spent his last night before being sent to death on the gallows, von Wächter retreated to the emptiness and escapism of his seventeenth-century castle in Austria with the long-term historical associations that allowed him, again, to evade confrontation with his father's past. Coming together in places where the fates of the three men's families had converged had served only, and despite all they had shared, to separate von Wächter entirely from agreement about the meaning of the past with the others.

The meanings for people who had themselves formerly been victims at these places of persecution are moreover quite different from those ascribed to the sites by people who come later to look and learn, and by people who lived alongside the sites or were relatively untouched. The reactions of local residents to the former women's concentration camp of Ravensbrück, for example, were strikingly at variance with some of the memories of former prisoners, as well as the commercial and municipal interests that surfaced at the time of controversy over the proposed opening of a supermarket at the edge of the current memorial site.[74] Young Germans doing alternative military service often work for organizations promoting reconciliation, such as Aktion Sühnezeichen: Friedensdienste (Action for Reconciliation: Service for Peace), assisting in the preservation of memorial sites. These activities are not without their critics; Ruth Klüger, for example, is somewhat bitter about the ways in which these generations, however well-meaning, could never really imagine or understand what had formerly gone on in such places.[75]

What is shown, what is selected for display and what suppressed—what can be "viewed"—varies according to personal memories and later viewpoints. Pierre Seel, imprisoned as a teenager by the Nazis for his homosexuality, returned with a group to visit the site of his torments in the former concentration camp of Schirmeck in Alsace in 1989, where he had been forced to watch his friend Jo, the love of his life, being torn apart and eaten alive by dogs. He was struck by the absence of physical traces in Schirmeck: the "reality of what had occurred in that place was hypocritically transformed into a symbolic plaque and sculpture; yet we are still haunted by the memory."[76] Seel made an immense personal contribution by bringing the plight of gay men to wider public attention. But the climate remained hostile, even in the 1990s. The only possibility for Seel was now that of purely personal and private remembrance:

> When I am overcome with rage, I take my hat and coat and defiantly walk the streets. I picture myself strolling through cemeteries that do not exist, the resting places of all the dead who barely ruffle the consciences of the living. And I feel like screaming....
> When I have finished wandering, I go home. Then I light the candle that permanently burns in my kitchen when I am alone. That frail flame is my memory of Jo.[77]

In large measure due to the courage of men like Seel and a tiny handful of gay survivors who were now prepared to speak openly—including in the few filmed interviews in *Paragraph 175*—things began to change. In 2003

Seel finally received official recognition as a victim of Nazism. And on the occasion of the French Holocaust Memorial Day in April 2005, just eight months before Seel's death in November that year, the French president Jacques Chirac first publicly mentioned homosexual victims of Nazism.

We find ourselves in an ambivalent and transitional situation. Remembrance of victims has not overcome fear and prejudice: antisemitism, homophobia, discrimination against "traveler" communities, and hostility toward "foreigners" and those seen on whatever grounds as "other" remain very much alive. Populist movements and parties continue to capitalize on social fragility. Nor, despite near universal condemnation of Nazism after its defeat, were the overwhelming majority of perpetrators brought to justice. Despite recent initiatives and renewed energy on this front, it is now definitively too late.

Yet public memorialization continues to mushroom and expand. Sites of remembrance operate within an increasingly transnational context. People travel more easily, and "Holocaust tourism" has taken off. The box office success of Holocaust films has turned some sites into a focus of interest. People of Polish-Jewish descent across the world frequently come to visit their families' former homeland as well as places where relatives suffered and died. Young Jews, including Israeli and American Jews with no direct personal connections, are brought to see Holocaust sites as part of their integration into the wider Jewish community. For many, Poland has in effect displaced Germany as the "hated other"; the record of Germans in terms of reparations, public education, and memorialization of the Holocaust seems to have had some effect, whereas the focus on sites of terror in Poland has brought the context of extermination more sharply into focus.[78]

Meanwhile, those in charge of conserving and developing relevant sites have become increasingly professionalized, participating in international trends and adapting exhibits to prevailing standards. Museums have raised new questions about "authentic" objects, "sacred relics," and how to remember with respect while also educating new generations, among a minefield of potential pitfalls.[79] There have been demands that the "memory" should itself become a shared European and indeed international phenomenon. In 2005, the United Nations designated January 27 an "annual International Day of Commemoration in memory of the victims of the Holocaust," the date also marked in the European Union.[80] Chosen because it marked the liberation of Auschwitz, this day was to be observed in remembrance of all victims of the Holocaust. Observance has been spreading, although knowledge about its significance—or indeed its very existence—varies markedly across European countries. On the occasion of the seventieth anniversary, in 2015, the British media devoted extensive space to remembrance ceremonies and the voices of survivors still able to mark it. Seeing the fewer than three hundred survivors gathered under a tent set up over the infamous ramp and rail tracks in Auschwitz-Birkenau, listening to the speeches and watching the lighting of candles, observers in 2015 could not help but be aware that this was a transitional moment. The inexorable disappearance of the ranks of the survivors from such events signifies the transformation from memory, among those who experienced the past, to education for the future.

But in the meantime, commemoration continued to grow, in an increasing variety of forms. Speeches, television series, public controversies, and other commemorations repeatedly ensured that interpretations of the past could never leave the public sphere, although with significant shifts in emphasis over the decades.[81] What was particularly significant was the growing confrontation between private or family discussions and public representations.

The wave of belated memorialization and associated sensitivities was not unique to Germany. Not only across Europe, where sites of terror and suffering increasingly received markers, but also across the United States numerous memorials were erected. The United States never experienced German invasion or occupation, but its population included significant numbers of families with relatives who were émigrés, refugees, and Holocaust victims as well as eighty thousand or so Jewish DPs who had made it there by the early 1950s. Despite the relatively small percentage of the United States population that is Jewish—around 2 percent, a little over or under according to definition—in terms of overall numbers the United States has one of the two largest Jewish populations in the world, approaching six million, again according to definition, comparable in size to that of Israel. The Holocaust has almost been incorporated as part of the American "heritage," part of the national narrative of diverse identities, challenges, and redemption. In Washington, DC, the United States Holocaust Memorial Museum was established against a backdrop of lengthy debates and controversies.[82] In towns and cities from Boston, Massachusetts, to Houston, Texas, from New Haven, Connecticut, to Los Angeles, California, memorials, museums, and educational centers were founded to ensure public remembrance of the Holocaust. Other victims of Nazi persecution tended to be rather less widely noticed in the United States, although from the 1980s the development of gay rights alongside the devastation caused by HIV/AIDS has led to heightened awareness. In the Pink Triangle Park in the Castro area of San Francisco, where many gay men lived and died when the HIV/AIDS epidemic first engulfed their community, a memorial to the homosexual victims of National Socialism was erected in 2001.

None of this remained uncontroversial. The writer Martin Walser, in his 1998 speech when awarded the Peace Prize of the German Book Trade in Frankfurt, began to voice new doubts about remembrance. Referring to what he called "the burden of our history, our everlasting disgrace," Walser critiqued "this unceasing presentation of our disgrace."[83] He favorably referred to characterizations of the Berlin Memorial to the Murdered Jews as "a nightmare the size of a football field," the "monumentalization of our disgrace."[84] Comments previously made only in private, suggesting that things could return to "normal" if only the victims would not repeatedly dredge up the past, were now accorded public legitimacy by a major author. The speech was enthusiastically received; only the chair of the Jewish Council in Germany, Ignatz Bubis, refused to applaud. In a lively speech on November 9, 1998 (the sixtieth anniversary of Kristallnacht), Bubis noted that while Walser had spoken of German "disgrace" (*Schande*) no fewer than four times, he had not even once mentioned German "crimes" (*Verbrechen*).[85] Bubis also acidly observed that rather than the Berlin Memorial being a "monumentalization of disgrace," it was the disgrace itself, namely, the crimes of the Nazis, that was truly monumental; these crimes were not first "monumentalized" by virtue of being remembered.[86] In 1979, Walser had commented that "victims and the perpetrators still stand on two different sides" and pointed to "organizations to promote reconciliation" as well as "attempts to prevent shame from turning into paralysis."[87] He had at that time, as in his 1965 essay reflecting on the Auschwitz trial, addressed issues of guilt.[88] But by the close of the century, Walser was seemingly tiring of the struggle. Yet again, it appeared that it was the victims who were to blame for raising the past to attention and causing discomfort, not the perpetrators whose crimes occasioned the need for memory.

Across Europe and far beyond, it was almost as if only an excess of belated and continually contested commemoration of victims could make up for the incapacity to deal appropriately with the perpetrators. Now is the moment to wonder, perhaps, how remembrance of victims could be accompanied by a more adequate portrayal of the full range of those responsible for making

Nazi persecution possible, and to highlight practices that continue to reinforce various forms of stigmatization, exclusion, and oppression.

The landscape of memorialization as we see it today is a product of the decades since the war ended: it does not adequately represent the realities and horrors of the past but rather those aspects people have sought, for a wide variety of reasons, to engage with, preserve, and portray. It reflects, as much as anything, continuing prejudices as well as disparate patterns of power and command of both material and symbolic resources. It is now almost impossible to gain an overview of the ever richer variety of memorials, museums, plaques, and places in which aspects of Nazi persecution and ever expanded groups of victims are brought to our attention.

To call this a landscape of "memory," as so many do, may be to do a further injustice to all those whose experiences were real and terrifying, whose memories have variously flickered and faded, and who are now passing away. For now, and in the future, awareness of the selectivity of remembrance and the significance of education will need to go hand in hand.

Conclusions

20

A Resonant Past

One word, "Auschwitz," has come to stand for *the* crime of modern times. In face of the enormity of Auschwitz, it is tempting to pause in bafflement, thinking there can be no answer to the questions of why and how cruelty on this scale was possible. But historians can at least clarify patterns of involvement in and responsibility for Nazi persecution and explore the implications both for those who lived through it and those who came after. It is essential not only to register the initial sense of incomprehensibility but also—precisely because this is such a significant and challenging past—to move beyond the first reaction of disbelief and think clearly about the many ramifications of living through and with this past.

There may be no answer to the question of "why"—or at least no answer accessible to historians. Answers to the question of "how" can be sought through a reconstruction of the ways in which wider social and political developments intersected with individual lives, such that large numbers of people were ultimately mobilized in service of a murderous cause, some more willingly than others. The system was willed by the few, sustained through the conformity and mobilization of the many, and backed up by the repression of those who opposed. There were pressures to conform, with rewards for some and sanctions for others. Outward behavior did not always correlate with inner views. And the dividing line between what people considered to be "legitimate" and "illegitimate" violence was a sliding one, varying with perspective, worldview, and circumstances. But whichever way this is approached, and for whatever combinations of reasons—individual outlooks, circumstances, opportunities—across Europe under Nazi rule the persecution and mass murder of the unwanted and excluded went far beyond the kinds of killing generally expected in warfare at the time.

This was a phenomenon on a scale that evades easy summary, that goes well beyond the experience of particular groups, that resists encapsulation in any one word—catastrophe, Shoah, Holocaust—restricting and defining as single words are. It engulfed not only those who were killed but all who lived through it, and it continued to affect generations born after.

In the Federal Republic of Germany, "the past" came to refer to the Nazi period above all. The historian Raul Hilberg, who was born in Vienna and whose family emigrated to America before the war, saw this usage as an attempt to make a clear demarcation between "then" and "now," to disassociate the rejected past from the reformed present. As he put it in 1961, in his still-classic work on the destruction of the European Jews: "Of all the terms used in postwar years to describe the actions of the Nazi regime, the most telling is the all-encompassing reference to the 'past' (*Vergangenheit*). It encloses the occurrence, disconnecting it from the present."[1] Yet any such attempt to "enclose" and "disconnect" the past was unsuccessful; despite all efforts to "draw a line under the past," its significance persisted. By the mid-1980s, a quarter of a century after Hilberg's observation, the German philosopher Ernst Nolte was dubbing the Nazi era the "past that refuses to pass away."[2] And this past has continued to pervade the present, in ways that have shifted over the decades.

Generations born well after the end of the Third Reich have grown up and lived in its long shadows. Whether people are consciously aware of it or not, the legacies of Nazi persecution have continued to resonate long after most of those who were perpetrators, or were survivors of persecution, or witnessed the crimes have passed away. The children and grandchildren of survivors, perpetrators, and witnesses have been affected by the consequences for their upbringing and for their relationships with members of their families and with others. The legacies have shaped their lifestyles, values, careers, even choice of friends and partners. It has influenced in turn the kinds of education they seek for their own children and the sorts of future they hope to build. Reactions to this past have played a role in building the landscapes of remembrance and historical environments we inhabit today, referencing and influencing political and moral outlooks on the contemporary world.

All who were involved in Nazi persecution were, in one way or another, contaminated by their degrees of exposure. And the toxicity has lingered over subsequent generations. This toxicity has a generational half-life, and its effects are now waning, with ever more diluted residues and distant echoes. In due course, no doubt, there will be barely any reverberations among new generations without personal connections to people touched by these times.

Even so, the violence unleashed by the Nazis was on a scale that renders it, in principle, of universal and abiding significance.

State-Sanctioned Violence and the Uneven Distribution of Guilt

Violence was integral to Nazi rule, and was so from the very beginning. With visible and audible brutality on the streets and in detention centers and early concentration camps, the reliance of the regime on terror was widely known from the outset. The rapid shift of many Germans into acquiescence, even enthusiasm, was accompanied by draconian repression of the rest through fear, imprisonment, and exile. With the expansion of the Nazi regime across Europe from 1938 onward, Nazi terror was exported—again, assisted by the collaboration and complicity of millions, and involving the savage oppression of millions of others.

Over the course of a mere dozen years, the Nazi regime developed a system of persecution that savagely attacked political enemies, brutally maltreated "undesirable" groups, and exploited and killed people designated as "inferior." Some of this was in the cause of political supremacy and the destruction of opposition, some in pursuit of an ideologically driven vision of "racial purity" and the elimination of people seen as polluting the "health" of the new society, and some related to ruthless exploitation in service of an economy geared for war and world mastery. Not all of these aims played an equal role, and some aspects were at times in conflict with others. Taken together, they constituted a bundle of multiple forms of persecution, collective violence, breaches of human rights, and a willingness to engage in murder on a breathtaking scale.

Although Hitler was central, this system—in which millions of civilians perished—was not based on the ideas and actions of one man, or even just a small circle. Hundreds of thousands of people were actively involved in one way or another in the practices and processes of exclusion, deportation, maltreatment, and killing, and millions more were knowledgeable about the violence and at least some aspects of the machinery of destruction. Yet later, many on the perpetrator side denied knowledge and claimed innocence through ignorance.

If we want to understand the long afterlife of the Nazi past, we need also to understand the distinctive features of the power structures and social processes through which people adapted to, sustained, and transformed the system. It was possible for people to experience a sense of unease, even to think that they were "internally opposed" to what they were doing, while at the same time obediently carrying out orders or even taking the initiative in fulfilling their roles. People could later present themselves as having been forced or constrained to act in the ways they did, bearing no personal responsibility for their actions.

Not all were equally guilty. People bore different degrees of responsibility, depending on specific roles and on whether they engaged voluntarily or were conscripted; they also varied in terms of individual attitudes and behaviors, once it became clear what sort of enterprise they were tangled up in. Some sought an exit, and a minority raised their voices in protest or actively tried to oppose or subvert the direction of events; many others became acclimatized, rationalized their situation in some way, and played their allotted roles to the full; a few were enthusiastic, out of whatever combination of commitment or careerism.

Some groups were directly involved at the front line: members of the ordinary police forces, the Gestapo, the SA and SS, the Einsatzgruppen, the camp guards, and innumerable others, including some in the army, engaged in violence against civilians that even they found hard to justify. A tiny minority of individuals from among these groups were later brought to account for their violent acts, becoming the focus of wider attention as "perpetrators." For a long time the direct killers were identified as the primary perpetrators, alongside those who gave orders and the most prominent men at the top of the hierarchy. Yet they were not the only ones to bear responsibility for what happened. Civilian administration was significant in putting policies into effect on the ground, both across the expanded Reich and in the occupied territories. The network of businesses and enterprises in which the concentration camp universe was embedded relied on common interests and cooperation in the exploitation of slave labor. Professionals, including medical doctors, lawyers, and population planners, played a variety of roles that propelled the machinery of destruction forward. The capitulation of a significant proportion of the highly educated in Germany to the inhumanity of Nazi practices is quite astounding. And both within the Reich and across Europe, many more people became involved as collaborators and beneficiaries of Nazi policies.

Social practices of discrimination and exclusion in everyday life were important in stigmatizing and isolating the victims of persecution; such informal practices could develop, more proactively, into targeted exploit-ation and willful profiting from radical injustice. Fear also played a signifi-cant role in transforming the landscape of persecution. Victims trapped in the Nazi net could not easily rely on former friends, neighbors, or others to support them in their plight or to provide assistance in hiding or flight. Despite the efforts of some committed individuals to engage in resistance and sabotage, the vast majority were neither sufficiently courageous (indeed potentially suicidal) nor necessarily even capable of such actions, given the overwhelming apparatus of terror and repression and the conflicting prior-ities of their own welfare and that of their families. The Third Reich was only finally brought down by massive external force in a World War.

This is not to condemn an entire "perpetrator society," as can so easily be done. An "Aryan" toddler sleeping in the cot of a Jewish child who had been deported was not herself guilty, even if she was, through no action of her own, a beneficiary of Nazi policies; there are limits to any useful notion of complicity.[3] Functionaries and active beneficiaries present a rather different picture.

The situation was certainly more ambiguous than it sometimes appears in the later accounts of those who were closely tangled up in the system. People could simultaneously be beneficiaries of the system, as in the use of slave labor, and yet feel they were in some way subverting it, as when they fed extra rations of bread to "their" laborers or were kinder to them than they thought they were supposed to be. They could later use such tales to make themselves feel good about their role in the past, while failing to acknowledge their simultaneous responsibility in having helped the system to function. Similarly, people could be victims of the Nazi regime, living in occupied countries, with their freedom constrained, their living standards reduced, their property taken away, and many of their compatriots coerced into forced labor; but, at the same time, they could be collaborators or perpetrators when it came to groups who were even lower in the hierarchy of victims, willingly betraying Jews or denouncing members of resistance groups, particularly where there were conflicts between opposing anti-Nazi forces. This was a system of many-sided violence from which it was difficult to come out clean.

There were also many people living within Nazi Germany and the occupied territories who neither benefited from nor sustained Nazi policies and who, if never actually engaging in any form of resistance or rescue, simply sought to survive. Whether such people can helpfully be termed "innocent bystanders" is another matter. In a system of collective violence persisting over a period of years, there is essentially no "outside" of the dynamics of violence.[4] Not to intervene in specific situations of conflict is itself a form of behavior affecting the outcome; and we need also to understand the dynamics and consequences of "nonintervention" over longer periods of time. Questions around the spectrum from willing complicity to unwilling capitulation or miserable accommodation to Nazi rule are complex. These people were, however, not the prime makers and actors of Nazi violence. And the latter were barely brought to reckon with a far more compromised past.

The Inadequacies of Justice and Communities of Experience after the War

Legal systems after the war were fundamentally ill equipped to deal with collective violence on this scale—not only physically but even conceptually. Indeed, the crime of genocide was only now conceived as such. Compared to the total numbers involved, only a small proportion of perpetrators of the whole gamut of Nazi crimes were even investigated, let alone brought to court and actually convicted; the vast majority escaped the net of justice entirely. This was not only because of the sheer scale of the crimes and the numbers involved, although it is true that, pragmatically, the task would have been insurmountable: any comprehensive legal reckoning would have burst the bounds of the courtrooms of Europe and stretched beyond the lifetimes of prosecutors. Nor was it because, as is so often suggested, former Nazis were essential to the running of new postwar states. There were other reasons, which varied according to place and time. These included the emergent dynamics of the Cold War and related considerations on the part of the Allies. Once new states had been established in succession to the dismembered Third Reich, contemporary social and political considerations in each state affected the selective prosecution of particular sorts of perpetrators, while they variously assisted the rehabilitation and reintegration of others.

Trials were as much about postwar history as they were attempts to reckon with the Nazi past. It was not only a matter of the "victor's justice" of the Nuremberg trials and the later big concentration camp trials. In the first few years immediately after the war, in each of the Third Reich successor states, hundreds of smaller trials dealt with issues relevant to current social and political priorities. In both East and West Germany, individual denunciations of fellow Germans were high on the list, reflecting fault lines rooted as much in personal frictions as in political divides. In East Germany, additionally, left-wing political causes—the brutal suppression of socialist and communist opponents of Nazism, as well as critiques of capitalists—figured high on the list of early priorities, while in West Germany violence against Germans in the closing months of the war as well as incidents associated with Kristallnacht in 1938 were significant issues. In all successor states, at first, euthanasia crimes were also a focus. So it initially seemed as if the chasms within German society under Nazi rule were being directly addressed in early trials. But very soon, rehabilitation of former Nazis took precedence, although with very different emphases in the East and the West. By the time later trials focused attention primarily on atrocities and mass killings in the East, the image of perpetrators had largely narrowed to physical thugs in the camps and those few giving orders in high places.

There are many ways of evaluating these developments—all somewhat hypothetical. Some argue that reintegration of those who had been mobilized in service of a murderous regime was the only way of ensuring the stability and efficiency of new states. But the stability of postwar states was not dependent solely (or even at all) on such reintegration; there were other factors involved in the stabilization of Austrian and West German democracy—and indeed of communist East Germany—than just the quiet integration of most former Nazis while scapegoating just a few. In West Germany, the government, administration, judiciary, and other professional groups could easily have functioned without reinstating so many individuals who had formerly sustained the Nazi regime. This does not necessarily mean that more perpetrators would have been prosecuted. But fewer people with tainted pasts would have been in positions to affect other ways in which a measure of justice was pursued, including compensation and recognition for former victims. The more general lesson, if there is one, is that following periods of massive state-sponsored collective violence, a great deal of thought has to be given to the restructuring of states, societies, and legal systems, and to the broader contexts as well as the specific ways in which perpetrators are brought to account.[5]

There are also implications on a more informal level. Large numbers of people had occupied roles or engaged in behavior that made mass murder and persecution possible. They later found ways of rationalizing and silencing their past. Evasive stories in perpetrator communities often painted a veiled picture of a past that was barely marked by any violence in which they might personally have been involved. Paradoxically, as the early trials addressing multiple crimes on German soil faded from view and the focus shifted to trials concerning sites of extermination in the East, it became ever easier for those who had been complicit in other ways to claim distance from Nazi atrocities. Everyday inhumanity was displaced by a focus on distant brutality.

By contrast, people who had been persecuted were affected for the rest of their lives. Despite their best efforts to make a new start, many survivors were inescapably tormented by their past, plagued by a sense of guilt, haunted by horrifying scenes and memories, pained by the losses of family, friends, and homelands. Bitter debates arose about failures of resistance and what more could have been done to save people; about who had suffered the most, who had failed to gain recognition or compensation, whose memories were being preserved and prioritized and whose marginalized or suppressed. These agonized reckonings with an unsettling past contrasted with the ways in which former oppressors evaded being brought to account. For some survivors, it was simply easier to try to forget, to move on, even to try to "forgive," for their own peace of mind; for others, this was simply impossible.

It is easy to feel a sense of moral outrage at the disproportionality here: so many perpetrators able to lead relatively untroubled postwar lives; so many of the persecuted damaged, displaced, disturbed for the rest of their lives by their experiences. So few perpetrators brought to account; so little justice.

There were also those who wanted to claim retrospectively the supposedly innocent status of "bystanders." For them, "not knowing," not having seen or heard about what was "really" going on, became a major element in retrospectively shoring up claims to innocence. Yet there were innumerable ways in which people were involved in, and benefited from, the Nazi regime. This was a regime that could not have functioned without the multiple links between businesses, industries, and forced labor; between local populations and enforcers of the new Nazi order; between functionaries fulfilling their official roles and the informal actions of everyday life. This was a system that was bottom-up as well as top-down, although in different ways depending on context. And the numerous beneficiaries of Nazi policies of oppression, exploitation, and expropriation, including the beneficiaries of "aryanization," the employers who directly exploited slave labor from concentration camps, even the Polish people who moved into the better houses and took the possessions of their murdered neighbors, similarly evaded both the postwar network of justice—such as it was—and also, for the most part, the spotlight of public attention. It was only very late that some of these issues began to emerge into larger discussions and controversies.

There was in this way a major mismatch between a system of state-sponsored persecution, with its intricate division of labor, and later attempts at reckoning with this past, both public and personal. For decades, while perpetrators were not brought to justice in any way commensurate with the scale of the crime, vested interests and continuing prejudices ensured that numerous claims by survivors to compensation were barely met, and some not at all; and some victims were still discriminated against, for much of the rest of their lives.

The Generational Half-Life of a Contaminated Past

One of the characters in *Liquidation*, a novel by Holocaust survivor Imre Kertész, relates how a friend described fellow victims of Nazi persecution: "Survivors represent a separate species.... That is what determines our perverse and degenerate mental world. Auschwitz. Then the forty years that we have put behind us since."[6] Those who had been persecuted were affected not only by what they had been through but also by the ways in which, over subsequent decades, they had to deal with what Kertész calls the "latter-day deformation of survival."[7] Less well understood—or at least far less thoroughly explored to date—are the ways in which those on the side of the perpetrators were also affected by the violence to which they had contributed. Even if privately tortured by memories or nightmares, most seem to have found ways of living with the knowledge of their past, silencing or reframing it in acceptable ways. No single metanarrative can encompass this complex past. There are many intertwined strands—in what is infinitely more complex than the double helix of DNA. Public and private developments interrelated but operated according to separate rhythms. Trials and public representations were crucially affected by national and international contexts that often bore little relation to the dynamics of family discussions and private reckonings.

Beyond the outlines of public debates and cultural representations of the past, there is a subterranean story, hard to capture, evading sharp and precise definition, of changing perceptions and the evolving recognition of the persecuted. This developed in three overlapping stages. At first, both during and immediately after the war, victims of Nazi persecution found few beyond the borders of their own communities who were willing to listen to their experiences and talked primarily among themselves. The "surviving remnant" of Jewish victims could more readily find others with whom to talk than could homosexual victims of persecution, for example. A second phase, overlapping with the first but coming fully into its own only fifteen or so years after the end of the war, was that of the "era of the witness," characterized by emergent communication across the borders of different communities—but frequently not in a manner geared toward greater understanding. A few survivors were brought into the public arena in confrontational settings, such as trials, to establish the guilt of defendants or in attempts to claim compensation—again, with higher visibility and success for some groups than others. Now the expanding interest in their testimony was not only to do with what had happened but also with who was responsible. During the period of the great trials that captured public attention, in the 1960s and 1970s, witnesses occupied a paradoxical position. They were listened to insofar as their testimony could assist in establishing the guilt or innocence of defendants; the focus was on the perpetrators' actions and mental states, on specific incidents and scenes of crime, and not on the victims and their lives in any wider sense. The classic "era of the witness," then, was not one that was very comfortable for those few survivors who felt strong enough and sufficiently determined to see justice done to devote their time and emotional energy to court cases.

From the later 1970s, what might be called the "era of the survivor" began, inaugurating a third phase, marked by the collection of ever more testimonies about the lives of the persecuted not only during but also before and after the catastrophe that had befallen so many. This coincided with the later life stages that survivors had now entered, marked for some by an increased willingness to talk. There were also new audiences in an altered climate of sympathy for victimhood and new technologies for the recording and transmission of testimony. The focus in survivor accounts now shifted from what victims could say about their former oppressors to what survivors could say about themselves.

A feature of particular significance in understanding the era of the survivor is that of generational change. No longer were those older people in

positions of power and influence who had formerly been implicated as perpetrators, collaborators, accessories, functionaries, beneficiaries, or not so
innocent bystanders. Younger generations who had grown up with a diffuse
sense of the burden of the past were now in positions to address this past—
not necessarily with a sense of "objective" distance, given the close connections to the past through people whom they knew personally and to whom
they were tied by emotional bonds, but at least with less at stake in either personal or professional terms. And, increasingly, members of younger generations
not only wanted to know about the past but could also begin to empathize
and seek to identify with the victims. Again, this took place differently according to context.

Alongside the rise of the survivor was the other, paradoxical, twist, the
second major shift in this part of the story: the decline of the victim as a key
witness in the courtroom. Just as the generation of perpetrators was dying
out and only a very few frail and elderly individuals from marginal positions
and lower ranks could be identified and brought to court, the role of the
witness in legal cases was dramatically altered. Their role was now one of
"bearing witness" in the widest sense: literally embodying the legacies of
Nazi persecution, bearing witness, in their very being and their suffering,
to the long-term significance of this past, rather than acting as a witness,
by virtue of specific knowledge, to the individual guilt of a particular
defendant.

The rise of the survivor as a person of interest in his or her own right,
and the decline of the key role of witness testimony in establishing guilt
in the courtroom, symbolized a broader transformation. This was the
growing need to understand what this past had done to the generations
who had lived through it as well as how it had influenced those who
came after.

Among members of the second generation, the aftermath also took some
unexpected twists. While some children of survivors sought to find roots
by curating parental memories, exploring the past and reconstructing their
family histories, others turned away, determined to build new lives with
minimal conscious engagement with the violent rupture on which their
families were founded. Among children of perpetrators, a few found ways
of seeking to "make amends," engaging in healing, educational, and restitu-
tive activities; many or most felt a diffuse sense of unease, even misplaced
guilt, and perhaps self-defensively chose to focus on the present and "not
know" too much about the parental past. On both sides, there were efforts
to break away from the past, sometimes focusing on quite different issues,

displacing feelings of unease, suppressing a nagging sense of responsibility for healing the wounds of a period through which they themselves had not lived.

From Cacophony to Chorus

The history of these multiple, diverse attempts at reckoning with the Nazi past is complex. We can seek to understand not only what happened during the Nazi era and its immediate impact but also the ways in which this past has continued to be of significance among members of subsequent generations.

The explosion of violence initially affected those at the epicenters of evil. Then contamination spread, affecting those immediately connected to the people directly involved in killing and being killed. With the passage of generations, the growth of global mobility, and new social movements and cultural outlooks, this cloud of fallout blew ever wider, dissipating and becoming diluted in potency, but affecting an ever-greater area.

With growing distance from the events, emergent narratives made it possible both to try to understand the past and to live with it in ways that were not entirely unbearable. Narratives varied with time, place, context, and community, and they carried with them different ambiguities and strains. Among some survivors, for example, a story of having actively fought to survive, of resistance and rescue, might be easier to tell than one that acknowledged utter helplessness and powerlessness, particularly where the audience might be more sympathetic to tales of heroism against the odds than ones of long drawn out misery and hopelessness, watching as loved ones faded away and died. But these sorts of stories, of agency and will, could not necessarily be sustained without a great deal of silencing and repression of other memories; and they might be combined with a deep sense of guilt about having failed to save others who perished in the ghettos and camps, the streets and marketplaces and ravines, the factories built on slavery, the gas chambers, or the death marches. For many survivors, no amount of selective talking by day, no amount of engagement or throwing oneself into activity, could necessarily silence the nightmares and flashbacks or quell the pain and depression that were the long-term consequences of their experiences. Which responses were possible, whether they were actively elicited or frowned upon, differed with context: public cultures of recognition of victim groups and popular responses to specific minorities were very different in Poland and Israel, in the United States and France; and they were very different in the Third Reich successor states during the decades when those who had earlier been complicit still dominated public life, compared to a later era when new generations had taken over in positions of power and influence.

Among the children and grandchildren of survivors, a "return" to a place they had never known might help to frame and contextualize their family stories and give them a previously missing sense of "emplacement"; but it might also raise again the utter senselessness of this suffering and sharply bring to attention the continuing pain for their parents of the loss of family members whom they themselves had never met, whom they could only faintly imagine, and whose fates they could only seek to reconstruct. The "resurrection" or at least remembrance of the lost could take place in physical sites of commemoration, or in reconstructions through talking and writing, putting together the pieces—but no amount of such puzzling together of the shards and fragments could ever make the picture whole again.

Among perpetrator communities, narrative dynamics were quite different. The original division of labor in the machinery of mass murder and oppression made it easier to disassociate oneself from what had happened. Narratives suggesting a "totalitarian state" in which no resistance was possible allowed a denial of personal agency to act otherwise. Selective stories about the past allowed self-distancing from anything really bad. The narrowing down of the focus to "Auschwitz" as the epitome of evil meant that acknowledgement of personal involvement in the system of violence and persecution all around could more easily be evaded.

For all the justified rejections by Germans of the notion of "collective guilt" after the war, there is a paradoxical twist to the later assumption—however much it stands on the moral high ground—of a notion of "collective responsibility." Quite apart from the burden this places on those who had not themselves been involved, this may provide a convenient means for the truly guilty to hide behind too large and vague a term. This was evidenced, for example, in the ways in which industries and companies that had benefited from slave labor later collaborated with others, more innocent, to make gesture payments rather than acknowledge liability for compensation. There is in fact a striking continuity between Adenauer's early assertion of responsibility without guilt in the early 1950s and the similar stance, some half a century later, underlying the symbolic payments made to former slave laborers by German firms as a moral gesture without any admission of legal liability.

Silencing of personal or family secrets—by the perpetrator generation and by those who were born later—could be combined with an energetic concern with "public history," with identification with the victims, with engagement in good causes. But the emotional economy of suppressed feelings of inchoate guilt or shame and attempts to redress the deficit could never quite balance here. At the level of official policies, a degree of restitution and compensation often had to be fought for by representatives of the victims, rather than being offered freely and readily by those who were keen only to claim the moral virtues of responsibility without acknowledging guilt. Moreover, any attempts to "make good again" could in principle never be successful; even without the foot dragging and the inadequate and often grotesquely belated gestures toward compensating the victims, nothing could actually make up for the wrongs inflicted, the mass suffering and deaths caused by Nazi persecution. No amount of memorialization, of "returning names" to previously anonymous victims, could return their lives to them or their presence to those who had loved them.

Some states, notably the Federal Republic of Germany, eventually gained a formidable reputation for "facing up to the past." Yet when we look more closely, there are significant complications to narratives of progress in this area. Remembering victims, celebrating resistance, and drawing wider moral lessons from the past were not necessarily accompanied by adequate naming and shaming of the guilty. And it was not states that were the key actors in energetically confronting the past; rather, it was individuals coming from particular communities of experience, connection, or identification who sought to address more actively the legacies of Nazi persecution, even as others sought to resist such reckonings.

This is where it becomes particularly important to recognize the conflicting and various narratives among different communities, and to understand that the currently prevailing chorus—which is not without discord, nor without challenge—is one that has developed over time, emerging out of an initial cacophony of competing voices. It is a chorus that has privileged certain notes and harmonies and drowned out others, allowing the condemnation, suppression, or non-recognition of alternative narratives. When we examine them a little more closely, we find that the "composers" of this chorus are members of particular communities, some with more power and control over the agenda than others, some who have had to fight hard to get their voices heard against considerable opposition. And quite different forces continually seek to revise interpretations of the Nazi past, and at times prove capable of mobilizing significant popular support for racist views, particularly in conditions of political, economic, and social uncertainty. This is an ever-changing kaleidoscope.

The paradox in West Germany was that the public culture of addressing the past, of repeatedly seeking to ensure that it should never be laid to rest, was established relatively early on, at precisely the same time as the tracks were laid for ensuring that the vast majority of those who were guilty were never really brought to account for their crimes. Members of a younger generation took up the baton of continuing confrontation with the past, but at a time when it was far too late to make good the earlier major sins of omission. The paradox in East Germany was that it gained such a poor reputation for political instrumentalization of the past that even the modest measure of success in bringing some—generally low-level—perpetrators to court was overlooked or discounted almost entirely, and a relatively guilt-free younger generation was more concerned with addressing the ills of the communist present than the evils of the Nazi past. With its demise in 1990, the GDR began to be seen as somehow a thing apart, a "footnote" or side-line in history, barely integrated into any longer view recognizing the con-tinuing personal significance as well as the political consequences of Nazi persecution. And for very different reasons, in Austria decades of failure to bring former Nazis to court were accompanied by a comparable failure to make much of the past in public monuments and memorials; while the latter is now being rectified, for the former it is too late. Younger gener-ations of Austrians could, by and large, continue to bask in the supposed innocence of their small and picturesque fatherland. Only relatively recently has this myth increasingly been challenged; the memorial landscape of Austria today does far more justice to the past than what its courts of law were able to achieve in the latter half of the twentieth century.

Whichever way it is approached, this is not an easy past. In surveying the legacies of Nazi persecution in the three-quarters of a century since the violence unleashed by Hitler swept across Europe, the most marked feature of the aftermath is the partial and selective disappearance of perpetrators. The vast majority of those who had been in some way complicit in mass murder by and large evaded the courts of justice; they also, despite the near obsession with Nazism in popular culture and the media, could not easily be dealt with in the museums and memorial sites that sprang up across

Europe. Whether in Eastern or Western Europe, the primary attention of memorial sites was on remembering victims: honoring their memory, providing them a degree of posthumous longevity, even if their ashes could not receive individual graves; paying respects; celebrating their lives; mourning their passing. Alongside the remembrance of victims was the celebration of heroism: memorials to the resisters, the rescuers, the liberators.

The content of memorials varied significantly with political context and changed over time, but nowhere was the identification of local collaborators, beneficiaries, or perpetrators a priority—and indeed, quite apart from the continuing frictions such naming and shaming would have caused, it might have been seen to sully what had in the meantime become sacred places. One view is that the "evil ones" are better kept as a largely anonymous breed of uniformed men and defunct organizations and not given human faces and personal profiles in sites of remembrance. Even in West Germany, with widespread concern to shoulder responsibility and bear the moral burden of the past, shame was primarily expressed in memorialization of victims, with only limited, belated, and partial identification of wider groups of perpetrators and facilitators. This increasingly became possible in united Germany from the 1990s, as the perpetrator generation was passing, but even so it remained underdeveloped. In places in Eastern Europe where collaborators were often locals, and where many had been beneficiaries of mass crimes, it would have been even more difficult to put names and faces of perpetrators near to memorials to victims. Sites of mass graves remain unmarked, the memory of their locations dying with the generations who participated in or personally witnessed these events, the people who knew the locations and those who were involved.

Shame may have fueled the efforts of members of the next generation in perpetrator communities to construct ever more memorials to the victims. A diffuse sense of unease as well as innumerable emotional ties to those who had been responsible for so much misery also kept the second generation from wanting to point a finger directly at the guilty while they remained alive. But now, with the passing not only of eyewitnesses and survivors but also—less widely noted—of the perpetrator generation, there is a new opportunity for reinserting a wider range of perpetrators into public narratives about the past. The chorus can begin to change again.

What, more generally, can we learn from engaging with this extraordinary period of history? It is almost inappropriate to suggest that any general conclusions could be drawn from analyzing diverse attempts to deal with such an immense sea of senseless suffering—but a few patterns do emerge.

Reckonings go beyond simple representations of a past that is genuinely over and done with; rather, they seek to rectify a perceived imbalance after a period of acute turmoil, and they seek to quell continuing disquiet arising from unresolved conflicts, both personal and societal. Reckonings can involve an individual accounting for past behaviors and experiences in order to restore a sense of an acceptable self, to retain or rebuild a measure of self-esteem, in quite different later circumstances. Reckonings can also be imposed from without, whether through courts of law or political and social processes or informal pressure in everyday life. Here, perceived injustices should in some way be rectified, punishments meted out, measures for compensation or restitution instituted. The pre-conflict situation can never be restored, but a sense of persisting injustice may perpetuate or ignite further conflicts.

In surveying a variety of ways of reckoning with the legacies of Nazi persecution, as these shifted among different groups and across place and time, some persisting imbalances are striking. Despite strenuous efforts among survivors to reconstruct damaged lives, and despite attempts by wider communities to mourn and remember the victims of persecution, there remains a serious imbalance. While an ever wider range of victims were remembered, former persecutors all too easily evaded being brought to account for their part in the crimes of the Nazi era. This continuing imbalance can now only be recognized, and no longer rectified.

The writings of those who recounted their experiences can help to illuminate some of the variations in the predicaments of victims of persecution. The profiles of just a few of the perpetrators who have generally remained out of the spotlight can help in understanding the distinctive distribution of guilt, and an appreciation of the sheer extent and escalating visibility of inhumanity, as well as expanding involvement in a system of collective violence provides crucial clues to the patterns of persecution and widespread later unease. Exploring the longer reverberations of this violence, we can begin to understand not only the persistence of a disturbing past, but also some of the ways in which it remains relevant—even in some sense alive—today.

In the twenty-first century the earlier cacophony of voices has begun to converge into a wider world chorus echoing the general message of "never again"—a message that is repeatedly challenged by resurgent violence and racist movements. For all the moral responsibility and civic awareness this demands, such a message runs the danger of overgeneralizing and failing to recognize historical specificities and differences. It is not some general, abstract message about tolerance, however laudable, but rather the detailed interactions between individuals and changing contexts on which we should focus if we want to understand the dynamics of this violent past and the continuing significance and legacies of persecution. This episode is one that has defined our times, and has done so in very particular ways.

The nature of specific circumstances, political structures, and social processes is crucial to understanding both how people were swept up in collective violence on this scale and how they lived afterward with what they had done or suffered. There were significant variations across place and time. But there is also a wider, more general point.

It is important to understand the distinctiveness of collective violence. It is not individual motivation or specific personality aberrations that explain how so many people became active participants in state-sanctioned persecution, nor did each individual perpetrator later think up, separately, ways of rationalizing former actions. These are collective, social phenomena that need to be looked at in larger contexts. We need therefore to focus not only on individual choices—and degrees of culpability—but also on the political, social, and institutional contexts in which violence is made possible and the changing circumstances in which subsequent reckonings take place. Such an approach may help in mitigating the impact of collective violence—a phenomenon that is perennial and continues to arise in many forms, many guises, across the world.

There are also implications for the ways in which we understand the continuing personal significance of this past. Cultural representations, political uses, and public controversies have received a great deal of attention in historical accounts of "coming to terms with the past." The psychological implications of this past for individuals and their families have often been left to the attention of those disciplines and professions focusing on individual persons, notably psychology and psychotherapeutic approaches as well as works of creative literature. But if we want to gain a more comprehensive understanding of the long-term significance and persisting legacies of a period of acute persecution, historians also have to develop ways of exploring individual experiences, ways of situating personal stories in the wider contexts that influenced both what happened and how people later were affected by, dealt with, and interpreted their experiences. This is the approach that I have sought to develop in this account—and there is far more to be explored in all the areas I have only been able to touch on here.

Circumstances shape ways of acting and understanding challenging situations and confronting their aftermath; we can identify patterns and variations. But they do not explain everything. Human beings make individual moral choices and have personal responsibility for their actions—even when they are forced to act in conditions not of their own choosing, and even when the range of choices available to them is unbelievably constrained and limited, or is perceived as such. At different stages, from different social backgrounds, and in a variety of positions, people have varying degrees of capacity to choose differently, to act differently, and even to think differently about past and present.

This means that we need to approach the past with a degree of precision. Analysis of responsibility has to be more specific than the generalized attributions of blame. Arguing for the abstract social and moral responsibility of a wider collective can serve to disguise specific locations of real guilt and legal responsibility. Such a sense of greater moral responsibility may be valuable and desirable, but it should complement, rather than displace, a more precise reckoning.

By exploring the legacies of the Nazi past in this way, we can begin to understand the immensity of the upheavals that not only shaped the last century but also continue to shape our present and ourselves.

Notes

CHAPTER I

1. "An Account by Szlamek," translated and reprinted in Łucia Pawlicka-Nowak, ed., *Chełmno Witnesses Speak* (Łódź: Council for the Protection of Memory of Combat and Martyrdom, and the District Museum in Konin, 2004), 101–18.
2. "An Account by Szlamek," 106.
3. "An Account by Szlamek," 107.
4. "An Account by Szlamek," 107.
5. Raul Hilberg's seminal work outlining the typology, or triad, includes under the section on bystanders chapters on such diverse historical actors as: "Nations in Adolf Hitler's Europe," "Helpers, Gainers and Onlookers," "Messengers," "The Jewish Rescuers," "The Allies," "Neutral Countries," and "The Churches." Raul Hilberg, *Perpetrators, Victims, Bystanders* (New York: HarperCollins, 1993). I have discussed approaches to this concept in M. Fulbrook, "Bystanders: Catchall Concept, Alluring Alibi, or crucial clue?" in M. Fulbrook, *Erfahrung, Erinnerung, Geschichtsschreibung: Neue Perspektiven auf die deutschen Diktaturen* (Göttingen, Germany: Wallstein, 2106), ch. 5 (despite the German book title, this essay is in English). The topic is explored further in M. Fulbrook, *Bystander Society: Nazi Germany on the Brink of Genocide* (in progress).
6. "An Account by Szlamek," 111.
7. "An Account by Szlamek," 112.
8. Yankel Wiernik, *A Year in Treblinka* (New York: American Representation of the General Jewish Workers' Union of Poland, 1945), 4, available at http://www.zchor.org/wiernik.htm, accessed January 24, 2016.
9. Tadeusz Borowski, *This Way for the Gas, Ladies and Gentlemen*, trans. Barbara Vedder (New York: Penguin, 1976).
10. Borowski, *This Way for the Gas*, 90.
11. Denise Dufournier, *Ravensbrück: The Women's Camp of Death*, trans. F. W. McPherson (London: George Allen & Unwin, 1948, vii; ellipsis in original.
12. Dufournier, *Ravensbrück*, vii–viii.

CHAPTER 2

1. The literature on the Third Reich is vast. Here and throughout, footnote references are kept to a minimum. For a summary, see Richard J. Evans, *The Third*

Reich in Power (London: Penguin, 2005) and *The Third Reich at War* (London: Penguin, 2008). On the Holocaust, see Saul Friedländer, *Nazi Germany and the Jews*, 2 vols. (London: Weidenfeld & Nicolson, 1997–2007).

2. During the Third Reich it was often people of mixed descent who were persecuted under the general designation "Gypsy," which embodied also assumptions about an itinerant lifestyle, while those of "pure" descent who led a settled life were less likely to be deported and murdered. There is, it should be noted at the outset, a problem with the terminology for many of these groups: to use Nazi terms such as "Gypsy" rather than "Roma and Sinti" or "Romanies" risks perpetuating the pejorative concepts of the Nazis. Usage varies among specialists in the area. Michael Zimmermann, *Verfolgt, vertrieben, vernichtet: Die nationalso-zialistische Vernichtungspolitik gegen Sinti und Roma* (Essen, Germany: Klartext, 1989), uses the word "Gypsy" (*Zigeuner*) when referring to Nazi policies and targets ("Zigeunerpolitik") and *Roma* and *Sinti* when referring to the self-designations of these groups. Julia von dem Knesebeck, *The Roma Struggle for Compensation in Post-War Germany* (Hatfield, UK: University of Hertfordshire Press, 2011), 1n2, points out the variations and suggests that the terms "Roma" and "Sinti" are more respectful. "Romanies" is the term, when not using Nazi language, preferred by Eve Rosenhaft, "Blacks and Gypsies in Nazi Germany: The Limits of the 'Racial State,'" *History Workshop Journal* 72 (2011): 161–70. Guenter Lewy, *The Nazi Persecution of the Gypsies* (Oxford: Oxford University Press, 2000), ix, writes that there is a "politically correct" insistence on using the terms "Roma" and "Sinti" but that "there is nothing pejorative per se about the word 'Zigeuner,' and several Gypsy writers have insisted on the uninterrupted use of the term in order to maintain historical continuity and express solidarity with those who were persecuted under this name." There is a wider question about the use of anachronistic language in the interests of historical accuracy while not using scare quotes across every page, as in discussing the Nazi "euthanasia" program of mass killing of those considered to be "life unworthy of life"—and even with respect to the term "Third Reich" itself, which many German authors treat with scare quotes. For some groups it is almost impossible not to use the label under which groups were persecuted, as with, for example, the heterogeneous category of "asocials."

3. Sebastian Haffner, *Geschichte eines Deutschen: Die Erinnerungen 1914–1933* (Munich: Deutscher Taschenbuch Verlag, 2002), translated into English under the title *Defying Hitler: A Memoir*.

4. See, e.g., Eckart Conze, Norbert Frei, Peter Hayes, and Moshe Zimmermann, *Das Amt und die Vergangenheit: Deutsche Diplomaten im Dritten Reich und in der Bundesrepublik* (Munich: Karl Blessing Verlag, 2010).

5. Christian Goeschel and Nikolaus Wachsmann, eds., *The Nazi Concentration Camps, 1933–1939* (Lincoln: University of Nebraska Press, 2012); Nikolaus Wachsmann, *KL: A History of the Nazi Concentration Camps* (London: Little, Brown, 2015).

6. Wachsmann, *KL*, 118–19.

7. Ruediger Lautmann, "Gay Prisoners in Concentration Camps as Compared with Jehovah's Witnesses and Political Prisoners," in *A Mosaic of Victims: Non-Jews Persecuted and Murdered by the Nazis*, ed. Michael Berenbaum (London: I. B. Tauris, 1990), 203; Albert Knoll, "Homosexuelle Häftlinge im KZ Dachau," in *Das Konzentrationslager Dachau: Geschichte und Wirkung nationalsozialistischer Repression*, eds. Wolfgang Benz and Angelika Königseder (Berlin: Metropol, 2008), 237–52.

8. Alan Steinweis, *Kristallnacht 1938* (Cambridge, MA: Belknap Press of Harvard University Press, 2009).

9. Ruth Andreas-Friedrich, *Berlin Underground, 1938–1945*, trans. Barrows Mussey (New York: Henry Holt, 1947), 25.

10. Evan Burr Bukey, *Hitler's Austria: Popular Sentiment in the Nazi Era, 1938–1945* (Chapel Hill: University of North Carolina Press, 2000), 22–24.

11. Harvard Houghton Library (henceforth HHL), b MS Ger 91 (4), Henry A., 62.

12. HHL, b MS Ger 91 (4), Henry A., 65.

13. HHL, b MS 91 (9), Miriam A., 37.

14. HHL, b MS 91 (9), Miriam A., 84.

15. Lewy, *Nazi Persecution of the Gypsies*, 14.

16. Raul Hilberg, *The Destruction of the European Jews*, 3rd ed. (New Haven, CT: Yale University Press, 2003), 3:1070–71.

17. Hilberg, *Destruction of the European Jews*, 3:1070–71.

18. Hilberg, *Destruction of the European Jews*, 3:1070.

19. *Anders als die Andern*, directed by Richard Oswald and co-written by Richard Oswald and Magnus Hirschfeld; a remastered version was shown at the German Historical Museum, Berlin, 2015.

20. David Fernbach, introduction to Heinz Heger, *The Men with the Pink Triangle*, trans. David Fernbach (London: Gay Men's Press, 1980), 11.

21. Felix Kersten, *The Kersten Memoirs, 1940–1945*, trans. Constantine Fitzgibbon and James Oliver (London: Hutchinson, 1956), 57.

22. Kersten, *Kersten Memoirs,* 58.

23. Yale Fortunoff Archive HVT-937, Hildegard W. (born 1912 in Berlin), interviewed on August 14, 1987, by Laurie Vlock.

24. Yale Fortunoff Archive HVT-95, Elisabeth D., interviewed on July 22, 1980, by Laurel Vlock. See also Mary Fulbrook, *Dissonant Lives: Generations and Violence through the German Dictatorships* (Oxford: Oxford University Press, 2011).

25. Wiener Library (henceforth WL), 055-EA-1034. P.III.H. no. 378, Ernest Platz, "Experiences in Berlin Gestapo Prisons and in Buchenwald," interviewed in Melbourne, 1956. Since he was both a journalist and resistance fighter, I have not preserved anonymity.

26. Hearing screaming forms a recurrent theme in the 2013 film by Anthea Kennedy and Ian Wiblin, *The View from our House.*

27. Gisela Faust, personal communications, Friends House, Berlin, 2013.

28. WL, 055-EA-1034. P.III.H. No.378, Ernest P., 4 (p. 2 of report).

29. WL, 055-EA-1034. P.III.H. No.378, Ernest P., 5 (p. 3 of report).

30. For fascinating texts, see Irene Eber, *Voices from Shanghai: Jewish Exiles in Wartime China* (Chicago: University of Chicago Press, 2008).

31. Mary Fulbrook, *Bystander Society* (in progress).

32. Frank Bajohr and Michael Wildt, eds., *Volksgemeinschaft: Neue Forschungen zur Gesellschaft des Nationalsozialismus* (Frankfurt am Main: Fischer Verlag, 2009); Detlef Schmiechen-Ackermann, ed., *"Volksgemeinschaft": Mythos, wirkungsmächtige soziale Verheißung oder soziale Realität im "Dritten Reich"?* (Paderborn, Germany: Ferdinand Schöningh, 2012); Martina Steber and Bernhard Gotto, eds., *Visions of Community in Nazi Germany* (Oxford: Oxford University Press, 2014); Michael Wildt, *Volksgemeinschaft als Selbstermächtigung: Gewalt gegen Juden in der deutschen Provinz 1919 bis 1939* (Hamburg: Hamburger Edition, 2007).

33. William Shirer, *Berlin Diary: The Journal of a Foreign Correspondent, 1934–1941* (London: Hamish Hamilton, 1941).

34. Particularly the pioneering works by Ian Kershaw, *Popular Opinion and Political Dissent in the Third Reich: Bavaria, 1933–45* (Oxford: Oxford University Press, 1983) and *The "Hitler Myth": Image and Reality in the Third Reich* (Oxford: Oxford University Press, 1987). See also *Deutschland-Berichte der Sozialdemokratischen Partei Deutschlands (Sopade) 1934–1940* (Frankfurt am Main: Verlag Petra Nettelbeck & Zweitausendeins, 1980), and Heinz Boberach, ed., *Meldungen aus dem Reich: Die geheimen Lageberichte des Sicherheitsdienstes der SS 1938–1945*, 17 vols. (Herrsching, Germany: Manfred Pawlak Verlag, 1984).

35. See further Fulbrook, *Dissonant Lives*.

36. Emmendingen, Deutsches Tagebuch Archive (henceforth DTA), 1035/II W. Fr. L., Briefe an Familie B., 1935–44, letter of July 22, 1935. Like other "ordinary Germans" in this book, "Herr Lorenz" is provided with anonymity through use of a pseudonym.

37. HHL, b MS 91 (158), Gerhard M., 12.

38. DTA, 1035/II W. Fr. L., Briefe an Familie B., 1935–44, December 22, 1935.

39. DTA, 1035/II W. Fr. L., Briefe an Familie B., 1935–44, February 16, 1936.

40. HHL, b MS 91 (35), Elisabeth B., 42.

41. HHL, b MS 91 (35), Elisabeth B., 48.

42. HHL, b MS 91 (35), Elisabeth B., 49.

43. HHL, b MS 91 (35), Elisabeth B., 62.

44. HHL, b MS 91 (35), Elisabeth B., 68.

45. HHL, b MS 91 (35), Elisabeth B., 69.

46. Melita Maschmann, *Fazit: Kein Rechtfertigungsversuch* (Stuttgart: dva, 1963).

47. WL, 051-EA-0789. P.III.e. No.727, K. G. R. interviewed by H. G. Adler, July 20, 1957, 1.

48. Irene Eber, *The Choice: Poland 1939–1945* (New York: Schocken, 2004), ch. 7, 177–208.

49. Introduction to Katharina Rauschenberger and Werner Renz, eds., *Henry Ormond—Anwalt der Opfer: Plädoyers in NS-Prozessen* (Frankfurt am Main: Campus Verlag, 2015), 7–28.

50. Marie Jalowicz Simon, *Gone to Ground*, trans. Anthea Bell (London: Profile, 2016); Inge Deutschkron, *Ich trug den gelben Stern* [I wore the yellow star] (Munich: dtv, 1978); Leonard Gross, *The Last Jews in Berlin* (New York: Carroll and Graf, 1999).

51. For a popular portrayal, see Peter Wyden, *Stella* (New York: Simon & Schuster, 1992).

CHAPTER 3

1. Many authors use quotation marks around "euthanasia" to indicate that there is little in common between the Nazi program and assisted dying. After highlighting the murderous character of this program, I shall drop the scare quotes.

2. Henry Friedlander, *The Origins of Nazi Genocide: From Euthanasia to the Final Solution* (Chapel Hill: University of North Carolina Press, 1997).

3. HHL b MS Ger 91 (35), E. B., writing in Long Island, New York, April 1, 1940; born 1918, Berlin.

4. HHL b MS Ger 91 (35), Elisabeth B., 16–17.

5. HHL b MS Ger 91 (35), Elisabeth B., 38.

6. HHL b MS Ger 91 (35), Elisabeth B., 38.

7. HHL b MS Ger 91 (35), Elisabeth B., 38.

8. HHL b MS Ger 91 (35), Elisabeth B., 39–40.

9. Michael Burleigh, *Death and Deliverance: "Euthanasia" in Germany, c. 1900–1945* (Cambridge: Cambridge University Press, 1994), 45.

10. Karl Binding and Alfred Hoche, *Die Freigabe der Vernichtung lebensunwerten Lebens: Ihr Maß und ihre Form* (Leipzig: Verlag von Felix Meiner, 1920).

11. Burleigh, *Death and Deliverance*, 21–25.

12. Götz Aly, "Medicine against the Useless," in *Cleansing the Fatherland: Nazi Medicine and Racial Hygiene*, by Götz Aly, Peter Chroust, and Christian Pross, trans. Belinda Cooper (Baltimore: Johns Hopkins University Press, 1994), 29–31.

13. The distinction between "eugenic" and "libertarian" approaches discussed in Michael Bryant, *Confronting the "Good Death": Nazi Euthanasia on Trial, 1945–1953* (Boulder: University Press of Colorado, 2005), 3–4.

14. Robert Jay Lifton, *The Nazi Doctors: Medical Killing and the Psychology of Genocide* (New York: Basic Books, 1986), 50–51.

15. Petitions were dealt with by Dr. Hans Hefelmann, while Department II of the KdF under Viktor Brack and his deputy, Werner Blankenburg, took general responsibility for the question of killing the very ill.

16. Ulf Schmidt, *Karl Brandt: The Nazi Doctor; Medicine and Power in the Third Reich* (London: Hambledon Continuum, 2007), 117–23.

17. Ernst Klee, ed., *Dokumente zur "Euthanasie"* (Frankfurt am Main: Fischer Taschenbuch Verlag, 1985).

18. In German, the *Reichsausschuss zur wissenschaftlichen Erfassung von erb- und anlagebedingten schweren Leiden*.

19. Cf. Karl Brandt's comments in Nuremberg, quoted by Alice Platen-Hallermund, *Die Tötung Geistes-Kranker in Deutschland: Aus der deutschen Ärztekommission beim amerikanischen Militärgericht* (Frankfurt am Main: Verlag der Frankfurter Hefte, 1948), 22–23.

20. Klee, *Dokumente zur "Euthanasie,"* 68.

21. A facsimile is reprinted, among other places, in Astrid Ley and Annette Hinz-Wessels, eds., *Morde an Kranken und Behinderten im Nationalsozialismus* (Berlin: Metropol Verlag, 2012), 51.

22. Thomas Schilter, "Horst Schumann—Karriere eines Arztes im National-sozialismus," in *Sonnenstein: Beiträge zur Geschichte des Sonnensteins und der Sächsischen Schweiz,* Vol. 3, 2001 (95–108), 97.

23. Quoted in Patrick Montague, *Chełmno and the Holocaust: The History of Hitler's First Death Camp* (London: I. B. Tauris, 2012), 10. See also Alexander Mitscherlich and Fred Mielke, eds., *Medizin ohne Menschlichkeit: Dokumente des Nürnberger Ärzteprozesses* (Frankfurt am Main: Fischer Taschenbuchverlag, 1960).

24. Bettina Winter and Hanno Loewy, foreword to Hanno Loewy and Bettina Winter, eds., *NS- "Euthanasie" vor Gericht: Fritz Bauer und die Grenzen juristischer Bewältigung* (Frankfurt am Main: Campus Verlag, 1996), 11.

25. Ernst Klee, *"Euthanasie" im Dritten Reich: Die "Vernichtung lebensunwerten Lebens,"* rev. ed. (Frankfurt am Main: Fischer Taschenbuch Verlag, 2010), 104–8; Friedlander, *Origins of Nazi Genocide,* 136–39.

26. Volker Rieß, "Christian Wirth—der Inspekteur der Vernichtungslager," in *Karrieren der Gewalt: Nationalsozialistische Täterbiographien,* ed. Klaus-Michael Mallmann and Gerhard Paul (Darmstadt, Germany: Wissenschaftliche Buchge-sellschaft, 2004), 239–51; Friedlander, *Origins of Nazi Genocide,* 86–88; and Burleigh, *Death and Deliverance.*

27. Dick de Mildt, ed., *Tatkomplex: NS-Euthanasie; Die ost- und westdeutschen Strafurteile seit 1945,* vol. 1 (Amsterdam: Amsterdam University Press, 2009), 346.

28. Nicholas Stargardt, *The German War: A Nation under Arms, 1939–1945* (London: Bodley Head, 2015), 144–54.

29. Margarete Buber-Neumann, *Under Two Dictators: Prisoner of Stalin and Hitler,* trans. Edward Fitzgerald (London: Pimlico, 2008), 210.

30. Buber-Neuman, *Under Two Dictators,* 210–11.

31. "Hungerhäuser," *Der Spiegel,* December 1, 1965, 82, commenting on the report by Gerhard Schmidt, *Selektion in der Heilanstalt 1939 bis 1945* (Stuttgart: Evangelisches Verlagsanstalt, 1965).

32. Markus Krischer, "Euthanasie: Die Mordbilanz von 1BE," *FOCUS Magazin,* June 26, 1995; Markus Krischer, "Euthanasie: Kundschaften aus der Hölle" *FOCUS Magazin,* October 16, 1995. "Wie Münchner Staatsanwaltschaft und bayerisches Justizministerium versuchten, Sewering mit falschen Ermittlungs-berichten zu entlasten."

33. Lutz Kaelber, "Tiegenhof [Dziekanka] (Landesheilanstalt Wojewodschafts-Anstalt für Psychiatrie Tiegenhof [Gnesen])," http://www.uvm.edu/~lkaelber/children/tiegenhof/tiegenhof.html.

34. Susan Benedict and Tessa Chelouche, "Meseritz-Obrawalde: A 'Wild Euthanasia' Hospital of Nazi Germany," *History of Psychiatry* 19, no. 1 (2008): 68–76; Susan Benedict, Arthur Caplan, and Traute Lafrenz Page, " 'Duty and 'Euthanasia': The Nurses of Meseritz-Obrawalde," *Nursing Ethics* 14, no. 6 (2007): 781–94; Friedlander, *Origins of Nazi Genocide*, 160–61.

35. Emphasized by Platen-Hallermund, *Die Tötung Geistes-Kranker.*

36. Thomas Vormbaum, ed., *"Euthanasie" vor Gericht: Die Anklageschrift des Generalstaatsanwalts beim OLG Frankfurt/M. gegen Dr. Werner Heyde u.a. vom 22. Mai 1962* (Berlin: Berliner Wissenschafts-Verlag, 2005), 323–36.

37. Vormbaum, *"Euthanasie" vor Gericht*, 333.

38. Vormbaum, *"Euthanasie" vor Gericht*, 335.

39. Friedrich Karl Kaul, *Nazimordaktion T4: Ein Bericht über die erste industriemäßig durchgeführte Mordaktion des Naziregimes* (Berlin: VEB Verlag Volk und Gesundheit, 1973), 104; Aly, Chroust, and Pross, *Cleansing the Fatherland*, 248.

40. De Mildt, *Tatkomplex: NS-Euthanasie*, 1:325–39.

41. De Mildt, *Tatkomplex: NS-Euthanasie*, 1:333.

42. Letters in the Bundesarchiv (henceforth BArch), DO 1/32563, e.g., Frau Ida H., report of February 25, 1946.

43. Feldpostsammlung Museum für Kommunikation (FMK), 3-2002-1248, letter of 1 August 1942, 12; and Wolfgang-D. Sch., "Vorbemerkung," p, 5. Further details in Mary Fulbrook, *Dissonant Lives: Generations and Violence through the German Dictatorships* (Oxford: Oxford University Press, 2011), 226–28.

44. Helga Schubert, *Die Welt da drinnen: Eine deutsche Nervenklinik und der Wahn vom "unwerten Leben"* (Frankfurt am Main: Fischer Taschenbuch Verlag, 2003), 88–98.

45. Sara Berger, *Experten der Vernichtung: Das T4-Reinhardt-Netzwerk in den Lagern Belzec, Sobibor und Treblinka* (Hamburg: Hamburger Edition, 2013), 14–15.

46. Ley and Hinz-Wessels (eds.), *Morde an Kranken*, 55.

47. Wolfgang Benz, "Verweigerte Erinnerung als zweite Diskriminierung der Opfer nationalsozialistischer Politik" in Margret Hamm, ed., *Ausgegrenzt! Warum? Zwangssterilisierte und Geschädigte der NS-Euthanasie in der Bundesrepublik Deutschland* (Berlin: Metropol, 2017) (15–22), 18.

CHAPTER 4

1. The historiography is vast. Cf., e.g., Richard J. Evans, *The Third Reich at War, 1939–1945* (London: Allen Lane, 2008); Ian Kershaw, *To Hell and Back: Europe, 1914–1949* (New York: Viking, 2015); Kershaw, *The End* (London: Penguin, 2011); Mark Mazower, *Hitler's Empire: Nazi Rule in Occupied Europe* (London: Allen Lane, 2008); Timothy Snyder, *Bloodlands: Europe between Hitler and Stalin* (London: Vintage, 2011); and Nicholas Stargardt, *The German War: A Nation under Arms, 1939–1945* (London: Bodley Head, 2015).

2. Jochen Böhler, *Auftakt zum Vernichtungskrieg: Die Wehrmacht in Polen 1939* (Frankfurt am Main: Fischer Taschenbuch Verlag, 2006); Alexander Rossino,

Hitler Strikes Poland: Blitzkrieg, Ideology and Atrocity (Lawrence: University Press of Kansas, 2003).

3. Martin Winstone, *The Dark Heart of Hitler's Europe: Nazi Rule in Poland under the General Government* (London: I. B. Tauris, 2015).

4. Jan Gross, *Neighbors: The Destruction of the Jewish Community in Jedwabne, Poland, 1941* (Princeton, NJ: Princeton University Press, 2003); Anthony Polonski and Joanna Michlic, eds., *The Neighbors Respond: The Controversy over the Jedwabne Massacre in Poland* (Princeton, NJ: Princeton University Press, 2003).

5. Anna Bikont, *The Crime and the Silence: A Quest for the Truth of a Wartime Massacre*, trans. Alissa Valles (London: William Heinemann, 2015).

6. Cf., e.g., Tim Cole, *Holocaust City: The Making of a Jewish Ghetto* (New York: Routledge, 2003).

7. See for example the stages of ghettoization in Będzin in Mary Fulbrook, *A Small Town Near Auschwitz: Ordinary Nazis and the Holocaust* (Oxford: Oxford University Press, 2012).

8. Alan Adelson, "One Life Lost," introduction to *The Diary of Dawid Sierakowiak: Five Notebooks from the Łódź Ghetto*, ed. Alan Adelson (New York: Oxford University Press, 1996), 3.

9. Catherine Epstein, *Model Nazi: Arthur Greiser and the Occupation of Western Poland* (Oxford: Oxford University Press, 2010); Michael Alberti, *Die Verfolgung und Vernichtung der Juden im Reichsgau Wartheland, 1939–1945* (Wiesbaden, Germany: Harrassowitz Verlag, 2006).

10. *Diary of Dawid Sierakowiak*, 47, Wednesday, October 4, 1939. This moving diary has also been discussed in Nicholas Stargardt, *Witnesses of War: Children's Lives under the Nazis* (London: Jonathan Cape, 2005), and Saul Friedländer, *Nazi Germany and the Jews*, vol. 2, *The Years of Extermination, 1933–45* (New York: HarperCollins, 2007).

11. Adelson, "One Life Lost," 7. See also Alan Adelson and Robert Lapides, eds., *Lodz Ghetto: Inside a Community under Siege* (New York: Viking, 1989), xvii.

12. Quoted in Adelson, "One Life Lost," 3.

13. Gordon Horwitz, *Ghettostadt: Łódź and the Making of a Nazi City* (Cambridge, MA: Harvard University Press, 2008).

14. See for example photographs in Lucjan Dobroszycki, ed., *The Chronicle of the Łódź Ghetto, 1941–1944*, trans. Richard Lourie, Joachim Neugroschel, and others (New Haven, CT: Yale University Press, 1984).

15. On the contrasts between "attritionists" and "productionists" and the role of Biebow, see Christopher Browning, *The Origins of the Final Solution: The Evolution of Nazi Jewish Policy, 1939–1942* (London: Heinemann, 2004), 111–68.

16. Emphasized in Horwitz, *Ghettostadt*.

17. *Diary of Dawid Sierakowiak*, 113.

18. Lucille Eichengreen, with Harriet Hyman Chamberlain, *From Ashes to Life* (San Francisco: Mercury House, 1994).

19. See the selection available at the website The Lodz Ghetto Photographs of Henryk Ross, http://agolodzghetto.com.

20. Jens-Jürgen Ventzki, *Seine Schatten, meine Bilder: Eine Spurensuche* (Innsbruck, Austria: Studien Verlag, 2011).

21. Dobroszycki, *Chronicle of the Łódź Ghetto*.

22. *Diary of Dawid Sierakowiak*, 90.

23. *Diary of Dawid Sierakowiak*, 91.

24. *Diary of Dawid Sierakowiak*, 94.

25. Anonymous girl, Łódź Ghetto, in Alexandra Zapruder, ed., *Salvaged Pages: Young Writers' Diaries of the Holocaust* (New Haven, CT: Yale University Press, 2002), 231, entry misdated February 24, 1942, but actually February 27.

26. Anonymous, in Zapruder, *Salvaged Pages*, 255–56.

27. Anonymous, in Zapruder, *Salvaged Pages*, 236.

28. Anonymous, in Zapruder, *Salvaged Pages*, 238.

29. *Diary of Dawid Sierakowiak*, 95.

30. *Diary of Dawid Sierakowiak*, 156.

31. *Diary of Dawid Sierakowiak*, 157.

32. Adelson, "One Life Lost," 14.

33. *Diary of Dawid Sierakowiak*, 268.

34. Ruth Andreas-Friedrich, *Berlin Underground, 1938–1945*, trans. Barrows Mussey (New York: Henry Holt, 1947), 70.

35. Dobroszycki, *Chronicle of the Łódź Ghetto*, 78n92.

36. Dobroszycki, *Chronicle of the Łódź Ghetto*, 85.

37. Dobroszycki, *Chronicle of the Łódź Ghetto*, 85–86.

38. Dobroszycki, *Chronicle of the Łódź Ghetto*, 86.

39. Dobroszycki, *Chronicle of the Łódź Ghetto*, 96.

40. Dobroszycki, *Chronicle of the Łódź Ghetto*, 96–97.

41. Dobroszycki, *Chronicle of the Łódź Ghetto*, 108.

42. Dobroszycki, *Chronicle of the Łódź Ghetto*, 141.

43. Andreas-Friedrich, *Berlin Underground*, 83.

44. Mary Berg, *Warsaw Ghetto: A Diary*, ed. S. L. Shneiderman (New York: L. B. Fischer, 1945), 57.

45. Berg, *Warsaw Ghetto*, 57–58.

46. Raul Hilberg, Stanislaw Staron, and Josef Kermisz, eds., *The Warsaw Diary of Adam Czerniakow: Prelude to Doom*, trans. Stanislaw Staron and staff of Yad Vashem (New York: Stein & Day, 1979), 384.

47. *Warsaw Diary of Adam Czerniakow*, 385.

48. *Warsaw Diary of Adam Czerniakow*, 385.

49. Josef Kermisz, introduction to *Warsaw Diary of Adam Czerniakow*, 70.

50. Berg, *Warsaw Ghetto*, 174.

51. See for example Lucille Eichengreen's autobiographical account, with Rebecca Camhi Fromer, *Rumkowski and the Orphans of Lodz* (San Francisco: Mercury House, 2000).

52. Rumkowski is quoted as saying: "A grievous blow has struck the ghetto. They are asking us to give up the best we possess—the children and the elderly. I never imagined I would be forced to deliver this sacrifice to the altar with my

own hands. In my old age, I must stretch out my hands and beg. Brothers and sisters: Hand them over to me! Fathers and mothers: Give me your children!" Available at the United States Holocaust Memorial Museum's online *Holocaust Encyclopedia*, http://www.ushmm.org/wlc/en/article.php?ModuleId= 10007282, accessed January 26, 2016. See Dobroszycki, *Chronicle of the Łódź Ghetto*, 250–55, for the reactions of ghetto inhabitants.

53. Isaiah Trunk, *Łódź Ghetto: A History*, trans. Robert Moses Shapiro (Bloomington: Indiana University Press, 2006), 104–47.

54. Melita Maschmann, *Fazit: Kein Rechtfertigungsversuch* (Stuttgart: dva, 1963), 90 and, on the Kutno and Łódź ghettos, 85–90.

55. In Hochberg-Mariańska and Grüss, *The Children Accuse*, nos. 1 and 2, 3–11.

56. Quoted in Heribert Schwan and Helgard Heindrichs, *Der SS-Mann: Josef Blösche—Leben und Sterben eines Mörders* (Munich: Droemer Knaur, 2003), 157, 163–64.

57. Jürgen Stroop, *Es gibt keinen jüdischen Wohnbezirk in Warschau mehr!*, facsimile in *Żydowska dzielnica mieszkaniowa w Warszawie już nie istnieje!*, ed. Andrzej Żbikowski (Warsaw: Instytut Pamięci Narodowej, 2009), available at http://www.pamiec.pl/ftp/ilustracje/Raport_STROOPA.pdf; English version: Jürgen Stroop, *The Stroop Report: The Jewish Quarter of Warsaw Is No More!*, trans. Sybil Milton, Andrzej Wirth (New York: Pantheon, 1979).

58. Brief summary in Wolfgang Benz and Barbara Distel, eds., *Der Ort des Terrors: Geschichte der nationalsozialistischen Konzentrationslager*, vol. 8 (Munich: C. H. Beck, 2008), 296–97.

59. BArch, DP 3/1587, Testimony of Bendet Gotdenker, (n.d., c. 1967), fo. 176.

60. Irene Eber, *The Choice: Poland 1939–1945* (New York: Schocken, 2004), 78.

61. Eber, *Choice*, 79.

62. Eber, *Choice*, 80.

63. Fortunoff Archive, HVT-69, Dr Hillel K., interviewed May 3, 1980 by Dori Laub and Laurel Vlock.

64. Fortunoff Archive, HVT-69, Hillel K.

65. Eber, *Choice*, 85.

66. Eber, *Choice*, 96–97.

67. Eber, *Choice*, 56.

68. BArch DP 3/1590, vol. 6, Letter of June 12, 1973 from Irma Zimmermann to the Generalstaatsanwalt der DDR, Dr. Streit, 2. See also Zimmermann's statement in BArch DP 3/1591.

69. Eber, *Choice*, 95.

70. Eber, *Choice*, 98.

71. Eber, *Choice*, 98.

72. Zimmermann's statements in BArch DP 3/1588, BArch DP 3/1589, and BArch DP 3/1591.

73. Eber, *Choice*, 10; Rochelle Saidel, *Mielec, Poland: The Shtetl that Became a Nazi Concentration Camp* (Jerusalem: Gefen, 2012), 56.

74. BArch DP 3/1588, fo. 248.
75. Yad Vashem, 033/1699, Record group 0.33, File number 1699.1, Jack (Icek) S., 3.
76. BArch DP 3/1588, fo. 247.
77. Eber, *Choice*, 9.
78. Yad Vashem, 033/1699, Jack (Icek) S., 3.
79. Yad Vashem, 033/1699, Jack (Icek) S., 3.
80. Yad Vashem, 033/1699, Jack (Icek) S., 3.
81. Adam Tooze, *The Wages of Destruction: The Making and Breaking of the Nazi Economy* (London: Penguin, 2007), 558–59.
82. Tooze, *Wages of Destruction*, 517.
83. Nikolaus Wachsmann, *KL: A History of the Nazi Concentration Camps* (London: Little, Brown, 2015), 392–443.
84. Tooze, *Wages of Destruction*, 513–551.
85. Richard Overy, *Goering: The "Iron Man"* (London: Routledge & Kegan Paul, 1984), ch. 7; Lutz Budrass, "Der Preis des Fortschritts: Ernst Heinkels Meistererzählung über die Tradition der deutschen Luftfahrtindustrie," in *Unternehmer und NS-Verbrechen: Wirtschaftseliten im "Dritten Reich" und in der Bundesrepublik Deutschland*, ed. Jörg Osterloh and Harald Wixforth (Frankfurt am Main: Campus Verlag, Wissenschaftliche Reihe des Fritz Bauer Instituts, 2014), 217–49.
86. Yad Vashem, Subsection M.21.3, File 35, Kriegsverbrecherrrefarat/War criminals section, Legal department at the Central Committee of Liberated Jews, Munich [IT Number 3692876], Testimony of Josef Kahane 2.L, 1947, fo. 50.
87. Budrass, "Der Preis des Fortschritts," 218.
88. Budrass, "Der Preis des Fortschritts," 218–19.
89. Budrass, "Der Preis des Fortschritts," 218.
90. Examples in Alicia Nitecki and Jack Terry, *Jakub's World: A Boy's Story of Loss and Survival in the Holocaust* (Albany: State University of New York Press, 2005), 35–47.
91. Reinhold Feix discussed in Nitecki and Terry, *Jakub's World*, 35–47. See also Ulrich Baron, "Sie haben uns nicht erwischt: Holocaust-Überlebende spielen auf in Deutschland; Jack Eisner erzählt die Geschichte der 'Happy Boys,'" *Die Welt*, August 14, 2004. There are differing stories about the fates of Feix and his son. Feix is variously supposed to have escaped justice and died quietly in his bed or to have died in Russian captivity, having lost a leg, and perhaps by committing suicide. His son almost certainly committed suicide, perhaps as a young man, or as late as 1980, when he would have been in his early forties. See for example Nitecki and Terry, *Jakub's World*, 116; contrasting story in Baron, "Sie haben uns nicht erwischt."
92. Jack Eisner, *The Survivor*, ed. Irving A. Leitner (New York: William Morrow, 1980), 247.
93. Eisner, *Survivor*, 247–50; Nitecki and Terry, *Jakub's World*, 35–47.
94. Eisner, *Survivor*, 250.
95. Nitecki and Terry, *Jakub's World*, 46–47.
96. Quoted in Nitecki and Terry, *Jakub's World*, 47.

97. George H. Stein, *The Waffen SS: Hitler's Elite Guard at War, 1939–1945* (Ithaca, NY: Cornell University Press, 1966), 109n47.

98. Volkhard Bode and Gerhard Kaiser, *Building Hitler's Missiles: Traces of History in Peenemünde*, trans. Katy Derbyshire (Berlin: Ch. Links Verlag, 2008), 59–61; Benjamin King and Timothy Kutta, *Impact: The History of Germany's V-Weapons in World War II* (Cambridge, MA.: Da Capo, 1998), 73–74. On Himmler, photograph at the HL Heidelager website, http://pustkow.republika.pl/historia. html, accessed October 27, 2014, and Christy Campbell, *Target London: Under Attack from the V-Weapons during WWII* (London: Hachette Digital, 2012), 143.

99. Biographical data supplied by his son in an interview held in the Kestenberg Archive, Jerusalem (henceforth KA) (257), 26–42, HM. "Peter Müller" did not enter the archival record as a "person of historical significance"; I have changed the names in order to preserve anonymity.

100. C. F. Rüter and D. W. de Mildt, eds., *Justiz und NS-Verbrechen: Sammlung deutscher Strafurteile wegen nationalsozialistischer Tötungsverbrechen, 1945–1999*, vol. 39, *Die vom 05.06.1973 bis zum 26.07.1974 ergangenen Strafurteile: Lfd Nr. 795–813* (Amsterdam: Amsterdam University Press and K. G. Saur Verlag München, 2008) Lfd. Nr. 802. Tatkomplex: NS-Gewaltverbrechen in Haftstätten/Tatort: ZAL Truppenübungsplatz Debica, 345.

101. Rüter and de Mildt, *Justiz und NS-Verbrechen*, 39:351.

102. Rüter and de Mildt, *Justiz und NS-Verbrechen*, 39:353.

103. University of Southern California, Visual History Archive (henceforth USC VHA), Norbert Friedman (b. 1922, Kraków), interviewed by Mark Goldberg on June 7, 1995, West Hempstead, NY.

104. Hochberg-Mariańska and Grüss, *The Children Accuse*, 15.

105. Jan Grabowski, *Hunt for the Jews: Betrayal and Murder in German-Occupied Poland* (Bloomington: Indiana University Press, 2013).

106. Zygmunt Klukowski, *Diary from the Years of Occupation 1939–44*, trans. George Klukowski, ed. Andrew Klukowski and Helen Klukowski May (Urbana: University of Illinois Press, 1993), 219.

107. Klukowski, *Diary*, 220.

108. Klukowski, *Diary*, 220.

109. Klukowski, *Diary*, 220.

100. Eber, *Choice*, 45–52, 114–16.

111. Eber, *Choice*, 114.

112. Benz and Distel, *Ort des Terrors*, 8:296.

CHAPTER 5

1. Horst Möller, foreword to Christian Hartmann, Johannes Hürter, and Ulrike Jureit, eds., *Verbrechen der Wehrmacht: Bilanz einer Debatte* (Munich: C. H. Beck, 2005), 12; Christian Hartmann, "Wie verbrecherisch war die Wehrmacht? Zur Beteiligung von Wehrmachtsangehörigen an Kriegs- und NS-Verbrechen," in Hartmann, Hürter, and Jureit, *Verbrechen der Wehrmacht*, 69–79.

2. The literature on this is massive. But for overviews see for example David Cesarani, *Final Solution: The Fate of the Jews, 1933–49* (London: Macmillan, 2016); Saul Friedländer, *Nazi Germany and the Jews*, vol. 2, *The Years of Extermination, 1933–45* (New York: HarperCollins, 2007); Dan Stone, ed., *The Historiography of the Holocaust* (Houndmills, UK: Macmillan, 2004); and, for insights into a less familiar area, Wendy Lower, *Hitler's Furies: German Women in the Nazi Killing Fields* (London: Vintage, 2014).

3. Donald Bloxham, "The Einsatzgruppen: An Overview," in *Einsatzgruppen C and D in the Invasion of the Soviet Union*, ed. Dieter Pohl and Andrej Angrick, Holocaust Educational Trust Research papers, vol. 1, no. 4 (London: Holocaust Educational Trust, 1999–2000), 4.

4. Ernst Klee, Willi Dressen, and Volker Riess, eds., *"The Good Old Days": The Holocaust As Seen by Its Perpetrators and Bystanders*, trans. Deborah Burnstone (New York: Free Press, 1991), 27.

5. Klee, Dressen, and Riess, *Good Old Days*, 32, see also 33.

6. Klee, Dressen, and Riess, *Good Old Days*, 34; see also 35.

7. The army's involvement was discussed by historians as early as the 1950s; e.g., Gerald Reitlinger, *The Final Solution: The Attempt to Exterminate the Jews of Europe 1939–1945*, 2nd ed. (South Brunswick, NJ: Thomas Yoseloff, 1961), 208–13.

8. Eyewitness accounts in Klee, Dressen, and Riess, *Good Old Days*, 63–68.

9. Nicholas Stargardt, *The German War: A Nation under Arms, 1939–1945* (London: Bodley Head, 2015), 233–67.

10. Pohl and Angrick, *Einsatzgruppen C and D*; Christopher Browning, *Ordinary Men: Reserve Police Battalion 101 and the Final Solution in Poland* (London: HarperCollins, 1992); Olaf Jensen and Claus-Christian Szejnmann, eds., *Ordinary People as Mass Murderers: Perpetrators in Comparative Perspectives* (Houndmills, UK: Palgrave Macmillan, 2008).

11. Klee, Dressen, and Riess, *Good Old Days*, 60.

12. Sönke Neitzel and Harald Welzer, *Soldaten: Protokolle vom Kämpfen, Töten und Sterben* (Frankfurt am Main: S. Fischer, 2011), 145.

13. Browning, *Ordinary Men*.

14. Klee, Dressen, and Riess, *Good Old Days*, 62.

15. Andrej Angrick, "Einsatzgruppe D," in Pohl and Angrick, *Einsatzgruppen C and D*, 23.

16. Klee, Dressen, and Riess, *Good Old Days*, 69.

17. Rudolf Höss, *Autobiography of Rudolf Höss*, in *KL Auschwitz Seen by the SS*, eds. Jadwiga Bezwińska and Danuta Czech, trans. Constantine Fitzgibbon (Oświęcim, Poland: Publications of Państwowe Muzeum w Oświęcimiu, 1972), 95.

18. Höss, *Autobiography*, 94.

19. Cf. Raul Hilberg, "Auschwitz and the 'Final Solution,'" in *Anatomy of the Auschwitz Death Camp*, ed. Yisrael Gutman and Michael Berenbaum (Bloomington: Indiana University Press, 1994), 81; Jonathan Huener, *Auschwitz, Poland, and the Politics of Commemoration, 1945–1979* (Athens: Ohio University Press, 2003), 15.

20. Huener, *Auschwitz*, 20. The figures are based on older work by Martin Gilbert, when exact numbers were not known. All estimates remain precisely that: estimates. The point is simply that numbers of survivors were very low, in single or double figures only, compared with the thousands surviving the Auschwitz complex.

21. See for example Jean Améry, *At the Mind's Limits: Contemplations by a Survivor of Auschwitz and Its Realities*, trans. Sidney and Stella P. Rosenfeld (Bloomington: Indiana University Press, 1980); Charlotte Delbo, *Auschwitz and After*, trans. Rose C. Lamont (New Haven, CT: Yale University Press, 1995); Wieslaw Kielar, *Anus Mundi: Five Years in Auschwitz*, trans. Susanne Flatauer (Harmondsworth, UK: Penguin, 1982); Primo Levi, *If This Is a Man*, trans. Stuart Woolf (London: Everyman's Library, 2000); Filip Müller, *Eyewitness Auschwitz: Three Years in the Gas Chamber* (Chicago: Ivan R. Dee, 1999); Miklós Nyiszli, *I Was Doctor Mengele's Assistant* (Oświęcim, Poland: Frap, 2001); the autobiographical stories of Tadeusz Borowski in his *This Way for the Gas, Ladies and Gentlemen* (London: Penguin, 1992); and autobiographical novels such as Imre Kertész, *Fateless*, trans. Tim Wilkinson (New York: Vintage International, 2004) and Elie Wiesel, *Night* (New York: Hill & Wang, 1960). There is a vast literature on Holocaust writing; see for example Ruth Franklin, *A Thousand Darknesses: Lies and Truth in Holocaust Fiction* (New York: Oxford University Press, 2011).

22. Father Patrick Desbois, *The Holocaust by Bullets: A Priest's Journey to Uncover the Truth behind the Murder of 1.5 Million Jews* (Houndmills, UK: Palgrave Macmillan, 2008).

23. For extensive photographic documentation, see Hans Citroen with Barbara Starzyńska, *Auschwitz—Oświęcim* (Rotterdam: Post Editions, 2011). Huener points out that the state museum covers 1.8 sq. km, "making it the largest memorial site of a former camp," but this is still "less than one-twentieth of the total area of the so-called Auschwitz 'area of interest' defined in 1941"; Jonathan Huener, *Auschwitz, Poland, and the Politics of Commemoration, 1945-1979* (Athens, Ohio: Ohio University Press, 2003), 253n42.

24. Andreas Plake, Babette Quinkert, and Florian Schmaltz, afterword to Hans Frankenthal, *The Unwelcome One: Returning Home from Auschwitz*, trans. John A. Broadwin (Evanston, IL: Northwestern University Press, 2002), 127–37.

25. Markus Roth, *Herrenmenschen: Die deutschen Kreishauptleute im besetzten Polen—Karrierewege, Herrschaftspraxis und Nachgeschichte* (Göttingen, Germany: Wallstein Verlag, 2009), 203–4.

26. Michael Bryant, *Confronting the "Good Death": Nazi Euthanasia on Trial, 1945–1953* (Boulder: University Press of Colorado, 2005), 98–104.

27. Yitzhak Arad, *Belzec, Sobibor, Treblinka: The Operation Reinhard Death Camps* (Bloomington: Indiana University Press, 1987); Robert Kuwałek, *Das Vernichtungslager Bełżec*, trans. Steffen Hänschen (Berlin: Metropol, 2013). The name is sometimes spelled "Operation Reinhardt" with a "t" at the end.

28. Kuwałek, *Vernichtungslager Bełżec*, 247–54.

29. Rudolf Reder, *Bełżec* (Kraków: Centralna Żydowska Komisja Historyczna przy C. K. Żydów Polskich, 1946); in English translation as *I Survived a Secret Nazi Extermination Camp*, ed. Mark Forstater (London: Psychology News, 2015). Hirszman's testimony, completed by his wife following his murder, is available at: https://kollublin.wordpress.com/2011/10/01/chaim-hirszman-testimo/, accessed January 25, 2015.

30. Reder, *I Survived*, 13

31. Reder, *I Survived*, 18.

32. Reder, *I Survived*, 23.

33. Reder, *I Survived*, 19.

34. Reder, *I Survived*, 20.

35. Reder, *I Survived*, 20.

36. Reder, *I Survived*, 30.

37. Reder, *I Survived*, 22.

38. Reder, *I Survived*, 35–36.

39. Reder, *I Survived*, 37–38.

40. Peter Witte et al., eds., *Der Dienstkalender Heinrich Himmlers 1941/42: Im Auftrag der Forschungsstelle für Zeitgeschichte in Hamburg* (Hamburg: Hans Christians Verlag, 1999), 310–11, details of the "Inspektionsreise" of January 7–8, 1942, including a "200 km" journey that probably went right past Bełżec, 311n26.

41. Himmler may have watched deportations while in Lemberg in August 1942. On Galicia, see Dieter Pohl, *Nationalsozialistische Judenverfolgung in Ostgalizien, 1941–1944* (Munich: Oldenbourg, 1996); and Thomas Sandkühler, *"Endlösung" in Galizien* (Bonn, Germany: Dietz Verlag, 1996).

42. Wendy Lower, *The Diary of Samuel Golfard and the Holocaust in Galicia* (Lanham, MD: AltaMira, 2011), 98–100.

43. Reder, *I Survived*, 38.

44. Reder, *I Survived*, 39.

45. Reder, *I Survived*, 39

46. Reder, *I Survived*, 40.

47. Pohl, *Nationalsozialistische Judenverfolgung*, 388.

48. Thomas (Toivi) Blatt, *Sobibor: The Forgotten Revolt; A Survivor's Report* (Issaquah, WA: HEP, 1997), 18.

49. Blatt, *Sobibor*, 17.

50. Blatt, *Sobibor*, 17.

51. Thomas (Toivi) Blatt, *From the Ashes of Sobibor: A Story of Survival* (Evanston, IL: Northwestern University Press, 1997), 96.

52. Blatt, *From the Ashes of Sobibor*, 232–33n13. See also Arad, *Belzec, Sobibor, Treblinka*; Blatt. *Sobibor*; Jules Schelvis, *Sobibór: A History of the Nazi Death Camp*, trans. Karin Dixon (Oxford: Berg, 2007).

53. Witold Chrostowski, *Extermination Camp Treblinka* (London: Vallentine Mitchell, 2004).

54. Shimon Goldberg, quoted in Arad, *Belzec, Sobibor, Treblinka*, 153.

55. Chil Rajchman, *Treblinka: A Survivor's Memory, 1942–1943*, trans. Solon Beinfeld (London: MacLehose, 2011), 50.

56. Yankel Wiernik, *A Year in Treblinka* (New York: American Representation of the General Jewish Workers' Union of Poland, 1945), 8. Available at http://www .zchor.org/wiernik.htm, accessed January 24, 2016.

57. Rajchman, *Treblinka*, 58.

58. Rajchman, *Treblinka*, 59.

59. Rajchman, *Treblinka*, 59.

60. Richard Glazar, *Trap with a Green Fence*, trans. Roslyn Theobald (Evanston, IL: Northwestern University Press, 1995), 56.

61. Glazar, *Trap with a Green Fence,* 64.

62. On Franz, see also Arad, *Belzec, Sobibor, Treblinka*, 189–91.

63. Wiernik, *Year in Treblinka*, 16.

64. Arad, *Belzec, Sobibor, Treblinka*, 40, 123.

65. Wiernik, *Year in Treblinka*, 12–13.

66. Wiernik, *Year in Treblinka*, 16.

67. Wiernik, *Year in Treblinka*, 13.

68. Wiernik, *Year in Treblinka*, 4.

69. Blatt, *Sobibor*, 91–92.

70. See for example Timothy Snyder, *Bloodlands: Europe between Hitler and Stalin* (London: Bodley Head, 2011).

71. Glazar, *Trap with a Green Fence*, 53.

72. Glazar, *Trap with a Green Fence*, 53.

73. Glazar, *Trap with a Green Fence*, 53.

74. Roth, *Herrenmenschen*; for the "war youth generation," see Michael Wildt, *Generation des Unbedingten: Das Führungskorps des Reichssicherheitshauptamtes* (Hamburg: Hamburger Edition, 2002), and Wildt, *Generation of the Unbound: The Leadership Corps of the Reich Security Main Office* (Jerusalem: Yad Vashem, 2002); see also Mary Fulbrook, *Dissonant Lives: Generations and Violence through the German Dictatorships* (Oxford: Oxford University Press, 2011).

75. Philippe Sands, "My father, the good Nazi," *Financial Times Magazine*, May 3, 2013, available at http://www.ft.com/cms/s/2/7d6214f2-b2be-11e2-8540-00144 feabdco.html, accessed January 31, 2016; see also Philippe Sands, *East West Street* (London: Weidenfeld & Nicolson, 2016).

76. BArch DP 3/2164, Bd. 31, Reservepolizeibataillon 41 (Kriegsverbrechen in Polen), 1980.

77. See for example Wolf Gruner, *Jewish Forced Labour under the Nazis: Economic Needs and Racial Aims, 1938–1944*, trans. Kathleen M. Dell'orto (Cambridge: Cambridge University Press, 2006), 214–29; Stephan Lehnstaedt, "Coercion and Incentive: Jewish Ghetto Labor in East Upper Silesia," *Holocaust and Genocide Studies* 24, no. 3 (Winter 2010): 400–430; Sybille Steinbacher, *"Musterstadt" Auschwitz: Germanisierungspolitik und Judenmord in Ostoberschlesien* (Munich: K. G. Saur, 2000), and Steinbacher, "In the Shadow of Auschwitz: The Murder

of the Jews of East Upper Silesia," in *Holocaust: Critical Concepts in Historical Studies*, ed. David Cesarani (London: Routledge, 2004), 110–36.

78. Jens-Christian Wagner, *Produktion des Todes: Das KZ Mittelbau-Dora* (Göttingen, Germany: Wallstein, 2001).

79. Bertrand Perz, *Projekt "Quarz": Der Bau einer unterirdischen Fabrik durch Häftlinge des KZ Melk für die Steyr-Daimler-Puch AG 1944–1945* (Innsbruck, Austria: Studien Verlag, 2012); Silvia Rief, *Rüstungsproduktion und Zwangsarbeit: Die Steyrer-Werke und das KZ Gusen* (Vienna: Studien Verlag, 2005).

80. Detailed figures in Florian Freund, Bertrand Perz, and Mark Spoerer, *Zwangsarbeiter und Zwangsarbeiterinnen auf dem Gebiet der Republik Österreich, 1939–1945* (Vienna: Oldenbourg Verlag, 2004).

81. Daniel Blatman, *The Death Marches: The Final Phase of Nazi Genocide* (Cambridge, MA: Belknap Press of Harvard University Press, 2011), 43.

82. Wachsmann, *KL*, ch. 8, "Economics and Extermination."

83. Michael Thad Allen, *The Business of Genocide: The SS, Slave Labor, and the Concentration Camps* (Chapel Hill: University of North Carolina Press, 2002), 167–71.

84. Perz, *Projekt "Quarz,"* 224–28.

85. Blatman, *Death Marches*, 31, 42. Also Wachsmann, *KL*, table 1: "Daily Inmate Numbers in the SS Concentration Camps, 1934–45," 627.

86. Gordon J. Horwitz, *In the Shadow of Death: Living outside the Gates of Mauthausen* (New York: Free Press, 1990), 9–10.

87. Horwitz, *In the Shadow of Death*, 35.

88. Horwitz, *In the Shadow of Death*, 43–44; 30. Gordon J. Horwitz, "Places Far Away, Places Very Near: Mauthausen, the Camps of the Shoah, and the Bystanders," in *The Holocaust and History: The Known, the Unknown, the Disputed, and the Reexamined*, ed. Michael Berenbaum and Abraham J. Peck (Bloomington: Indiana University Press, 1998), 409–20.

89. Blatman, *Death Marches*, 37, 370.

90. Simone Erpel, ed., *Im Gefolge der SS: Aufseherinnen des Frauen-KZ Ravensbrück* (Berlin: Metropol Verlag, 2007); Sarah Helm, *If This Is a Woman: Inside Ravensbrück: Hitler's Concentration Camp for Women* (London: Little, Brown, 2015).

91. Jack C. Morrison, *Ravensbrück: Everyday Life in a Women's Concentration Camp, 1939–45* (Princeton, NJ: Markus Wiener, 2000), 24–25.

92. Margarete Buber-Neumann, *Under Two Dictators: Prisoner of Stalin and Hitler*, trans. Edward Fitzgerald (London: Pimlico, 2008), 175.

93. Buber-Neumann, *Under Two Dictators*, 176.

94. Buber-Neumann, *Under Two Dictators*, 232.

95. Buber-Neumann, *Under Two Dictators*, 232.

96. Buber-Neumann, *Under Two Dictators*, 232–33.

97. Christian Streit, *Keine Kameraden: Die Wehrmacht und die Sowjetischen Kriegsgefangenen, 1941–1945* (Bonn, Germany: Dietz Verlag, 1991).

98. Horwitz, *In the Shadow of Death*, 21.

99. Blatman, *Death Marches*.
100. Contrast Blatman, *Death Marches*, with Daniel Jonah Goldhagen, *Hitler's Willing Executioners: Ordinary Germans and the Holocaust* (London: Little, Brown, 1996).
101. Lucille Eichengreen, with Harriet Hyman Chamberlain, *From Ashes to Life* (San Francisco: Mercury House, 1994).
102. David P. Boder interviews: Sigmund Reich; August 26, 1946; Genève, Switzerland: Voices of the Holocaust Project, http://voices.iit.edu/interviewee?doc=reichS.
103. Yad Vashem, YV 069/310, testimony of Mark Stern (Markus, Maniek), Pittsburgh, PA, June 1981, "specifically, for the World Gathering of Holocaust Survivors in Israel," 12.
104. Yad Vashem, record group 0.3, file no. 12865, Nathan Gottlieb, born 1925, Radom, Poland, interviewed February 2, 2007, by Esther Hagar, 54.
105. Jack Eisner, *The Survivor*, ed. Irving A. Leitner (New York: William Morrow, 1980), 266.
106. Alicia Nitecki and Jack Terry, *Jakub's World: A Boy's Story of Loss and Survival in the Holocaust* (Albany: State University of New York Press, 2005).
107. Sven Felix Kellerhoff, "Der SS-Mörder von Gardelegen blieb straflos," *Die Welt*, April 13, 2015, available online at http://www.welt.de/geschichte/zweiter-weltkrieg/article139484279/Der-SS-Moerder-von-Gardelegen-blieb-straflos.html, accessed February 1, 2016.
108. BArch, DO 1/32699, Bericht vom 25.6.50, Betr: Gräberfund auf der Flur Spohla—Wittichanau, Landesbehörde der Volkspolizei Sachsen, fos. 58–62.
109. BArch, DO 1/32574 Bd 1, fos. 243–44, testimony of Gertrud L.
110. For East German reports, see BArch, DO 1/32574 Bd. 1; BArch, BArch, DO 1/32574 Bd. 2.; BArch, DO 1/32577.

CHAPTER 6

1. Jack Terry, "Ich fühle noch den Schmerz," *Der Spiegel*, March 18, 2009, available at http://www.spiegel.de/einestages/kz-ueberlebender-jack-terry-a-949757.html, accessed November 30, 2015.
2. Fortunoff Archive, HVT-1521, Aaron S. (born 1909), interviewed by Bernard Weinstein and Susanna Rich, March 28 and April 5, 1989.
3. Sarah Kaplan, " 'I'm Still There—In My Dreams', Said Thomas Blatt, Survivor of Daring Escape from Nazi Death Camp," *Washington Post*, November 3, 2015, available at https://www.washingtonpost.com/news/morning-mix/wp/2015/11/03/thomas-blatt-vocal-survivor-of-rare-revolt-at-nazi-death-camp-dies-at-88/, accessed December 17, 2015.
4. Cf. Guenter Lewy, *The Nazi Persecution of the Gypsies* (New York: Oxford University Press, 2000), 219–28, and Anton Weiss-Wendt, introduction to Anton Weiss-Wendt, ed., *The Nazi Genocide of the Roma: Reassessment and Commemoration* (New York: Berghahn, 2013), 1–26.

5. Denise Dufournier, *Ravensbrück: The Women's Camp of Death*, trans. F. W. McPherson (London: George Allen & Unwin, 1948), viii.

6. Autobiographical novel, in the third person: Cordelia Edvardson, *Gebranntes Kind sucht das Feuer*, trans. Anna-Liese Kornitzky (Munich: Carl Hanser Verlag, 1986).

7. Primo Levi, *If This Is a Man*, trans. Stuart Woolf (London: Random House, 2000).

8. Cordelia Edvardson, *Die Welt zusammenfügen*, trans. Jörg Scherzer and Anna-Liese Kornitzky (Munich: Deutscher Taschenbuch Verlag, 1991), 11.

9. Judith Kestenberg Archive (henceforth KA), Hebrew University of Jerusalem, interview no. (257) 24–15, Eva S., 2–3.

10. KA, (257) 24-15, Eva S., 8.

11. KA, (257) 24-15, Eva S., 8.

12. KA, (257) 24-15, Eva S., 8.

13. KA, (257) 24-15, Eva S., 8.

14. Fortunoff Archive, HVT-87, Niusia A. (born 1924 in Kraków), interviewed on November 5, 1979 by Laurel Vlock in Israel.

15. Denise Dufournier, *Ravensbrück: The Women's Camp of Death*, trans. F. W. McPherson (London: George Allen & Unwin, 1948), 16.

16. Yankel Wiernik, *A Year in Treblinka* (New York: American Representation of the General Jewish Workers' Union of Poland, 1945), 12, available at http://www.zchor.org/wiernik.htm, accessed January 24, 2016.

17. Yad Vashem (YV) 069/310, Mark Stern, June 1981.

18. Margarete Buber-Neumann, *Under Two Dictators: Prisoner of Stalin and Hitler*, trans. Edward Fitzgerald (London: Pimlico, 2008), 185.

19. Buber-Neumann, *Under Two Dictators*, 185.

20. Buber-Neumann, *Under Two Dictators*, 173.

21. Gilbert Michlin, *Of No Interest to the Nation: A Jewish Family in France, 1925–1945* (Detroit, MI: Wayne State University Press, 2004), 73–74.

22. Fortunoff Archive, HVT-210, Alex H., interviewed July 16, 1983 by Rosemary Balsam and Paul Schwaber.

23. Ella Lingens-Reiner, *Prisoners of Fear* (London: Victor Gollancz, 1948), 50–53 and passim.

24. Richard Glazar, *Trap with a Green Fence*, trans. Roslyn Theobald (Evanston, IL: Northwestern University Press, 1995); Thomas (Toivi) Blatt, *Sobibor: The Forgotten Revolt; A Survivor's Report* (Issaquah, WA: HEP, 1997).

25. Peter Michael Lingens, *Ansichten eines Außenseiters* (Vienna: Verlag Kremayr & Scheriau, 2009), 38.

26. KA, (257) 24-15, Eva S., 31.

27. KA, (257) 24-15, Eva S., 35.

28. KA, (257) 24-15, Eva S., 73.

29. Hans Frankenthal, with Andreas Plake, Babette Quinkert and Florian Schmaltz, *The Unwelcome One: Returning home from Auschwitz*, trans. John A. Broadwin (Evanston, IL: Northwestern University Press, 2002), 50.

30. Frankenthal, *Unwelcome One*, 51.
31. Lingens-Reiner, *Prisoners of Fear*, 50–53.
32. Bruno Bettelheim, "Individual and Mass Behavior in Extreme Situations," *Journal of Abnormal Social Psychology* 38 (1943): 417–52.
33. Heinz Heger, *The Men with the Pink Triangle*, trans. David Fernbach (London: Gay Men's Press, 1980), 32. The prisoner was actually called Josef Kohout; Hans Neumann, using the pen name of Heinz Heger, wrote the book on the basis of extensive interviews with Kohout. This account was significant in raising awareness of the plight of gay men during and after the war.
34. Heger, *Men with the Pink Triangle*, 101.
35. Heger, *Men with the Pink Triangle*, 35.
36. Heger, *Men with the Pink Triangle*, 44–45.
37. Heger, *Men with the Pink Triangle*, 45.
38. Heger, *Men with the Pink Triangle*, 101.
39. Wiener Library (henceforth WL), 049-EA-0666, P.III.b.Np.1178, Janka Galambos, recorded by Alexander Szanto, London, February 1960, 6.
40. Fortunoff Archive, HVT-2836, Henry K. (born 1923), interviewed by Steven Gonzer and Judith Melman, February 28, 1995.
41. Heger, *Men with the Pink Triangle*, 75.
42. Marie Jalowicz Simon, *Gone to Ground*, trans. Anthea Bell (London: Profile Books, 2016).
43. Thomas (Toivi) Blatt, *From the Ashes of Sobibor: A Story of Survival* (Evanston, IL: Northwestern University Press, 1997), xxii.
44. Wiernik, *Year in Treblinka*, 14.
45. Wiernik, *Year in Treblinka*, 17–18.
46. Buber-Neumann, *Under Two Dictators*, 193.
47. Buber-Neumann, *Under Two Dictators*, 195.
48. Buber-Neumann, *Under Two Dictators*, 195.
49. USC VHA, 3022, Norbert Friedman (born 1922, Krakow), interviewed by Mark Goldberg, June 7, 1995, West Hempstead, NY.
50. USC VHA, 3022, Norbert Friedman.
51. Michlin, *Of No Interest to the Nation*, 93.
52. Mémorial de la Shoah, Center of Contemporary Jewish Documentation (CDJC) CMXXI-45, Témoignage de Robert Francès; letter dated August 8, 1945.
53. Blatt, *Sobibor*, 47.
54. Blatt, *Sobibor*, 47–48.
55. Fortunoff Archive, HVT-69, Dr. Hillel K., interviewed May 3, 1980 by Dori Laub and Laurel Vlock.
56. Fortunoff Archive, HVT-69, Hillel K.
57. Viktor Frankl, *Man's Search for Meaning*, trans. Ilse Lasch (London: Rider, 2004), 48–52, 73.
58. Gerd Fleischmann, "'Jedem das Seine': Eine Spur vom Bauhaus in Buchenwald," in *Franz Ehrlich: Ein Bauhäusler in Widerstand und Konzentrationslager*, eds. Volkhard

Knigge and Harry Stein (Weimar, Germany: Stiftung Gedenkstätten Buchenwald & Mittelbau-Dora, 2009), 112.

59. Ehrlich evidenced several Bauhaus influences: following Joost Schmidt, he used a narrow J with a short straight top, and following Herbert Bayer, there is a rounded m and n, in universal typeface; the n has the serif, while only the m is in the sans-serif Grotesk font; Fleischmann, "Jedem das Seine," 113.

60. Karl Schnog, *Jedem das Seine: Satirische Gedichte* (Berlin: Ulenspiegel-Verlag, 1947), 54, reprinted in Knigge and Stein, *Franz Ehrlich*, 175.

61. I was privileged to be able to interview Alice Sommer when she was "only" 106 years old, living independently, and still eager to accentuate the positive. See also Melissa Muller and Reinhard Piechocki, *A Garden of Eden in Hell: The Life of Alice Herz-Sommer* (London: Pan, 2008), and Alan Rusbridger, "Life Is Beautiful," A 2006 Interview with Alice Sommer, *Guardian*, December 13, 2006, available at http://www.theguardian.com/music/2006/dec/13/classicalmusicandopera. secondworldwar, accessed January 26, 2016.

62. Hannah Arendt, *Eichmann in Jerusalem: A Report on the Banality of Evil* (London: Penguin, 2006).

63. Till Bastian, *Sinti und Roma im Dritten Reich: Geschichte einer Verfolgung* (Munich: Verlag C. H. Beck, 2001), 62.

64. See for example the family of US congressman Tom Lantos, depicted in the documentary film directed by James Moll, *The Last Days* (Steven Spielberg and Shoah Visual History Foundation, 1998).

65. Dufournier, *Ravensbrück*, 130–31.

66. Dufournier, *Ravensbrück*, 150.

67. Michlin, *Of No Interest to the Nation*, 1.

68. Saul Friedländer, *Nazi Germany and the Jews: The Years of Extermination* (London: Penguin, 2007), 663.

69. Edvardson, *Die Welt zusammenfügen*, 13.

70. Edvardson, *Die Welt zusammenfügen*, 13–14.

71. Edvardson, *Die Welt zusammenfügen*, 42.

72. Edvardson, *Die Welt zusammenfügen*, 39.

73. Pierre Seel, *I, Pierre Seel, Deported Homosexual*, trans. Joachim Neugroschel (New York: Basic Books, 2011).

74. Seel, *I, Pierre Seel*, 25–26.

75. Seel, *I, Pierre Seel*, 42, 43.

76. Seel, *I, Pierre Seel*, 43.

77. Seel, *I, Pierre Seel*, 43.

78. Seel, *I, Pierre Seel*, 43–44.

CHAPTER 7

1. David Cesarani and Eric J. Sundquist, eds., *After the Holocaust: Challenging the Myth of Silence* (London: Routledge, 2012).

2. Robert Moeller, *War Stories: The Search for a Usable Past in the Federal Republic of Germany* (Berkeley: University of California Press, 2003); Norbert Frei, *Adenauer's Germany and the Nazi Past*, trans. Joel Golb (New York: Columbia University Press, 2002); Jeffrey Herf, *Divided Memory: The Nazi Past in the Two Germanys* (Cambridge, MA: Harvard University Press, 1997).

3. Mark Spigelman, "And you shall dream all the days of your life," in *The Words to Remember It: Memoirs of Child Holocaust Survivors*, ed. Survivors Group (Sydney: Scribe, 2009), 48–49.

4. Yael Danieli, "The Treatment and Prevention of Long-term Effects and Intergenerational Transmission of Victimization: A Lesson from Holocaust Survivors and their Children," in *Trauma and Its Wake*, vol. 1, *The Study and Treatment of Post-Traumatic Stress Disorder*, ed. Charles R. Figley (New York: Brunner/Mazel, 1985), 298–99.

5. Lisa Appignanesi, *Losing the Dead* (London: Chatto & Windus, 1999); Anne Karpf, *The War After: Living with the Holocaust* (London: Heinemann, 1996); Ruth Klüger, *Weiter leben: Eine Jugend* (Göttingen, Germany: Wallstein Verlag, 1992).

6. Eva Hoffman, *After Such Knowledge: A Meditation on the Aftermath of the Holocaust* (London: Vintage, 2004), 9.

7. KA (257) 24-15, Eva S., 46.

8. KA (257) 24-15, Eva S., 66.

9. KA (257) 24-15, Eva S., 66.

10. Jan T. Gross, *Fear: Antisemitism in Poland after Auschwitz* (Princeton, NJ: Princeton University Press, 2006).

11. Cordelia Edvardson, *Gebranntes Kind sucht das Feuer*, trans. Anna-Liese Kornitzky (Munich: Carl Hanser Verlag, 1986); Cordelia Edvardson, *Die Welt zusammenfügen*, trans. Jörg Scherzer and Anna-Liese Kornitzky (Munich: Deutscher Taschenbuch Verlag, 1991), 52–53.

12. Jacques Semelin, *Persécutions et entraides dans la France occupée* (Paris: Éditions du Seuil, 2013).

13. See for example testimonies in Mémorial de la Shoah, Center of Contemporary Jewish Documentation (CDJC), including CDJC CMXXI-42, Fella Isboutsky, saved by two French women, Marinette Guy and Juliette Vidal, or CDJC CMXXI-43, Eva Mendelsson, and CDJC DLXI-36.

14. Gilbert Michlin, *Of No Interest to the Nation: A Jewish Family in France, 1925–1945* (Detroit, MI: Wayne State University Press, 2004), 103.

15. Michlin, *Of No Interest to the Nation*, 104.

16. Michlin, *Of No Interest to the Nation*, 105.

17. Michlin, *Of No Interest to the Nation*, 105.

18. Gerhard Durlacher, *Stripes in the Sky: A Wartime Memoir*, trans. Susan Massotty (London: Serpent's Tale, 1991), 100.

19. Durlacher, *Stripes in the Sky*, 100.

20. Durlacher, *Stripes in the Sky*, 99.

21. Durlacher, *Stripes in the Sky*, 100.

22. Durlacher, *Stripes in the Sky*, 100.

23. KA (257) 26-24, Dagmar B., 25–26, 30.

24. KA (257) 26-24, Dagmar B., 27.

25. KA (257) 26-24, Dagmar B., 27.

26. KA (257) 26-24, Dagmar B., 27.

27. KA (257) 26-24, Dagmar B., 28.

28. KA (257) 26-24, Dagmar B., 28.

29. KA (257) 26-24, Dagmar B., 29.

30. Hans Frankenthal, with Andreas Plake, Babette Quinkert, and Florian Schmaltz, *The Unwelcome One: Returning home from Auschwitz*, trans. John A. Broadwin (Evanston, IL: Northwestern University Press, 2002), 78.

31. Frankenthal, *Unwelcome One*, 82.

32. Frankenthal, *Unwelcome One*, 82.

33. Frankenthal, *Unwelcome One*, 84.

34. Frankenthal, *Unwelcome One*, 90.

35. Frankenthal, *Unwelcome One*, 91.

36. Frankenthal, *Unwelcome One*, 92.

37. Frankenthal, *Unwelcome One*, 92.

38. Tom Segev, *The Seventh Million: The Israelis and the Holocaust*, trans. Haim Watzman (New York: Holt, 2000).

39. David Grossman, *See Under: Love*, trans. Betsy Rosenberg (London: Vintage, 1999), "Momik."

40. Dagi Knellesen, "Momentaufnahmen der Erinnerung: Juristische Zeugenschaft im ersten Frankfurter Auschwitz-Prozess—Ein Interviewprojekt," in *Zeugenschaft des Holocaust: Zwischen Trauma, Tradierung und Ermittlung*, ed. Fritz Bauer Institut (Frankfurt; Campus Verlag, 2007), 123–24.

41. Bernhard Rammerstorfer, *Unbroken Will: The Extraordinary Courage of an Ordinary Man* (New Orleans: Grammaton, 2004).

42. Rammerstorfer, *Unbroken Will*, 163–64.

43. Gilad Margalit, *Germany and its Gypsies: A Post-Auschwitz Ordeal* (Madison: University of Wisconsin Press, 2002).

44. Luisa Passerini, "Memories between Silence and Oblivion," in *Memory, History, Nation: Contested Pasts*, ed. Katharine Hodgkin and Susannah Radstone (New Brunswick, NJ: Transaction publishers. 2006), 238–54. But see the autobiographical account by Ceija Stojka, *Wir leben im Verborgenen: Aufzeichnungen einer Romni zwischen den Welten*, ed. Karin Berger (Vienna: Picus Verlag, 2013).

45. Yale Fortunoff Archive HVT-2805, Karl W., interviewed July 22, 1991, by Gabrielle Tyrnauer.

46. Christian Reimisch, *Vergessene Opfer des Nationalsozialismus? Zur Entschädigung von Homosexuellen, Kriegsdienstverweigerern, Sinti und Roma und Kommunisten in der Bundesrepublik Deutschland* (Berlin: Verlag für Wissenschaft und Kultur, 2003).

47. Examples from Niko Wahl, *Verfolgung und Vermögensentzug Homosexueller auf dem Gebiet der Republik Österreich während der NS-Zeit: Bemühungen um Restitution,*

Entschädigung und Pensionen in der Zweiten Republik (Munich: Oldenbourg Verlag, 2004), 83–88.

48. Heinz Heger, *The Men with the Pink Triangle*, trans. David Fernbach (London: Gay Men's Press, 1980), 114.

49. Zoe Waxman, *Writing the Holocaust: Identity, Testimony, Representation* (Oxford: Oxford University Press, 2006); Alexandra Garbarini, *Numbered Days: Diaries and the Holocaust* (New Haven, CT: Yale University Press, 2006).

50. Raul Hilberg, Stanislaw Staron, and Josef Kermisz, eds., *The Warsaw Diary of Adam Czerniakow: Prelude to Doom*, trans. Stanislaw Staron and staff of Yad Vashem (New York: Stein & Day, 1979); Dawid Sierakowiak, *The Diary of Dawid Sierakowiak: Five Notebooks from the Łódź Ghetto*, ed. Alan Adelson (New York: Oxford University Press, 1996).

51. Alexandra Zapruder, ed., *Salvaged Pages: Young Writers' Diaries of the Holocaust* (New Haven, CT: Yale University Press, 2002); Michał Grynberg, *Words to Outlive Us: Eyewitness Accounts from the Warsaw Ghetto*, trans. Philip Boehm (London: Granta, 2004).

52. Samuel D. Kassow, *Who Will Write Our History? Rediscovering a Hidden Archive from the Warsaw Ghetto* (London: Penguin, 2007).

53. Zygmunt Klukowski, *Diary from the Years of Occupation, 1939–44* (Urbana: University of Illinois Press, 1993).

54. Bernard Goldstein, *Five Years in the Warsaw Ghetto: (The Stars Bear Witness)*, trans. and ed. Leonard Shatzkin (Oakland, CA: AK Press/Nabat, 2005).

55. Mary Berg, *Warsaw Ghetto: A Diary*, ed. S. L. Shneiderman (New York: L. B. Fischer, 1945).

56. Jennifer Schuessler, "Survivor Who Hated the Spotlight," *New York Times*, November 10, 2014, available at http://www.nytimes.com/2014/11/11/arts/survivor-who-hated-the-spotlight.html?_r=0, accessed August 1, 2015; Amy Rosenberg, "What Happened to Mary Berg?," *Tablet*, July 17, 2008, available at http://www.tabletmag.com/jewish-news-and-politics/981/what-happened-to-mary-berg, accessed August 1, 2015; Mike Argento, "Holocaust Diary Author Mary Berg Lived in York County for Years," *York Daily Record*, December 23, 2014, available at http://www.ydr.com/local/ci_27170657/holocaust-diary-author-mary-berg-lived-york-county, accessed August 12, 2015.

57. Richard Glazar, *Trap with a Green Fence*, trans. Roslyn Theobald (Evanston, IL: Northwestern University Press, 1995), viii.

58. Chil Rajchman, *Treblinka: A Survivor's Memory, 1942–1943*, trans. Solon Beinfeld (London: MacLehose, 2011); Yankel Wiernik, *A Year in Treblinka* (New York: American Representation of the General Jewish Workers' Union of Poland, 1945), 8, available at http://www.zchor.org/wiernik.htm, accessed January 24, 2016.

59. Thomas (Toivi) Blatt, *From the Ashes of Sobibor: A Story of Survival* (Evanston, IL: Northwestern University Press, 1997), xxi–xxii.

60. Thomas (Toivi) Blatt, *Sobibor: The Forgotten Revolt; A Survivor's Report* (Issaquah, WA: HEP, 1997); Blatt, *From the Ashes of Sobibor*.

61. Elie Wiesel, *Night*, trans. Marion Wiesel (London: Penguin, 2006), x.
62. See for example Alexander Cockburn, "Did Oprah Pick Another Fibber? Truth and Fiction in Elie Wiesel's *Night*: Is Frey or Wiesel the Bigger Moral Poseur?," *CounterPunch*, April 1–3, 2006, noting that Raul Hilberg pointed out that Wiesel's literary account was not a reliable historical source. Revisionists associated with Holocaust denial have attacked Wiesel's credentials; cf., e.g., Nikolaus Grüner, *Stolen Identity: Research* (self-published, 2007).
63. Primo Levi, *If This Is a Man*, trans. Stuart Woolf (London: Random House, 2000), was first published in Italian in 1947 as *Se questo è un uomo* and first appeared in English in 1958; it was published in the United States as *Survival in Auschwitz*.
64. Charlotte Delbo, *Auschwitz and After*, trans. Rosette Lamont (New Haven, CT: Yale University Press, 1995).
65. See for example Imre Kertész, *Fateless*, trans. Tim Wilkinson (London: Vintage, 2006); Kertész, *Fiasco*, trans. Tim Wilkinson (Brooklyn, NY: Melville House, 2011); Kertész, *Liquidation*, trans. Tim Wilkinson (London: Vintage, 2007); Kertész, *Kaddish for an Unborn Child*, trans. Tim Wilkinson (London: Vintage, 2010); and Kertész, *Dossier K.*, trans. Tim Wilkinson (Brooklyn, NY: Melville House, 2013).
66. On some of the key characteristics of "testimony," see Horace Engdahl, "Philomela's Tongue: Introductory Remarks on Witness Literature," in *Witness Literature: Proceedings of the Nobel Centennial Symposium*, ed. Horace Engdahl (New Jersey: World Scientific, 2002), 1–14.
67. Laura Jokusch, *Collect and Record! Jewish Holocaust Documentation in Early Postwar Europe* (Oxford: Oxford University Press, 2012).
68. Maria Hochberg-Mariańska and Noe Grüss, eds., *The Children Accuse*, trans. Bill Johnstone (London: Vallentine Mitchell, 1996).
69. Donald L. Niewyk, *Fresh Wounds: Early Narratives of Holocaust Survivors* (Chapel Hill: University of North Carolina Press, 1998); Alan Rosen, *The Wonder of Their Voices: The 1946 Holocaust Interviews of David Boder* (Oxford: Oxford University Press, 2010); online collection at http://voices.iit.edu.
70. Rosen, *Wonder of Their Voices*, 239–40.
71. David Boder, *I Did Not Interview the Dead* (Chicago: University of Illinois Press, 1949).
72. Mary Fulbrook, "East Germans in a Post-Nazi State: Communities of Experience, Connection and Identification," in *Becoming East German: Socialist Structures and Sensibilities after Hitler*, ed. Mary Fulbrook and Andrew Port (New York: Berghahn, 2013), and Fulbrook, *Dissonant Lives: Generations and Violence through the German Dictatorships* (Oxford: Oxford University Press, 2011).
73. Yaffa Eliach, *Hasidic Tales of the Holocaust* (New York: Oxford University Press, 1982).
74. BArch DO 1/32563, letter of April 27, 1949, fo. 26.
75. The voices of former forced laborers were elicited in the massive transnational oral history project led by Alexander von Plato and colleagues at the Institute for History and Biography, Fernuniversität Hagen, in Germany: Alexander von

Plato, Almut Leh, and Christoph Thonfeld, eds., *Hitler's Slaves: Life Stories of Forced Labourers in Nazi-Occupied Europe* (New York: Berghahn, 2010).

76. Hochberg-Mariańska and Grüss, *Children Accuse.*

77. On experiences in DP camps see for example Dan Stone, *The Liberation of the Camps: The End of the Holocaust and Its Aftermath* (New Haven, CT: Yale University Press, 2015); Atina Grossmann, *Jews, Germans and Allies: Close Encounters in Occupied Germany* (Princeton, NJ: Princeton University Press, 2007).

78. Available at http://voices.iit.edu/interview?doc=joseph&display=joseph_en, accessed November 25, 2015.

79. Niewyk, *Fresh Wounds*, 5–6.

80. See for example DTA Emmendingen, 386, Heinrich R., "Nicht in der Gnade der späten Geburt."

81. Pertti Ahonen et al., *People on the Move: Forced Population Movements in Europe in the Second World War and Its Aftermath* (Oxford: Berg, 2008); Pertti Ahonen, *After the Expulsion: West Germany and Eastern Europe, 1945–1990* (Oxford: Oxford University Press, 2003); Michael Schwartz, *Vertriebene und "Umsiedlerpolitik": Integrationskonflikte in den deutschen Nachkriegs-Gesellschaften und die Assimilationsstrategien in der SBZ/DDR, 1945–1961* (Munich: Oldenbourg, 2004); Philipp Ther and Ana Siljak, eds., *Redrawing Nations: Ethnic Cleansing in East-Central Europe, 1944–1948* (Lanham, MD: Rowman & Littlefield, 2001); Alexander von Plato and Wolfgang Meinicke, *Alte Heimat—Neue Zeit: Flüchtlinge, Umgesiedelte, Vertriebene in der Sowjetischen Besatzungszone und in der DDR* (Berlin: Verlags-Anstalt Union, 1991).

82. See the archive of diaries, letters, autobiographies and memoirs collected by Walter Kempowski and now held in the Berlin Academy of Arts (henceforth referred to as Kempowski BIO), including for example Kempowski BIO 4517, Anni A., Tagebuch 01.06.45–27.07.46, and 1947 essay "Flucht, Heimkehr und Zwangsevakuierung" in "1784–1984. Kirche und Kirchgemeinde Poischwitz. Anfang und Abschied. Zwei Dokumente"; Kempowski BIO A 933/7, letters from Rita O., 1945–47; Kempowski BIO 5674, Heinz E., "Die Hölle von Lamsdorf. Dokumentation über eine polnisches Vernichtungslager [*sic*]," published by the Landsmannschaft der Oberschlesier e/V/Bundesverband, Bonn, Kaiserstr 173 (1969); DTA Emmendingen, 735/I.1 and 735/I.2, Marianne O.-B.

83. For example Kempowski BIO 3105, Christiane K., Tagebuch 1947–50, entry of October 16, 1946.

84. For example: Kempowski BIO 4166, Margarete K., Briefwechsel mit Bekannten in Polen (Filehne/Posen) 1946, who discusses her time in Łódź/Litzmannstadt, complaining about the ways in which Poles treated her, but with no mention of the ghetto, and Kempowski BIO 5910, Helmut F., "Weisser Jahrgang 28: Eine Jugend 1943–1947."

85. Melita Maschmann, *Fazit: Kein Rechtfertigungsversuch* (Stuttgart: dva, 1963), translated as *Account Rendered: A Dossier on My Former Self* (London: Abelard-Schuman, 1965).

86. Maschmann, *Fazit*, 85–90.

87. James Joll, "Review: The Conquest of the Past: Some Recent German Books on the Third Reich," *International Affairs* 40, no. 3 (July 1964): 487.

88. For example, extensive use in Richard J. Evans, *The Coming of the Third Reich: How the Nazis Destroyed Democracy and Seized Power in Germany* (London: Penguin 2004), 225, 313; Evans, *The Third Reich in Power* (London: Penguin, 2006), 98, 166, 275, 367, 492, 549–50, 553, 587, 696; Evans, *The Third Reich at War* (London: Penguin, 2008), 9, 39–41, 65–66, 189–90, 679, 721, 731, 752. Maschmann is also used in Claudia Koonz, *Mothers in the Fatherland: Women, the Family and Nazi Politics* (London: Jonathan Cape, 1987), 162–63, 194, 195, 399, and Daniel Jonah Goldhagen, *Hitler's Willing Executioners* (New York: Knopf, 1996), 88–89, 103, 429. But see the nuanced analysis of strategies of self-representation in Elizabeth Harvey, " 'We Forgot All Jews and Poles': German Women and the 'Ethnic Struggle' in Nazi-Occupied Poland," *Contemporary European History* 10, no. 3 (November 2001): 455.

89. "Afterword, as told by Marianne Schweitzer Burkenroad to Helen Epstein," appended to the English edition of *Account Rendered: A Dossier on My Former Self* (Kindle edition); Helen Epstein, "I Was a Nazi, and Here's Why," *New Yorker*, May 29, 2013, available at http://www.newyorker.com/books/page-turner/ i-was-a-nazi-and-heres-why, accessed May 21, 2014.

90. Account given by the Seidels' son Hans-Joachim Seidel, reported in Rudi Kübler, "Die doppelte Verfolgung," *Südwest Presse*, January 3, 2014, available at http://www.swp.de/2381825 accessed August 28, 2015.

91. I write here from personal knowledge. Rele Seidel was a close friend of my mother, having been in the same school class in Berlin in the early 1930s. We stayed with the Seidel family in Stuttgart every summer on our way to family holidays in Bavaria. I recall Hans Seidel from my then child's-eye view, including memories of occasions marked by his silence and barely eating at the evening meal, and later wandering around in the night, apparently plagued by insomnia. I have also discussed the wider school group in Fulbrook, *Dissonant Lives*; see also Mary Fulbrook, *A Small Town near Auschwitz: Ordinary Nazis and the Holocaust* (Oxford: Oxford University Press, 2012).

CHAPTER 8

1. Otto Dov Kulka, *Landscapes of the Metropolis of Death: Reflections on Memory and Imagination* (London: Allen Lane, 2013), 48.

2. Kulka, *Landscapes of the Metropolis of Death*, 49.

3. Tom Segev, *The Seventh Million: The Israelis and the Holocaust*, trans. Haim Watzman (New York: Holt, 1991), 140–52; David Cesarani, *Final Solution: The Fate of the Jews, 1933–49* (London: Macmillan, 2016), 782–83.

4. See for example Eva Mozes Kor, with Guido Eckart, *Die Macht des Vergebens* (Wals bei Salzburg, Austria: Benevento, 2016); and Candles, an organization she

founded for survivors of Mengele's twins experiments, whose website is at http://www.candlesholocaustmuseum.org, accessed November 9, 2015.

5. Jon Elster, *Closing the Books: Transitional Justice in Historical Perspective* (Cambridge: Cambridge University Press, 2004).

6. On the wider contexts, see for example István Deák, Jan Gross, and Tony Judt, eds., *The Politics of Retribution in Europe* (Princeton, NJ: Princeton University Press, 2000); Jeffrey Herf, *Divided Memory: The Nazi Past in the Two Germanys* (Cambridge, MA: Harvard University Press, 1997); Norman Naimark, *The Russians in Germany* (Cambridge, MA: Harvard University Press, 1995); and for a European overview Tony Judt, *Postwar: A History of Europe since 1945* (London: Heinemann, 2006).

7. Susan Benedict, Arthur Caplan, and Traute Lafrenz Page, "Duty and 'Euthanasia': The Nurses of Meseritz-Obrawalde," *Nursing Ethics* 14, no. 6 (2007): 781–94.

8. Michael C. Steinlauf, *Bondage to the Dead: Poland and the Memory of the Holocaust* (Syracuse, NY: Syracuse University Press, 1997), 32–33; Barbara Engelking, *Holocaust and Memory: The Experience of the Holocaust and Its Consequences: An Investigation Based on Personal Experiences*, ed. Gunner S. Paulsson, trans. Emma Harris (London: Leicester University Press, 2001), 276.

9. Martin Winstone, *The Dark Heart of Hitler's Europe: Nazi Rule in Poland under the General Government* (London: I. B. Tauris, 2015), 247; also Jan Gross, *Fear: Anti-Semitism in Poland after Auschwitz* (Princeton, NJ: Princeton University Press, 2006).

10. Thomas (Toivi) Blatt, *Sobibor: The Forgotten Revolt; A Survivor's Report* (Issaquah, WA: HEP, 1997), 103.

11. Thomas (Toivi) Blatt, *From the Ashes of Sobibor: A Story of Survival* (Evanston, IL: Northwestern University Press, 1997), 155–225.

12. Blatt, *From the Ashes of Sobibor*, 223.

13. Richard Glazar, *Trap with a Green Fence*, trans. Roslyn Theobald (Evanston, IL: Northwestern University Press, 1995).

14. Raul Hilberg, *The Destruction of the European Jews*, 3rd ed. (New Haven, CT: Yale University Press, 2003), 3:1170; Bogdan Musial, "NS-Kriegsverbrecher vor polnischen Gerichten," *Vierteljahrshefte für Zeitgeschichte* 47 (1999): 25–56.

15. Claudia Kuretsidis-Haider, Irmgard Nöbauer, Winfried Garscha, Siegfried Sanwald, and Andrzej Selerowicz, eds., *Das KZ-Lublin-Majdanek und die Justiz: Strafverfolgung und verweigerte Gerechtigkeit; Polen, Deutschland und Österreich im Vergleich* (Graz, Austria: CLIO, 2011), 53.

16. Michael Bazyler and Frank Tuerkheimer, *Forgotten Trials of the Holocaust* (New York: New York University Press, 2014), 101–27.

17. Gordon J. Horwitz, *Ghettostadt: Łódź and the Making of a Nazi City* (Cambridge, MA: Harvard University Press, 2008), 317–18.

18. Cf., e.g., Norbert Frei, ed., *Transnationale Vergangenheitspolitik: Der Umgang mit deutschen Kriegsverbrechern in Europa nach dem Zweiten Weltkrieg* (Göttingen, Germany: Wallstein, 2006); Richard J. Golsan, "Crimes-Against-Humanity Trials in France and their Historical and Legal Contexts," in *Atrocities on Trial:*

Historical Perspectives on the Politics of Prosecuting War Crimes, ed. Patricia Heberer and Jürgen Matthäus (Lincoln: University of Nebraska Press, 2008), 247–61; Richard J. Golsan, ed., *Memory, the Holocaust and French Justice: The Bousquet and Touvier Affairs* (Hanover, NH: University Press of New England, 1996); Julian Jackson, *France: The Dark Years, 1940–44* (Oxford: Oxford University Press, 2001), 570–632; Claudia Kuretsidis-Haider and Winfried Garscha, eds., *Keine "Abrechnung": NS-Verbrechen, Justiz und Gesellschaft in Europa nach 1945* (Leipzig: Akademische Verlagsanstalt, 1998); Ahlrich Meyer, *Täter im Verhör: Die "Endlösung der Judenfrage" in Frankreich, 1940–1944* (Darmstadt, Germany: Wissenschaftliche Buchgesellschaft, 2005); Devin O. Pendas, "Seeking Justice, Finding Law: Nazi Trials in Postwar Europe," *Journal of Modern History* 81, no. 2 (June 2009): 347–68; and Nathan Stoltzfus and Henry Friedlander, eds., *Nazi Crimes and the Law* (Cambridge: Cambridge University Press, 2008).

19. Cf. Dan Stone, *The Liberation of the Camps: The End of the Holocaust and its Aftermath* (New Haven, CT: Yale University Press, 2015), 179–80.

20. Michael Bazyler, "The Jewish *Kapo* Trials in Israel: Is There a Place for the Law in the Gray Zone?" in Bazyler and Tuerkheimer, *Forgotten Trials of the Holocaust*, 195–225.

21. Melita Maschmann, *Fazit: Kein Rechtfertigungsversuch* (Stuttgart: dva, 1963).

22. Lutz Niethammer, *Die Mitläuferfabrik: Die Entnazifizierung am Beispiel Bayerns* (Berlin: Dietz, 1982), remains a classic study. For the Soviet zone see for example Damian van Melis, *Entnazifizierung in Mecklenburg-Vorpommern: Herrschaft und Verwaltung, 1945–1948* (Munich: Oldenbourg Verlag, 1999); Timothy Vogt, *Denazification in Soviet-Occupied Germany: Brandenburg, 1945–1948* (Cambridge, MA: Harvard University Press, 2001). For Austria in comparative perspective: Walter Schuster and Wolfgang Weber, eds., *Entnazifizierung im regionalen Vergleich* (Linz, Austria: Archiv der Stadt Linz, 2002), and Robert Knight, "Denazification and Integration in the Austrian Province of Carinthia," *Journal of Modern History* 79, no. 3 (2007): 572–612, critiquing the approach taken by Dieter Stiefel, *Entnazifizierung in Österreich* (Vienna: Europaverlag, 1981).

23. See for example Ulrike Weckel, *Beschämende Bilder: Deutsche Reaktionen auf alliierte Dokumentarfilme über befreite Konzentrationslager* (Stuttgart: Franz Steiner Verlag, 2012); Mary Fulbrook, *Dissonant Lives: Generations and Violence through the German Dictatorships*, vol. 2, *From Nazism through Communism* (Oxford: Oxford University Press, 2017).

24. Cf., e.g., Donald Bloxham, *Genocide on Trial: War Crimes Trials and the Formation of Holocaust History and Memory* (Oxford: Oxford University Press, 2001).

25. Dubost quoted in Lynne Viola, "The Question of the Perpetrator in Soviet History," *Slavic Review* 72, no. 1 (Spring 2013): 4. See also Lawrence Douglas, *The Memory of Judgment: Making Law and History in the Trials of the Holocaust* (New Haven, CT: Yale University Press, 2001), 91.

26. There is a large literature. See further, for example, Kim Priemel, *The Betrayal: The Nuremberg Trials and German Divergence* (Oxford: Oxford University Press,

2016); documents in *Der Prozess gegen die Hauptkriegsverbrecher:Vor dem Internationalen Militärgerichtshof Nürnberg* (Nuremberg, 1948); and selections in English in Michael Marrus, ed., *The Nuremberg War Crimes Trial, 1945-46: A Documentary History* (Boston: Bedford, 1997).

27. Michael Bazyler, *Holocaust, Genocide, and the Law: A Quest for Justice in the Post-Holocaust World* (New York: Oxford University Press, 2016), 69-108.

28. Available through the Yale Law School Avalon Project at http://avalon.law.yale.edu/imt/01-28-46.asp.

29. Cf. Gitta Sereny, *Albert Speer: His Battle with the Truth* (London: Macmillan, 1995).

30. Karl Jaspers, *Die Schuldfrage (und) Für Völkermord gibt es keine Verjährung* (Munich: Piper, 1979), 93.

31. Jaspers, *Schuldfrage*, 92-93.

32. Jaspers, *Schuldfrage*, 46-47.

33. Jaspers, *Schuldfrage*, 52-53.

34. Heike Krösche, "Abseits der Vergangenheit: Das Interesse der deutschen Nach-kriegsöffentlichkeit am Nürnberger Prozess gegen die Hauptkriegsverbrecher 1945/46," in *NS-Prozesse und deutsche Öffentlichkeit: Besatzungszeit, frühe Bundesrepublik und DDR*, ed. Jörg Osterloh and Clemens Vollnhals (Göttingen, Germany: Vandenhoeck & Ruprecht, 2011), 96, 105.

35. DTA Emmendingen, 1828, Hugo M., "Briefe an einen vermissten Sohn (1943-1971)," letter of October 20, 1946.

36. Kempowski BIO, 25/1-3, Ursula E. diary, entry of June 20, 1945, 41.

37. Kempowski BIO, 25/1-3, Ursula E. diary, entry of October 8, 1946, 57-58.

38. Kempowski BIO, 25/1-3, Ursula E., diary entry of October 8, 1946, 57-58.

39. DTA 3853-1 Ingrid P., July 26, 1946.

40. DTA 3853-1 Ingrid P., September 19, 1946.

41. DTA 3853-1 Ingrid P., October 15, 1946.

42. Donald Bloxham, "Milestones and Mythologies. The Impact of Nuremberg," in *Atrocities on Trial: Historical Perspectives on the Politics of Prosecuting War Crimes*, Patricia Heberer and Jürgen Matthäus (Lincoln: University of Nebraska Press, 2008), 270-71; Anna J. Merritt and Richard L. Merritt, eds., *Public Opinion in Occupied Germany: The OMGUS Surveys* (Urbana: University of Illinois Press, 1970).

43. Bazyler, *Holocaust, Genocide, and the Law*, 83-85.

44. Bloxham, *Genocide on Trial*; Bob Carruthers, ed., *SS Terror in the East: The Einsatzgruppen on Trial* (Barnsley, UK: Pen & Sword Military, 2013); Hilary Earl, *The Nuremberg SS-Einsatzgruppen Trial, 1945-1958: Atrocity, Law and History* (Cambridge: Cambridge University Press, 2009); Kim Priemel and Alexa Stiller, eds., *Reassessing the Nuremberg Military Tribunals: Transitional Justice, Trial Narratives, and Historiography* (New York: Berghahn, 2012); Ulf Schmidt, *Justice at Nuremberg: Leo Alexander and the Nazi Doctors' Trial* (Houndmills, UK: Palgrave Macmillan, 2004).

45. On Herta Oberheuser, see Kathrin Kompisch, *Täterinnen: Frauen im National-sozialismus* (Cologne: Böhlau Verlag, 2008), 143–44.

46. Felicja Karay, *Death Comes in Yellow: Skarżysko-Kamienna Labor Camp*, trans. Sara Kitai (Amsterdam: Harwood Academic Publishers, 1996), 1.

47. Robert S. Wistrich, *Who's Who in Nazi Germany* (London: Routledge, 2013), 61.

48. Bernd Boll, "*Fall 6*: Der IG-Farben Prozeß," in *Der Nationalsozialismus vor Gericht: Die alliierten Prozesse gegen Kriegsverbrecher und Soldaten, 1943–52*, ed. Gerd R. Ueberschär (Frankfurt am Main: Fischer Taschenbuch Verlag, 1999), 133–43; Sebastian Brünger, "Der Vergangenheit eine Form geben: Mentale Kontinuitäten nach 1945 am Beispiel des IG-Farben Prozesses und Fritz ter Meers," in *Unternehmer und NS-Verbrechen: Wirtschaftseliten im "Dritten Reich" und in der Bundesrepublik Deutschland*, ed. Jörg Osterloh and Harald Wixforth, Wissenschaftliche Reihe des Fritz Bauer Instituts 23 (Frankfurt am Main: Campus Verlag, 2014), 183–216).

49. Bazyler and Tuerkheimer, *Forgotten Trials*, 129.

50. See particularly Norbert Frei, *Vergangenheitspolitik: Die Anfänge der Bundesrepublik und die NS-Vergangenheit* (Munich: C. H. Beck, 1996); available in English as *Adenauer's Germany and the Nazi Past: The Politics of Amnesty and Integration*, trans. Joel Golb (New York: Columbia University Press, 2002).

51. Anette Kretzer, *NS-Täterschaft und Geschlecht: Der erste britische Ravensbrück-Prozess 1946/47 in Hamburg* (Berlin: Metropol, 2009), and Bazyler and Tuerkheimer, *Forgotten Trials*, 129–57.

52. Albert Kesselring, *Kesselring: A Soldier's Record* (New York: William Morrow, 1954), 353; Kerstin von Lingen, *Kesselring's Last Battle: War Crimes Trials and Cold War Politics, 1945–1960*, trans. Alexandra Klemm (Lawrence: University Press of Kansas, 2009); Richard Raiber, *Anatomy of Perjury: Field Marshal Albert Kesselring, Via Rasella, and the Ginny Mission*, ed. Dennis E. Showalter (Newark: University of Delaware Press, 2008); Alessandro Portelli, *The Order Has Been Carried Out: History, Memory, and Meaning of a Nazi Massacre in Rome* (New York: Palgrave Macmillan, 2003).

53. Kesselring, *Kesselring*, 354.

54. Kesselring, *Kesselring*, 366.

55. Von Lingen, *Kesselring's Last Battle*, 6, 294.

56. Kesselring, *Kesselring*, 374n1.

57. Annette Leo, "Antifaschismus," in *Erinnerungsorte der DDR*, ed. Martin Sabrow (Munich: C. H. Beck, 2009), 38–39.

58. Christoph Höschler, *NS-Verfolgte im "antifaschistischen Staat": Vereinnahmung und Ausgrenzung in der ostdeutschen Wiedergutmachung, 1945–1989* (Berlin: Metropol, 2002), 232.

59. Robert Moeller, *War Stories: The Search for a Usable Past in the Federal Republic of Germany* (Berkeley: University of California Press, 2001); Axel Schildt, "The Long Shadows of the Second World War: The Impact of Experiences and Memories of War on West German Society," in *Experience and Memory: The Second*

World War in Europe, ed. Jörg Echternkamp and Stefan Martens (New York: Berghahn, 2010), 197–213; Dorothee Wierling, "The War in Postwar Society: the Role of the Second World War in Public and Private Spheres in the Soviet Occupation Zone and Early GDR," in Echternkamp and Martens, *Experience and Memory*, 214–28; Christian Morina, *Legacies of Stalingrad: Remembering the Eastern Front in Germany since 1945* (Cambridge: Cambridge University Press, 2011).

60. Personal discussion, Helene B., December 2015.

61. Gerald Reitlinger, *The SS: Alibi of a Nation 1922–1945* (London: Arms & Armour, 1981).

62. Kesselring, *Kesselring*, 376.

63. Kesselring, *Kesselring*, 111.

64. Kesselring, *Kesselring*, 270–71.

65. Kesselring, *Kesselring*, 271.

66. Kesselring, *Kesselring*, 271.

67. Kesselring, *Kesselring*, 271.

68. Von Lingen, *Kesselring's Last Battle*, 302.

69. Hartmut Berghoff, "Zwischen Verdrängung und Aufarbeitung: Die bundesdeutsche Gesellschaft und ihre nationalsozialistische Vergangenheit in den Fünfziger Jahren," *Geschichte in Wissenschaft und Unterricht* 49, no. 2, (1998): 108.

70. See also Norbert Frei, ed., *Hitlers Eliten nach 1945* (Munich: dtv, 2003).

71. Fritz ter Meer, *Die I. G. Farben Industrie Aktiengesellschaft: Ihre Entstehung, Entwicklung und Bedeutung* (Düsseldorf: Econ-Verlag, 1953).

72. Ter Meer, *I. G. Farben Industrie Aktiengesellschaft*, 113.

73. Ter Meer, *I. G. Farben Industrie Aktiengesellschaft*, 114.

74. Ter Meer, *I. G. Farben Industrie Aktiengesellschaft*, 92.

75. Ter Meer, *I. G. Farben Industrie Aktiengesellschaft*, 115.

76. See further Brünger, "Der Vergangenheit eine Form geben."

77. Ernst Heinkel, *Stürmisches Leben* (Stuttgart: Mundus Verlag, 1953), available in English as *He 1000*, ed. Jürgen Thorwald, trans. Mervyn Savill (London: Hutchinson, 1956). The book was reprinted three times in the first year of publication; licensed for two hundred thousand members of the European Book Club in 1955; published in English the following year; reprinted twice in 1959; and saw new editions in 1963, 1977, and 1998. Lutz Budrass, "Der Preis des Fortschritts: Ernst Heinkels Meistererzählung über die Tradition der deutschen Luftfahrtindustrie," in Osterloh and Wixforth, *Unternehmer und NS-Verbrechen*, 221.

78. Heinkel, *He 1000*, 147.

79. Heinkel, *He 1000*, 232.

80. Heinkel, *He 1000*, 270.

81. Heinkel, *He 1000*, 274.

82. Heinkel, *He 1000*, 276.

83. Heinkel, *He 1000*, 276.

84. Heinkel, *He 1000*, 276.

85. Heinkel, *He 1000*, 276.
86. Heinkel, *He 1000*, 277–78.
87. See also Benjamin B. Ferencz, *Less than Slaves: Jewish Forced Labor and the Quest for Compensation* (Cambridge, MA: Harvard University Press, 1979).
88. Oliver Schröm, with Andrea Röpke, *Stille Hilfe für braune Kameraden: Das geheime Netzwerk der Alt- und Neonazis* (Berlin: Chr. Links Verlag, 2001).
89. Kestenberg Archive, Jerusalem (KA) (257) 26-42, HM, 13.
90. KA (257) 26-42, HM, 14.
91. KA (257) 26-42, HM, 9.
92. Case studies in Christina Ullrich, *"Ich fühl' mich nicht als Mörder": Die Integration von NS-Tätern in die Nachkriegsgesellschaft* (Darmstadt, Germany: Wissenschaftliche Buchgesellschaft, 2011).

CHAPTER 9

1. *Neues Deutschland*, September 29, 1987; press clipping in BArch DP 3/2273.
2. Andreas Eichmüller, *Keine Generalamnestie: Die Strafverfolgung von NS-Verbrechen in der frühen Bundesrepublik* (Munich: Oldenbourg Wissenschaftsverlag, 2012), 5.
3. Andreas Eichmüller, "Die Strafverfolgung von NS-Verbrechen durch westdeutsche Justizbehörden seit 1945: Eine Zahlenbilanz," *Vierteljahrshefte für Zeitgeschichte* 4 (2008): 634; C. F. Rüter with L. Hekelaar Gombert and D. W. de Mildt, eds., *Justiz und NS-Verbrechen: Sammlung deutscher Strafurteile wegen nationalsozialistischer Tötungsverbrechen, 1945–2012*, 49 vols. (Amsterdam: Amsterdam University Press, 1968–2012), and C. F. Rüter and D. W. de Mildt, *DDR-Justiz und NS-Verbrechen: Sammlung Ostdeutscher Strafurteile wegen Nationalsozialistischer Tötungsverbrechen, 1945–1998*, 14 vols. (Amsterdam: Amsterdam University Press, 2002–2010).
4. C. F. Rüter, "Die Ahndung von NS-Tötungsverbrechen: Westdeutschland, Holland und die DDR im Vergleich; Eine These," in *Keine "Abrechnung": NS-Verbrechen, Justiz und Gesellschaft in Europa nach 1945*, eds. Claudia Kuretsidis-Haider and Winfried Garscha (Leipzig: Akademische Verlagsanstalt, 1998), 180–84.
5. "Die Schande nach Auschwitz," *Der Spiegel*, August 25, 2014, 31.
6. Crime categories and statistics derived from Rüter and de Mildt, *DDR-Justiz und NS-Verbrechen*, Register und Dokumente (2010), available at http://www1.jur.uva.nl/junsv/ddr/DDRTatkengfr.htm, accessed December 13, 2014. For statistical analysis and discussion of Rüter's categories, see Raimond Reiter, *30 Jahre Justiz und NS-Verbrechen: Die Aktualität einer Urteilssammlung* (Frankfurt am Main: Peter Lang, 1998).
7. Rüter, "Ahndung von NS-Tötungsverbrechen," 183.
8. Dick de Mildt, *In the Name of the People: Perpetrators of Genocide in the Reflections of Their Post-War Prosecution in West Germany; The "Euthanasia" and "Aktion Reinhard" Trial Cases* (The Hague: Martinus Nijhoff, 1996), 21.

9. Statistics compiled from the index by crime category in Rüter and de Mildt, *Justiz und NS-Verbrechen,* summary available at http://www1.jur.uva.nl/junsv/brd/Tatkdeufr.htm, accessed December 13, 2014.

10. Edith Raim, *Nazi Crimes against Jews and German Post-War Justice: The West German Judicial System during Allied Occupation, 1945–1949* (Berlin: De Gruyter Oldenbourg, 2015), on which this paragraph is based.

11. Eichmüller, "Die Strafverfolgung von NS-Verbrechen," 624–25.

12. Raim, *Nazi Crimes,* 152.

13. Eichmüller, "Die Strafverfolgung von NS-Verbrechen," 628. See also Alan Steinweis, *Kristallnacht 1938* (Cambridge, MA: Belknap Press of Harvard University Press, 2009).

14. Raim, *Nazi Crimes,* 186–301.

15. Raim, *Nazi Crimes,* 262.

16. For a range of cases, see BArch, DP/3/1804.

17. BArch, DO 1/32729, fols. 94 ff.

18. Joachim Käpper, *Erstarrte Geschichte: Faschismus und Holocaust im Spiegel der Geschichtswissenschaft und Geschichtspropaganda der DDR* (Hamburg: Ergebnisse Verlag, 1999), 63, quoting the 1949 publication *Die Hölle von Kamienna.*

19. For an academic dissertation written by a survivor, see Felicja Karay, *Death Comes in Yellow: Skarżysko-Kamienna Labor Camp,* trans. Sara Kitai (Amsterdam: Harwood Academic Publishers, 1996).

20. BArch, DO 1/32729, fo. 105.

21. BArch, DO 1/32729, twelve-page document paginated only within itself.

22. BArch, DO 1/32729, 5.

23. BArch, DO 1/32729, 7.

24. BArch DP 3/1614, Henry Schmidt, Oberstes Gericht der DDR, 1. Strafsenat 1 OSB 8/87, "Urteil im Namen des Volkes! In der Strafsache gegen den ehemaligen Kriminalkommissar der Geheimen Staatspolizei und SS Obersturmführer Henry Schmidt," meetings of December 21 and 22, 1987; biography on 3–4.

25. Kim Christian Priemel, "Arbeitsverwaltung vor Gericht: Das Reichsarbeitsministerium und die Nürnberger Prozesse 1945–1949," in *Das Reichsarbeitsministerium im Nationalsozialismus: Verwaltung—Politik—Verbrechen,* ed. Alexander Nützenadel (Göttingen, Germany: Wallstein Verlag, 2017), 492.

26. Winfried Garscha and Claudia Kuretsis-Haider, "Die strafrechtliche Verfolgung nationalsozialistsicher Verbrechen—eine Einführung," in *Holocaust und Kriegsverbrechen vor Gericht: Der Fall Österreich,* ed. Thomas Albrich, Winfried Garscha, and Martin Polaschek (Innsbruck, Austria: Studien Verlag, 2006), 11–12.

27. Garscha and Kuretsis-Haider, "Die strafrechtliche Verfolgung nationalsozialistsicher Verbrechen," 17–18.

28. Claudia Kuretsidis-Haider, "Die Rezeption von NS-Prozessen in Österrreich durch Medien, Politik und Gesellschaft im ersten Nachkriegsjahrzehnt," in *NS-Prozesse und deutsche Öffentlichkeit: Besatzungszeit, frühe Bundesrepublik und*

DDR, ed. Jörg Osterloh and Clemens Vollnhals (Göttingen, Germany: Vanden-hoeck & Ruprecht, 2011), 426.

29. Dieter Skiba and Reiner Stenzel, *Im Namen des Volkes: Ermittlungs- und Gerichtsverfahren in der DDR gegen Nazi- und Kriegsverbrecher* (Berlin: Edition Ost, 2016).

30. For a strong view, see Ingo Müller, *Furchtbare Juristen: Die unbewältigte Vergangenheit der deutschen Justiz*, 2nd ed. (Berlin: Klaus Bittermann, 2014), Part 3, 255–399.

31. Mary Fulbrook, *The People's State: East German Society from Hitler to Honecker* (Oxford: Oxford University Press, 2005).

32. Berger, *Experten der Vernichtung*, 363–64.

33. Nationalrat der Nationalen Front des Demokratischen Deutschland, ed., *Braunbuch: Kriegs- und Naziverbrecher in der Bundesrepublik* (Berlin: Staatsverlag der Deutschen Demokratischen Republik, 1960–68).

34. Jens Gieseke, "Antifaschistischer Staat und postfaschistische Gesellschaft: Die DDR, das MfS und die NS-Täter," *Historical Social Research* 35, no. 3 (2010): 79–94, available at http://nbn-resolving.de/urn:nbn:de:0168-ssoar-310694.

35. Henry Leide, *NS-Verbrecher und Staatssicherheit: Die geheime Vergangenheitspolitik der DDR*, 2nd ed. (Göttingen, Germany: Vandenhoeck & Ruprecht, 2006), 109.

36. Leide, *NS-Verbrecher und Staatssicherheit*.

37. Skiba and Stenzel, *Im Namen des Volkes*, 40–41.

38. BArch DP 3/1861.

39. BArch DP 3/1861, fo. 3.

40. BArch DP 3/1861, fo. 3.

41. BArch DP 3/1861, fo. 3.

42. BArch DP 3/1861, fo. 3.

43. BArch DP 3/1861, fo. 3.

44. See Leide, *NS-Verbrecher und Staatssicherheit*; Gieseke, "Antifaschistischer Staat und postfaschistische Gesellschaft."

45. Greve, "Täter oder Gehilfen?," 202.

46. Annette Weinke, *Eine Gesellschaft vermittelt gegen sich selbst: Die Geschichte der Zentralen Stelle Ludwigsburg, 1958–2009* (Darmstadt, Germany: Wissenschaftliche Buchgesellschaft, 2008). Eichmüller, *Keine Generalamnestie*, sees the foundation of Ludwigsburg less as a turning point than a milestone marking a shift that began in the mid-1950s.

47. Marc von Miquel, *Ahnden oder amnestieren? Westdeutsche Justiz und Vergangenheitspolitik in den sechziger Jahren* (Göttingen, Germany: Wallstein Verlag, 2004); Michael Greve, *Der justitielle und rechtspolitische Umgang mit NS-Gewaltverbrechen in den sechziger Jahren* (Frankfurt am Main: Peter Lang, 2001).

48. Historians disagree on this.

49. Ronen Steinke, *Fritz Bauer, oder Auschwitz vor Gericht* (Munich: Piper, 2013), 274–76; Ulrich Herbert, *Best: Biographische Studien über Radikalismus, Weltanschauung und Vernunft, 1903–1989* (Bonn: Dietz Verlag, 1996), 537, calls this the most far-reaching amnesty for NS perpetrators in West German history.

50. Michael Bryant, *Eyewitness to Genocide: The Operation Reinhard Death Camp Trials, 1955–1966* (Knoxville: University of Tennessee Press, 2014); Norbert Frei, *Vergangenheitspolitik: Die Anfänge der Bundesrepublik und die NS-Vergangenheit* (Munich: C. H. Beck'sche Verlagsbuchhandlung, 1996); Ingo Müller, *Hitler's Justice: The Courts of the Third Reich*, trans. Deborah Lucas Schneider (London: I. B. Tauris, 1991).

51. De Mildt, *In the Name of the People*, 22–23.

52. Herbert, *Best*, 535–36. On Best's postwar activities, see Part 6, "Fall und Wiederaufstieg," 403–76, and Part 7, "Vergangenheit und Gegenwart," 477–521.

53. Andreas Eichmüller, "Die strafrechtliche Verfolgung von NS-Verbrechen und die Öffentlichkeit in der frühen Bundesrepublik Deutschland 1949–1958," in Osterloh and Vollnhals, *NS-Prozesse und deutsche Öffentlichkeit*, 53–73.

54. Frei, *Adenauer's Germany and the Nazi Past*, 23–25.

55. Frei, *Adenauer's Germany and the Nazi Past*, 67–91.

56. Frei, *Adenauer's Germany and the Nazi Past*, 54.

57. Markus Roth, *Herrenmenschen: Die deutschen Kreishauptleute im besetzten Polen— Karrierewege, Herrschaftspraxis und Nachgeschichte* (Göttingen, Germany: Wallstein Verlag, 2009), 434–38.

58. Christian Dirks, *"Die Verbrechen der Anderen": Auschwitz und der Auschwitz-Prozess der DDR; Das Verfahren gegen den KZ-Arzt Dr. Horst Fischer* (Paderborn, Germany: Ferdinand Schöningh, 2004), 53–72.

59. Michael Bryant, *Eyewitness to Genocide: The Operation Reinhard Death Camp Trials, 1955–1966* (Knoxville: University of Tennessee Press, 2014), 191–221.

60. Müller, *Furchtbare Juristen*, Part 3.

61. Wolfram Wette, "Der KZ-Kommandant Josef Schwammberger und die deutsche Justiz," foreword to Almut Greiser, *Der Kommandant: Josef Schwammberger: Ein NS-Täter in der Erinnerung von Überlebenden* (Berlin: Aufbau Verlag, 2011), 12–13. See also Müller, *Hitler's Justice*; Kerstin Freudiger, *Die juristische Aufarbeitung von NS-Verbrechen* (Tübingen, Germany: J. C. B. Mohr Paul Siebeck, 2002); Jörg Friedrich, *Freispruch für die Nazi-Justiz: Die Urteile gegen NS-Richter seit 1948; Eine Dokumentation* (Berlin: Ullstein, 1998); Annette Weinke, *Die Verfolgung von NS-Tätern im geteilten Deutschland: Vergangenheitsbewältigungen 1949–1989, Oder: Eine deutsch-deutsch Beziehungsgeschichte im Kalten Krieg* (Paderborn, Germany: Ferdinand Schöningh, 2002), 339, 343.

62. Michael Greve, "Täter oder Gehilfen? Zum strafrechtlichen Umgang mit NS-Gewaltverbrechern in der Bundesrepublik Deutschland," in *"Bestien" und "Befehlsempfänger": Frauen und Männer in NS-Prozesse nach 1945*, eds. Ulrike Weckel and Edgar Wolfrum (Göttingen, Germany: Vandenhoeck & Ruprecht, 2003), 194–221.

63. Guenter Lewy, *The Nazi Persecution of the Gypsies* (Oxford: Oxford University Press, 2000), 209.

64. L. G. Verden (Rüter vol. 18, 567), quoted in Greve, "Täter oder Gehilfen?," 214.

65. Ruth Bettina Birn, "Book Reviews," *Journal of International Criminal Justice* 12 (2014): 639–51.

66. It is notable that the men staffing the Reinhard camps who were later brought to trial were predominantly from the lower middle class: see Yitzhak Arad, *Belzec, Sobibor, Treblinka: The Operation Reinhard Death Camps* (Bloomington: Indiana University Press, 1987), 198. The notion of "normative demarcation" is argued by Norbert Frei, *Adenauer's Germany and the Nazi Past: The Politics of Amnesty and Integration*, trans. Joel Golb (New York: Columbia University Press, 2002).

67. Andreas Plake, Babette Quinkert, and Florian Schmaltz, afterword to Hans Frankenthal, *The Unwelcome One: Returning Home from Auschwitz*, trans. John A. Broadwin (Evanston, IL: Northwestern University Press, 2002), 129–35.

68. Fritz ter Meer, *Die I. G: Farben Industrie Aktiengesellschaft: Ihre Entstehung, Entwicklung und Bedeutung* (Düsseldorf: Econ-Verlag, 1953).

69. Katharina Rauschenberger and Werner Renz, introduction to Katharina Rauschenberger and Werner Renz, eds., *Henry Ormond—Anwalt der Opfer: Plädoyers in NS-Prozessen* (Frankfurt am Main: Campus Verlag, 2015), 7–28.

70. Benjamin B. Ferencz, *Less than Slaves: Jewish Forced Labor and the Quest for Compensation* (Cambridge, MA: Harvard University Press, 1979), 174–77; Joachim R. Rumpf, "Die Entschädigingsansprüche deutscher Zwangsarbeiter," in *Rüstung, Kriegswirtschaft und Zwangsarbeit im "Dritten Reich,"* ed. Andreas Heusler, Mark Spoerer and Helmuth Trischler (Munich: Oldenbourg Verlag, 2010), 269–94.

71. "Entschädiging: Sklaven des Reichs," *Der Spiegel*, May 13, 1964, 59–61; list reproduced on 61.

72. Ferencz, *Less than Slaves*, 182–83.

73. Weinke, *Die Verfolgung von NS-Tätern*.

74. On Austria, see for example Bertrand Perz, "Österreich," in *Verbrechen erinnern: Die Auseinandersetzung mit Holocaust und Völkermord*, ed. Volkhard Knigge and Norbert Frei (Munich: C. H. Beck, 2002), 150–62, and David Art, *The Politics of the Nazi Past in Germany and Austria* (Cambridge: Cambridge University Press, 2006), 101–44.

75. Evan Burr Bukey, *Hitler's Austria: Popular Sentiment in the Nazi Era, 1938–1945* (Chapel Hill: University of North Carolina Press, 2000), 228.

76. Bukey, *Hitler's Austria*, 230.

77. Anton Pelinka, *Austria: Out of the Shadow of the Past* (Boulder, CO: Westview, 1998), 184. More than half of Austrian Jews escaped before deportations started; the number murdered in the Holocaust is 65,459.

78. Pelinka, *Austria*, 190.

79. Peter Eichelsberger, " 'Mauthausen vor Gericht'. Die österrreichischen Prozesse wegen Tötingsdelikten im KZ Mauthausen und seinen Außenlagern," in Albrich, Garscha and Polaschek, *Holocaust und Kriegsverbrechen vor Gericht*, 198–228.

80. Garscha and Kuretsis-Haider, "Die strafrechtliche Verfolgung nationalsozialistsicher Verbrechen."

81. Lewy, *Nazi Persecution of the Gypsies*, 208.
82. Albrich, Garscha, and Polaschek, *Holocaust und Kriegsverbrechen vor Gericht*; Winfried Garscha, "The Trials of Nazi War Criminals in Austria," in *Nazi Crimes and the Law*, ed. Nathan Stoltzfus and Henry Friedlander (New York: Cambridge University Press, 2008), 139–50.
83. Garscha, "Trials of Nazi War Criminals," 147.
84. Claudia Kuretsidis-Haider, "Die Rezeption von NS-Prozessen in Österrreich durch Medien, Politik und Gesellschaft im ersten Nachkriegsjahrzehnt," in Osterloh and Vollnhals, *NS-Prozesse und deutsche Öffentlichkeit*, 403.
85. Garscha and Kuretsis-Haider, "Die strafrechtliche Verfolgung nationalsozialistsicher Verbrechen," 13.
86. Garscha and Kuretsis-Haider, "Die strafrechtliche Verfolgung nationalsozialistsicher Verbrechen," 23–24.
87. Garscha, "Trials of Nazi War Criminals," 142.
88. Adalbert Rückerl, *The Investigation of Nazi Crimes, 1945-1978*, trans. Derek Rutter (Hamden, CT: Archon, 1980), 74.
89. Garscha, "Trials of Nazi War Criminals."
90. Wiesenthal was notorious for storytelling, embellishment of details, and providing conflicting accounts even of his own life. See Tom Segev, *Simon Wiesenthal: The Life and Legends* (London: Jonathan Cape, 2010), and Guy Walters, *Hunting Evil: How the Nazi War Criminals Escaped and the Hunt to Bring Them to Justice* (London: Bantam, 2009).
91. Segev, *Simon Wiesenthal*, 244ff.
92. Art, *Politics of the Nazi Past*, 115ff.

CHAPTER 10

1. Gerald Reitlinger, *The Final Solution: The Attempt to Exterminate the Jews of Europe, 1939–1945*, 2nd ed. (South Brunswick, NJ: Thomas Yoseloff, 1961), 551.
2. Günter Dahl, "Hände, die töteten, statt zu heilen," *Die Zeit*, February 27, 1958.
3. Susanne Benzler and Joachim Perels, "Justiz und Staatsverbrechen: Über den juristischen Umgang mit der NS-'Euthanasie,'" in *NS-"Euthanasie" vor Gericht: Fritz Bauer und die Grenzen juristischer Bewältigung*, ed. Hanno Loewy and Bettina Winter (Frankfurt am Main: Campus Verlag, 1996), 18–19.
4. Bettina Winter and Hanno Loewy, foreword to Loewy and Winter, *NS-"Euthanasie" vor Gericht*, 11.
5. Willi Dreßen, "NS-'Euthanasie'-Prozesse in der Bundesrepublik Deutschland im Wandel der Zeit," in Loewy and Winter, *NS-"Euthanasie" vor Gericht*, 36.
6. Martin Achrainer and Peter Ebener, "'Es gibt kein unwertes Leben': Die Strafverfolgung der 'Euthanasie'-Verbrechen," in *Holocaust und Kriegsverbrechen vor Gericht: Der Fall Österreich*, ed. Thomas Albrich, Winfried Garscha, and Martin Polaschek (Innsbruck, Austria: Studien Verlag, 2006), 57–86.
7. Achrainer and Ebener, "Es gibt kein unwertes Leben," 82.

8. Patricia Heberer, "Justice in Austrian Courts? The Case of Josef W. and Austria's Difficult Relationship with Its Past," in *Atrocities on Trial: Historical Perspectives on the Politics of Prosecuting War Crimes*, ed. Patricia Heberer and Jürgen Matthäus (Lincoln: University of Nebraska Press, 2008), 240–41; see also "The Long Shadow of Nazi Psychiatry: The Case of Dr Heinrich Gross," available online at http://gedenkstaettesteinhof.at/en/exibition/17-long-shadow-nazi-psychiatry, and John Silverman, "Gruesome Legacy of Dr Gross," BBC News, May 6, 1999, available online at http://news.bbc.co.uk/1/hi/world/europe/336189.stm.

9. Joachim S. Hohmann, *Der "Euthanasie"-Prozeß Dresden 1947: Eine zeitgeschichtliche Dokumentation* (Frankfurt am Main: Peter Lang, 1993); Boris Böhm and Gerald Hacke, eds., *Fundamentale Gebote der Sittlichkeit: Der "Euthanasie"-Prozess vor dem Landgericht Dresden 1947* (Dresden: Sandstein Verlag, 2008).

10. Thomas Müller, " 'Ein Prozess, dem das stärkste Allgemeininteresse entgegengebracht wurde'—Der Dresdner 'Euthanasie'-Prozess und die Öffentlichkeit," in Böhm and Hacke, *Fundamentale Gebote der Sittlichkei*, 79–80.

11. Boris Böhm and Agnes Muche, "Zeugenschaft der NS-'Euthanasie'—Angehörige der Opfer im Prozess," in Böhm and Hacke, *Fundamentale Gebote der Sittlichkeit*, 85–94.

12. Sara Berger, *Experten der Vernichtung: Das T4-Reinhardt-Netzwerk in den Lagern Belzec, Sobibor und Treblinka* (Hamburg: Hamburger Edition, 2013), 370.

13. Dick de Mildt, ed., *Tatkomplex NS-Euthanasie: Die ost- und westdeutschen Strafurteile seit 1945*, vol. 1 (Amsterdam: Amsterdam University Press, 2009), 325–39.

14. De Mildt, *Tatkomplex: NS-Euthanasie*, 1:341–50.

15. De Mildt, *Tatkomplex NS-Euthanasie*, 1:343.

16. De Mildt, *Tatkomplex NS-Euthanasie*, 1:348–49.

17. Ute Hoffmann, " 'Das ist wohl ein Stück verdrängt worden…' Zum Umgang mit den 'Euthanasie'-Verbrechen in der DDR," in *Vielstimmiges Schweigen: Neue Studien zum DDR-Antifaschismus*, ed. Annette Leo and Peter Reif-Sirek (Berlin: Metropol Verlag, 2001), 51–66; Hohmann, *Der "Euthanasie"-Prozeß Dresden 1947*.

18. Leide, *NS-Verbrecher und Staatssicherheit*, 332–47.

19. Kerstin Freudiger, *Die juristische Aufarbeitung von NS-Verbrechen* (Tübingen, Germany: J. C. B. Mohr Paul Siebeck, 2002), 110–13; Michael Bryant, *Confronting the "Good Death": Nazi Euthanasia on Trial, 1945–1953* (Boulder: University Press of Colorado, 2005), 118–20.

20. Andreas Eichmüller, "Die Strafverfolgung von NS-Verbrechen durch westdeutsche Justizbehörden seit 1945: Eine Zahlenbilanz," *Vierteljahrshefte für Zeitgeschichte* 4 (2008): 637.

21. Bryant, *Confronting the "Good Death,"* 121–28.

22. Patricia Heberer, "Early Postwar Justice in the American Zone: The 'Hadamar Murder Factory' Trial," in Heberer and Matthäus, *Atrocities on Trial*, 25–47.

23. Dreßen, "NS-'Euthanasie'-Prozesse in der Bundesrepublik Deutschland, 38. See also Bryant, *Confronting the "Good Death,"* 128–35, and Bettina Winter, Gerhard Baader, Johannes Cramer, et al., *"Verlegt nach Hadamar": Die Geschichte*

einer NS- "Euthanasie"-Anstalt, Historische Schriften des Landeswohlfahrtverbandes Hessen, Kataloge, 2 (Kassel, Germany: Landeswohlfahrtverbandes Hessen, 2009), 166–81.

24. Heberer, "Early Postwar Justice in the American Zone," 40.
25. Quoted in Heberer, "Early Postwar Justice in the American Zone," 41.
26. Benzler and Perels, "Justiz und Staatsverbrechen," 15–34.
27. Matthias Meusch, "Der Düsseldorfer 'Euthanasie'-Prozess und die juristische Exkulpation von NS-Tätern," in Böhm and Hacke, *Fundamentale Gebote der Sittlichkeit*, 172–89.
28. Benzler and Perels, "Justiz und Staatsverbrechen," 31.
29. De Mildt, *Tatkomplex NS-Euthanasie*, 1:363–78.
30. De Mildt, *Tatkomplex NS-Euthanasie*, 1:363–78, 376.
31. De Mildt, *Tatkomplex NS-Euthanasie*, 1:373.
32. De Mildt, *Tatkomplex NS-Euthanasie*, 1:378.
33. See also Patrick Montague, *Chełmno and the Holocaust: The History of Hitler's First Death Camp* (London: I. B. Tauris, 2012), 10, and Alexander Mitscherlich and Fred Mielke, eds., *Medizin ohne Menschlichkeit: Dokumente des Nürnberger Ärzteprozesses* (Frankfurt am Main: Fischer Taschenbuchverlag, 1960).
34. Dreßen, "NS-'Euthanasie'-Prozesse," 43–46; Freudiger, *Die juristische Aufarbeitung von NS-Verbrechen*, 272–78; Ernst Klee, *Das Personenlexikon zum Dritten Reich: Wer war was vor und nach 1945*, 2nd ed. (Frankfurt am Main: Fischer Taschenbuch Verlag, 2007), 458.
35. Dreßen, "NS-'Euthanasie'-Prozesse in der Bundesrepublik Deutschland," 40–43.
36. See also Friedrich Karl Kaul, *Nazimordaktion T4: Ein Bericht über die erste industriemäßig durchgeführte Mordaktion des Naziregimes* (Berlin: VEB Verlag Volk & Gesundheit, 1973).
37. Werner Catel, *Grenzsituationen des Lebens: Beitrag zum Problem der begrenzten Euthanasie* (Nuremberg: Glock & Lutz, 1962).
38. "Aus Menschlichkeit töten? Spiegel-Gespräch mit Professor Dr. Werner Catel über Kinder-Euthanasie," *Der Spiegel*, February 19, 1964, 41–47, interview with Spiegel journalist Hermann Renner.
39. Ernst Klee, *Was sie taten—was sie wurden: Ärzte, Juristen und andere Beteiligte am Kranken- oder Judenmord* (Frankfurt am Main: Fischer Taschenbuch Verlag, 1986), 98–107.
40. Dreßen, "NS-'Euthanasie'-Prozesse," 50–51.
41. Dreßen, "NS-'Euthanasie'-Prozesse," 52.
42. Dreßen, "NS-'Euthanasie'-Prozesse," 52–54.
43. Dreßen, "NS-'Euthanasie'-Prozesse," 46–48; *Süddeutsche Zeitung* quoted here, 48.
44. Kaul, *Nazimordaktion T4*.
45. Kurt Nowak, *"Euthanasie" und Sterilisierung im "Dritten Reich": Die Konfrontation der evangelischen und katholischen Kirche mit dem Gesetz zur Verhütung erbkranken Nachwuchses und die "Euthanasie"-Aktion* (Göttingen, Germany: Vandenhoeck & Ruprecht, 1978).

46. Ernst Klee, ed., *Dokumente zur "Euthanasie"* (Frankfurt am Main: Fischer Taschenbuch Verlag, 1985); Klee, *Was sie taten—was sie wurden.*

47. Winter and Loewy, foreword to Loewy and Winter, *NS-"Euthanasie" vor Gericht*, 13.

48. There were conflicting rumors that Bauer's heart attack was caused by an overdose of sleeping pills or brought on by overwork and stress; see Ronen Steinke, *Fritz Bauer, oder Auschwitz vor Gericht* (Munich: Piper, 2013), 268–77.

49. Michael Greve, *Der justitielle und rechtspolitische Umgang mit NS-Gewaltverbrechen in den sechziger Jahren* (Frankfurt am Main: Peter Lang, 2001), 387–93; Steinke, *Fritz Bauer*, 274–76.

50. See Hilary Earl, *The Nuremberg SS-Einsatzgruppen Trial, 1945–1958: Atrocity, Law and History* (Cambridge: Cambridge University Press, 2009).

51. Annette Weinke, *Eine Gesellschaft vermittelt gegen sich selbst: Die Geschichte der Zentralen Stelle Ludwigsburg 1958–2009* (Darmstadt, Germany: Wissenschaftliche Buchgesellschaft, 2008).

52. BArch DP 3/1878, vol. 47, file on Erwin Schüle 1965.

53. Annette Weinke, *Die Verfolgung von NS-Tätern im geteilten Deutschland: Vergangenheitsbewältigungen 1949–1989; Oder, Eine deutsch-deutsch Beziehungsgeschichte im Kalten Krieg* (Paderborn, Germany: Ferdinand Schöningh, 2002), 341–43.

54. C. F. Rüter, "Die Ahndung von NS-Tötungsverbrechen: Westdeutschland, Holland und die DDR im Vergleich; Eine These," in *Keine "Abrechnung": NS-Verbrechen, Justiz und Gesellschaft in Europa nach 1945*, ed. Claudia Kuretsidis-Haider and Winfried Garscha (Leipzig: Akademische Verlagsanstalt, 1998), 183; Henry Leide, *NS-Verbrecher und Staatssicherheit* (Göttingen, Germany: Vandenhoeck & Ruprecht, 2006); Joachim Käpper, *Erstarrte Geschichte: Faschismus und Holocaust im Spiegel der Geschichtswissenschaft und Geschichtspropaganda der DDR* (Hamburg: Ergebnisse Verlag, 1999), 97ff.

55. Steinke, *Fritz Bauer*, 13–27.

56. Michael Bazyler, *Holocaust, Genocide, and the Law: A Quest for Justice in a Post-Holocaust World* (Oxford: Oxford University Press, 2016), 143, 132–33.

57. Attorney general's opening speech, session no. 6, April 17, 1961 (morning), from the trial transcript, courtesy of the Nizkor Project, available at http://www.nizkor.org/ftp.cgi/people/e/eichmann.adolf/transcripts/ftp.cgi?people/e/eichmann.adolf/transcripts/Sessions/Session-006-007-008-01, accessed April 20, 2014.

58. Attorney general's opening speech, at http://www.nizkor.org/ftp.cgi/people/e/eichmann.adolf/transcripts/ftp.cgi?people/e/eichmann.adolf/transcripts/Sessions/Session-006-007-008-01.

59. Some argue that its significance within Israel may have been overstated. Cf. Boaz Cohen, *Israeli Holocaust Research: Birth and Evolution*, trans. Agnes Vazsonyi (London: Routledge, 2013), 269–78.

60. Quoted in Saul Friedländer, *Nazi Germany and the Jews*, vol. 2, *The Years of Extermination, 1933–45* (New York: HarperCollins, 2007), 325–26.

61. Tom Segev, *The Seventh Million: The Israelis and the Holocaust*, trans. Haim Watzman (New York: Holt, 1991), 140–52; David Cesarani, *Final Solution: The Fate of the Jews, 1933–49* (London: Macmillan, 2016), 782–83.

62. Hannah Arendt, *Eichmann in Jerusalem: A Report on the Banality of Evil* (New York: Penguin, 1977); see also Deborah E. Lipstadt, *The Eichmann Trial* (New York: Schocken, 2011).

63. Raul Hilberg, *The Politics of Memory: The Journey of a Holocaust Historian* (Chicago: Ivan R. Dee, 1996).

64. Bettina Stangneth, *Eichmann before Jerusalem: The Unexamined Life of a Mass Murderer*, trans. Ruth Martin (New York: Alfred Knopf, 2014), challenges Arendt's portrayal of Eichmann.

65. Peter Krause, "'Eichmann und wir': Die bundesdeutsche Öffentlichkeit und der Jerusalemer Eichmann-Prozess 1961," in *NS-Prozesse und deutsche Öffentlichkeit: Besatzungszeit, frühe Bundesrepublik und DDR*, ed. Jörg Osterloh and Clemens Vollnhals (Göttingen, Germany: Vandenhoeck & Ruprecht, 2011), 306; see also Peter Krause, *Der Eichmann-Prozess in der deutschen Presse* (Frankfurt am Main: Campus Verlag, 2002).

66. "Deutsche und Weltmeinung über den Eichmann-Prozess," in *Der Eichmann-Prozeß in der deutschen öffentlichen Meinung*, ed. Hans Lamm (Frankfurt-am-Main: Ner-Tamid Verlag, 1961), 71.

67. Lamm, *Eichmann-Prozeß*, 72.

68. Hartmut Berghoff, "Zwischen Verdrängung und Aufarbeitung: Die bundesdeutsche Gesellschaft und ihre nationalsozialistische Vergangenheit in den Fünfziger Jahren," *Geschichte in Wissenschaft und Unterricht* 49, no. 2 (1998): 110.

69. Ernst Wilm, "Eichmann und wir," *Kirche und Mann*, April 1961, reprinted in Lamm, *Der Eichmann-Prozeß*, 16.

70. Wilm, *Kirche und Mann*, 16–17.

CHAPTER 11

1. Devon O. Pendas, *The Frankfurt Auschwitz Trial, 1963–1965: Genocide, History, and the Limits of the Law* (Cambridge: Cambridge University Press, 2006); Rebecca Wittmann, *Beyond Justice: The Auschwitz Trial* (Cambridge, MA: Harvard University Press, 2005). More broadly: Nathan Stoltzfus and Henry Friedlander, eds., *Nazi Crimes and the Law* (Cambridge: Cambridge University Press, 2008); Thomas Albrich, Winfried Garscha, and Martin Polaschek, eds., *Holocaust und Kriegsverbrechen vor Gericht: Der Fall Österreich* (Innsbruck, Austria: Studien Verlag, 2006).

2. Peter Reichel, *Vergangenheitsbewältigung in Deutschland: Die Auseinandersetzung mit der NS-Diktatur in Politik und Justiz*, 2nd ed. (Munich: C. H. Beck, 2007), 10.

3. Hans Buchheim, *Anatomie des SS-Staates*, vol. 1, *Die SS—das Herrschaftsinstrument: Befehl und Gehorsam* (Munich: Deutscher Taschenbuch Verlag, 1967), first produced as an expert report for the Frankfurt Auschwitz trial in 1964; Martin Broszat, Hans-Adolf Jacobsen, and Helmut Krausnick, *Anatomie des SS-Staates*,

vol. 2, *Konzentrationslager, Kommissarbefehl, Judenverfolgung* (Munich: Deutscher Taschenbuch Verlag, 1967), first produced as three expert reports for the Frankfurt Auschwitz trial in 1964.

4. Boaz Cohen, *Israeli Holocaust Research: Birth and Evolution*, trans. Agnes Vazsonyi (London: Routledge, 2013).

5. Raul Hilberg, *The Destruction of the European Jews* (New Haven, CT: Yale University Press, 2003), for which he initially had difficulty finding a publisher; Helmut Eschwege, ed., *Kennzeichen J. Bilder, Dokumente, Berichte zur Geschichte der Verbrechen des Hitlerfaschismus an den deutschen Juden, 1933–1945*, 2nd ed. (Berlin: VEB Deutscher Verlag der Wissenschaften, 1981). For difficulties of initial publication in East Germany, see Helmut Eschwege, *Fremd unter meinesgleichen: Erinnerung eines Dresdner Juden* (Berlin: Ch. Links Verlag, 1991), 184–211.

6. Sabine Loitfellner, "Auschwitz-Verfahren in Österreich: Hintergründe und Ursachen eines Scheiterns," in Albrich, Garscha, and Polaschek, *Holocaust und Kriegsverbrechen vor Gericht*, 183.

7. Hermann Langbein, *Der Auschwitz-Prozess: Eine Dokumentation* (Vienna: Europa-Verlag, 1965), 2:993–1005, for a list of all trials and judgments relating to crimes committed at Auschwitz.

8. Gerhard Werle and Thomas Wandres, *Auschwitz vor Gericht: Völkermord und bundesdeutsche Strafjustiz* (Munich: Verlag C. H. Beck, 1995), 43.

9. Christian Dirks, *"Die Verbrechen der anderen": Auschwitz und der Auschwitz-Prozeß der DDR; Das Verfahren gegen den KZ-Arzt Dr. Horst Fischer* (Paderborn, Germany: Ferdinand Schöningh, 2006).

10. Christian Dirks, " 'Vergangenheitsbewältigung' in der DDR: Zur Rezeption des Prozesses gegen den KZ-Arzt Dr. Horst Fischer 1966 in Ost-Berlin," in *NS-Prozesse und deutsche Öffentlichkeit: Besatzungszeit, frühe Bundesrepublik und DDR*, ed. Jörg Osterloh and Clemens Vollnhals (Göttingen, Germany: Vandenhoeck & Ruprecht, 2011), 369–70.

11. Dirks, " 'Vergangenheitsbewältigung' in der DDR," 370–74.

12. Werle and Wandres, *Auschwitz vor Gericht*, 42.

13. Werner Renz, "Der 1. Frankfurter Auschwitz-Prozess 1963–65 und die deutsche Öffentlichkeit: Anmerkungen zur Entmythologisierung eines NSG-Verfahrens," in Osterloh and Vollnhals, *NS-Prozesse und deutsche Öffentlichkeit*, 361, citing Jürgen Wilke, Birgit Schenk, Akiba A. Cohen, and Tamar Zemach, *Holocaust und NS-Prozesse: Die Presseberichterstattung in Israel und Deutschland zwischen Aneignung und Abwehr* (Cologne: Böhlau Verlag, 1995), 53.

14. Norbert Frei, *Adenauer's Germany and the Nazi Past: The Politics of Amnesty and Reintegration*, trans. Joel Golb (New York: Columbia University Press, 2002).

15. Ronen Steinke, *Fritz Bauer, oder Auschwitz vor Gericht* (Munich: Piper, 2013).

16. Hermann Langbein, *People in Auschwitz*, trans. Harry Zohn (Chapel Hill: University of North Carolina Press, 2004).

17. Werner Renz, *Fritz Bauer und das Versagen der Justiz: Nazi-Prozesse und ihre "Tragödie"* (Hamburg: CEP Europäische Verlagsanstalt, 2015).

18. Dagi Knellesen, "Momentaufnahmen der Erinnerung: Juristische Zeugenschaft im ersten Frankfurter Auschwitz-Prozess—Ein Interviewprojekt," in *Zeugenschaft des Holocaust: Zwischen Trauma, Tradierung und Ermittlung*, ed. Fritz Bauer Institut (Frankfurt am Main: Campus Verlag, 2007), 133; Werle and Wandres, *Auschwitz vor Gericht*, 43; Hermann Langbein, *Der Auschwitz-Prozess: Eine Dokumentation* (Vienna: Europa-Verlag, 1965), 2:993ff.

19. Knellesen, "Momentaufnahmen der Erinnerung," 127, gives the figure of 211 survivors called to give evidence; Werle and Wandres, *Auschwitz vor Gericht*, 41, give the somewhat higher figure of 248 former Auschwitz prisoners out of a total of 359 witnesses altogether.

20. Irmtrud Wojak, ed., *Auschwitz-Prozess 4 Ks 2/63: Frankfurt am Main* (Cologne: Snoeck, 2004), Vrba on 299–319.

21. Knellesen, "Momentaufnahmen der Erinnerung," 128–29.

22. Wittmann, *Beyond Justice*, 83–87.

23. Letter of March 2, 1959, quoted in Wittmann, *Beyond Justice*, 86.

24. Detailed reports by Bernd Naumann, originally in the *Frankfurter Allgemeine Zeitung*: Bernd Naumann, *Der Auschwitz-Prozess: Bericht über die Strafsache gegen Mulka u.a. vor dem Schwurgericht Frankfurt am Main, 1963–1965*, rev. ed. (Hamburg: CEP Europäische Verlagsanstalt, 2013). The Fritz Bauer Institute has made available taped recordings and transcripts, available at http://www.auschwitz-prozess.de, accessed January 1, 2015.

25. Lingens, in Naumann, *Der Auschwitz-Prozess*, 103.

26. Sybille Bedford, "The Worst That Ever Happened: The Trial of Twenty-Two Former Staff of Auschwitz Concentration Camp, Frankfurt, West Germany," *Saturday Evening Post*, October 22, 1966, 29–33; reprinted in Sybille Bedford, *As It Was: Pleasures, Landscapes and Justice* (London: Picador, 1990), 219.

27. Bedford, "Worst That Ever Happened," 238.

28. Hans Buchheim, Martin Broszat, Hans-Adolf Jacobsen, and Helmut Krausnick, *Anatomie des SS-Staates* (Munich: Deutscher Taschenbuch Verlag, 1967).

29. Langbein, *Auschwitz-Prozess*, 2:833–35.

30. Wojak, *Auschwitz-Prozess 4 Ks 2/63*, 283.

31. Wojak, *Auschwitz-Prozess 4 Ks 2/63*, 283.

32. Wojak, *Auschwitz-Prozess 4 Ks 2/63*, 284.

33. Wojak, *Auschwitz-Prozess 4 Ks 2/63*, 289.

34. Wojak, *Auschwitz-Prozess 4 Ks 2/63*, document dated August 12, 1942, 292.

35. Klehr, quoted in Naumann, *Der Auschwitz-Prozess*, 85.

36. Klehr, quoted in Naumann, *Der Auschwitz-Prozess*, 85.

37. Scherpe, quoted in Naumann, *Der Auschwitz-Prozess*, 91–93.

38. Bedford, "Worst That Ever Happened," 222.

39. Christoph Busch, Stefan Hördler, and Robert Jan van Pelt, eds., *Das Höcker-Album: Auschwitz durch die Linse des SS* (Darmstadt, Germany: Wissenschaftliche Buchgesellschaft, Philipp von Zabern, 2016); see also "Auschwitz through the Lens of the SS: The Album," at the United States Holocaust Memorial Museum website, https://www.ushmm.org/wlc/en/article.php?ModuleId=10007435.

40. Neubert, quoted in Naumann, *Der Auschwitz-Prozess*, 95–96.
41. Bednarek, quoted in Naumann, *Der Auschwitz-Prozess*, 96–97.
42. Naumann, *Der Auschwitz-Prozess*, 87.
43. Langbein, *Der Auschwitz-Prozess* 1:565.
44. Reproduced in Jadwiga Bezwińska and Danuta Czech, comps., *KL Auschwitz seen by the SS*, trans. Constantine Fitzgibbon (Oświęcim, Poland: Publications of the Państwowe Muzeum w Oświęmcu, 1972).
45. Naumann, *Der Auschwitz-Prozess*, 127.
46. Werle and Wandres, *Auschwitz vor Gericht*, 64–65; Langbein, *Der Auschwitz-Prozess*.
47. Hans Laternser, *Die andere Seite im Auschwitz-Prozess, 1963–65: Reden eines Verteidigers* (Stuttgart: Seewald Verlag, 1966); Naumann, *Der Auschwitz-Prozess*; and Langbein, *Der Auschwitz-Prozess*.
48. Sabine Horn, *Erinnerungsbilder: Auschwitz-Prozess und Majdanek-Prozess im westdeutschen Fernsehen* (Essen, Germany: Klartext, 2009).
49. Hans Frankenthal, with Andreas Plake, Babette Quinkert, and Florian Schmaltz, *The Unwelcome One: Returning Home from Auschwitz*, trans. John A. Broadwin (Evanston, IL: Northwestern University Press, 2002), 100.
50. Bedford, "Worst That Ever Happened," 259.
51. Norbert Frei, "Die Aufklärer und die Überlebenden," in *Zeitgenossenschaft: Zum Auschwitz-Prozess 1964*, Martin Warnke (Zürich: Diaphanes, 2014), 57.
52. Bedford, "Worst That Ever Happened," 239.
53. Knellesen, "Momentaufnahmen der Erinnerung."
54. Knellesen, "Momentaufnahmen der Erinnerung," 121.
55. Knellesen, "Momentaufnahmen der Erinnerung," 121–22.
56. Knellesen, "Momentaufnahmen der Erinnerung," 122.
57. Knellesen, "Momentaufnahmen der Erinnerung," 122.
58. Knellesen, "Momentaufnahmen der Erinnerung," 123.
59. "Was haben wir gelernt? Zum Urteil im Majdanek-Prozess in Düsseldorf (1981)," in Gerhard Mauz, *Die großen Prozesse der Bundesrepublik Deutschland*, ed. Gisela Friedrichsen (Springe, Germany: zu Klampen Verlag, 2005), 47–48.
60. Langbein, *Der Auschwitz-Prozess*, 2:1002–5.
61. Langbein, *Der Auschwitz-Prozess*, 2:1003. See also Claudia Kuretsidis-Haider, Johannes Laimighofer, and Siegfried Sanwald, "Auschwitz-Täter und die österreichische Nachkriegsjustiz," *Täter: Österreichische Akteure im Nationalsozialismus*, ed. Dokumentationsarchiv des österreichischen Widerstandes (Vienna: Dokumentationsarchiv des österreichischen Widerstandes, 2014), 13–39.
62. Loitfellner, "Auschwitz-Verfahren in Österreich"; Michael Thad Allen, "Realms of Oblivion: The Vienna Auschwitz Trial," *Central European History* 40 (2007): 397–428.
63. Quoted in Loitfellner, "Auschwitz-Verfahren in Österreich," 190.
64. Loitfellner, "Auschwitz-Verfahren in Österreich," 192–93.
65. Loitfellner, "Auschwitz-Verfahren in Österreich," 194.
66. Cf. Annette Wieviorka, *The Era of the Witness*, trans. Jared Stark (Ithaca, NY: Cornell University Press, 2006).

67. Patrick Montague, *Chełmno and the Holocaust: The History of Hitler's First Death Camp* (Chapel Hill: University of North Carolina Press, 2012), 179–80; C. F. Rüter and D. W. de Mildt, eds., *Justiz und NS-Verbrechen: Sammlung deutscher Strafurteile wegen nationalsozialistischer Tötungsverbrechen 1945–1999*, vol. 21, Lfd. no. 594.

68. Sara Berger, *Experten der Vernichtung: Das T4-Reinhardt-Netzwerk in den Lagern Belzec, Sobibor und Treblinka* (Hamburg: Hamburger Edition, 2013).

69. Michael Bryant, *Eyewitness to Genocide: The Operation Reinhard Death Camp Trials, 1955–1966* (Knoxville: University of Tennessee Press, 2014).

70. Adalbert Rückerl, ed., *NS-Vernichtungslager im Spiegel deutscher Strafprozesse* (Munich: dtv, 1977), 89–90.

71. Bryant, *Eyewitness to Genocide*, 35–70.

72. Rückerl, *NS-Vernichtungslager*, 83.

73. The original Polish version of Reder's testimony includes photographs and drawings; see Rudolf Reder, *Bełżec* (Kraków: Centralna Żydowska Komisja Historyczna przy CK Żydów Polskich, 1946), translated into English as *I Survived a Secret Nazi Extermination Camp*, ed. Mark Forstater (London: Psychology News Press, 2013).

74. Berger, *Experten der Vernichtung*, 374.

75. Belzec-Prozess—Urteil, LG München I, 21.1.1965, 110 Ks 3/64; Kerstin Freudiger, *Die juristische Aufarbeitung von NS-Verbrechen* (Tübingen, Germany: J. C. B. Mohr Paul Siebeck, 2002), 163–67.

76. Belzec-Prozess—Urteil, LG München I vom 21.1.1965, 110 Ks 3/64.

77. Rückerl, ed., *NS-Vernichtungslager*, 81.

78. Bryant, *Eyewitness to Genocide*, 94.

79. Bryant, *Eyewitness to Genocide*, 103–4.

80. Bryant, *Eyewitness to Genocide*, 100–101. Zabecki also testified at trials in 1966, 1968, and 1970 (Stangl).

81. Gitta Sereny, *Into that Darkness: From Mercy Killing to Mass Murder* (London: Pimlico, 1995).

82. Bryant, *Eyewitness to Genocide*, 124–89.

83. BArch, DO 1/32572, "Das Vernichtungslager Sobibor," report by the "Presse-Agentur Zachodnia Agencja Prasowa" sent by Dr. Rudi Goguel on April 7, 1970, to Heinz Schumann, Ministry of the Interior, GDR, 9.

84. Bryant, *Eyewitness to Genocide*.

85. Claudia Kuretsidis-Haider, "NS-Verbrechen vor österreichischen und bundesdeutschen Gerichten. Eine blianzierende Betrachtung," in Albrich, Garscha, and Polaschek, *Holocaust und Kriegsverbrechen vor Gericht*, 347.

86. Winfried Garscha, "The Trials of Nazi War Criminals in Austria," in *Nazi Crimes and the Law*, ed. Nathan Stoltzfus and Henry Friedlander (New York: Cambridge University Press, 2008), 141.

87. Berger, *Experten der Vernichtung*, 377–80.

88. Cf. Wieviorka, *Era of the Witness*.

89. Rückerl, *NS-Vernichtungslager*, 85.
90. Rückerl, *NS-Vernichtungslager*, 86.
91. Rückerl, *NS-Vernichtungslager*, 88–89.
92. Rückerl, *NS-Vernichtungslager*, 89.
93. BArch, DO 1/32629, "Ein Report aus Anlass des Majdanek-Prozesses in Düsseldorf," VVN Bund der Antifaschisten and published by the VVN Präsidium in Frankfurt/Main, compiled by Karl Sauer, Leiter des Referates NS-Verbrechen beim Präsidium der VVN—Bunde der Antifaschisten, foreword by Werner Stertzenbach, Vorsitzender des Kreis der Antifaschisten Düsseldorf, 15–16.
94. Horn, *Erinnerungsbilder*, 243–49.
95. Heiner Lichtenstein, *Majdanek: Reportage eines Prozesses: Mit einem Nachwort von Simon Wiesenthal* (Frankfurt am Main: Europäische Verlagsanstalt, 1979), 129–40.
96. Lichtenstein, *Majdanek*, 140.
97. Lichtenstein, *Majdanek*, 141–51.
98. Ernst Klee, *Was sie taten—was sie wurden: Ärzte, Juristen und andere beteiligte am Kranken- oder Judenmord* (Frankfurt am Main: Fischer Taschenbuch Verlag, 1986), 239.
99. Lichtenstein, *Majdanek*, 140.
100. See also Claudia Kuretsidis-Haider, Irmgard Nöbauer, Winfried Garscha, Siegfried Sanwald, Andrzej Selerowicz, eds., *Das KZ-Lublin-Majdanek und die Justiz: Strafverfolgung und verweigerte Gerechtigkeit; Polen, Deutschland und Österreich im Vergleich* (Graz, Austria: CLIO, 2011).
101. Eberhard Fechner, *Der Prozess*. Eine Darstellung des sogenannten "Majdanek-Verfahrens gegen Angehörige des Konzentrationslagers Lublin/Majdanek" in Düsseldorf von 1975 bis 1981 in drei Teilen von Eberhard Fechner. Erstsendung am 21.November 1984. Teil 1: "Anklage," Teil 2: "Beweisaufnahme," Teil 3: "Urteile."
102. Quoted by John Vinocur, "Ex-New Yorker Gets Life for Crimes in Nazi Camp," *New York Times*, July 1, 1981.
103. Kuretsidis-Haider et al., *Das KZ-Lublin-Majdanek und die Justiz*, 321–442.
104. Garscha, "Trials of Nazi War Criminals," 140.
105. Peter Eichelsberger, "'Mauthausen vor Gericht': Die österreichischen Prozesse wegen Tötingsdelikten im KZ Mauthausen und seinen Außenlagern," in Albrich, Garscha and Polaschek, *Holocaust und Kriegsverbrechen vor Gericht*, 222.

CHAPTER 12

1. In German, Zentralstelle für die Bearbeitung von nationalsozialistischen Verbrechen bei dem Generalstaatsanwalt Berlin.
2. BArch DP 3/1587, fols. 1–5.
3. BArch DP 3/1587, 15.10.1966, fol. 15.

4. BArch DP 3/1591, draft protocol of Zimmermann's statement, fo. 14.

5. BArch DP 3/1591, draft protocol of Zimmermann's statement, fo. 23.

6. BArch DP 3/1589, fo. 532.

7. BArch DP 3/1589, fo. 551.

8. BArch DP 3/1589, fo. 539.

9. BArch DP 3/1589, fo. 539.

10. BArch DP 3/1589, fo. 539.

11. BArch DP 3/1589, fo. 597.

12. BArch DP 3/1589, fo. 597.

13. BArch DP 3/1589, fo. 598.

14. BArch DP 3/1587, letter of April 26, 1968, from Parteisekretär Schlenker of Karl-Marx-Schule (Erweiterte Oberschule), fo. 225.

15. BArch DP 3/1587, letter of May 9, 1968, from Friedrich, Staatsanwalt, to Genossen Schlenker, Parteiorganisation of the Karl-Marx-Schule (Erweiterte Oberschule), fos. 226–7.

16. BArch DP 3/1590, fo. 604.

17. BArch DP 3/1590, letter of June 12, 1973, from Irma Zimmermann, to the General State Prosecutor (Generalstaatsanwalt) of the GDR, Dr. Streit, 4–5.

18. *Husumer Tageszeitung*, February 24, 1967; *Heilbronner Stimme*, February 24, 1967; *Pforzheimer Zeitung*, February 24, 1967.

19. BArch DP 3/1587, fo. 141.

20. BArch DP 3/1587, fo. 139.

21. BArch DP 3/1587, fo. 139.

22. BArch DP 3/1587, fos. 27–35.

23. BArch DP 3/1587, fo. 142.

24. BArch DP 3/1587, fo. 148.

25. BArch DP 3/1587, fos. 146–7.

26. BArch DP 3/1587, fo. 147.

27. BArch DP 3/1587, fo. 147.

28. *Badisches Tagblatt*, December 7, 1966; Berlin *Tagesspiegel*, December 7, 1966; repeated in similar words in others, including the *Weser-Kurier*, December 7, 1966.

29. *Badisches Tagblatt*, December 7, 1966.

30. *Basler Nachrichten,* December 7, 1966.

31. *Badische Zeitung*, December 7, 1966.

32. *Die Welt*, December 7, 1966.

33. *Westdeutsche Allgemeine*, December 7, 1966.

34. Zimmermann also recalls Glamann participating in shootings: BArch DP 3/1588, fo. 229.

35. *Badische Zeitung*, December 16, 1966.

36. *Badische Zeitung*, December 20, 1966.

37. *Badische Zeitung*, January 14, 1967.

38. See also Michael Greve, "Täter oder Gehilfen? Zum strafrechtlichen Umgang mit NS-Gewaltverbrechern in der Bundesrepublik Deutschland," in *"Bestien"*

und "Befehlsempfänger": Frauen und Männer in NS-Prozesse nach 1945, ed. Ulrike Weckel und Edgar Wolfrum (Göttingen, Germany: Vandenhoeck & Ruprecht 2003), 194–221; on the Thormeyer case, 219–21.

39. C. F. Rüter and D. W. de Mildt, eds., *Justiz und NS-Verbrechen: Sammlung deutscher Strafurteile wegen nationalsozialistischer Tötungsverbrechen 1945–1999*, vol. 26, *Die vom 16.03.1967 bis zum 14.12.1967 ergangenen Strafurteile. Lfd. Nr. 648–662* (Munich: K. G. Saur Verlag, 2001), 385.

40. Rüter and de Mildt, *Justiz und NS-Verbrechen*, 385.

41. Ulrich Herbert, *Best: Biographische Studien über Radikalismus, Weltanschauung und Vernunft, 1903–1989* (Bonn: Dietz Verlag, 1996), 498–500.

42. Karsten Wilke, *Die "Hilfsgemeinschaft auf Gegenseitigkeit" (HIAG) 1950–1990: Veteranen der Waffen-SS in der Bundesrepublik* (Paderborn: Ferdinand Schöningh, 2011).

43. C. F. Rüter and D. W. de Mildt, eds., *Justiz und NS-Verbrechen: Sammlung deutscher Strafurteile wegen nationalsozialistischer Tötungsverbrechen 1945–1999, Vol 39, Die vom 05.06.1973 bis zum 26.07.1974 ergangenen Strafurteile. Lfd Nr. 795–813* (Amsterdam: Amsterdam University Press and K.G. Saur Verlag München, 2008) Lfd. Nr. 802, Tatkomplex: NS-Gewaltverbrechen in Haftstätten/Tatort: ZAL Truppenübungsplatz Debica (313–462).

44. KA (257) 26–42, interview with HM, 2 February 1994.

45. KA (257) 26–42, interview with HM, 2 February 1994, 34–35.

46. KA (257) 26–42, interview with HM, 2 February 1994, 35.

47. Rüter and de Mildt, *Justiz und NS-Verbrechen*, 39:386.

48. Rüter and de Mildt, *Justiz und NS-Verbrechen*, 39:386.

49. Rüter and de Mildt, *Justiz und NS-Verbrechen*, 39:330–64.

50. Rüter and de Mildt, *Justiz und NS-Verbrechen*, 39:455.

51. Heribert Schwan and Helgard Heindrichs, *Der SS-Mann: Josef Blösche—Leben und Sterben eines Mörders* (Munich: Droemer Knaur, 2003); Dieter Skiba and Reiner Stenzel, *Im Namen des Volkes: Ermittlungs- und Gerichtsverfahren in der DDR gegen Nazi- und Kriegsverbrecher* (Berlin: Edition Ost, 2016), 36–40.

52. BArch, DP 3/1577, fos. 2–3, letter of April 6, 1966; Jacek Andrzej Młynarczyk, "Vom Massenmörder zum Lebensversicherer. Dr. Ludwig Hahn und die Mühlen der deutschen Justiz," in *Die Gestapo nach 1945: Karrieren, Konflikte, Konstruktionen*, ed. Klaus-Michael Mallmann and Andrej Angrick (Darmstadt, Germany: Wissenschaftliche Buchgesellschaft, 2009), 136–50.

53. For Stenzel's account of interrogating Blösche, see Skiba and Stenzel, *Im Namen des Volkes*, 36–40. See also Schwan and Heindrichs, *Der SS-Mann*, 17–21.

54. BArch, DP 3/1577, fo. 20, letter of January 31, 1967.

55. BArch DP 3/1578, fos. 402–11, "Vernehmungsprotokoll," March 24, 1969.

56. BArch DP 3/1578, fos. 493–505.

57. See Młynarczyk, "Vom Massenmörder zum Lebensversicherer."

58. BArch, DP 3/1577, fo. 9, letter of June 27, 1966 from the Hamburg regional court to the GDR state prosecutor.

59. Młynarczyk, "Vom Massenmörder zum Lebensversicherer," 145, citing *Stern* magazine.

60. Josef Wulf, *Das Dritte Reich und seine Vollstrecker* (Berlin: Arani, 1961).

61. BArch, DP 3/1577, fos. 61–65.

62. BArch DP 3/1578, fo. 393, internal note of March 20, 1969; fo. 434, *Neues Deutschland*, May 4, 1969; fo. 444, envelope containing photographs of the trial.

63. BArch DP 3/1578, fos. 512–18.

64. BArch DO 1/32778, newspaper clippings, 1985–90, including the Heinz Barth case in *Neues Deutschland*, June 8, 1983.

65. Beate Meyer, "Der 'Eichmann von Dresden': 'Justizielle Bewältigung' von NS-Verbrechen in der DDR am Beispiel des Verfahrens gegen Henry Schmidt," in *Deutsche, Juden, Völkermord: Der Holocaust als Geschichte und Gegenwart*, ed. Jürgen Matthäus and Klaus-Michael Mallmann (Darmstadt, Germany: Wissenschaftliche Buchgesellschaft, 2006), 275–91; deportation trials figures on 275.

66. Meyer, "Der 'Eichmann von Dresden,'" 281–83.

67. BArch DP 3/1614; BArch DP 3/1615.

68. BArch DP 3/1614, Oberstes Gericht der DDR, 1. Strafsenat, 1 OSB 8/87, 21.

69. BArch DP 3/1614, Oberstes Gericht der DDR, 1. Strafsenat, 1 OSB 8/87, 18.

70. Horst Busse and Udo Krause, *Lebenslänglich für den Gestapokommissar: Der Prozeß gegen den Leiter des Judenreferats bei der Dresdener Gestapo, SS-Obersturmführer Henry Schmidt, vor dem Bezirksgericht Dresden vom 15. bis 28. September 1987* (Berlin: Staatsverlag der Deutschen Demokratischen Republik, 1988), 11.

71. *Neues Deutschland*, September 24, 1987, BArch DP 3/2273.

72. *Neues Deutschland*, September 29, 1987, BArch DP 3/2273.

73. "Büßen für die Sauberkeit: Inhaftierte NS-Verbrecher in der DDR hoffen auf Gnade," *Der Spiegel*, March 5, 1990, 150–51, available at http://www.spiegel.de/spiegel/print/d-13497256.html, accessed August 20, 2013.

74. "Büßen für die Sauberkeit," 150.

75. Almut Greiser, *Der Kommandant: Josef Schwammberger; Ein NS-Täter in der Erinnerung von Überlebenden* (Berlin: Aufbau Verlag, 2011); Gerhard Mauz, *Die großen Prozesse der Bundesrepublik Deutschland*, ed. Gisela Friedrichsen (Springe, Germany: zu Klampen Verlag, 2005); Oliver Schröm with Andrea Röpke, *Stille Hilfe für braune Kameraden: Das geheime Netzwerk der Alt- und Neonazis* (Berlin: Chr. Links Verlag, 2001); Aaron Freiwald with Martin Mendelsohn, *The Last Nazi: Josef Schwammberger and the Nazi Past* (New York: W. W. Norton, 1994).

76. BArch, DP 3/2078, Bd. 14.

77. USC VHA Mielec, Norbert Friedman (b. 1922, Kraków), interviewed by Mark Goldberg on June 7, 1995, in West Hempstead, NY.

78. Greiser, *Der Kommandant*; Freiwald, *The Last Nazi*; Gerhard Steinacher, *Nazis on the Run: How Hitler's Henchmen Fled Justice* (Oxford: Oxford University Press, 2011), chs. 2 and 3.

79. BArch, DP 3/2078.

80. Greiser, *Der Kommandant*, 31.

81. Greiser, *Der Kommandant*, 188.

82. Greiser, *Der Kommandant*, 196.

83. Greiser, *Der Kommandant*, 189–98.

84. Greiser, *Der Kommandant*, 196.

85. Gerhard Mauz, "Stellvertretend für das System: Über den NS-Prozess gegen Josef Schwammberger in Stuttgart (1992)," in Mauz, *Die großen Prozesse*, 58.

86. Mauz, "Stellvertretend für das System," 63.

87. Hans Schueler, "Schuldig ist nur, wer grausam mordet," *Die Zeit*, May 22, 1992.

CHAPTER 13

1. On this topic see for example: Henning Borggräfe, *Zwangsarbeiterentschädigug* (Göttingen, Germany: Wallstein Verlag, 2014); Constantin Goschler, *Schuld und Schulden: Die Politik der Wiedergutmachung für NS-Verfolgte seit 1945* (Göttingen, Germany: Wallstein Verlag, 2005); Christoph Höschler, *NS-Verfolgte im "antifaschistischen Staat": Vereinnahmung und Ausgrenzung in der ostdeutschen Wiedergutmachung (1945–1989)* (Berlin: Metropol, 2002); Jürgen Lillteicher, *Raub, Recht und Restitution: Die Rückerstattung jüdischen Eigentums in der frühen Bundesrepublik* (Göttingen, Germany: Wallstein Verlag, 2007).

2. Hans Frankenthal, in collaboration with Andreas Plake, Babette Quinkert, and Florian Schmaltz, *The Unwelcome One: Returning Home from Auschwitz*, trans. John A. Broadwin (Evanston, IL: Northwestern University Press, 2002), 95.

3. For a comparison including Germany, France, and Switzerland, see Regula Ludi, *Reparations for Nazi Victims in Postwar Europe* (Cambridge: Cambridge University Press, 2012), particularly ch. 4, "Germany: Hitler's Many Victims and the Survivors of Nazi Persecution," 76–144.

4. See for example David Art, *The Politics of the Nazi Past in Germany and Austria* (Cambridge: Cambridge University Press, 2006).

5. Michael Bazyler, *Holocaust, Genocide, and the Law: A Quest for Justice in the Post-Holocaust World* (New York: Oxford University Press, 2016), ch. 5.

6. See for example Robert Moeller, *War Stories: The Search for a Usable Past in the Federal Republic of Germany* (Berkeley: University of California Press, 2001), ch. 2.

7. Frankenthal, *Unwelcome One*, 96.

8. Frankenthal, *Unwelcome One*, 96.

9. Frankenthal, *Unwelcome One*, 97.

10. Guenter Lewy, *The Nazi Persecution of the Gypsies* (Oxford: Oxford University Press, 2000), 199–217; Gilad Margalit, *Germany and Its Gypsies: A Post-Auschwitz Ordeal* (Madison: University of Wisconsin Press, 2002). See also Julia von dem Knesebeck, *The Roma Struggle for Compensation* (Hatfield, UK: University of Hertfordshire Press, 2011).

11. Till Bastian, *Sinti und Roma im Dritten Reich: Geschichte einer Verfolgung* (Munich: Verlag C. H. Beck, 2001), 83.

12. Margalit, *Germany and Its Gypsies*.

13. Quoted in Lewy, *Nazi Persecution of the Gypsies*, 203.
14. José Brunner, Norbert Frei, and Constantin Goschler, "Komplizierte Lernprozesse: Zur Geschichte und Aktualität der Wiedergutmachung," in *Die Praxis der Wiedergutmachung: Geschichte, Erfahrung und Wirkung in Deutschland und Israel*, ed. N. Frei, J. Brunner, and C. Goschler (Göttingen, Germany: Wallstein Verlag, 2009), 41.
15. Lewy, *Nazi Persecution of the Gypsies*, 203–4.
16. Lewy, *Nazi Persecution of the Gypsies*, 204.
17. Brunner, Frei, and Goschler, "Komplizierte Lernprozesse," 40.
18. Wahl, *Verfolgung und Vermögensentzug Homosexueller*, 89–90.
19. Pierre Seel, *I, Pierre Seel, Deported Homosexual*, trans. Joachim Neugroschel (New York: Basic Books, 2011), 134.
20. Seel, *I, Pierre Seel*, 139.
21. Henning Borggräfe, "Deutsche Unternehmen und das Erbe der NS-Zwangsarbeit: Verlauf und Folgen des Streits um Entschädigung seit den 1990er Jahren," in *Unternehmer und NS-Verbrechen: Wirtschaftseliten im "Dritten Reich" und in der Bundesrepublik Deutschland*, ed. Jörg Osterloh and Harald Wixforth, Wissenschaftliche Reihe des Fritz Bauer Instituts (Frankfurt am Main: Campus Verlag, 2014), 368.
22. Borggräfe, "Deutsche Unternehmen und das Erbe der NS-Zwangsarbeit."
23. Goschler, *Schuld und Schulden*, 480–81.
24. Borggräfe, "Deutsche Unternehmen und das Erbe der NS-Zwangsarbeit," 386.
25. Alexander von Plato, Almut Leh, and Christoph Thonfeld, eds., *Hitler's Slaves: Life Stories of Forced Labourers in Nazi-Occupied Europe* (New York: Berghahn, 2010), ix.
26. Borggräfe, "Deutsche Unternehmen und das Erbe der NS-Zwangsarbeit," 384–85.
27. Brunner, Frei, and Goschler, "Komplizierte Lernprozesse," 32.
28. Brunner, Frei, and Goschler, "Komplizierte Lernprozesse," 45.
29. Brunner, Frei, and Goschler, "Komplizierte Lernprozesse," 14.
30. Goschler, *Schuld und Schulden*, 477; Lutz Niethammer, "Converting Wrongs to Rights? Compensating Nazi Forced Labor as Paradigm," in *Restitution and Memory: Material Restoration in Europe*, ed. Dan Diner and Gotthard Wunberg (New York: Berghahn, 2007); Stuart Eizenstat, *Imperfect Justice: Looted Assets, Slave Labor, and the Unfinished Business of World War II* (New York: Public Affairs, 2003).
31. Angelika Benz, *Der Henkersknecht: Der Prozess gegen John (Iwan) Demjanjuk in München* (Berlin: Metropol Verlag, 2011); Robert D. Mcfadden, "John Demjanjuk, 91, Dogged by Charges of Atrocities as Nazi Camp Guard, Dies," *New York Times*, March 17, 2012, available at http://www.nytimes.com/2012/03/18/world/europe/john-demjanjuk-nazi-guard-dies-at-91.html?_r=0, accessed August 19, 2015.
32. Raul Hilberg, *The Destruction of the European Jews*, 3rd ed. (New Haven, CT: Yale University Press, 2003), 1171.

33. Lawrence Douglas, *The Right Wrong Man: John Demjanjuk and the Last Great Nazi War Crimes Trial* (Princeton, NJ: Princeton University Press, 2016), 260, terms this "the simple, terrible, and great insight" of the courts in the Demjanjuk and Gröning cases.

34. Peter Huth, ed., *Die letzten Zeugen: Der Auschwitz-Prozess von Lüneberg 2015; Eine Dokumentation* (Berlin: Reclam, 2015).

35. *Auschwitz: The Nazis and the Final Solution*, written and produced by Laurence Rees, BBC, 2005; Laurence Rees, *Auschwitz: The Nazis and the Final Solution* (London: BBC Books, 2005).

36. Quoted in "Oskar Gröning to Stand Trial for Being Auschwitz Guard in Case That Could Make German Legal History," *Independent*, February 14, 2015.

37. Miklós Nyiszli, *I Was Doctor Mengele's Assistant*, trans. Witold Zbirohowski-Kościa (Oświęcim, Poland: Frap-books, 2001); this was originally published in Hungarian; this is a translation of the Polish translation.

38. The CANDLES website, http://www.candlesholocaustmuseum.org, accessed July 20, 2015.

39. "Oskar Gröning trial: British Auschwitz survivor takes the stand," *Guardian*, May 13, 2015, available at http://www.theguardian.com/world/2015/may/13/oskar-groning-trial-british-auschwitz-survivor-susan-pollack, accessed July 20, 2015.

40. Judith Kalman, "Victim Impact Statement at the Trial of Oskar Gröning," available at http://judithevakalman.com/nazi-war-crime-trial-testimony/court-transcript/, accessed July 20, 2015.

41. See now https://candlesholocaustmuseum.org, and formerly http://www.candlesholocaustmuseum.org/sites/default/files/Statement%20on%20sentenc-ing%20of%20Groening%20-%2015%20July%202015.pdf, accessed July 20, 2015.

42. There is a vast literature on public debates, media controversies, and political and cultural interventions, particularly on West Germany. Peter Reichel, *Vergangenheitsbewältigung in Deutschland: Die Auseinandersetzung mit der NS-Diktatur in Politik und Justiz*, 2nd ed. (Munich: C. H. Beck, 2007) provides a selective overview. On West Germany's hidden "second guilt," for example, see Ralph Giordano, *Die zweite Schuld: Oder von der Last ein Deutscher zu sein* (Hamburg: Rasch & Röhring, 1993); Ralph Giordano, ed., *"Wie kann diese Generation eigentlich noch atmen?" Briefe zu dem Buch Die zweite Schuld, oder Von der Last Deutscher zu sein* (Hamburg: Rasch & Röhring, 1990). See also the "biographical approach" in Donald M. McKale, *Nazis after Hitler: How Perpetrators of the Holocaust Cheated Justice and Truth* (Lanham, MD: Rowman & Littlefield, 2012); critiqued by Peter Hayes, *German Studies Review* 36, no. 3 (October 2013): 728–30.

43. Kate Connolly, "'Accountant of Auschwitz' Jailed for the Murder of 300,000 Jews," *Guardian*, July 15, 2015.

44. Figures given by Michael Greve, "Täter oder Gehilfen? Zum strafrechtlichen Umgang mit NS-Gewaltverbrechern in der Bundesrepublik Deutschland," in *"Bestien" und "Befehlsempfänger": Frauen und Männer in NS-Prozesse nach 1945,*

eds. Ulrike Weckel und Edgar Wolfrum (Göttingen, Germany:Vandenhoeck & Ruprecht, 2003), 202.

45. Andreas Eichmüller, "Die Strafverfolgung von NS-Verbrechen durch west-deutsche Justizbehörden seit 1945: Eine Zahlenbilanz," *Vierteljahrshefte für Zeitgeschichte* 4 (2008): 624–25.

46. Eichmüller, "Die Strafverfolgung von NS-Verbrechen," 634.

47. Eichmüller, "Die Strafverfolgung von NS-Verbrechen," 637.

48. Eichmüller, "Die Strafverfolgung von NS-Verbrechen," 636.

49. While the GDR population remained relatively static, with minor fluctuations, the population of the West grew from around fifty million at the time of its foundation, to sixty million in the late 1960s, to nearly sixty-four million just prior to unification. Numbers of sentences taken from Adalbert Rückerl, *The Investigation of Nazi Crimes, 1945–1978*, trans. Derek Rutter (Hamden, CT: Archon, 1980), 72–73.

50. Figures from C. F. Rüter, *DDR-Justiz und NS-Verbrechen: Sammlung Ostdeutscher Strafurteile wegen Nationalsozialistischer Tötungsverbrechen, Register und Dokumente* (Munich: K. G. SaurVerlag, 2010), 97–98.

CHAPTER 14

1. Cf., e.g., Peter Novick, *The Holocaust and Collective Memory* (London: Bloomsbury, 2000), and Theodore S. Hamerow, *Why We Watched: Europe, America and the Holocaust* (New York: W. W. Norton, 2008), 452–78. See also the controversial Norman Finkelstein, *The Holocaust Industry: Reflections on the Exploitation of Jewish Suffering*, 2nd ed. (New York:Verso, 2003).

2. On changing approaches to trauma, Didier Fassin and Richard Rechtman, *The Empire of Trauma: An Inquiry into the Condition of Victimhood*, trans. Rachel Gomme (Princeton. NJ: Princeton University Press, 2009), chs. 1–4.

3. Gilad Margalit, *Germany and Its Gypsies: A Post-Auschwitz Ordeal* (Madison: University of Wisconsin Press, 2002), 180ff.

4. Alexander von Plato, "Geschichte ohne Zeitzeugen? Einige Fragen zur 'Erfahrung' im Übergang von Zeitgeschichte zur Geschichte," in *Zeugenschaft des Holocaust: Zwischen Trauma, Tradierung und Ermittlung*, ed. Fritz Bauer Institut (Frankfurt am Main; Campus Verlag, 2007), 141–42.

5. Dina Porat, *Israeli Society, the Holocaust and Its Survivors* (London: Vallentine Mitchell, 2008), 389.

6. Werner Weinberg, quoted in Peter Novick, *The Holocaust and Collective Memory: The American Experience* (London: Bloomsbury, 2001), 66.

7. Finkelstein, *The Holocaust Industry*, 81, 83.

8. See for example the account in Judith Miller, *One by One by One: Facing the Holocaust* (New York: Simon & Schuster, 1990).

9. Raul Hilberg, *The Destruction of the European Jews*, 3rd ed. (New Haven, CT:Yale University Press, 2003), 3:1142.

10. Robert Paxton, *Vichy France: Old Guard and New Order, 1940–44* (New York: Columbia University Press, 1972). See also: Robert Gildea, *Marianne in Chains: Daily Life in the Heart of France during the German Occupation* (New York: Henry Holt, 2002); Julian Jackson, *France: The Dark Years, 1940–1944* (Oxford: Oxford University Press, 2001); Adam Nossiter, *France and the Nazis: Memories, Lies and the Second World War* (London: Methuen, 2001); Henry Rousso, *The Vichy Syndrome: History and Memory in France since 1944*, trans. Arthur Goldhammer (Cambridge, MA: Harvard University Press, 1991); and Olivier Wieviorka, *Divided Memory: French Recollections of World War II from the Liberation to the Present*, trans. George Holoch (Stanford, CA: Stanford University Press, 2012).

11. Serge Klarsfeld, *Memorial to the Jews Deported from France, 1942–1944: Documentation of the Deportation of the Victims of the Final Solution in France* (New York: B. Klarsfeld Foundation, 1983).

12. Serge Klarsfeld, "Author's Preface," in *French Children of the Holocaust: A Memorial*, ed. Susan Cohen, Howard M. Epstein, and Serge Klarsfeld; trans. Glorianne Depondt and Howard M. Epstein (New York: New York University Press, 1996), xi.

13. Pierre Nora, *Realms of Memory*, trans. Arthur Goldhammer (New York: Columbia University Press, 1998), 3:609–37.

14. See the autobiographical account by one of the pioneers, Annette Leo, "Oral History in der DDR: Eine sehr persönliche Rückschau," in *Es gilt das gesprochene Wort: Oral History und Zeitgeschichte heute,* ed. Knud Andresen, Linde Apel and Kirsten Heinsohn (Göttingen, Germany: Wallstein, 2015).

15. First published in *Tygodnik Powszechny*, January 11, 1987.

16. Tom Segev, *The Seventh Million: The Israelis and the Holocaust* (New York: Hill & Wang, 1991); Porat, *Israeli Society*, ch. 19.

17. Porat, *Israeli Society*, 388–403.

18. Lawrence Langer, *Holocaust Testimonies: The Ruins of Memory* (New Haven, CT: Yale University Press, 1993).

19. For the Fondation pour la Mémoire de la Shoah see http://www.fondationshoah .org.

20. Transcripts of the Fruchtmann interviews in Karl Fruchtmann, *Zeugen: Aussagen zum Mord an einem Volk* (Cologne: Kiepenheuer & Witsch, 1982); Claude Lanzmann, *Shoah: An Oral History of the Holocaust* (New York: Pantheon, 1985). The Visual History Archive at the University of Southern California curates the collection initiated by Spielberg; see http://sfi.usc.edu.

21. Filip Müller, *Sonderbehandlung: Drei Jahre in den Krematorien und Gaskammern von Auschwitz* (Munich: Stenhausen, 1979); Filip Müller, *Eyewitness Auschwitz: Three Years in the Gas Chambers* (Chicago: Ivan R. Dee, 1999); Gerhard Zwerenz, "Auf Bertelsmanns Spuren: Der Fall Filip Müller," available at http://www .poetenladen.de/zwerenz-gerhard-sachsen48-filip-mueller.htm.

22. Andreas Plake, Babette Quinkert, and Florian Schmaltz, afterword to Hans Frankenthal, with Andreas Plake, Babette Quinkert, and Florian Schmaltz,

The Unwelcome One: Returning Home from Auschwitz, trans. John A. Broadwin (Evanston, IL: Northwestern University Press, 2002), 127–37.

23. *Woman in Gold*, 2015, directed by Simon Curtis and written by Alexi Kaye Campbell, explicitly acknowledged that it was based on the earlier documentary *Stealing Klimt*.

24. Binjamin Wilkomirski, *Fragments: Memories of a Wartime Childhood*, ed. Carol Brown Janeway (New York: Shocken, 1996).

25. Jack Eisner, *The Survivor*, ed. Irving A. Leitner (New York: William Morrow, 1980), 266, where he claims that the gate said "Jedem das Seine. Arbeit Macht Frei."

26. Frankenthal, *Unwelcome One*.

27. Ruth Klüger, *Weiter leben* (Göttingen, Germany: Wallstein, 1992).

28. Ann Kirschner, *Sala's Gift: My Mother's Holocaust Story* (New York: Free Press, 2006).

29. Doris Martin, with Ralph S. Martin, *Kiss Every Step* (privately published, 2009).

30. See for example Sam Pivnik, *Survivor: Auschwitz, the Death March and My Fight for Freedom* (London: Hodder & Stoughton, 2012). It does not take away from the authenticity of the experience, suffering, and courage of the survivor to note that ghostwriters played an increasing role in bringing survivor accounts to a public whose appetite appeared virtually insatiable.

31. Josef Baumgarten, USC VHA, Interview Code 10509; born Będzin July 7, 1925; interviewed San Diego, CA, by John Kent, December 22, 1995.

32. Bernhard Rammerstorfer, *Unbroken Will: The Extraordinary Courage of an Ordinary Man* (New Orleans: Grammaton, 2004), 164.

33. Rammerstorfer, *Unbroken Will*, 174.

34. Rammerstorfer, *Unbroken Will*, 177.

35. Stefanie Westermann, Tim Ohnhäuser, and Richard Kühl, " 'Euthanasie'-Verbrechen und Erinnerung," in *NS- "Euthanasie" und Erinnerung: Vergangenheits-aufarbeitung—Gedenkformen—Betroffenenperspektiven*, ed. Stefanie Westermann, Richard Kühl, and Tim Ohnhäuser (Berlin: LitVerlag, 2011), 7–15.

36. Alfred Fleßner, "Zur Aufarbeitung der NS-'Euthanasie' in den Familien der Opfer," in Westermann, Kühl, and Ohnhäuser, *NS- "Euthanasie" und Erinnerung: Vergangenheitsaufarbeitung*, 195–207.

37. Margalit, *Germany and Its Gypsies*, ch. 8. See also, for example, Wolfgang Wippermann, *"Wie die Zigeuner": Antisemitismus und Antiziganismus im Vergleich* (Berlin: Elefanten, 1997).

38. Interviews by Gabrielle Tyrnauer and held at the Yale Fortunoff Video Archive (YVA), particularly: HVT 2802, August D., July 21, 1991; HVT 2805, Karl W., July 22, 1991; HVT 2769, Martha E., July 21, 1991; HVT 2810, Agnes B., July 21, 1991; HVT 2812, Gertrud B., July 22, 1991; HVT 2807, Friedrich L., July 19, 1991.

39. Guenter Lewy, *The Nazi Persecution of the Gypsies* (New York: Oxford University Press, 2000), 227.

40. Christian Reimesch, *Vergessene Opfer des Nationalismus? Zur Entschädigung von Homosexuellen, Kriegsdienstverweigeren, Sinti und Roma und Kommunisten in*

der Bundesrepublik Deutschland (Berlin: Verlag für Wissenschaft und Kultur, 2003), 173.

41. Yale Fortunoff Archive, HVT 2769, Martha E., July 21, 1991, 20:55.
42. But see Eve Rosenhaft, "At Large in the 'Gray Zone': Narrating the Romany Holocaust," in *Unsettling History: Archiving and Narrating in Historiography*, ed. Sebastian Jobs and Alf Lüdtke (Frankfurt am Main: Campus, 2010); Eve Rosenhaft, "Blacks and Gypsies in Nazi Germany: The Limits of the 'Racial State,' " *History Workshop Journal* 72 (2011): 161–70.
43. Heinz Heger, *The Men with the Pink Triangle*, trans. David Fernbach (London: Gay Men's Press, 1980).
44. Pierre Seel, *I, Pierre Seel, Deported Homosexual: A Memoir of Nazi Terror*, trans. Joachim Neugroschel (New York: Basic Books, 2011); Frank Rector, ed., *The Nazi Extermination of Homosexuals* (New York: Stein & Day, 1981); Gad Beck with Frank Heibert, *An Underground Life: The Memoirs of a Gay Jew in Nazi Berlin*, trans. Allison Brown (Madison: University of Wisconsin Press, 1999); Niko Wahl, *Verfolgung und Vermögensentzug Homosexueller auf dem Gebiet der Republik Österreich während der NS-Zeit: Bemühungen um Restitution, Entschädigung und Pensionen in der Zweiten Republik* (Munich: Oldenbourg Verlag, 2004).

CHAPTER 15

1. Primo Levi, *The Drowned and the Saved*, trans. Raymond Rosenthal (London: Michael Joseph, 1988), 12.
2. Primo Levi, *Drowned and the Saved*, 11–12.
3. Charlotte Delbo, *Auschwitz and After*, 2nd ed., trans. Rosette C. Lamont (New Haven, CT: Yale University Press, 2014).
4. Otto Dov Kulka, *Landscapes of the Metropolis of Death: Reflections on Memory and Imagination* (London: Penguin, 2013), 11.
5. Kulka, *Landscapes*, 56–71.
6. Saul Friedländer, *When Memory Comes*, trans. Helen Lane (New York: Farrar, Straus & Giroux, 1979); Kulka, *Landscapes*; Ruth Klüger, *Weiter leben* (Munich: Deutscher Taschenbuch Verlag, 1994).
7. Imre Kertész, *Fateless*, trans. Tim Wilkinson (London: Vintage, 2006;), also published as *Fatelessness*; Imre Kertész, *Dossier K.*, trans. Tim Wilkinson (Brooklyn, NY: Melville House, 2013).
8. Yitzhak Arad, *Belzec, Sobibor, Treblinka: The Operation Reinhard Death Camps* (Bloomington: Indiana University Press, 1987).
9. Kulka, *Landscapes*, 75.
10. Kulka, *Landscapes*, 75.
11. Kulka, *Landscapes*, 75, 77.
12. Gerhard Durlacher, *Stripes in the Sky: A Wartime Memoir*, trans. Susan Massot (London: Serpent's Tale, 1991).
13. Kertész, *Fateless*, 261.
14. Kertész, *Fateless*, 262.

15. Kulka's reflections have been challenged by Anna Hájková, "Israeli Historian Otto Dov Kulka Tells Auschwitz Story of a Czech Family That Never Existed," *Tablet*, October 30, 2014, available at http://tabletmag.com/jewish-arts-and-culture/books/186462/otto-dov-kulka, accessed May 9, 2015. Hájková's critique raises questions about historians' intrusions on personal privacy.

16. Irene Eber, *The Choice: Poland 1939–1945* (New York: Schocken, 2004), 24.

17. Resilience is emphasized by Aaron Hass, *The Aftermath: Living with the Holocaust* (Cambridge: Cambridge University Press, 1996). Dori Laub, working with severely disturbed people, sees the difficulties in narrating traumatic experiences. See for example Dori Laub, "From Speechlessness to Narrative: The Cases of Holocaust Historians and of Psychiatrically Hospitalized Survivors," *Literature and Medicine* 24, no. 2 (Fall 2005): 253–65.

18. A point made particularly by Hass, *Aftermath*.

19. Quoted in Amy Rosenberg, "What Happened to Mary Berg?," *Tablet*, July 17, 2008, available at http://www.tabletmag.com/jewish-news-and-politics/981/what-happened-to-mary-berg, accessed October 2, 2015.

20. Available on the United States Holocaust Memorial Museum website, http://www.ushmm.org/online/film/display/detail.php?file_num=5090, accessed December 29, 2015.

21. Available on the United States Holocaust Memorial Museum website, http://collections.ushmm.org/search/catalog/irn513313, accessed December 27, 2015, here spelled as Richard Glazer (not Glazar).

22. Richard Glazar, *The Trap with a Green Fence: Survival in Treblinka*, trans. Roslyn Theobald (Evanston, IL: Northwestern University Press, 1992).

23. Gerhard Durlacher, *The Search: The Birkenau Boys*, trans. Susan Massotty (London: Serpent's Tail, 1998), 62–79.

24. Pierre Seel, *I, Pierre Seel, Deported Homosexual: A Memoir of Nazi Terror*, trans. Joachim Neugroschel (New York: Basic Books, 2011).

25. Fortunoff Video Archive for Holocaust Testimonies, Yale University Library (YVA), HVT-111, Mila P., interviewed by Dori Laub and Laurel Vlock, February 23, 1980.

26. Kestenberg Archive (henceforth KA), (257) 30-85, "Rachel P." (not her real name), born Poland 1936, interviewed in Sweden, 1.

27. KA (257) 30-85, "Rachel P." 3.

28. KA (257) 24-9, Paulette G., born Paris, March 1938; resident in Australia, interviewed 1994, 18–19.

29. KA (257) 24-9, Paulette G., 37.

30. KA (257) 24-9, Paulette G., 38.

31. KA (257) 24-9, Paulette G., 41.

32. KA (257) 24-9, Paulette G., 41–42.

33. KA (257) 24-9, Paulette G., 20.

34. KA (257) 24-9, Paulette G., 20.

35. KA (257) 24-15, Eva S., 67.

36. KA (257) 24-15, Eva S., 32.

37. YVA, HVT-210, Alex H., interviewed 16 July 1983 by Rosemary Balsam and Paul Schwaber.

38. YVA, HVT-210, Alex H.

39. YVA, HVT-1521, Aaron S., interviewed by Bernard Weinstein and Susanna Rich, 28 March 1989 and 5 April 1989.

40. YVA, HVT-111, Mila P.

41. KA (257) 24-9, Paulette G., 19.

42. KA (257) 24-9 Paulette G., 19.

43. KA (257) 24-9 Paulette G., 20.

44. KA (257) 24-9 Paulette G., 35.

45. KA (257) 24-15, Eva S. (born 1931 Bratislava), 62.

46. KA (257) 24-15, Eva S., 62.

47. KA (257) 24-15, Eva S., 62.

48. KA (257) 24-15, Eva S., 65.

49. KA (257) 30-85, "Rachel P." 3.

50. KA (257) 30-85, "Rachel P." 3.

51. KA (257) 30-85, "Rachel P." 3.

52. KA (257) 30-85, "Rachel P." 3.

53. YVA, HVT-1521, Aaron S.

54. YVA, HVT-111, Mila P.

55. YVA, HVT-2705, Olga S., born 1929 in Czechoslovakia (now Ukraine), interviewed by Naomi Rappaport, November 4, 1993.

56. Yad Vashem, 069/310, Testimony of Mark Stern (Markus, Maniek), June 1981, 18.

57. Friedländer, *When Memory Comes*, 85.

58. Friedländer, *When Memory Comes*, 75.

59. Friedländer, *When Memory Comes*, 88.

60. Mark Spigelman, "And You Shall Dream All the Days Of Your Life," in *The Words To Remember It: Memoirs of Child Holocaust Survivors*, ed. Sydney Child Holocaust Survivors Group (Sydney: Scribe, 2010). Spigelman, who is a cousin of the artist Art Spiegelman (despite the difference in spelling), appears as the three-year-old bawling "Waah! I'm hungry!" in Art Spiegelman, *The Complete Maus* (London: Penguin, 2003), 125.

61. YVA, HVT-2705, Olga S.

62. YVA, HVT-1285, Evelore Sch., born 1921 in Frankfurt am Main, interviewed November 13, 1989.

63. Susan Rubin Suleiman, "The 1.5 Generation: Thinking about Child Survivors and the Holocaust," *American Imago* 59, no. 3 (Fall 2002): 277. See also Susan Rubin Suleiman, *Crises of Memory and the Second World War* (Cambridge, MA: Harvard University Press, 2006), 178–214.

64. Anna Bikont, *The Crime and the Silence: A Quest for the Truth of a Wartime Massacre*, trans. Alissa Valles (London: Penguin, 2015), 11–12.

65. Bikont, *Crime and Silence*, 12.
66. See for example: Danielle Bailly, ed., *The Hidden Children of France 1940–1945: Stories of Survival*, trans. Betty Becker-Theye (Albany: State University of New York Press, 2010); Sharon Kangisser Cohen, *Child Survivors of the Holocaust in Israel: "Finding their Voice"; Social Dynamics and Post-War Experiences* (Brighton, UK: Sussex Academic Press, 2005); Wiktoria Śliwowska, ed., *The Last Eyewitnesses: Children of the Holocaust Speak*, trans. and ed. Julian Bussgang and Fay Bussgang (Evanston, IL: Northwestern University Press, 1998); Sydney Child Holocaust Survivors Group, *Words To Remember It*.
67. KA (257) 26-24.
68. KA (257) 26-24, 20.
69. KA (257) 26-24, 23.
70. KA (257) 26-24, 24.
71. KA (257) 26-24, 24.
72. KA (257) 26-24, 24.
73. KA (257)30-85, Rachel P., interviewed in Swedish in 1993, English translation, 1; transcription copied here without correcting errors.
74. KA (257)30-85, Rachel P., 1.
75. KA (257)30-85, Rachel P., 1.
76. KA (257)30-85, Rachel P., 2.
77. KA (257)30-85, Rachel P., 2.
78. Spigelman, "And You Shall Dream."
79. Mark Spigelman, personal conversation with the author, Jerusalem, April 30, 2014.
80. Spigelman, "And You Shall Dream."
81. KA (257) 15–20, Lilo C, 3.
82. KA (257) 15–20, Lilo C, 13.
83. Eber, *Choice*, 175.
84. Eber, *Choice*, 176.
85. Sylvia Ruth Gutmann's account available on her website at https://sylviaruthgutmann.com/my-story, and Paul Haist, "Survivor Credits Foundations for Saving Her Life," *Jewish Review*, February 15 2000.
86. Friedländer, *When Memory Comes*.
87. Friedländer, *When Memory Comes*, 33–34.

CHAPTER 16

1. Frank Bajohr and Dieter Pohl, *Der Holocaust als offenes Geheimnis: Die Deutschen, die NS-Führung und die Alliierten* (Munich: C. H. Beck, 2006); Bernward Dörner, *Die Deutschen und der Holocaust: Was niemand wissen wollte, aber jeder wissen konnte* (Berlin: Ullstein, 2007); Peter Longerich, *"Davon haben wir nichts gewusst!" Die Deutschen und die Judenverfolgung, 1933–1945* (Munich: Siedler Verlag, 2006); Nicholas Stargardt, *The German War: A Nation under Arms, 1939–1945* (London: Bodley Head, 2015).

2. Cf., e.g., Christabel Bielenberg, *The Past Is Myself* (London: Chatto & Windus, 1968).

3. Letter reprinted in Heiner Lichtenstein and Michael Schmid-Ospach, eds., *Holocaust: Briefe an den WDR* (Wuppertal, Germany: Peter Hammer Verlag, 1982), 84.

4. DTA Emmendingen, 386, Heinrich R., b. 1925, "Nicht in der Gnade der späten Geburt," 1998–99, 27.

5. Harald Welzer, "Die Konstruktion des 'anderen Nazis': Über die dialogische Verfertigung der Vergangenheit in einem Zeitzeugeninterview," in *Aus einem deutschen Leben: Lesarten eines biographischen Interviews*, ed. Christian Geulen and Karoline Tschuggnall (Tübingen, Germany: Edition Diskord, 2000), 77–78.

6. Gudrun Schwarz, *Eine Frau an seiner Seite: Ehefrauen in der "SS-Sippengemeinschaft"* (Hamburg: Hamburger Edition, 1997), 282.

7. Harald Welzer, Robert Montau, and Christine Plaß, *"Was wir für böse Menschen sind!" Der Nationalsozialismus im Gespräch zwischen den Generationen* (Tübingen, Germany: Edition Diskord, 1997), 14.

8. Cf. Günter Grass, *Beim Häuten der Zwiebel* (Göttingen, Germany: Steidl Verlag, 2006), 125–27.

9. Lingens quoted in Bernd Naumann, *Der Auschwitz-Prozess: Bericht über die Strafsache gegen Mulka u. a. vor dem Schwurgericht Frankfurt am Main 1963–1965*, rev. ed. (Hamburg: CEP Europäische Verlagsanstalt, 2013), 103–4.

10. Kempowski Bio (KB), 2910/2, Ursula B. diary. For a more detailed discussion, see Mary Fulbrook, "East Germans in a Post-Nazi State: Communities of Experience, Connection and Identification," in *Becoming East German: Socialist Structures and Sensibilities after Hitler*, ed. Mary Fulbrook and Andrew Port (New York: Berghahn, 2013), ch. 2.

11. Sabine Moller, *Vielfache Vergangenheit: Öffentliche Erinnerungskulturen und Familienerinnerungen an die NS-Zeit in Ostdeutschland* (Tübingen, Germany: Edition Diskord, 2003).

12. See for example: Sabine Bode, *Kriegsenkel: Die Erben der vergessenen Generation* (Stuttgart: Klett-Cotta, 2009); Bill Niven, ed., *Germans as Victims: Remembering the Past in Contemporary Germany* (Houndmills, UK: Palgrave Macmillan, 2006).

13. Cf. Eric Johnson and Karl-Heinz Reuband, *What We Knew: Terror, Mass Murder and Everyday Life in Nazi Germany* (London: Hodder, 2005); Alan Steinweis, *Kristallnacht 1938* (Cambridge, MA: Harvard University Press, 2009), 77, 82ff., 150.

14. DTA Emmendingen, 463, Marianne B., "Bericht über die Dienstzeit als Gymnasiallehrerin in Auschwitz (1.9.43—21.1.1945)."

15. This latter point, the persistence of Nazi ways of thinking, is the one particularly emphasized by Norbert Frei, *1945 und wir: Das Dritte Reich im Bewußtsein der Deutschen* (Munich: C. H. Beck, 2005), 156–59.

16. DTA Emmendingen, 463, 21, 47.

17. DTA Emmendingen, 463, 20–21.

18. DTA Emmendingen, 463, 9; italics and bold in original.

19. DTA Emmendingen, 463, 10.

20. DTA Emmendingen, 463, 22–23.
21. DTA Emmendingen, 463, 65–68.
22. DTA Emmendingen, 463, 21.
23. DTA Emmendingen, 463, 21.
24. DTA Emmendingen, 463, 15.
25. DTA Emmendingen, 463, 15.
26. DTA Emmendingen, 463, 21.
27. DTA Emmendingen, 463, 15–16; italics and bold in original.
28. Cf. also Welzer, Montau, and Plaß, *Was wir für böse Menschen sind*.
29. Cf. Harold Welzer, Sabine Moller, and Karoline Tschuggnall, *Opa war kein Nazi: Nationalsozialismus und Holocaust im Familiengedächtnis* (Frankfurt am Main: S. Fischer Verlag, 2002).
30. Sönke Neitzel and Harald Welzer, *Soldaten: Protokolle vom Kämpfen, Töten und Sterben* (Frankfurt am Main: S. Fischer Verlag, 2011).
31. Interview with Franz Schalling, Claude Lanzmann Shoah Collection, RG-60.5034, Accession Number 1996.166, Film ID 3355, 3356, available at the United States Holocaust Memorial Museum website, USHMM, https://collections.ushmm.org/search/catalog/irn1004244.
32. Hilary Earl, *The Nuremberg SS-Einsatzgruppen Trial, 1945–1958* (New York: Cambridge University Press, 2009), ch.2; Bob Carruthers, ed., *SS Terror in the East: The SS-Einsatzgruppen on Trial* (Barnsley, UK: Pen & Sword Military, 2013), 368ff.
33. Interview in Ahrensburg, Germany, 1979. Available through the United States Holocaust Memorial Museum, Claude Lanzmann Shoah Collection (subsequently USHMM), Heinz Schubert, Story RG-60.5013, Film IDs 3216, 3217, 3218, 3219.
34. USHMM, Story RG-60.5013, Film ID 3218.
35. USHMM, Story RG-60.5013, Film ID 3218.
36. USHMM, Story RG-60.5013, Film ID 3218.
37. USHMM, Story RG-60.5013, Film ID 3219.
38. See also Sue Vice, "Claude Lanzmann's Einsatzgruppen Interviews," in *Representing Perpetrators in Holocaust Literature and Film*, ed. Jenni Adams and Sue Vice (London: Vallentine Mitchell, 2013), 47–68.
39. USHMM, Interview with Karl Kretschmer, Film IDs 3246, 3247.
40. USHMM, Film ID 3247.
41. BArch DP 3/1588, Protocol by Rudolf Zimmermann, Berlin, April 25, 1968, fos. 228–29, fo. 248.
42. BArch DP 3/1588, fos. 249–52.
43. BArch DP 3/1587, Helmut Hensel, October 6, 1967, fos. 207–211, fo. 210.
44. BArch DP 3/1587, fo. 210.
45. Rudolf Höss, *Autobiography of Rudolf Höss*, in *KL Auschwitz Seen by the SS*, ed. Jadwiga Bezwińska and Danuta Czech, trans. Constantine Fitzgibbon (Oświęcim, Poland: Publications of Państwowe Muzeum w Oświęcimiu, 1972), 43.

46. 1. Frankfurter Auschwitz-Prozess "Strafsache gegen Mulka u.a.," 4 Ks 2/63, Landgericht Frankfurt am Main, 22.Verhandlungstag, 2.3.1964 und 23.Verhandlungstag, 5.3.1964, Vernehmung des Zeugen Hans Wilhelm Münch. Available from the Fritz Bauer Institute at http://www.auschwitz-prozess.de, accessed February 8, 2015.

47. 1. Frankfurter Auschwitz-Prozess "Strafsache gegen Mulka u.a.," 4 Ks 2/63.

48. Robert Jay Lifton, *The Nazi Doctors* (New York: Basic, 1986), 418–29.

49. Bruno Schirra, "Die Erinnerung der Täter," *Der Spiegel*, September 28, 1998, 90–100; available at http://www.spiegel.de/spiegel/print/d-8001833.html, accessed February 8, 2015; Imre Karacs, "Is Dr Munch a Confused Old Man or a Defiant Nazi?," *Independent*, November 8, 1998.

50. Juozas Aleksynas interview, United States Holocaust Memorial Museum online exhibit, "Some Were Neighbors," http://somewereneighbors.ushmm.org/#/exhibitions/workers/un2991, accessed 2 July 2015.

51. Regina (Kirvelaitytė) Prudnikova interview, "Some Were Neighbors," http://somewereneighbors.ushmm.org/#/exhibitions/neighbors/un2916 accessed July 2, 2015.

52. Jan Gross, *Fear: Anti-Semitism in Poland after Auschwitz* (New York: Random House, 2006).

53. BArch DP 3/2164, Bd. 31, Reservepolizeibataillon 41 (Kriegsverbrechen in Polen) 1980, testimony of Kazimierz K., Fol. 341b.

54. See further Mary Fulbrook, "Bystanders: Catchall Concept, Alluring Alibi, or Crucial Clue?" in *Erfahrung, Erinnerung, Geschichtsschreibung: Neue Perspektiven auf die deutschen Diktaturen* (Göttingen, Germany: Wallstein, 2106), ch. 5.

55. Michael Steinlauf, *Bondage to the Dead: Poland and the Memory of the Holocaust* (Syracuse, NY: Syracuse University Press, 1997), ch. 7.

56. Jan Gross, *Neighbors: The Destruction of the Jewish Community in Jedwabne, Poland, 1941* (London: Arrow, 2003); Antony Polonsky and Joanna Michlic, eds., *The Neighbors Respond: The Controversy over the Jedwabne Massacre in Poland* (Princeton, NJ: Princeton University Press, 2004).

57. Anna Bikont, *The Crime and the Silence: A Quest for the Truth of a Wartime Massacre*, trans. Alissa Valles (London: William Heinemann, 2015).

CHAPTER 17

1. *Speer und Er* (*Speer and Hitler: The Devil's Architect*), directed by Heinrich Breloer (2005).

2. This section is based on an interview in Altenburg with Rudi Zimmermann's son, Klaus, and Klaus's wife, Sabine, on August 5, 2016. I am immensely grateful to Klaus and Sabine Zimmermann for being willing to talk, for the time they gave me, and for the understanding they showed, despite the difficulty of the topic.

3. Details of Zimmermann's trial above, ch. 12. For a published version of the judgment, see C. F. Rüter, with L. Hekelaar Gombert and D. W. de Mildt,

DDR-Justiz und NS-Verbrechen: Sammlung Ostdeutscher Strafurteile wegen National-sozialistischer Tötungsverbrechen, vol. 2, *Die Verfahren Nr. 1031–1963 der Jahre 1965-1974* (Munich: K. G. Saur Verlag, 2002), 463–93.

4. See for example Oliver von Wrochem, with Christine Eckel, *Nationalsozialistische Täterschaften: Nachwirkungen in Gesellschaft und Familie* (Berlin: Metropol, 2016).

5. KA (257) 26-42, HM (born 1941).

6. KA (257) 26-42, HM, 1.

7. KA (257) 26-42, HM, 2.

8. C. F. Rüter and D. W. de Mildt, eds., *Justiz und NS-Verbrechen: Sammlung deutscher Strafurteile wegen nationalsozialistischer Tötungsverbrechen 1945–1999*, vol. 39, *Die vom 05.06.1973 bis zum 26.07.1974 ergangenen Strafurteile* (Amsterdam: Amsterdam University Press, 2008), 313–462.

9. KA (257) 26-42, HM, transcript 12, where he says that his "Vater einen besonderen Wert darauf legte, kranke Stücke auszuschießen."

10. Cf., e.g., Stephan Lebert and Norbert Lebert, *My Father's Keeper: The Children of the Nazi Leaders—An Intimate History of Damage and Denial*, trans. Julian Evans (Boston: Little, Brown, 2001); originally published as *Denn Du trägst meinen Namen* (Munich: Karl Blessing Verlag, 2000); Peter Sichrovsky, *Born Guilty: The Children of the Nazis*, trans. Jean Steinberg (London: I. B. Tauris, 1988); Gerald Posner, *Hitler's Children* (London: Heinemann, 1991).

11. Dan Bar-On, *Legacy of Silence: Encounters with Children of the Third Reich* (Cambridge, MA: Harvard University Press, 1989), ch. 5; Renate Wald, *Mein Vater Robert Ley: Meine Erinnerungen und Vaters Geschichte* (Nümbrecht, Germany: Galunder, 2004).

12. Bar-On, *Legacy of Silence*, ch. 8. Although the identity of Martin A. Bormann (originally named Adolf Martin Bormann) was not revealed in the book, he later spoke extensively about his experiences: Martin Bormann, *Leben gegen Schatten: Gelebte Zeit, geschenkte Zeit* (Paderborn, Germany: Bonifatius, 1996).

13. *The Decent One* (2014).

14. Oliver Schröm and Andrea Röpke, *Stille Hilfe für braune Kameraden* (Berlin; Christoph Links Verlag, 2001); Lebert and Lebert, *My Father's Keeper,* 194.

15. Lebert's expression, Lebert and Lebert, *My Father's Keeper*, 180, and on Gudrun Himmler's interview, 154–96.

16. Thomas Harding, *Hanns and Rudolf: The German Jew and the Hunt for the Kommandant of Auschwitz* (London: Random House, Windmill Books, 2014).

17. Lebert and Lebert, *My Father's Keeper,* 83.

18. Niklas Frank, *In the Shadow of the Reich*, trans. Arthur S. Wensinger (New York: Alfred Knopf, 1991); originally *Der Vater: Eine Abrechnung* (Munich: C. Bertelsmann, 1987).

19. Frank's comment quoted in Lebert and Lebert, *My Father's Keeper,* 151.

20. Niklas Frank, *Meine deutsche Mutter* (Munich: C. Bertelsmann, 2005) and *Bruder Norman! "Mein Vater war ein Naziverbrecher, aber ich liebe ihn"* (Bonn: Dietz, 2013).

21. Daniel Goldhagen, *Hitler's Willing Executioners: Ordinary Germans and the Holocaust* (New York: Knopf, 1996).

22. Philippe Sands, *My Nazi Legacy* (BFI, 2015). See also Philippe Sands, "My Father, the Good Nazi," *Financial Times Magazine*, May 3, 2013, available at http://www.ft.com/cms/s/2/7d6214f2-b2be-11e2-8540-00144feabdc0.html, accessed January 31, 2016.

23. Lebert and Lebert, *My Father's Keeper*, 107–21; Bar-On, *Legacy of Silence*, Ch. 8.

24. Lebert and Lebert, *My Father's Keeper*, 120–21.

25. Lebert and Lebert, *My Father's Keeper*, 121.

26. Werner Oder, *Battling with Nazi Demons* (West Horsley, UK: Onwards & Upwards, 2011).

27. Bar-On, *Legacy of Silence*, ch. 5.

28. Wald, *Mein Vater Robert Ley*.

29. Richard J. Evans, *The Third Reich in Power* (London: Penguin, 2006), 462–65.

30. On Speer's own contentious reckoning, see Albert Speer, *Erinnerungen* (Frankfurt am Main: Ullstein, 1969), and Gitta Sereny, *Abert Speer: His Battle with the Truth* (New York: Alfred Knopf, 1995).

31. Hilde Schramm's speech, February 15, 2009, available at the Zurückgeben website, http://www.stiftung-zurueckgeben.de/69.html, accessed November 2, 2014.

32. "I feel ashamed"—Hilde Schramm interview with Henrik Hamrén, "How It Really Feels to Be the Daughter of Albert Speer," *Guardian*, April 18, 2005, available at http://www.theguardian.com/world/2005/apr/18/secondworldwar.gender/print (accessed October 7, 2013).

33. Ilka Piepgras, "In vielen Wohnzimmern steht von den Nazis beschlagnahmter Besitz—eine Stiftung will auf das Unrecht aufmerksam machen. Schnäppchen mit dem Hausrat deportierter Juden," *Berliner Zeitung*, February 16, 1995, available at http://www.berliner-zeitung.de/archiv/in-vielen-wohnzimmern-steht-von-den-nazis-beschlagnahmter-besitz---eine-stiftung-will-auf-das-unrecht-aufmerksam-machen-schnaeppchen-mit-dem-hausrat-deportierter-juden,10810590,8915128.html#plx1317477401, accessed October 27, 2015.

34. Irene Anhalt. "Farewell to My Father," in *The Collective Silence: German Identity and the Legacy of Shame*, eds. Barbara Heimannsberg and Christoph Schmidt, trans. Cynthia Oudejans Harris and Gordon Wheeler (San Francisco: Jossey-Bass, 1993), 47.

35. Anhalt. "Farewell to My Father," 47.

36. Anhalt. "Farewell to My Father," 40.

37. Anhalt. "Farewell to My Father," 43.

38. Anhalt. "Farewell to My Father," 44.

39. Anhalt. "Farewell to My Father," 46.

40. Anhalt. "Farewell to My Father," 48.

41. Malte Ludin, dir., *2 oder 3 Dinge, die ich von ihm weiß: Die Gegenwart der Vergangenheit in einer deutschen Familie*, 2004.

42. Alexandra Senfft, *Schweigen tut weh: Eine deutsche Familiengeschichte* (Berlin: Ullstein, 2007).

43. Katrin Himmler, *The Himmler Brothers: A German Family History*, trans. Michael Mitchell (London: Macmillan, 2007), 307–8.

44. Bar-On, *Legacy of Silence*, 144.

45. Bar-On, *Legacy of Silence*, 155.

46. See for example Konstantinos Lianos, "Auschwitz Commander's Grandson: Why My Family Call Me a Traitor," *Daily Telegraph*, November 20, 2014, available at http://www.telegraph.co.uk/news/worldnews/europe/germany/ 11241714/Auschwitz-commanders-grandson-Why-my-family-call-me-a-traitor .html, accessed July 13, 2017.

47. Jens-Jürgen Ventzki, *Seine Schatten, meine Bilder: Eine Spurensuche* (Innsbruck, Austria: Studien Verlag, 2011), 32ff.

48. Ventzki, *Seine Schatten, meine Bilder*, 33.

49. See her discussion in two documentaries, *Inheritance* (2006) and *Hitler's Children* (2011), and also her autobiographical account, with Matthias Kessler, *Ich muß doch meinen Vater lieben, oder? Die Lebensgeschichte von Monika Göth, Tochter des KZ-Kommandanten aus "Schindlers Liste"* (Frankfurt am Main: Eichborn, 2002).

50. Thomas Keneally, *Schindler's Ark* (London: Hodder & Stoughton, 1982).

51. See for example Olaf Jensen, *Geschichte machen: Strukturmerkmale des intergenera-tionellen Sprechens über die NS-Vergangenheit in deutschen Familien* (Tübingen, Germany: Edition Diskord, 2004); Sabine Moller, *Vielfache Vergangenheit: Öffentliche Erinnerungskulturen und Familienerinnerungen an die NS-Zeit in Ostdeutschland* (Tübingen, Germany: Edition Diskord, 2003); Margit Reiter, *Die Generation danach: Der Nationalsozialismus im Familiengedächtnis* (Innsbruck, Austria: Studienverlag, 2006); Gabriele Rosenthal, ed., *The Holocaust in Three Generations: Families of Victims and Perpetrators of the Nazi Regime* (London: Cassell, 1998); Harold Welzer, Sabine Moller, and Karoline Tschuggnall, *Opa war kein Nazi: Nationalsozialismus und Holocaust im Familiengedächtnis* (Frankfurt am Main: S. Fischer Verlag, 2002); and Harald Welzer, Robert Montau and Christine Plaß, unter Mitarbeit von Martina Piefke, *"Was wir für böse Menschen sind!" Der Nationalsozialismus im Gespräch zwischen den Generationen* (Tübingen, Germany: Edition Diskord, 1997).

52. KA (257) 26-25, DH.

53. KA (257) 26-25, DH, 23.

54. KA (257) 26-25, DH, 24.

55. KA (257) 26-25, DH, 24.

56. KA (257) 26-25, DH, 3.

57. KA (257) 26-25, DH, 3.

58. KA (257) 26-25, DH, 3.

59. DTA Emmendingen, Handbibliothek T Lutt 1a, Horst Lutter, *Tagebücher meiner Mutter*, 202.

60. DTA Emmendingen, 301, Rainer L., "Zwölf Jahre" (written 1994–98).

61. DTA Emmendingen, 301, Rainer L., "Zwölf Jahre," 10.

62. DTA Emmendingen, 301, Rainer L., "Zwölf Jahre," 11.

63. Bar-On, *Legacy of Silence*, ch. 9. On the "1929ers" more generally, see Mary Fulbrook, *Dissonant Lives: Generations and Violence through the German Dictatorships* (Oxford: Oxford University Press, 2011).

64. See for example Björn Krondorfer, "Eine Reise gegen das Schweigen," in *Das Vermächtnis annehmen: Kulturelle und biographische Zugänge zum Holocaust—Beiträge aus den USA und Deutschland*, eds. Brigitte Huhnke and Björn Krondorfer (Gießen, Germany: Psycho-Sozial Verlag, 2002), 315–44.

65. Bar-On, *Legacy of Silence*, 257.

66. Bar-On, *Legacy of Silence*, 26–41.

67. Bar-On, *Legacy of Silence*, 330.

68. Bar-On, *Legacy of Silence*, 160–78.

69. Dörte von Westernhagen, *Die Kinder der Täter: Das Dritte Reich und die Generation danach* (Munich: Kösel, 1987), 102–7.

70. KA (257) 24-21: "HK."

71. KA (257) 24-21: "HK," 5.

72. KA (257) 24-21: "HK," 51–52.

73. KA (257) 24-21: "HK," 41.

74. KA (257) 24-21: "HK," 37.

75. KA (257) 24-21: "HK," 39.

76. See for example Krondorfer, "Eine Reise gegen das Schweigen."

77. Cf. e.g. Vamik D. Volkan, *A Nazi Legacy: Depositing, Transgenerational Transmission, Dissocation, and Remembering through Action* (London: Karnac, 2015).

78. Bar-On, *Legacy of Silence*, 74.

79. Cf. Reiter, *Die Generation danach*, 262–91.

80. For theoretical considerations, see Dorothee Wierling, " 'Zeitgeschichte ohen Zeitzeugen': Vom kommunikativen zum kulturellen Gedächtnis—drei Geschichten und zwölf Thesen," *BIOS* 21, no. 1 (2008): 28–36.

81. Reiter, *Die Generation danach*.

82. Annette Leo, "Antifaschismus," in *Erinnerungsorte der DDR*, ed. Martin Sabrow (Munich: C. H. Beck, 2009), 38–39. See also the account by her son, Maxim Leo, *Red Love: The Story of an East German Family*, trans. Shaun Whiteside (London: Pushkin, 2013).

83. BArch DC 4/305, Zentralinstitut für Jugendforschung, Dr. Wilfried Schubarth, "Zum Geschichtsbewusstsein von Jugendlichen der DDR."

84. Konrad Brendler, "Die NS-Geschichte als Sozialisationsfaktor und Identitätsballast der Enkelgeneration," in *"Da ist etwas kaputtgeggangen an den Wurzeln...": Identitätsformen deutscher und israelischer Jugendlicher im Schatten des Holocaust*, eds. Dan Bar-On, Konrad Brendler, and A. Paul Hare (Frankurt am Main: Campus, 1997), 54.

85. Annette Leo, "Das Problem der nationalsozialistischen Vergangenheit," in *Zweierlei Geschichte: Lebensgeschichte und Geschichtsbewußtsein von Arbeitnehmern in West- und Ost-Deutschland*, ed. Bernd Faulenbach, Annette Leo, and Klaus Weberskirch (Essen, Germany: Klartext Verlag, 2000), 300–340.

86. For an interesting example, see Bettine Völter and Gabriele Rosenthal, "We Are the Victims of History: The Seewald Family," in Rosenthal, *Holocaust in Three Generations*, 264–84.

87. Moller, *Vielfache Vergangenheit*, 82–105; Iris Wachsmuth, *NS-Vergangenheit in Ost und West: Tradierung und Sozialisation* (Berlin: Metropol, 2008).

88. Simone Scherger und Martin Kohli, "Eine Gesellschaft—zwei Vergangenheiten? Historische Ereignisse und kollektives Gedächtnis in Ost- und Westdeutschland," *BIOS* 18, no. 1 (2005): 3–27.

89. Jensen, *Geschichte machen*, 382.

90. Jensen, *Geschichte machen*, 379–80.

91. Jensen, *Geschichte machen*, 380–81.

92. Moritz Pfeiffer, *Mein Großvater im Krieg, 1939–1945: Erinnerung und Fakten im Vergleich* (Bremen, Germany: Donat Verlag, 2012), particularly 148–63.

93. Uwe Timm, *Am Beispiel meines Bruders* (Munich: Kiepenheuer & Witsch, 2003).

94. Pfeiffer, *Mein Großvater im Krieg*, 173–75.

CHAPTER 18

1. Helen Epstein, *Children of the Holocaust: Conversations with Sons and Daughters of Survivors* (London: Penguin, 1979).

2. Epstein, *Children of the Holocaust*, 16.

3. Epstein, *Children of the Holocaust*, 16.

4. Epstein, *Children of the Holocaust*, 16.

5. Epstein, *Children of the Holocaust*, 16.

6. Epstein, *Children of the Holocaust*, 16.

7. Arlene Stein, *Reluctant Witnesses: Survivors, Their Children and the Rise of Holocaust Consciousness* (Oxford: Oxford University Press, 2014), 75–76; Stephen Cohen, ed., "The Holocaust: Our Generation Looks Back," special issue, *Response: A Contemporary Jewish Review* 25 (Spring 1975).

8. Lucy Y. Steinitz, "A Personal Foreword," in *Living after the Holocaust: Reflections by Children of Survivors in America*, ed. Lucy Y. Steinitz, 2nd ed. (New York: Bloch, 1979), iii.

9. Atina Grossmann, *Jews, Germans, and Allies: Close Encounters in Occupied Germany* (Princeton, NJ: Princeton University Press, 2007), 184–235.

10. See for example Stefanie Westermann, Tim Ohnhäuser, and Richard Kühl, "'Euthanasie'—Verbrechen und Erinnerung," in *NS-"Euthanasie" und Erinnerung: Vergangenheitsaufarbeitung—Gedenkformen—Betroffenenperspektiven*, ed. Stefanie Westermann, Richard Kühl, and Tim Ohnhäuser (Berlin: Lit Verlag, 2011), 7–15, and Alfred Fleßner, "Zur Aufarbeitung der NS-'Euthanasie' in den Familien der Opfer," in Westermann, Ohnhäuser, and Kühl, *NS-"Euthanasie" und Erinnerung*, 195–207.

11. Peter Michael Lingens, *Ansichten eines Außenseiters* (Vienna: Verlag Kremayr & Scheriau, 2009).

12. Lingens, *Ansichten eines Außenseiters*, 83.

13. Steinitz, *Living after the Holocaust*.

14. Alan L. Berger and Naomi Berger, eds., *Second Generation Voices: Reflections by Children of Holocaust Survivors and Perpetrators* (Syracuse, NY: Syracuse University Press, 2001), 3.

15. Anne Karpf, *The War After: Living with the Holocaust* (London: Minerva, 1997), 250, 219.

16. An online listing of UK companies, http://www.companieslist.co.uk/03294539 -second-generation-trust, accessed January 4, 2014, gives the date of incorporation as December 19, 1996, and the date of dissolution as May 22, 2012.

17. This is discussed by Aaron Hass, *In the Shadow of the Holocaust: The Second Generation* (Cambridge: Cambridge University Press, 1996).

18. Paula S. Fass, *Inheriting the Holocaust: A Second-Generation Memoir* (New Brunswick, NJ: Rutgers University Press, 2009), 145.

19. Eva Hoffman, *After Such Knowledge: A Meditation on the Aftermath of the Holocaust* (London: Vintage, 2004), 10.

20. Gabriele Rosenthal, Michal Dasberg, and Yael Moore, "The Collective Trauma of the Lodz Ghetto: The Goldstern Family," in *The Holocaust in Three Generations: Families of Victims and Perpetrators of the Nazi Regime*, ed. Gabriele Rosenthal (London: Cassell, 1998), 51–68.

21. Rosenthal, Dasberg, and Moore, "The Collective Trauma of the Lodz Ghetto," 58–59.

22. Hoffman, *After Such Knowledge*, 11.

23. Yael Danieli, "The Treatment and Prevention of Long-term Effects and Inter-generational Transmission of Victimization: A Lesson from Holocaust Survivors and Their Children," in *Trauma and Its Wake*, vol. 1, *The Study and Treatment of Post-Traumatic Stress Disorder*, ed. Charles R. Figley (New York: Brunner/Mazel, 1985), 295–313.

24. See fascinating vignettes in Hass, *In the Shadow of the Holocaust*.

25. Cf., e.g., Helen Thomson, "Study of Holocaust Survivors Finds Trauma Passed On to Children's Genes," *Guardian*, August 21, 2015, available at http://www .theguardian.com/science/2015/aug/21/study-of-holocaust-survivors-finds-trauma-passed-on-to-childrens-genes, accessed August 24, 2015.

26. Fass, *Inheriting the Holocaust*, 5.

27. Karpf, *War After*, 146.

28. Fass, *Inheriting the Holocaust*, 109.

29. Hoffman, *After Such Knowledge*, 3.

30. Hoffman, *After Such Knowledge*, 3.

31. Hoffman, *After Such Knowledge*, 6.

32. Hoffman, *After Such Knowledge*, 16.

33. Dina Wardi, *Memorial Candles: Children of the Holocaust* (London: Routledge, 1992).

34. Wardi, *Memorial Candles*.

35. Wardi, *Memorial Candles*, 46.

36. Wardi, *Memorial Candles*, 28.

37. Wardi, *Memorial Candles*, 36.
38. Wardi, *Memorial Candles*, 221.
39. Wardi, *Memorial Candles*, 222.
40. Marianne Hirsch, *Generation of Postmemory: Writing and Visual Culture after the Holocaust* (New York: Columbia University Press, 2012), 5; Marianne Hirsch, *Family Frames: Photography, Narrative and Postmemory* (Cambridge, MA: Harvard University Press, 1997).
41. Hoffman, *After Such Knowledge*, x.
42. Hoffman, *After Such Knowledge*, xv.
43. Karpf, *War After*, 4.
44. Karpf, *War After*, 5.
45. Judith Kalman, "Victim Impact Statement at the Trial of Oskar Gröning," available at http://judithevakalman.com/nazi-war-crime-trial-testimony/court-transcript/, accessed August 24, 2015.
46. Kalman, "Victim Impact Statement."
47. Hoffman, *After Such Knowledge*, 9–10.
48. Lisa Appignanesi, *Losing the Dead: A Family Memoir* (London: Random House, 2000), 32–33.
49. Appignanesi, *Losing the Dead*, 49–52.
50. Berger and Berger, *Second Generation Voices*, 1.
51. Kalman, "Victim Impact Statement."
52. Lisa Reitman-Dobi, "Once Removed," in Berger and Berger, *Second Generation Voices*, 19.
53. Fass, *Inheriting the Holocaust*, 109.
54. Fass, *Inheriting the Holocaust*, 111.
55. Fass, *Inheriting the Holocaust*, 113–19.
56. Fass, *Inheriting the Holocaust*, 109.
57. Dan Bar-On, *Legacy of Silence: Encounters with Children of the Third Reich* (Cambridge, MA: Harvard University Press, 1989), 4.
58. Tom Segev, *The Seventh Million: The Israelis and the Holocaust*, trans. Haim Watzman (New York: Henry Holt, 1991).
59. Also in works of fiction, e.g., David Grossman, *See Under: Love*, trans. Betsy Rosenberg (London: Vintage, 1989), and Aharon Appelfeld, *The Immortal Bartfuss*, trans. Jeffrey Green (New York: Grove, 1988).
60. Carol. A. Kidron, "Silent Legacies of Trauma: A Comparative Study of Cambodian Canadian and Israeli Holocaust Trauma Descendant Memory Work," in *Remembering Violence: Anthropological Perspectives on Intergenerational Transmission*, ed. Nicholas Argenti and Katharina Schramm (New York: Berghahn, 2010), 193–228.
61. Jaclyn Blumenfeld, "Conscription and the Marginalization of Military Values in Modern Israeli Society (1982–2010)" (honors thesis, Emory University, 2010), 17.
62. The term is occasionally used for people with a drug addiction or suffering from severe emotional disturbance. See for example "The Magical Mystery

Tour (2 of 2)," *Haaretz*, December18, 2003, available at http://www.haaretz .com/the-magical-mystery-tour-2-of-2-1.109095, accessed June 14, 2012).

63. Dina Wardi, "Familial and Collective Identity in Holocaust Survivors and the Second Generation," in *A Global Perspective on Working with Holocaust Survivors and the Second Generation*, ed. John Lemberger (Jerusalem: JDC-Brookdale Institute in cooperation with the World Council of Jewish Communal Service, 1995), 331–40.

64. Karpf, *War After*.

65. Maria Orwid, Ewa Domagalska-Kurdziel, and Kazimierz Pietruszewski, "Psychosocial Effects of the Holocaust on Survivors and the Second Generation in Poland: Preliminary Report," in Lemberger, *Global Perspective*, 205–42.

66. See for example Piotr Madajczyk, "Experience and Memory: The Second World War in Poland," in *Experience and Memory: The Second World War in Europe*, ed. Jörg Echternkamp and Stefan Martens (New York: Berghahn, 2010), 70–85.

67. Art Spiegelman, *Maus: A Survivor's Tale* (New York: Pantheon, 1997); Jonathan Safran Foer, *Everything Is Illuminated* (Boston: Houghton Mifflin, 2002); Daniel Mendelsohn, *The Lost: A Search for Six of Six Million* (New York: HarperCollins, 2006).

68. Fass, *Inheriting the Holocaust*, 7.

69. *Die Wohnung*, dir. Arnon Goldfinger, 2011.

70. See for example Monika Maron, *Pawels Briefe* (Frankfurt am Main: Fischer, 1999) and Mendelsohn, *Lost*. See also Erin McGlothlin, *Second-Generation Holocaust Literature: Legacies of Survival and Perpetration* (Rochester, NY: Camden House, 2006); Irene Kacandes, " 'When Facts Are Scarce': Authenticating Strategies in Writing by Children of Survivors," in *After Testimony: The Ethics and Aesthetics of Holocaust Narrative for the Future*, ed. Jakob Lothe, Susan Rubin Suleiman, and James Phelan (Columbus: Ohio State University Press, 2012), 179–97.

71. Fass, *Inheriting the Holocaust*, 28.

72. Solly Kaplinski, *Lost and Found: A Second Generation Response to the Holocaust: A Polish Experience* (Cape Town: Creda, 1992).

73. Kaplinski, *Lost and Found*, 9.

74. Wardi, *Memorial Candles*, 214–15, discusses how in the last stage of therapy "memorial candles" begin to be able to leave their designated roles and "drop the burden of unworked grief and depression." They are often able to achieve this by exploring the locations from which their families came and "discovering that the towns, villages and houses they heard fragmented stories about actually existed, with real people living in them. They no longer have trouble imagining past figures, families and communities. The world of the past acquires gestalt and meaning."

75. Lucille Eichengreen, with Harriet Hyman Chamberlain, *From Ashes to Life: My Memories of the Holocaust* (San Francisco: Mercury House, 1994). Barry Eichengreen wrote a chapter on the European economy in Mary Fulbrook, ed., *The Short*

Oxford History of Europe: Europe since 1945 (Oxford: Oxford University Press, 2000), and despite the fact that we spoke about central European émigré backgrounds, I do not recall him discussing his mother's experiences in any detail.

76. Personal interview; excerpts may be seen in my film on Będzin, available on YouTube at http://www.youtube.com/watch?v=iHyRb3ctnxo.

77. Bar-On, *Legacy of Silence*, 291.

78. Peter Sichrovsky, *Born Guilty: The Children of the Nazis*, trans. Jean Steinberg (London: I. B. Tauris, 1988).

79. Dörte von Westernhagen, *Die Kinder der Täter: Das Dritte Reich und die Generation danach* (Munich: Kösel, 1987).

80. Norbert Lebert and Stephan Lebert, *Denn Du trägst meinen Namen: Das schwere Erbe der prominenten Nazi-Kinder* (Munich: Karl Blessing Verlag, 2000).

81. Rosenthal, *Holocaust in Three Generations*.

82. Gertrud Hardtmann, "Auf der Suche nach einer unbeschädigten Identität," in *"Da ist etwas kaputtgeggangen an den Wurzeln . . ." Identitätsformen deutscher und israelische Jugendlicher im Schatten des Holocaust*, ed. Dan Bar-On, Konrad Brendler, and A. Paul Hare (Frankfurt am Main: Campus, 1997), 106–7.

83. Harold Welzer, Sabine Moller, and Karoline Tschuggnall, *Opa war kein Nazi: Nationalsozialismus und Holocaust im Familiengedächtnis* (Frankfurt am Main: S. Fischer Verlag, 2002); Harald Welzer, Robert Montau, and Christine Plaß, *"Was wir für böse Menschen sind!" Der Nationalsozialismus im Gespräch zwischen den Generationen* (Tübingen, Germany: Edition Diskord, 1997).

84. *Eine unmögliche Freundschaft*, prod. Michael Richter, Provobis, 1998.

85. Samson Munn, "The Austrian Encounter," available at http://nach.ws/SummarySamson.html, accessed January 4, 2014.

86. Mona Weissmark, *Justice Matters: Legacies of the Holocaust and World War II* (Oxford: Oxford University Press, 2004).

87. See for example *NBC Dateline*, "Journey to Understanding," part 2, 2011, available at http://www.youtube.com/watch?v=IcWeufEszyo.

88. Cf., e.g., Samson Munn, "The Austrian Encounter," available at http://nach.ws/SummarySamson.html, accessed January 4, 2014.

89. Berger and Berger, *Second Generation Voices*, 10.

90. See for example Naftali Bendavid and Harriet Torry, "How Grandson of Auschwitz Boss Is Trying to Remake Family Name," *Wall Street Journal*, January 26, 2015, available at http://www.wsj.com/articles/how-grandson-of-auschwitz-boss-is-trying-to-remake-family-name-1422243182, accessed August 24, 2015.

CHAPTER 19

1. As with all the issues discussed in this book, there is a vast literature that cannot be adequately referenced here. But for a wider context see for example Peter Reichel, *Politik mit der Erinnerung: Gedächtnisorte im Streit um die nationalsozialistische Vergangenheit* (Munich: Hanser, 1995); James E. Young, ed., *The Art of*

Memory: Holocaust Memorials in History (Munich: Prestel-Verlag, 1994); and James E. Young, *Stages of Memory. Reflections on Memorial Art, Loss, and the Spaces Between* (Amherst: University of Massachusetts Press, 2016).

2. Piotr Trojański, academic advisor to the International Center for Education about Auschwitz and the Holocaust, Memorial and Museum Auschwitz-Birkenau, at a workshop organized by University College London at Auschwitz, September 19, 2013.

3. Jonathan Huener, *Auschwitz, Poland, and the Politics of Commemoration, 1945–1979* (Athens: Ohio University Press, 2003).

4. According to Huener, "Even as the pope's words and deeds at the site legitimized the Polish-national commemorative paradigm, they also marked the beginning of its dissolution." Huener, *Auschwitz*, 30.

5. Cf. the photograph in Mary Fulbrook, *A Concise History of Germany*, 2nd ed. (Cambridge: Cambridge University Press, 2004), 203, taken when I visited in 1988.

6. Trojański, September 19, 2013.

7. Trojański, September 19, 2013.

8. E.g., Anne Karpf, *The War After* (London: Heinemann, 1996).

9. Mary Fulbrook *A Small Town near Auschwitz: Ordinary Nazis and the Holocaust* (Oxford: Oxford University Press, 2012), ch. 12.

10. Michael Steinlauf, *Bondage to the Dead: Poland and the Memory of the Holocaust* (Syracuse, NY: Syracuse University Press, 1997), 48.

11. Steinlauf, *Bondage to the Dead*, 49.

12. Quoted in Steinlauf, *Bondage to the Dead*, 73.

13. Thomas (Toivi) Blatt, *Sobibor: The Forgotten Revolt; A Survivor's Report* (Issaquah, WA: HEP, 1997).

14. Blatt, *Sobibor*, 130.

15. Blatt, *Sobibor*, 131.

16. Blatt, *Sobibor*, 131.

17. Robert Kuwałek, *Das Vernichtungslager Bełżec*, trans. Steffen Hänschen (Berlin: Metropol Verlag, 2013), 307–34.

18. Hirszman's testimony in English accessible at https://kollublin.wordpress.com/2011/10/01/chaim-hirszman-testimo/, accessed January 25, 2015; see also Rudolf Reder, *Bełżec* (Kraków: Centralna Żydowska Komisja Historyczna przy C. K. Żydów Polskich, 1946), in English translation in *I Survived a Secret Nazi Extermination Camp*, ed. Mark Forstater (London: Psychology News Press, 2013). Members of Forstater's family perished in the Lublin area, giving him a sense of personal connection.

19. Kuwałek, *Vernichtungslager Bełżec*, 327.

20. "Growing Number of Visitors to the State Museum at Majdanek," January 12, 2017, available at http://www.belzec.eu/en/news/growing_number_of_visitors_to_the_state_museum_at_majdanek/758, accessed July 18, 2017.

21. Łucja Pawlicka-Nowak, "Events Commemorating the Former Extermination Camp at Chełmno-on-Ner (until 1995)" and "Events Commemorating Chełmno

(1995–2004)," in *Chełmno Witnesses Speak*, ed. Łucia Pawlicka-Nowak (Lodz: Council for the Protection of Memory of Combat and Martyrdom, District Museum in Konin, 2004), 32–39, 40–41.

22. Lisa Appignanesi, *The Memory Man* (London: Arcadia, 2004).

23. Jan T. Gross, *Neighbors: The Destruction of the Jewish Community in Jedwabne, Poland, 1941* (London: Arrow, 2003); Antony Polonsky and Joanna Michlic, eds., *The Neighbors Respond: The Controversy over the Jedwabne Massacre in Poland* (Princeton, NJ: Princeton University Press, 2004).

24. Anna Bikont, *The Crime and the Silence* (New York: Farrar, Straus, and Giroux, 2015).

25. Robert Kuwalek, *From Lublin to Bełżec: Traces of Jewish presence and the Holocaust in South-Eastern Part of the Lublin Region* (Lublin, Poland: Ad Rem, n.d.), 13.

26. Irene Eber, *The Choice: Poland, 1939–1945* (New York: Schocken, 2004), 43–45.

27. Eber, *Choice*, 44.

28. Eber, *Choice*, 44.

29. Eber, *Choice*, 45.

30. Eber, *Choice*, ch. 4.

31. Alfred Konrad, speech on May 11, 2013, *Leseprobe aus dem Mitteilungsblatt, Hl. Band*, June 2013, available at http://www.galizien-deutsche.de/hochgeladen/dateien/Leseprobe-Juni2013-Ansprache-A.Konrad.pdf, accessed January 26, 2015.

32. Heinz Heger, *The Men with the Pink Triangle*, trans. David Fernbach (London: Gay Men's Press, 1980), 50.

33. See for example Brian Ladd, *The Ghosts of Berlin* (Chicago: University of Chicago Press, 1997); Uta Staiger, Henriette Steiner, and Andrew Webber, eds., *Memory Culture and the Contemporary City: Building Sites* (London: Palgrave Macmillan, 2009); Karen E. Till, *The New Berlin: Memory, Politics, Place* (Minneapolis: University of Minnesota Press, 2005).

34. Daniel Jonah Goldhagen, *Hitler's Willing Executioners* (New York: Alfred A. Knopf, 1996); Hannes Heer and Klaus Naumann, eds., *Vernichtungskrieg: Verbrechen der Wehrmacht, 1941–1944* (Hamburg: Hamburger Edition HIS Verlag, 1995).

35. Micha Brumlik, "Der Sinn des Holocaustdenkmals zu Berlin," in *Umkämpftes Vergessen: Walser-Debatte, Holocaust-Mahnmal und neuere deutsche Geschichtspolitik*, by Micha Brumlik, Hajo Funke, and Lars Rensmann (Berlin: Verlag Das Arabische Buch, 1999), 175–76; Wolfgang Thierse, "Warum ist es notwendig, in Berlin einen Erinnerungsort an die Opfer des Holocaust zu haben?," in *Was hat der Holocaust mit mir zu tun? 37 Antworten*, ed. Harald Roth (Munich: Pantheon, 2014), 224–28.

36. But see Cem Özdemir, "Was geht mich das an? Erinnerungskultur in der Einwanderungsgesellschaft," in Roth, *Was hat der Holocaust mit mir zu tun?*, 234–36.

37. See the website for Gunter Demnig's Stolpersteine project, http://www.stolpersteine.eu/start/.

38. See also, for example, Caroline Pearce, "Visualising 'Everyday Evil': The Representation of Nazi Perpetrators in German Memorial Sites," in *Representing Perpetrators in Holocaust Literature and Film*, ed. Jenni Adams and Sue Vice (London: Vallentine Mitchell, 2013), 207–30.

39. The distinction between sites associated with perpetrators and "memorial sites" for victims is made by Markus Urban, "Memorialization of Perpetrator Sites in Bavaria," in *Memorialisation in Germany since 1945*, ed. Bill Niven and Chloe Paver (Houndmills, UK: Palgrave Macmillan, 2010), 103. See also Neil Gregor, *Haunted City: Nuremberg and the Nazi Past* (New Haven, CT: Yale University Press, 2008).

40. Oliver von Wrochem, ed., *Nationalsozialistische Täterschaften: Nachwirkingungen in Gesellschaft und Familie* (Berlin: Metropol Verlag, 2016).

41. Gregor Holzinger, ed., *Die zweite Reihe: Täterbiografien aus dem Konzentrationslager Mauthausen*, Mauthausen-Studien 10 (Vienna: New Academic Press, 2016).

42. Bertrand Perz, *Projekt "Quarz": Der Bau einer unterirdischen Fabrik durch Häftlinge des KZ Melk für die Steyr-Daimler-Puch AG, 1944–1945* (Innsbruck, Austria: Studien Verlag, 2012), 551–53.

43. E.g., Martin Pollack, *Kontaminierte Landschaften* (Vienna: Residenz Verlag, 2014).

44. Patrick Desbois, *The Holocaust by Bullets: A Priest's Journey to Uncover the Truth behind the Murder of 1.5 Million Jews* (Houndmills, UK: Palgrave Macmillan, 2008).

45. Jens Nagel, "Remembering Prisoners of War as Victims of National Socialist Persecution and Murder in Post-War Germany," in Niven and Paver, *Memorialisation*, ch. 2.5.

46. Mary Fulbrook, *Anatomy of a Dictatorship: Inside the GDR, 1949–1989* (Oxford: Oxford University Press, 1995).

47. Albert Knoll, "Homosexuelle Häftlinge im KZ Dachau," in *Das Konzentrationslager Dachau: Geschichte und Wirkung nationalsozialistischer Repression*, ed. Wolfgang Benz and Angelika Königseder (Berlin: Metropol, 2008), 237–52; Harold Marcuse, *Legacies of Dachau: The Uses and Abuses of a Concentration Camp, 1933–2001* (Cambridge: Cambridge University Press, 2001).

48. Christopher Isherwood, *The Berlin Stories* (New York: New Directions, 1945).

49. E.g., Rudolf Brazda, *Itinéraire d'un Triangle rose* (Paris: Massot, 2010), and Alexander Zinn *"Das Glück kam immer zu mir": Rudolf Brazda—Das Überleben eines Homosexuellen im Dritten Reich* (Frankfurt am Main: Campus Verlag, 2011).

50. Reactions summarized in "Homo-Denkmal in Berlin eröffnet," *Medrum*, http://www.medrum.de/content/homo-denkmal-berlin-eroeffnet.

51. See for example Elizabeth Olson, "Gay Focus at Holocaust Museum," *New York Times*, January 4, 2003.

52. Jonathan Danilowitz, "Remembering the '175ers,'" *Jerusalem Post*, January 23, 2014.

53. Patricia Pientka, *Das Zwangslager für Sinti und Roma in Berlin-Marzahn: Alltag, Verfolgung und Deportation* (Berlin: Metropol Verlag, 2013), 197–202.

54. "Nazi Graffiti Mars Berlin Memorial to Roma," *Deutsche Welle*, October 20, 2015, available at http://www.dw.com/en/nazi-graffiti-mars-berlin-monument-to-roma/a-18814597, accessed January 13, 2016.

55. See for example: Melissa Eddy, "Monument Seeks to End Silence on Killings of the Disabled by the Nazis," *New York Times*, September 2, 2014.

56. Gerrit Hohendorf, "Informations- und Gedenkort Tiergartenstrasse 4 in Berlin—Der Appell des Arbeitskreises vom 14. Juni 2010 und die Stellungnahme von 8. Dezember 2010," in *Den Opfern ihre Namen geben: NS-"Euthanasie"- Verbrechen, historisch-politische Verantwortung und Erinnerungskultur: Fachtagung vom 13. bis 15. Mai 2011 in Kloster Irsee*, ed. Arbeitskreis zur Erforschung der nationalsozialistischen "Euthanasie" und Zwangssterilisation, Berichte des Arbeitskreises 7 (Münster, Germany: Klemm & Oelschläger, 2011); see also the letter to the German president, Parliament, and key individuals of December 8, 2010, reproduced here, 70–74.

57. Arbeitskreis, *Den Opfern ihre Namen geben*, 69.

58. Henry Friedlander, *The Origins of Nazi Genocide: From Euthanasia to the Final Solution* (Chapel Hill: University of North Carolina Press, 1992), 88–89.

59. Boris Böhm, "Der Umgang mit der NS-'Euthanasie'-Verbrechen in der DDR," in *25 Jahre Aufarbeitung der NS-"Euthanasie" in Pirna*, ed. Kuratorium Gedenkstätte Sonnenstein e.V. (Pirna, Germany: Kuratorium Gedenkstätte Sonnenstein e.V., 2014), 13.

60. See the website of Fördervereines der Gedenkstätte für die Opfer der NS-"Euthanasie" Bernburg e.V., http://www.gedenkstaette-bernburg.de, and 'Bernburg 'Euthanasia' Centre," http://www.dark-tourism.com/index.php/germany/15-countries/individual-chapters/357-bernburg-euthanasia-centre, accessed September 15, 2014.

61. Thomas Schilter, "Persönliche Erinnerungen," in Kuratorium Gedenkstätte Sonnenstein, *25 Jahre Aufarbeitung*, 18–21.

62. Bernd Richter, "Erinnerungen des Pfarrers der Gemeinde Pirna-Sonnenstain," in Kuratorium Gedenkstätte Sonnenstein, *25 Jahre Aufarbeitung*, 22–25.

63. Kurt Nowak, "Krankenmorde im NS-Staat: Die Vernichtung 'lebensunwertes Lebens' in den psychiatrischen Anstalten Sachsens 1939/40–1945," in Kuratorium Gedenkstätte Sonnenstein, *25 Jahre Aufarbeitung*, 33–46.

64. Gedenkstätte Pirna-Sonnenstein website, https://www.stsg.de/cms/pirna/startseite, accessed September 15, 2014.

65. Thomas Schilter, "Persönliche Erinnerungen," in Kuratorium Gedenkstätte Sonnenstein., *25 Jahre Aufarbeitung*, 18–21.

66. Bettina Winter, Gerhard Baader, Johannes Cramer, et al., *"Verlegt nach Hadamar": Die Geschichte einer NS-"Euthanasie"-Anstalt*, Historische Schriften des Landeswohlfahrtverbandes Hessen, Kataloge, 2 (Kassel, Germany: Landeswohlfahrtverbandes Hessen, 2009).

67. Gedenkstätte Hadamar website, http://www.gedenkstaette-hadamar.de/webcom/show_article.php/_c-618/_nr-1/_p-1/i.html, accessed September 15, 2014.

68. Susanne Knittel, "Remembering Euthanasia: Grafeneck in the Past, Present and Future," in Niven and Paver, *Memorialisation*, 124–33.

69. Gedenkstätte Grafeneck website, http://www.gedenkstaette-grafeneck.de/265.htm, accessed September 15, 2014; see now http://s522790709.online.de/265.htm.

70. Hartmut Reese and Brigitte Kepplinger, "Das Gedenken in Hartheim," in *Tötungsanstalt Hartheim*, ed. Brigitte Kepplinger, Gerhart Marckhgott, and Hartmut Reese (Linz, Austria: Oberösterreichisches Landesarchiv and Lern- und Gedenkort Schloss Hartheim, 2013), 523–48; see also Bizeps—Zentrum für Selbstbestimmtes Leben, ed., *Wertes/unwertes Leben* (Vienna: Bizeps—Zentrum für Selbstbestimmtes Leben, 2012).

71. Official website at http://www.schloss-hartheim.at/index.php/en/memorial-site-exhibition/exhibition-value-of-life, accessed September 9, 2016.

72. See http://de.nationalfonds.org, accessed September 15, 2014.

73. *My Nazi Legacy* (BFI, 2015).

74. Klaus Neumann, *Shifting Memories: The Nazi Past in the New Germany* (Ann Arbor: University of Michigan Press, 2000), ch. 9; Annette Leo, *"Das ist so'n zweischneidiges Schwert hier unser KZ..." Der Fürstenberger Alltag und das Frauenkonzentrationslager Ravensbrück* (Berlin: Metropol, 2007).

75. Ruth Klüger, *Weiter leben* (Göttingen, Germany: Wallstein Verlag, 1992).

76. Pierre Seel, *I, Pierre Seel, Deported Homosexual: A Memoir of Nazi Terror*, trans. Joachim Neugroschel (New York: Basic Books, 2011), 134.

77. Seel, *I, Pierre Seel*, 140.

78. Erica Lehrer, "Relocating Auschwitz: Affective Relations in the Jewish-German-Polish Troika," in *Germany, Poland, and Postmemorial Relations: In Search of a Livable Past*, ed. Kristin Kopp and Joanna Niżyńska (New York: Palgrave Macmillan, 2012), 213–37.

79. Cf., e.g., Jennifer Hansen-Glucklich, *Holocaust Memory Reframed: Museums and the Challenges of Representation* (New Brunswick, NJ: Rutgers University Press, 2014).

80. United Nations General Assembly, October 26, 2005, Sixtieth session, Agenda item 72, A/60/L.12, available as a PDF on the Yad Vashem website at http://www.yadvashem.org/yv/en/remembrance/international/pdf/un_decision.pdf, accessed November 1, 2013.

81. E.g., Bill Niven and Chloe Paver, introduction to Niven and Paver, *Memorialisation*, 5, arguing that by the end of the century "the interest in German victimhood is (by and large) free of the resentment and politicization which characterized it in the 1950s."

82. Cf., e.g., Judith Miller, *One by One by One* (New York: Simon & Schuster, 1990).

83. English translation of the speech in Martin Walser, "Experiences while Composing a Sunday Speech (1998)," in *The Burden of the Past: Martin Walser on Modern German Identity: Texts, Contexts, Commentary*, by Thomas Kovach and Martin Walser (Rochester, NY: Camden House, 2008, 89).

84. Walser, "Experiences while Composing a Sunday Speech," 91.
85. Ignatz Bubis, "Rede des Präsidenten des Zentralrates der Juden in Deutschland am 9. November 1998 in der Synagoge Ryketsrasse in Berlin, 9.11.1998," in *Die Walser-Bubis-Debatte: Ein Dokumentation*, ed. Frank Schirrmacher (Frankfurt am Main: Suhrkamp, 1999), 109.
86. Bubis, "Rede," 112.
87. Martin Walser, "No End to Auschwitz (1979)," in Kovach and Walser, *Burden of the Past*, 26.
88. Walser, "No End to Auschwitz," 26. See also Martin Walser, "Our Auschwitz (1965)," in Kovach and Walser, *Burden of the Past*, 7–18.

CHAPTER 20

1. Raul Hilberg, *The Destruction of the European Jews*, 3rd ed. (New Haven, CT: Yale University Press, 2003), 3:1134.
2. Ernst Nolte, "Die Vergangenheit, die nicht vergehen will: Eine Rede, die geschrieben, aber nicht gehalten werden konnte," *Frankfurter Allgemeine Zeitung*, June 6, 1986, also in *"Historikerstreit": Die Dokumentation der Kontroverse um die Einzigartigkeit der nationalsozialistischen Judenvernichtung* (Munich: Piper, 1987).
3. Here I part company with Götz Aly, *Hitlers Volksstaat* (Frankfurt am Main: Fischer Verlag, 2005), according to which all beneficiaries were contaminated by collective guilt.
4. See further Mary Fulbrook, "Bystanders: Catchall Concept, Alluring Alibi, or Crucial Clue?" in *Erfahrung, Erinnerung, Geschichtsschreibung: Neue Perspektiven auf die deutschen Diktaturen*, by Mary Fulbrook (Göttingen, Germany: Wallstein, 2016), ch. 5.
5. For well-founded skepticism about "lessons" from history, see Michael Marrus, *Lessons of the Holocaust* (Toronto: University of Toronto Press, 2016). Cf. Timothy Snyder, *Black Earth: The Holocaust as History and Warning* (New York: Tim Duggan, 2015), 319–43.
6. Imre Kertész, *Liquidation*, trans. Tim Wilkinson (London: Vintage, 2007), 18.
7. Kertész, *Liquidation*, 18.

Index